Craig Miller
July 2010

Cape Cod

Martha's Vineyard
& Nantucket

Photo by Lynette Molnar

Cape Cod

Martha's Vineyard
& Nantucket

Kim Grant
with photographs by the author

The Countryman Press ✳ Woodstock, Vermont

EIGHTH EDITION

We welcome your comments and suggestions. Please contact Explorer's Guide Editor, The Countryman Press, P.O. Box 748, Woodstock, VT 05091, or e-mail countrymanpress@wwnorton.com.

ISBN: 978-0-88150-857-4

Cover and text design by Bodenweber Design
Cover photograph and interior photographs © Kim Grant
Maps by Paul Woodward, © The Countryman Press
Text composition by PerfecType, Nashville, TN

Published by The Countryman Press, P.O. Box 748, Woodstock, Vermont 05091

Distributed by W. W. Norton & Company, Inc., 500 Fifth Avenue, New York, NY 10110

Printed in the United States of America

10 9 8 7 6 5 4 3 2

For all the readers who helped along the way
with their opinions

EXPLORE WITH US!

Welcome to the eighth edition of the most comprehensive guide to Cape Cod, Martha's Vineyard, and Nantucket. I have been highly selective but broadly inclusive, based on years of repeated visits, cumulative research, and ongoing conversations with locals. All entries—attractions, inns, and restaurants—are chosen on the basis of personal experience.

I hope that the organization of this guide makes it easy to read and use. The layout has been kept simple; the following pointers will help you get started.

WHAT'S WHERE

In the beginning of the book you'll find an alphabetical listing of special highlights and important information that you can reference quickly. You'll find advice on everything from where to find the best art galleries and lighthouses, to where to take a whale-watching excursion.

LODGING

Prices: Please don't hold us or the respective innkeepers responsible for the rates listed as of press time. Changes are inevitable. At the time of this writing, the state and local room tax was 9.7 percent. Please also see Lodging in "What's Where on Cape Cod, Martha's Vineyard, and Nantucket."

RESTAURANTS

In most sections, note the distinction between Dining Out and Eating Out. Restaurants listed under Eating Out are generally inexpensive and more casual; reservations are often suggested for restaurants in Dining Out. A range of prices for main dishes is included with each entry.

GREEN SPACE

In addition to trails and walks, "green space" also includes white and blue spaces, that is, beaches and ponds.

KEY TO SYMBOLS

❋ The "off-season" icon appears next to appealing year-round lodging or attractions.

⑤ The "special-value" icon appears next to lodging entries, restaurants, and activities that combine exceptional quality with moderate prices.

🐾 The "pet-friendly" icon appears next to lodgings where pets are welcome.

✎ The "child and family interest" icon appears next to lodging entries, restaurants, activities, and shops of special appeal to youngsters and families.

☂ The "rainy-day" icon appears next to things to do and places of interest that are appropriate for foul-weather days.

Ⓨ The "martini glass" icon appears next to restaurants and entertainment venues with good bars.

♿ The "handicap" symbol indicates lodging and dining establishments that are truly wheelchair accessible.

⬙ᵢ⬙ The "WiFi" symbol indicates which establishments offer free WiFi Internet.

Please visit my Web sites (kimgrant.com and capecodeg.com) for up-to-the-minute reviews and to add your voice to the growing chorus of Explorers.

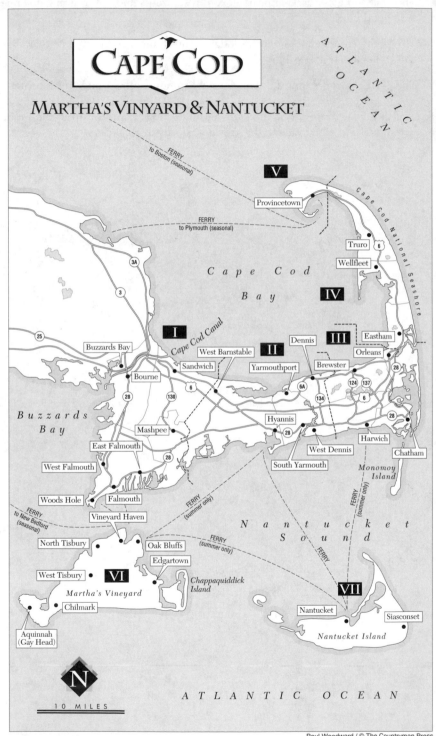

CAPE COD

MARTHA'S VINYARD & NANTUCKET

CONTENTS

LIST OF MAPS

INTRODUCTION

Welcome to the eighth edition of *Cape Cod, Martha's Vineyard & Nantucket: An Explorer's Guide*.

With the Web, you have infinite information at your fingertips. What I provide here, in a nutshell, in an old-fashioned print guide, is a reasoned assessment of all those choices. These days, I spend my precious word count on why you should visit one place over another, why one place is right for you and not for your sister. I see my job as providing "decision assistance," as my colleague Tom Brosnahan likes to say.

During one sojourn or another, I have personally visited every place in this guide—and many, many more that don't make it into this guide. Selection is key; the very fact that a place is in this guide means it has been chosen over its brethren for any number of reasons. I hope it helps you determine where best to spend your hard-earned dollars and precious vacation time. Unlike a standalone Web review of a single hostelry, for instance, my reviews appear within a context of knowing what the other 10 or 20 hostelries in town are like.

In my position, I ferret out the great from the good. I assess those intangible qualities that make a vacation memorable. What I am looking for when I research a place to stay, for instance, is how personable and friendly the innkeepers are; how service-oriented the staff is; how clean the rooms are. Those factors can't be measured through surfing Web pages. Thankfully, you seem to sense and appreciate that; sales of this guide continue to increase nicely with each edition. We can tell that you value independent assessment. And we're grateful.

The publishers and I take reader feedback seriously (to comment, please see the "Explore with Us!" page). In fact, I attribute and embed many of my reader's comments (after verifying the information). Some of you have mentioned that you want even more restaurant reviews. So I have provided more. But there are dozens and dozens of eateries along Route 28, for instance, that I don't review. You can trust that I've investigated almost every single one of them and have chosen the best in each range, from budget to expensive, from family-friendly establishments to places for a romantic rendezvous.

One other significant way this guide differs from the competition is that I alone have researched and written it since 1994. What that means to you, the reader, is that when I say a place is the best clam shack on the Cape, you know that I have visited them all. Many other guidebooks dispatch a team of researchers to various parts of the Cape; when these authors write that a place is the best clam shack on the Cape, what they really mean is, "This is the best clam shack in the territory I was assigned for this edition." Furthermore, because I have written every edition of this book since its inception, you will benefit from insights I have gained over the course of many years of research.

By most accounts and calculations, almost 120,000 cars cross the Cape Cod Canal every day in July and August, and the ferries to Martha's Vineyard and Nantucket transport more than 2.4 million people each summer. So it would be a stretch of the imagination to say that these fragile parcels of prized real estate are undiscovered or unexplored. In fact, sometimes it seems there isn't a grain of sand that hasn't been written about.

But just when I think I've seen it all, a ray of bright, clear sunlight will hit the Provincetown dune shacks in such a way as to make them seem new again. I'll strike up a conversation with a historical society curator, and she'll regale me with stories about town affairs at the turn of the 19th century. I'll walk down a trail in October that I previously walked in May and hear different birds and see different plants.

There is certainly no lack of information about Cape Cod, Martha's Vineyard, and Nantucket. But the way I see it, there are a few big problems with the material. Some stem from its abundance. Many of the print and Web compilations are overwhelming and undiscriminating. Much of what passes for editorial recommendation is actually just paid advertising copy. And finally, many of the special-interest brochures—for antiquing or kids' activities, for instance—cover the entire area. So if you're just visiting one town or concentrating on one region, you must wade through a lot of extraneous information.

Quite honestly, this guidebook is intended to be many things to many people. The publishers and I have set our sights to include a wide audience. This book is written for people who live close enough, or are fortunate enough, to be able to make many short trips to the Cape throughout the year—people who know that the region takes on a whole different character from Labor Day weekend to Memorial Day weekend. (It is a common misconception that the region closes down from mid-October to mid-May.) It will prove valuable, as well, to year-rounders who must give advice to a steady stream of summer guests. It's for Cape residents who may live on the Upper Cape, but don't know much about the Lower Cape. It's for people whose only trip to the Cape or the islands is their annual summer holiday—people who have always vacationed in Wellfleet, let's say, but are ready to explore other places. My highest hope, though, is to introduce the *other* Cape and islands to that segment of the traveling public that assumes traffic jams, crowded beaches, and tacky souvenir shops define the region.

This book is the result of years of research, conversation, observation,

Photo by Lynette Molnar

pleasure reading, and personal exploration. I am a Bostonian who spent youthful summer vacations on Cape Cod, bicycling at the Cape Cod National Seashore, eating saltwater taffy in Provincetown, and camping on Martha's Vineyard. My introduction to Nantucket came later, in the mid-1980s; by then I was old enough to appreciate the island's sophisticated culinary treats and rich history all the more.

Since I am also a professional photographer, I am pleased to supplement my written observations and recommendations with a visual portrait. I have intentionally emphasized the region's tranquility, since conventional wisdom already associates the Cape with masses of humanity. But the photos are proof, really, that there are beaches where you can walk alone on a sunny September day.

Traveling, and writing about it, is a nice lifestyle; there's no doubt about that, and I'm grateful for the opportunity to do it. But it is work (as my friends and family, temporarily abandoned in favor of my laptop computer, will attest). The book wouldn't have been possible without the encouragement, guidance, and firsthand experience of many people who appreciate the Cape and the islands from many different perspectives.

As much as I love both four-star dining and a bucket of fried clams from a shack on the pier, I just can't eat everywhere for every edition. I have called upon my innkeeper friends, who benefit from the collective opinions of dozens of guests who eat in dozens of places night after night and then discuss their experiences the next morning over breakfast. Likewise, it is impossible to sleep in every room in every B&B, but I can assure you that I have personally visited and inspected every establishment in this guide.

As with all editions, this one benefits from the accumulated knowledge that fellow explorers have shared with me, through letters and over breakfast at B&Bs.

The folks at The Countryman Press (a division of W. W. Norton) epitomize everything that's good about the publishing industry. I appreciate their responsiveness to and respect for writers, as well as their commitment to providing a quality guidebook to the book-buying public.

I welcome readers' thoughtful comments, criticisms, and suggestions for the next edition of *Cape Cod, Martha's Vineyard & Nantucket: An Explorer's Guide*.

Feel free to contact me at my e-mail address (cceg@kimgrant.com) or add your voice to the forum on my Web site (capecodeg.com). You may also purchase black-and-white note cards of Cape Cod through the Bindu Press section of kimgrant.com.

SUGGESTED ITINERARIES

IF YOU HAVE 3 DAYS

Special thanks for buying this book. It contains far more information than you'll ever be able to use. We hope you will pass this book along to a friend after it serves you well.

IF YOU HAVE 5 DAYS

You'll need to be efficient. Visit the village of Sandwich, poke around antiques and artisan shops on Route 6A, and drive down scenic bayside roads north of Route 6A, spending 2 nights mid-Cape. On the third morning, pop down to Main Street and the lighthouse in Chatham, and then head to the Outer Cape and the famed Cape Cod National Seashore beaches, stopping at the Salt Pond Visitor Center in Eastham. Spend 2 nights on the Outer Cape (or in Orleans): Visit galleries in Well-fleet, walk the Atlantic beaches and short nature trails, and take a day trip to Provincetown.

IF YOU HAVE 7 DAYS

You'll end up with a very enjoyable trip. Spend 3 nights mid-Cape and 3 on the Outer Cape. Do all of the above, plus linger longer in Sandwich, visiting the Glass

Museum and/or Heritage Museums & Gardens. Add a beach walk at Barnstable's Sandy Neck Beach and/or Nauset Beach in Orleans. Visit the Cape Cod Museum of Natural History in Brewster and/or the Wellfleet Bay Wildlife Sanctuary. Spend a day and a half in Provincetown—watching people, walking Commercial Street, ducking into art museums and the informative Provincetown Museum, taking in a sunset from Race Point or Herring Cove, heading out on a whale-watching excursion.

IF YOU HAVE 10 DAYS

You'll be very happy. Allot the entire 3 additional days (from the above plan) to Martha's Vineyard. (Trying to see the Vineyard in a day borders on silliness.) Or add a night or two in the diverse Falmouth–Woods Hole area and a day trip to Nantucket. Back on the Cape, get out on the water with a trip to Monomoy Island in Chatham or some other boat tour. Add a couple of whistle-stops at the Cape's small, sweet, historic museums.

IF YOU HAVE 2 WEEKS

You're really lucky. Allot 3 days to one of the islands. Add a quiet canoe or kayak paddle somewhere. Take a leisurely bike ride or an aerial sightseeing flight. Get tickets to summer stock and cheer on the home team at a free baseball game. Slip into a parking space at the Wellfleet Drive-In. Investigate an old cemetery. Take an art class. Visit Mashpee's South Cape Beach State Park.

IF YOU LIVE ON THE CAPE AND ISLANDS

You're the luckiest of all. Scribble comments in the margins of this book and lend it to visiting friends so you don't have to keep repeating yourself. Explore something new at least once a week. Isn't that one reason you live here?

A PERFECT DAY IN . . .

These town-by-town, hour-by-hour tours will get you started on how best to dip into a town. But a word of caution: If you try to do everything mentioned, you might not feel like you're on a vacation. Use them merely as a guide.

WHAT'S WHERE ON CAPE COD, MARTHA'S VINEYARD & NANTUCKET

AREA CODE The area code for the region of Cape Cod, Martha's Vineyard, and Nantucket is **508**.

AIRPORTS AND AIRLINES There is regularly scheduled air service from Boston to Provincetown. Hyannis is reached by air from Boston, Providence, and New York. Nantucket and Martha's Vineyard enjoy regularly scheduled year-round service; **Cape Air** (800-352-0714; flycapeair.com) offers the most flights. Sightseeing by air is best done in Chatham, Barnstable, and Provincetown.

ANTIQUARIAN BOOKS Among the many shops on Route 6A, two are great: **Titcomb's Book Shop** in Sandwich and Parnassus Book Service in Yarmouth Port. I also highly recommend **Isaiah Thomas Books & Prints** in Cotuit.

ANTIQUES Antiques shops are located all along Route 6A, on the 32-mile stretch from Sandwich to Orleans, but there is an especially dense concentration in Brewster, often called Antique Alley. You'll also find a good concentration of antiques shops in Barnstable, Dennis Port, Chatham, and Nantucket. (It's never made sense to me to buy antiques on an island, but folks do!)

Look for the free directory published by the **Cape Cod Antique Dealers Association**, available at on-Cape antiques stores.

AQUARIUMS The **Woods Hole Science Aquarium** is small, but it's an excellent introduction to marine life. There is also the small **Maria Mitchell Association Aquarium** on Nantucket.

ART GALLERIES Wellfleet and Provincetown are the centers of fine art on the Cape. Both established and emerging artists are well represented in dozens of diverse galleries. Artists began flocking to Provincetown at the turn of the 20th century, and the vibrant community continues to nurture creativity. The islands also attract large numbers of artists, some of whom stay to open their own studios and galleries. Chatham, Nantucket, and Martha's Vineyard also have many fine galleries. Look for the outstanding color booklet *Arts & Artisans Trails* (sponsored by CapeCodChamber .org)—and then don't leave home without it.

ATTIRE The Cape and the islands are casual for the most part; a jacket is required at only one or two places. At

the other end of the spectrum, you'll always need shoes and shirts at beach-front restaurants.

AUCTIONS Estate auctions are held throughout the year: check the news-papers; check out **Sandwich Auction House**. Great benefit auctions include the **Fine Arts Work Center Annual Benefit Auction**, the **AIDS Support Group's Annual Silent and Live Auction** in Provincetown, and the celebrity-studded **Possible Dreams Auction** on Martha's Vineyard.

Y BARS Look for the Y symbol next to restaurants and entertainment ven-ues that have more than a few bar stools.

BASEBALL The 10-team **Cape Cod Baseball League** (capecodbaseball .org) was established in 1946. Only players with at least one year of colle-giate experience are allowed to partici-pate. Wooden bats are supplied by the major leagues. In exchange for the opportunity to play, team members work part time in the community, live with a community host, and pay rent. Carlton Fisk and the late Thurman Munson are just two alumni of the Cape Cod League who succeeded in the majors. Currently, about almost 250 major-league players are former league players. Games are free and

played from mid-June to mid-August; it's great fun. In relevant chapters, baseball venues are listed under *To Do*.

BEACHES Cape Cod National Seashore (CCNS; nps.gov/caco) beaches are the stuff of dreams: long expanses of dune-backed sand. In fact, you could walk with only a few natural interruptions (breaks in the beach), as Henry David Thoreau did, from Chatham to the tip of Provincetown. My favorites on the Cape include **Sandy Neck Beach** in West Barnsta-ble; **Nauset Beach** in Orleans; **Old Silver Beach** in North Falmouth; **Chapin Memorial Beach** in Dennis; **West Dennis Beach**; **Craigville Beach** near Hyannis; and all the **Outer Cape** ocean beaches. Practical-ly all of Nantucket's beaches are pub-lic, and although the same cannot be said for Martha's Vineyard, there are plenty of places to lay your towel.

A daily parking fee is enforced from mid-June to early September; many of the smaller beaches are open only to residents and weekly cottage renters. CCNS offers a seasonal parking pass for its beaches. There is no overnight parking at beaches. Four-wheel-drive vehicles require a permit, and their use

is limited. Open beach fires require a permit. Greenhead biting flies plague non–Outer Cape beaches in mid- to late July; they disappear with the first high tide at the new or full moon in August, when the water level rises, killing the eggs.

Generally, beaches on **Nantucket Sound** have warmer waters than the Outer Cape Atlantic Ocean beaches, which are also pounded by surf. **Cape Cod Bay** beaches are shallower than Nantucket Sound beaches, and the bay waters are a bit cooler. Because of the proximity of the warm Gulf Stream, you can swim in Nantucket Sound waters well into September.

BICYCLING The Cape is generally flat, and there are many paved, off-road bike trails. The 26-mile **Cape Cod Rail Trail** runs along the bed of the Old Colony Railroad from Route 134 in Dennis to Wellfleet; bike trails can be found along both sides of the **Cape Cod Canal**; the **Shining Sea Bike Path** runs from Falmouth to

Woods Hole; and bike trails can be found within the **Cape Cod National Seashore (CCNS)** in Provincetown and Truro. Nantucket is ideal for cycling, with six routes emanating from the center of town and then circling the island. Bicycling is also great on the Vineyard, but stamina is required for a trip up-island to Aquinnah. For more information, consult *Backroad Bicycling on Cape Cod, Martha's Vineyard, and Nantucket* by Susan Milton and Kevin and Nan Jeffrey (Backcountry Guides).

Rubel Bike Maps (bikemaps.com) are the most detailed maps available for the Cape and islands. Rubel produces a combination Nantucket and Vineyard map, as well as another that includes the islands, Cape Cod, and the North Shore.

BIRD-WATCHING The **Bird Watcher's General Store** in Orleans is on every birder's list of stops. Natural areas that are known for bird-watching include **Monomoy National Wildlife Refuge** off the coast of Chatham; **Wellfleet Bay Wildlife Sanctuary** (massaudubon.org); **Felix Neck Wildlife Sanctuary** in Vineyard Haven; **Ashumet Holly and Wildlife Sanctuary** in East Falmouth; and on Nantucket, **Coatue–Coskata–Great Point**. The **Maria Mitchell Association** and **Eco Guides**, both in Nantucket, offer bird-watching expeditions, as do **Wellfleet Bay Wildlife Sanctuary** and **Monomoy National Wildlife Refuge**. Scheduled bird walks are also offered from both Cape Cod National Seashore (CCNS) visitor centers: **Salt Pond Visitor Center** in Eastham and **Province Lands Visitor Center** in Provincetown. The **Cape Cod Museum of Natural History** in Brewster is always an excellent source of information for all creatures within the animal kingdom residing on the Cape.

BUS SERVICE The **Plymouth & Brockton bus line** (508-778-9767; p-b.com) serves some points along Route 6A and the Outer Cape from Boston. **Bonanza/Peter Pan** (800-751-8800; peterpanbus.com) serves Bourne, Falmouth, Woods Hole, and Hyannis from Boston, Providence, and New York City.

CAMPING No camping is permitted on Nantucket, but there is still one campground on Martha's Vineyard. The Cape offers dozens of private campgrounds, but only those in natural areas are listed; the best camping is in **Nickerson State Park** (mass.gov/dcr) in Brewster and in Truro.

CANOEING AND KAYAKING For guided naturalist trips and lessons there is no better outfitter than **Goose Hummock** in Orleans (508-255-0455; goose.com). Also look for the book *Paddling Cape Cod: A Coastal Explorer's Guide* by Shirley and Fred Bull (Backcountry Guides). There are also very good venues and outfitters in Falmouth and Wellfleet, and on Martha's Vineyard and Nantucket.

CAPE COD NATIONAL SEASHORE Established on August 7, 1961, through the efforts of President John F. Kennedy, the Cape Cod

National Seashore (CCNS; nps.gov/caco) stretches over 40 miles through Eastham, Wellfleet, Truro, and Provincetown. It encompasses more than 43,500 acres of land and seashore. Sites within the CCNS that are listed in this guide have been identified with "CCNS" at the beginning of the entry. The **Salt Pond Visitor Center** in Eastham and **Province Lands Visitor Center** in Provincetown are excellent resources and offer a variety of exhibits, films, and ranger-led walks and talks. The CCNS is accessible every day of the year, although you must pay to park at the beaches in summer.

✎ CHILDREN, ESPECIALLY FOR Within this guide a number of activities and sites that have special "child appeal" are identified by the crayon symbol.

CLASSES AND WORKSHOPS Want to "improve" yourself on vacation, or brush up on some long-lost creative artistic urges? There are more programs in **Provincetown**, the **Vineyard**, and **Nantucket** than I can list here; see *To Do* under each town or region. Also see the sidebar "Artistic Outlets during Vacation" in "Truro" for offerings at the **Truro Center for the Arts at Castle Hill**. The other Outer Cape sidebar, "Trails, Birds, Seals & Classes" in "Wellfleet," discusses the **Wellfleet Bay Wildlife Sanctuary Adult Field School**.

COUNTRY STORES Old-fashioned country stores still exist on Cape Cod and the islands. Aficionados can seek out **The Brewster Store** in Brewster and **Alley's General Store** in West Tisbury on the Vineyard.

CRAFTS Craftspeople have made a living on the Cape and the islands since they began making baskets, ships, and furniture 300 years ago. The tradition continues with artists emphasizing the aesthetic as well as the functional. Today's craftspeople are potters, jewelers (particularly in Dennis), scrimshaw and bird carvers, weavers, glassblowers, clothing designers, and barrel makers. Look for the highly coveted (and pricey) lightship baskets in Nantucket and glass objects in Sandwich, Bourne, and Brewster. A partial list of the particularly noteworthy shops would include **Woods Hole Handworks**; **Pewter Crafter of Cape Cod** in Harwich Port; and the **Orleans Carpenters**. There are too many artisans in Provincetown, Chatham, Nantucket, and Martha's Vineyard to detail

here. Look for the outstanding color booklet *Arts & Artisans Trails* (sponsored by CapeCodChamber.org)—and then don't leave home without it.

CRANBERRIES The cranberry is one of only three major native North American fruits (the other two are Concord grapes and blueberries). Harvesting began in Dennis in 1816 and evolved into a lucrative industry in Harwich Port. Harvesting generally runs from mid-September to mid-October, when the bogs are flooded and ripe red berries float to the water's surface. Before the berries are ripe, the bogs look like a dense green carpet, separated by 2- to 3-foot dikes. **Nantucket** has two bogs but only 180 of their 240 acres are harvested; most lie fallow due to a glut in supply. Harwich, which lays claim to having the first commercial cranberry bog, celebrates with a **Cranberry Harvest Festival** (harwichcranberryfestival.org) in mid-September. Most on-Cape bogs are located on the Mid- and Lower Cape.

DINING Perhaps the biggest surprise to folks is the high quality of cuisine on the Cape these days. Modernity and urbane sophistication are no longer rare breeds once you cross the canal bridges. Indeed, locals are so supportive that many fine restaurants stay open through the winter. During the off-season, many chefs experiment with creative new dishes and offer them at moderate prices. With the exception of July and August (when practically all places are open nightly), restaurants are rarely open every night of the week. The major problem for a travel writer (and a reader relying on the book) is that this schedule is subject to the whims of weather and foot traffic. To avoid disappointment, phone ahead before setting out for a much-anticipated meal.

Expect to wait for a table in July and August. Always call for reservations at *Dining Out* establishments. Remember that many restaurants are staffed by college students who are just learning the ropes in June and who may depart before Labor Day weekend, leaving the owners short-handed. Smaller seasonal establishments don't take credit cards.

Consult CapeCodRestaurants.com, CapeCodDining.com, and CapeCod DiningGuide.com.

ECOSYSTEM This narrow peninsula and these isolated islands have a delicate ecosystem. Remember that dunes are fragile, and beaches serve as nesting grounds for the endangered piping plover. Avoid the nesting areas when you see signs directing you to do so.

Residents conserve water and recycle, and they hope you will do likewise.

EMERGENCIES Call **911** from anywhere on Cape Cod. Major hospitals are located in Falmouth (508-548-5300) and Hyannis (508-771-1800).

EVENTS The largest annual events are listed within each chapter of this book. Otherwise, invest in the *Cape Cod Times* (508-775-1200; capecodon line.com). It features a special section about the day's events and a Friday calendar supplement.

FERRIES There are fast and slow ferries to Provincetown from Boston and a day-tripper from Plymouth. To reach Martha's Vineyard, the car ferry departs from Woods Hole, and passenger ferries depart from Woods Hole, Falmouth, Hyannis, and New Bedford. There is a seasonal inter-island ferry. There are high-speed and regular ferries to Nantucket from Hyannis (car and passenger) and Harwich (passenger). See the appropriate chapter for details on schedules.

FISHING You don't need a license for saltwater fishing, but you do for freshwater. Get a state license at various

Town Halls or bait and tackle shops.

Charter boats generally take up to six people on 4- or 8-hour trips. Boats leave from the following harbors on Cape Cod Bay: Barnstable Harbor in West Barnstable; Sesuit Harbor in Dennis; Rock Harbor in Orleans; Wellfleet Harbor; and Provincetown. On Nantucket Sound, head to Hyannis Harbor, Saquatucket Harbor in Harwich Port, and Chatham. You can also fish from the banks of the Cape Cod Canal and surf-fish on the Outer Cape. There are also plenty of opportunities for fishing off the shores of Nantucket and the Vineyard. **Goose Hummock** (goose.com) in Orleans offers lots of very good trips, as does **Chatham Family Charters** (chathamfamily charters.com).

FLEA MARKETS **Wellfleet Flea Market** (at the Drive-In) is the biggie.

GOLF There are about 50 courses on the Cape and the islands, and because of relatively mild winters, many stay open all year (although perhaps not every day). **Highland Golf Links** in Truro is the Cape's oldest course; it's also very dramatic.

& HANDICAP ACCESS Look for the & icon in the margin to find establishments that are *truly* wheelchair accessible.

HIGH SEASON Memorial Day weekend in late May kicks things off, then there is a slight lull until school lets out in late June. From then on, the Cape is in full swing through Labor Day (early September). There are two exceptions to this, though, and they're the best-kept secrets for planning a Cape Cod vacation: The Cape is relatively quiet during the week following the July 4 weekend and the week prior to Labor Day weekend. You will find B&B vacancies and no lines at your favorite restaurant. As a rule, traveling to the Cape or the islands without reservations in high season is not recommended. Accommodations—especially cottages, efficiencies, and apartments—are often booked by January for the upcoming summer. The Cape and islands are also quite busy from Labor Day to Columbus Day (mid-October). It's fairly common for B&Bs to be booked solid on every autumn weekend.

HIGHWAYS Route 6, also called the Mid-Cape Highway, is a speedy, four-lane, divided highway until Exit 9½, when it becomes an undivided two-laner. After the Orleans rotary (Exit 13), it becomes an undivided four-lane highway most of the way to Provincetown.

Scenic Route 6A, also known as Old King's Highway and Main Street, runs from the Sagamore Bridge to Orleans. It is lined with sea captains' houses, antiques shops, bed & breakfasts, and huge old trees. Development along Route 6A is strictly regulated by the Historical Commission. Route 6A links up with Route 6 in Orleans. Without stopping, it takes an extra 30 minutes or so to take Route 6A instead of Route 6 from Sandwich to Orleans.

Route 28 can be confusing. It's an elongated, U-shaped highway that runs from the Bourne Bridge south to Falmouth, then east to Hyannis and Chatham, then north to Orleans. The problem lies with the Route 28 directional signs. Although you're actually heading north when you travel from Chatham to Orleans, the signs will say ROUTE 28 SOUTH. When you drive from Hyannis to Falmouth, you're actually heading west, but the signs will say ROUTE 28 NORTH. Ignore the north and south indicators, and look for towns that are in the direction you want to go.

HISTORIC HOUSES Every town has its own historical museum or house, but some are more interesting than others. Among the best are **Hoxie House** in Sandwich; **Centerville Historical Museum** and **Osterville Historical Society Museum**, both in Barnstable; and the **Truro Historical Museum**. The center of Nantucket has been designated a historic district, so there are notable houses everywhere you turn; the oldest

is the **Jethro Coffin House**. The **Nantucket Historical Association** publishes a walking guide to its properties. Don't miss the **Martha's Vineyard Museum** on Martha's Vineyard.

HORSEBACK RIDING There are a surprising number of riding facilities and trails on the Cape. Look for them

in Falmouth and Brewster, and on Martha's Vineyard.

INFORMATION For those coming from the Boston area, Cape-wide information can be obtained at the tourist office on Route 3 (Exit 5) in Plymouth. If you're coming from the south or west, stop at the information and rest area on Route 25, 3 miles east of the Bourne Bridge. Both are open, at a minimum, daily 9–5 year-round.

There is also a year-round **Cape Cod Chamber of Commerce Welcome Center** at Exit 6 off Route 6 (508-362-3225 ext. 528 or 518; 888-332-2732; CapeCodChamber.org).

INTERNET Free wireless Internet is readily available at most lodging places, libraries, and chambers of commerce. Additionally many towns are experimenting with service that blankets part of their downtowns. You should have little trouble getting online almost everywhere. Having said that, I have indicated with the symbol "❝❶❞ " where you can log on with assurance.

LIBRARIES The Cape and the islands boast a few libraries with world-class maritime collections and works pertaining to the history of the area: **Sturgis Library** in Barnstable; **William Brewster Nickerson Memorial Room** at Cape Cod Community College in West Barnstable; the **Atheneum** and **Nantucket Historical Association Research Library**, both in Nantucket; and the **Martha's Vineyard Museum** in Edgartown on Martha's Vineyard. I have also included all town and village libraries, most of which provide free WiFi ("❶ "). In addition to being great community resources, libraries also make great rainy-day (☂) destinations.

LIGHTHOUSES It's a toss-up as to whether the most picturesque lighthouse is **Nobska Light** in Woods Hole or **Great Point Light** on Nantucket. (Nobska is certainly more accessible.) But there are also working lighthouses in Chatham, Eastham, Truro, and Provincetown. Nantucket and Martha's Vineyard, too, have their share of working lighthouses. For a really

unusual trip, the lighthouses at **Race Point** in Provincetown and on **Monomoy Island** off Chatham are available for overnight stays by advance reservation; see *Lodging* under each town.

LODGING There are many choices—from inns and bed & breakfasts to cottages, apartments, and efficiencies. Rates quoted are for two people sharing one room. Cottages are generally rented from Saturday to Saturday. Most inns and bed & breakfasts don't accept children under 10 to 12 years of age. All accept credit cards unless otherwise noted. None allows smoking unless otherwise noted. Pets are not accepted unless otherwise noted by our 🐾 icon in the margin. So many places require a 2-night minimum stay during the high season that I have not included that information unless it deviates significantly. Holiday weekends often require a 3-night minimum stay.

LYME DISEASE Ticks carry this disease, which has flu-like symptoms and may result in death if left untreated. Immediately and carefully remove any ticks that may have migrated from dune grasses to your body. Better yet, wear long pants, tuck pants into socks, and wear long-sleeved shirts whenever possible when hiking. Avoid hiking in grassy and overgrown areas of dense brush.

MAPS I love the *Cape Cod Street Atlas (Includes Martha's Vineyard and Nantucket)*, Third Edition ($14.95, DeLorme; delorme.com). I'm forever searching out bodies of water or shorelines that look interesting on the map and always finding scenic roads that I didn't expect.

MOVIES In addition to the standard multiplex cinemas located across the

Cape, the **Wellfleet Drive-In** remains a much-loved institution. The **Cape Cinema** in Dennis is a special venue; check it out. The **Nantucket Film Festival** and **International Film Festival** in Provincetown, both held in mid-June, are relatively new "must-see" events for independent-film buffs. Because moviegoing is a popular vacation activity, I have listed mainstream movie theaters under *Entertainment*.

MUSEUMS People who have never uttered the words *museum* and *Cape Cod* in the same breath don't know what they're missing. Don't skip the **Glass Museum** and **Heritage Museums & Gardens**, both in Sandwich; **Museums on the Green** in Falmouth; **Aptucxet Trading Post and Museum** in Bourne Village; **Cahoon Museum of American Art** in Cotuit; **John F. Kennedy Hyannis Museum**; **Cape Cod Museum of Art** in Dennis; **Cape Cod Museum of Natural History** in Brewster; **Provincetown Art Association & Museum**, the **Pilgrim Monument & Provincetown Museum**, and the **Old Harbor Lifesaving Station**, all in Provincetown; **Martha's Vineyard Museum** in Edgartown on Martha's Vineyard; and the **Nantucket Whaling Museum** and **Shipwreck and Lifesaving Museum** on Nantucket.

Children will particularly enjoy the **Railroad Museum** in Chatham and the **Thornton W. Burgess Museum** in Sandwich.

MUSIC Outdoor summertime band concerts are now offered by most towns, but the biggest and oldest is held in Chatham at **Kate Gould Park**. Sandwich offers a variety of outdoor summer concerts at **Heritage Museums & Gardens**.

The **Nantucket Musical Arts Society** and the **Vineyard's Cham-** ber Music Society are also excellent, albeit with much shorter seasons.

The 85-member **Cape Symphony Orchestra** (508-362-1111; capesym phony.org) performs classical, children's, and pops concerts year-round.

There are a couple of regular venues for folk music, including the **Woods Hole Folk Music Society** and the **First Encounter Coffee House** in Eastham.

This edition lists many more venues with live music; see the *Entertainment* headings under each town.

NATURE PRESERVES There are walking trails—around salt marshes, across beaches, through ancient swamps and hardwood stands—in every town on the Cape and the islands, but some traverse larger areas and are more "developed" than others. For a complete guide, look for the excellent *Walks & Rambles on Cape Cod and the Islands* by Ned Friary and Glenda Bendure (Backcountry Publications). Watch for poison ivy and deer ticks; the latter carry Lyme disease. And pick up a copy of *Wildflowers of Cape Cod & the Islands* by Kate Carter to help make the most of any walk.

To find some Upper Cape green space, head to **Green Briar Nature**

Center & Jam Kitchen in Sandwich; **Lowell Holly Reservation** in Mashpee; and **Ashumet Holly and Wildlife Sanctuary** and **Waquoit Bay National Estuarine Research Reserve**, both in East Falmouth. In the mid-Cape area, you'll find **Sandy Neck Great Salt Marsh Conservation Area** in West Barnstable. The Lower Cape offers **Nickerson State Park** in Brewster and **Monomoy National Wildlife Refuge** off the coast of Chatham. The **Cape Cod National Seashore** (CCNS) has a number of short interpretive trails on the Outer Cape, while Wellfleet has the **Wellfleet Bay Wildlife Sanctuary** and **Great Island Trail**.

On Martha's Vineyard you can escape the crowds at **Felix Neck Wildlife Sanctuary** in Vineyard Haven; **Cedar Tree Neck Sanctuary** and **Long Point Wildlife Refuge**, both in West Tisbury; and **Cape Pogue Wildlife Refuge** and **Wasque Reservation** on Chappaquiddick.

Nantucket boasts conservation initiatives that have protected 45 percent of the land from development, including the areas of **Coatue–Coskata–Great Point**, **Eel Point**, **Sanford Farm**, **Ram Pasture**, and the **Woods**.

NEWSPAPERS AND PERIODICALS

The *Cape Cod Times* (capecod online.com), with Cape- and island-wide coverage, is published daily. The *Cape Codder*, published on Friday in Orleans, focuses on the Lower and Outer Cape. The *Falmouth Enterprise* is published every Tuesday and Friday. Provincetown's weekly *Provincetown Banner* (provincetownbanner.com) is noteworthy, as are the *Vineyard Gazette* (mvgazette.com) and Nantucket's *Inquirer and Mirror* (ack.net).

In addition to its bimonthly magazine, *Cape Cod Life* publishes an annual guide and a "Best of the Cape & Islands" within its June edition.

❄ **OFF-SEASON** In an attempt to get people thinking about visiting the Cape and the islands off-season, I have put the ❄ symbol next to activities, lodging, and restaurants that are open and appealing in the off-season.

🐾 **PETS** Look for the 🐾 icon to find lodgings where your pet is welcome. But always call ahead; there may be additional fees associated with bringing your pet, and there may be special rooms reserved for pets and their owners.

PHOTOGRAPHY For tips about how and where to take perfect photos, pick up a copy of *The Photographer's Guide to Cape Cod & the Islands* by Chris Linder. As you'll see, it *is* possible to shoot in places that are not overrun with tourists in the summertime.

PONDS Supposedly there are 365 freshwater ponds on Cape Cod, one for every day of the year. As glaciers retreated 15,000 years ago and left huge chunks of ice behind, depressions in the earth were created. When the ice melted, "kettle ponds" were born. The ponds are a refreshing treat, especially in August when salty winds kick up beach sand.

POPULATION More than 210,000 people live year-round on the Cape and the islands. No one has a truly accurate count of how many people visit in summer, but it is well into the millions.

RADIO WOMR (92.1 FM) in Provincetown has diverse and great programming. Tune in to National Public Radio with WCCT (90.3 FM). On the Vineyard tune to WMVY (92.7

FM); on Nantucket, WNAN (91.1 FM); and on the Cape try WCOD (106.1 FM), WFCC (107.5 FM), and WQRC (99.9 FM).

☂ RAINY-DAY ACTIVITIES

Chances are, if it were sunny every day we would start taking the sunshine for granted. So when the clouds move in and the raindrops start falling on your head, be appreciative of the sun and look for the ☂ icon in this book, which tells you where to head indoors.

RECOMMENDED READING ABOUT CAPE COD
Henry Beston's classic *The Outermost House: A Year of Life on the Great Beach of Cape Cod* recounts his solitary year in a cabin on the ocean's edge. Cynthia Huntington's marvelous *The Salt House* updates Beston's work with a woman's perspective in the late 20th century. Also look for *The House on Nauset Marsh* by Wyman Richardson (The Countryman Press). Henry David Thoreau's naturalist classic *Cape Cod* meticulously details his mid-1800s walking tours. Josef Berger's 1937 Works Progress Administration (WPA) guide, *Cape Cod Pilot*, is filled with good stories and still-useful information. I devoured the excellent *Nature of Cape Cod* by Beth Schwarzman, as well as everything by poet Mary Oliver. Pick up anything by modern-day naturalists Robert Finch (including *The Primal Place*) and John Hay. Finch also edited a volume of writings by others about the Cape, *A Place Apart* (with a black-and-white cover photo by yours truly). Another collection of writings about Cape Cod is *Sand in Their Shoes*, compiled by Edith and Frank Shay. Look for *Cape Cod, Its People & Their History* by Henry Kittredge (alias Jeremiah Digges) and *The Wampanoags of Mashpee* by Russell Peters. Mary Heaton Vorse, a founder of the

Provincetown Players, describes life in Provincetown from the 1900s to the 1950s in *Time and the Town: A Provincetown Chronicle*. And for children, Kevin Shortsleeve has written an illustrated history book, *The Story of Cape Cod*. Look also for Admont Clark's *Lighthouses of Cape Cod, Martha's Vineyard, and Nantucket: Their History and Lore* and photographer Joel Meyerowitz's *A Summer's Day* and *Cape Light*.

RECOMMENDED READING ABOUT MARTHA'S VINEYARD
Start with the *Vineyard Gazette Reader*, a marvelous "best-of" collection edited by Richard Reston and Tom Dunlop; it will give you an immediate sense of the island. *On the Vineyard II* contains essays by celebrity island residents, including Walter Cronkite, William Styron, and Carly Simon, with photographs by Peter Simon (Carly's brother). *Martha's Vineyard* and *Martha's Vineyard, Summer Resort*, are both by Henry Beetle Hough, Pulitzer Prize–winning editor of the *Vineyard Gazette*. Photographer Alfred Eisenstaedt, a longtime summer resident of the Vineyard, photographed the island for years. Contemporary *Vineyard Gazette* photographer Alison Shaw has two Vineyard books to her credit: the black-and-white *Remembrance and Light* and the color collection *Vineyard Summer*.

RECOMMENDED READING ABOUT NANTUCKET Edwin P. Hoyt's *Nantucket: The Life of an Island* is a popular history, and Robert Gambee's *Nantucket* is just plain popular. Architecture buffs will want to take a gander at *Nantucket Style* by Leslie Linsley and Jon Aron and the classic *Early Nantucket and Its Whale Houses* by Henry Chandler Forman. Photography lovers will enjoy *On Nantucket*, with photos by Gregory Spaid.

ROTARIES When you're approaching a rotary, cars already within the rotary have the right-of-way.

SEAL CRUISES A colony of seals lounges around Monomoy, and there is no shortage of outfits willing to take you out to see them. See listings in "Chatham" and "Wellfleet" for detailed information. Chief among the operators is the **Wellfleet Bay Wildlife Sanctuary**.

SHELLFISHING Permits, obtained from local Town Halls, are required for the taking of shellfish. Sometimes certain areas are closed to shellfishing due to contamination; it's always best to ask.

SHOPPING Chatham and Falmouth's Main Streets are well suited to walking and shopping. Commercial Street in Provincetown has the trendiest shops. Mashpee Commons features a very dense and increasingly fine selection of shops. Shopping on the Vineyard and Nantucket is a prime activity.

SMOKING Smoking in bars and restaurants is not permitted in the state of Massachusetts.

SURFING AND SAILBOARDING Surfers should head to **Nauset Beach** in Orleans, **Coast Guard** and **Nauset**

Light beaches in Eastham, and **Marconi Beach** in Wellfleet. Sailboarders flock to Falmouth. Vineyard beaches are also good for sailboarding.

SWIMMING POOLS For a fee, you can swim at the **Willy's Gym** in Eastham, the **Nantucket Community Pool**, and at the **Mansion House** in Vineyard Haven on the Vineyard. Swimming at the **Provincetown Inn** is free.

THEATER Among the summer-stock and performing arts venues are **Cape Playhouse** in Dennis; **Cape Repertory Theatre** in Brewster; **Monomoy Theatre** in Chatham; **Academy Playhouse** in Orleans; **Wellfleet Harbor Actors Theater**; **Provincetown Repertory Theatre** and **Provincetown Theatre Co.**; **College Light Opera Company** in Falmouth; **Barnstable Comedy Club**; **Harwich Junior Theatre**; the **Theatre Workshop of Nantucket**; and the **Vineyard Playhouse** on Martha's Vineyard.

TIDES Tides come in and go out twice daily; times differ from day to day and from town to town. At low tide, the sandy shore is hard and easier to walk on; at high tide, what little sand is visible is more difficult to walk on. Since tides vary considerably from one spot to another, it's best to stop in at a local bait-and-tackle shop for a tide chart. For **Cape Cod Canal** tide information, call 508-759-5991. Log onto boatma.com/tides/tides_capecod .html.

TRAFFIC It's bad in July and August no matter how you cut it. It's bumper-to-bumper on Friday afternoon and evening when cars arrive for the weekend. It's grueling on Sunday afternoon and evening when they return home. And there's no respite on Saturday when all the weekly cottage renters have to vacate their units and a new set of renters arrives to take their places. Consult **Smart Traveler** (617-374-1234; or 511 on your cell phone; smartraveler.com) for up-to-the-minute information on traffic. This service uses remote cameras and airplanes to report current traffic conditions.

TRAINS The **Cape Cod Central Railroad** runs between Sandwich and Hyannis, alongside cranberry bogs and the Sandy Neck Great Salt Marsh. It turns into a dinner train at night (see *Where to Eat* in "Hyannis").

✦ VALUE The ✦ symbol appears next to entries that represent an exceptional value.

WALKING Cape Cod Pathways (508-362-3828; capecodcommission .org/pathways/trailguide.htm), a growing network of trails linking open space in all 15 Cape Cod towns from Falmouth to Provincetown, is coordinated by the Cape Cod Commission in Barnstable.

Also see *Walks & Rambles on Cape Cod and the Islands* by Ned Friary and Glenda Bendure (Backcountry Publications). Also consult cctrails.org.

WEATHER You really can't trust Boston weather reports to provide accurate forecasts for all the microclimates between Route 28 and 6A, from the canal to Provincetown. If you really want to go to the Cape, just go. There'll be plenty to do even if it's cloudy or rainy. When in doubt, or when it really matters, call the radio station WQRC, 99.9 FM (508-771-5522), or consult capecodweather.net.

WEB SITES Web addresses are listed throughout. Also, consult my sites (capecodexplorersguide.com and kim grant.com).

WHALE-WATCHING Whale-watching trips leave from Provincetown, including the excellent **Dolphin Fleet Whale Watch** (508-240-3636), but you can also catch the **Hyannis *Whale***

Watcher **Cruises** (508-362-6088) out of Barnstable Harbor.

⟨ɪ⟩ WIFI The special symbol " ⟨ɪ⟩ " indicates which establishments offer free wireless Internet.

WINERIES The Cape and islands are not Napa and Sonoma, but you could drop in for tastings at **Truro Vine-yards of Cape Cod** in Truro and the **Cape Cod Winery** in East Falmouth. The **Nantucket Vineyard** (are you confused?) imports grapes to make wine.

YOUTH HOSTELS Good youth hostels (usahostels.org/cape) are located on Martha's Vineyard and Nantucket, and in Eastham and Truro.

The Upper Cape 1

BOURNE

SANDWICH

FALMOUTH AND WOODS HOLE

MASHPEE

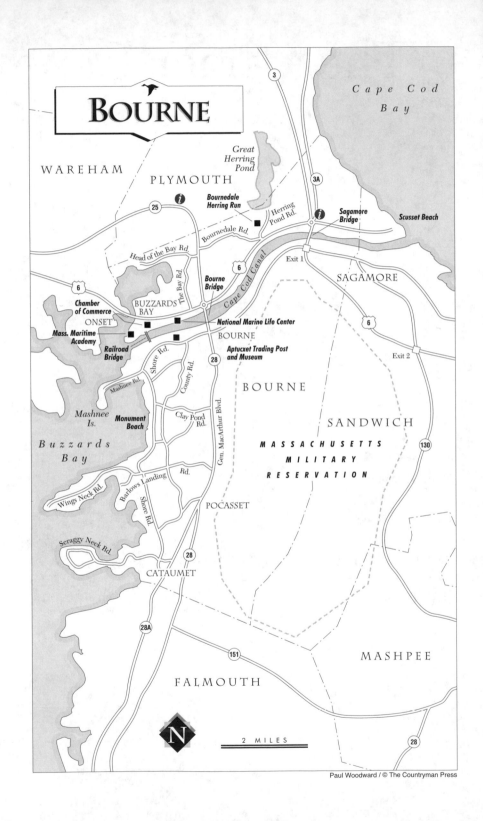

BOURNE

BOURNE

Despite summertime traffic tie-ups approaching the Sagamore and Bourne bridges, there's something magical about the first glimpse of them, a sure sign that you're entering a place separate from where you've been. All travelers, except those arriving by plane or boat, must pass through Bourne, over the bridges and the Cape Cod Canal.

Bourne straddles the canal, nips at the heels of Sandwich on the Cape Cod Bay side, and follows the coastline south toward Falmouth along Route 28. (All the land to the immediate east of Route 28 belongs to the Massachusetts Military Reservation.) Bourne is often completely bypassed—especially now that the so-called flyover has been completed—as travelers head south to catch the Vineyard ferry from Falmouth or Woods Hole. Indeed, there is some justification for not spending a monthlong holiday here. Bourne is predominantly inhabited by year-rounders, enjoying a quiet, rural, unhurried existence and tending their gardens and lives. But perhaps of the entire Cape, Bourne remains the most unexplored area. The back roads off County and Shore roads are lovely for bicycling, as are the peninsulas reached by Scraggy Neck Road and Wings Neck Road. Fishing, walking, and bicycling are prime activities along the Cape Cod Canal. In fact, there are over 1,695 acres of protected land along the canal for your enjoyment.

When Sandwich refused to grant Bourne its independence, the state legislature incorporated it in 1884. Originally known for its fishing wharves, shipbuilding, and factories, Bourne quickly attracted prominent vacationers to its sandy shores. Named for an affluent resident who made his fortune during the whaling heyday, Bourne encompasses 40 square miles and consists of nine tiny villages.

Sagamore, on both sides of the canal and on Cape Cod Bay, has more in common with Sandwich; it even has a renowned glassmaking factory. Bournedale, on the "mainland" and wedged between the two bridges, has a diminutive old red schoolhouse and a picturesque herring pond. And although Buzzards Bay, north and west of the Bourne Bridge, is the region's commercial center, it also offers some lovely glimpses of Buttermilk Bay. (Buzzards Bay, by the way, was misnamed by inexperienced birders. If the original settlers had gotten it right, it would be called Osprey Bay today.) On the western end of the canal, the Massachusetts Maritime Academy affords nice views of the canal as well as of handsome summer homes on the other side.

Across the 2,384-foot Bourne Bridge (almost twice as long as the Sagamore Bridge), the Cape villages of Monument Beach, Bourne Village, Gray Gables,

Pocasset, and Cataumet are tranquil in summer and downright sleepy in winter, although 20,000 people live there year-round. The first Summer White House was in Gray Gables, where President Grover Cleveland spent the season fishing during the 1890s. Monument Beach, Cataumet, and Pocasset are pleasant, residential, seaside towns with old houses, just west of Route 28. Residents don't take much notice of visitors; they just go about their business, fishing, shopping, raising children, and commuting to work.

Cataumet Pier was the site of the nation's first labor strike, when dockworkers demanded a 100 percent pay raise in 1864, from 15¢ per hour to 30¢.

GUIDANCE ❊ **Cape Cod Canal Region Chamber of Commerce** (508-759-6000; capecodcanalchamber.org), 70 Main Street, Buzzards Bay. Open 9–5 weekdays. This town booklet has a good regional map.

Herring Run Visitors Center (508-833-9678), Route 6 on the mainland side of the canal, about a mile south of the Sagamore Bridge. Open 10–5 daily late June to late October.

Cape Cod Canal Recreation Hotline (508-759-5991). A 24-hour number with up-to-date tide, weather, and canal recreation information provided by the U.S. Army Corps of Engineers.

PUBLIC RESTROOMS Located at the chamber office and Herring Run Visitors Center.

PUBLIC LIBRARY ❊ ✎ ⚲ ⚐ **Jonathan Bourne Public Library** (508-759-0644; bournelibrary.org), 19 Sandwich Road, Bourne. Open Tuesday through Saturday. Story hour and children's programs.

GETTING THERE *By car:* To reach Sagamore, take Exit 1 onto Route 6A from the Sagamore Bridge. To reach Bournedale and Buzzards Bay, take Route 6 west at the Sagamore Bridge. To reach the other villages, take the Bourne Bridge across the canal, and at the rotary take Shore Road. You can also whiz down Route 28 and head west to Pocasset, Cataumet, and Monument Beach.

By bus: **Bonanza/Peter Pan** (888-751-8800; peterpanbus.com) operates buses from Bourne to Boston as well

as Providence, New York City, and other points south and west of the Cape. The bus stops at the Tedeschi Food Shop at the Bourne Bridge rotary.

GETTING AROUND Bourne is quite spread out, so you'll need a car. The Cape Cod Canal has a great bicycle trail (see *To Do*).

MEDICAL EMERGENCY Call **911**.

It's not an "emergency" (the kind you'd expect under this category, anyway), but many area water wells have been contaminated by years of training with grenades and other live munitions at the Massachusetts Military Reservation. I drink bottled water on the Upper Cape.

✳ To See

Massachusetts Maritime Academy (508-830-5000; maritime.edu), Taylors Point, off Main Street, Buzzards Bay. The academy's presence explains why you'll see so many young men with close-cropped hair jogging along the canal bicycle trail. Although tours of the 55-acre campus are no longer conducted for the general public, you can arrange to tag along on a tour for prospective merchant-marine cadets. Not only will you see the oldest continuously operating maritime academy in the country (established in 1891) from an insider's perspective, but, if you're lucky, you'll also get to tour the cadets' training ship (the *Enterprise*) and eat in the cadets' dining hall overlooking the canal. Contact the Admissions office to arrange a tour.

Aptucxet Trading Post and Museum (508-759-9487), 24 Aptucxet Road, Bourne. From the Cape-side Bourne Bridge, follow signs for Mashnee Village, then Shore Road and Aptucxet Road. Open 10–4 daily May to mid-October. English settlers thought this location, near two rivers, was perfect for a post to promote trade with their neighbors, the Wampanoag Indians and the Dutch from New Amsterdam. Furs, sugar and other staples, tools, glass, tobacco, and cloth were bought and sold; wampum (carved quahog shells made into beads) served as currency. Cape Cod commerce was born.

The trading post you see today was built in 1927 by the Bourne Historical Society on the foundations of the original; a few bricks from the fireplace date to the Pilgrims. The hand-hewn beams and wide floor planks came from a 1600s house in Rochester, Massachusetts. On the grounds a small Victorian railroad station was used solely by President Grover Cleveland when he summered at his Gray Gables mansion in Monument Beach. You'll also find a Dutch-style windmill (which was intended merely "to add interest and beauty to the estate"), an 18th-century saltworks, an herb garden, a gift shop, and a shaded picnic area. Curator Eleanor Hammond is a treasure. Adults $4, children $2.

❧ **Bournedale Herring Run** (508-759-4431), Route 6, about a mile south of the Sagamore Bridge. Mid-April to early June. After the canal destroyed the natural herring run into Great Herring Pond, local engineers created an elaborate artificial watercourse to allow mature herring to migrate back to their birthplace. Each twice-daily tide brings thousands of the bony fish slithering upstream, navigating the pools created by wooden planks. In total, hundreds of thousands of herring pass through the Bournedale run annually. Kids really get a kick out of this spring ritual.

⚓ **National Marine Life Center**
(508-759-8722; nmlc.org), 120 Main
Street, Buzzards Bay. Open daily 10–5
late May to early September. In late
2008 a marine-animal rehabilitation
hospital opened to aid whales, dol-
phins, sea turtles, and seals that wash
ashore on Cape Cod and require medical attention before they can be set
free again. A Discovery Center offers
saltwater pools, interactive exhibits,
and a small science museum where
one learns about the impact of
humankind on the ocean.

BRIGGS MCDERMOTT HOUSE

Briggs McDermott House & Blacksmith Shop (508-759-6120), 522 Sandwich
Road, Bourne. Open 1–4 Tuesday, mid-June to late September. This early-19th-
century Greek Revival home—complete with period gardens, a carriage house
with quite a collection of carriages, and a granite-walled barn—is maintained by
the Bourne Society for Historic Preservation. Take a guided tour, on which docents
might discuss local architecture or former neighbor Grover Cleveland. Blacksmiths
operate a restored forge on site—complete with artifacts, tools, and a wagon—
where President Cleveland's horses were shod. Donations.

Mashnee Island. From the Cape side of the Bourne Bridge, take Shore Road and
follow signs for Mashnee Island. From the 2-mile-long causeway, there are lovely
views of summer homes dotting the shoreline, sailboats on the still waters, and the
distant railroad bridge and Bourne Bridge. Parking is nonexistent in summer, and
as the island is private, you'll have to turn around at the end of the causeway.

Massachusetts Military Reservation (Otis Air National Guard Base) (508-
968-4003), off the rotary at Routes 28 and 28A. The 21,000 acres east of Route 28
are a closed installation that contains Camp Edwards Army National Guard Training Site, Otis Air National Guard Base, the U.S. Coast Guard Air Station, the State
Army Aviation complex, and the PAVE PAWS radar station. The latter detects
nuclear missiles and tracks satellites (it was established during the cold war).

BOURNE RAILROAD BRIDGE

Although you won't read about it in
most guidebooks, the MMR has been
designated by the Pentagon as a federal environmental Superfund site since
1989. In 2007 there was discussion
about removing *portions* of the MMR
from the list. Most experts agreed that
it would take decades to clean up the
toxic cold war–era pollutants that are
contaminating an estimated 8 million
gallons of groundwater a day. Others
suggested it may be impossible to clean
up all the underground chemical
plumes that resulted from various
training exercises, landfill leaks, and oil

OUR VERY OWN PANAMA CANAL

The **Cape Cod Canal** (7.5 miles long) separates the mainland from Cape Cod. The canal, between 480 and 700 feet wide at various points, is the world's widest ocean-level canal. In 1623 Captain Myles Standish, eager to facilitate trade between New Amsterdam (New York City) and Plymouth Colony, was the first to consider creating a canal, which also would eliminate the treacherous 135-nautical-mile voyage around the tip of the Cape. George Washington brought up the idea again in the late 18th century as a means to protect naval ships and commercial vessels during war, but the first serious effort at digging a canal was not attempted until 1880, by the Cape Cod Canal Company.

For a few months, the company's crew of 500 immigrants dug with hand shovels and carted away the dirt in wheelbarrows. Then, in 1899, New York financier Augustus Belmont's Boston, Cape Cod, and New York Canal Company took over the project with more resolve. They began digging in 1909, and the canal opened to shipping 5 years later, on July 30, 1914. (It beat the Panama Canal opening by a scant 17 days.) On hand at the opening was then Assistant Secretary of the Navy Franklin D. Roosevelt. But the enterprise wasn't a financial success, because the canal was too narrow (it could handle only one-way traffic) and early drawbridges caused too many accidents. In 1928 the federal government purchased the canal, and the U.S. Army Corps of Engineers (USACE) built the canal we know today. The USACE has overseen the canal ever since. The canal provides a north–south shortcut for some 30,000 vessels each year, hundreds daily in summer. Water currents in the 32-foot-deep canal change direction every six hours.

The Buzzards Bay Vertical Railroad Bridge (western end of the canal at the **Buzzards Bay Recreation Area**) is the third longest vertical railway bridge in the world. (It stands 270 feet high and 540 feet long, but those in Chicago, Illinois, and on Long Island, New York, beat it.) The railroad bridge was completed the same year as the Sagamore and Bourne bridges. When trains approach, it takes 2 or 3 minutes for the bridge to lower and connect with the tracks on either side of it. The most reliable times (read: it's not so reliable) to witness this event are at 9:30 and 5 (more or less), when trains haul trash off-Cape. You might see the morning lowering at 7 AM too. Free parking. This is a good place to start the **bicycle trail** on this side of the canal.

There is great bicycling, fishing, boating, and walking from the canal shores. See the appropriate sections under *To Do*.

spills. The Environmental Protection Agency has mandated a cleanup, which will cost in the hundreds of millions of dollars.

SCENIC DRIVE See **Mashnee Island**, above.

✳ To Do

BICYCLING/RENTALS ✿ **Cape Cod Canal**. The canal is edged by level, well-maintained service roads perfect for biking. The mainland side has almost 7 miles of trail; the Cape side has 6.5 miles. Access points along the mainland side of the canal include Scusset State Park off Scusset Beach Road; the Sagamore Recreation Area off Canal Road at the Sagamore Bridge; near the Bournedale Herring Run in Bournedale; and beneath the Bourne Bridge. On the Cape side of the canal, there are access points from the Sandcatcher Recreation Area off Tupper Road in Sandwich; from Pleasant Street in Sagamore; and from the Bourne Bridge. If you want to cross the canal with your bike, use the Sagamore Bridge—its sidewalk is safer.

✳ **Sailworld Cape Cod** (508-759-6559; www.sailworld.com), 139 Main Street, Buzzards Bay. Bikes rent for $10 hourly, $18 for 3 hours, and $25 daily.

BOAT EXCURSIONS/RENTALS ✐ **Cape Cod Canal Cruises** (508-295-3883), off Routes 6 and 28 at the Onset Bay Town Pier (a few miles west of the mainland-side Bourne Bridge rotary), Onset. Operated by Hy-Line Cruises, these 2- and 3-hour tours—with running commentary—are conducted from May to mid-October. $14–20 adults, $7.50–10.50 children 5–12. There are also sunset cocktail cruises Tuesday through Thursday; moonlight and music cruises Friday and Saturday (21 and over only); jazz trips and dance cruises on Sunday afternoon; and a discounted family trip (children ride for free) every day at 4 PM. Reservations only accepted for jazz and moonlight cruises, or parties of 20 or more. These tours fill up, so book in advance.

FISHING Freshwater licenses are available from the clerk's office at the Bourne Town Hall (508-759-0600, ext. 505 on Perry Avenue. **Flax Pond** in Pocasset offers freshwater fishing.

For saltwater fishing, the banks of the Cape Cod Canal provide plenty of opportunities for catching striped bass, bluefish, cod, and pollack. Just bait your hook and cast away; no permits are required if you're fishing with a rod and line from the shore. Lobstermen pull traps from the shoreline. But there is no fishing, lobstering, or boat trolling permitted in the canal.

Maco's Bait and Tackle (508-759-9836), at Routes 6 and 28, Buzzards Bay. Open daily April through October.

See also **Bournedale Herring Run** under *To See*.

FOR FAMILIES ✐ **Water Wizz Water Park** (508-295-3255; waterwizz.com), Routes 6 and 28, a few miles west of the Bourne Bridge, Wareham. Open 10–6:30 daily, mid-June to early September. Southern New England's largest water park has it all: a 50-foot-high water slide with tunnels, tube rides, a hanging rope bridge, a wave pool, three kiddie water parks, and a river ride. As my dear friend Beth Anderson (who held a recent birthday party here for her son Charlie) said,

"It's a bit older and in need of some updates to the slides and physical plant, but it's very clean, organized, and well-run. And you can let kids run around without too much worry; the park is so heavily staffed with lifeguards that it's very safe for kids older than 5 or 6. It's much less expensive than larger parks, and the food selection and quality are good." If you're taller than 4 feet, tickets $30; otherwise, it's $15. Reduced admission after 4:30 PM.

✔ **Cartland of Cape Cod** (508-295-8360), 3044 Routes 6 and 28, East Wareham. Open daily in summer, weekends in spring and fall. Bumper boats, go-carts, air cannon, slip track, game room, batting cages, and mini-golf.

❋ ✔ **Ryan Family Amusements** (508-759-9892), 200 Main Street, Buzzards Bay. Bowling, a game room, and facilities for birthday parties.

See also **Cataumet Arts Center** under *Selective Shopping*.

HORSEBACK RIDING ❋ **Grazing Fields Farm** (508-759-3763), 201 Bournedale Road, off Head of the Bay Road, Buzzards Bay. Private and semiprivate lessons are offered.

ICE-SKATING **John Gallo Ice Arena** (508-759-8904, galloarena.com), 231 Sandwich Road, Buzzards Bay. Call or check the Web site for a highly variable public skating schedule.

SPECIAL PROGRAMS ✔ **U.S. Army Corps of Engineers** (508-833-9678; capedcodcanal.us), 60 Ed Moffitt Drive, Sandwich. Junior ranger programs (for ages 6–10) are usually offered free on Tuesday afternoons at 1 PM in July and August. Call for meeting place.

See also **Cataumet Arts Center** under *Selective Shopping*.

TENNIS Public courts are located at the old schoolhouse, County Road in Cataumet; at Chester Park, across from the old railroad station in Monument Beach; behind the Town Hall on Perry Avenue in Buzzards Bay; at the community center off Main Street in Buzzards Bay; and behind the fire station on Barlows Landing Road in Pocasset Village.

❋ Green Space

BEACHES The canal moderates considerable differences in tides between Buzzards Bay (4 feet) and Cape Cod Bay (9½ feet on average). Because of the swift currents caused by tides and because of heavy boat traffic, swimming is prohibited in the Cape Cod Canal.

Scusset and **Sagamore beaches**, Cape Cod Bay, Sagamore. Both beaches are located near the Sagamore Bridge via Scusset Beach Road. Facilities include changing areas, restrooms, and a snack bar. Parking fee.

Monument Beach, Buzzards Bay, on Emmons Road off Shore Road, Monument Beach. The warm waters of Buzzards Bay usually hover around 75 degrees in summer. This small beach has restrooms, a snack bar, and a lifeguard. Parking fee.

WALKS ❧ **Cape Cod Canal**. The U.S. Army Corps of Engineers (508-833-9678 or 508-759-4431, ext 622; capecodcanal.us), 60 Ed Moffitt Drive, Sandwich, offers numerous and excellent 1- to 2-hour guided programs from early July to mid-October. Look for walks and talks on Sagamore Hill history, managing canal maritime traffic, Bournedale history, astronomy, and dune-beach exploration. There is also biking and hiking along the canal. Call for meeting place. Free.

Red Brook Pond, Thaxter Road off Shore Road, Cataumet. Forty acres of wooded conservation land.

See also **Cape Cod Canal** under *To Do*.

✳ Lodging

There really aren't many places to stay in this quiet corner.

BED & BREAKFAST �֎ 😺 🌼 ⁛ᵀᵎ
Wood Duck Inn (508-564-6404; woodduckinnbb.com), 1050 County Road, Cataumet. This rustic 1848 farmhouse, less than 1 mile from the Vineyard ferry shuttle, sits on a rural road, has a sweeping lawn overlooking a cranberry bog, is a short walk to the harbor, and offers one- and two-room suites with private entrances. There are also miles of conservation paths near the inn and around the bog. Tree Tops, an efficiency unit with a kitchenette and geared to a family (if you don't mind a rollaway bed and fold-out couch), has a little balcony overlooking said bog. In the morning, innkeepers Dawn Champagne and Phil Duddy deliver a continental breakfast-in-a-basket. Children under 13 free. May through October $129–149; off-season $99–119. No credit cards.

CAMPGROUNDS ⁛ᵀᵎ **Bayview Campgrounds** (508-759-7610; bayviewcampground.com), 260 Route 28 (1 mile south of the Bourne Bridge). Open May to mid-October. Since only 21 of the 140 transient sites are set up for tenters, RVers make up the majority of guests. Season-long campers have settled into 250 more sites. $49–52 daily in-season, depending on electrical needs.

⁛ᵀᵎ **Bourne Scenic Park Campground** (508-759-7873; bournescenicpark.com), Route 6 on the mainland side of the canal, Buzzards Bay. Open late March to late October. Camping ($29–31 daily for tent sites, more for sites with electricity) is practically underneath the pylons of the Bourne Bridge. The same is true for the five rustic cabins ($50 daily, $250 weekly). Reservations recommended from late May to early September; required for cabins.

✳ Where to Eat

Despite the region's drive-through feel, there are a number of places to sit down.

♈ **Chart Room** (508-563-5350), Shipyard Lane off Shore Road at the Cataumet Marina. Open for lunch and dinner daily, early June to early September; weekends in May and October. It's bustling and boisterous and the wait is long, but the Chart Room epitomizes summertime dining on the Cape—with a great salty atmosphere and a cast of regulars. For the best sunset views from picturesque Red Brook Harbor, get a table on the edge of the outer dining room. The Chart Room serves killer mudslides and reliable sandwiches and seafood standards, including lobster salad (ask for it even if it's not on the menu), seafood bisque, and grilled swordfish. You won't find any fried seafood on the menu here. Vinny McGuiness and Tom Gordon have been co-chefs since the early 1980s. Live piano and bass duo nightly in summer. Lunch $10–26, dinner $10–36.

Y **Beachmoor Restaurant** (508-759-7522; beachmoor.com), Buttermilk Way, Taylor's Point, Buzzard's Bay.

Open for dinner Wednesday through Saturday, brunch on Sunday, April through December. This ocean-view fine dining establishment, located next to Massachusetts Maritime Academy and in business since 1995, offers traditional seafood dishes like broiled sea scallops and surf and turf. Dine fireside or on the waterside deck. If you're in the area, it's a nice place for a sunset drink. Dinner $13–28.

Y **Mashnee Island Grill** (508-759-9390; mashneeislandgrill.com), 162 Leeward Road, Bourne, to the left once you get on the island. Open lunch and dinner (various days) April through October. The cinder block beach bar doesn't look like much from the outside, but if you want to know something that not many locals know about, this is your chance. Nosh on burgers or black bean hummus with a margarita, watch Buzzards Bay from both sides (or watch a Red Sox game), and count yourself lucky.

✳ ✎ ♿ Y **The Courtyard** (508-563-1818; courtyardcapecod.com), Route 28A and County Road, Cataumet. Open for lunch and dinner. The outdoor summertime bar and courtyard are hopping. And the food is pretty good, too: lunchtime sandwiches and fish-and-chips, lighter salads, and whopping prime rib dinner specials. Entertainment nightly in the summer. Lunch $7–12, dinner $8–20.

✳ **Stir Crazy** (508-564-6464; stircrazyrestaurant.com), 626 Route 28, Pocasset. Open Tuesday through Sunday for dinner, Friday for lunch. This small, welcoming Asian restaurant features homemade Cambodian noodle dishes with fresh spices and vegetables. Request the level of spiciness you can take. Everything is prepared from scratch here, thanks to owner Bopha Samms. Lunch $5–8, dinner $13–16.

✎ **Lobster Trap** (508-759-3992; lobstertrap.net), 290 Shore Road, Bourne. Open for lunch and dinner daily, May through October. Every town has one restaurant that overlooks water and has the requisite nautical paraphernalia; this is Bourne's. The menu features daily specials, fried seafood, seafood rolls, and seafood plates. Lunch $9–19, dinner $11–30.

you see, but it won't be the last—there are five more on the Cape. This is the place where "everyone loves a bargain," and they've gone all out to get your attention: You can't miss the revolving windmill and thatched roof—made from Canadian marsh grass and so authentic that thatchers come from England and Ireland every other year

✳ Selective Shopping

❄ Unless otherwise noted, all shops are open year-round.

Pairpoint Crystal (508-888-2344; 800-899-0953; pairpoint.com), 851 Route 6A, Sagamore. Retail shop open daily; glassmaking 10–4 weekdays. This place has existed under one name or another since 1837. Thomas Pairpoint, a glass designer in the 1880s, used techniques created by Deming Jarves, and master craftspeople still employ these techniques here today. Clear or richly colored glass is hand blown, hand sculpted, or hand pressed on a 19th-century press. Through large picture windows you can watch the master glassblowers working on faithful period reproductions and candlesticks or more modern lamps, paperweights, and vases.

✦ **Cataumet Arts Center** (508-563-5434; cataumet-arts.org), 76 Scraggy Neck Road, off County Road and Route 28A, Cataumet. This community arts center has ever-changing exhibits; artists' studios to rent; classes for children, adults, printmakers, and others; and an airy gallery showcasing crafts, paintings, wearable art, and whimsical wooden sculptures. It's a beloved resource.

❦ **Christmas Tree Shops** (508-888-7010; christmastreeshops.com), on the Cape side of the Sagamore Bridge, Exit 1 off Route 6; open daily. This may be the first Christmas Tree Shop

to make repairs. As for the merchandise, it has little to do with Christmas. It revolves around inexpensive housewares, random gourmet food items, or miscellaneous clothing accessories. By the way, it's been owned by Bed, Bath, and Beyond since 2003.

✳ Special Events

Mid-September: **Bourne Scallop Festival**, Buzzards Bay Park (508-759-6000). A weekend celebration with games, concerts, and restaurants and vendors offering dishes that celebrate—what else?—the scallop. Rain or shine, as the eating takes place under a big tent; since 1969.

Early December: **Christmas in Old Bourne Village** (508-759-8167). A traditional holiday celebration with tree lighting.

SANDWICH

Sandwich is calm, even in the height of summer. Many visitors whiz right by it, eager to get farther away from the "mainland." Even people who know about delightful Sandwich Village often hop back onto Route 6 without poking around the rest of Sandwich—the back roads and historic houses off the beaten path. Those who take the time to explore will find that Sandwich is a real gem.

You could spend a day wandering the half-mile radius around the village center, a virtual time capsule spanning the centuries. Antiques shops, attractive homes, and quiet, shady lanes are perfect for strolling. Shawme Duck Pond, as idyllic as they come, is surrounded by historic houses (including one of the Cape's oldest), an old cemetery on the opposite shore, a working gristmill, swans and ducks, and plenty of vantage points from which to take it all in. A museum dedicated to the naturalist Thornton W. Burgess, a town resident and the creator of Peter Cottontail, also sits pondside. Both children and adults delight in the museum and in the Green Briar Nature Center & Jam Kitchen down the road. Sandwich's greatest attraction lies just beyond the town center: Heritage Museums & Gardens, a 76-acre horticulturist's delight with superb collections of Americana and antique automobiles.

Beyond the town center, the Benjamin Nye Homestead is worth a visit; have a look-see, even if it's closed, because it sits in a picturesque spot. East of town on Route 6A, past densely carpeted cranberry bogs (harvested in autumn), you'll find a few farm stands, antiques shops, and artisans' studios. At the town line with Barnstable, you'll find one of the Cape's best beaches and protected areas: Sandy Neck Beach (see the "Barrier Beach Beauty" sidebar in "Barnstable") and Sandy Neck Great Salt Marsh Conservation Area (see *Green Space* in "Barnstable"). The marina, off Tupper Road, borders the Cape Cod Canal with a recreation area. The often-overlooked town beach is nothing to sneeze at, either, and there are numerous conservation areas and ponds for walking and swimming.

Although a surprising number of Sandwich's 23,000 year-round residents commute to Boston every morning, their community dedication isn't diminished. A perfect example took place after fierce storms in August and October 1991 destroyed the town boardwalk, which had served the community since 1875. To replace it, townspeople purchased more than 1,700 individual boards, each personally inscribed, and a new boardwalk was built within eight months.

The oldest town on the Cape, Sandwich was founded in 1637 by the Cape's first permanent group of English settlers. The governor of Plymouth Colony had given

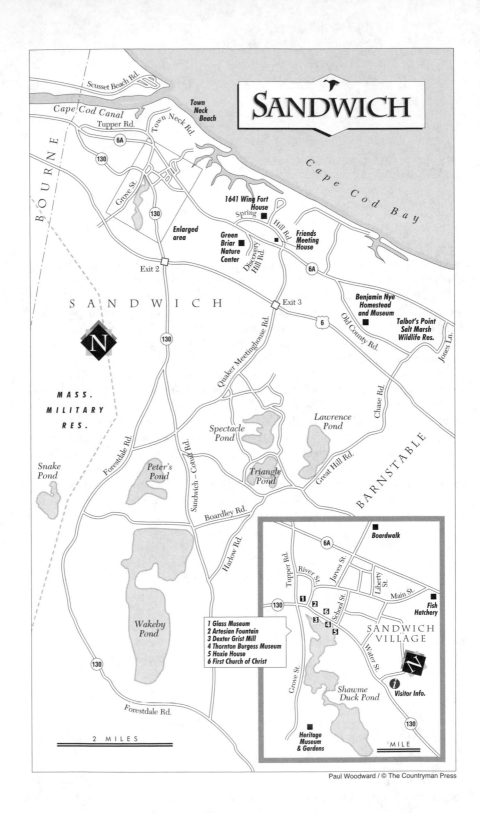

SANDWICH

Scusset Beach Rd.

Cape Cod Canal

Tupper Rd.

Town Neck Rd.

Town Neck Beach

6A

130

BOURNE

Grove St.

130

Enlarged area

Exit 2

1641 Wing Fort House

Spring

Hill Rd.

Friends Meeting House

Green Briar Nature Center

Discovery Hill Rd.

6A

Cape Cod Bay

SANDWICH

130

N

MASS. MILITARY RES.

Exit 3

6

Benjamin Nye Homestead and Museum

Old County Rd.

Talbot's Point Salt Marsh Wildlife Res.

Jones Ln.

Quaker Meetinghouse Rd.

Spectacle Pond

Lawrence Pond

Chase Rd.

Great Hill Rd.

BARNSTABLE

Snake Pond

Forestdale Rd.

Peter's Pond

Sandwich–Cotuit Rd.

Triangle Pond

Boardley Rd.

Harlow Rd.

Wakeby Pond

130

Forestdale Rd.

2 MILES

Tupper Rd.

River St.

Jarves St.

6A

Boardwalk

Liberty St.

Main St.

School St.

1
2
6
3
4
5

130

Grove St.

Water St.

SANDWICH VILLAGE

N

Fish Hatchery

1 Glass Museum
2 Artesian Fountain
3 Dexter Grist Mill
4 Thornton Burgess Museum
5 Hoxie House
6 First Church of Christ

Shawme Duck Pond

i Visitor Info.

130

Heritage Museum & Gardens

1 MILE

permission to "tenn men from Saugust" (now Lynn, Massachusetts) to settle the area with 60 families. Sandwich was probably chosen for its close proximity to the Manomet (now Aptuxcet) Trading Post (see *To See* in "Bourne") and for its abundant salt-marsh hay, which provided ready fodder for the settlers' cows. Agriculture supported the community until the 1820s, when Deming Jarves, a Boston glass merchant, decided to open a glassmaking factory. The location couldn't have been better: There was a good source of sand (although more was shipped in from New Jersey), sea salt was plentiful, salt-marsh hay provided packaging for the fragile goods, and forests were thick with scrub pines to fuel the furnaces. But by the 1880s, midwestern coal-fueled glassmaking factories and a labor strike shut down Sandwich's factories. The story is told in great detail at the excellent Sandwich Glass Museum. Today, glassblowers work in a few studios in town.

Sandwich was named, by the way, for the English town, not for the sandwich-creator earl, as many think. (That Earl of Sandwich was born 81 years after this town was founded.)

GUIDANCE ❊ "ı" **Sandwich Visitor Information Center** (508-833-9755; sand wichchamber.com), 4 Water Street. Information Center open 10–4 Monday through Saturday, 1–4 Sunday, mid-May to mid-October. Located within the Thornton W. Burgess Museum (see *To See*), these folks offers helpful advice. You can also find a good village walking guide at many shops in town. FYI: the chamber, a distinct entity, is open year round 9–5 weekdays.

U.S. Army Corps of Engineers (USACE) Visitors Center (508-833-9678), Ed Moffit Drive, east of the Sandwich Marina. Open Thursday through Sunday mid-May to late June; daily late June to late October. Staffed by USACE personnel, the office dispenses information about boating, fishing, camping, and other canal activities. Highlights of the center include historic photos, interactive monitors, and a small theater showing films on canal history, critters, and wildflowers. Inquire about their hikes, lectures, and other programs.

PUBLIC RESTROOMS Seasonal restrooms are located across from Town Hall and at Russell's Corner.

PUBLIC LIBRARY ❊ ✂ ↑ "ı" **Sandwich Public Library** (508-888-0625; sand wichpubliclibrary.com), 142 Main Street. Open Tuesday through Saturday year round, and 1–5 Sunday early September to late May. You can borrow toys and videos here.

GETTING THERE *By car:* Take the Sagamore Bridge to Route 6 east to Exit 2 (Route 130 North) and travel 2 miles to Main Street. From Exit 1 and Route 6A, you can take Tupper Road or Main Street into the village center.

By bus: There is no bus service to Sandwich proper, but **Plymouth & Brockton** (508-778-9767; p-b.com) buses bound for Boston stop at the Sagamore Bridge, behind McDonald's in the commuter parking lot. For points south and west (off Cape, **Bonanza** (888-751-8800; peterpanbus.com) buses stop nearby in Bourne.

GETTING AROUND Sandwich Village is perfect for strolling, but you'll have to get back in your car to reach the marina and Heritage Museums & Gardens (see *To See*).

MEDICAL EMERGENCY Call **911**.

It's not an "emergency" (the kind you'd expect under this category, anyway), but many area water wells have been closed in recent years. They've been contaminated by years of training with grenades and other live munitions at the Massachusetts Military Reservation. I drink bottled water on the Upper Cape.

✳ To See

In Sandwich Village

✑ **Dexter Grist Mill** (508-888-1173), on Shawme Duck Pond, Water Street. Open 10–5 Monday through Saturday and 1–5 Sunday, mid-June to mid-October. The circa-1640 mill has had a multiuse past, and the site wasn't always as quaint as it is now. The mill was turbine powered during Sandwich's glassmaking heyday; it then sat idle until 1920, when it was converted into a tearoom. After adjacent mills were torn down in the late 1950s, it was opened to tourists in 1961, with the cypress waterwheel you see today. On-site miller Harold Shurtleff describes the intricacies of the milling process. You can purchase stone-ground cornmeal—great for muffins, Indian pudding, and polenta. Adults $3; children 5–15, $2; under 5, free. Combination ticket with Hoxie House: adults $5; children 5–15, $3.

✑ **Thornton W. Burgess Museum** (508-888-4668; thorntonburgess.org), 4 Water Street. Open 10–4 Monday through Saturday and 1–4 Sunday, May through October. This Sandwich native and renowned children's author and naturalist wrote more than 15,000 stories and 170 books featuring the escapades of Jimmy Skunk, Grandfather Frog, and the beloved Peter Cottontail (not to be confused with Beatrix Potter's Peter Rabbit). The house features Burgess's books, original Harrison Cady illustrations, and exhibits honoring Burgess's life and work. Don't miss story time, which takes place on Monday, Wednesday, and Saturday mornings at 10:30 on the lawn in July and August; $1 per person. The Thornton Burgess Society was begun by local bookseller Nancy Titcomb (see *Selective Shopping*) in 1974 to celebrate the centennial of Burgess's birth. Suggested donations: adults $2, children $1. (See also Green Briar Nature Center & Jam Kitchen under *Green Space*.)

Artesian fountain, between the gristmill and Town Hall. Join residents by filling water jugs with what some consider the Cape's best water, reportedly untainted by the plume of pollution that affects Upper Cape tap water.

✇ **Hoxie House** (508-888-1173), 18 Water Street. Open 10–5 Monday through Saturday and 1–5 Sunday, mid-June to mid-October. For a long time this circa-1640 structure was thought to be the Cape's oldest saltbox, but it's impossible to know definitively since the Barnstable County Courthouse deeds were lost in a fire. Nonetheless, the house has a rare saltbox roofline, small diamond-shaped leaded windows, and a fine vantage above Shawme Duck Pond. Thanks to loaner furniture from Boston's Museum of Fine Arts, the restored interior looks much as it did during colonial times. One of the most

DEXTER GRIST MILL ON SHAWME POND

SAND TRANSFORMED

🐾 ✎ 🍽 **Sandwich Glass Museum** (508-888-0251; sandwichglassmuseum .org), 129 Main Street. Open 9:30–5 daily, April through December; 9:30–4 Wednesday through Sunday, February through March. If you're in the habit of skipping town historical museums, break the habit this time; you won't be disappointed. During the 19th century, Sandwich glassmaking flourished at Deming Jarves's Boston & Sandwich Glass Company (1825–1888) and the Cape Cod Glass Works (1859–1869). Today this internationally known museum, operated by the Sandwich Historical Society, chronologically displays thousands of decorative and functional glass objects, which became increasingly more elaborate and richly colored as the years progressed. Many displays are dramatically backlit by natural light streaming through banks of windows. Check out the elaborate table setting featuring Hannah Rebecca Burgess's late-1800s collection; a 20-minute multimedia presentation that describes the first 200 years of Sandwich's history; and a diorama with voiceovers showing and telling how the glass was made. You'll also enjoy glassblowing demonstrations, and the contemporary gallery with changing exhibits. Adults $5; children 6–14, $1.25.

remarkable facts about this house is that it was occupied without electricity or indoor plumbing until the 1950s. The house was named for Abraham Hoxie, who purchased it in 1860 for $400. The Reverend John Smith lived here in 1675 when he came to be minister of the First Parish Church. The rather fun tours include more of a social historical view rather than emphasizing dates. Adults $3; children 5–15, $2. Combination ticket with Dexter Grist Mill: adults $5; children 5–15, $3.

First Church of Christ, 136 Main Street. This Christopher Wren–inspired church with a tall white spire was built in 1847, but its brass bell, cast in 1675, is thought to be the country's oldest.

Town Hall (508-888-5144), 130 Main Street. Sandwich has certainly gotten its money's worth out of this Greek Revival building. It was constructed at a cost of little more than $4,000 in 1834 and still serves as the center for town government.

Old Town Cemetery, Grove Street, on the shore opposite the Hoxie House and Thornton W. Burgess

Museum. You'll recognize the names on many gravestones (including those of Burgess, Bodfish, and Bourne) from historic houses and street signs around town. Although the oldest marker dates to 1683, most are from the 1700s; many are marked with a winged skull, a common Puritan design.

Elsewhere around town

❋ ❧ **Heritage Museums & Gardens** (508-888-3300; heritagemuseumsand gardens.org), 67 Grove Street. Open 10–5 daily early April to late October. Established in 1969 by Josiah K. Lilly III, a descendant of the founder of the pharmaceutical firm Eli Lilly and Company, this place is an oasis for garden lovers, antiques and vintage-car buffs, and Americana enthusiasts. These 100 acres are planted with outstanding collections of rhododendrons, including the famous Dexter variety, which blooms from late May to early June. (Charles O. Dexter was the estate's original owner, and he experimented with hybridizing here.) There are also impressive collections of holly bushes, heathers, hostas, hydrangeas, and over 1,000 daylilies, which bloom from mid-July to early August. Don't miss the labyrinth or the Hart family maze garden. The estate is equally pleasant for an autumn walk.

The **American History Museum** features an extensive collection of bird carvings by Elmer Crowell in addition to a large array of hand-painted miniatures, while the J. K. Lilly III **Antique Automobile Museum**, in the replica **Shaker Round Barn**, houses the museum's outstanding vintage-car collection. A 1930 Duesenberg built for Gary Cooper and President Taft's White Steamer (the first official auto of the White House) are a two of the mint-condition classics.

The **Art Museum** features folk art, scrimshaw, cigar-store figures, weather vanes, and Currier & Ives lithographs. Also on the grounds you'll find an 1800 windmill, an operational Coney Island–style 1912 carousel, and the **Carousel Café**. The alfresco café has a limited but more-than-adequate menu of overstuffed sandwiches, salads, and desserts. A trolley can transport people around the grounds, but it is neither intended for sightseeing nor always available. Keep your eyes peeled for museum special events, including plant sales, concerts, and car shows. Gift and garden shop at the entrance. Adults $12; seniors $10; youths 4–16, $6.

Benjamin Nye Homestead and Museum (508-888-2368; nyefamily.org), 85 Old County Road, East Sandwich. Open noon–4:30 Tuesday through Saturday, mid-June to mid-October. Off Route 6A, this 1685 homestead belonged to one of Sandwich's first settlers and has undergone many structural changes over the years. Although it began life as a small narrow house with a central chimney, an addition turned it into a saltbox. A second floor created the full Colonial you see today. Although the interior is hardly a purist restoration, you'll see some of the original construction, early paneling, 18th-century wallpaper, a rosewood melodeon built the Nye in the 1850s, a spinning wheel, and hand-woven sheets. Adults $3, children $1.

1641 Wing Fort House, 69 Spring Hill Road (off Route 6A), East Sandwich. Open 10–4 Tuesday through Saturday. The Wing house is the country's oldest home continuously inhabited by the same family. This circa-1646 house began as a one-room cottage when Stephen Wing, descendant of the Reverend John Wing, arrived with his new bride. In the mid-1800s, a second house was added to it to create the current three-quarter Colonial. Nominal admission.

Friends Meeting House, Quaker Road, off Spring Hill Road (from Route 6A),

East Sandwich. Meetings Sunday at 10 AM. The building standing today was built in 1810, the third Quaker meetinghouse on this site. The congregation has been meeting since 1657, which makes it the oldest continuous meeting in North America. The interior is simple, with pews and a wood-burning stove stoked in winter for 25 or so congregants.

❊ ♪ **Sandwich Fish Hatchery** (508-888-0008), Route 6A at Old Main Street. Open 9–3 daily. More than 200,000 trout at various stages of development are raised to stock the state's ponds. Throw in pellets of food (bring quarters for the vending machines) and watch 'em swarm.

♪ **Boardwalk**, Harbor Street off Factory Street. The boardwalk crosses marshland, Mill Creek, and low dunes to connect to Town Neck Beach (see *Green Space*). Depending on the season, you might see teens jumping into the creek (1½ hours before and after high tide) or blue heron poking around the tidal pools and tall grasses. There are expansive views at the end of the 1,350-foot walkway.

❊ To Do

BLUEBERRY PICKING **The Blueberry Bog**, Spring Hill off Route 6A. In the 1940s, this former cranberry bog was turned into a blueberry farm. Today there are about 400 bushes on more than 4 acres. The fruit matures from early to mid-July through August; pick your own by the quart or pound.

BICYCLING **Sandwich Cycles** (508-833-2453), 40 Route 6A. Open April to early November. Standard bikes rent for $5 hourly, $20 daily, and $70 weekly. This is the only bike shop on the Cape that rents recumbents.

CANOEING **Shawme Duck Pond**, Water Street (Route 130), is actually linked to two other ponds, so you can do a lot of canoeing here.

Scorton Creek. Head east on Route 6A, turn right onto a gravel road before reaching the Scorton Creek Bridge. This is a good place for picnics, too.

Wakeby Pond, off Cotuit Road, South Sandwich.

A PERFECT DAY IN SANDWICH

  8:15 Swivel at counter seats at the diner-style Marshland Restaurant.

  9:30 Locate 17th-century gravestones at the Old Town Cemetery.

10:30 Fill glass containers with clear water from the artesian fountain.

10:45 Feed ducks, geese, and swans at Shawme Pond.

11:15 Visit one of a remarkable trio of houses dating to the mid–17th century: Wing Fort House, Hoxie House, or Benjamin Nye Homestead.

12:45 Gather bread, cheese, and wine from the Brown Jug.

  2:00 Peruse used, rare, and new tomes at Titcomb's Book Shop.

  3:00 Learn about the process of glassmaking, and see stunning examples of antique glass, at the fine Sandwich Glass Museum.

  6:30 Dine at Aqua Grille or Amari, depending on your mood.

  8:30 Indulge in a hot fudge sundae from Twin Acres Ice Cream.

FISHING Freshwater fishing licenses and regulations can be procured from the Town Clerks Office (508-888-0340), Main Street.

For saltwater fishing (no permit required), **Sandcatcher Recreation Area** (at the Sandwich Marina) and **Scusset Beach State Reservation** Pier (off Scusset Beach Road from the rotary on the mainland side of the canal) are good places to cast a line into the Cape Cod Canal.

GOLF ✳ **Holly Ridge** (508-428-5577), off Route 130, South Sandwich. An 18-hole, 3,000-yard, par-54 course.

✳ **Sandwich Halls Golf Club** (508-888-3384), Exit 3 (off Round Hill Road) off Route 6, East Sandwich. An 18-hole, par-71 course.

MINI-GOLF ✐ **Sandwich Minigolf** (508-833-1905), 159 Route 6A. Open weekends mid-May to mid-October and daily in summer. This course, which has a cult-like following, is set on a cranberry bog and boasts a floating raft for a green! An honest-to-goodness stream winds around many of the 34 holes. Unable to verify prices at press time.

SCENIC RAILROAD ✐ **Cape Cod Central Railroad** (508-771-3800; 888-797-7245; capetrain.com), 252 Main Street (Main and Center streets). Weekends in late May, June, September, and late October; daily in July and August. The 48-mile trip takes 2 hours and passes alongside cranberry bogs and the Sandy Neck Great Salt Marsh. Since there are typically two trains daily, you can take the first one from Hyannis, hop off in Sandwich, walk around Sandwich center for 3 hours, and then catch the next train back to Hyannis. The best part of this trip is the local narration—unless you've never been on a train before, in which case, the simple act of taking a train will tickle you more. Adults $20; seniors $18; children 12 and under, $16.

TENNIS Public courts are located at **Wing Elementary School** on Route 130, **Oak Ridge School** and Sandwich High school, both off Quaker Meetinghouse Road, and **Forestdale School** off Route 130.

CAPE COD CENTRAL RAILROAD

✳ Green Space

✐ **Green Briar Nature Center & Jam Kitchen** (508-888-6870; thornton burgess.org), 6 Discovery Hill Road off Route 6A, East Sandwich. Trails open year-round. Open 10–4 Monday through Saturday and 1–4 Sunday, April through December; 10–4 Tuesday through Saturday, January through March. Guided tours, plus a dessert featuring berries, at 10:30 on Tuesday and Thursday (adults $5, children $3). Jam-cooking demonstrations most days April through December. Even in an area with so many tranquil spots,

Green Briar rises to the top. It's run by the **Thornton W. Burgess Society** "to re-establish and maintain nature's fine balance among all living things and to hold as a sacred trust the obligation to make only the best use of natural resources." Located on Smiling Pond and adjacent to the famous Briar Patch of Burgess's stories, these 57 acres of conservation land have many short interpretive nature trails (less than a mile long), a lovely wildflower garden, and an educational facility that rehabilitates injured animals. The society hosts natural history classes, lectures, nature walks, and other programs. Young children enjoy creeping along marsh creeks in search of hermit crabs, while older children take canoeing expeditions and learn Native American crafts and lore. Donations suggested.

SANDWICH BOARDWALK

The **Jam Kitchen** was established in 1903 by Ida Putnam, who used her friend Fanny Farmer's recipes to make jams, jellies, and fruit preserves. Step inside the old-fashioned, aromatic, and homey place to see mason jars filled with apricots and strawberries and watch fruit simmering on vintage-1920 Glenwood gas stoves. Two-hour workshops on preserving fruit and making jams and jellies are also held. About this place, Burgess said to Putnam in 1939, "It is a wonderful thing to sweeten the world which is in a jam and needs preserving." Different berry festivals are held throughout summer: look for strawberries in June, blueberries in August, and cranberries in September.

✍ **Shawme Duck Pond**, Water Street (Route 130), in the village center. Flocks of ducks, geese, and swans know a good thing when they find it. And even though this idyllic spot is one of the most easily accessible on the Cape, it remains a tranquil place for humans and waterfowl alike. Formerly a marshy brook, the willow-lined pond was dammed prior to the gristmill operating in the 1640s. It's a nice spot to canoe.

❋ 🐾 ✍ **Shawme-Crowell State Forest** (508-888-0351; 877-422-6762 reservations; reserveamerica.com), Route 130. You can walk, bicycle, and camp ($12–14 nightly) at 285 sites on 742 acres. When the popular Nickerson State Park (see the sidebar "A Supreme State Park" in "Brewster") is full of campers, there are often dozens of good sites still available here. There are also four yurts—reservations required.

❋ 🐾 ✍ **Scusset Beach State Reservation** (508-888-0859; 877-422-6762 reservations; reserveamerica.com), on Cape Cod Bay, off Scusset Beach Road from the mainland side of the canal. The 380-acre reservation offers about 100 campsites (primarily used by RVers, but 5 tent sites are also available) in-season, bicycling, picnicking, and walking opportunities. Facilities include in-season lifeguard, restrooms, changing rooms, and a snack bar. Parking $7. Camping $20–22 nightly.

See also **Giving Tree Gallery and Sculpture Gardens** under *Selective Shopping*.

BEACHES Town Neck Beach, on Cape Cod Bay, off Town Neck Road and Route 6A. This pebble beach extends 1.5 miles from the Cape Cod Canal to Dock Creek. Visit at high tide if you want to swim; at low tide, it's great for walking. Parking $10; free after 3 PM; the lot rarely fills up.

See also **Scusset Beach State Reservation**, above.

PONDS Wakeby Pond (off Cotuit Road), South Sandwich, offers freshwater swimming and picnicking.

WALKS Talbot's Point Salt Marsh Wildlife Reservation, off Old County Road from Route 6A. This little-used, 1.52-mile (roundtrip) hiking trail winds past red pines, beeches, and a large salt marsh.

See also **Green Briar Nature Center & Jam Kitchen** and **Shawme-Crowell State Forest**.

✳ Lodging

☙ Sandwich's historic hostelries provide great diversity, something for everyone—from an incredibly impressive church conversion to a large motor inn.

RESORT MOTOR INN ✳ ✎ ⁍T⁌
Dan'l Webster Inn & Spa (508-888-3622; 800-444-3566; danlwebsterinn.com), 149 Main Street. Modeled after an 18th-century hostelry where Revolutionary patriots met, today's motor inn has a certain colonial charm that's vigilantly maintained by the Catanias, owners since 1980. Most of the 48 traditionally decorated rooms and suites are of the top-notch motel/hotel variety. A minority are more distinctively innlike and found in two separate older houses; an attractive pool is well sited behind the inn; touring motor coaches are part of the parking lot landscape. Amenities include turndown service, room service, daily newspaper at your door, the **Beach Plum Spa** (with massages, pedicures, manicures, and body treatments), and five well-regarded dining rooms (see *Dining Out*). Guests also have privileges at the nearby

Sportsite Health & Racquet Club. Children under 12 free. June to mid-October $189–389; off-season $129–299; off-season packages.

INNS ✳ ⁍T⁌ **Belfry Inne** (508-888-8550; 800-844-4542; belfryinn.com), 8 Jarves Street. Innkeeper Chris Wilson lords over the center of town with a circa-1900 **Abbey**, a circa-1879 **Painted Lady**, and the 1830s Federal-style **Village House**. Between the three, about 30 guest rooms are outfitted with fine antiques and tasteful furnishings. Abbey rooms are downright spectacular: outfitted with stained glass, flying buttresses, fancy linens, bold colors, beds made from pews, gas fireplaces, Jacuzzis, and balconies. Chris and his architect deserve awards for this spectacular conversion. Most Painted Lady rooms have whirlpools, while Village House rooms are relatively modest with hardwood floors (some bleached) and down comforters. Both the Abbey and Painted Lady offer dining to the public (see *Dining Out*). Because of the size of the operation, service can sometimes be uneven. Full breakfast included. Abbey $315, Painted Lady $215, Village House $179; less from December through April.

BED & BREAKFASTS ❄ "ᵼ" **Isaiah Jones Homestead** (508-888-9115; 800-526-1625; isaiahjones.com), 165 Main Street. This Victorian gem in the middle of the village deserves your full attention. Filled with killer antiques and showing lots of elegant decorating prowess, there isn't one single room I'd hesitate to recommend. Although the Web site photos may seem too fussy, it's not at all the case. The delightful innkeepers Katherine and Don Sanderson, presiding since 2007, serve a 3-course candlelit breakfast and outfit their seven rooms with cable TV/DVD and a fireplace or gas stove. For more privacy, choose the adjacent carriage house with whirlpool tubs, robes, and upscale amenities. Children over 12 welcome. Mid-June through October $190–300; off-season $165–200.

❄ "ᵼ" **Annabelle Bed and Breakfast** (508-833-1419; annabellebedandbreakfast.com), 4 Grove Street. Although I didn't get a chance to see this romantic and elegant B&B for this edition, its reputation preceded it with practically everyone I spoke with who overnighted in Sandwich. Paula and Brian Murphy, innkeepers since 2006, offer six rooms, two of which can be converted into a suite with a shared bath. Most have a whirlpool for soaking; all have flat-screen TVs and fine linens. Perched on a private knoll within a few hundred yards of the gristmill, the location of this contemporary (but architecturally significant) house couldn't be better. A full breakfast and evening wine are included, and spa services are available. Children over 12 welcome, Early May to late October $165–235; off-season $155–195.

Bay Beach (508-888-8813; 800-475-6398; baybeach.com), 3 Bay Beach Lane. Open early May to late October. You'd be hard pressed to sleep closer to dune grass than at this B&B. Located right smack on a private beach, with floor-to-ceiling views of the Cape Cod Canal's east entrance, Emily and Reale Lemieux's contemporary house has three luxurious rooms with air-conditioning, fresh flowers daily, refrigerators, outdoor decks, lots of sliding doors, whirlpools, and gas fireplaces. Upon arrival you'll receive a welcome basket with wine and cheese, and while there is no fixed breakfast, the refrigerator is stocked with breakfast items. No children under 16. Rooms $245–285.

❄ "ᵼ" **1750 Inn at Sandwich Center** (508-888-6958; 800-249-6949; innatsandwich.com), 118 Tupper Road. Expert service and hospitality are the watchwords at this five-room inn operated by lovely innkeepers Jan and Charlie Preus. They serve fancy breakfasts (like macadamia nut French toast or quichettes served in individual ramekins) in the keeping room—complete with a beehive oven—or on the patio. And they set out brandy and cookies in the evening. Guests gather in the living room surrounded by period architectural details and are regaled with vivid stories about the inn's history. The two choice guest rooms, painted in soothing colors, are the upper floor front rooms. Come off-season to best enjoy the fireplaces (in most rooms). Loaner bikes available; children over 12 welcome. Mid-June to mid-October $149–179; off-season $119–149.

❄ 🐾 **Wingscorton Farm Inn** (508-888-0534), 11 Wing Boulevard, East Sandwich. A throwback to another era, this circa-1758 working farm, on 13 acres of orchards and woods, is a rare bird, a truly astonishing piece of craftsmanship. Once a stop on the Underground Railroad, the house features low ceilings, wainscoting, wide-plank floors, rich paneling, and wood-burning fireplaces in the guest rooms. Along with two living rooms (one of which has the largest hearth in New England), guests enjoy three suites (each with refrigerator, fine period antiques, Oriental carpets, and canopy bed) and a two-story carriage house with a private deck and patio, full

INN AT SANDWICH CENTER

kitchen, and woodstove. Innkeeper Sheila Weyers includes a multicourse breakfast, which is served at a long harvest table. Dogs and cats roam around the property, which is also home to pygmy goats, horses, and sheep. Free-range chickens and fresh eggs are sold from the barn. Walk to the inn's private bay beach. Smoking permitted. Rooms $190–235; $25–50 nightly per child.

COTTAGES & MOTELS **Pine Grove Cottages** (508-888-8179; pinegrovecottages.com), 358 Route 6A, East Sandwich. Open May to early November. These 10 tidy cottages with kitchens (freshly painted white) come in various sizes: from tiny one-rooms to small and larger one-bedrooms to "deluxe" two-bedroom cottages, which are about 20 feet by 24 feet. Although guests spend most of their time at the beach, there is also a pool and play area in the pine grove. Mid-June to early September $400–775 weekly for two to four people; off-season $50–85 nightly.

❄ "🍴" **Spring Garden Inn** (508-888-0710; 800-303-1751; springgarden.com), 578 Route 6A, East Sandwich. Reserve early if you can; this is one of the best motels on Route 6A. Although modest from the street, the bilevel motel overlooks a salt marsh and the Scorton River, particularly beautiful at sunset. The peaceful backyard is dotted with lawn chairs, grills, and picnic tables. Owners Linda Gruberski and Jesse Hawkins have eight carpeted rooms with knotty-pine paneling, two double beds, air-conditioning, refrigerator, and telephone. In addition, there are two efficiencies and a two-room suite with a private deck. An outdoor pool is nicely shielded from Route 6A. Children under 12 free. June through August $105–130; off-season $79–99; continental breakfast included.

ISIAH JONES HOMESTEAD

❉ 🐾 **Shadynook Inn & Motel** (508-888-0409; 800-338-5208; shadynookinn
.com), 14 Route 6A. This spiffy, shaded motel (with 30 units) has lush land-scaping and a heated outdoor pool. The large rooms are typically appoint-ed as far as motel rooms go, only a bit nicer, while some of the two-room suites are more like efficiencies. In 2007 kitchens were remodeled and hardwood floors added. Children under 12, free. Mid-June to early September $109–142 for two to four people; off-season $75–95.

CAMPGROUND 🐾 "ℐ" **Peters Pond Park** (508-477-1775; peterspond.com),

185 Cotuit Road. Open mid-April to mid-October. The park offers 463 well-groomed campsites, walking trails, summertime children's activities, a ballfield, 2 beaches, a campfire ring, and a popular spring-fed lake for trout and bass fishing, boating, and swim-ming. Campsites $35–75 in-season, cottages $850 weekly in-season, $150 daily off-season. Rental rowboats, pad-dleboats, and kayaks are also available.

See also **Shawme-Crowell State Forest** and **Scusset Beach State Reservation** under *Green Space*.

RENTAL HOUSES AND COTTAGES
Beach Realty (800-886-4998; beachrealtycapecod.com), 133 North Shore Boulevard, East Sandwich.

❉ Where to Eat

Sandwich eateries run the gamut, from fine dining in a former church to casu-al eating in a tiny tea shop.

DINING OUT ❉ 🦞 ✐ ℐ **Amari** (508-375-0011; amarirestaurant.com), Route 6A, East Sandwich. Open for dinner. On the town line with Barnstable and near Sandy Neck Beach, this upscale but comfortable eatery has a little something for everyone. Dine within sight of an open kitchen, surrounded by lots of mahogany, on Italian cooking with a contemporary flair. Try a wood oven pizza, antipasti like tomato and mozzarella, pasta specialties like *zuppa de pesce*, classics like scampi, or grilled specialties like a 15-ounce steak! Owner Craig Austin has presided over this neighborhoody place since open-ing it in 1999. Dinner $14–23.

❉ ℐ ⅙ **Belfry Bistro** (508-888-8550; belfryinn.com), 8 Jarves Street. Open for dinner. The quiet setting (inside a converted church) is divinely dramat-ic—with soaring beadboard ceilings, stained glass, interior flying buttresses,

	King	King	Queen	Queen	Double	Twins	Double	Double	
	170	170	160	140	100	130	75	75	

a confessional converted into a tasteful bar, and a former altar set with tables. It's also elegant—with candlelight, damask-covered tables, high-backed leather chairs, and a wood-burning fireplace. Tasteful al fresco terrace dining is available, but it seems a waste not to sit indoors here. For me, it's more about the setting than the food, which can seem pricey. Having said that, the menu features dishes like sautéed lobster and gulf shrimp and oven roasted rack of lamb. Early specials. Dinner $18–34.

❋ ✍ ♿ **Dan'l Webster Inn** (508-888-3622; danlwebsterinn.com), 149 Main Street. Open for breakfast, lunch, dinner, and Sunday brunch. Chef Steve Chausse's kitchen serves (surprisingly) contemporary creative and classic American dishes in comfortable dining rooms. The sunlit and elegant Conservatory is an indoor oasis; the Music Room is more intimate and traditional; and the Tavern is delightfully casual and has lighter fare. The menu changes seasonally and includes entrées that you can order in either full or half sizes. Look for Green Palate selections, featuring organic and more health-conscious dishes; there's

also a Saturday evening piano player. By the way, the inn has an excellent water-filtration system, and its water is perhaps the best tasting on the Cape. Early specials. Breakfast $5–18, lunch $8–20, dinner $9–34.

EATING OUT ♨ ✍ ☕ ♿ **Aqua Grille** (508-888-8889; aquagrille.com), 14 Gallo Road, at the marina. Open for lunch and dinner mid-April to late October. Quite good (especially for the money), the Aqua Grille's eclectic regional American menu features ubiquitous fried seafood and lobster, but also pasta dishes, grilled meats, and fish prepared in a variety of ways. Since Chef Gert Rausch spent many years in Austin and Aspen, look for modern interpretations of quesadillas (with smoked chicken and corn, perhaps). The grille is a spacious, pleasant, and modern place with aqua walls, and some Naugahyde, banquette-style booths. The marina and canal are visible from most tables. Brought to you by the owners of the Paddock in Hyannis, these folks know what they're doing—witness the low staff turnover! (So when a waiter suggests you *not* have something, listen to him or her.) Early specials; entertainment on Friday nights. Lunch $7–16, dinner $9–22; prime rib night on Wednesdays $21.

The Brown Jug (508-888-0053; thebrownjug.com), 1 Jarves Street. Open daily mid-April to mid-January, except closed Monday off-season. Proprietors Michael Johnston and Steven Cox taste everything they sell at the store. And what taste they have! Bostonians and New Yorkers whizzing to points elsewhere have all the reason they need to detour in Sandwich: artisan cheese, patés, dozens of kinds of salt, caviar, pastas, gravlax, breads, and more. Furthermore, the wine store is one of the best I've wandered, with bottles in the

THE BROWN JUG

$10–100 range; they even carry my favorite and little-known Gruet champagne from New Mexico. Miss it at your peril.

❋ ❧ **Bee-Hive Tavern** (508-833-1184; thebeehivetavern.com), 406 Route 6A, East Sandwich. Open for lunch and dinner daily and for Sunday breakfast. Dine at this old-fashioned eatery for the atmosphere. Low ceilings, barnboard, and booths make this dark, Colonial-style tavern a comfortable (if simple) choice year-round. If you're tired of eating in "quaint" clam shacks, this place might do the trick. Dine with the locals on homemade soups, pasta, sandwiches, and burgers, or dig into chef-owner Stephen Davies's more substantial prime rib and lobster pie. Seagrass martinis spice up the evening. Sunday breakfast $3–10, lunch $7–20, dinner $8–40.

❋ **Painted Lady Café** (508-888-8550; belfryinn.com), 8 Jarves Street. Open for lunch and dinner daily except Monday, mid-April to mid-October. Part of Chris Wilson's empire (along with the Belfry, *above*), this ladies-who-lunch café serves eclectic comfort food (like three cheese macaroni, grilled veggie wraps, chicken pot pie, and grilled shrimp). Outside porch seating makes it more special. If you're not careful, it can end up being more pricey than it's worth here. Dishes $10–22.

❋ **Dunbar Tea Room & Gift Shop** (508-833-2485; dunbarteashop.com), 1 Water Street. Open 11–4:30 daily. This tiny English tearoom, in a slightly rustic, American-style country setting, has bustled since the day it opened in 1991. Try the authentic ploughman's lunch, specials like seafood quiche (which sells out fast), or scones and Scottish shortbread. Afternoon English tea ($12 plus tea) includes scones, finger sandwiches, and desserts. In summer, garden tables are an oasis; in winter, the fireplace makes it cozy indoors. Lunches average about $8–12.

❧ ❧ ♿ **Seafood Sam's** (508-888-4629; seafoodsams.com), Coast Guard Road. Open for lunch and dinner daily, early March to mid-November. This casual spot near the marina serves fried and broiled seafood, seafood sandwiches, and seafood salad plates. Early specials. Lunch $8–11, dinner $14–18.

❋ ❧ ❧ **Marshland Restaurant** (508-888-9824; marshlandrestaurant.com), 109 Route 6A. Open daily for all three meals. It's primarily locals who frequent this small, informal roadside place for coffee and a breakfast muffin—or lunch specials like homemade meat loaf, quiche with great salads, and chicken club sandwiches. They serve real mashed potatoes for dinner, too, along with prime rib. Eat at one of the Formica booths or on a swiveling seat at the U-shaped counter. Beer and wine only. Breakfast $6, lunch specials $7, dinner $8–15.

DRINKS ♟ **Hemisphere** (508-888-6166; hemispherecapecod.com), 98 Town Neck Road. Open daily April to late October. This airy, contemporary, and boisterous beachfront eatery is a nice place for an afternoon drink on the deck; views are spectacular. Then head elsewhere for dining.

ICE CREAM ✍ **Twin Acres Ice Cream** (508-888-0566), 21 Route 6A. Open April to mid-October. The best in the area. The shop also boasts a lush lawn, a little oak grove, and plenty of tables and chairs. (It sure beats standing in a parking lot!) It's lit at night, too. My only complaint: There's so much colorful signage describing the offerings that it's overwhelming. To compensate, I've returned often enough to memorize the menu. Generous servings; banana boats, hot fudge sundaes, and an ample grill menu (served 11–3 only).

✳ Entertainment

Heritage Museums & Gardens (508-888-3300; heritageplantation.org), 67 Grove Street, sponsors outdoor concerts—from big band to jazz, from chamber singers to ethnic ensembles. Mid-June to early September.

✍ **Band concerts**, at the Wing School off Route 130, are given by the Sandwich Town Band on Thursday evenings at 7:30 in July and August.

✳ Selective Shopping

✳ Unless otherwise noted, all shops are open year-round. (Still, don't expect many to be open midweek during the winter.)

ANTIQUES Sandwich Antiques Center (508-833-3600), 131 Route 6A. Open daily. A multidealer shop worth your time . . . if you treasure the hunt.

Maypop Lane (508-888-1230), Route 6A at Main Street. Open daily. With many dealers under one roof, there's a broad selection: decoys, quilts, jewelry,

sterling, copper, brass, glass, furniture, and other collectibles and antiques.

AUCTIONS Sandwich Auction House (508-888-1926; sandwich auction.com), 15 Tupper Road. Consignment estate sales are held Wednesday in summer and Saturday off-season. Once a month (call for dates) they hold a superduper Oriental rug auction.

BOOKSTORE 🏷 ✍ ☂ **Titcomb's Book Shop** (508-888-2331; titcombs bookshop.com), 432 Route 6A, East Sandwich. Open daily. Titcomb's beacon draws you in: It's hard to miss the life-sized statue of a colonial man holding a book and walking stick. Book enthusiasts won't be disappointed; rare-book lovers will be even happier. This three-story barn is filled with more than 30,000 new, used, and rare books for adults and children, a good selection of Cape and maritime books, educational toys and puzzles, and cards by Tasha Tudor. Personalized service is exceptional: the Titcombs have owned and staffed the shop since 1969 and, with the help of their eight children, have made hundreds of yards of shelves. It's a charming place, promoting browsing. By the way, owner Nancy Titcomb helped resurrect interest in Thornton W. Burgess, and, as you might imagine, she offers a great selection of his work. Titcomb's was recently selected by the International Booksellers Federation as one of 50 unique bookshops around the world. Check the Web site for book signings and other special events.

SPECIAL SHOPS ✐ **Giving Tree Gallery and Sculpture Gardens** (508-888-5446; givingtreejewelry.com), 550 Route 6A, East Sandwich. Open April through January. The gallery's motto might as well be "Where Art and Nature Meet." It's a wonderful and aesthetically pleasing place. Outdoor sculpture is exhibited on acres of marshland with nature paths, perennial gardens, and a bamboo grove. And the rope suspension bridge out to the marsh is fun for kids. But don't overlook the indoor gallery, featuring mainly the work of hundreds of jewelry artists.

Glass Studio (508-888-6681), 470 Route 6A, East Sandwich. Open daily except Tuesday, April through Decem-

GIVING TREE GALLERY

ber; every day in July and August; call for winter hours. Artist Michael Magyar offers a wide selection of glass made with modern and centuries-old techniques. He's been glassblowing since 1980, and you can watch him work Thursday through Sunday. Choose from graceful Venetian goblets, square vases, bud vases, handblown ornaments, and "sea bubbles" glassware, influenced by the water around him.

Salt Meadow Gallery (508-833-8808; saltmeadowgallery.com), 598 Route 6A, East Sandwich. Open daily in-season, Wednesday through Sunday mid-October to mid-April. With so many little galleries dotting this highway, it's hard to know where to stop. Well, stop here for a good selection of sculpture, blown and stained glass, and painting in many media.

The Weather Store (508-888-1200; theweatherstore.com), 146 Main Street. Open daily except Sunday. If it relates to measuring or predicting weather, it's here: weather vanes, sun dials, and weather sticks to indicate when a storm is headed your way.

Home for the Holidays (508-888-4388), 154 Main Street. Open late May through December. Each room of this 1850 house is filled with decorations and gifts geared to specific holidays or special occasions. Items in one room are changed every month, so there's always a room devoted to the current holiday.

Horsefeathers (508-888-5298), 454 Route 6A, East Sandwich. This small shop sells linens, lace, Victoriana, teacups, and vintage christening gowns.

Collections Unlimited (508-833-0039), 365 Route 6A, East Sandwich. Open daily. Handcrafted items—wood objects, pottery, baskets, stained glass, and the like—from members of the

Cape's longest-running cooperative (since 1990).

Mrs. Mugs (508-362-6462), 680 Route 6A, East Sandwich. Reader Janet Grant (no relation) and my mother (relation) write passionately about this place, which has mugs (of course) but also some specialty foods, unique watches, locally made jewelry, and what has to be the largest selection of Crocs on the Cape. The beloved owner, Lori Simon, offers gifts for all price ranges.

Crow Farm (508-888-0690), Route 6A, East Sandwich. In addition to jams, jellies, corn, summer squash, native peaches, and bread, the farm stand also offers cornmeal ground at the local grist mill.

See also **Green Briar Nature Center & Jam Kitchen** under *Green Space* and the Brown Jug under *Eating Out*.

✳ Special Events

Mid-September: **Boardwalk Celebration**. A road race and walk, a kite festival, and a beachgoers' parade.

Early December: **Christmas in Sandwich** (508-759-6000). A weeklong festival with caroling, hot cider served at open houses, trolley tours, and crafts sales.

FALMOUTH AND WOODS HOLE

The Cape's second largest town, Falmouth has more shore and coastline than any other town on the Cape. In fact, it has 14 harbors, 12 miles of public beaches, and more than 30 ponds. Saltwater inlets reach deep into the southern coastline, like fjords—only without the mountains. Buzzards Bay laps at the western shores of quiet North and West Falmouth and bustling Woods Hole. Falmouth's eight distinctive villages accommodate about 105,000 summer people, which is triple the year-round population.

The villages differ widely in character. Quiet, restful lanes and residents who keep to themselves characterize Sippewissett and both North and West Falmouth. The West Falmouth Harbor (off wooded, scenic Route 28A) is tranquil and placid, particularly at sunset. Although Falmouth Heights is known for its opulent, turn-of-the-20th-century shingled houses on Vineyard Sound, its beach is a popular gathering spot for 20-somethings—playing volleyball, sunbathing, flying kites, and enjoying the relatively warm water and seaside condos that line Grand Avenue and Menauhant Road. Falmouth Heights has early ties to the Kennedys: Rose Fitzgerald was vacationing here with her family when Joe Kennedy came calling.

East Falmouth is a largely residential area. There are several motels and grand year-round and summer homes lining the inlets of Green Pond, Bourne's Pond, and Waquoit Bay. Historic Danville was once home to whaling-ship captains and has a strong Portuguese and Cape Verdean fishing community and farming heritage.

The center of Falmouth, with plentiful shops and eateries, is busy year-round. And the village common, picture-perfect with historic houses (converted to beautiful bed & breakfasts) encircling the tidy green space, is well worth a stroll. Falmouth's Inner Harbor is awash with restaurants, boatyards, a colorful marina, and moderate nightlife. Two passenger ferries to Martha's Vineyard operate from here.

Four miles south of Falmouth, Woods Hole is more than just a terminus for the Steamship Authority auto and passenger ferries to the Vineyard. It is also home to three major scientific institutions: the National Marine Fisheries Service ("the Fisheries"), Woods Hole Oceanographic Institution (or WHOI, pronounced *hooey*), and the Marine Biological Laboratory (MBL).

Woods Hole, named for the "hole" or passage between Penzance Point and Nonamessett Island, was the site of the first documented European landing in the New World. Bartholomew Gosnold arrived here from Falmouth, England, in 1602.

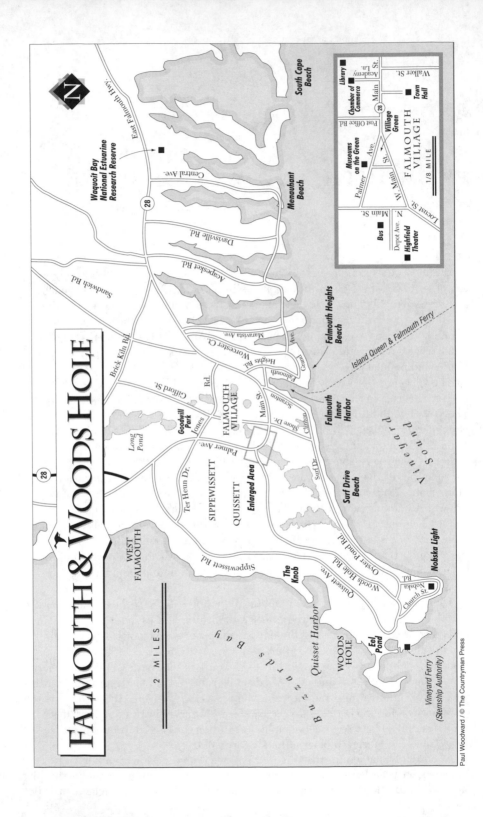

FALMOUTH & WOODS HOLE

N

2 MILES

WEST FALMOUTH

Long Pond

Goodwill Park

Brick Kiln Rd.

Sandwich Rd.

Gifford St.

Ter Heun Dr.

Jones Rd.

Palmer Ave.

SIPPEWISSETT

QUISSETT

Enlarged Area

Sippewissett Rd.

The Knob

Quisset Harbor

Quisset Ave.

Buzzards Bay

WOODS HOLE

Eel Pond

Vineyard Ferry
(Steamship Authority)

Nobska Light

Church St.

Nobska Rd.

Woods Hole Rd.

Oyster Pond Rd.

Surf Drive Beach

Surf Dr.

Shore Dr.

Main St.

Scranton

Clinton

FALMOUTH VILLAGE

Falmouth Inner Harbor

Falmouth Heights

Grand Ave.

Falmouth Heights Beach

Worcester Ct.

Maravista Ave.

Heights Rd.

Island Queen & Falmouth Ferry

Vineyard Sound

Acapesket Rd.

Davisville Rd.

Central Ave.

East Falmouth Hwy.

Waquoit Bay
National Estuarine
Research Reserve

Menauhant Beach

South Cape Beach

28

28

FALMOUTH VILLAGE

1/8 MILE

Library

Chamber of Commerce

Post Office Rd.

Museums on the Green

W. Main St.

Palmer Ave.

N.

Main St.

Bus

Depot Ave.

Highfield Theater

Locust St.

Village Green

Academy Ln.

Walker St.

Main St.

Town Hall

28

GUIDANCE ❄ ⓘ **Falmouth Chamber of Commerce** (508-548-8500; 800-526-8532; falmouth-capecod.com and woodshole.com), 20 Academy Lane, Falmouth. Open 8:30–5 weekdays year-round; 9–4 Saturdays, mid-May through October. This knowledgeable office also has Woods Hole information, good foldout street maps, a WiFi hot spot map since so much of town is "hot," and a historical walking-tour brochure.

MEDIA The *Falmouth Enterprise* (508-548-4700; 800-286-7744; capenews.net), published every Tuesday and Friday at noon, has local news and gossip.

The *Falmouth Visitor* (508-548-3047; falmouthvisitor.com), geared toward repeat and long-term visitors, is a great and free publication that gets beneath Falmouth's outer shell.

PUBLIC RESTROOMS *In Falmouth:* Chamber of Commerce on Academy Lane; Peg Noonan Park and Town Hall on Main Street; and the harbormaster's office at Marina Park on Scranton Avenue.

In Woods Hole: At the Steamship Authority.

PUBLIC LIBRARIES ❄ ✆ ♁ ⓘ The area has five libraries (falmouthpublic library.org); call each for its own hours:

Falmouth Public Library (508-457-2555), 300 Main Street, is excellent.

East Falmouth Public Library (508-548-6340), 310 Route 28 (Library Lane).

North Falmouth Public Library (508-563-2922), Chester Street, above the ball field; no WiFi.

West Falmouth Library (508-548-4709), 575 Route 28A.

Woods Hole Library (508-548-8961), 581 Woods Hole Road, Woods Hole. As you might imagine, there are lots of scientists and NPR *Science Friday* types at this branch.

GETTING THERE *By car:* Via Route 28 South, Falmouth is 15 miles from the Bourne Bridge and 20 miles from the Sagamore Bridge. Route 28 turns into Main Street. In northern Falmouth, Route 28A parallels Route 28 and is much more scenic. Route 28 leads directly to Locust Street and Woods Hole Road for Woods Hole.

The directional signposts for Route 28 are a tad confusing from this point on. Although Hyannis and Chatham are east of Falmouth, the signpost from Falmouth to Chatham says Route 28 South. This is because Route 28 originates in Bourne and does indeed head south to Falmouth before jogging east.

By bus: **Bonanza/Peter Pan** (888-751-8800; peterpanbus.com) has service to Falmouth (Depot Avenue

terminal) and Woods Hole (Steamship Authority) from New York, Providence, Connecticut, western Massachusetts, and Boston. Some Logan Airport buses connect with Vineyard ferries, although the ferry won't wait for a late bus. The roundtrip fare from Boston's South Station to Woods Hole is $42 and from Logan Airport it's $47.)

GETTING AROUND Whoosh (800-352-7155; thebreeze.info), whose trolleys are equipped with bike racks, travels between Falmouth and Woods Hole. Tourists can hop on and off downtown and at shops and beaches; flag it down when you see it. Whoosh operates about 9–7 daily, late May to early September; tickets cost $2 adults, $1 seniors and children. Look for schedules and route maps at the chamber, the Steamship Authority, and some local shops. Parking is extremely limited in Woods Hole, and roads are congested, so take Whoosh if you're just visiting for the afternoon.

Trolley Tours (508-548-4857). Sponsored by the Falmouth Historical Society, this narrated 2-hour trip covers 10 miles and illuminates Falmouth's almost 350 years of maritime ties and rich history. Trips depart from the Julia Wood House on the village green on Wednesday in September. Tickets $15.

GETTING TO MARTHA'S VINE-YARD There is year-round automobile and passenger ferry service to Martha's Vineyard from Woods Hole; there are two seasonal passenger ferry services to the Vineyard from Falmouth Harbor. See *Getting There* in "Martha's Vineyard."

MEDICAL EMERGENCY Falmouth Hospital (508-548-5300), 100 Ter Heun Drive (off Route 28), Falmouth. Open 24/7.

Falmouth Walk-In Medical Center (508-540-6790), 309 Route 28, Teaticket Highway. Walk-ins taken 8–4 weekdays.

It's not an "emergency" (the kind you'd expect under this category, anyway), but many area water wells have been contaminated by years of training with grenades and other live munitions at the Massachusetts Military Reservation. I drink bottled water on the Upper Cape.

✳ To See

In Falmouth
Village Green. The green is bordered by Colonial, Federal, Italianate, and Greek Revival homes, many built for wealthy ship captains and then converted to B&Bs. Designated as public land in 1749 and now on the National Register of Historic Places, this large triangle of grass is enclosed by a white fence, surely as pastoral a sight today as it was more than 250 years ago. It's not difficult to imagine local militiamen practicing marches and drills and townspeople grazing horses—in fact,

A PERFECT DAY IN FALMOUTH

8:00   Down a double espresso at "Coffee O" with other groove-meisters.

8:45   Appreciate one person's generosity at the waterfront Spohr Gardens.

10:00   Find the Punch Bowl kettle pond at Beebe Woods and take a dip.

11:45   Learn a little something at the Museums on the Green.

1:00   Enjoy lunch from the harborfront Clam Shack.

2:30   Kayak around Waquoit Bay and over to Washburn Island.

6:00   Drive the back roads to Quissett Harbor and walk around the Knob.

8:00   Enjoy huge portions at RooBar.

10:00   Sing along at Liam Maguire's Irish Pub.

a local militia reenacts maneuvers on July 4. Free walking tours around the green and old cemetery depart on Tuesday at 10 from the Hallett Barn Visitors Center at the **Falmouth Historical Society**. The tour returns by a secret back route. Call 508-548-4857 for recommended reservations.

First Congregational Church, 68 Main Street, on the green. This quintessential New England church—with its high steeple and crisp white lines—is graced by a bell (which still rings) commissioned by Paul Revere. The receipt for the bell—from 1796—is on display; the inscription on the bell reads: THE LIVING TO THE CHURCH I CALL, AND TO THE GRAVE I SUMMON ALL. Today's church was built on the foundations of the 1796 church.

🦞 ✂ **Museums on the Green** (508-548-4857; falmouthhistoricalsociety.org), 55–65 Palmer Avenue, just off the village green. Open 10–4 Tuesday through Saturday, mid-June through September; archives open Tuesday and Thursday morning and by appointment year-round. Operated by the Falmouth Historical Society. **The Conant House** (a circa-1760 structure) contains sailors' valentines, scrimshaw, and old tools. One room honors Katharine Lee Bates, a Wellesley College professor and author of the lyrics for "America the Beautiful," who was born nearby in 1859 at 16 Main Street (not open to the public). I suspect most Falmouth residents would lend support to the grassroots movement in the United States to change the national anthem from "The Star-Spangled Banner" to Bates's easier-to-sing, less militaristic song.

FALMOUTH HISTORICAL SOCIETY

Next door, look for a formal Colonial-style garden and a *Nimrod* cannon from HMS; the replicated 100-year-old **Hallett Barn**, with an educational center with hands-on exhibits; and the late-18th-century **Julia Wood House**, home to Dr. Francis Wicks, known for his work with smallpox inoculations. Adults $5; children under 13, free; tours by trained guides are included. See also *Getting Around* for historical society trolley tours. If it's a Friday during July and August, and your pod constitutes a family, head here for tailor-made, well-done, hands-on history activities. Or if it's a Thursday, make a beeline for Afternoon Tea in Julia's Garden ($12, which includes museum admission; reservations recommended.)

The Dome, Woods Hole Road, Woods Hole. When Buckminster Fuller was teaching at MIT, he patented the geodesic dome design in 1954. One of his domes, which "epitomize doing more with less," is just north of town. Although the exterior is in bad shape, it's still worth a look.

Cape Cod Winery (508-457-5592; capecodwinery.com), 681 Sandwich Road, East Falmouth. Open weekends, early May to early December; 11–4 Thursday through Sunday, July and August. Summer weekend tours at 2 PM. Come for tastings of fruity wines, a blanc de blancs blend, cabernet, pinot grigio, and merlot. During harvest time in late September and early October, visitors may pick grapes in exchange for a gift certificate redeemable for that particular vintage. Once the wine is bottled, it includes a custom label that indicates the names of the harvesters.

See also **Bourne Farm** under *Green Space.*

In Woods Hole

❋ ❦ ✎ **Woods Hole Science Aquarium** (508-495-2001; aquarium.nefsc.noaa .gov), Water Street. Open 11–4 weekdays, September through May; 11–4 Tuesday through Saturday June through August. When it opened in 1871, this was the first aquarium in the country. Today it's a fun place to learn about slippery fish, living shellfish (rather than the empty shells we're all accustomed to seeing), and other lesser-known creatures of the deep. Visitors delight in observing and interacting with lobsters, hermit crabs, and other crawling sea critters in a several tanks, including two touch tanks, a seal pool, and shallow pools of icy-cold bubbling seawater. Donations; adults need picture ID.

❦ **Woods Hole Oceanographic Institution (WHOI) and Ocean Science Exhibit Center** (508-289-2663; 508-289-2252 for tour reservations; whoi.edu), 15 School Street. Open 10–4:30 Monday through Saturday May through October; also open 10–4:30 Tuesday through Friday, November through December. Closed January through March. A Rockefeller grant of $2.5 million got WHOI off the ground

---

A PERFECT DAY IN WOODS HOLE

8:30   Enjoy pastry and java from Pie in the Sky.

9:30   Watch the Eel Pond drawbridge go up and down.

9:45   Support local artists at Woods Hole Handworks.

10:30   Feel smart after taking a walking tour with WHOI or MBL.

11:45   Support a wider net of artists at Woods Hole Gallery.

12:30   Dine waterfront on creative dishes at Captain Kidd.

2:30   Contemplate quietude from St. Mary's Garden after climbing to the top of St. Joseph's Bell Tower.

4:00   Ride the Shining Sea Bike Path out to Nobska Light and beyond.

6:30   Enjoy Cambodian noodles at the waterfront Phusion Grille.

in 1930, and since then its annual budget has grown to about $140 million. It is the largest independent oceanography lab in the country. About 1,000 students and researchers from all over the world are employed here year-round. During World War II, WHOI worked on underwater explosives and submarine detection. Today scientists study climate issues, undersea volcanoes, ocean and coastal pollution, deep-sea robotics and

acoustics, and large and small marine life. Relatively unpolluted waters and a deep harbor make Woods Hole an ideal location for this work.

WHOI buildings cover 200 acres. One-hour guided walking tours are offered weekdays at 10:30 AM and 1:30 PM from July through August. The tour covers a lot of ground and is geared to adults and teenagers. The small exhibit center shows excellent videos and has an interactive display with marine-mammal sounds and a fascinating display of *Alvin*, the tiny submarine that allowed WHOI researchers to explore and photograph the *Titanic* in 1986. While you're at it, don't miss the exhibit on the *Titanic*. Suggested exhibit donation $2; walking tour free, but reservations required.

❊ **Marine Biological Laboratory** (MBL; 508-289-7623 tour reservations; mbl .edu), 127 Water Street. Tours (at 1, 2, and 3 PM only) are very popular and restricted in size, so reservations are required at least a week in advance. Visitors center open 10–4 weekdays June through August, and 10–3 Saturday in July and August. Founded in 1888 as "a non-profit institution devoted to research and education in basic biology," the MBL studies more than fish. It studies life at its most basic level, with an eye toward answering the question, "What is life?" And marine creatures tend to be some of the most useful animals in that quest. Scientists (including 49 Nobel laureates over the years) study the problems of infertility, hypertension, Alzheimer's, AIDS, and other diseases. It's not hyperbole to say there's no other institution or academy like it in the world. Guides lead excellent tours that include a video about what goes on at the MBL. History buffs will be interested to note that one of the MBL's granite buildings was a former factory that made candles with spermaceti (whale oil). Free. Not appropriate for children under age 5.

St. Joseph's Bell Tower, Millfield Street (north shore of Eel Pond). To encourage his colleagues not to become too caught up in the earthly details of their work and lose their faith in the divine, an MBL student designed this pink-granite Romanesque bell tower in 1929. He arranged for its two bells to ring twice a day to remind the scientists and townspeople of a higher power. (One bell is named for Gregor Mendel, the 19th-century botanist, the other for Louis Pasteur.) Nowadays the bells ring three times, at 7 AM, noon, and 6 PM. Do we need that much more reminding these days? The meticulously maintained **St. Mary's Garden** surrounds the tower with flowers, herbs, a bench, and a few chairs. Right on the harbor, this is one of the most restful places in the entire area.

Church of the Messiah, Church Street. Nine Nobel Prize winners are buried in the churchyard. This 1888 stone Episcopal church is admired by visiting scientists, tourists, and towns-folk alike. The herb meditation garden is a treasure.

🦞 𝒪 **Woods Hole Historical Collection and Museum** (508-548-7270; woodsholemuseum.org), 579 Woods Hole Road. Open 10–4 Tuesday through Saturday, mid-June to mid-October. Archives open 10–2 Tuesday and Thursday year-round. This is a little gem. Located at the end of Woods Hole Road, near the Woods Hole Library, this museum has two galleries with changing exhibits of local historical interest. It also maintains a good library on maritime subjects, more

WOODS HOLE HISTORICAL MUSEUM

than 500 local oral histories, and a scale model of Woods Hole in the late 1800s. Dr. Yale's actual 1890s workshop is in a separate building. The adjacent Swift Barn exhibits small historic boats that plied these local waters long ago. Try to make time for the staff's free 60-minute **walking tour** around Eel Pond on Tuesday at 4 during July and August. And if you're around on Saturday mornings, drop by to watch volunteers help restore boats in the collection. Donations.

SCENIC DRIVE Take Route 28A to Old Dock Road to reach placid West Falmouth Harbor. Then double back and take Route 28A to Palmer Avenue, to Sippewissett Road, to hilly and winding Quissett Avenue, and to equally tranquil **Quissett Harbor**. At the far edge of the harbor you'll see a path that goes up over the hill of the **Knob**, an outcrop that's half wooded bird sanctuary and half rocky beach. Walk out to the Knob along the water and back through the woods. It's great for picnicking and sunset watching. Sippewissett Road takes you past **Eel Pond** and **Woods Hole** via the back way. Surf Drive from Falmouth to **Nobska Light** is also picturesque.

✳ To Do

BASEBALL 𝒪 **Fuller Field**, just off Main Street, Falmouth. The **Commodores**, one of 10 teams in the Cape Cod Baseball League, play in July and August. Check online (capecodbaseball.org) for schedules and team information.

BICYCLING/RENTALS 🦞 **Shining Sea Bike Path**. The easygoing and level 4-mile (one-way) trail is one of Falmouth's most popular attractions. Following the old Penn Central Railroad line between Falmouth and Woods Hole, the path parallels unspoiled beaches, marshes, and bird sanctuaries. It was named in honor of Katherine Lee Bates, composer of "America the Beautiful." The last line of her song—"from sea to shining sea"—is a fitting description of the trail, which offers lovely views of Vineyard Sound, Martha's Vineyard, and Naushon Island.

The trail connects with several other routes: from Falmouth to Menauhant Beach in East Falmouth; from Woods Hole to Old Silver Beach in North Falmouth; and from Woods Hole to Quissett and Sippewissett. There is a trailhead and parking

WATERFRONT BEAUTIES

Nobska Light, Church Street, off Woods Hole Road. Open sporadically for free tours on Thursdays and Saturdays in summer. Built in 1828, rebuilt in 1876, and automated in 1985, the beacon commands a high vantage point on a bluff. The light is visible from 17 miles out at sea. It's a particularly good place to see the "hole" (for which Woods Hole was named), the Elizabeth Islands, and the north shore of Martha's Vineyard, and to watch the sunset. Some 30,000 vessels—ferries, fully rigged sailing ships, and pleasure boats—pass by annually, as does the internationally regarded Falmouth Road Race.

NOBSKA LIGHTHOUSE—WOODS HOLE

Spohr Gardens (508-548-0623; spohrgardens.org), Fells Road off Oyster Pond Road from Woods Hole Road or Surf Drive; park on Fells Road. Thanks to Charles and Margaret Spohr (Charles won the citizen-of-the-year award in 1993), this spectacular 6-acre private garden is yours for the touring. More than 100,000 daffodils bloom in spring, followed by lilies, azaleas, magnolias, and hydrangeas. (You'll share the wide path with geese and ducks.) Don't miss the iris garden by the water; remarkably, it's maintained by only two people! Donations.

SPOHR GARDENS

Consider bicycling here via the **Shining Sea Bike Path** (see *To Do*), which also has great water views.

lot on Locust Street (at Mill Road) in Falmouth, as well as access points at Elm Road and Oyster Pond Road. Park here; it's very difficult to park in Woods Hole.

Holiday Cycles (508-540-3549), 465 Grand Avenue, Falmouth Heights. Along with a wide variety of bikes (including tandems and surreys) and equipment (from child seats to locks), Holiday Cycles offers free parking. Ask for details about the **23-mile Sippewissett route**.

SKETCHING AT QUISSETT HARBOR

❊ **Corner Cycle** (508-540-4195; cornercycle.com), 115 Palmer Avenue, Falmouth, also rents a variety of bicycles. It's a couple of hundred yards from the Shining Sea Bike Path.

BOAT EXCURSIONS/RENTALS ⚓ **Ocean Quest** (508-385-7656; 800-376-2326; oceanquestonline.org), Water Street, Woods Hole. Mid-June through September; in spring and fall individuals may be able to tag along with schools or nonprofit groups. Founder and director Kathy Mullin offers hands-on marine education for the entire family on her boat the *Venture Inn II*. Kathy, a science teacher and naturalist, and her staff of educators and mariners give a brief overview of oceanography. The 90-minute trip costs $22 for adults, $17 for children 4–12, $5 for children under 4. The boat departs four times daily and twice on Saturday in July and August. They also offer full-day Cuttyhunk Island cruises on Sundays from late July to September. On this trip, the naturalist guide gives a history of the island, or you can go for the unguided option, $53–60 per person. Advance reservations necessary. Or for a real treat, the boat is available for private charters ($500 per hour with a 2-hour minimum). On July 4th, their cruise is a great way to guarantee getting a good spot to view the annual fireworks display over Falmouth Harbor; book early.

❊ ✿ **Patriot Party Boats,** *Liberté* (508-548-2626; patriotpartyboats.com), 227 Clinton Avenue at Scranton Avenue, Falmouth. This excellent outfit operates 2- and 3-hour sails during July and August on the *Liberté*, a 74-foot, 3-masted schooner that carries 49 passengers; adults $20–30; children 12 and under, $15–20. Free parking. The Tietje (pronounced *teegee*) family has been chartering boats since the mid-1950s, and they know the local waters like the backs of their hands. Patriot also has a year-round **ferry shuttle service** to Oak Bluffs on Martha's Vineyard. Although they primarily service commuters, you can catch a ride for $9 one-way.

CANOEING AND KAYAKING ❊ ✿ **Cape Cod Kayak** (508-563-9377; capecod kayak.com), 1270 Route 28A, Cataumet. Exploring salt marshes, tidal inlets, freshwater ponds, and the ocean shoreline from the vantage point and speed of a kayak is a great way to experience the Cape. When you rent by the week, delivery is included; 1- and 2-seaters are available. If you want to go kayaking but don't know where to go, owner Kim Fernandes will recommend spots or locations suited to your interests and level of ability. She organizes tours with about six people per guide; $35–75 per person.

See also **Waquoit Bay National Estuarine Research Reserve** under *Green Space*.

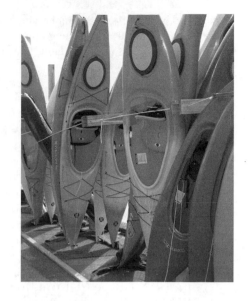

FISHING/SHELLFISHING Eastman's Sport & Tackle (508-548-6900), 783 Main Street. Open 7–7:30 daily. Head to this knowledgeable shop for fishing licenses, regulations, local fishing information, and rod and reel rental, too.

 **Patriot Party Boats** (508-548-2626; patriotpartyboats.com), 227 Clinton Avenue, Falmouth. Sport- and bottom-fishing from late May to mid-October. Bottom-fishing aboard the *Patriot II* costs $40–50 for adults for a half day; $25–30 for children 6–12; full-day rates are $60 adults, $38 children. Bait and tackle are included. Sportfishing is offered every day aboard the custom-outfitted *Minuteman*; call for reservations and times of departure.

Susan Jean (508-548-6901), Eel Pond, off Water Street, Woods Hole. From late May to mid-October, Captain John Christian's 22-foot Aquasport searches for trophy-sized striped bass. This trip is for the serious angler—John usually departs in the middle of the night (well, more like 4 AM) because of the tides. $600 for a 7-hour trip to Cuttyhunk Island and the Elizabeth Islands for one to three people.

Fish for trout, smallmouth bass, chain pickerel, and white perch at the town landing on **Santuit Pond** and on the **Quashnet River**. Surf-casting is great on **Surf Drive**.

The chamber of commerce (see *Guidance*) publishes a very good (free) fishing map and guide.

GOLF ❋ **Ballymeade Country Club** (508-540-4005; ballymeade.com), 125 Falmouth Woods Road, North Falmouth. A tough 18-hole, par-72 semiprivate course.

❋ **Cape Cod Country Club** (508-563-9842; capecodcountryclub.com), off Route 151, North Falmouth. A scenic 18-hole, par-71 course with great variety.

❋ **Paul Harney Golf Club** (508-563-3454), off Route 151, East Falmouth. This 18-hole, 3,700-yard, par-59 course offers somewhat narrow fairways but generally within the ability of weekend golfers.

❋ **Falmouth Country Club** (508-548-3211; falmouthcountryclub.com), 630 Carriage Shop Road off Route 151, East Falmouth. Two courses: an 18-hole, par-72 course with a good mix of moderate and difficult pars, and a 9-hole, par-37 course.

HORSEBACK RIDING ❋ **Haland Stables** (508-540-2552), 878 Route 28A, West Falmouth. Open 9–5 Monday through Saturday; reservations absolutely necessary. Haland offers excellent English instruction, individual and group lessons, and guided trail rides through pine wood groves, fields, a bird sanctuary, cranberry bogs, and salt-marsh land. Pony rides by appointment.

ICE-SKATING ✔ **Falmouth Ice Arena** (508-548-0275; falmouthicearena.com), 9 Skating Lane, off Palmer Avenue, Falmouth. Call for public skating times; $5 per person. Rental $4 through the nearby prICE's Pro Shop (508-548-6940).

PICK-YOUR-OWN ✔ **Andrew's Farm Stand** (508-548-4717), 394 Old Meeting House Road, East Falmouth. Open daily, mid-June through December, since 1935. Strawberries, strawberries everywhere, and other produce, too, all reasonably priced (especially if you pick your own). From the looks of it, East Falmouth was once the strawberry center of the world! Strawberry season runs from early June to early July, more or less. You can also pick your own peas in June, tomatoes in August, sunflowers from July to October, and pumpkins in late September and October. Call ahead for availability.

SAILBOARDING **Cape Cod Windsurfing** (508-801-3329; capecodwindsurfing .com), 350 Quaker Road, North Falmouth, adjacent to the Sea Crest Hotel (off Route 28A, North Falmouth) on Old Silver Beach. Open seasonally. Old Silver Beach gets a good, predominantly southwestern wind, so there is good sailboarding here. You can take lessons or rent nonmotorized vessels like kayaks, canoes, and windsurfers. This outfit also has radio communication helmets for students so instructors can be in constant touch with them. Since the Sea Crest Hotel only offers parking to hotel guests, and the nearby public (fee) lot fills up quickly, get there early.

TENNIS ❋ The following courts are public: **elementary school**, Davisville Road, East Falmouth; **Lawrence School**, Lakeview Avenue, Falmouth; the **high school**, Gifford Street Extension, Falmouth; **Nye Park**, North Falmouth; **Blacksmith Shop Road**, behind the fire station, West Falmouth; **Taft's Playground**, Bell Tower Lane, Woods Hole.

Ballymeade Country Club (508-540-4005; ballymeade.com), 125 Falmouth Woods Road, North Falmouth. Six outdoor Har-Tru and four hard courts; lessons and clinics.

Falmouth Sports Center (508-548-7433), Highfield Drive, Falmouth. Six indoor and three outdoor courts; rental rates depend on the time you play and how many people want to participate.

✳ Green Space

Ashumet Holly and Wildlife Sanctuary (508-362-1426; massaudubon.org), 286 Ashumet Road (off Route 151), East Falmouth. Open daily sunrise to sunset. Local philanthropist Josiah K. Lilly III (of Heritage Museums & Gardens fame; see *To See* in "Sandwich") purchased and donated the land in 1961 after the death of Wilfred Wheeler, who cultivated most of these plants and had been very concerned about holiday overharvesting of holly. Crisscrossed with self-guided nature trails, this 45-acre Massachusetts Audubon Society sanctuary overflows with holly: There are more than eight species, 65 varieties, and 1,000 trees (from America,

Europe, and Asia). More than 130 bird species have also been sighted here: Since 1935, nesting barn swallows have made their home in the rafters of the barn from mid-April to late August. Other flora and fauna thrive as well. Rhododendrons and dogwoods bloom in spring. Large white franklinia flowers (named for Benjamin Franklin) make a show in autumn, and in the summer Grassy Pond might overflow (depending on water levels) with rare wildflower blossoms. The sanctuary also offers nature trips to Cuttyhunk Island and guided bird walks. Pick up the informative trail map before setting out. Adults $4; children $3; members free.

Waquoit Bay National Estuarine Research Reserve (508-457-0495; waquoit bayreserve.org), 149 Waquoit Highway, East Falmouth. Headquarters open 10–4 weekdays year-round, plus Saturdays in July and August. Part of a national system dedicated to research and education regarding coastal areas and estuaries, Waquoit Bay has four components: **South Cape Beach State Park** (see also *Green Space* in "Mashpee"), **Washburn Island**, **Quashnet River Property**, and the **headquarters** (which houses watershed exhibits). More than 3,000 acres of delicate barrier beaches, pine barrier beaches, and marshlands surround lovely Waquoit Bay. Stop in at the headquarters for a trail map and schedule of guided walks in July and August. In summer look for "Evenings on the Bluff" talks as well as other activities like the Watershed Block Party in August, with hands-on activities and demonstrations about the bay that are perfect for kids and families. Within South Cape Beach State Park is the little-used, mile-long Great Flat Pond Trail (accessible year-round). It winds past salt marshes, bogs, and wetlands and along coastal pine forests. Pine-filled, 330-acre, Washburn Island is accessible year-round if you have a boat. The 11 primitive island campsites require reservations and a permit.

Falmouth Moraine Trail (508-540-0876). These 10 miles of trails are part of Cape Cod Pathways (508-362-3828; capecodcommission.org), "a growing network of walking paths linking open space in all 15 Cape Cod towns." Pick up the excellent trail map at the chamber of commerce (see *Guidance*) and set out. The lower section of the trail circles Long Pond (3.5 miles) and then heads north along Route 28 (more or less), without doubling back. Park at these spots, which are east off Route 28 (from north to south): Route 151 at the rotary; Thomas Lander's Road; the Service Road off Brick Kiln Road; and Goodwill Park adjacent to Grews Pond (the closest spot for Long Pond).

See also the **Knob** under *To See*.

BEACHES Along Buzzards Bay and Vineyard Sound, 12 miles of Falmouth's 68-mile shoreline are accessible to the public via four beaches. (There are eight additional town beaches.) Generally, waters are a bit warmer off Falmouth than off northside beaches because of the Gulf Stream. Weeklong cottage renters qualify to purchase a beach sticker, obtainable at the Surf Drive Beach Bathhouse 9–4 daily in summer. The permit costs $60 for one week, $70 for two. Some innkeepers

provide beach stickers. Otherwise, you may pay a daily fee to park at the following beaches. (The **Falmouth Beach Department** (508-548-8623) has further details.)

& **Menauhant Beach**, on Vineyard Sound, off Route 28 and Central Avenue, East Falmouth. The best Sound beach, by far. Waters are less choppy on Vineyard Sound than they are on the Atlantic. Facilities include restrooms, lifeguard, and snack bar. Parking is $10.

& **Old Silver Beach**, on Buzzards Bay, off Route 28A and Quaker Road, North Falmouth. One of the sandiest beaches in town, this is a good one for children, as an offshore sandbar creates shallow tidal pools. Facilities include a lifeguard and a snack bar. Parking is $20.

& **Surf Drive Beach**, on Vineyard Sound, on Surf Drive, off Main and Shore streets, Falmouth. This beach attracts sea kayakers, walkers, and swimmers who want to escape "downtown" beach crowds. It's accessible via the Shining Sea Bike Path (see *To Do*); by foot it's 15 minutes from the center of Falmouth. Facilities include a bathhouse, snack bar, and lifeguard. Parking is $10.

Falmouth Heights Beach, on Vineyard Sound, Grand Avenue, Falmouth Heights. Although there is no public parking, the beach is public and popular. Facilities include restrooms, a lifeguard, and lots of snack bars.

PONDS *&* **Grews Pond**, off Gifford Street at Goodwill Park, Route 28, West Falmouth. Lifeguard in-season, as well as picnic and barbecue facilities and a playground. There are also hiking trails all around the pond.

WALKS 🐾 **Beebe Woods**, access from Ter Heun Drive off Route 28A or Highfield Drive off Depot Avenue, behind the College Light Opera Company (see *Entertainment*), Falmouth. The Beebes, a wealthy family originally from Boston, lived in Falmouth from the late 1870s to the early 1930s. Generous town benefactors, they were among the first to purchase land in Falmouth. **Highfield Hall** (508-495-1878; highfieldhall.org), built in 1878, was the centerpiece of the property and has been magnificently restored with the vision of Friends of Highfield. (They hold concerts, exhibits, and workshops here, all with marvelous acoustics. If you have an opportunity to get inside, seize it!) The 383 acres around it contain miles of public trails for walking, mountain biking, dog walking, and bird-watching. In autumn especially it seems like the whole town takes the trail to the **Punch Bowl** (a kettle pond). It's particularly pretty in May when the lady's slippers bloom.

EEL POND DRAWBRIDGE

Waterfront Park, Water Street near the MBL, with shaded benches and a sundial from which you can tell time to within 30 seconds.

Eel Pond, off Water Street. The harborlike pond has a drawbridge that grants access to Great Harbor for fishing boats, yachts, and research vessels moored here. (The walk around the shore is lovely.) The little bridge goes up and down on demand; in summer boats line up to pass through.

🐾 **Bourne Farm** (508-548-8484), Route 28A, North Falmouth. Bucolic grounds open year-round; house open by appointment. Owned by the nonprofit Salt Pond Areas Bird Sanctuaries, Inc., this 1775 historic landmark includes a restored and furnished farmhouse, a bunkhouse (now a private residence), a barn, and 49 acres of orchards, fields, and wooded trails. It's a perfectly tranquil spot overlooking **Crocker Pond**, complete with a picnic area under a grape arbor. It's about as relaxing as it gets anywhere on the Cape! Donations for trail fees. The property and barn are available for wedding rentals.

See also **Spohr Gardens** under the sidebar "Waterfront Beauties" and **Ashumet Holly and Wildlife Sanctuary, Grews Pond** and **Waquoit Bay National Estuarine Research Reserve** under Green Space.

✳ Lodging

Falmouth boasts as wide a variety of places to stay as anywhere on the Cape but, unfortunately, many of its family motels have been converted to time-share units. Generally, your lodging dollars will go a long way around here.

BED & BREAKFASTS

In Falmouth Heights

✳ 🐾❝↑❞ **Inn on the Sound** (508-457-9666; 800-564-9668; innonthesound .com), 313 Grand Avenue. As good as it gets anywhere on Cape Cod, Janet Campbell and Howard Grosser's place welcomes with contemporary grace, sophistication, and warmth. And it's waterfront to boot! They have a per-

INN ON THE SOUND

fectly attuned sense of what people want: Fabrics are fashionable but not overdone; sitting areas are comfortable and substantial but seaside-breezy; and the turn-of-the-20th-century B&B is elegantly upscale yet casual. Eight of the 10 bedrooms, each with an utterly tasteful aesthetic, have direct and expansive ocean views. Five have a private deck with those same ocean views. A lavish breakfast (served at individual tables) includes an artful array of breads, fruits, and perhaps an egg dish like *huevos oceaneros.* April through October $120–325; mid-June to mid-September $195–325; November through March $120–195; other months $145–285.

🐾 ❝↑❞ **Bailey's by the Sea** (508-548-5748; 866-548-5748; baileysbythesea .com), 321 Grand Avenue. Open mid-May through October. Whenever I visit, it always feels like a bunch of friends has taken over this nicely renovated waterfront B&B. It's a testimony to the accommodating innkeepers, Liz and Jerry Bailey, who offer six rooms with fabulous ocean views. The first-floor living space helps too: it boasts a wraparound porch with a dozen picture windows and plenty of rocking chairs. In the comfortable guest rooms (with flat-screen TVs), decor ranges from

Victorian to Japanese to traditional. Families should inquire about adjoining rooms at special rates. Third-floor rooms are particularly spacious. A full breakfast, served on the porch, might include poached peaches with white cheese mousse, a rolled omelet, and freshly baked bread; Bailey's blended juice drinks are a specialty. And in case you're wondering, Baileys Irish Cream is available in the evening. Mid-May through October $180–265.

On or near the Falmouth Green

❋ ⓣ **Mostly Hall** (508-548-3786; mostlyhall.com), 27 Main Street. If you want to be close to the action downtown but a world away, this Georgian plantation-style house—the only one of its kind on Cape Cod—is set back from the road in the heart of the historic district. (It was built in the 1800s for the original owner's southern bride.) Innkeepers Charlene and René Poirer (René is fluent in French and is quite a storyteller) have outfitted the six spacious corner rooms with queen-sized canopy beds and comfortable armchairs. Guest rooms are large enough not to be overwhelmed by tall, shuttered casement windows, while the living room, with its impressively high ceilings, is decorated with period furnishings. The backyard parklike gardens and a gazebo are visible from the wraparound porch. Full breakfast at one long table included. No children under age 18. Rooms $125–225, depending on the season.

❋ 🐾 ♿ ⓣ **Palmer House** (508-548-1230; 800-472-2632; palmerhouseinn .com), 81 Palmer Avenue. Innkeepers Pat and Bill O'Connell run an upscale Victorian B&B that's chock full of period appointments and fanciful decor right in the middle of town. The main house is a Queen Anne beauty with stained-glass windows, shiny hardwood floors, and front-porch rockers. I particularly like the rooms, many with gas fireplace, in the adjacent guesthouse because they afford greater privacy. In all, the O'Connells preside over 16 "bedchambers" and one cottage suite, all with robes, lots of lace, TV, flowers, air-conditioning, triple sheeting, and turndown service. Breakfast is elaborate and full, served at individual tables. Loaner bikes are available. Children permitted in cottage. Mid-June to mid-October $199–295; off-season $109–265; midweek specials throughout the year.

✎ ⓣ **Captain Tom Lawrence House** (508-540-1445; 800-266-8139; captaintomlawrence.com), 75 Locust Street. Open February through December. This 1861 former sea captain's home with an impressive spiral staircase is a pleasant and friendly B&B operated by Anne Grebert and Jim Cotter. The inn, set back from the road, offers six comfortable rooms with air-conditioning, mini-fridges, showers (as opposed to bath tubs), and carpeting (to keep down the noise). A few of the bathrooms are small, so if you are large, inquire. Families might appreciate the efficiency apartment with private entrance; children over age 6 allowed. A full breakfast (perhaps omelets and Irish soda bread) is served at two tables in the combo living/dining room. Mid-May through October $140–180 rooms, $220 apartment; off-season $110–155.

In West Falmouth

❋ ✎ ⓣ **Chapoquoit Inn** (508-540-7232; 800-842-8994; chapoquoit.com), 495 Route 28A. Innkeepers since 1999, Kim and Tim McIntyre are constantly upgrading their Quaker homestead, one of the first 26 built in Falmouth. On my last visit I was very impressed with the new decor and amenities. Set on 3½ acres a couple of miles from the village center and less than 0.5 mile from Chapoquoit Beach, the inn has five rooms in the main house and two cozy cottages—the latter with a refrigerator, sitting area, and gas fireplace. (Of those, Captain's Quarters is my favorite.) Main guest rooms are spacious and delightfully uncluttered, with crisp linens and bedding, and decorated with quilts and local artwork. A full breakfast—perhaps spiced lemon pancakes stuffed with cream cheese with a side of Tim's homemade granola—is served on white linen tablecloths. Complimentary bicycles, beach paraphernalia, and tennis equipment are available. Children over age 12 welcome. Mid-June through September $225–275; off-season $150–200.

❋ 🏵 🐾 ♂ '¶' **Beach Rose Inn** (508-540-5706; 800-498-5706; thebeach roseinn.com), 17 Chase Road (off Route 28A). Ever since Douglas and Sheryll Reichwein bought this inn in 2006 they've been going gangbusters with renovations and upgrades. From the outdoor water features, fire pit, outdoor patio (for breakfast), and hot tub to the indoor massage room and feng shui–inspired guestrooms, they're hitting their stride. Eight rooms in the main inn and carriage house have been freshened with canopy beds, gas fireplaces, and whirlpools. As for the 19th-

century farmhouse itself, it sits on a delightfully quiet back road. A full breakfast may include homemade granola, apple oatcakes, and baked egg, cheese, and crab. Families might appreciate the low-key housekeeping cottage since it has a large front yard. Some rooms have cable TV with DVD; all rooms have access to the hospitality room, which has a computer. Mid-June to mid-September $160–225; April to mid-June and late September through December $125–180; cottage $1,350 weekly in-season, $1,080 off-season.

In Woods Hole

❋ ♂ '¶' **Woods Hole Passage** (508-548-9575; 800-790-8976; woodshole passage.com), 186 Woods Hole Road. There are few more welcoming inns on Cape Cod, thanks to innkeeper Deb Pruitt. On the road connecting Woods Hole and Falmouth, this quiet B&B has a delightful feel. Its 2 acres of gardens are best enjoyed from the hammock or from the plentiful lounge chairs. The attached barn has five renovated guest rooms; second-floor rooms are more spacious, with vaulted ceilings and exposed beams. Decor is crisp country-modern, and each room has a bold splash of color. A full breakfast (served on the relaxing back patio) is included, as are loaner bikes, beach chairs, beach towels, and use of the outdoor shower. The B&B is within walking distance of a beach. Children are accommodated by advance arrangement. Mid-May through October $125–195; off-season $120–190.

Woods Hole Inn (508-495-0248; visit woodsholeinn.com), 6 Luscombe Ave. Open February through December. New to the lodging scene in 2008 and smack in the middle of town, this 1870s inn (overseen by resident manager Sally) has been completely renovated with everything from soundproof windows to appealing front-porch rockers

BEACH ROSE INN

WOODS HOLE PASSAGE

to floor-to-ceiling interior spaces. The four rooms and the two-room suite are seaside-breezy, with a sophisticated and contemporary aesthetic. One has a water view. Upscale amenities include iPod docking stations, flat-screen TVs, pillow-top mattresses, and luxe linens. Inquire about the three-bedroom cottage near the water. Five more second-floor suites, even more upscale than the first floor's, should be ready by summer 2010. Mid-June to early September $225–275, off-season $99–225.

OTHER PLACES TO STAY ♿ ⁗ẏ⁗
Sands of Time (508-548-6300; 800-841-0114; sandsoftime.com), 549 Woods Hole Road, Woods Hole. Open April to mid-November. This motel has been in Susie Veeder's family since the mid-1960s, and you'd be hard pressed to find as much family pride elsewhere. Who stays? Some guests missed the last ferry; others know it's a convenient place for exploring Woods Hole (a five-minute walk away). And the rooms? There are 20 air-conditioned motel units (most with a delightful view of Little Harbor and two with kitchenettes), an apartment, and 15 nice and large innlike rooms in an adjacent 1870s house (many with a harbor view and working fireplace). Fresh flowers, morning coffee and

donuts, a small heated pool, and morning newspapers set this place apart. It's also a short walk to the beach and is adjacent to the Shining Sea Bikeway. June through September $165–225; off-season $100–170.

❄ ✿ ⅌ ⁗ẏ⁗ **Seaside Inn** (508-540-4120; 800-827-1976; seasideinnfalmouth .com), 263 Grand Avenue, Falmouth Heights. Across from Falmouth Heights Beach (see *Green Space*) and playing fields, this family-oriented motel has 23 rooms. Rates vary widely and are based on the degree of water view and amenities; whether the room has access to a deck, full kitchen, or kitchenette; and if the deck is shared or private. Rooms in the back building are the nicest, but the reservation folks won't guarantee a particular room. Too bad, since the third-floor rooms are the best. Late May through September $149–304; off-season $69–89.

By the way, the **British Beer Company** (508-540-9600; britishbeer.com) is on the premises. It's a fine place for an authentic stout or ale on tap. If you're not in a hurry, wait for some fish-and-chips or a burger for lunch or dinner. Lunch $7–20, dinner $7–25; live music on weekends.

✿ **Mariner's Point Resort** (508-457-0300; marinerspointresort.com), 425 Grand Avenue, Falmouth. Open April to late October. This bilevel time-share offers 37 efficiency studios and apartments within a short stroll of Falmouth Heights Beach (see *Green Space*). Most of the four-person units overlook the pool area; a few have unobstructed views of Vineyard Sound and a town-owned park popular with kite fliers. WiFi is available in the office. May through September $180 studio, $245 up to six people; off-season $115–190.

❄ ✿ ⁗ẏ⁗ **Coonamessett Inn** (508-548-2300), Jones Road and Gifford Street, Falmouth. Although billed as an inn, complete with a foyer-style living room, the 27 units with outside entrances more closely resemble motel rooms. Choose between suites overlooking picturesque Jones Pond, two-bedroom apartment-style accommodations, or one self-contained cottage. With 7 acres of meticulously landscaped lawns, the Coonamessett hosts its share of weddings and conferences. The inn is filled with the late Cotuit artist Ralph Cahoon's whimsical, neoprimitive paintings. Expanded continental breakfast included. Late June to early September $170–280 rooms, $195–250 two-bedroom suite, $220–280 cottage; off-season $89–150.

RENTAL HOUSES AND COTTAGES

Real Estate Associates (capecod-houses.com), in North Falmouth (508-563-7173), West Falmouth (508-540-3005), Falmouth (508-548-0200), or Pocasset (508-563-5266).

CAMPGROUNDS 🐾 ⁽¹⁾ **Sippewissett Campground and Cabins** (508-548-2542; sippewissett.com), 836 Palmer Avenue, Falmouth. Open mid-May to mid-October. This well-run, private campground has 11 cabins and 100 large campsites for tents, trailers, and RVs; clean, large bathrooms and showers; and free shuttles to Chapoquoit Beach, the ferry to Martha's Vineyard, and other Falmouth-area locations. In-season camping $37 daily, cabins $425–815 weekly; in-season teepees $58. Pets permitted prior to Memorial Day and after Labor Day, but not in cabins.

See also **Waquoit Bay National Estuarine Research Reserve** under *Green Space.*

✷ Where to Eat

Falmouth and Woods Hole restaurants satisfy all palates and budgets—through upscale bistro dining, waterfront fish houses, taverns, and diners.

DINING OUT

In Falmouth

✷ ♈ **RooBar of Falmouth** (508-548-8600; theroobar.com), 285 Main Street. Open for lunch on weekends (in summer) and dinner daily (year-round). As they say in their advertising, "Life is too short to eat boring food." I couldn't agree more. Portions are also quite substantial. Vibrant and buzzy, with more of an urban feel than a Cape Cod vibe, this hip place has an open kitchen that churns out a world-influenced menu of contemporary coastal cuisine. In other words, it's not your grandfather's (or even your mother's probably) seafood eatery. Look for dishes like the gorgonzola-encrusted filet mignon, or Kona coffee–crusted pork tenderloin, served by a staff who knows the difference between sea and bay scallops. Pizzas $10–15, lunch $5–14, dinner $20–34.

Osteria La Civetta (508-540-1616; osterialacivetta.com), 133 Main Street. Open for dinner daily and lunch Wednesday through Saturday; closed February. When you want to linger, this Old World and family-style trattoria has few equals—partly because service is so "relaxed" and partly because that's the way things are done in the home country. Of the six or seven main dishes, half of them were made completely from scratch. Come hungry and do it up with all four courses: antipasti, primi, secondi, and contorni. And yes, the pasta tastes like it was made minutes ago because it was! (The proprietors, a daughter and her parents, hail from Emilia Romagna in northern Italia.) There's also a retail component with take-away luncheon meats and cheeses, just like in the Old Country. Lunch $7–15, dinner secondi $16–23.

❊ **La Cucina Sul Mare** (508-548-5600; lacucinasulmare.com), 237 Main Street. Open for lunch and dinner daily. Northern Italian and Mediterranean cuisine is stupendous on the Upper Cape. And you'll rarely encounter portions so large as you do here; think about sharing dishes or having leftovers for lunch. To make matters even better, the husband and wife team of Cynthia and Mark Cilfone do a super job of making it feel like one giant dinner party here. Intimate, charming, and villa-like, La Cucina has been offering fresh, old-world pasta and seafood specials since 2002. Lunch $5–12, dinner $14–25; half portions available for kids; outdoor seating available.

❊ ♈ **Firefly Woodfire Grill & Bar** (508-548-7953; fireflywoodfiregrill .com), 271 Main Street. Open for lunch and dinner daily in summer; dinner off-season. Come for a happening bar scene and stay for appetizer noshing (wings and ribs, anyone?) and more. This eclectic, contemporary, and lively place appeals to both visitors and locals, who appreciate a relaxed yet up-market menu of grilled steaks, blue corn tostadas, pizzettas, and oven-roasted salmon. Most everything (including romaine in their Caesar salad) is grilled or oven roasted! Live entertainment on Sunday; early evening specials most nights. If you're grazing around Falmouth, consider stopping by for a glass of wine and dessert too. Dinner $12–34.

❊ ♨ ♈ ♿ **Chapoquoit Grill** (508-540-7794; chapoquoitgrill.com), 410 West Falmouth Highway, West Falmouth. Open for dinner daily. From the moment this eclectic New American bistro opened in 1993, it was a success. (Readers from Mississauga, Ontario, suggest a double value symbol!) You can spot the regulars who appreciate

innovative cooking with a low-key atmosphere: They order from the nightly specials menu. Swordfish and seafood dishes are always superb. The popular wood-fired, super-thin-crust pizzas are also excellent. No reservations are taken, so get there when it opens (5 PM) or be prepared for a wait in the convivial bar. Dinner $8–20.

❊ ♈ **Café Villaggio** (508-540-6400; villaggiocapecod.com), 188 Main Street. Open for lunch Friday through Sunday and dinner nightly. This Tuscan steakhouse has lots of competition, but what sets it apart is alfresco sidewalk dining. Dishes are hearty and large, martinis are strong, and the vibe is convivial and contemporary. Try my faves: mussels pomodoro and eggplant rollatini. Early specials; dinner $14–35.

In Woods Hole

❊ ♪ ♈ ♿ **Fishmonger's Café** (508-540-5376), 56 Water Street. Open for all three meals daily. The beloved 'Monger was sold in 2007 and my one-person jury is still out on the new chef-owner (partly because change isn't easy and partly because of execution). The somewhat Mediterranean menu features surf and turf, grilled seafood, black bean chili, mussels, and some Armenian dishes. What hasn't changed? The classic Popeye chicken breasts, the location overlooking the Eel Pond Bridge, and the 1970s retro modern atmosphere. And even though the 'Monger is always bustling, the friendly staff keep it comfortable. Evenings sparkle, thanks to candle-light, shiny wooden tables, and lots of little windowpanes. Friendly bar. Breakfast, $5–14, lunch $9–15, dinner $9–30.

♪ ♿ **Phusion Grille** (508-457-3100; phusiongrille.com), 71 Water Street, Woods Hole. Open for lunch weekdays, dinner daily, and brunch on weekends, mid-April through October.

This sure is different and exotic for Cape Cod; foodies will love it here. Think along the lines of oven-roasted halibut. Sounds simple enough? Wrong—when it's served with shitake-lemongrass risotto, heirloom tomato vinaigrette, and white truffle oil drizzle. Wraparound windows and decks greatly enhance the (indoor) fine-dining atmosphere at this waterside restaurant. In good weather, you'll definitely want to eat outdoors beside the Eel Pond drawbridge. There's entertainment on weekends. Lunch $8–15, dinner $19–30.

EATING OUT

In Falmouth
❋ ✿ ♿ **The Quarterdeck** (508-548-9900), 164 Main Street. Open for lunch and dinner daily. This beloved neighborhood place, operated by the successful Chart Room entrepreneurs in Bourne, makes a great lobster salad (and lobster anything, for that matter). When I don't feel like lobster, I gravitate toward the daily specials . . . or

swordfish tips, day-boat scallops, and scrod from the regular menu. Do you get the idea that seafood dishes are big here? It feels particularly cozy in winter. Piano music nightly. Lunch $8–11 dinner $14–27.

❋ ✿ **Pi Pizza & Bistro** (508-495-5553; pipizzabistro.com), 75 Davis Straits (the continuation of Main Street). Open 11–midnight daily. This American-style neighborhood bistro features a brick oven and an open kitchen where you can watch the chef preparing bistro fare. Try their fig and prosciutto pizza. Dishes $8–18.

✿ **Clam Shack** (508-540-7758), 227 Clinton Avenue. Open 11:30–7:45 daily, late May to early September. The father and son duo of Jim and Jim Limberakis have expertly operated this busy clam shack since 1962. There is rarely enough room inside, but it's just as well—head to the back deck to munch on fried clams, scallops, and fish while watching pleasure boats and fishing boats come and go. Dishes $8–19.

CLAM SHACK

❋ ❧ **Pies a la Mode** (508-540-8777; piesalamode.com), 352 Main Street, near White Hen Pantry. Open 10–5 or 6 daily. I love this hidden gem, which makes everything from scratch and on premises. Take their chicken pot pies and Cornish pasties to the beach, to the green, or home and count yourself lucky to have found them! Excellence continues with dessert pies and gelato too. Pies $9–30.

❋ **Golden Swan** (508-540-6580), 323 Main Street. Open for lunch and dinner daily. When you tire of New American cuisine or seafood, you won't be disappointed with the Indian cuisine here—unless you hail from Bangalore. The extensive menu has mild, medium, and hot dishes and lots of vegetarian options. Too bad the interior is so dark. Dishes $12–20.

❋ ⚅ **Peking Palace** (508-540-8204; pekingpalacefalmouth.com), 452 Main Street. Open from "lunchtime until late" daily. If you're hankering for takeout from your favorite Chinese restaurant at home, the Peking Palace offers the best on the Upper Cape and mid-Cape. Along with sushi, there must be 200 Mandarin, Szechuan, and Cantonese dishes on the menu. Lunch $7–9, dinner $9–16.

❋ ❧ **Betsy's Diner** (508-540-0060), 457 Main Street, East Falmouth. Open for all three meals daily. This old-fashioned 1957 Mountain View Diner was transported in 1992 from Pennsylvania to Main Street, and placed on the site of another diner. The boxy addition isn't historic, just functional. The place is packed with locals and families who come for the inexpensive fare: club sandwiches, breakfast specials, or perhaps the famous roast turkey dinner. Specials are generally excellent and portions large. Breakfast is served all day to tunes from the '60s. Breakfast $3–9, lunch $5–8, dinner $7–10.

❋ ❧ **Mary Ellen's Portuguese Bakery** (508-540-9696), 829 Main Street. Open 5 AM–2 PM daily. In addition to traditional Portuguese offerings like kale soup and malasadas, these friendly (and family-friendly) folks offer breakfast omelets throughout the day and cheeseburgers, too. Prices $6–8.

❋ **Dana's Kitchen** (508-540-7900; danas-kitchen.com), 881 Palmer Avenue. Open for breakfast and lunch. Formerly Peach Tree Circle, this overgrown farm stand with outdoor seating offers sandwiches, salads, and pastries in a tranquil, country-style setting. Dishes $5–10.

❋ **Artie's Café** (508-457-0100; artiescafe.com), 281 Main Street. Open for lunch and dinner daily, breakfast on weekends. When you want a quick meal with good food at good prices, think of Artie's. It's nothing fancy, but you can feed a family of four without mortgaging your future. From burgers, pasta, and hotdogs to fried seafood platters, wings, and sandwiches, you'll be pleased with this friendly joint. Dishes $5–13.

❋ ❧ **Moonakis Café** (508-457-9630), 460 Route 28, Waquoit. Open for breakfast and lunch Monday through Saturday, breakfast only Sunday. Paul Rifkin and Ellen Mycock run a great breakfast joint. Specialties include homemade corned beef hash and chowder, as well as fresh-fruit waffles, crabcakes, and Reubens. Ellen is family-friendly: Upon request, she'll make simple, small dishes for kids. By the way, *moonakis* means "beautiful water" in the Wampanoag language. Breakfast and lunch dishes $3–9.

❧ ⚅ ♟ **Flying Bridge** (508-548-2700), 220 Scranton Avenue (west side of Inner Harbor). Open 11:30–9 or 11 daily, mid-April through October. This enormous, 600-seat restaurant overlooks the *Island Queen* dock and the busiest area of Falmouth's Inner Harbor. The view is the main attraction, so ask for a table on the deck. I usually munch on appetizers or get a salad and sandwich. Lunch $10–26, dinner $10–30.

❊ ⍩ **Casino Wharf Fx** (508-540-6160; casinowharffx.com), 286 Grand Avenue. Open for lunch and dinner daily, except closed Monday, November through March. When this two-story upscale place supplanted one with wet T-shirt contests, everyone breathed a sigh of relief—the stunning waterfront location was accessible to all once again. I go for lunch served at one of two beachfront decks; the interior has soaring ceilings but rather conservative decor. The bar plays a central role in the dining room. Lunch $9–19, dinner $9–28.

🦞 ✂ & & **Seafood Sam's** (508-540-7877; seafoodsams.com), Route 28/Palmer Avenue. Open daily March through November. Ignore the plastic silverware and focus on the crispy, crunchy fried fish. Lunch specials $8–11, dinner $11–18.

See also **Nimrod**, **Liam Maguire's**, and **Boathouse** under *Entertainment* and the **British Beer Company** at the Seaside Inn under *Lodging*.

In Woods Hole
🦞 ✂ & **Shuckers World Famous Raw Bar & Café** (508-540-3850; shuckersrb.com), 91A Water Street. Open for lunch and dinner May through October. Sit on the deck overlooking Eel Pond and enjoy twin lobsters (on Tuesday evening), lobster bisque, lobster rolls, stuffed tomatoes with lobster, and stuffed lobster. Do you get the idea that lobster is a specialty? Of course, there is also raw and steamed seafood, and even mesquite-grilled fish and chicken. It's a fun place, kept consistent by the vision of a longtime chef-owner. The dockside

patio is heated on cool spring and fall evenings. Lunch $9–16, dinner $12–24.

❊ ✂ ⍩ **Captain Kidd** (508-548-8563; thecaptainkidd.com), 77 Water Street. The tavern is open for lunch and dinner daily; the fancier waterfront section overlooking Eel Pond is open for dinner daily, mid-June to early September. This local watering hole is named for the pirate who supposedly spent a short time in the environs of Woods Hole on the way to his execution in England. As such, a playful pirate mural hangs above barrel-style tables across from the long, hand-carved mahogany bar. The Kidd, as it's affectionately called, offers specialty pizzas, burgers, sandwiches, fish-and-chips, scrod, steaks, and blackboard fish specials. It's all very good these days, and it remains an institution. The glassed-in patio with a woodstove is a cozy place to be in winter. The only drawback here: the staff are at times more attentive to the TV at the bar than they are to patrons. Tavern dishes $9–14, waterfront dining $9–22.

✂ ⍩ & **Landfall** (508-548-1758), 2 Luscombe Avenue. Open 11–10 daily,

LANDFALL

April through November. The Landfall, in the Estes family since 1946, is
better for soaking up local atmosphere
than for dining on creative cuisine:
Both preppies and weather-beaten
fishermen are regulars here. Bedecked
with seafaring paraphernalia and built
with salvaged materials, the large dining room is also cozy with hurricane
lamps. The waterfront location is
excellent: Ask for a table overlooking
the ferry dock. Traditional fare
includes lobster and seafood like
swordfish, cod, and scallops. Entertainment on weekends during the summer.
Lunch $8–13, dinner $20–28.

❊ **Pie in the Sky** (508-540-5475;
woodshole.com/pie), 10 Water Street.
Open 363 days a year (5 AM–10 PM in
summer, 6–9 in winter). This funky—
in a good way—institution has strong
coffee (they roast it themselves), good

handmade pastries, hearty sandwiches,
and homemade soups. There are a few
tables inside and garden/streetside. In
summer, frequent patio entertainment
packs a crowd that extends up the hill-
side. It's inevitably my first and last
stop in Woods Hole.

COFFEE, ICE CREAM & MARKETS

❊ "1" **Coffee Obsession** (508-540-
2233), 110 Palmer Avenue, Falmouth;
and in Woods Hole Village. Open at
least 7 AM–7:30 PM daily. Caffeine
addicts flock to "Coffee O" for bracing
espressos, a slice of coffee cake, and a
smidgen of counterculture à la Falmouth and Woods Hole. Eggnog,
apple cider, and other seasonal bever-
ages, too. A retail shop serves all your

COFFEE OBSESSION

chai- and coffee-related needs.

❊ **Windfall Market** (508-548-0099),
77 Scranton Avenue, Falmouth. Open
daily. Prepared foods, a deli section,
trout, lobsters, homemade breads, and
a fine wine selection with knowledgeable staff.

❊ **Ben & Bill's Chocolate Emporium** (508-548-7878), 209 Main Street,
Falmouth. This old-fashioned sweets
shop is lined with walls of confections,
some made on the premises. The

excellent store-made ice cream is tasty and served in abundant quantities.

✴ Entertainment

✎ **Band concerts**, July and August. The Falmouth Town Band performs at **Marina Park**, on the west side of the Inner Harbor, on Thursday evenings at 7:30 or 8. Bring a chair or a blanket and watch the kids dance to simple marches and big-band numbers. Or wander around and look at the moored boats. There are also free Friday concerts at 6:30 PM at **Peg Noonan Park** on Main Street in July and August.

✎ **Movies Under the Stars** (508-548-9888), Peg Noonan Park on Main Street, Falmouth. June through August. Family friendly movie starts at dusk every Wednesday. It's a charming way to spend the evening—rather like a drive-in of yore, except without the car! Free.

College Light Opera Company (508-548-0668; collegelightopera.com), Highfield Theatre, Depot Avenue, Falmouth. Mid-June to late August. Performances Tuesday through Saturday at 8 PM and Thursday at 2 PM. Founded in 1969, this talented and energetic company includes music majors and theater arts students from across the country. They perform nine shows in nine weeks; tickets cost $30 for those age 5 and older. Reserve early as these performances sell out quickly.

Highfield Hall (508-495-1878; high fieldhall.org). After a $6.5 million labor of love, this magnificently restored 1878 manse opened as a community cultural center. It holds concerts, exhibits, and workshops, all with marvelous acoustics. Check the local papers to see what's going on.

Woods Hole Folk Music Society (508-540-0320), Community Hall, 30 Water Street, Woods Hole. Well-known folkies generally play on the first and third Sunday of each month, early October to early May. Tickets $12.

Cape Cod Theatre Project (508-457-4242; capecodtheatreproject.org), Falmouth Academy, Highfield Drive, Falmouth. Established by two New York actors who were vacationing in Woods Hole in 1994, the project stages readings of new American plays in July. Donations.

See also **Highfield Hall** under Beebe Woods in *Green Space*.

MOVIES ✴ ❦ ↑ **Regal (Hoyts) Cinemas Nickelodeon 5** (508-563-6510), Route 151, North Falmouth.

❡ **NIGHTLIFE** ✴ **Liam Maguire's Irish Pub & Restaurant** (508-548-0285; liammaguire.com), 273 Main Street, Falmouth. Open for lunch and dinner. It doesn't get any more fun than this unless you go to South Boston or Dublin. Irish students serve shepherd's pie, Irish beef stew, or fish-and-chips in beer batter for $15. Food is average, the sandwiches a bit better. Come for beer (Guinness on draft) and live entertainment year-round (including sing-alongs). Liam himself plays some nights.

✴ **The Nimrod** (508-540-4132; then imrod.com), 100 Dillingham Avenue, Falmouth. Open for dinner daily, lunch Wednesday through Friday, and Sunday brunch. This is a great townie place to listen to jazz—piano, trios, and piano bar sing-along nightly. Grab a seat at the bar or order traditional fare like shrimp scampi or a grilled chicken club sandwich. Off-season, you'll probably appreciate one of the three working fireplaces. Sunday brunch $13, lunch specials $5–13, dinner $13–29.

The Boathouse (508-548-7800), 88 Scranton Avenue, Falmouth. Open late

April to mid-October. An attractive and decent restaurant by day, the Boathouse jumps with live music and lively crowds nightly in summer (on weekends in spring and fall). Early specials, but lobster for $12 is always a bargain! Lunch $6–11, dinner $18–25.

✳ Selective Shopping

✳ In recent years, the quality of Main Street stores in Falmouth has risen, sidewalks have been repaved, benches added, and flower beds and boxes are overflowing. You can pass a couple of hours here easily. Most shops are open year-round.

ART GALLERIES **Gallery 333** (508-564-4467; gallery333.com), 333 Old Main Road (near the intersection of Routes 151 and 28A), North Falmouth. Open afternoons Wednesday through Sunday, June through September. Arlene Hecht's gallery is housed in a wonderful 19th-century home that has been expanded over the last 200 years. Once the site of an asparagus farm, the house now showcases a medley of works by over 40 local, regional, national and international artists (both abstract and representational). Look for paintings, drawings, photography, ceramics, sculpture, and limited-edition prints. Don't miss the sculpture garden. On many Saturdays in summer, the gallery holds meet-the-artists receptions.

Woods Hole Gallery (508-548-4329), 14 School Street, Woods Hole. Open late June through September. Owner, curator, and all-around arbiter of fine art Edie Bruce has operated this gallery since 1963. It's hardly a pristine environment; the old house has low ceilings, walls are in need of a paint job. But amid the general feeling of clutter, with paintings stacked everywhere, you will find some real gems. Some are inexpensive; some are pricey. But any way you look at it, you can trust Edith's expertise about area artists.

Falmouth Artists Guild (508-540-3304; falmouthart.org), Gifford Street. Open Tuesday through Sunday. This nonprofit guild (active since the 1950s) holds 8 to 13 exhibitions annually, a few of which are juried. They host a big Arts Alive Festival in mid-June and Cape Art and Soul (a fund-raising auction) in July. Since these digs are temporary, you'll want to call for class and exhibition information. See Special Events for the sand sculpture contest.

ARTISANS **Woods Hole Handworks** (508-540-5291), 68 Water Street, Woods Hole. Open daily early June to mid-September. This tiny artisans' cooperative, perched over the water near the drawbridge to Eel Pond, has a selection of fine handmade jewelry, scarves, weaving, and beadwork.

Under the Sun (508-540-3603), 22 Water Street, Woods Hole. An eclectic selection of handcrafted jewelry, pottery, glass, and wood. Although the quality is somewhat uneven, the very good far outweighs the all right.

BOOKSTORES 🐿 ✒ **Eight Cousins Children's Books** (508-548-5548; eightcousins.com), 189 Main Street. Long before it won the equivalent of the Pulitzer Prize for children's bookstores in 2002, this excellent shop enjoyed broad and deep roots in the community. Named for one of Louisa May Alcott's lesser-known works, Eight Cousins stocks more than 17,000 titles and is a great resource, whether you're a teacher or a gift buyer, or entertaining a child on a rainy afternoon. It continues to excel with kids' programs, regular story times, and great service. Don't miss artist Sarah Peters's Alphabet Chair metal sculpture in front of store. It's a favorite with kids *and* adults, who love to sit on it and feel the different textures of the individual letters that make up the throne.

🐿 **Inkwell Bookstore** (508-540-0039; inkwellbookstore.com), 199 Main Street. This is arguably the best independent bookseller on Cape Cod.

Booksmith (508-540-6064), Falmouth Plaza, Route 28. This is a fine general (independent) bookstore.

CLOTHING Maxwell & Co. (508-540-8752), 200 Main Street. Absolutely fine men's and women's clothing.

Liberty House (508-548-7568), 89 Water Street, Woods Hole; 119 Palmer Avenue (508-548-3900), Falmouth. Open mid-April through December. Good taste and reasonable prices for linen shorts and slacks, sundresses, stacks of cotton T-shirts, and gifts.

FARMERS' MARKET, Peg Noonan Park, 10–5 every Thursday mid-June to mid-October.

MALL Falmouth Mall (508-540-8329), Route 28. A smaller version of the nearby Cape Cod Mall in Hyannis.

SPECIAL SHOPS Oolala (508-495-3888), 45 North Main Street. A hip and funky store with great gifts: fun greeting cards, candles, soaps, journals, jewelry, bags.

Rosie Cheeks (508-548-4572), 233 Main Street. Women's clothing and home accents.

Twigs (508-540-0767), 178 Main Street. Practical, decorative, and functional accessories for the home and garden.

Bojangles (508-548-9888), 239 Main Street. This wonderfully tactile shop appeals to all the senses with a nostalgic feel. But the goods are modern, funky, and contemporary. Stop in for high-end gifts: scarves, perfume bottles, hats, throws, candles, glassware, loose-hanging women's clothing, specialty place settings, unusual utensils.

✳ Special Events

Mid-June: **Amateur Sand Sculpture Contest**, Surf Drive Beach, Falmouth. Fee parking, but registration is $5.

Late June: **Arts Alive Festival** (508-540-3304; falmouthart.org), at Peg Noonan Park. Featuring artists' demonstrations, a "wet auction" of paintings made around town by local artists that morning, and local bands.

July 4: **Bike and Carriage Parade**, Main Street, Village Green. The parade starts at 11, but there are also spectacular evening fireworks over Vineyard Sound.

Early–mid-July: **Arts and Crafts Street Fair**. A fund-raising auction for Falmouth Artists Guild. Beginning at 10 AM, Main Street fills with crafts, artisans, and food stalls.

Late July–early August: **Woods Hole Film Festival** (508-495-3456; woods holefilmfestival.com). About 50 films by established and new filmmakers have been screened at various locations since the early 1990s.

Mid-August: **Annual Antiques Show**, Falmouth Historical Society; since 1970. **Falmouth Road Race** (508-540-7000; falmouthroadrace.com). The event of the year in Falmouth: an internationally renowned 7-mile seaside footrace, limited to 9,500 participants. Get your registration in before May 15th or you won't have a chance of running. Reserve your lodging ASAP—like when you send in your registration!

Early October: **Jazz Fest**, Arts Foundation of Cape Cod, Marina Park.

Late October: **The Cape Cod Marathon** (508-540-6959; capecod marathon.com). A high-spirited event, beginning and ending on Falmouth's village green, and attracting several thousand long-distance runners and relay teams. Commit by September or you'll be disappointed.

Early December: **Christmas by the Sea**. Tree lighting, caroling at the lighthouse and town green, and a significant Christmas parade. Popular house tours are operated by the West Falmouth Library (508-548-4709).

✐ FAIRS AND POWWOWS

Early July: **Powwow** (508-477-0208, Wampanoag Tribe; mashpeewampanoag tribe.com), 483 Great Neck Road South, Mashpee. The People of the First Light's Mashpee Wampanoag Powwow has been open to the public since before 1924, and the Mashpee Wampanoag Tribal Council has sponsored it since 1974. The powwow attracts Native Americans in full regalia from nearly every state as well as from Canada, Mexico, and some Central and South American countries. These traditional gatherings provide an opportunity for tribes to exchange stories and to discuss common problems and goals. Dancing, crafts demonstrations, storytelling, pony rides, a "fire ball," a clambake, and vendor booths. Kids are encouraged to join in the dancing and nearly constant percussive music. Adults $8; children 5–12, $5; seniors $5.

Late July: **Barnstable County Fair** (508-563-3200), 1220 Nathan Ellis Highway, East Falmouth. A popular weeklong family tradition. Local and national musical acts, a midway, livestock shows, and horticulture, cooking, and crafts exhibits and contests. Over age 12, $10; otherwise free.

MASHPEE

Just east of Falmouth, fast-growing Mashpee (which means "land near the great cove") is one of two Massachusetts towns administered by Native Americans (the other is Aquinnah on Martha's Vineyard). For 1,000 years prior to the colonists' arrival, native Wampanoag Indians had established summer camps in the area, but with the settlement of Plymouth Colony, they saw larger and larger pieces of their homeland taken away from them and their numbers decimated by imported disease. In 1617, three years after Captain John Smith explored the area, six Native Americans were kidnapped and forced into slavery. By 1665, the missionary Reverend Richard Bourne appealed to the Massachusetts legislature to reserve about 25 square miles for the Native Americans. The area was called Mashpee Plantation (or Massapee or Massipee, depending on who's doing the translating), in essence the first Native American reservation in the United States. In 1870, the plantation was incorporated as the town of Mashpee. When the *Mayflower* arrived at Plymouth, the Wampanoag population was an estimated 30,000; there are about 1,200 Wampanoag in Mashpee today.

Mashpee wasn't popular with wealthy 19th-century settlers, so there are few stately old homes here. The Wampanoag maintain a museum and church, both staffed by knowledgeable tribespeople. In the 1930s classic *Cape Cod Ahoy!* Arthur Wilson Tarbell observed something about Mashpee that could still be said today: It's "retiring, elusive, scattered, a thing hidden among the trees."

The largest developed area of Mashpee is New Seabury, a 2,300-acre resort of homes, condos, restaurants, golf courses, shops, and beaches. When developers won their lengthy legal battle with the Wampanoag, the tribe—and the town—lost much of its prettiest oceanfront property. The only noteworthy beach is South Cape Beach, a relatively pristine barrier beach with several miles of marked nature trails and steady winds that attract sailboarders. Compared with its neighbors, Mashpee is a quiet place, with a year-round population of 13,000, plenty of commuters (into Boston), and an upscale outdoor mall, Mashpee Commons.

GUIDANCE ❉ **Mashpee Chamber of Commerce** (508-477-0792; 800-423-6274; mashpeechamber.com), 520 Main Street (Route 130), Mashpee. Open 10–4 weekdays, 9–3 weekends, mid-June to early September. Off season hours unavailable.

PUBLIC RESTROOMS Mashpee Commons (see *Selective Shopping*); South Cape Beach and Johns Pond have seasonal facilities.

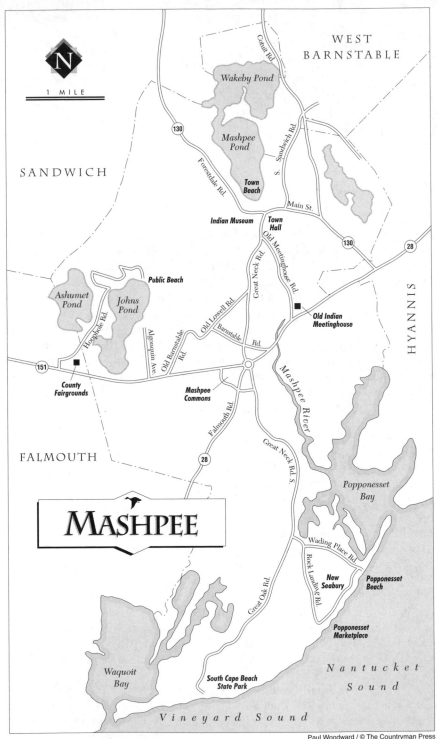

N

1 MILE

WEST BARNSTABLE

SANDWICH

Cotuit Rd.

Wakeby Pond

Mashpee Pond

S. Sandwich Rd.

130

Forestdale Rd.

Town Beach

Main St.

Indian Museum

Town Hall

130

28

Old Meetinghouse Rd.

Great Neck Rd.

HYANNIS

Public Beach

Ashumet Pond

Johns Pond

Old Lowell Rd.

Old Indian Meetinghouse

Hooppole Rd.

Algonquin Ave.

Old Barnstable Rd.

Barnstable Rd.

151

County Fairgrounds

Mashpee Commons

Mashpee River

Falmouth Rd.

28

Great Neck Rd. S.

Popponesset Bay

MASHPEE

Great Oak Rd.

Wading Place Rd.

Rock Landing Rd.

New Seabury

Popponesset Beach

Popponesset Marketplace

FALMOUTH

Nantucket Sound

Waquoit Bay

South Cape Beach State Park

Vineyard Sound

Paul Woodward / © The Countryman Press

PUBLIC LIBRARY ❋ ✦ ⚓ 🛈 **Mashpee Public Library** (508-539-1435; friends ofmashpeelibrary.org), 5 Joy Street in South Cape Village. Open Monday through Saturday. In mid-2010 the library relocates to Route 151 across from Mashpee Commons.

GETTING THERE *By car:* From the Sagamore Bridge, take Route 6 east to Route 130 south to North Great Neck Road to the Routes 151/28 Mashpee rotary. The Mashpee Commons shopping area at the rotary acts as Mashpee's hub.

MEDICAL EMERGENCY **Mashpee Family Medicine** (508-477-4282), Mashpee Health Center, 5 Industrial Drive at Route 28, accepts walk-ins 9–11 weekdays, 8–noon Saturday.

It's not an "emergency" (the kind you'd expect under this category, anyway), but many area water wells have been contaminated by years of training with grenades and other live munitions at the Massachusetts Military Reservation. I drink bottled water on the Upper Cape.

❋ To See and Do

HISTORIC HOUSES **Mashpee Indian Meetinghouse** (508-477-0208, Wampanoag Tribal Council; mashpeewampanoagtribe.com), Meetinghouse Way off Route 28. Under reconstruction for quite some time and located on the edge of what was once a Wampanoag-only cemetery ("They even took our burial ground away from us and made it theirs," laments a volunteer guide), this is the Cape's oldest surviving meetinghouse. It was built in 1684 and moved to its present spot in 1717.

Mashpee Wampanoag Museum (508-477-0208; mashpeewampanoagtribe.com), on Route 130 across from Lake Avenue. This small, early-19th-century house was built by Richard Bourne, minister and missionary to the Mashpee Wampanoag. (Check out the herring run at the end of the parking lot.)

FISHING/SHELLFISHING Obtain freshwater fishing and shellfishing licenses from the town clerk (508-539-1416), Town Hall, 16 Great Neck Road North. Open 8:30–4:30 weekdays.

Fish for trout, smallmouth bass, chain pickerel, and white perch at **Mashpee–Wakeby Pond** and the **Mashpee River** (access from Quinnaquissett Avenue). Surf-casting is great at **South Cape Beach State Park** (see *Green Space*).

FOR FAMILIES ❋ ✦ ⚓ **Cape Cod Children's Museum** (508-539-8788; capecodchildrensmuseum.org), 577 Great Neck Road South. Open 10–5 Monday through Saturday, noon–5 Sunday (shorter daily hours September to late May). Toddlers love the castle, puppet theater, and 30-foot pirate ship;

kids of all ages love arts and crafts. Check out the Starlab Planetarium and high-tech submarine with a working periscope, too. Ages 1–59, $6; seniors $5. Memberships, providing unlimited visits, cost $75 for a family of four.

GOLF ✳ **Quashnet Valley Country Club** (508-477-4412), Old Barnstable Road, off Great Neck Road. This semiprivate course winds around woods and cranberry bogs; ponds and marshes surround 12 of 18 holes; par 72.

TENNIS **Mashpee High School**, 500 Old Barnstable Road (off Route 151), has public courts.

✳ Green Space

BEACH **South Cape Beach State Park** (508-457-0495; waquoitbayreserve.com), on Vineyard Sound, Great Neck Road. Open dawn to dusk, late May to early September. Headquarters open daily year-round. The 432-acre state park boasts a lovely mile-long, dune-backed barrier beach, boardwalks, and nature trails. In-season facilities include restrooms and a handicap ramp onto the beach. Parking $7 daily in-season; free off-season (but you'll have to access through the Mashpee Town Beach parking lot).

PONDS **Mashpee** and **Wakeby ponds**, off Route 130. Combined, these ponds create the Cape's largest freshwater body, wonderful for swimming, fishing, and boating. This area was a favorite fishing spot of both patriot Daniel Webster and President Grover Cleveland.

✳ WALKS **Lowell Holly Reservation** (508-679-2115; thetrustees.org), off Sandwich Road from Route 130. Open year-round, dawn to dusk. Ranger on duty 9–5 PM weekends and holidays, late May to early September. Donated by Harvard University's president Abbott Lawrence Lowell to the Trustees of Reservations in 1942, this tranquil 135-acre preserve contains an untouched forest of native American beeches and more than 100 varieties of wild hollies, as well as white pines, rhododendrons, and wildflowers. There is a small bathing beach (no lifeguard) and 4 miles of walking trails and former carriage paths. $6 parking fee for non-members.

Mashpee River Woodlands/South Mashpee Pine Barrens. Parking on Quinnaquissett Avenue (off Route 28 just east of the rotary) and at the end of River Road off Great Neck Road South. The 8-mile hiking trail winds along the Mashpee River, through a quiet forest, and along marshes and cranberry bogs. Put in your canoe at the public landing on Great Neck Road. Free.

Jehu Pond Conservation Area. Established in 1997, there are almost 5 miles of trails here on almost 80 acres

encompassing woodlands, marshes, an abandoned cranberry bog, two islands, and Atlantic white cedar swamplands. Take Great Neck Road South toward South Cape Beach and follow the CONSERVATION AREA signs.

Great Flat Pond Trail, at South Cape Beach State Park. This easy-grade trail, a little less than a mile long, winds through woodland and wetland. Park at South Cape Beach ($7 in summer).

See also **South Cape Beach State Park** under *Beach*.

✳ Lodging

Family-style accommodations rule in Mashpee.

✳ ♪ **New Seabury Resort** (508-477-9400; newseabury.com), 20 Red Brook Road. This self-contained resort is scattered across 2,300 acres fronting Nantucket Sound. The 13 "villages" of small, gray-shingled buildings offer a variety of rental accommodations. Sea Quarters consists of one- and two-bedroom town houses; Maushop Village resembles Nantucket, with its lanes of crushed shells and weathered buildings; Tidewatch is a 1960s-style hotel near the golf course; Mews consists of contemporary California-influenced units. Some units overlook golf courses; some are oceanfront; others have more distant water views. Facilities include two restaurants, 16 tennis courts, two private golf courses, a well-equipped health club, two outdoor pools, 3 miles of private beach on Nantucket Sound, a small shopping mall, and mini-golf. You needn't leave the grounds. Late June through August $330 one-bedroom, $498–630 two-bedroom; rates less off-season.

✳ ♪ **Cape Cod Holiday Estates** (508-477-3377; 866-969-8222; 8664myvacation.com), 97 Four Seasons Drive. These 32 upscale time-share houses are airy two-bedroom and two-bath units with a full modern kitchen, Jacuzzi, central air-conditioning, separate living and family room, and private patio. On-premise activities and facilities include an indoor pool, shuffleboard, playground, tennis, basketball, and a putting green. Late June to early September $260 nightly, $1,650 weekly; off-season $120–140 nightly, $600–790 weekly.

RENTAL HOUSES AND COTTAGES
Century 21 Regan Realtors (508-539-2121; century21reganrealtors .com), 18 Steeple Street in Mashpee Commons, Routes 151 and 28.

✳ Where to Eat

There aren't many choices in Mashpee, but the ones here are good. If you're not satisfied with these, stop at Mashpee Commons shopping area to see if any new restaurants recently opened.

DINING OUT ✳ **Heather** (508-539-0025; restaurantheather.com), 20 Joy Street, in the South Cape Village shopping area. Open daily for dinner April through December; call for winter hours. Run, don't walk, to Heather, who burst out with an eponymous bistro in 2007. Since she'd been cooking at the renowned Regatta for years, she knows what she's doing; devoted patrons quickly followed. The setting is theatrical and romantic: high ceilings, halogen lighting, dramatic sprays of orchids, fine linens, and stemware. There's limited outdoor seating, but inside is so much more special. As for the cuisine, it's high art without the pretense. On a recent visit, I was wowed with crispy lacquered half duckling and roasted salmon with Boursin cheese, potato gnocchi, and crispy leeks. Top it off with Theresa's s'more, like nothing you ever had around a campfire. Service is as professional and seamless as you'd expect. Three-course prix fixe dinner (a bargain at $23) Sunday through Thursday, otherwise dinner $20–40.

❄ ✎ ♿ **Bleu** (508-539-7907; bleurestaurant.com), Mashpee Commons. Open for lunch and dinner daily; jazz brunch on Sundays in the winter. I really love Bleu—from the very cool blue interior to the cushy seats where you could sit all afternoon to the side-alley alfresco dining. It's upscale but casual and definitely stylin' with a smart waitstaff decked out in all black. French chef-owner Frederic Feufeu excels in both inspired bistro and contemporary cuisine, from regional French classics like *cassoulet* and duck confit to seafood specialties. There's a nice wine selection too. Lunch $9–18, dinner $16–30.

❄ ✎ ♿ **Siena Italian Bar & Grill** (508-477-5929; siena.us), Mashpee Commons. Open for lunch and dinner daily. Graham Silliman's spacious Italian ristorante features a contemporary, sophisticated menu that's been well executed by Pierce Capell from an open kitchen since 2006. Try the perfectly cooked seared scallops on a skewer, an addictive Caesar salad, stuffed Italian meatloaf, or the Cotuit oysters and clams that hail from waters less than 3 miles away. Thin-crust pizzas are sublime and always reliable. As an added bonus, Siena offers discounted movie tickets, under the guise of Cinema Siena, to patrons who are heading to a flick at Mashpee Commons. Although I like the buzz and the booths in the dining room, there is also popular patio dining in the summer. Either way, the bartender is known for margaritas and pomegranate martinis; wines are poured liberally. Lunch $8–13, dinner $13–28.

EATING OUT ♿ **The Raw Bar** (508-539-4858; therawbar.com), Popponessett Marketplace, New Seabury. Open mid-June to late October (weekends only in spring and fall). You know this tiny place has something going for it because locals outnumber tourists. Part Cape Cod, part Caribbean, the raw bar boasts loyal staff and fresh seafood. Since 1985 this little joint has been offering casual fare from hotdogs to lobster. In fact, their lobster salad may be the best on Cape Cod! Grab a picnic table outside and chow down. Lunch and dinner, $2–40.

Popponessett Marketplace, New Seabury. If you're staying in the neighborhood, this little collection of shacks and seashell-lined pathways also has a good coffee joint and a pizza place.

🏵 ✎ ♿ **Cooke's Seafood** (508-477-9595; cookesseafood.com), 7 Ryan's Way, off Great Neck Road North adjacent to Mashpee Commons. Open for lunch and dinner seasonally. The best area fried clams, along with other seafood, of course, and lighter fare. Lunch $6–8, dinner $10–22.

✳ **Persy's Place** (508-477-6633), 62 Route 28 on the town line with Hyannis. Open for breakfast daily. They bill this place as having something like 300 breakfast items on their menu, and although I didn't count them, I believe it. The closest thing you'll come to a New York City diner, Persy's doesn't disappoint (except for the coffee.) Go all out with a king of the sea omelet made with a quarter pound of lobster and doused with hollandaise sauce. Dishes $5–17.

The Tea Shoppe (508-477-7261), Mashpee Commons. Open for light, pick-me-up lunch fare of quiches or sandwiches, stop here between shopping expeditions. Afternoon English tea, too, with scones and Devonshire cream ($16.50). Otherwise, dishes $6–9.

✳ Entertainment

Mashpee Commons (508-477-5400; mashpeecommons.com), Routes 151 and 28, Mashpee. Dozens of performances, including some free concerts, take place here. Keep your eyes peeled for current listings.

✳ ✿ ↑ **Regal Mashpee Commons 6** (508-477-7333), Mashpee Commons, 15 Steeple Street (Routes 151 and 28).

✳ Selective Shopping

✳ **Mashpee Commons** (508-477-5400; mashpeecommons.com), Routes 151 and 28. Open daily. If you're familiar with Seaside, the planned community of architectural note in Florida, you may recognize elements of this 30-acre outdoor shopping mall–cum–new town center. It's located at what the Wampanoag used to call "pine tree corner," back when Mashpee was quieter than it is today. Developers have won numerous awards for transforming a strip mall into a veritable downtown commercial district. It's one of the most concentrated shopping venues on the Cape, boasting several good clothing stores, specialty boutiques, a movie theater, restaurants, cafés, and free outdoor entertainment in summer. Shops range from the Gap, Coldwater Creek, Origins, Ann Taylor, and Starbucks to more one-off shops like **Market Street Bookshop** (which is an excellent independent; 508-539-6985; marketstreetbookshop.com) and **M Brann** (508-477-0299;mbrann.com).

✳ Special Events

See the "Fairs and Powwows" sidebar in "Falmouth and Woods Hole."

Late July: **Mashpee Night at the Pops** (508-539-2345), Mashpee Commons. Hosted by the Mashpee Community Concert Committee (MCCC) since 1992, an outdoor concert by the Cape Symphony Orchestra, capped off by spectacular fireworks. Over 15,000 people pack this free event, but you can also purchase reserved seats; just make sure you do it by March, as they sell out quickly.

Mid-Cape 2

BARNSTABLE

HYANNIS

YARMOUTH

DENNIS

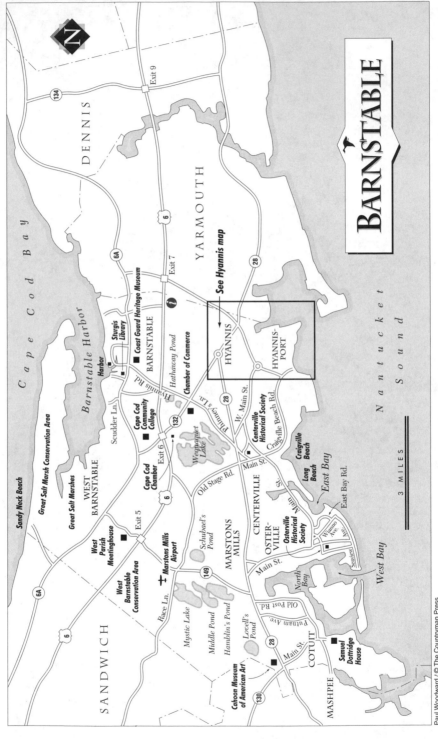

BARNSTABLE

The Cape's largest town covers 60 square miles and is home to 48,000 year-round souls. It's also the Cape's second oldest town, incorporated two years after Sandwich, in 1639. Barnstable actually comprises seven distinct villages—Cotuit, Marstons Mills, Osterville, Centerville, and Hyannis along Route 28, and West Barnstable and Barnstable along Route 6A. (Barnstable is sometimes referred to as Barnstable Village to distinguish it from Barnstable County, which embraces the whole of the Cape.)

On the bayside, Route 6A (also called Old King's Highway and Main Street) winds through West Barnstable and Barnstable Village. Development—or lack thereof—is rigidly controlled by the Old King's Highway Historical Commission, which regulates signage and does not allow gas stations, chain stores, or unconventional restorations within sight of the road. Sandy Neck, a haven for naturalists and beachgoers, is located off Route 6A, as are stately homes now converted into B&Bs.

On the southside, off Route 28, you'll find Centerville, Osterville, and Cotuit—parts of which front Nantucket Sound. Centerville's Main Street is full of handsome old homes built during the 19th century by affluent sea captains and businessmen. Osterville boasts some of the Cape's largest summer mansions, all with Nantucket Sound as their front yard. Osterville's Main Street is lined with upscale shops. At the turn of the 20th century, Cotuit was dubbed Little Harvard, as it was home to many academicians. Cotuit's Main Street is lined with impressive Federal, Greek Revival, and Queen Anne houses, with American flags and Adirondack chairs dotting the lawns. The popular Craigville Beach dominates this side of Barnstable.

Landlocked and wedged between Routes 28 and 6, Marstons Mills is tiny, quiet, and residentially developed. It was founded by the Marston family, who built and ran the mills driven by the Goodspeed River.

Barnstable was founded by English Congregationalist minister John Lothrop and a small band of religious renegades who felt that Plymouth Colony was a bit too settled for them. The neighborhood of Oysterville, as it was called, was purchased from the Native Americans in 1648 for "two copper kettles and some fencing." The area then was called Mattakeese, which translates as "plowed fields"—indeed, the land had already been cleared—but the settlers eventually named it for a similar harbor in Barnstaple, England.

GUIDANCE ❋ **Hyannis Area Chamber of Commerce** (508-362-5230; hyannis
.com), 397 Main Street, Hyannis. Open 9–5 Monday through Saturday, noon–5
Sunday, late May to late October; 10–4 Monday through Saturday, noon–4 Sunday,
typically, November through April, but hours may vary during winter. The Hyannis
chamber has information about all Barnstable villages.

MEDIA The weekly *Barnstable Patriot* (508-771-1427; barnstablepatriot.com) has
local news and gossip.

PUBLIC LIBRARY ⁰ʇ⁰ **Osterville Free Library** (508-428-5757; ostervillefree
library.org), 43 Wianno Avenue, Osterville. Call for hours.

Also see **Sturgis Library** under *To See and Do.*

GETTING THERE *By car:* Barnstable is 15 miles from the Cape Cod Canal. Take
Route 6 to Exit 5 for West Barnstable (Route 149 North) and Marstons Mills,
Cotuit, and Osterville (Route 149 South). Take Exit 6 for Barnstable Village (Route
132 West) and Centerville (Route 132 East).

By bus: The **Plymouth & Brockton** bus line (508-778-9767; p-b.com) connects
Barnstable with other Cape towns, as well as with Boston's Logan Airport. The bus
stops at the big commuter parking lot at Burger King, Exit 6 off Route 6 at Route
132.

GETTING AROUND *By shuttle:* The **Barnstable Villager** (800-352-7155;
capecodtransit.org) connects Barnstable's Route 6A (at the courthouse) with the
malls in Hyannis on Route 132, the Hyannis Transportation Center bus terminal,
and the Barnstable harbor. Schedules are available from the chamber of commerce
(see Guidance). Purchase tickets on board; fares are $2 over age 5, half price for
seniors.

MEDICAL EMERGENCY **Cape Cod Hospital** (508-771-1800), 27 Park Street,
Hyannis. Open 24/7.

❋ To See

Along or near Route 6A
West Parish Meetinghouse, 2049 Meetinghouse Road, off Route 149, West
Barnstable. Open 10–4 daily, late May to early September; Sunday services at 10.
This fine example of early Colonial architecture is the second oldest surviving
meetinghouse on Cape Cod. Don't miss it. (The oldest, the 1684 Old Indian Meetinghouse, is in Mashpee.) Its members belong to the oldest Congregationalist
church fellowship in America, established in 1639 and descended from London's
First Congregational Church. Founding pastor John Lothrop and his small band of
followers erected their first meetinghouse in 1646. By 1715 the Congregational
church had become so popular that Barnstable split into two parishes; the building
you see today was constructed in 1717. Its bell tower, topped by a gilded rooster,
holds a bell cast in Paul Revere's foundry in 1806; it still rings. Until 1834 the
meetinghouse doubled as a town hall—so much for separation of church and state!
In the 1950s, the meetinghouse was fully restored to its original modest, neoclassi-
cal beauty. Donations.

West Barnstable Cemetery, at Routes 6A and 149. Near the stone wall along Route 6A, look for a large granite memorial bearing the following inscription: "In this cemetery lie the mortal remains of Capt. John Percival known as 'Mad Jack.' Born April 3, 1779. Died September 17, 1862 in command of *Old Ironsides* around the world 1844–1846."

✷ ⚓ **William Brewster Nickerson Memorial Room at Cape Cod Community College** (508-362-2131; capecod.edu/library), 2240 Route 132, West Barnstable. Open 8:30–4 Monday, Wednesday, and Friday. Rainy day or not, visitors with more than a passing interest in the social history, literature, institutions, and people of the Cape and islands owe it to themselves to stop at the 4Cs. Students voted in 1966 to set up this collection to honor the college's second president's son, a Vietnam War hero and Mayflower descendant. The significant collection contains more than 5,000 documents: religious treatises, biographies, autobiographies, oral histories, letters by dune poet Harry Kemp, scrimshaw, ship registers and logs, early diaries, U.S. Lifesaving Service reports, telephone directories from 1886 on, and aerial photographs. The place is a treasure trove for researchers; several excellent books have been written solely using these materials.

✷ ✎ ⚓ "ℐ" **Sturgis Library** (508-362-6636; sturgislibrary.org), 3090 Route 6A, Barnstable Village. Open 10–5 Monday, Wednesday, Thursday, and Friday; 1–8 Tuesday; 10–4 Saturday. Researchers from all over the country (including entrepreneurs looking for information about shipwrecks) visit the country's oldest public library. It boasts one of the finest collections of genealogical records, dating to the area's first European settlers; an original 1605 Lothrop Bible; more than 1,500 maps and charts; and archives filled with other maritime material. William Sturgis, by the way, was born in the original part of the building, went off to sea at age 15 when his father died, and returned four years later as a ship's captain. Although he received no formal education, this self-made man obtained reading lists from a Harvard-educated friend and deeded the building to the town as a library. Use of the collections is free, though donations are welcome. The library also has a very good children's area.

Barnstable County Courthouse (508-362-2511), 3195 Route 6A, Barnstable Village. Open 8–4:30 weekdays. Built in 1831–1832, this imposing granite Greek Revival building is one of few reminders that tranquil Barnstable is the county seat for the Cape (and has been since 1685). Look for original murals and a pewter codfish in the main courtroom. On the front lawn, a bronze sculpture commemorates James Otis Jr., a West Barnstable "patriot" who wrote the famous 1761 Writs of Assistance speech. President John Adams said that Otis was the "spark by which the child of Independence was born." And on the side lawn, a memorial stands to Mercy Otis Warren, who self-published her Revolutionary War memoirs.

Lothrop Hill Cemetery, Route 6A, just east of Barnstable Village. Slate head-stones are scattered across this little hillock, where John Lothrop and other Barnstable founders rest.

Barnstable Harbor, Mill Way Road off Route 6A. Fishing charters and whale-watching trips depart from this small harbor.

✍ ↑ ⚒ **Coast Guard Heritage Museum (Old Customs House)** (508-362-8521), 3353 Route 6A, Barnstable Village. Open 10–3 Tuesday through Saturday, early May to early November. Before Barnstable Harbor filled with silt around 1900, it was the Cape's busiest port. The Old Customs House was built in 1856 to oversee the enormous stream of goods passing through the harbor. When harbor activity diminished, the brick Italian Renaissance Revival building served as a post office, until the Barnstable Historical Commission made it their headquarters in 1959. The commission restored the beautiful building, painted it deep red, and opened this museum complex. On the grounds you'll find the Coast Guard Heritage Museum (showcasing the history of the Coast Guard and the lighthouse service), a blacksmith shop, and a circa-1690 jail cell (the oldest in the U.S. but closed because of a fire), complete with colonial "graffiti." Adults $4; children under 10, free.

Off Route 28

❄ ⚘ ↑ **Cahoon Museum of American Art** (508-428-7581; cahoonmuseum.org), 4676 Route 28, Cotuit. Open 10–4 Tuesday through Saturday; 1–4 Sunday, February through December. This magnificent 1775 Georgian Colonial farmhouse was once a stagecoach stop on the Hyannis-to-Sandwich route. Today it houses a permanent collection of 19th- and early-20th-century American art, and features the whimsical and often humorous paintings of the late neoprimitive artists Martha and Ralph Cahoon. The building's low ceilings, wide floorboards, fireplaces, and wall stenciling provide an intimate backdrop for the artwork. Don't miss it. The museum also offers summer workshops and classes. Gallery talks are held on many Tuesday mornings at 11. Docent tours are conducted on Friday mornings at 11. Adults $4; children under 12, free.

✍ ↑ **Centerville Historical Museum** (508-775-0331; centervillehistorical museum.org), 513 Main Street, Centerville. Open noon–4 Tuesday through Saturday, May to mid-December. The 1850s Mary Lincoln House (no relation to Abraham) was built by Mary's father, Clark, a local tinsmith. Then along came Charles Ayling, a wealthy Cape businessman and philanthropist, who endowed a wing and assembled an entire Cape Cod colonial kitchen, complete with large open fireplace and dozens of iron utensils. The 14 rooms are filled with rare Sandwich glass, Civil War artifacts, maritime artifacts, historic quilts, costumes from 1750 to 1950, children's toys and games, perfume bottles, and A. E. Crowell's miniature duck carvings. Exhibits change throughout the season. Adults $5; children under 12, free.

❄ **The 1856 Country Store** (508-775-1856; 1856countrystore.com), 555

OSTERVILLE HISTORICAL SOCIETY MUSEUM

Main Street, Centerville. With the exception of the original wooden floors, the store is more picturesque outside than inside. Crowds do flock here for the selection of cutesy country and perfumed things.

Osterville Historical Society Museum (508-428-5861; osterville.org), 155 West Bay Road, Osterville. Open 1:30–4:30 Thursday through Sunday, mid-June to mid-September. The society maintains three properties, well worth a visit. The **Captain Jonathan Parker House**, built circa 1824, contains period art, antiques, furniture, and dolls, as well as paintings and porcelain from the China trade. The one-room-deep **Cammett House**, a simple Cape Cod farmhouse built circa 1790, is furnished with period pieces. And the **Boat Shop Museum** showcases the famous Crosby-designed catboat *Cayuga*, built in 1928, and the *Wianno Senior* and *Junior.* Half models, tools, and historic Osterville waterfront photographs are also displayed. Don't miss the period Colonial gardens maintained by the Osterville Garden Club. Adults $3, children free.

Samuel B. Dottridge House (508-428-0461), 1148 Main Street, Cotuit. Open 2–5 Thursday through Sunday, June to early September; Saturday until mid-October. Owned by the Historical Society of Sansuit and Cotuit, this 1790 house contains historical but otherwise fairly unremarkable objects pertaining to daily 19th-century life. Adults $1, children 50¢.

SPECIAL PROGRAMS ✿ **Tales of Cape Cod** (508-362-8927; talesofcapecod .org), 3018 Route 6A at Rendezvous Lane, Barnstable Village. This simple, white-clapboard building served as the Barnstable County Courthouse from 1772 to 1832, when the "new" granite structure down the road was built. The secular Olde Colonial Courthouse then became a Baptist church until it was purchased in 1949 by Tales of Cape Cod, a nonprofit organization that preserves Cape folklore and oral histories. The organization sponsors an excellent lecture series Tuesday evenings at 7:30 in July and August. Subjects range from Inventors, Entrepreneurs, and Opportunists of Cape Cod to Cape Cod Attics: Antique Appraisal Evening, Whale Rescues, Shipwrecks, and Growing Up on Cape Cod in the 1930s. Talks are delivered by knowledgeable townspeople. Adults $5, children free. (Refreshments alone are worth the price of admission.)

See also **Barnstable Comedy Club** under *Entertainment.*

SCENIC DRIVES From the center of Centerville, take South Main Street toward Osterville. Turn left on East Bay, which will wind around and become Seaview; follow that to the end. Double back and turn left on Eel River, then turn left onto Bridge. You will not be able to go very far on this road (it empties into a gated community), but it does cross a sparkling waterway. After turning around, follow West Bay back to Main Street.

You can also take Main Street off Route 28 in Santuit (as you head toward Falmouth on Route 28, turn left onto Main Street just before the Mashpee town line). Follow Main Street through

Cotuit center, jog left onto Ocean View overlooking Nantucket Sound, then jump back onto Main Street and follow it to the end for more pond and Sound views.

✳ To Do

AIRPLANE RIDES ✳ **Cape Cod Soaring Adventures** (508-420-4201; 800-660-4563; capecodsoaring.com), Marstons Mills Airport, Route 149, Marstons Mills. Open 10–5 daily, weather permitting; reservations recommended at least 24 hours in advance. Flying aboard Randy Charlton's glider at 5,000 feet and 40 mph, you'll see butterflies, seagulls, and hawks. The unrestricted views and the quietness are like nothing you've probably ever experienced. Fall is perhaps the best time to fly, with spring a close second. On a sunny winter day, you can see for 80 miles, far better than on an average hazy summer day, when visibility peaks at about 5 miles. The key is low humidity and seasonably cool days. Of the three tours, Seagull takes 20 minutes and is best for inexperienced flyers ($105). The longer trips are 30 ($140) and 45 minutes ($175).

✳ **Mills Air Service** (508-428-8732), Marstons Mills Airport, Route 149, Marstons Mills. These scenic tours, from the Cape's only grass-strip airport, can go virtually anywhere on the Cape. Chris takes you on airplane rides around the area ($150; reservations recommended; any age allowed).

BASEBALL ✐ The **Cotuit Kettleers** (capecodbaseball.org) play at Lowell Park in Cotuit from mid-June to mid-August.

BICYCLING If you don't have a friend with a summer place in the exclusive Wianno section of town, the best way to enjoy the village of Osterville is to cycle or drive along Wianno Avenue to Seaview Avenue, then turn right onto Eel River Road to West Bay Road and head back into town.

A PERFECT DAY IN BARNSTABLE

8:00 Break bread with fellow guests at your B&B.

9:30 Head up, up and away with a tour from Cape Cod Soaring Adventures.

11:15 Pour over centuries-old primary sources of Cape Cod history at the Nickerson Memorial Room at Cape Cod Community College.

12:30 Duck into the anglicized and Japanese-style St. Mary's Church garden.

1:15 Enjoy waterside dining at Mattakeese Wharf.

2:30 Drop some cash at Route 6A antiques and specialty stores like Blacks' Handweaving Shop or West Barnstable Tables.

7:00 Dine on seafood with the locals at the taverny Dolphin.

9:00 Appreciate seasonal, fleeting beach plum ice cream from Four Seas.

FISHING/SHELLFISHING Get freshwater fishing licenses from the town clerk's office (508-790-6240) in Town Hall, 367 Main Street, Hyannis. Shellfishing permits are required and may be obtained from the Department of Natural Resources (508-790-6272), 1189 Phinney's Lane (which runs between Routes 28 and 132), Centerville. You can also get freshwater fishing permits here.

Wequaquet Lake in Centerville has plenty of largemouth bass, sunfish, and northern pike to go around. Park along Shoot Flying Hill Road. Marstons Mills has three ponds stocked with small-mouth bass, trout, and perch: **Middle Pond**, Race Lane; **Hamblin's Pond**, Route 149; and **Schubael's Pond**, Schubael Pond Road off Race Lane.

Barnstable Harbor Charter Fleet (508-362-3908), 186 Millway, off Route 6A. Late May to early October. A fleet of four boats takes up to six passengers each for 4-, 6-, and 8-hour fishing expeditions in Cape Cod Bay.

FOR FAMILIES ❄ ᗌ **Cape Cod YMCA** (508-362-6500; ymcacapecod .org), Route 132, West Barnstable. In addition to a fitness and cardiovascular center, the YMCA offers a number of programs that welcome short-term visitors: open swims daily. During the school year, they offer Saturday evening Teen Nights and Friday Kids' Night Out. Drop off the children and go out to dinner while they do arts and crafts. The Y also has a summer camp with weekly sessions.

ᗌ **Main Street Playground**, adjacent to the recreation building, Centerville. Built by local volunteers in 1994, there are swings slides, a fancy jungle gym, sand for digging and building, climbing rings, and picnic tables.

GOLF ❄ **Cotuit Highground Country Club** (508-428-9863), 31 Crocker Neck Road, Cotuit. A popular nine-hole, 1,240-yard, par-28 course.

Olde Barnstable Fairgrounds Golf Course (508-420-1142), 1460 Route 149, Marstons Mills. An 18-hole course (par 70) so close to the airport that you can see the underbellies of approaching planes from the driving range.

TENNIS Public courts are located at the **Centerville Elementary School** on Bay Lane; at the **Cotuit Elementary School** on Highland Avenue; at the **Marstons Mills East Elementary School** on the Osterville–West Barnstable Road; and at the **Barnstable–West Barnstable Elementary School** on Route 6A.

WHALE-WATCHING ᗌ **Hyannis *Whale Watcher* Cruises** (508-362-6088; 888-942-5392; whales.net), Mill Way off Route 6A, Barnstable Harbor. Daily departures, mid-May to mid-October. A convenient mid-Cape location and a fast boat make this a good choice for whale-watching. An onboard naturalist provides commentary. There are also occasional sunset cruises (adults $43, children $26) in summer.

BEACHES Millway Beach, just beyond Barnstable Harbor. Although a resident parking sticker is needed in summer, you can park and look across to **Sandy Neck Beach** (see the "Barrier Beach Beauty" sidebar) in the off-season.

✍ **Craigville Beach**, on Nantucket Sound, Centerville. This crescent-shaped beach—long and wide—is popular with college crowds and families. Facilities include restrooms, changing rooms, and outdoor showers. Parking $15 daily, $50 weekly.

Long Beach, on Nantucket Sound, Centerville. Centerville residents favor Long Beach, at the western end of Craigville Beach; walk along the water until you reach a finger of land between the Sound and the Centerville River. Long Beach is uncrowded, edged by large summer shore homes and a bird sanctuary on the western end. Although a resident sticker is required, I include it anyway because it's the nicest beach, and Explorers can check it out off-season.

PONDS Hathaway Pond, Phinney's Lane, Barnstable Village, is a popular freshwater spot with a bathhouse and lifeguard. The following freshwater locations require a resident sticker: **Lovell's Pond**, off Newtown Road from Route 28, Marstons Mills; **Hamblin's Pond**, off Route 149 from Route 28, Marstons Mills; and **Wequaquet Lake**, off Shoot Flying Hill Road from Route 132, Centerville.

WALKS Sandy Neck Great Salt Marsh Conservation Area (508-362-8300), West Barnstable; trailhead from the parking lot near the gatehouse off Sandy Neck Road. First things first: Hike off-season when it's not so hot. It takes about 6 hours to do the whole circuit. The 12-mile (roundtrip) trail to Beach Point winds past pine groves, wide marshes, low blueberry bushes, and 50- to 100-foot dunes. It'll be obvious that this 3,295-acre marsh is the East Coast's second largest. Beginning in June, be on the lookout for endangered piping plovers nesting in the sand. Eggs are very difficult to see and, therefore, easily crushed. If you're into camping they have a **primitive campground** open May to mid-October with four sites. Hike in the 3.1 miles with your gear; they provide wood, water, and bathroom facilities. Fee is $20 per day. Parking $15 per day.

TIDAL FLATS

St. Mary's Church Gardens, 3005 Route 6A (across from the library), Barnstable Village. Locals come to these peaceful, old-fashioned gardens to escape summer traffic swells on Route 6A. In spring, the gardens are full of crocuses, tulips, and daffodils. A small stream, crisscrossed with tiny wooden bridges, flows through the property; the effect is rather like an anglicized Japanese garden.

Tidal flats, Scudder Lane, off Route 6A, West Barnstable. At low tide you can walk onto the flats and almost across to the neck of Sandy Neck.

West Barnstable Conservation Area, Popple Bottom Road, off Route 149 (near Route 6), West Barnstable. Park at the corner for wooded trails.

Armstrong-Kelley Park, Route 28 near East Bay Road, Osterville. This lovely 8½-acre park has shaded picnic tables, flowers blooming throughout the summer, wooded walking trails with specimens identified, and wetland and woodland walkways. Look for rare trees like the umbrella magnolia and the Camperdown elm. This park claims to be the oldest and largest private park on the Cape.

BARRIER BEACH BEAUTY

Sandy Neck Beach, on Cape Cod Bay, off Route 6A, West Barnstable. One of the Cape's most stunning beaches. The entrance to this 6-mile-long barrier beach is in Sandwich. Encompassing almost 4,500 acres, the area is rich with marshes, shellfish, and bird life. Sandy Neck dunes protect Barnstable Harbor from the winds and currents of Cape Cod Bay. Sandy Neck was the site of a Native American summer encampment before the colonists purchased it in 1644 for three axes and four coats. Then they proceeded to harvest salt-marsh hay and boil whale oil in tryworks on the beach. Today a private summertime cottage community occupies the far eastern end of the beach. Known locally as the Neck, the former hunting and fishing camps, built in the late 19th century and early 20th, still rely on water pumps and propane lights.

Beach facilities include restrooms, changing rooms, and a snack bar. Parking costs $15 daily. You can purchase four-wheel-drive permits at the gatehouse (508-362-8300). But six items must be in your car when the permit is issued: a spare tire, jack, jack pad, shovel, low-pressure tire gauge, and something to tow the car. If you live outside Barnstable, the cost is $50 from early September to mid-April, or $140 per calendar year.

✳ Lodging

While a number of historic B&Bs line Route 6A, I've included only a select few because each offers exceptional hospitality and are all quite different. To get off the beaten path, head "inland" to Cotuit or Centerville; you won't be disappointed. Barnstable's only beachfront option is a motel.

BED & BREAKFASTS ✳ "ᵀ"

Honeysuckle Hill (508-362-8418; 866-444-5522; honeysucklehill.com), 591 Route 6A, West Barnstable. Arguably the most welcoming innkeepers on the Cape, Freddy and Ruth Riley have applied their considerable talents to making this 1810 farmhouse—filled with floral scents—a favorite. Their four rooms and two-bedroom suite (an extremely good value) have feather bedding, robes, fine English toiletries, flat-screen TVs, and marble baths. Friendly, elegant, and modestly furnished with a mix of white wicker and antiques, they're a breath of fresh air. I particularly like Wisteria, the largest, with a king bed, blue toile decor, and its own entrance. What's not to love? Fred, ever the Englishman, has planted a garden that boasts woodland walks, sitting areas, a barbecue area, and a spa tub with outdoor shower. Guests gather in the large screened-in porch for warm snacks and full afternoon bar or for convivial pre-breakfast scones. From there, guests are escorted inside for a four-course breakfast—set at a formal but inviting table—that might include fruit, Belgian waffles, and eggs Benedict with asparagus. May through October $179–194 rooms, $259 suite (for two to four—kids must be over age 12); off-season $139–199; November through April $149–209.

✳ ⬡ "ᵀ" **Josiah Sampson House** (508-428-8383; josiahsampson.com), 40 Old King's Road, Cotuit. The most fun part of my job is discovering places and sharing them. Well, here's one: The sophisticated duo of Richard Thomas and Joe Gergyes seem to have opened up their Federal-style manse because they really want to share it. Richard is a true breakfast gourmand, and on my last visit, I dined on the back deck on the best French toast (with a spicy Spanish orange sauce) and sun-dried chicken sausage I have ever had the privilege of tasting. As for the six guest rooms, they're comfortable and spacious, with every detail attended to. The living room is elegant without being stuffy and features a working player piano (with plenty of rolls); the dining room is handsome and contemporary; the deep backyard has a hammock, a gazebo, and a hot tub; and the inn is about a mile from the bay. Loaner bicycles are perfect for in-town use. All in all, this B&B represents one of the best values on the Cape. Not appropriate for children. May to September $179; summer holidays $199; off-season $129–159.

✳ "ᵀ" **Beechwood** (508-362-6618; 800-609-6618; beechwoodinn.com), 2839 Route 6A, Barnstable Village. The primary reason why guests overnight here is a toss-up: Debbie's championship golden retrievers and

BEECHWOOD

their pups, Ken's exuberant personality (actually, both Traugots are consummate concierges), or the high Victorian, character-filled guest rooms. Whatever sways you, the inn offers six romantic guest rooms all furnished quite differently. All are recommended. So . . . are you more interested in a canopy bed, marble fireplace, or steeply angled walls? (If the last, try the Garret Room, tucked under third-floor eaves.) There are two more reasons to stay at this 1853 Queen Anne–style house: the stunning weeping copper beeches flanking it are rare specimens—rather like the dining room's tongue-and-groove paneling and a pressed-tin ceiling. Debbie's multi-course full breakfasts (perhaps an egg and cheese blintz soufflé) prepare you for the day like few other places. Late May through October $185–210; November to late May $135–150.

❄ 🐾 ✂ ⁙ᵀ⁙ **Lamb and Lion Inn** (508-362-6823; 800-909-6923; lambandlion .com), 2504 Route 6A, Barnstable. Proprietors Alice Pitcher and Tom Dott know a little something about service and hospitality: they operated a Relais & Château restaurant in the Hudson Valley before coming here. This transformed inn consists of 10 guestrooms (including the Lamb's

Retreat **cottage** and "Barn-Stable" that can accommodate families) surrounding an open-air heated swimming pool and hot tub. Long hallways are brightened with sky murals, and the diverse rooms are pleasant with wicker and antiques. I particularly like room 9, which gets great afternoon sun, and the suite with a private deck, hot tub, and kitchenette. Although rooms are quite different, they all have flat-screen TVs and air-conditioning; most have a fireplace, half have a kitchenette, and most have a spiffy motel-style bathroom. Before leaving, ask to see the rare, triple-sided fireplace in the original 1740 house. A fine expanded continental breakfast is included. Children over 8 welcome. Mid-May through October $189–275 rooms, $250–295 cottage/suite/barn; off-season $125–225.

❄ ⁙ᵀ⁙ **Acworth Inn** (508-362-3330; 800-362-6363; acworthinn.com), 4352 Old Kings Highway, Cummaquid. Innkeeper Lisa Callahan's comfortable B&B has five romantic rooms (including one suite) that make you feel at home because of their restful colors, hand-painted furniture, and fluffy robes. Two of the rooms feature whirlpool tubs. A full breakfast with fruit, freshly baked bread, and, perhaps, fruit-covered waffles, is served on the backyard deck in summer. Mid-May through October $150–219; off-season $90–175.

RENTAL HOUSES ✂ **Craigville Realty** (508-775-3174; craigville beach.com), 648 Craigville Beach Road, West Hyannisport.

CAMPGROUND **Sandy Terraces Nudist Family Campground** (508-428-9209; sandyterraces.com), Marstons Mills. Open May to mid-October. Geared toward couples and families, this 10-acre campground has

12 wooded sites, a sandy beach on a mile-long lake, a redwood sauna, and lots of activities and cookouts. Call or write in advance of your visit.

✳ Where to Eat

Barnstable doesn't have a plethora of restaurants, but it does have two fine ones, a waterfront restaurant, an excellent local tavern, and the best home-made ice cream on the Cape. What else could you want?

DINING OUT ✳ ✿ ⅋ **The Regatta** (508-428-5715; regattaofcotuit.com), 4613 Route 28, Cotuit. Open for dinner. Housed in a 200-year-old Federal mansion—a former stagecoach stop—the Regatta is romantic, elegant, and relaxed with six intimate dining rooms. Chef-owner Weldon Fizell, who took over from longtime owner Brantz Bryan in Spring 2007, has had big shoes to fill at this beloved institution. He's featuring Asian- and European-inspired pairings of traditional New England meats and seafood. Because of consistency of execution and pricing, I'm beginning to prefer the more casual, lighter menu from the expanded taproom (aka bar). Either way, plan on ending your gastronomic romp with Chocolate Seduction with *sauce framboise.* Or get the sampler plate of three desserts—a bargain at $16. Dinner $25–36, including a sorbet course and scrumptious side dishes; taproom menu $12–38.

✳ ⅋ **Five Bays Bistro** (508-420-5559; fivebaysbistro.com), 825 Main Street, Osterville. Open for dinner; call for off-season schedule. Named for the five bodies of water that surround Osterville, this buzzy (or noisy, depending on your sensibilities) little place is urban and stylish—befitting a neighborhood awash with patrons sizing each other up and keeping up with the Joneses. As for the sophisticated fusion cuisine, it gets very good reviews across the board. Local seafood (perhaps done with an Asian twist) and fish (like grilled Chilean sea bass) are always a good bet. Dinner $22–34.

✳ ⌀ ⅋ ⅋ **Dolphin** (508-362-6610; the dolphinrestaurant.com), 3250 Route 6A, Barnstable. Open for lunch and dinner. This friendly watering hole, in chef-owner Nancy Jean Smith's family for three generations, features extensive seafood selections. At midday you'll find everything from crabcakes and oysters to salads, specialty sandwiches, and baked and fried seafood. At dinner it's a bit more elaborate, with grilled swordfish, braised salmon, home-roasted duck, and lamb chops. Still, if you're looking for cutting-edge food, the knife might seem in need of sharpening here. The Dolphin, complete with a long bar separated from the main dining room, is heavily patronized by locals who know a good thing when they taste it. It's also staffed by folks just as loyal. Early specials. Lunch $6–18, dinner $15–25.

EATING OUT ⅋ **Keepers Restaurant** (508-428-6719), 330 West Bay Road (on the harbor at the Crosby Boat Yard), Osterville. Open for lunch and dinner June through September. Wanna know a secret? Find Keepers.

Comments from locals are consistent: this place is really decent, they all say with enthusiasm and earnestness. Located in the old Crosby boatyard, this small and kinda contemporary restaurant not only offers local standards like lobster rolls, baked cod, oysters, and ribs, it also affords views of the old wooden Crosby Cats alongside million-dollar yachts. It's rather like a smaller version of the Chart Room (see *Where to Eat*, in "Bourne"). Lunch $8–19, dinner $20–32; off-season entertainment.

❉ ♉ **Barnstable Restaurant and Tavern** (508-362-2355; barnstable restaurant.com), 3176 Route 6A, Barnstable Village. Open for lunch and dinner. This old tavern in Barnstable's historic district, under new ownership since 2005, has been resurrected into a fine choice—whether for a burger and beer in the tavern or a more substantial meal of fried seafood (calamari, sole, scrod, clams) or daily specials like sautéed sea scallops in the main dining room. Salads are always a good choice. Lunch $13–15, dinner $16–20.

Mattakeese Wharf (508-362-4511; mattakeese.com), 271 Mill Way, Barnstable Harbor. Open 11:30–10 daily, May through October. Few places beat this quintessential harborside location for $64 million water views. Get a table an hour before sunset so you can watch the fishing boats and pleasure craft come and go in this quiet harbor. Prices are high relative to the quality, but you're here for the views, right? Right. Tried-and-true main dishes include bouillabaisse, large burgers, scrod, and boiled lobster. Bob Venditti has owned Mattakeese since 1968, and chef Ken La Casse has run the kitchen since the early 1980s. Lunch $6–12, dinner $14–25.

❉ **Craigville Pizza & Mexican** (508-775-2267), Craigville Beach Road, Centerville. Open for lunch and dinner. A favorite of readers Dan and Judie Dunham Spiritus, it's a no-frills place, but you can't beat it for these parts. Pies $8 to 14.

❉ **Osterville Cheese Shop** (508-428-9085), 29 Wianno Avenue, Osterville. Open daily. Osterville residents and summer folks order imported and domestic cheeses and other gourmet goodies for their cocktail parties here. Enjoy a thick sandwich, soup, breakfast pastries and breads, a slice of chicken pie, or a pint of pasta salad, all wrapped up to take away.

❉ **Cotuit Grocery** (508-428-6936), 737 Main Street, Cotuit. This old multiuse building would go unnoticed in Vermont, but on the Cape it's an anomaly. It's a convenience store–cum–wine shop–cum–grille. Sandwiches under $10.

✳ Entertainment

Barnstable Comedy Club (508-362-6333; barnstablecomedyclub.com), 3171 Route 6A, across from the Barnstable Restaurant and Tavern, Barnstable Village. Performances November through May. Let's get something straight right off the bat: This is not an actual comedy club! Founded in 1922, the state's oldest amateur theater group performs more than comedies in this 200-seat theater—look for musicals and straight (though not heavy or provocative) theater. Since 1922 its motto has been "To produce good plays and remain amateurs." (Kurt Vonnegut got his feet wet here and was the club's first president.) Tickets $16–18.

♉ **Kettle Ho Restaurant & Tavern** (508-428-1862), 12 School Street, Cotuit. Open nightly. When you want to hang out with locals for a beer or mixed drink, this friendly place is *the* place. Blink and you'll miss it since

Cotuit only consists of four or five buildings. Even though it's recently been refurbished, it still feels divey—in a good way.

Y Joe's Twin Villa (508-428-9861), 195 Old Mill Road, Osterville. Open seasonally. The neighborhoody Sloppy Joe's, as it's affectionately known, reigns as another supreme dive bar. Patrons run the gamut from rags to riches, and the live music rocks.

✳ Selective Shopping

❊ All shops are open year-round unless otherwise noted. Osterville center, with a number of upscale shops, is good for a short stroll.

ANTIQUES Harden Studios (508-362-7711), 3264 Route 6A, Barnstable Village. This late-17th-century house was beautifully restored by Charles M. Harden in 1993 and now functions as an antiques shop and gallery. It's a true family affair: Harden's son Charles operates an etching press and art gallery in the adjacent shed, and son Justin researches the fine antiques collection. The collection includes American antiques from the early 1700s to the 1840s; Empire and Federal pieces; Oriental rugs, lamps, and chandeliers.

Sow's Ear Antiques (508-428-4931), Route 28 at Route 130, Cotuit. Americana and primitive folk art and furniture sold from an 18th-century house; some garden antiques, too.

Cotuit Antiques (508-420-1234), 70 Industry Road, behind Cotuit Landing off Route 28, Cotuit. Henry Frongillo enjoys people and keeping his shop folksy. Since he buys whole estates, you never know what you'll find. Primarily, though, he offers fine furniture, collectibles, some art, pottery, and lots of great old signage and advertising memorabilia.

Glass Workshop (508-362-0175), 4039 Route 6A, Cummaquid. This contemporary gallery has distinctive, artistic glass pieces like earrings and sculptures. As one Explorer says, there's "no crummy, touristy stuff" here.

ART GALLERIES Cape Cod Art Association (508-362-2909; capecodartassoc.org), 3480 Route 6A, Barnstable Village. This nonprofit was founded in 1948 and displays a fine range of juried art and artists in a beautiful and airy gallery. Shows change monthly. Indoor and outdoor classes and workshops are offered.

Tao Water Art Gallery (508-375-0428), 1989 Route 6A, West Barnstable. This contemporary Asian gallery, representing more than 45 artists from post–Cultural Revolution China and the States, runs the gamut from exceptional abstract painting to landscapes, sculpture, and Chinese contemporary art. One of the largest galleries on the Cape, with over 5,600 square feet, Tao Water also sells antique furniture and handmade crafts and gifts from all over Asia.

See also **Harden Studios** under *Antiques.*

ARTISANS Oak and Ivory (508-428-9425), 1112 Main Street, Oster-

SINFUL SCOOPS

🦞 🍴 ♿ **Four Seas Ice Cream** (508-775-1394), 360 South Main Street, at Centerville Four Corners. Open 9 AM–10:30 PM daily, mid-May to mid-September; sandwiches served 10–2:30. Founded in 1934 and celebrating its 75th anniversary in 2009, Four Seas was, until recently, owned by Doug Warren, who took over from his father—who had owned it since 1960, when he (in turn) bought it from the folks who had given him a summer job as a college student. Did you get that? The walls of this funky place, a former blacksmith's shop, are lined with photos of preppy summer crews, newspaper articles about Four Seas (it wins national ice-cream awards every year), and poems penned in honor of past anniversaries. You can see that this place really inspires folks! It's named for the four "seas" that surround the Cape: Buzzards Bay, Cape Cod Bay, the Atlantic Ocean, and Nantucket Sound. Oh yes, about that ice cream: The Cape's absolute best is made almost daily, using the freshest ingredients. Try the coconut or black raspberry. Lobster salad sandwiches are great, too.

ville. If you've always wanted a Nantucket lightship basket but haven't made it to Nantucket, this is the off-island place for you. The baskets are expensive (from about $700 to several thousand dollars), reflecting the fine craftsmanship and 35–45 hours of work that go into each delicate piece. Basket makers Bob and Karen Marks (he a Nantucketer, she a wash-ashore) also offer traditional 18th-century coastal New England artwork and gifts like scrimshaw, Wedgwood china with lightship basket patterns, sailors' valentines, and hand-carved shorebirds. They've expanded into reproduction furniture, carpets, tabletop lamps, and jewelry, too.

BOOKSTORES ❋ **Isaiah Thomas Books & Prints** (508-428-2752), 4632 Falmouth Road, at Routes 28 and 130, Cotuit. Open daily June through September; closed Mondays in the shoulder seasons; open weekends January through March. Jim Visbeck offers more than 60,000 antiquarian, first-edition, and slightly used books,

including books for children. They're divided by age group and interest. He also offers appraisals, search services, and archival materials. The Cape's only antiquarian bookseller is simply marvelous; you could easily spend an afternoon here. (Well, I have.)

SPECIAL SHOPS West Barnstable Tables (508-362-2676), Route 149, West Barnstable. Open daily. This showroom features the work of a dozen master craftsmen and artists, including that of Dick Kiusalas. Since it's difficult (not to mention prohibitively expensive) to find antique tables anymore, Dick makes tables using salvaged 18th- and 19th-century wood. His creations are exquisite and worth admiring even if you don't have a couple of thousand dollars to spare. Less expensive pieces include windowpane mirrors, primitive cupboards made with old painted wood and found objects, and Windsor and thumb-back chairs.

Margo's (508-428-5664), 27 Wianno Avenue, Osterville. Unusual picture frames, serving pieces, furniture, home accessories, bed linens, gifts, and interior design services.

✳ Special Events

Mid-July: **Osterville Village Day** (talk to Gail at 508-428-6327). Always the third Saturday; includes a crafts and antiques fair, a road race, children's events, and a parade.

July 4: **Hyannis Village Parade**, Main Street, Hyannis.

July 5: **Fireworks** over Lewis Bay at dusk; view from Veteran's Beach. The Cape Symphony Orchestra plays at Aselton Park before the display.

✐ Late July: **Barnstable County Fair** (508-563-3200; barnstablecountyfair .org), Route 151, East Falmouth. Local and national music acts, a midway, livestock shows (including horse, ox, and pony pulls), and horticulture, cooking, and crafts exhibits and contests. A weeklong tradition, especially for teens and families. Over age 12, $10; otherwise, free.

Mid-August: **Centerville Old Home Week**. Main Street open houses; until 1994 this event hadn't been held for 90 years.

Mid-October: **Osterville Village Fall Festival Day** (talk to Gail at 508-428-6327). Wine tasting, entertainment, an antiques show, a dog show, and food. Typically held on the Saturday of Columbus Day weekend.

Mid-December: **Osterville Christmas Open House and Stroll** (talk to Gail at 508-428-6327). Since 1972, the village has gussied itself up with traditional decorations for New England's second oldest stroll. Upwards of 2,000 to 3,000 participate in Friday-evening festivities, which include hayrides, trolley rides, wine tastings, and more.

HYANNIS

Hyannis is the Cape's commercial and transportation hub: Just under 1 million people take the ferry from Hyannis to Nantucket every year. Most Cape visitors end up in Hyannis at some point, whether by choice or by necessity.

Among Cape visitors, Hyannis seems to be everyone's favorite whipping post: A sigh of sympathy is heard when someone mentions he "has" to go into Hyannis in July or August. Yes, traffic is gnarly and Route 28 is overbuilt, but those same Cape residents and off-Cape visitors who moan about congestion in Hyannis couldn't live as easily without its services, including many fine restaurants. They come to buy new cars, embark to the islands, visit doctors, and shop at malls. Thus, because it is so distinct from the rest of Barnstable, I have given it its own chapter even though Hyannis is technically one of Barnstable's seven villages.

Hyannis's harborfront and Main Street began to be revitalized in the 1990s, thanks in part to the encouragement of the late Ben Thompson, architect of Boston's Quincy Market shopping complex and other successful urban waterfront development projects. And in 2006 it received another phased face-lift. It's a downright pleasant place these days. Boating activity on Lewis Bay is active. Main Street is a study in contrasts: Lined with benches and hanging flower baskets, in an attempt to attract strollers, it also has lots of T-shirt shops, some vacant storefronts, and a growing crop of congregating youth and shops geared to them. (Hyannis is, after all, the closest thing to a "city" that the Cape has.) Look for the Walkway to the Sea—a nice, spiffy link between Main Street and the waterfront—and harborfront "shacks" from which artists sell their goods.

Hyannis has a bit of everything: discount outlets, upwards of 60 eating establishments in the waterfront district alone, some quiet cottages and guesthouses, plenty of motels geared to overnight visitors waiting for the morning ferry, harbor tours, and lots of lively bars and nightlife.

Then there's the Kennedy mystique. Hyannisport—a neighborhood within Hyannis but quite distinct from Hyannis—will forever be remembered as the place where, in the early 1960s, President John F. Kennedy and Jacqueline sailed offshore and played with Caroline and John. Visitors who come in search of the "Kennedy compound," or in hopes of somehow experiencing the Kennedy aura, will find only an inaccessible, residential, Yankee-style community of posh estates.

Lastly, let's talk historical perspective for a paragraph or two. Hyannis's harbor area was inhabited about 1,000 years ago by ancestors of the Eastern Algonquian Indians, who set up summer campsites south of what is now Ocean Street. The

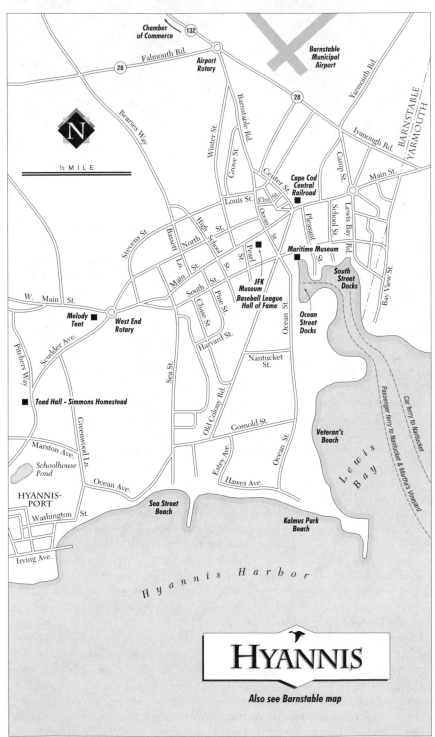

Chamber of Commerce

132

Falmouth Rd.

28

Airport Rotary

Barnstable Municipal Airport

28

Yarmouth Rd.

BARNSTABLE
YARMOUTH

Bearses Way

Winter St.

Barnstable Rd.

Grove St.

Iyanough Rd.

Camp St.

Main St.

N

½ MILE

Center St.

Cape Cod Central Railroad

Louis St.

Elm St.

School St.

Lewis Bay Rd.

Stevens St.

Bassett Ln.

High School St.

North St.

Ocean St.

Pleasant

Bay View St.

Main St.

South St.

Pearl St.

Maritime Museum

South Street Docks

W.   Main   St.

Melody Tent

West End Rotary

Sea St.

Chase St.

Pine St.

JFK Museum
Baseball League
Hall of Fame

Ocean St.

Ocean Street Docks

Pitchers Way

Scudder Ave.

Harvard St.

Nantucket St.

Toad Hall - Simmons Homestead

Greenwood Ln.

Old Colony Rd.

Gosnold St.

Veteran's Beach

L e w i s   B a y

Passenger ferry to Nantucket & Martha's Vineyard

Car ferry to Nantucket

Marston Ave.

Schoolhouse Pond

Ocean Ave.

Estey Ave.

Ocean St.

Hawes Ave.

HYANNIS-PORT

Washington   St.

Sea Street Beach

Kalmus Park Beach

Irving Ave.

H y a n n i s   H a r b o r

HYANNIS

Also see Barnstable map

first European to reach Cape Cod, Bartholomew Gosnold, anchored in the harbor in 1602. Shortly thereafter, settlers persuaded Native American sachem Yanno to sell them what is now known as Hyannis and Centerville for £20 and two pairs of pants.

Main Street was laid out in 1750, and by the early 1800s Hyannis was already known as the Cape's transportation hub. The harbor bustled with two- and three-masted schooners. When the steam-train line was extended from Barnstable in 1854, land-based trade and commerce supplanted the marine-based economy. Tourists began arriving in much greater numbers by the end of the 19th century. Yachts filled the harbor by the 1930s, until John Kennedy (who tied up at the Hyannisport Yacht Club) renewed interest in traditional local sailboats, known as catboats, in the 1950s.

GUIDANCE ❄ "ⓘ" **Hyannis Area Chamber of Commerce** (508-362-5230; hyannis.com), 397 Main Street, Hyannis. Open 9–5 Monday through Saturday, noon–5 Sunday, late May to late October; 10–4 Monday through Saturday, noon–4 Sunday, typically, November through April (but hours may vary during winter). The Hyannis chamber has information about all Barnstable villages. A visitor booth at the JFK Hyannis Museum on Main Street is staffed in summer only.

MEDIA The daily *Cape Cod Times* (508-775-1200; capecodonline.com) is published in Hyannis (319 Main Street).

PUBLIC RESTROOMS At beaches (see *Green Space*), behind the JFK Hyannis Museum on Main Street, and at the Ocean Street Docks (Bismore Park).

PUBLIC LIBRARY ❄ ✐ ⓣ "ⓘ" **Hyannis Public Library** (508-775-2280; hyannis library.org), 401 Main Street. This charming little house has a much larger facility tacked onto the rear. It's open weekdays from early June to mid-September, and Tuesday through Thursday and Saturday off-season. Buy your paperbacks here to benefit the library.

GETTING THERE *By car:* To reach Hyannis, about 30 minutes from the Cape Cod Canal, take Exit 6 off Route 6; follow Route 132 south to the airport rotary (at the junction of Routes 28 and 132). Take the second right off the rotary onto Barnstable Road, which intersects with Main, Ocean, and South streets (for the harbor).

By bus: The **Plymouth & Brockton** bus line (508-778-9767; p-b.com) connects Hyannis with other Cape towns, as well as with Boston's Logan Airport. **Bonanza/ Peter Pan** (888-751-8800; peterpanbus.com) connects Hyannis to Providence, T. F. Green Airport, and New York City. Both buses operate out of the Hyannis Transportation Center (at Center and Main streets). In-season there are six daily trips to and from New York City. The trip takes about 7 hours, and coaches are equipped with movies.

❄ *By air:* **Barnstable Municipal Airport** (508-775-2020), at the rotary junction of Route 28 and Route 132, Hyannis. Small carriers flying in and out of Hyannis include **Cape Air** and **Nantucket Air** (508-790-1980; 800-352-0714; flycapeair .com).

GETTING AROUND *By car:* Hyannis suffers from serious summer traffic problems. Parking on Main Street is free if you can get a space. If not, try North Street, one block north of Main Street and parallel to it. Main Street (one-way) is geared to strolling, but it's a long walk from end to end.

For rentals, call the big agencies based at the airport: **Hertz** (800-654-3131; hertz.com), **Avis** (800-331-1212; avis.com), and **Budget** (800-527-0700; budget .com). **Thrifty** (508-771-0450; 800-367-2277; thrifty.com) is across from the airport. **Trek** (508-771-2459; 800-776-8735; trekrentacar.com) is near the bus terminal, but they'll pick you up from the airport.

By shuttle: ✳ The **H₂O** (800-352-7155; capecodtransit.org) bus line, used more by locals than visitors, travels along Route 28 between Hyannis and Orleans daily except Sunday. Its terminus is the Hyannis Transportation Center.

Yarmouth Shuttle (800-352-7155; capecodtransit.org) operates late June to early September. The shuttle begins at the Hyannis Transportation Center and runs along Route 28 to various family-oriented points (including beaches) in Yarmouth. Flag down the driver, who will pull over to pick you up. (It sure beats sitting in traffic.) $2 one-way; $3 one-day passes; tickets are purchased aboard the trolley or at the chamber of commerce (see *Guidance*).

Hyannis Trolley (800-352-7155; capecodtransit.org). Operating daily, every half hour, from late June to early September; daily except Sunday in the winter. The summertime beach trolley makes a loop down Main Street to Sea Street, the beaches, and South Street. Fare $1 or $2.

The **Sealine** connects Hyannis to Barnstable, Mashpee, Falmouth, and Woods Hole. One-way ride $1 or $2. Pick up a schedule at the chamber of commerce (see *Guidance*) or Hyannis Transportation Center.

GETTING TO THE ISLANDS From Hyannis, there is year-round auto and passenger service to Nantucket from Hyannis and seasonal passenger service to Martha's Vineyard. For complete information, see *Getting There* in "Martha's Vineyard" and "Nantucket." You can also fly to the islands.

MEDICAL EMERGENCY Cape Cod Hospital (508-771-1800), 27 Park Street. Open 24/7.

STEAMSHIP AUTHORITY FERRY

✳ To See

John F. Kennedy Hyannis Museum (508-790-3077; jfkhyannismuseum .org), 397 Main Street. Open 9–5 Monday through Saturday, noon–5 Sunday, mid-April through October (with slightly shorter hours November, December, and mid-February to mid-April); closed January to mid-February. This museum opened in 1992 to meet the demands of visitors making the pilgrimage to Hyannis in search of JFK. People wanted to see "something," so the chamber gave them a museum that focuses on JFK's time in Hyannisport and on Cape Cod. The museum features more than 100 photographs of Kennedy from 1931 to 1963, arranged in themes: JFK's friends, his family, JFK the man. He said, "I always go to Hyannisport to be revived, to know the power of the sea and the master who rules over it and all of us." (If you want to learn something about the president and his administration, head to the JFK Museum in Boston.) In 2007 a new statue of JFK, sculpted by native Cape Codder David Lewis, was unveiled in front of the museum. Adults $5; children 10–16, $2.50; seniors $3.

Baseball League Hall of Fame (508-790-3077), ground floor of the JFK Hyannis Museum. Hours same as museum, above. Celebrating the 10 teams in the Cape Cod Baseball League, the museum displays autographed bats and balls, old photos, baseball cards of players drafted by the majors, and other memorabilia. If you're a real fan of America's favorite pastime, this will be of interest to you. If you're more interested in peanuts and cracker jacks, go to a game instead. Adults $5; children 10–16, $2.50; seniors $3.

JFK Memorial, Ocean Street. The fountain, behind a large presidential seal mounted on a high stone wall, is inscribed: "I believe it is important that this country sail and not sit still in the harbor." There is a nice view of Lewis Bay from here.

JFK MEMORIAL

Kennedy compound. Joe and Rose Kennedy rented the Malcolm Cottage in Hyannisport from 1926 to 1929 before purchasing and remodeling it to include 14 rooms, nine baths, and a private movie theater in the basement. (It was the first private theater in New England.) By 1932 there were nine children scampering around the house and grounds, which included a private beach, dock, tennis court, and pool. In 1956, then Senator John Kennedy purchased an adjacent house (at the corner of Scudder and Irving avenues), which

KENNEDY COMPOUND

JFK MEMORIAL

came to be known as the Summer White House. Bobby bought the house next door, which now belongs to his widow, Ethel. Senator Edward Kennedy's former house (it now belongs to his ex-wife, Joan) is on private Squaw Island. Eunice (Kennedy) and Sargent Shriver purchased a nearby home on Atlantic Avenue.

It was at Malcolm Cottage that JFK learned he'd been elected president, at Malcolm Cottage that Jacqueline and the president mourned the loss of their infant son, at Malcolm Cottage that the family mourned the deaths of the president and Bobby Kennedy, at Malcolm Cottage that Senator Edward Kennedy would annually present his mother with a rose for each of her years, and at Malcolm Cottage that matriarch Rose Kennedy died in 1995 at the age of 104. Although Kennedy sightings are rare, the Kennedys are still Hyannis's number one "attraction."

If you drive or walk around this stately area, you'll see nothing but high hedges and fences. Those who can't resist a look-see will be far better off taking a boat tour (see *To Do*); some boats come quite close to the shoreline and the white frame houses.

St. Francis Xavier Church, 347 South Street. When Rose Kennedy's clan was in town, they worshiped here. The pew used by JFK is marked with a plaque, while the altar is a memorial to JFK's brother, Lieutenant Joe Kennedy Jr., killed during World War II. More recently, Maria Shriver and Governor Arnold Schwarzenegger were wed here.

❄ **Cape Cod Maritime Museum** (508-775-1723; capecodmaritimemuseum.org), 135 South Street. Open 10–4 Monday through Saturday, noon–4 Sunday. New in 2004, this harborfront museum offers interactive exhibits, lectures, and classes (in ship model making, maritime archaeology, and boat building). It also displays boats that illuminate the region's past, present, and forthcoming connections with the sea. After the traditional catboat *Sarah* was built on the premises (quite a production), she was launched in Lewis Bay in 2007 and set out on excursions from ports between Chatham and Woods Hole. Don't miss a chance to go cruising with her; $10 per person. Adults $5; children 6–18, $4; seniors $4.

❄ ♪ ☂ **Cape Cod Potato Chip Factory** (508-775-7253 or 508-775-3358; capecodchips.com), 100 Breed's Hill Road, Independence Park, off Route 132. Open 9–5 weekdays. After Chatham resident Steve Bernard began the company in 1980 and parlayed it into a multimillion-dollar business, he sold it to corporate giant Anheuser-Busch in 1986, and moved on to the business of purveying Chatham Village Croutons. But in late 1995, when Anheuser-Busch wanted to sell or close it, Bernard bought the company back, saving about 100 year-round jobs. Take the 15-minute self-guided tour of the potato-chip-making process, then sample the rich flavor and high crunchability resulting from all-natural ingredients cooked in small kettles. Free.

🚣 **Cape Cod Central Railroad** (508-771-3800; 888-797-7245; capetrain.com), 252 Main and Center streets. Weekends in late May, June, September, and late October; daily in July and August. The 48-mile trip takes 2 hours and passes cranberry bogs, the Sandy Neck Great Salt Marsh, and the Cape Cod Canal. Since there are typically two trains daily, you take the first one, hop off in Sandwich, walk into the picturesque village (it's about a 10-minute walk), and then catch the next train back to Hyannis. The best part of this trip is the local narration—unless you've never been on a train before, in which case, the simple act of taking a train will tickle you more. See *Where to Eat* for information on their dinner train. Adults $20; children 12 and under, $16; seniors $18.

Town green, adjacent to the JFK Hyannis Museum. Note the life-sized bronze of the sachem Iyanough, chief of the Mattakeese tribe of Cummaquid and friend to the Pilgrims, created in 1995 by Osterville sculptor David Lewis.

Weeping beech tree, in the courtyard behind Plush & Plunder (605 Main Street). To the town's knowledge, this is one of seven remaining weeping beeches in the entire country. (Another is in Yarmouth.) It's an awesome, magnificent 200-plus-year-old specimen.

❋ **Toad Hall—Simmons Homestead Antique Car Collection** (508-778-4999; simmonshomesteadinn.com), 288 Scudder Avenue. Open 11–5 daily. Bill Putman relishes his quirkiness, and it's on full display here with an impressive collection of classic red sports cars—56 at last count. They're packed into a low-slung, garage-style barn, complete with fake oriental carpets lining the gravel pathways between the cars. Bill's a collector at heart: he also probably has 31 orange cats and the largest single malt scotch collection in America—almost 600 bottles, but who's counting? Adults $8; children 10–15, $4.

SCENIC DRIVE Hyannisport is by far the loveliest section of Hyannis, but don't come expecting to see the Kennedys. The "compound" is wedged between Scudder and Irving avenues. From Main Street, turn left onto Sea Street, right onto Ocean Avenue, left onto Hyannis Avenue, left onto Iyanough Road (Route 132), right onto Wachusett Avenue, and left onto Scudder Avenue.

❋ To Do

BASEBALL 🚣 The **Hyannis team** plays from mid-June to early August under the lights at McKeon Park. (Take South Street to High School Road and turn right.)

BICYCLING/RENTALS ❋ **Cascade Motor Lodge** (508-775-9717; cascade motorlodge.com), 201 Main Street. One block north of the harbor and 1½ blocks east of the bus and train stations, Cascade rents mountain and three-speed bikes daily from May to late October. Bicycles cost $12–20 daily; $8–14 half day; helmets are $2 (free for children under 12).

SIMMONS HOMESTEAD ANTIQUE CARS

A PERFECT DAY IN HYANNIS

9:00   Go for an early-morning swim at Veteran's Beach.

10:45   Relive or discover Camelot at the JFK Hyannis Museum.

1:00   Eat on the harbor at Spanky's Clam Shack.

2:30   See kettle chips roll off the assembly line at CC Potato Chip Factory.

4:00   Get out on the water with Hyannisport Harbor Cruises.

6:00   Order a sublime seafood dish at the Naked Oyster.

8:00   Take in an outdoor concert at the Cape Cod Melody Tent.

10:30   Sit beneath a rare 200-year-old weeping beech tree.

CRUISING OUT OF HYANNIS HARBOR PAST A LIGHTHOUSE

BOAT EXCURSIONS/RENTALS ✍ **Hyannisport Harbor Cruises** (508-778-2600; hy-linecruises.com), 138 Ocean Street. Mid-April to late October. Lewis Bay and Hyannis Harbor are beautiful, and the best way to appreciate them is by water. Also, if you're like 85,000 other visitors each season and you want the best possible view of the Kennedy compound, take this hour-long Hy-Line excursion. The boat comes within 500 feet of the shoreline compound—which is closer than you can get by foot or car. Hy-Line also offers a special deal for families: From mid-April to mid October, children ride free early morning until noon. During the height of summer, there's also a Sunday-afternoon family cruise with Ben & Jerry's ice-cream sundaes. Adults $12–15; children 5–12, $8–9.

Cape Cod Duckmobiles (508-790-2111; 888-225-3825; capecodduckmobile .com), 437 Main Street. Weekends Mid-April through May; daily mid-June to mid-September. These amphibious tours last 45 minutes, go splashing around Hyannis Harbor, and then roll along the street, rather like ducks out of water. Adults $17; seniors $14; children (under 5) $5.

✍ **Pirate Adventures** (508-430-0202; pirateadventures.com), Ocean Street Docks, Hyannis. Trips daily mid-June to early September. Particularly fun for children age 2–10, this swashbuckling trip begins with face painting on the dock. Then kids sign on to the pirate ship as crew, take a pirate oath, search for sunken treasure, and fire water cannons against renegade pirates. On the return voyage, the

booty is shared and pirates celebrate with song and dance. $21 per person. Reservations required.

Cat Boat (508-775-0222; catboat .com), Ocean Street Docks. Mid-April to late November. Look for the big cat on the sail. Eventide has a full complement of trips, including 90-minute excursions and private charters; head down to the dock to see what they offer.

FISHING/SHELLFISHING Freshwater fishing licenses are obtained from the town clerk's office (508-790-6240) in Town Hall, 367 Main Street, Hyannis. Shellfishing permits are required and may be obtained from the Department of Natural Resources (508-790-6272), 1189 Phinney's Lane (which runs between Routes 28 and 132), Centerville. You can also get freshwater fishing permits here.

❋ **Sports Port** (508-775-3096), 149 West Main Street. Surely you've seen the statue of a yellow guy in a red rowboat? That means the store is open. References for charters and tours; supplies for freshwater, saltwater, and fly-fishing; shellfish permits; and ice-fishing details, too.

Hy-Line Fishing Trips (508-790-0696; hy-linecruises.com), Ocean Street Docks. Bottom-fishing and deep-sea fishing for fluke and blues from mid-June to early September. Half-day trips cost $38 adults, $33 children; rod rental $5. Reservations strongly recommended.

❋ The supercruiser **Helen-H** (508-790-0660; helenh.com), Pleasant Street Docks, goes in search of big fish, too. You'll find cod all year long, bottom fish in the spring, and blues in summer.

GOLF ❋ **Hyannis Golf Club** (508-362-2606; hyannisgc.com), Route 132. An 18-hole, par-71 course.

❋ **Twin Brooks Golf Course** (508-862-6980; twinbrooksgolf.net), 35 Scudder Avenue, West End Circle. The Resort and Conference Center at Hyannis's par-3 course is 18 holes and 2,621 yards

ICE-SKATING Kennedy Memorial Skating Rink (508-790-6346; town .barnstable.ma.us), 141 Bassett Lane off Bearses Way. Public skating mid-October through March. Adults $6, children $4, seniors $2; skate rental $4.

SPECIAL PROGRAMS ❋ **Eastern Mountain Sports (EMS)** (508-362-8690; ems.com), 1513 Route 132. Open daily. In addition to renting kayaks (great for navigating herring rivers, creeks, and inlets), the Cape's

largest purveyor of outdoor gear offers free instructional clinics every couple of weeks. Topics range from outdoor cooking to mastering compass skills.

TENNIS Public courts are located at **Barnstable High School** off of West Main Street.

✳ Green Space

🕊 **BEACHES** Weekly cottage renters can purchase beach stickers at the Kennedy Memorial Skating Rink (508-790-6346), 141 Bassett Lane, Bearses Way.

Kalmus Park Beach, on Nantucket Sound, at the end of Ocean Street. This beach is good for sailboarding. The land, by the way, was donated by Technicolor inventor Herbert Kalmus, who also owned the Fernbrook estate in Centerville. Facilities include a restroom, picnic area, lifeguards, snack bar, and bathhouse. Parking $15.

🐟 **Veteran's Beach**, on Hyannis Harbor (Lewis Bay), off Ocean Street. This is a good beach for children because the waters are fairly shallow and calm, and it's a fine place to watch harbor sailboats (because the Hyannis Yacht Club is next door). Facilities include a restroom, a bathhouse, lifeguards, a snack bar, swings, grills, and a big wooded area with picnic tables. Parking $15.

Sea Street Beach, on Nantucket Sound, off Sea Street. Facilities include a restroom, lifeguards, snack bar and bathhouse. Parking $15.

✳ Lodging

Hyannis has hordes of nondescript motels and many good family-oriented cottages. If you want a good B&B, stay in one of Barnstable's other villages.

RESORT MOTOR INNS ✳ 🐟 🕊 ⁌¶⁌
Cape Codder Resort & Spa (508-771-3000; 888-297-2200; capecodder resort.com), 1225 Route 132 at Bearses Way. About 2 miles from the center of town, this two-story destination property was under reconstruction at press time by the Catania family, who are pouring millions into it. (The Catanias have long owned the venerable Dan'l Webster Inn in Sandwich and the Cape-wide, family-style Hearth & Kettle restaurants.) When it's done, the ultra-family-friendly resort will have 257 rooms, an indoor wave pool (complete with 2½-foot waves and waterslides), an outdoor pool, a 3-story medi-spa, two restaurants, a wine bar, a large fitness center, a game room, and tennis. Fifteen fractional ownership residences were also being built at

press time. Mid-June through August $193–279; off-season $109–199; children under age 17, free; inquire about various packages.

BED & BREAKFASTS ❄ "1"

Sea Breeze Inn (508-771-7213; seabreezeinn.com), 270 Ocean Avenue. These 10 rooms (some with two beds) are within a stone's throw of the beach. Although the old-fashioned rooms aren't fancy or filled with antiques, they are certainly comfortable, clean, and pleasant. Expanded continental breakfast included. Inquire about the family-friendly cottage with a Jacuzzi and kitchenette (rented nightly for $350 and weekly for $2000.) Mid-June to mid-September $98–150; off-season $70–105.

🐾 "1" **Sea Beach Inn** (508-775-4612), 388 Sea Street, Hyannis. Open mid-May to mid-October. This family-friendly inn, hosted by Neil and Elizabeth Carr, boasts ten cozy and comfortable guest rooms (some with refrigerator and most with private bath). The best part? The circa-1860 inn, once a sea captain's home, is within ear shot of Nantucket Sound (a two-minute walk to be exact) and within walking distance of downtown (if you like to walk). The resident golden retriever, Gracie, greets guests upon arrival. Continental breakfast included. $90–100 inn rooms; $100–150 carriage house rooms.

COTTAGES AND TOWNHOUSES

🐾 🖉 **Harbor Village** (508-775-7581; harborvillage.com), 160 Marstons Avenue, Hyannisport. Open early May to late October. Delightfully off the beaten path but still centrally located, Bob and Shirley Palardy's one- to four-bedroom cottages can sleep up to nine people. They're set on a private, wooded, 17-acre compound, within a 2-minute walk of Quahog Beach. It

doesn't get much better than this. Each of the 10 cottages has a living room, dining area, fully equipped kitchen, individual heat, a fireplace, a deck or patio with grill, and cable TV. A few have central air and washer/dryer; most have a dishwasher. You'll need to bring your own beach towels and chairs, though. Late June to early September from $1,825 weekly for a two-bedroom, $1,900 for a three-bedroom, $2,100 for a four-bedroom. Cottages have a 3-night minimum off-season: from $165 for a two-bedroom per night, $190 for a three-bedroom. Service charge of $50 weekly added; no credit cards; pets for an additional fee with prior approval.

🐾 🖉 **The Breakwaters** (508-775-6831; thebreakwaters.com), 432 Sea Street Beach. Open May to mid-October. Within a sandal shuffle of Sea Street Beach, these 18 well-maintained cottages accommodate two to six people. Kitchens are small but complete and updated. All cottages have a private deck or patio; most have ocean views. Even though it's on the beach, Breakwaters also has a heated pool with a lifeguard. Late June through August $1,350 weekly for a one-bedroom, $2,100 for a two-bedroom, $3,000 for a three-bedroom; off-season $490–625, $800–1,075, and $1,015–1,375, respectively. No credit cards.

HARBOR VILLAGE

❄ ⚓ "I" **Capt. Gosnold Village** (508-775-9111; captaingosnold.com), 230 Gosnold Street. In a residential area near the harbor, the family-friendly Capt. Gosnold's is a short walk to three beaches. And children will also enjoy the wooded and grassy grounds with a fenced-in pool and lifeguard, lawn games, and a play area. All rooms have been redecorated, and most of the 24 cottages are spacious and have a private deck and a gas grill. Request a newer cottage with three bedrooms and you'll also get three bathrooms and four TVs. While you can expect maid service Monday through Saturday and fully equipped kitchens, you'll have to bring your own beach towels. Late June to early September $100–350; off-season $60–200. Three-night minimum in cottages. Gosnold's adds a $6–12 nightly gratuity, depending on the number of people in your party.

❄ ⚓ **The Yachtsman** (508-771-5454; 800-695-5454; yachtsmancondo.com); rental office at 500 Ocean Street, Apt. 14. These privately owned townhouse condominiums, with their own private stretch of beach between Kalmus and Veteran's beaches (see *Green Space*), are right on Lewis Bay. During the summer, about 40 of the 125 units are available for rent. Although the decor varies from one unit to another, all meet certain standards. Multilevel units have a full kitchen, 2½ baths, private sundeck, sunken living room, and two to four bedrooms. About half have water views; half overlook the heated pool. Late June to early September $1,725–3,125 weekly; about $1,295–2,345 off-season. No credit cards.

✳ Where to Eat

With more than 60 eateries, Hyannis offers everything from mod seafood to romantic Italian. Unless otherwise noted, all restaurants are open year-round.

DINING OUT ❄ ♈ **Naked Oyster** (508-778-6500; nakedoyster.com), 20 Independence Drive, off Route 132. Open for lunch Tuesday through Friday and dinner nightly. My favorite area eatery, this cosmopolitan and sophisticated bistro is thankfully (slightly) off the beaten path. Savor palate-pleasing seafood and steaks complemented by a wonderful selection of wines by the glass. In addition to excellent raw bar choices, try appetizers like Thai shrimp, tuna tartar, lobster salad, and an oyster sampler. Mains like halibut with lobster meat, swordfish chops, and filet mignon take center stage at night. Whatever you do, don't miss their silk chocolate martini (it's a hip bar) and chocolate crème brûlée (arguably the best on the Cape). Hip and hopping hats off to owner Florence Lowell, owner since 2006. Early specials off-season. Lunch $8–14, dinner $18–32.

❄ ⚓ ♈ ♿ **RooBar City Bistro** (508-778-6515; theroobar.com), 586 Main Street. Open for dinner. This is one happening place, especially when the bar crowd reappears. Along with an exposed kitchen, high ceilings, and

CAPT. GOSNOLD VILLAGE

steel-based art, Tony Thind's innovative bistro offers internationally influenced New American fusion prepared by chef Sean McEachern. Think Wellfleet oysters, wood-roasted native cod, and shrimp scampi, wood-oven pizza with whole wheat crust. They even make homemade chicken fingers for the kids. Enjoy live jazz on Saturday nights. Pizzas $12–15, dinner $18–28.

❀ ✿ ♿ **Alberto's Ristorante** (508-778-1770; albertosristorante.com), 360 Main Street. Open for lunch and dinner daily. Thanks to chef-owners Felis and Donna Barreiro, Alberto's has been consistently fabulous, catering to a loyal following since 1984. Elegant and romantic, done up with faux marble and off-white colors, it may look formal but it doesn't project an ounce of stuffiness. The service is delightfully professional. The extensive Northern Italian menu features large portions of homemade pasta and regional specialties. Look for sublime eggplant *parmigiana*, lobster *fra diavolo*, rich seafood ravioli, and sesame-encrusted and seared tuna. Nightly seasonal additions are surprising in their breadth and execution. Alberto's, deeply deserving of their fine reputation, always does an excellent job. Despite not having room, I still top off my meal with a

ALBERTO'S RESTAURANT

ROADHOUSE CAFÉ

rich cappuccino and a decadent dessert sampler. Sidewalk tables are pleasant in the summer, as is the pianist (Joe Delanney) or jazz on Thursday and Friday evenings. Early dinner specials. Dinner $15–30.

❀ ▼ ♿ **Roadhouse Café** (508-775-2386; roadhousecafe.com), 488 South Street. Open for dinner nightly. This charming and pleasant place—with polished floors, Oriental carpets, hanging plants, tongue-and-groove ceilings with paddle fans, candlelight, and two fireplaces—is also very dependable, thanks to the long tenure of owner Dave Colombo and chef Ken VanBurren. Come for a romantic interlude or with a group for some fun. The extensive Italian and seafood menu features large portions. Consider splitting a simple main dish and pairing it with a couple of appetizers. Creative, thin-crust pizzas are offered in the Back Door Bistro (see *Entertainment*), which has a clubby feel with dark paneling and a mahogany piano bar. It also has a large selection of wine by the glass and 30 brands of beer. Dinner $19–38; early specials many nights.

❀ ▼ **Hannah's Fusion Bar and Bistro** (508-778-5565; hannahsbistro.com), 615 Main Street. Open for dinner nightly, lunch daily in-season and Friday and Saturday off-season. Although I didn't get a chance to eat here for this edition, I can heartily recommend Hannah's based on trusted innkeeper feedback. Look for Asian, Thai, and Vietnamese fusion dishes from chef-owner (and CIA graduate) Binh Phu, who understands how to push the envelope just enough. The cool, upscale environs reflect the contemporary cuisine, and there's a nice bar for hanging out. Lunch $8–12, dinner $25–33.

❄ **Colombo's** (508-790-5700), 544 Main Street. Open for lunch and dinner daily. Brought to you by the successful Roadhouse Café owner, this spacious and new (in 2008) mainstream eatery has a little something for everyone. From outside dining to an indoor bar and gelato case, from lunchtime sandwiches and salads to intermediate offerings like pizza and pasta to more hefty nighttime selections like grilled salmon and chicken parmesan, this might just be what Main Street was lacking. Time will tell. Dishes $8–24.

✍ ⚒ **The Paddock** (508-775-7677; paddockcapecod.com), 20 Scudder Avenue, West End rotary. Open for lunch and dinner April to mid-November. If you're in the mood for New England cuisine, the main dining room's Victorian surroundings provide the requisite backdrop. It sports dark beams, mahogany paneling, frosted glass, linen-covered tables, and fresh-cut flowers. And it attracts an older crowd and families. For lunch, stick to salads, chowder, and sandwiches. For dinner, try the steak au poivre, pan-seared sea scallops with mushroom risotto, roast rack of lamb, or parmesan-encrusted halibut with an artichoke-tomato ragout. When there's an event at the Melody Tent, stay away until after 8 PM. The Zartarian family has operated this institution since 1970, and John Anderson has been the chef since 1973. The wine list is excellent, and Ray Rasicot works the piano lounge like few others. In the spring and fall, the Paddock's "Neighborhood

Nights" menu features $15 mains; it's a great deal. Otherwise, lunch $7–13, dinner $17–30.

❄ ❀ ✍ **Ardeo on Main** (508-790-1115; ardeocapecod.com), 644 Main Street. Open 11:30–10 daily. Part of a successful local chain, this branch opened in 2006 with the same formula that worked so well in the original location: family-friendly offerings for good prices, an extensive Mediterranean and Greek menu, and citified surroundings. Wood oven pizzas, burgers, paninis, wrapped sandwiches, pasta dishes, and sampler plates (of grape leaves, baba ghanouj, and hummus) keep prices below stratospheric levels. It's always a good standby. Dinner $13–23.

EATING OUT **Spanky's Clam Shack** (508-771-2770), 138 Ocean Street. Open 11–10 daily mid-April to mid-October. Right on the harbor near where the sightseeing boats launch, this casual seafood place is the best of the fry bunch. Portions are huge, the prices are right, and you have a choice of inside or outside dining. Dishes $11–25.

✍ ⚑ **Baxter's Boat House Club and Fish 'n Chips** (508-775-4490; baxters capeod.com), 177 Pleasant Street. Open for lunch and dinner, mid-April to mid-October. It's as much about location as it is food here, and even though they serve the same menu throughout the day, I prefer going at lunchtime. Built on an old fish-packing dock near the Steamship Authority terminal, Baxter's has attracted a crowd since 1956, from beautiful people tying up at the dock to singles meeting at the bar, from families to folks who don't mind eating on paper plates on a harborfront picnic table. It's really the best waterfront table in town. The fried and broiled seafood is consistent, too, if not exemplary. Lunch and dinner $10–25.

❋ **Brazilian Grille** (508-771-0109; braziliangrille-capecod.net), 680 Main Street. Open for lunch and dinner. You'd have to fly to Rio for more authentic *churrascaria rodizio*, a traditional, elaborate all-you-can-eat barbecue buffet of skewered meats. Come hungry or don't bother. And then don't bother eating for the rest of the week. The atmosphere isn't anything to write home about, but the servers sure are friendly. Buffet $8–26.

❋ 🍷 **Ying's Sushi Bar** (508-790-2432), 59 Center Street. Open for lunch and dinner. Ying's boasts very good pad Thai, Japanese and Korean dishes, noodles, and sushi. The atmosphere here is tranquil, rather like an indoor garden. Sushi is half price on Monday. Lunch specials $7–9, dinner $10–16.

❋ 🍴 **Common Ground Café** (508-778-8390; hyanniscommonground .com), 420 Main Street. Open for lunch and dinner Monday through Thursday and Sunday, lunch only on Friday. When you step inside, let your eyes adjust to the darkness for a minute: You'll find hand-hewn booths resembling hobbit houses and an old-fashioned community (a religious collective actually) of folks serving honest food. The menu includes a few wholesome sandwiches and wraps, soups, salads, and daily specials. Everything is made from scratch. There is also a juice bar upstairs. Dishes $5–15.

❋ 🍷 ♿ **Sam Diego's** (508-771-8816; samdiegos.com), 950 Route 132. Open 11:30 AM–1 AM. Decorated with colored lights, colorful serapes, toucans, and sombreros, this huge and hopping place is often full of families. They come for reliable southwestern- and Mexican-inspired fare like chicken fajitas, barbecued ribs, burritos, enchiladas, and daily blackboard specials. In warm weather, dine on the large outdoor patio. For weekday lunches, try the all-you-can eat chili, soup, and taco bar for a mere $7 (less for children). Dishes $5–20.

❋ 🍷 ♿ **Harry's** (508-778-4188; harrys bluesbar.com), 700 Main Street. Open for lunch and dinner daily. This small, local bar-hangout (in new digs adjacent to the old ones since 2007) features Cajun dishes, BBQ, and homemade soups. Lunch leans heavily toward New Orleans with "hoppin' John" (rice with black-eyed peas), jambalaya, and blackened chicken. Now that JC is back as the chef, all is right with the world. The joint jumps with live blues nightly. Lunch $5–10, dinner $9–20.

ICE CREAM Katie's (508-790-2600), 568 Main Street. Open April to mid-October. Everyone seems to end up at this little shop sometime during the day or night for homemade scoops.

DINNER TRAIN 🍴 **Cape Cod Dinner Train** (508-771-3800; 888-797-7245; capetrain.com), 252 Main Street. Operates early May through December with a highly variable schedule. These vintage-1920s cars run at "soup speed" for a 3-hour trip to the canal and back. The train gets good reviews from diners, who appreciate that the

CAPE COD DINNER TRAIN

food is cooked on board, and who enjoy fancy white linens, candlelight, crystal, and china. Tables are set for four, so if you want to dine alone as a couple when it's crowded, you'll have to pay a hefty surcharge. Here's another tip: If you care about seeing scenery during the latter part of the trip, schedule a train ride in summer, when the days are longer. $66 per person; alcohol and tipping additional. Summertime family or Sunday brunch trains cost $40 adults, $30 children under 12. The former includes children's entertainment. Reservations required for all.

✳ Entertainment

♪ **Cape Symphony Orchestra** (508-362-1111; capesymphony.org). Performances September through April. The orchestra performs about 15 concerts for children and adults at the 1,400-seat Barnstable High School, 744 West Main Street in Hyannis.

✳ ☂ ↑ **Regal Mall Cinema Stadium 12** (508-771-7460), 739 Routes 132 and 28, at the Cape Cod Mall. The Cape's only stadium-seating megacomplex, with 12 screens.

Ÿ **Back Door Bistro** at the Roadhouse Café (508-775-2386; roadhouse cafe.com), 488 South Street. Jazz on Monday night year-round, jazz by Lou Colombo Monday and Tuesday in summer, and piano on Friday and Saturday off-season. It's de rigueur for Hyannis.

Ÿ **The Island Merchant** (508-771-1337; theislandmerchant.com), 302 Main Street. Open 4 PM-midnight or 1 AM Wednesday through Monday. Along with islandy comfort food and $2 burgers (after 10 PM), this bar features microbrews, espresso, and sandwiches. There's a full calendar of live entertainment scheduled too. Dishes $5–28.

See also **Naked Oyster**, **Ardeo's**, and **RooBar**, under *Dining Out*; and **Harry's** and **Baxter's** under *Eating Out*.

✳ Selective Shopping

❋ Unless otherwise noted, all shops are open year-round.

ART GALLERIES AND CRAFTS
Spectrum (508-771-4554; spectrum america.com), 342 Main Street. Textiles, jewelry, lamps, glass objects, wooden boxes and business-card holders, musical instruments, and ceramics—all creatively handcrafted by contemporary American artists.

Artist Shanties (508-862-4678; har boryourarts.com), Bismore Park, on the waterfront. Open late May to mid-October (daily in summer and weekends in the shoulder season). Taking a page out of the playbook of Nantucket's waterfront area, these little shacks are occupied by 15 juried artists, including one revolving one. Mediums vary from watercolors and pastels to tapestries and jewelry to calligraphy and photography. It really livens up the area, whether or not you're waiting for a ferry.

Red Fish Blue Fish (508-775-8700), 374 Main Street. The most fun and whimsical "gallery" in town carries unusual gifts and crafts. When it's not too busy, you can watch owner Jane Walsh making handblown glass jewelry in the store.

Guyer Barn Gallery and Arts Center (508-790-6370), 250 South Street. The Barnstable Arts and Humanities Council established this art gallery in 1986, and in addition to new monthly shows, the center offers workshop and classes.

BOOKSTORES **Barnes & Noble** (508-862-6310), Cape Cod Mall, Route 132, north of the airport rotary.

Borders (508-862-6363), Cape Cod Mall, Route 132, north of the airport rotary.

CLOTHING **Plush & Plunder** (508-775-4467), 605 Main Street. Open daily. Vintage and eccentric used clothing adorns those marching to an offbeat drummer, including fabled customers like Cyndi Lauper, Joan Baez, and Demi Moore. You don't have to be an entertainer to shop here, although you'll end up entertained and entertaining (if you purchase something), while searching for gold lamé, a boa, or other retro accessories. Don't miss this place.

FACTORY OUTLETS **Christmas Tree Shops** (508-778-5521; christmas treeshops.com), between Route 28 and Route 132, next to the Cape Cod Mall. This is the largest of the six Christmas Tree Shops on the Cape.

FARMER'S MARKET **Mid-Cape Farmer's Market**, 232 Main Street, Hyannis. Open 8–noon Wednesday, mid-June to early September.

MALL ♪ **Cape Cod Mall** (508-771-0200; simon.com), Routes 132 and 28. Open daily. The Cape's only "real" mall—as distinguished from a plethora of strip malls—is anchored by big retailers and supplemented by more than 100 other stores, a huge food court, and an ultramodern movie theater. To keep kids occupied, there is an arcade and a Venetian carousel, too.

SPECIAL SHOPS **Cellar Leather** (508-771-5458), 592 Main Street. Quality coats, vests, shoes, clogs, sandals, briefcases, hats, and wallets—if you have any money left over.

Play It Again Sports (508-771-6979), 25 Route 28. Whether it's new or used equipment you're after, this shop has it all.

All Cape Cook's Supply (508-790-8908), 237 Main Street. Useful gadgets for pros and amateurs.

Kandy Korner Gifts (508-771-5313), 474 Main Street. Closed January. Watch chocolates and fudge being

---

STARSTRUCK

♪ **Cape Cod Melody Tent** (508-775-5630; melodytent.com), 21 West Main Street. Shows June through September. When this big white tent with a revolving stage was erected in 1950, entertainment was limited to Broadway musicals. Today (despite the occasional, less-than-perfect sound and acoustics) it's the Cape's biggest and best venue for top-name musicians. Look for the likes of Mary Chapin Carpenter, the Indigo Girls, Shawn Colvin, Melissa Etheridge, Tony Bennett, Julio Iglesias, and Lyle Lovett. It's only "big" by Cape standards; you'll be surprised at how close you are to your favorite stars here—about 20 rows max. That translates to about 50 feet. Look into once-weekly **children's shows** in July and August. Profits are poured into arts programs and education on the Cape and Boston's South Shore.

made in the front windows before heading in to indulge your sweet tooth.

✳ Special Events

May: **Annual Figawi Sailboat Race Weekend**. The largest sailboat race in New England goes from Hyannis to Nantucket.

Late July: **Regatta**. At the Hyannis Yacht Club since the early 1940s.

Early August: **Pops by the Sea** (arts foundationcapecod.org). Boston Pops Esplanade Orchestra on the town green. In the past, guest conductors have included Mike Wallace, Julia Child, Olympia Dukakis, and Walter Cronkite. Reserved-seating and general-admission tickets.

Early December: **Harbor Lighting and Boat Parade**. Bismore Park, Ocean Street. Parade of boats includes the arrival of Santa; entertainment with a holiday theme.

YARMOUTH

Yarmouth, like neighboring Dennis, stretches from Cape Cod Bay to Nantucket Sound; it unfolds along quiet Route 6A *and* congested Route 28. It's a family-oriented town, with golf courses, tennis courts, and town-sponsored sailing lessons, as well as quite a few southside oceanfront resorts.

Although Yarmouth's 5.3-mile section of Route 28 was planted with more than 350 trees in 1989 (on its 350th birthday), the road is still a wall-to-wall sea of mini-golf courses, shops, fast-food places, and family-style attractions like a combination zoo-aquarium, a billiards emporium, and boating on the Bass River. A larger-than-life plastic polar bear, a lunging shark, and an elephant epitomize the Cape's kitschier side. They're alternately viewed as icons and eyesores.

It's difficult to imagine that Route 28 was once open land dotted with small farms and that Yarmouth's ports bustled in the 19th century: Packets sailed to New York City and Newark from South Yarmouth at Bass River. Today the scenic Bass River and South Yarmouth Historic District provide a delightful detour south of Route 28.

On the northside, Route 6A was settled in the 1600s, was traveled by stagecoaches in the 1700s, and reached its height of prosperity in the 1800s, when it was lined with houses built for and by rope makers, sea captains, bankers, and shipbuilders. At one time, a mile-long section of Yarmouth Port was referred to as Captain's Row, as it was home to almost 50 sea captains. Many former sea captains' houses are now attractive B&Bs.

Stephen Hopkins, a *Mayflower* passenger, built the first house in Yarmouth in 1638 (off Mill Lane) and the town was incorporated just one year later. Today Yarmouth is the third most populous town on the Cape, with 24,000 year-round residents. Meander along tranquil Route 6A and you'll find crafts and antiques shops, a quiet village green, a couple of fine historic houses open to the public, walking trails, and an antiquarian bookstore. Take any lane off Route 6A to the north, and you'll find picturesque residential areas and the bay, eventually.

GUIDANCE ✳ **Yarmouth Area Chamber of Commerce** (508-778-1008; 800-732-1008; yarmouthcapecod.com), 424 Route 28, West Yarmouth. Open 9–5 Monday through Saturday and 10–3 Sunday, early May to mid-October; 9–5 weekdays mid-October to early May. Along with a helpful chamber staff, the office has two self-guided historical tours of Yarmouth and Old South Yarmouth.

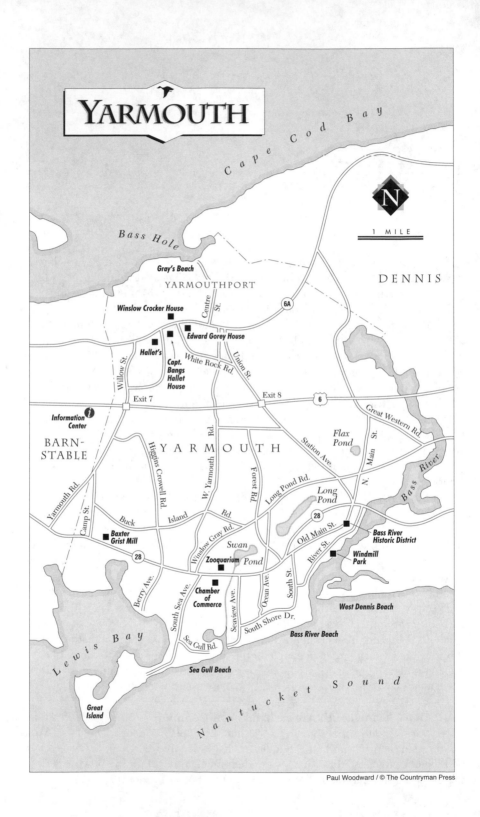

YARMOUTH

Cape Cod Bay

Bass Hole

Gray's Beach

YARMOUTHPORT

DENNIS

N

1 MILE

Winslow Crocker House

Centre St.

6A

Edward Gorey House

Hallet's

White Rock Rd.

Capt. Bangs Hallet House

Union St.

Willow St.

Exit 7

Exit 8

6

Information Center

BARN-STABLE

YARMOUTH

Great Western Rd.

W. Yarmouth Rd.

Flax Pond

N. Main St.

Higgins Crowell Rd.

Station Ave.

Bass River

Yarmouth Rd.

Forest Rd.

Long Pond Rd.

Long Pond

Camp St.

Buck

Island

Rd.

Winslow Gray Rd.

28

Baxter Grist Mill

Old Main St.

Bass River Historic District

28

Zooquarium

Swan Pond

River St.

Windmill Park

Berry Ave.

South Sea Ave.

Chamber of Commerce

Seaview Ave.

Ocean Ave.

South St.

West Dennis Beach

Sea Gull Rd.

South Shore Dr.

Bass River Beach

Lewis Bay

Sea Gull Beach

Nantucket Sound

Great Island

MEDIA The weekly *Register* (508-375-4945) lists local happenings.

PUBLIC RESTROOMS On Route 6 between exits 6 and 7, and at Gray's Beach (open seasonally, off Centre Street from Route 6A).

PUBLIC LIBRARIES ✳ ✒ ♈ ⁗Ⅰ⁗ Call ahead because of variable hours:

South Yarmouth Library (508-760-4820; yarmouthlibraries.org), 312 Old Main Street.
West Yarmouth Library (508-775-5206), 391 Route 28.
Yarmouth Port Library (508-362-3717), 297 Route 6A.

GETTING THERE *By car:* Yarmouth is 26 miles from the Cape Cod Canal; take Route 6 to Exit 7 for the northside (Yarmouth Port and Route 6A). For points along Route 28 on the southside, take Exit 7 south to Higgins Crowell Road for West Yarmouth. Take Exit 8 south for South Yarmouth and the Bass River.

GETTING AROUND *By shuttle:* **Yarmouth Shuttle** (800-352-7155; capecod transit.org) operates late June to early September. The shuttle begins at the Hyannis Transportation Center and runs along Route 28 to various family-oriented points (including beaches) in Yarmouth; flag down the driver. $2 one-way; $6 all-day pass. Tickets are purchased aboard the trolley or at the chamber of commerce (see *Guidance*).

MEDICAL EMERGENCY Call **911**.

Bass River Healthcare Associates (508-394-1353; bassriverhealthcare.com), 833 Route 28, South Yarmouth. Open Monday through Saturday. Dr. Reida, an extraordinary chiropractor, is full of quiet wisdom.

✳ To See

✳ ✒ **Edward Gorey House** (508-362-3909; edwardgoreyhouse.org), 8 Strawberry Lane, Yarmouth Port. Open mid-April to late December; call for specific hours. *Curious, surreal, bizarre, whimsical,* and *quirky*: These have all been used to describe Gorey. His masterful pen-and-ink illustrations, as well as his offbeat sense of humor, endeared him to a wide audience. And the reputation he earned by doing the introductory credit for PBS's *Mystery* propelled him even farther. So did the Tony Award he won for costume design for the Broadway production of *Dracula*. Closer to home, when Gorey moved to the Cape full time in the early 1980s, he contributed greatly to local theater productions. The restored house contains exhibits celebrating this marvelous artist, who lived here and died in 2000. Adults $5; seniors $3; children 6–12, $2.

🍦 ♈ **Hallet's** (508-362-3362; hallets.com), 139 Route 6A, Yarmouth Port. Open daily April through December, although at press time hours were uncertain. Hallet's has been a community fixture since it was built as an apothecary in 1889 by Thacher Taylor Hallet. His great-grandson Charles owns and operates the store, which boasts an old-fashioned oak counter and a marble-topped soda fountain. As time stands still, sit on a swivel stool or in one of the wrought-iron, heart-shaped chairs beneath the tin ceiling, and relax over a ice-cream soda (the food's not much to write home about). The second floor has been turned into something of a museum, documenting Yarmouth's history as seen through one family's annals and attic treasures. In addition to being a pharmacist (old medicine bottles are on display), T. T. Hallet was a postmaster (during his tenure, only 15 families had mail slots), selectman (the second floor was used as a meeting room from 1889 to the early 1900s), and justice of the peace. The charming displays include store posters from the last 100 years and historical photographs. Tours: $6 per person, suggested donation.

Village pump, Route 6A near Summer Street, Yarmouth Port. This wrought-iron pump has served the community since 1886. It's located just west of the Old Yarmouth Inn, the oldest inn (and stagecoach stop) on the Cape, dating from 1696. The pump's iron frame, decorated with birds, animals, and a lantern, is supported by a stone trough from which horses drank. Horse-drawn carriages traveling from Boston to Provincetown stopped here.

↑ **Captain Bangs Hallet House** (508-362-3021; hsoy.org), 11 Strawberry Lane (park behind the post office on Route 6A), Yarmouth Port. Open for tours at 1, 2, and 3 Thursday through Sunday, mid-June to mid-October. The original section of this Greek Revival house was built in 1740 by town founder Thomas Thacher, but it was substantially enlarged by Captain Henry Thacher in 1840. Captain Hallet and his wife, Anna, lived here from 1863 until 1893. The house, maintained by the Historical Society of Old Yarmouth, is decorated in a manner befitting a prosperous sea captain who traded with China and India. Note the original 1740 kitchen, and don't miss the lovely weeping beech behind the house or the 1850 **Gorham Cobbler Shop** (open 9:30–3 Tuesday and Thursday year-round) serves an archival research center. Adults $3; children 12 and under, 50¢.

🐾 ↑ **Winslow Crocker House** (617-227-3957; historicnewengland.org), 250 Route 6A, Yarmouth Port. Tours hourly 11–4 on the second and fourth Saturday of each month, June to mid-October. Set back from Route 6A, this two-story Georgian home was built in 1780 with 12-over-12 small-paned windows and rich interior paneling. The house was constructed for a wealthy 18th-century trader and land speculator and moved to its present location in 1936 by Mary Thacher. Thacher, a descendant of Yarmouth's original land grantee, was an avid collector of 17th-, 18th-, and 19th-century furniture, and she used the house as a backdrop for her magnificent collection. The house was donated to Historic New England and is the only such property on Cape Cod. Adults $4; members and Yarmouth Port residents, free.

✍ **Baxter Grist Mill**, Route 28, West Yarmouth. Call Town Hall (508-398-2231, ext. 292) for opening hours. The original mill was built in 1710 with an exterior waterwheel. But in 1860, when water levels in Mill Pond became so low that the wheel froze, an indoor water turbine was added. (This is the Cape's only mill with an indoor water turbine.) Kids can help grind corn with "the Mill Man." Free.

Windmill Park, off River Street from Old Main Street, South Yarmouth. This eight-sided windmill on the Bass River was built in 1791 and moved here in 1866. This scenic spot also has a small swimming beach.

✳ To Do

BASEBALL ✍ The Cape League (capecodbaseball.org) sponsors the **Yarmouth-Dennis Red Sox**. Games are held from mid-May to early August typically at 5 PM at the Dennis-Yarmouth High School, Station Avenue, South Yarmouth.

A PERFECT DAY IN YARMOUTH

  8:30 Order an Irish farmhouse breakfast from the Keltic Kitchen.

10:00 Cruise Route 28 and take your pick among trampolines at Jump On Us, mini-golf at Pirate's Cove Adventure Golf, sea creatures at Zooquarium, and bowling at Ryan Family Amusement Center.

12:30 Satisfy everyone in your party at Ardeo Mediterranean Tavern.

  2:00 Life is short; relax with coffee at Seven Beans.

  3:00 Buy inflatable beach toys on Route 28 and head to Sea Gull Beach.

  6:30 Have a relaxing and unusual dinner at the creative Inaho.

FISHING/SHELLFISHING Shellfishing permits and freshwater fishing licenses are required.

❋ **Truman's Bait & Tackle** (508-771-3470), 608 Route 28, West Yarmouth. One-stop shopping for rod rentals, repairs, freshwater licenses, and local maps and charts.

❋ **Riverview Bait & Tackle** (508-394-1036), 1273 Route 28, South Yarmouth. Among other services, the staff will direct you to local fishing spots, including the Bass River and High Bank Bridges, Sea Gull Beach at Parker's River off South Shore Drive, and Smugglers Beach off South Street.

FOR FAMILIES ✐ **Zooquarium of Cape Cod** (508-775-8883; zooquariumcape cod.net), 674 Route 28, West Yarmouth. Open 9:30–5 daily July and August; call for off-season hours. Part zoo (with a petting area), part aquarium (with performing sea lions), Zooquarium is packed on cloudy days; but if you come at the beginning or end of a sunny beach day, you can avoid the crowds. Although the place may conjure up thoughts of the movie Free Willy, keep in mind that many of these animals would have died if they hadn't been brought here. Some arrive injured or blind. With the exception of the farm animals, all land and sea creatures are native. Small endangered animals will educate small children at the **Zoorific Theater**. Children 10 and older $9.75; children 2–9, $6.75.

✐ **Jump On Us** (508-775-3304), 260 Route 28, West Yarmouth. This trampoline center is open daily in July and August, and some holiday weekends off-season.

✐ **Flax Playground** is on Center Street in South Yarmouth; another is in **Old Townhouse Park** on Old Townhouse Road in South Yarmouth. **Sandy Pond Playground**, off of Buck Island Road, WestYarmouth, has no swings. **Long Pond Playground**, at Indian Memorial Drive off Station Avenue in South Yarmouth, does.

✐ **Classical Billiards** (508-771-5872), 657B Route 28, West Yarmouth. Open daily. This family-oriented billiards room has lots of tables, darts, foosball, video games, and table tennis.

❋ ✐ ⚲ **Ryan Family Amusement Center** (508-394-5644; ryanfamily.com), 1067 Route 28, South Yarmouth. Open daily. When rain strikes, head indoors to bowl away the blues. Ten-pin and candlepin.

GOLF **King's Way** (508-362-8870; kingswaygolfinc.com), off Route 6A, Yarmouth Port. Open April through November. A challenging 18-hole, 4,100-yard, par-60 course designed by Cornish and Silva.

Bayberry Hills (508-394-5597; golfyarmouthcapecod.com), off West Yarmouth Road, West Yarmouth. Open early April to late November. A town-owned, 27-hole, par-72 course with driving range.

❊ **Bass River Golf Course** (508-398-9079; golfyarmouthcapecod.com), 622 Highbank Road, South Yarmouth. Open year-round, weather permitting. A town-owned, 18-hole, par-72 course with great views of the Bass River.

❊ **Blue Rock Golf Course** (508-398-9295; bluerockgolfcourse.com), 48 Todd Road, off Highbank Road, South Yarmouth. Open year-round, weather permitting. A short 18-hole, par-54 course.

MINI-GOLF ✍ **Pirate's Cove Adventure Golf** (508-394-6200; piratescove.net), 728 Route 28, South Yarmouth. Open daily mid-April to late October. At the granddaddy of all Cape mini-golf courses, kids have their choice of two 18-hole courses complete with lavish pirate-themed landscaping, extravagant waterfalls, and dark caves. Kids receive eye patches, flags, tattoos, and a jaunty pirate hat.

✍ **Bass River Sports World** (508-398-6070; bassriversportsworld.com), 928 Route 28 at Long Pond Road, South Yarmouth. Open weekends April to mid-May and daily mid-May to early October. In addition to a "Swiss Family Treehouse" adventure mini-golf, Bass River lures families with baseball and softball batting cages, soccer cages, a game room, go-carts, and a driving range.

SOCCER **The Cape Cod Crusaders** (mpsbr.com), the Cape's only pro team, play from late May to early August on many Saturdays at 7 PM at various area fields. Check Web site for start time and locations. Adults $8, children $5.

TENNIS The public can play at **Flax Pond**, which has 4 courts (off North Main Street from Route 28 in South Yarmouth); at **Sandy Pond**, which has 4 courts (from Route 28 in West Yarmouth, take Higgins Crowell Road to Buck Island Road); and at **Dennis-Yarmouth High School**, which has 10 courts (from Route 28, take Station Avenue to Regional Avenue in South Yarmouth). All are free.

✳ Green Space

BEACHES Some lodging places offer discounted daily beach stickers; don't forget to ask. Weekly stickers for cottage renters are available for $50 at beach gates or resident stickers at Town Hall (508-398-2231), 1146 Route 28, South Yarmouth. If you take the Yarmouth Shuttle (see *Getting Around*), though, there is no fee to walk onto the beach.

Sea Gull Beach, off South Sea Avenue from Route 28, West Yarmouth. This is the longest, widest, and nicest of Yarmouth's southside beaches, which generally tend to be small, narrow, and plagued by seaweed. The approach to the beach is lovely, with views of the tidal river. (The blue boxes you see, by the way, are fly traps—filled with Octenol—a chemical derived from oxen breath, they attract the dreaded biting greenhead flies that terrorize sunbathers in July.) Parking $12–15; facilities include a bathhouse, restrooms, and food service.

WALKS Botanical Trails of the Historical Society of Old Yarmouth, behind the post office and Captain Bangs Hallet House, off Route 6A, Yarmouth Port. This 1.5-mile trail, dotted with benches and skirting 60 acres of pines, oaks, and a pond, leads past rhododendrons, holly, lady's slippers, and other delights. The trail begins at the gatehouse, which has a lovely herb garden. A spur trail leads to the profoundly simple **Kelley Chapel**, built in 1873 as a seaman's bethel (a sacred space for sailors) by a father for his daughter, who was mourning the untimely death of her son. The interior contains a few pews, an old woodstove, and a small organ. It may be rented (508-375-6424) for small weddings and special events.

Taylor-Bray Farm, Bray Farm Road South, off Route 6A near the Dennis town line, Yarmouth Port. Open dawn to dusk. The Bray brothers purchased this land in the late 1800s and created a successful shipyard and farm. Now town-owned con-

---

SCENIC DRIVES

South Yarmouth and the Bass River Historic District, on and around Old Main Street (off Route 28), South Yarmouth. The Pawkannawkut Indians (a branch of the Wampanoag tribe) lived, fished, and hunted on a tract of land Yarmouth set aside for them along Long Pond and the Bass River in 1713. But by the 1770s, a smallpox epidemic wiped out most of the Native population. In 1790 David Kelley (a Quaker) acquired the last remaining Pawkannawkut land from the last surviving Pawkannawkut, Thomas Greenough. Quakers then settled the side streets off Old Main Street near Route 28 and built handsome homes. The Historical Society of Old Yarmouth publishes a walking-tour brochure to Old South Yarmouth, which you can get at the chamber of commerce (see *Guidance*). Note the simple traffic rotary at River and Pleasant streets; it's thought to be the oldest in the country.

Yarmouth Port. From Route 6A, turn onto Church Street across from the village green. Follow it around to Thacher Shore Drive and Water Street. When Water Street turns left, head right down a dirt road for a wide-open view of marshland. Continue on Water Street across Keveney Bridge, which crosses Mill Creek; Keveney Lane takes you back to Route 6A. Turn left to head east, back into Yarmouth Port. This scenic loop is nice for a quiet walk, a bicycle ride, or an early-morning jog.

servation land, this working farm offers a short walking trail and tidal-marsh views. It's a nice place for a picnic. You can't help but take a deep breath of fresh air here.

Captain's Mile. The Historical Society of Old Yarmouth has printed a booklet (look for it at the chamber of commerce or Captain Bangs Hallet house) that covers three walking tours of local sea captain's houses along Route 6A. It's an informative brochure and gives some perspective about the area.

Meadowbrook Road Conservation Area, off Route 28, West Yarmouth. This recommendation originally came from Joseph Molinari, a longtime Explorer from New Jersey. A peaceful place to relax, this area has a 310-foot boardwalk with an observation deck that overlooks a swamp and salt marsh. Take Winslow Gray Road north from Route 28 in West Yarmouth. After a few miles, take Meadowbrook Lane to the right and park at the end.

See also **Bass Hole (or Gray's) Beach** in the sidebar "Boardwalk, Not Park Place." And, don't forget about the **walking-tour** brochure published by the Historical Society of Old Yarmouth (see *Guidance*).

BOARDWALK, NOT PARK PLACE

🔗 ♿ **Bass Hole (or Gray's) Beach**, off Centre Street from Route 6A, Yarmouth Port. The small, protected beach is good for children, but the real appeal lies in the **Bass Hole Boardwalk**, which extends across a marsh and a creek. From the benches at the end of the boardwalk, you can see across to Chapin Memorial Beach in Dennis. It's a great place to be at sunset, although you won't be alone. The 2.5-mile **Callery-Darling Trail** starts from the parking lot and crosses conservation lands to the salt marsh. As you walk out into the bay, a mile or so at low tide, recall that this former harbor used to be deep enough to accommodate a schooner shipyard in the 18th century. Free parking; handicap ramp.

✴ Lodging

Route 6A is lined with lovely B&Bs, while the southside generally appeals to families (with a couple of notable exceptions).

RESORT ✐ ❝Ⰱ❞ **Red Jacket Beach Resort** (508-398-6941; 800-672-0500; redjacketbeach.com), South Shore Drive, South Yarmouth. Open early April through October. Occupying 7 acres wedged between Nantucket Sound and the Parker's River, this extensive complex courts families. Amenities include a large private beach, heated indoor and outdoor pools, a kiddie pool with water features, a supervised children's program, tennis, parasailing, kayaks, and jet skis. A family-style restaurant serves all three meals. All accommodations (150 rooms and 14 cottages) have their own deck or patio and in-room fridge. Rates vary considerably, according to view: near the hotel entrance, riverside or poolside, ocean view, and ocean-front (from least to most expensive). Mid-July to late August $290–430; off-season $130–270; two children under age 12 free in parent's room; (cots $15).

BED & BREAKFASTS ✳ ❀ ♿ ❝Ⰱ❞ **Liberty Hill Inn** (508-362-3976; 800-821-3977; libertyhillinn.com), 77 Route 6A, Yarmouth Port. Innkeepers John Hunt and Kris Srihadi offer the best bang for the buck in Cape Cod lodging. It's certainly got a lot going for it. The former 1825 whaling tycoon's home is nicely set back from Route 6A on a knoll. It features five comfortable rooms in the elegant main house and four in the adjacent post-and-beam-style carriage house. Light and airy rooms in the main inn benefit from lofty ceilings, floor-to-ceiling windows, a dramatic spiral staircase, and

MUD FLATS AT GRAY'S BEACH

restored bathrooms. Crisp linens, triple sheeting, and arrival snack baskets are the norm. Next door, rooms might have a whirlpool, fireplace, or canopy bed. A sumptuous breakfast (served at individual tables) is included. Mid-June to mid-September $140–225; off-season $100–200.

✳ ❀ ❝Ⰱ❞ **Inn at Lewis Bay** (508-771-3433; 800-962-6679; innatlewisbay .com), 57 Maine Avenue, West Yarmouth. I really like this place because it's so down to earth and represents real value. In a seaside residential neighborhood near a small, protected beach, this delightful Dutch Colonial has six comfy guest rooms

THE INN AT CAPE COD

(two with ocean view). Innkeepers Janet and Dave Vaughn include a full breakfast (perhaps featuring eggs with crabmeat), afternoon refreshments, beach towels and chairs, and a flower filled front porch perfect for relaxing. The beds are graced with homey quilts, and quilters should inquire about quilting weekends. Children 12 and above welcome. Mid-May to mid-September $138–148; off-season $98–108.

❄ ❝❡❞ **The Belvedere** (508-398-1950; belvederebb.com), 167 Old Main Street, South Yarmouth. There may only be three antique-filled rooms and a carriage house suite here, but what rooms they are: the early-19th-century house has been outfitted with the luxuries of the 21st century. They (and the whole house) have been completely renovated and restored with a casual elegance and historical charm that's hard to match. Robert Alexander (a sixth-generation Cape Codder from Dennis) and Sue have been here since 2006, and they know a thing or two about the hospitality business; it's evident everywhere you turn. Not to be outshone, Rusty the golden retriever and Stanley the family cat are the official greeters. A full breakfast is typically served on the screened-in porch. Call about the inn's child policy. July

INN AT LEWIS BAY

through September $200; off-season $150.

❄ ❝❡❞ **The Inn at Cape Cod** (508-375-0590; 800-850-7301; innatcapecod .com), 4 Summer Street, Yarmouth Port. Helen and Mike Cassels, innkeepers since 2006, have brought this 1820s gem back to life through keen decorating skills and quintessential British hospitality. I love being surprised, and their attention to this southern plantation-style inn blew my socks off. The seven guestrooms and two suites (the latter with a separate sitting room and private balcony) are lovely and elegant. Each is equipped with flat-screen TV and gas fireplace, and each features spacious, high ceilings. A 4-course breakfast is served at individual tables in the sunny breakfast room or terrace. As you might expect, afternoon tea served fireside with homemade treats is worth returning for. There's plenty of additional guest space, including elegant gardens, porches, and a sitting room with fireplace. Kids over 16 welcome. June through October $175–315; off-season $160–250.

❄ ✐ ❝❡❞ **One Centre Street Inn** (508-362-9951; onecentrestreetinn .com), One Centre Street at Route 6A, Yarmouth Port. This homey and humble 1824 inn has four guest rooms and one suite (the latter which is good for families), overseen by owners Mary Singleton and Judy Murphy since 2005. Mary has an open-kitchen policy so guests can chat with her and drink coffee as she cooks; a full breakfast is served in the adjacent three-season porch (or at the formal dining room in cooler months, at individual tables or a communal one.) Rooms feature flat-screen TVs; at pres time DVD players were on the way. Kids 11 and over welcome. April through October $150–235; off-season $135–225.

🦞 🍴 "🛏" **Village Inn** (508-362-3182; thevillageinncapecod.com), 92 Route 6A, Yarmouth Port. Open May through December. If you want to understand genuine hospitality, look up the dictionary entry for innkeeper Karen Hickey learned it from her mother-in-law, Esther, who died in mid-2008 after operating this historic, colonial landmark since 1952. Theirs is a profoundly basic idea: provide a modest but spic-n-span place for travelers to relax and interact. To that end, the inn has two comfortable living rooms, a wicker-filled, screened-in porch (with Astroturf lest anyone get the wrong idea), and a full, cooked-to-order breakfast. The ten delightfully old-fashioned guest rooms (including one suite) are modestly furnished and all have private bath. Quite simply, they don't make 'em like this anymore. When you're looking for honest value, look no further. And when you're here, walk five minutes down the adjacent lane to the old wharf on the water. Rooms $90–160.

❄ "🛏" **Captain Farris House** (508-760-2818; 800-350-9477; captainfarris.com), 308 Old Main Street, South Yarmouth. Because I was not shown rooms for this edition, I only know what used to be true. Located within a small pocket of historic homes off Route 28, the 1845 Captain Farris House offers understated elegance and luxurious modern amenities. Lovely window treatments, fine antiques, fine linens, and Jacuzzi tubs fill the guest rooms. Of the 10 rooms, 4 are suites, 5 have a fireplace, a few have a private deck, and most have a private entrance. A fancy three-course breakfast is served at individual tables in the courtyard or at one formal dining-room table. Mid-February to early January $140–295.

🍴 ♿ "🛏" **Seaside** (508-398-2533; seasidecapecod.com), 135 South Shore Drive, South Yarmouth. Open May to late October. These 41 one- and two-room cottages, built in the 1930s but nicely upgraded and well maintained, are very popular for their oceanfront location. Reserve by mid-March if possible; otherwise, cross your fingers. Sheltered among pine trees, the shingled and weathered units are clustered around a sandy barbecue area and sit above a 500-foot stretch of private beach. (A playground is next door.) Kitchens are fully equipped, and linens are provided, as is daily maid service. Many of the tidy units have a working fireplace. The least-expensive units (without views) are decorated in 1950s style. Don't bother with the motel efficiencies. Mid-June to early September $1,050–1,960 weekly for one-room and two-room units; off-season $85–170 daily.

🦞 🍴 ♿ "🛏" **Beach House at Bass River** (508-394-6501; 800-345-6065), 73 South Shore Drive, Bass River. Open early April through October. This tasteful bi-level motor inn, built in the 1970s by Cliff Hagberg (who still operates it), sits on a 110-foot stretch of private Nantucket Sound beach. Each of the 26 rooms in the tidy complex is decorated differently with country antiques and wicker; generally the oceanfront rooms are a bit spiffier, with country-pine furnishings. All rooms have private balcony or patio and a refrigerator. An expansive buffet breakfast is included. Late June to early September $190–275; off-season $110–220; 10 percent off for seniors; children under 10 free in parent's room (plus free cribs and use of microwave).

🍴 "🛏" **Ocean Mist** (508-398-2633; 800-248-6478), 97 South Shore Drive,

South Yarmouth. Open early May to mid-November. This shingled three-story complex fronting a 300-foot private Nantucket Sound beach offers 32 rooms and 32 loft suites. Each of the contemporary rooms has a wet bar or full efficiency kitchen, two double beds, and air-conditioning. Loft suites feature an open, second-floor sitting area—many of the rooms have ocean views, all have a sofa bed; many of these have skylights and two private balconies. There's also an indoor pool on the premises. Smoking allowed in some rooms. June to early September $189–309; off-season $69–179; three children up to age 15 stay free in parent's room.

RENTAL HOUSES ✍ **Great Island Ocean Club** (508-775-0985; greatis landoceanclub.com), off South Sea Avenue, West Yarmouth. Open April through November. This gated residential community has about 30 rental homes, fully equipped houses with one to six bedrooms. Best of all, they're located on or within a quarter mile of a private Nantucket Sound beach. Off by itself, it's a real find, perfect for families. Shared facilities include tennis courts and a pool. Reservations by mail only, until mid-March. Mid-June to early September $1,500–2,200 weekly for two bedrooms, $2,200–4,200 for three bedrooms; about 40 percent lower off-season.

✍ **Century 21–Sam Ingram Real Estate** (508-362-8844; 800-697-3340; summerrentalscapecod.com), 938 Route 6A, Yarmouth Port.

✳ Where to Eat

Route 6A has a couple of excellent restaurants, and while Route 28 is lined with dozens, most are not discernible from one another. I have reviewed only the few that are. If you're staying on the southside, and want more choice, check the entries in "Dennis."

DINING OUT ✳ 🦞 ♿ **Inaho** (508-362-5522; inahocapecod.com), 157 Route 6A, Yarmouth Port. Open for dinner nightly except Sunday. Year in and year out, this remains on my Top 10 Cape Cod list! Masterful chef-owner and sushi-maker Yuji Watanabe continues to give patrons plenty of reason to remain loyal, offering some of the most sophisticated and authentic Japanese cuisine east of Tokyo. While fearless diners are handsomely rewarded with spicy handrolls and creative specials like volcano shots, the less adventurous revel in traditional tofu, teriyaki (the best I've had), bento box combinations, and miso soup. Then there is tempura, an exemplary metaphor for life: Wait too long to partake, and the fleeting, perfect moment passes by. Meanwhile, over at the bar, intense concentration is focused on the Zen of sushi preparation. Save room for banana tempura or ginger ice cream. Dinner $15–25.

✳ ✍ ♿ **Old Yarmouth Inn** (508-362-9962; oldyarmouthinn.com), 223 Route 6A, Yarmouth Port. Open for lunch Tuesday through Saturday, dinner nightly, and a very popular and extensive Sunday buffet brunch. You have a choice to make at this 1696 inn, the oldest on the Cape: casual pub dining or fine dining in one of three dining rooms. The fireplaces and white linens in the main dining rooms create a cozy elegance, but I often end up at the low-key tavern, a former stagecoach stop. It's just the perfect place for a grilled chicken Caesar, cup of clam chowder, or great burger. In addition to lighter fare, you can get serious with lobster ravioli with a fresh tomato and cream sauce or a broiled seafood platter. Chef David Woodbury has been at the helm since 2004, garnering Wine Spectator awards and whipping up specialties like black and white sesame ahi with wasabi mashed potatoes. Early specials nightly except Saturday. Lunch $8–15, brunch $18, dinner $15–30.

✳ ✿ ⑆ **Ardeo Mediterranean Tavern** (508-760-1500; ardeocapecod .com), Union Station Plaza (Exit 8 off Route 6), 23V Whites Path, South Yarmouth. Open for lunch and dinner. A fun place for noshing with friends, this sleek eatery has creative woodstove pizzas, specialties with a Mediterranean flair, excellent Middle Eastern appetizers (based on recipes from the owner's grandmother), sandwiches made with sun-dried tomato bread, panini, homemade pastas, and creative mains (but I go for the former rather than the latter). Ignore its strip-mall location. Lunch $6–9, dinner $10–22.

✳ ⑆ **Gerardi's Café** (508-394-3111), 902 Route 28, South Yarmouth. Open for dinner. This cute and casual place, with wooden booths, wooden chairs, a gas fireplace, and Oriental carpets, packs a big punch relative to its size. Thanks to chef Diego Gerardi, raised by restaurateurs in Boston's North End and trained at the Costigliole d'Asti at the Italian Culinary Institute for Foreigners, you can look with assurance

for authentic Italian dishes like chicken marsala and fettuccine alfredo. You gotta love a place that knows what it is, doesn't overreach, and executes with aplomb. Dinner $12–29.

EATING OUT ✳ ✿ ✿ **Keltic Kitchen** (508-771-4835; thekeltickitchen.com), 415 Route 28, West Yarmouth. Open for breakfast all day (6 or 7 AM–2 PM). Chef-owner and Irishman Dave Dempsey and his staff still sport thick brogues from the old country when they take your orders. How about an Irish farmhouse breakfast with rashers and black and white pudding or Keltic Bennys with poached eggs on an English muffin and corned beef hash? And despite having no ties to Ireland, the cranberry french toast, made with Portuguese bread, is a favorite. This friendly and cozy place is a family operation—Dave's father did trompe l'oeil artwork on walls. Come once and I bet you'll come back again. Try the beef and barley soup for lunch. And dine outside in fine weather. Dishes $3–10.

✳ ⑆ **Cape & Island Thai Food** (508-771-2489), 594 Route 28, South Yarmouth. Open for lunch and dinner daily. Don't let the strip-mall location fool or dissuade you: this authentic Thai food will be memorable. Try their tamarind duck and special fried rice— the latter is a meal in and of itself. Perhaps not surprisingly, this family-owned restaurant also has very attentive and efficient service. Dishes $7–18.

✿ ⑆ **Stefani's Restaurant** (508-760-2929), at the Bayberry Hills Golf Course, 635 West Yarmouth Road, West Yarmouth. Open 6–6 daily April through November. Longtime caterer and restaurateur Stefani Wright offers home-baked goodies that are gobbled up quickly, great clam chowder, chicken BLT roll-ups, burgers, and grilled roast beef with horseradish mayo. Try the Red Onion sandwich, with turkey, sun-dried tomato pesto, mayo, gruyère cheese, red onion, and green apple on a rustica roll. While the pleasant concessionaire overlooks the course with outdoor seating, this place isn't just for golfers. Sandwiches $7.

✳ ♪ ♿ **Oliver's & Planck's Tavern** (508-362-6062; oliverscapecod.com), Route 6A, Yarmouth Port. Open for lunch and dinner daily. Oliver's offers generous portions in cozy, tavernlike surroundings (or on the outdoor deck in summer). Chef-owner Dale Ormon attracts an older crowd at lunchtime; longtime Cape residents who like to keep things simple; and families who need to satisfy everyone. Specialties include seafood flatbread and broiled seafood, but hearty sandwiches, steak tips, and fettuccini are also quite popular. Live entertainment on weekends. Lunch $8–20, dinner $10–20.

✳ ♞ ♪ **Jack's Outback** (508-362-6690), 161 Route 6A, Yarmouth Port. Open for breakfast daily and lunch daily except Sunday. Classic American down-home cooking is served from an exposed, dinerlike kitchen. Get there early for fluffy omelets, pancakes, and popovers or be prepared to wait. Breakfast and lunch $4–15.

♞ ♪ **Seafood Sam's** (508-394-3504; seafoodsams.com), 1006 Route 28, South Yarmouth. Open for lunch and dinner, February through early December. You can always count on Sam's for reliable, informally presented, reasonably priced fried or broiled seafood. Lunch specials $5–10, dinner $8–15.

✳ **Seven Beans** (508-771-0335), 582 Route 28, West Dennis. As their tag line says: Life is too short—stay awake for it! Serving Caribou Coffee (and various teas) this independent place is a comfy alternative to Starbuck's.

✳ Entertainment

♪ **Band concerts** (508-778-1008), Mattachesse Middle School band shell, Higgins Crowell Road, West Yarmouth. Monday night at 7 in July and August; since 1970.

✳ ♞ ↑ **Patriot Square Cinemas** (508-394-1100), Patriot Square Mall, Route 134, South Dennis.

✳ Selective Shopping

✳ Unless otherwise noted, all shops are open year-round.

BOOKSTORE **Parnassus Book Service** (508-362-6420; parnassus books.com), 220 Route 6A, Yarmouth Port. Deliberately avoiding signs and categories, proprietor Ben Muse wants people to browse and dig around, perhaps finding a first edition James or Melville among the stacks. Specializing in maritime, Cape Cod, and ornithology, Muse has been selling new, used, and rare books since the mid-1950s. Shelves line the wall outside, where the books are available for browsing or purchase on a 24/7 honor system. In its former incarnations, this 1840 building served as a general store and as a church; it was once home to the Yarmouth Society of the New Jerusalem. This really is one unique shop.

SPECIAL SHOPS **Bass River Boatworks** (508-398-4883), 1361 Route 28, South Yarmouth. Barely west of the Bass River, this crammed shop will satisfy nautical fanatics. Look for copper weather vanes, lightship baskets, marine antiques, custom-made glass display cases, lighthouse models, and the largest number of ship-model kits on the Cape. They also do lots of ship-model restoration.

Design Works (508-362-9698), 159 Route 6A, Yarmouth Port. Open daily. Scandinavian country antiques, home furnishings, and accessories like throws, pillows, and linens.

Peach Tree Designs (508-362-8317), 173 Route 6A, Yarmouth Port. Open daily. Homebodies will delight in this two-floor shop filled to the brim with an assortment of decorative accessories for gracious living.

Town Crier (508-362-3138), 153 Route 6A, Yarmouth Port. Open May to mid-October. Four dealers share this space, where you can find plates, glassware, collectibles, silver, brass, and small furniture.

✳ Special Events

Late May–late September: **Art shows**. The Yarmouth Art Guild sponsors outdoor shows at the Cape Cod Cooperative Bank (Route 6A in Yarmouth Port) on many Sundays (10–5).

Mid-October: **Seaside Festival**. Begun in 1979, this festival features jugglers, clowns, fireworks, field games, a parade, sand-castle competitions, arts and crafts, and bicycle, kayak, and road races.

✐ *Early December:* **Yarmouth Port Christmas Stroll**. Tree lighting on the village common, caroling, and special children's activities; wreaths for sale.

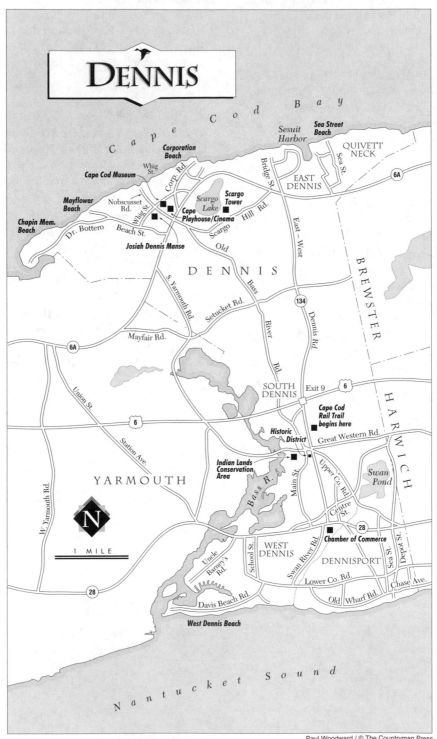

DENNIS

Cape Cod Bay

Cape Cod Bay

Sesuit Harbor

Sea Street Beach

QUIVETT NECK

Corporation Beach

Whig St.

Cape Cod Museum

Corp. Rd.

Bridge St.

EAST DENNIS

Sea St.

6A

Mayflower Beach

Nobscusset Rd.

Scargo Lake

Scargo Tower

Scargo Hill Rd.

Chapin Mem. Beach

Whig St.

Cape Playhouse/Cinema

East – West

Dr. Bottero

Beach St.

Scargo

BREWSTER

Josiah Dennis Manse

Old

DENNIS

S. Yarmouth Rd.

Setucket Rd.

Bass

River

Rd.

134

Dennis Rd.

Mayfair Rd.

6A

Union St.

SOUTH DENNIS

Exit 9

6

HARWICH

6

Cape Cod Rail Trail begins here

Station Ave.

Historic District

Great Western Rd.

Indian Lands Conservation Area

Swan Pond

YARMOUTH

Bass Rd.

Main St.

Upper Co. Rd.

N

Centre St.

28

1 MILE

W. Yarmouth Rd.

Chamber of Commerce

Uncle Barney's Rd.

School St.

WEST DENNIS

Swan River Rd.

DENNISPORT

Sea St.

Depot St.

Chase Ave.

28

Davis Beach Rd.

Lower Co. Rd.

Old Wharf Rd.

West Dennis Beach

Nantucket Sound

Nantucket Sound

DENNIS

Located at the Cape's geographic center, Dennis is a convenient base for day trips. Some visitors are drawn to Dennis for fine summer theater; others come for family-style attractions along Route 28. Indeed, to outsiders (including the 42,000 or so summer visitors), Dennis suffers from a split personality. Luckily, the 14,000 year-round residents have long since reconciled the village's conflicting natures.

On the north side of town, Route 6A continues along its scenic way, governed by a historical commission. Skirting Dennis and East Dennis, Route 6A is lined with a smattering of antiques shops, crafters, and sea captains' gracious homes. (During the 19th century, more than 400 sea captains called Dennis home.) Colonial side roads off Route 6A lead to beach communities, Quivett Neck (settled in 1639), and Sesuit Marsh and Sesuit Harbor, where the fishing industry once flourished and fishing charters now depart. Note the streets in this area, named for methods of preserving fish: Cold Storage Road and Salt Works Road.

The Cape's oldest cranberry bog is also off Route 6A; Dennis resident Henry Hall cultivated the first cranberries in 1807. He discovered that the berries grow much better when covered with a light layer of sand. His brother, Isaiah, a cooper, patented the barrels used to transport the harvest. It wasn't until the 1840s, when sugar became more readily available, that anyone could do much with these tart berries, though.

The center of Dennis has a quintessential white steeple church, town green, and bandstand.

On the southern side of town, the 6-mile-long Bass River is the largest tidal river on the eastern seaboard. It serves as a natural boundary between Yarmouth and Dennis, offering numerous possibilities for exploration, fishing, and birding. Although it has never been proved, it's widely believed that Viking explorer Leif Eriksson sailed up the Bass River about 1,000 years ago, built a camp, and stayed awhile. Follow Cove Road off Route 28 and Main Street for nice views of the Bass River and sheltered Grand Cove. (The villages of South Dennis and West Dennis were once connected by a bridge here.) In Dennis Port, kids will enjoy the smaller Swan River in a paddleboat.

Each side of Dennis has its own nice, long beach: Chapin Memorial Beach on Cape Cod Bay and West Dennis Beach on Nantucket Sound. Head to Scargo Tower for an expansive view.

GUIDANCE ❋ "ℹ" **Dennis Chamber of Commerce** (508-398-3568; dennis chamber.com), 238 Swan River Road (near Routes 134 and 28), West Dennis. Open 10–4 Monday through Saturday, late May to mid-October; 9–5 weekdays, mid-October to late May. Chamber staff are quite knowledgeable.

PUBLIC RESTROOMS Sesuit Harbor in East Dennis; Town Hall, Main Street, South Dennis.

PUBLIC LIBRARIES ❋ ✎ ↑ "ℹ" Call for hours at the five village libraries (town .dennis.ma.us/dept/library/libraries).

Dennis Memorial Library (508-385-2255), 1020 Old Bass River Road.

Dennis Public Library (508-760-6219; dennispubliclibrary.org), 5 Hall Street.

Jacob Sears Memorial Library (508-385-8151; jacobsearsmemoriallibrary.org), 23 Center Street, East Dennis.

South Dennis Free Public Library (508-394-8954), 389 Main Street.

West Dennis Free Public Library (508-398-2050; wdlibrary.com), 260 Main Street.

GETTING THERE *By car:* From the Cape Cod Canal, take Exit 9 off the Mid-Cape Highway (Route 6). Head north on Route 134 to Route 6A for Dennis and East Dennis. Head south on Route 134 to Route 28 for West Dennis and Dennis Port. The tiny historic district of South Dennis is just west of Route 134 as you head south. Depending on traffic, it takes 20 to 30 minutes to get to various points in Dennis from the canal.

GETTING AROUND As the crow flies, Dennis is only about 7 miles wide from Cape Cod Bay to Nantucket Sound. When navigating, keep a couple of things in mind: South Dennis is actually the geographic center of Dennis, and Dennis Port (the southeastern portion of town) doesn't have a harbor on the ocean as you might expect (given its name!). In general, there isn't much to interest travelers between Routes 6A and 28. Year-rounders make their homes here, visit doctors' and lawyers' offices, and buy food and gardening supplies. Concentrate your meandering north off Route 6A and around the tiny historic district on Main Street in South Dennis.

MEDICAL EMERGENCY Call **911**.

❋ To See

❋ ✎ ↑ **Cape Cod Museum of Art** (508-385-4477; ccmoa.org), Route 6A, Dennis. Open 10–5 Monday through Saturday, noon–5 Sunday, and open until 8 on Thursday; late May to mid-October). The museum is a winner, with eight exhibition spaces, a glassed-in sculpture court, and the Weny Education Center. At the CCMA, Cape Cod's important, historical and contemporary artists—both living and dead—are represented by almost 2,000 works on paper and canvas as well as sculpture. It should definitely be at the top of your list of things to do. The museum also sponsors lectures and art classes for adults and children, and features first-run independent and foreign films in their Screening Room. One of the most popular events is a Secret Garden Tour in late June, which features local artists painting scenes inspired by the Cape's most lovely gardens; tickets $75, including lunch and transportation (see *Special Events*). Adults $8; kids under 18, free; Thursday by donation.

⚭ **Scargo Tower**, Bass Hill Road, Dennis. (Bass Hill Road is just off Scargo Hill Road from Route 6A.) The 30-foot stone tower sits 160 feet above sea level atop the area's tallest hill, and on a clear day the panoramic view extends all the way to Provincetown. Even on a hazy day you can view the width of the Cape: from Nantucket Sound to Cape Cod Bay. **Scargo Lake** (see *Green Space*), a glacial kettle pond, is directly below the tower.

⚭ **Josiah Dennis Manse Museum** and **Old West Schoolhouse** (508-385-2232; 385-3528 for tours), 77 Nobscusset Road at Whig Street, Dennis. Open 10–noon Tuesday and 2–4 Thursday, late June through August. This 1736 saltbox was home to the Reverend Mr. Dennis, for whom the town is named. Today it's set up much as it would have been during the reverend's time, with a keeping room, child's room, maritime wing, and spinning exhibit in the attic. Costumed interpreters are on hand to answer questions. The 1745 one-room schoolhouse, filled with wooden and wrought-iron desks, was moved to its present location in the mid-1970s. Donations.

Congregational Church of South Dennis (508-394-5992), 234 Main Street, South Dennis. The 1835 church itself is not open, but the office is (9–noon Monday and Thursday), and staff are happy to let folks inside. What's there? The chapel features a chandelier made with Sandwich glass and a 1762 Snetzler pipe organ, the country's oldest, which is still in use every Sunday morning. The church is also called the Sea Captain's Church because more than 100 of its founding members were sea captains.

❋ *⚭* **Jericho House and Barn Museum** (508-398-6736), Trotting Park Road and Old Main Street, West Dennis. Open by appointment (when there are enough volunteers.) The 1801 full-Cape-style house contains period furnishings, and the 1810 barn is filled with antique tools, carriages, and a fanciful collection of folk art animals (a veritable "driftwood zoo") crafted in the 1950s by Sherman Woodward. Donations.

SCENIC DRIVES The **South Dennis Historic District**, on and around Main Street from Route 134, gets wonderful afternoon light and relatively little traffic. Escape the crowds and head for this little gem; it's worth a short drive or quiet walk. Note the South Dennis Free Public Library (circa 1858) on Main Street, a cottage-style building covered with wooden gingerbread trim. Liberty Hall is also noteworthy; it was used for concerts, fairs, lectures, and balls when the second story was added in 1865. Edmond Nickerson, founder of the Old South Dennis Village Association, deserves much of the credit for initiating fund-raising drives and overseeing restoration projects.

For a pleasant alternative to Route 134, which also connects the north- and south-sides, take Old Bass River Road, which turns into Main Street in the South Dennis Historic District.

✳ To Do

BICYCLING/RENTALS The **Cape Cod Rail Trail** is a well-maintained asphalt bikeway that follows the Old Colony Railroad tracks for 26 miles from Dennis to Wellfleet. The trail begins off Route 134 in South Dennis across from Hall Oil.

Parking and bike rentals are available at the trailhead from **Barbara's Bike and Sports Equipment** (508-760-4723; barbsbikeshop.com), 430 Route 134. Bikes with helmets are about $12 for 2 hours, $24 daily. The shop stays open from late March to late December. On the southside, you can rent from the even more seasonal **Pizazz** (508-760-3888), 633 Route 28, Dennis Port, about 1.5 miles from the rail trail.

BOAT EXCURSIONS/RENTALS ✍ **Water Safari's Starfish** (508-362-5555; capecodrivercruise.com), 109 Main Street, Route 28, West Dennis. These worth-while 90-minute narrated trips of the Bass River, the largest tidal river on the East Coast, operate late May to mid-October. Along the shoreline you'll see windmills, luxurious riverfront estates, sea captains' homes, and lots of birds. The flat-bottomed aluminum boat (which has an awning) accommodates almost 50 people. Adults $18; children age 1–11, $7. They also rent kayaks for $20 to $65 for a half day.

✍ **Cape Cod Waterways** (508-398-0080), Route 28 near Route 134, Dennis Port. Open May to mid-October. The small and winding Swan River heads about 0.75

A PERFECT DAY IN DENNIS

7:30 Wax nostalgic over breakfast at the old-fashioned waterfront Lighthouse Inn.

9:30 Rent an electric paddleboat (or a kayak) from Cape Cod Waterways.

1:00 Chow down on a lobster roll aboard a lobster boat at Sesuit Harbor Café.

2:15 Tour the Cape Cod Museum of Art, featuring important area artists.

3:45 Browse at the Arm Chair Bookstore with a devoted following.

4:45 Climb Scargo Tower on a clear day to see Provincetown.

5:15 Skip stones on Scargo Lake, a freshwater kettle pond.

7:30 Immerse yourself in garlic with any dish at Gina's by the Sea.

10:00 Order mocha chip ice-cream cone at the Ice Cream Smuggler.

mile north to the 200-acre Swan Pond and 2 miles south to Nantucket Sound. Cape Cod Waterways rents electric and manual paddleboats, canoes, and kayaks that can accommodate a family with two small children.

FISHING/SHELLFISHING Freshwater fishing for smallmouth bass and trout is good at **Scargo Lake**. Obtain a state fishing license at Town Hall (508-394-8300), Main Street, South Dennis. Shellfishing permits are required and can also be obtained through the Natural Resources Office at Town Hall.

Bass River Bridge, Route 28, West Dennis. Park on one side and try your luck; or just stop and watch. Although fishing is not officially not allowed here, the rule is not enforced.

A number of competitively priced, seasonal fishing charters depart from Sesuit Harbor, off Route 6A in East Dennis. But it's best to contact the chamber for specifics.

FOR FAMILIES ✔ **Cartwheels** (508-394-6755; capecodcartwheels.com), 11 South Gages Way, across from Tony Kent Arena, South Dennis. Open 10–10 daily in the summer. "Indy-style" go-carts, batting cages, an arcade, moon walk, Italian ice, and ice cream.

GOLF ✲ **Dennis Highlands** (508-385-8347; dennisgolf.com), Old Bass River Road, Dennis. An 18-hole, par-71 course that's wider and more forgiving; great driving range and practice putting greens.

✲ **Dennis Pines** (508-385-8347; dennisgolf.com), off Route 134 at the end of Golf Course Road, East Dennis. A tight and flat 18-hole, par-72 course that's more competitive than Highlands.

✲ **The Longest Drive** (508-398-5555), 131 Great Western Road, South Dennis. A driving range with covered enclosures, lessons, and clinics.

ICE-SKATING ✲ **Tony Kent Arena** (508-760-2415; tonykentarena.com), 8 South Gages Way, South Dennis. Off Route 134, this rink served as Olympic silver medalist Nancy Kerrigan's training ground back in the early 1990s. Call ahead for public skating hours; rental skates available.

MINI-GOLF ✔ **Holiday Hill** (508-398-8857), Route 28, Dennis Port. Open late April to mid-October. Route 28 is lined with mini-golf courses similar in quality, but can others claim that they plant more than 10,000 flowers annually, as Holiday Hill can?

SAILING ✔ **West Dennis Yacht Club** (508-398-9757; wdyc.org), 259 Loring Way. Sailing school for kids 5–14. The 3-hour morning and afternoon classes are geared to "pre-sailors," beginners, and advanced students.

TENNIS ❄ **Sesuit Tennis Centre**
(508-385-2200; sesuittennis.com), 1389 Route 6A, East Dennis. Open year-round, depending on weather. The center offers three Har-Tru clay courts, a ball machine, open tournaments, and instruction.

❋ Green Space

BEACHES Cottage renters may purchase a weekly parking pass for $55 at Town Hall (508-394-8300), Main Street, South Dennis. Day-trippers can pay a daily fee of $15 to park at the following beaches:

❡ ⅄ **West Dennis Beach** (off Davis Beach Road) on Nantucket Sound is the town's finest and longest beach (it's more than a mile long). Like many Nantucket Sound beaches, though, it's also rather narrow. While there's parking for more than 1,000 cars, the lot rarely fills. If you drive to the western end, you can usually find a few yards of beach for yourself. The eastern end is for residents only. Facilities include 10 lifeguard stations, a snack bar at the eastern end, showers, and restrooms. It's difficult to imagine that fishing shanties, fish weirs, and dories once lined the shores of West Dennis Beach. But they did.

Chapin Memorial Beach, off Chapin Beach Road on Cape Cod Bay, is open to four-wheel-drive vehicles. It's a nice, long, dune-backed beach. As you drive up to Chapin, you'll probably notice an incongruous-looking building plunked down in the marshes and dunes. In fact, it's the headquarters for the Aquaculture Research Corporation (known as the Cultured Clam Corp.), the only state-certified seller of shellfish seed. Begun in 1960, the company is a pioneer in the field of aquaculture. There's no better place to study shellfish. Facilities at the beach include restrooms and a snack bar.

⅄ **Corporation Beach**, off Corporation Road on Cape Cod Bay, is backed by low dunes and was once used as a packet-ship landing by a group of town residents who formed the Nobscusset Pier Corporation (hence its name). The crescent-shaped beach has concession stands, a play and picnic area, lifeguards, and restrooms.

❡ ⅄ **Mayflower Beach**, off Beach Street on Cape Cod Bay, has a boardwalk, restrooms, and a concession stand. **Sea Street Beach**, off Sea

Street, and **Howes Street Beach**, off Howes Street and backed by low dunes; both have boardwalks. The Sea Street parking lot fills up by noon. These three beaches are relatively small and good for families with young children because the water is shallow. As at Corporation and Chapin Memorial beaches, at low tide you can walk a mile out into the bay.

There are about eight other public beaches on Nantucket Sound, but all are quite small.

PONDS/LAKES **Scargo Lake**, a deep, freshwater kettle hole left behind by retreating glaciers, has two beaches: **Scargo Beach** (off Route 6A) and **Princess Beach** (off Scargo Hill Road). Princess Beach has a picnic area; bathers at Scargo Beach tend to put their beach chairs in the shallow water or on the narrow, tree-lined shore. There are two legends concerning the lake's creation—you decide which you prefer: Did an Indian princess have the lake dug for fish that she received as a present? Or did a giant named Maushop dig the hole as a remembrance of himself to the local Native Americans?

Swan Pond Overlook, off Centre Street from Searsville Road and Route 134. Beach, picnic area, and bird-watching area.

WALKS **Indian Lands Conservation Area**, behind Town Office on Main Street, South Dennis. This easy, 2-mile roundtrip walk skirts the banks of the upper Bass River. In winter you'll see blue herons and kingfishers; lady's slippers bloom in May. From the northern end of the Town Hall parking lot on Main Street, follow the power-line right-of-way path for half a mile to the trailhead.

✳ Lodging

Dennis lodging establishments represent very good values; one of my all-Cape favorite places is located in South Dennis. One place off Route 6A *really* stands out on the northside, while the southside is loaded with family places (with one noteworthy exception). Most southside places are on or quite close to the beach.

RESORT ✿ ♿ "🐾" **Lighthouse Inn** (508-398-2244; lighthouseinn.com), Lighthouse Inn Road, West Dennis. Open mid-May to mid-October. They don't make them like this anymore! This classic Cape Cod, family-friendly resort on Nantucket Sound has 68 rooms and tidy cottages on 9 grassy, waterfront acres. The resort, expertly operated by the Stones since 1938, has lots of amenities: supervised children's activities, special children's dinners, a

heated pool, tennis, shuffleboard, mini-golf, volleyball, and the Sand Bar Club and Lounge. On rainy days guests gather in the common rooms of the lodge-style main building, stocked with games, books, and a TV. Oriental carpets lend it a delightful, old-shoe, Adirondack camp feel. And a staff of over 100 hustle around keeping guests happy. Lunch is served on the deck or

LIGHTHOUSE INN

poolside (see *Dining Out*). A full breakfast is included. Its Bass River Lighthouse is the only privately owned working lighthouse in the country. July and August $248–322; off-season $168–242. Children are additional $45 nightly. Ask about rates including meals and about bundled activity packages.

BED & BREAKFASTS ❀ ❝❡❞

Isaiah Hall Bed and Breakfast Inn (508-385-9928; 800-736-0160; isaiahhallinn.com), 152 Whig Street, Dennis. On a quiet street off Route 6A, innkeeper Jerry and Judy Neal's rambling 1857 farmhouse is one of the most comfortable and welcoming places on Cape Cod. It feels like one big non-stop social event here, with guests lingering in the pass-through kitchen and hanging around in the "great room." Main inn guest rooms are furnished with country-style antiques, while rooms in the attached carriage house are newer, each decorated with stenciling, white wicker, and knotty-pine paneling. Check out the newer Isaiah Hall Suite, a jewel of a two-bedroom suite with a fireplace. All 12 rooms are air-conditioned and equipped with flat-screen TVs, DVDs, and 600-thread count sheets. There is plenty of indoor and outdoor common

ISAIAH HALL BED & BREAKFAST INN

space, including that cathedral-ceilinged great room (with a guest computer), a delightfully relaxing garden, and a deep lawn that leads to the Cape's oldest cranberry bog. A full breakfast is served at one long, extraordinarily convivial table. Children over age 7 welcome; 3-night minimum in summer. Mid-June to mid-September $145–350; off-season $100–185.

❀ **Shady Hollow Inn** (508-394-7474; shadyhollowinn.com), 370 Main Street, South Dennis. I could go on and on with accolades for this favorite place, but space limits my words. Suffice it to say, if I operated a B&B it would probably look like this. This off-the-beaten-path B&B, with a tranquil side garden, is a graciously renovated sea captain's house that dates to 1839. The four guest rooms (three with private bath and a fourth that completes a family/friends suite), with mission-style furnishings and quilts, are also outfitted with TV/VCRs, a hefty dose of attention, soothing color palettes, and tasteful bathroom renovations. Hearty vegetarian breakfasts, with organic ingredients as often as possible, are included. (Great care is taken to accommodate dietary restrictions.) Hosts—Ann Hart and David Dennis—also offer use of two loaner bicycles, two kayaks, and a divine outdoor shower. Join them, on the occasional cool summer evening, as they enjoy their outdoor chimenia. It's always a treat to find places like this. Children over age 10 welcome. Late May to mid-October $130–220, off-season $110–185.

♿ ❝❡❞ **An English Garden B&B** (508-398-2915; 888-788-1908; an englishgardenbb.com), 32 Inman Road, Dennis Port. Open mid-April through October. This is a very good, comfortable, contemporary choice. Within a 2-minute walk of the beach, this guesthouse has nine tasteful rooms and two suites. Each boasts hardwood floors, quilts, and a deck or small balcony; some have a whirlpool or ocean view. Both airy living rooms are perfect for reading on a rainy afternoon. A full breakfast (perhaps a vegetable omelet and an assortment of breads) is served at individual tables in a spacious and bright breakfast room. Ask innkeepers Joe and Anita Sangiolo about their refurbished two-bedroom guesthouse that has a full kitchen and rents for $1300 weekly in the summer. I also like the master bedroom with a private entrance in the main house. Children over age 10 are welcome in main inn. Mid-June to early September $150–165 nightly for rooms, $1,400–1,500 weekly for suites; off-season $80–120 rooms, $975 weekly or $140–160 nightly for suites (with a 3-night minimum).

✍ ᴄ **By the Sea Guests B&B** (508-398-8685; 800-447-9202; bythesea guests.com), 57 Chase Avenue at Inman Road, Dennis Port. Open early May through December. You can't get closer to Inman Beach than this. Each of the 12 large rooms, with refrigerator and cable TV, is basically but pleasantly outfitted. Look for well-maintained 1950s-style cottage furniture, white cotton bedspreads, and white curtains. It's all very summery, charming, and breezy. On rainy days, B&B guests can head to the enclosed porch overlooking the private beach (just steps away) or to the large living room with books, games, and a ready supply of snacks. There are also five contemporary, fully equipped one- and two-bedroom suites that can accommodate four to six people for weekly stays. Full breakfast included with B&B rooms: July to early September $175–275; off-season $102–145. Suites (in-season): $1,865–2,795 weekly, $295 nightly. (Ask about minimum stays and the service change for suites.)

COTTAGES ✍ ᴄ "ı" **Dennis Seashores** (508-398-8512; dennis seashores.com), 20 Chase Avenue, Dennis Port. Open May through October. These 32 housekeeping cottages are some of the best on Nantucket Sound; make reservations a year in advance. The two-, three-, and four-bedroom shingled cottages, with knotty-pine paneling and fireplaces, are decorated and furnished in a "Cape Cod Colonial" style. Cottages, with fully equipped kitchens, towels, and linens, are either beachfront or nestled among pine trees; each has a grill and picnic table. The resort's private stretch of beach is well tended. Early July to late August $1,290–5,495; off-season $550–4,195. Three-night rentals are available in the shoulder seasons.

RENTAL HOUSES ✍ **Peter McDowell Associates** (508-385-9114; capecodproperties.com), 585 Route 6A in Dennis.

✳ Where to Eat

Dennis has an embarrassing riches of good and great restaurants to satisfy every budget and whim. Surrounding towns should be so lucky.

DINING OUT ᴄ **Red Pheasant Inn** (508-385-2133; redpheasantinn.com), Route 6A, Dennis. Open for dinner (except during January). Chef-owner Bill Atwood and his wife, Denise, have been going strong since 1980 and still receive consistently glowing reviews. Low ceilings, wood floors, exposed beams, and linen-draped tables set a rustic and romantic tone. Located in a 200-year-old renovated barn (actually, a former ship chandlery on Corporation Beach), the elegant restaurant enjoys a fine reputation for attentive service, first-rate cuisine, and a well-chosen (and a very well priced) wine list. Prime cuts of lamb, beef, and game with regional American influences are offered. Lobster and other seafood are always popular, and their rack of lamb could compete head to head anywhere! In a nod to changing palates, they've added a bistro menu in the bar. Off-season early specials. Dinner $20–34.

♠ ♈ **Ocean House** (508-394-0700; oceanhouserestaurant.com), 421 Old Wharf Road, at the end of Depot Street, Dennis Port. Open for dinner nightly except Monday mid-March to early January. Everyone loves the Ocean House, but don't let appearances deceive you: The boxy brick building belies the ocean views that await. Go before sunset to drink in the views; it's half the fun. The other half is artful chef Anthony Silvistri, who prepares seasonal, contemporary, New American dishes with a local influence. Look for fusion dishes like cedar roasted teriyaki salmon, grilled Hawaiian tuna steak, or a 12oz. Wolfneck's Farm ribeye. If you don't want to wait for a table, dine at the bar on gourmet pizzas and appetizers. Definitely save room for distinctive desserts, and consider starting with a signature martini. Off-season, the prix fixe meal (nightly except Saturday) is a terrific bargain at $25. Service is quite knowledgeable. Otherwise, small plates $9–20, dinner $20–36.

❄ ✎ ♈ ♿ **The Oyster Company Raw Bar & Grille** (508-398-4600; the oystercompany.com) 202 Depot Street, Dennis Port. Open for dinner; call for off-season schedule. This is one hip and happening place to nosh with pals. And to think, too, you don't have to drive to Wellfleet to enjoy magnificently fresh oysters any more! Although the Oyster Company offers other fishy temptations besides briny delicacies, the 95¢ oysters (available from 5–6:30)

really pack 'em in. Oysters are harvested daily from Quivet Neck in Dennis. Try summertime oysters barely broiled in cilantro and butter. The regular menu is fairly limited because the chef relies on the daily catch for inspiration. Dinner $8–25.

♈ ♿ **Gina's by the Sea** (508-385-3213; ginasbythesea.com), 134 Taunton Avenue, Dennis. Open for dinner Thursday through Sunday, April through November. Gina's is a very friendly and fun place, with a low-key bar, knotty-pine walls, a fireplace, and exposed beams. A fixture in this beachside enclave since 1938 (chef Chris Lemmer has been cooking since 1990), Gina's really is as consistently good as everyone says. Its northern Italian menu features signature dishes like garlicky shrimp scampi, mussels marinara, and chicken "gizmondo." Because the restaurant is small, very popular, and doesn't take reservations, arrive early or wait until after 9 PM. Otherwise, put your name on the waiting list and take a walk on nearby Chapin Memorial Beach or have a drink and watch the sunset. A trip to Gina's epitomizes the essence of summer, and a trip to Dennis wouldn't be the same without it. Dinner $9–22.

Gracie's Table (508-385-5600; graciestablecapecod.com), 800 Route 6A,

BUCKIES BISCOTTI & CO.

Dennis. Open for dinner; call for exact days. Although I didn't get a chance to eat at this hot little Spanish tapas restaurant for this edition, I understand from devoted readers (Wellfleet's Marje Sparrow among them) that this chef-owned Basque eatery is worth your money and time. Have a cocktail at the copper bar while you wait. Tapas $3–14, mains $19.

❀ ❦ **Blue Moon Bistro** (508-385-7100; bluemoonbistro.net), 605 Route 6A, Dennis. Open for dinner Tuesday through Sunday, late May to mid-October; closed Sunday and Mondays off-season. Chef-owner Peter Hyde runs a well-respected neighborhood bistro featuring bold flavors and Mediterranean-influenced dishes like cedar planked organic salmon with balsamic glazed cippolini onions, sautéed spinach, and wild and basmati risotto-style rice. It's all so sophisticated without being stuffy, outfitted with soft lighting and soothing colors. The martini and wine selection is enough to keep you coming back. Dinner $16–32.

❀ 🐾 ✿ ♿ **Scargo Café** (508-385-8200; scaragocafe.com), Route 6A, Dennis. Open for lunch and dinner. The friendly staff here are particularly adept at getting patrons to Cape Playhouse shows (see *Entertainment*) on time without hurrying them. If you're really late, light bites and finger foods

such as shrimp martini and calamari are served in the pleasant bar. Otherwise, dependable specials include seafood strudel topped with shrimp, a vegetable-and-brie sandwich, rack of lamb, and lobster risotto. As for the atmosphere, the bustling, renovated former sea captain's house is awash in wood: paneling, wainscoting, and floors. Brothers Peter and David Troutman have presided over the extensive and well-executed menu since 1987. It's hard to beat the prices and quality here. Off-season early specials. Lunch $6–14, dinner $7–22.

✿ ♿ **Lighthouse Inn** (508-398-2244; lighthouseinn.com), 1 Lighthouse Road, off Lower County Road, on the road to West Dennis Beach. Open for breakfast and dinner, mid-May to mid-October, and for lunch in July and August. The decor here, as well as the cuisine, is decidedly old-fashioned. Indoor tables are draped with white linen, and the service is professional; it's the kind of place you might expect in the Catskills, à la 1950. Except this is seaside. Along with peaked ceilings and knotty-pine paneling, the large and open dining room features a full wall of windows overlooking the ocean. I prefer their casual luncheons, served on the oceanfront deck; the seaside setting is a treat. Keep it simple with sandwiches, seafood and pasta combos, burgers, and light salads. The extensive dinner menu is reasonably priced, and steamed lobster is always a popular choice. Breakfast is a hot or cold buffet ($11 and $7, respectively). Lunch $7–13, dinner $20–30.

❀ ✿ **Chapin's** (508-385-7000; chapins restaurant.com), 85 Taunton Avenue, Dennis. Open for lunch and dinner daily. Near the beach, this newly constructed, casual eatery has something for everyone, which generally means the food isn't gourmet quality but it also means that most folks will walk away fairly happy. There's a lot to be said for that. From a salad bar to a raw bar, Chapin's also offers chicken, local seafood, lobster, steaks, sandwiches, prime rib, and pasta dishes. See what I mean? This noisy place is wildly popular in the winter when they offer value-laden specials to keep locals coming back. The outdoor deck is pleasant. Dishes $6–22.

EATING OUT 🦞 🍴 **Sesuit Harbor Café** (508-385-6134; 508-385-2442; sesuitharborcafe.com), on Sesuit Harbor. Open for lunch and dinner seasonally. Wildly, wildly popular with good reason, this café offers excellent lobster rolls and trips aboard a retrofitted **lobster boat** (lobsterrollcruises .com; 508-385-1686). If you prefer to keep your feet on terra firma, make a beeline through the marina and boatyard for their simple harborfront shack. It's nothing to look at, but the raised herb beds augur well for quality ingredients. Order off the blackboard menu and eat at picnic tables, inside or outside, with mismatched umbrellas. Lunch $5–15, dinner $5–22.

❄ 🦞 🍴 ♿ **Marshside** (508-385-4010), 28 Bridge Street, East Dennis. Open

SESUIT HARBOR CAFÉ

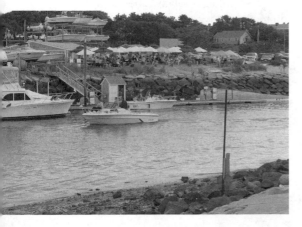

for lunch and dinner daily. Marshside went from a homey, beloved little place with a soul in 2007 to a more institutional one in 2008, albeit one that's shiny, new, and spacious. During my recent visit, the transformation seemed to have brought some growing pains (with less than stellar service). It's still noted for a casual atmosphere, home-style dishes (shrimp scampi, lobster, salads, sandwiches, and veggie melts), and reasonable prices. And it's still a family-oriented restaurant that provides coloring placemats and toys for children. All the tables overlook the namesake marsh, with a view of Sesuit Harbor. Lunch $5–20, dinner $10–35.

Wee Packet (508-394-6595; weepack et2.com), 79 Depot Street, Dennis Port. Open 8 AM—9 PM early May to late October. Recently under new management, this small and sweet place serves full Irish breakfasts, tons of egg dishes, clam chowder, great scallops, and fish and chips (but not at the same time of day!) Dishes $4–16.

Center Stage Café (508-385-7737; centerstagedennis.com), 36 Hope Lane, behind the Cape Playhouse, Dennis. Open for dinner mid-April to late November. Head to the backstage pub side for a before-or-after theater martini and burger or a mojito and pizza. Early three-course specials. Dinner $11–24.

❄ **Lost Dog Pub** (508-385-6177), 1374 Route 134, East Dennis. Open daily for lunch and dinner. I wouldn't waste good daylight hours at this tavern at lunchtime, but this place makes a cozy spot after dark—when you just want something homey and decent, with good service. Their burgers and pizza are good; seafood, fishcakes, and clam chowder are specialties. Lunch specials $5–8, dinner $9–14.

❄ 🍴 **The Breakfast Room** (508-398-0581; breakfastroomcapecod.com), 675

Route 28, West Dennis. Open for breakfast and lunch daily April through December, weekends January through March. This place is classic, a local fixture. In addition to griddle cakes, you can order no-nonsense egg dishes or go whole hog and chow down on steak, eggs, and potatoes. They have cran-nut pancakes, eggs Benedict, and french toast, too. Dishes $4–10.

❦ ✎ ♿ **Captain Frosty's** (508-385-8548; captainfrosty.com), 219 Route 6A, Dennis. Open 11–8 or 9 daily, mid-April to mid-October. Since 1976, Mike and Pat Henderson have run one of the Cape's best no-frills roadside clam shacks. Because they use premium ingredients like hooked (not gill-netted) Chatham cod, Gulf shrimp, native clams, lobster, and small sea scallops, you'll want to look for daily specials. Also try grilled salmon sandwiches, black Angus burgers, and grilled scallop Caesar salads. And rest assured that the seafood and onion rings are deep-fried in 100 percent canola oil. Choose between the casual dining room or outdoor seating at a brick patio surrounded by rhododendrons. Save room for the Cape's best soft-serve ice cream. Dishes $3–14.

✎ ♿ **Swan River Seafood** (508-394-4466), 5 Lower County Road, Dennis Port. Open for lunch and dinner, mid-May to mid-October. Family owned and operated, this casual restaurant's appeal is fresh, fresh, hook-caught fish, thanks to the attached fish market. Keep it simple with lobster, clams, oysters, and the catch of the day. Arrive early to secure a table overlooking a river, a marsh, Nantucket Sound, and a windmill. Outdoor dining too. Lunch $10–20, dinner $15–25.

✎ ♉ **Clancy's Fish 'n Chips and Beach Bar** (508-394-6900; clancys fishnchips.com), 228 Lower County Road, Dennis Port. Open for lunch and dinner early May to early September. You can count on very reliable seafood in pleasant, noisy, and casual surroundings here. Large portions of food arrives in plastic baskets at outdoor tables under canvas umbrellas, within the screened-in porch, or at shiny wooden tables with directors' chairs. Try the boneless Buffalo wings. Expect to long lines or try bellying up to the convivial bar. Wines by the glass tend to be generous pours. Dishes $7–22.

✎ **Kream 'n' Kone** (508-394-0808; kreamnkone.com), 961 Route 134 and Route 28, West Dennis. Open early March through October. This place dishes honest-to-goodness kitsch, not kitsch imported from any consultant who says kitsch is cool. Come for self-serve fried seafood, ice cream, and clams. Although it's campy, it is not necessarily cheap; a family can easily spend $60 here. Lunch and dinner $4–19.

❦ ♿ **The Dog House** (508-398-7774), 189 Lower County Road, Dennis Port. Open daily except Tuesday 11:00–8:30 mid-May to early October. This old-fashioned hot dog stand dispenses dogs with sauerkraut or bacon and cheese or lots of other combinations for $2–10. After you've ordered from the take-out window, have a seat at one of a few covered picnic tables.

COFFEE AND SWEETS ✴ ❦ **Buckies Biscotti & Co.** (508-385-4700 and 508-398-9700; buckiebiscotti.com), 780 Route 6A, Dennis; and 281 Route 28, Dennis Port. Open 6:30 AM to at least 5 PM daily. For excellent espresso, authentic Italian cookies, biscotti, and cannoli, and savory sandwiches and panini, it's tough to beat Buckies. Long live entrepreneurs like baker Alyson Bucchiere. The Dennis location is on the grounds of the playhouse and behind the post office, while the Dennis Port location is in a groovy building worth stopping at on Route 28. It's got concrete floors, high ceilings, and big pane windows.

❋ **Stage Stop Candy** (508-394-1791), 411 Main Street, Dennis Port. Ray and Donna Hebert originated the ultimate chocolate-covered cranberry. You gotta try it. They'll make chocolates in any shape, including computer boards and TV remote controls.

Sundae School Ice Cream Parlor (508-394-9122), 381 Lower County Road, Dennis Port. Open mid-April to mid-October, until 11 PM in summer for that late-night fix. This old-fashioned parlor is replete with a marble soda fountain, marble tables, tin signage, and a nickelodeon. Some confections are delightfully modern, though: Frozen yogurt and ice cream are made with two-thirds less fat. I refuse to take a stand, by the way, in the Sundae School versus Smuggler debate of which is better. You can't make me walk the plank one that one; I can't win!

P&D Fruit, 349 Lower County Road, Dennis Port. Open mid-May to mid-September. Who says the southside of Cape Cod is so commercialized that you can't find a decent farm stand? Look no further.

P & D FRUIT

&. **Ice Cream Smuggler** (508-385-5307), 716 Route 6A, Dennis. Open April to mid-October. Homemade ice cream—including a great mocha chip—and frozen yogurt.

✳ Entertainment

🦞 ♪ ♼ &. **Cape Playhouse** (508-385-3911; capeplayhouse.com), Route 6A, Dennis. Shows Monday through Saturday, mid-June to early September. The Cape Playhouse was established in 1927 by Californian Raymond Moore, who initially went to Provincetown to start a theater company but found it too remote. Moore's attitude when he purchased this former 1830s Unitarian meetinghouse for $200 was, "If we fix it up, they will come." Sure enough, the playhouse proudly claims the title of the country's oldest continuously operating professional summer theater and the Cape's only full Equity theater. Basil Rathbone starred in the company's first production, *The Guardsman*. Over the years, the playhouse has featured the likes of Helen Hayes, Julie Harris, Olivia de Havilland, and Jessica Tandy, when they were already "stars." Henry Fonda, Bette Davis, Humphrey Bogart, and Gregory Peck acted here before they were "discovered." On Thursday and Friday mornings in July and August there is **children's theater**. If you make it to only one summer production, let it be here. Tickets $25–50; children's theater $8–9.

♪ **Band concerts**, whether the music be country or American classics, are held on both town greens in July and August. Head to Dennis on Route 6A on Mondays and Dennis Port off Route 28 on Tuesdays. Check with the chamber (see *Guidance*) for an exact schedule of places and times.

✳ 🦞 ♼ **Entertainment Cinemas 12** (508-394-1100), 2–6 Enterprise Road, Patriot Square Mall, South Dennis. Take Exit 9 off Route 6.

✳ Unless otherwise noted, all shops are open year-round. **The Dennis Art Walk** (dennisartwalk.com) is sponsored by the chamber on Thursday and Saturday evenings.

ANTIQUES Dennis Port center is a quiet place for year-round antiques browsers. Chief among the half dozen shops "downtown" is the **Main Street Antique Center** (508-760-5700), 691 Main. With more than 100 dealers, it's just one of many retailers trying to revitalize the little district.

Antiques Center of Cape Cod (508-385-6400), 243 Route 6A, Dennis. With more than 150 dealers, this two-story (former) building supply store is the Cape's largest cooperative, offering curios large and small. Don't miss it or the giant warehouse next door. Most objects sell for under $200 and are classified as "old," "vintage," or "collectible" rather than "antique."

✳ **O'Shea's Olde Inne** (508-398-8887; osheasoldeinne.com), 348 Route 28, West Dennis. It's too packed to deal with in the summer, the food portions are smallish, and screaming kids can ruin the experience for some, but I recommend O'Shea's off-season for deeply authentic, serious Irish music on weekends. The smell of whiskey shots fills the air. If you're hungry, order a kid's portion of something. (The prices make more sense.)

See also **Cape Cinema**, in the "Heavenly Screenings," sidebar and **Cape Cod Museum of Art** under *To See.*

HEAVENLY SCREENINGS

✳ **Cape Cinema** (508-385-2503; capecinema.com), 35 Hope Lane, off Route 6A, Dennis. Screenings daily. Built in 1930 as a movie theater, Cape Cinema continues to bring fine art films, foreign films, and independent productions to Cape audiences. The exterior was designed after the Congregational church in Centerville, while the interior ceiling was designed by Rockwell Kent to represent his view of heaven, filled with comets and constellations. When Kent refused to set foot in Massachusetts because he was protesting the 1921 verdict in the Sacco and Vanzetti trial, Jo Mielziner supervised the painting and installation of the 6,400-square-foot art deco mural, which was done by the Art Students League in a New York theater and shipped by train to the Cape. There are about 300 seats in this theater, which was chosen to premiere *The Wizard of Oz* in 1940. Don't miss catching a flick here; screening times are usually 4:30, 7, and 9. Tickets $8.50 adults, $6.50 seniors.

ART GALLERIES AND ARTISANS

Kate Nelson (at **Ross Coppelman**) (508-385-7900), 1439 Route 6A, East Dennis. Kate's work is some of the most sophisticated abstraction I've seen on the Cape. Her nonrepresentational paintings and prints are extraordinary and, as she says, "ever-changing, like the path to the outgoing tide on the Brewster flats." She continues to fuse the experience of exterior landscape with the "inscape," the inner landscape of psyche and spirit.

Michael Baksa Studio (508-385-5733), 766 Route 6A, Dennis, and Ross Coppelman (508-385-7900), 1439 Route 6A, East Dennis, have fashioned stunning designs as goldsmiths for more than 20 years. Both men work on the premises. Ross's shop is a special-occasion kind of place; his creations have lots of zeros on the price tags. If you're serious about having a stone set or buying something in gold or silver, don't overlook **Jewelry by Etta** (508-394-8964), 530 Route 28, West Dennis. Many people who don't venture to the southside are unaware of Etta and unwittingly bypass this fine, singular shop.

Fritz Glass (508-394-0441; fritzglass.com), 36 Upper County Road, Dennis Port. Open most days; call to confirm. Although this is primarily a wholesale glassblowing operation, the colorful and striking showroom is filled with extraordinarily decorative, functional creations. You can watch Fritz Lauenstein work, and check out the inventory of fun and intricate marbles (sold in museums around the country) and sand dollars, honey pots and bud vases. Chances are that Fritz's wife, June, and daughter Coco will be in the shop, too.

❄ **Scargo Pottery** (508-385-3894; scargopottery.com), 30 Dr. Lord Road South, off Route 6A, Dennis. Open daily. Down a path through the woods, potter Harry Holl and his four daughters (Tina, Kim, Mary, and Sarah) make whimsical and decidedly untraditional birdhouses, fountains, and architectural sculptures, among other things. The "gallery" is a magical world that you won't want to miss: Pieces hang from tree branches and sit on tree stumps. The work isn't cheap, but it isn't run-of-the-mill, either. There's no question that this is pottery as art. Harry has been working here since 1952.

A Touch of Glass (508-398-3850), 711 Route 28, West Dennis. These stained-glass lamps and lampshades have been created using the same techniques employed by Tiffany.

AUCTIONS Eldred's Auctions (508-385-3116; eldreds.com), 1483 Route 6A, East Dennis. This high-end auction house—the Cape's largest—moves magnificent collections. In July the weekly auctions concentrate on books, collectibles, marine items, and paintings. During August there is an Americana auction the first week; contemporary Cape Cod art auction the second week; and a weeklong Asian auction late in the month. In spring and fall, call about the monthly specialty auctions.

Tobey Farm, 352 Route 6A, Dennis. This colorful farm has been in the same family since 1681, when it was given to Thomas Tobey for his service during King Philip's War.

✐ **Pizazz** (508-760-3888), 633 Route 28, Dennis Port. Giant blowup beach toys and summer novelties. There are dozens of other similar shops, but they just don't have pizzazz, so to speak.

✳ Special Events

Mid- to late June: **Secret Garden Tour**, sponsored by the Cape Cod Museum of Art (508-385-4477, ext. 19). Tour gardens and watch artists paint their inspiration.

BOOKSTORES 🐾 **Arm Chair Bookstore** (508-385-0900; armchairbookstore.com), 619 Route 6A, Dennis. Open daily. This fantastic, independent bookshop has a devoted following, with obvious reason: There isn't a more inviting bookstore on the Cape.

SPECIAL SHOPS Arm Chair Cottage (508-385-4808), 611 Route 6A, Dennis. Search no more for that distinctive summery cottage look. Loaded with Maine cottage furniture and Cape Cod gifts, this fun store appeals to all budgets. Offerings are built around colors, which makes shopping all that much easier, and harder to resist.

Grandma Daisy's (508-394-3373), 444 Lower County Road, Dennis Port. Open early May to mid-November. This former blacksmith's barn is loaded with tasteful gifts for any occasion, books, and distinctive home accessories. It's great browsing and buying.

The Lower Cape   3

BREWSTER

HARWICH

CHATHAM

ORLEANS

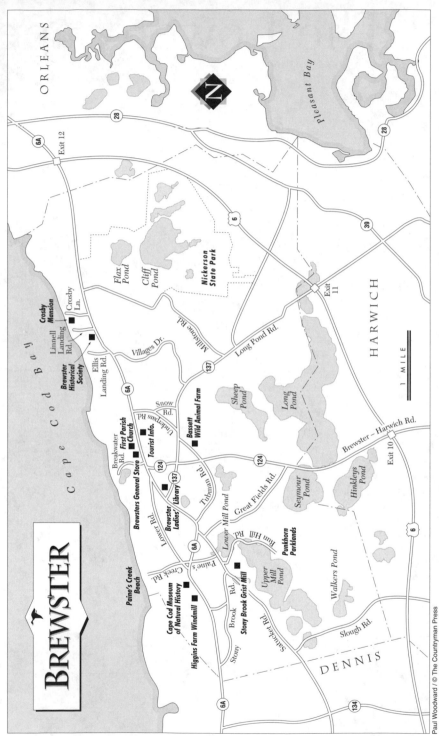

BREWSTER

ORLEANS

Pleasant Bay

28

6A
Exit 12

28

28

6

39

Flax
Pond

Cliff
Pond

Nickerson State Park

Exit
11

HARWICH

Crosby Mansion

Crosby
Ln.

Linnell
Landing
Rd.

Brewster Historical Society

Ellis
Landing Rd.

Villages Dr.

Millstone Rd.

Long Pond Rd.

137

Sheep
Pond

Long
Pond

1 MILE

Cape Cod Bay

6A

Snow
Rd.

Underpass Rd.

Bassett
Wild Animal Farm

Breakwater
Rd.

First Parish
Church

Tourist Info.

124

Brewsters General Store

137

Brewster
Ladies'
Library

124

Tubman Rd.

Great Fields Rd.

Lower Mill Pond

124

Brewster – Harwich Rd.

Exit 10

Hinkleys
Pond

Seymour
Pond

6

Lower Rd.

6A

Paine's
Creek Rd.

Paine's Creek Beach

Cape Cod Museum
of Natural History

Higgins Farm Windmill

Tun Hill Rd.

Punkhorn
Parklands

Upper
Mill
Pond

Walkers Pond

Stony Brook Grist Mill

Stony
Brook
Rd.

Setucket Rd.

Slough Rd.

DENNIS

6A

134

Paul Woodward / © The Countryman Press

BREWSTER

Y ou could spend a charmed week in Brewster with plenty to occupy you. While the 2,000-acre Nickerson State Park boasts facilities for a dozen outdoor activities, there is also Punkhorn Parklands, an undeveloped, 800-acre parcel of conservation land in town. Although Brewster has only 10,500 year-round residents, it has more than its share of attractions, including two good golf courses, horseback-riding trails, an outstanding museum of natural history, and exceptional dining choices.

Brewster's section of Route 6A is a vital link in the 80-square-mile Old King's Highway Historic District. Known for its selection of fine antiques shops, Brewster also attracts contemporary artists, who are drawn to a landscape more evocative of the countryside than the seaside—the land south of Route 6A is dotted with ponds, hills, and dales.

Brewster, settled in 1659 and named for *Mayflower* passenger Elder William Brewster, wasn't incorporated until 1803, when it split from Harwich. By then the prosperous sea captains who'd built their homes on the bay side wanted to distance themselves from their less-well-off neighbors to the south. Between 1780 and 1870, 99 sea captains called Brewster home (although they sailed their clipper ships out of Boston and New York), a fact that even Henry David Thoreau commented on during his 1849 trip. Many of these beautiful houses on Route 6A have been converted to B&Bs and inns.

In the early 1800s, Breakwater Beach was a popular landing for packet ships, which transported salt and vegetables to Boston and New York markets and brought tourists to the area. Salt making was big business in 1837, when more than 60 saltworks dotted Brewster beaches. Windmills pumped seawater into 36-by-18-foot vats, where it was left to evaporate (this process was developed in Dennis). During the late 18th and early 19th centuries, Brewster's Factory Village sold cloth, boots, and food to people all over the Cape.

GUIDANCE **Brewster Visitor Information Center** (508-896-3500; brewster capecod.org), 2198 Route 6A, about half a mile east of Route 124, on the ground floor of Town Hall. Open 9–3 daily June to early September; 10–2 the rest of the year. Staff are very friendly and quite knowledgeable but how can they realistically close at 3 PM?

PUBLIC RESTROOMS Nickerson State Park and the Visitor Information Center, both on Route 6A.

PUBLIC LIBRARY See **Brewster Ladies' Library** under *To See*.

GETTING THERE *By car:* Brewster is 30 minutes from the Cape Cod Canal (take Route 6 east to Exit 9, to Route 134, to Route 6A); it is 45 minutes from Provincetown, at the tip of the peninsula.

GETTING AROUND It's very easy to get around in Brewster. There's no real "center" to the town; places of interest are strung along Route 6A.

MEDICAL EMERGENCY Call **911**.

✳ To See

✎ ⚲ **Cape Cod Museum of Natural History** (508-896-3867; ccmnh.org), 869 Route 6A. Open 10–4 Wednesday through Sunday April and May, 9:30–4 daily June through September, and Wednesday through Sunday October through March. Founded by naturalist John Hay (along with seven local educators) in 1954, this is a terrific resource for learning about the Cape's natural world. And it's doing a splendid job these days. The museum takes its mission seriously: to "inspire and foster an understanding and appreciation of our environment through education, and a means to sustain it." Check out marine tanks (containing upwards of 65 creatures: crabs, lobsters, mollusks, turtles, eels, and frogs), a live "osprey cam" which shows a bird family nesting behind the museum), whale displays, a natural history library, as well as many interactive, hands-on exhibits for children. The gift shop is packed with fun and educational toys, books, and games. The Wing's Island Trail—just one trail traversing the museum's 80 acres of marshes, beaches, and woodland—begins from here (see *Green Space*). Adults $8; children 3–12, $3.50; seniors $7; fee for some programs. (Also see Summer camps under *For Families*.)

Stony Brook Grist Mill and Herring Run (508-896-1734), Stony Brook Road. Open Saturdays in July and

STONY BROOK GRIST MILL

August; corn grinding on Saturdays. This millside pond is one of the Cape's most picturesque places, especially during the spring migration (mid-April to early May), when the herring are "running" and the natural "ladders" are packed with the silver-backed fish. In 1663 America's first water-powered mill stood on this location. The present gristmill, constructed on 1873 woolen mill foundations (part of the 19th-century Factory Village), contains old milling equipment and a 100-year-old loom on which age-old techniques are demonstrated by special request (508-896-6194). The museum, where cornmeal is for sale, was redone in 2006 and includes early American artifacts and Indian arrowheads. Donations.

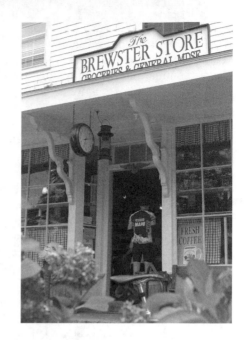

❋ **The Brewster Store** (508-896-3744; brewsterstore.com), 1935 Route 6A at Route 124. Open daily. Purveying groceries and general merchandise since 1866, this quintessentially Cape Cod store was built in 1852 as a Universalist church. Since then, four generations of families have relied on the store. As always, locals and visitors sit outside on old church pews, sip coffee, read the morning newspaper, eat penny candy and ice cream, and watch the world go by. Upstairs has been re-created with memorabilia from the mid-1800s to the mid-1900s; downstairs has a working antique nickelodeon and oft-used peanut roaster.

❋ ✿ ♟ "♟" **Brewster Ladies' Library** (508-896-3913; brewsterladieslibrary.org), 1822 Route 6A. Open at least 10–5 Tuesday through Saturday. In 1852 two teenage Brewster girls established this "library," which began as a shelf of books lent from the girls' houses. After local sea captains donated funds in 1868, the ever-expanding library moved to a handsome red Victorian building. The two original front-parlor rooms—each with a fireplace, stained-glass windows, and armchairs—are still filled with portraits of sea captains and ships. Not just for ladies, the modern library has a large children's area, videos, DVDs, CDs, periodicals, newspapers, and word processing equipment. Call for current information about musicals, lectures, and art exhibits.

BREWSTER LADIES' LIBRARY

Brewster Historical Society Museum (508-896-9521; brewsterhistorical society.org), 3171 Route 6A. Open 1–4 Thursday through Saturday mid-July to mid-September. Highlighting Brewster's rich heritage, this small museum has an 1884 barbershop, an 1830s sea captain's room, dolls and toys, the old East Brewster Post Office, and antique gowns. Special summertime exhibits feature some little-known aspect of Brewster history. There are plans afoot to move an old blacksmith shop to the property too. A walking trail originates from the house (see Spruce Hill Conservation Area under *Green Space*). Donations.

Crosby Mansion (508-896-1744), Crosby Lane off Route 6A. This Colonial Revival structure, once the elegant home of Albert and Matilda Crosby, sits on 19 acres of bayside property. Massachusetts acquired the land (and the house by default) by eminent domain in 1985 so that the public could access Cape Cod Bay from Nickerson State Park. Because the state couldn't afford to maintain it (the 28-room mansion requires millions in repairs), a volunteer group, the Friends of Crosby Mansion, stepped in. They've done an impressive job repairing the worst structural damage and much of the interior.

Once upon a time, Albert Crosby owned the Chicago Opera House and fell in love with one of the showgirls, Matilda. When she came to live in Albert's modest turn-of-the-20th-century house, she was so unhappy that Albert had a mansion built for her—around his original four-room house! (Kids compare stepping into the smaller house to what Alice must have felt like in Wonderland.) Matilda is said to have entertained in the larger mansion while Albert stayed in his interior boyhood home. The mansion is open 5 days per season—the first and third Sunday in July and August (10–3)—but you can always peek in the oversized windows.

♪ **First Parish Church** (508-896-5577; fpbuu.org), 1969 Route 6A, on the town green (aka the Egg because of its shape and natural depression). Gothic windows and a bell tower mark the church's 1834 clapboard exterior, while interior pews are marked with names of prominent Brewster sea captains. Wander around the graveyard behind the church, too.

Higgins Farm Windmill and Harris-Black House (508-896-9521), 785 Route 6A, Drummer Boy Park. Open 1–4 Thursday, Friday, and Saturday. Members of the Brewster Historical Society are on hand to tell you personal anecdotes like how a family raised 10 children in the one-room house (possibly the "last remaining primitive one-room house on the Cape"). The1795 windmill is known for its octagonal design, while its top resembles a boat's hull. Free.

A PERFECT DAY IN BREWSTER

  8:00 Read the morning paper on the front porch of the Brewster Store.
  9:30 Traverse some 80 acres of marshland, beaches, and woodlands at the Cape Cod Museum of Natural History.
12:30 Dine outdoors at Cobie's or El Guapo's.
  2:00 Poke around the Stony Brook Grist Mill and Herring Run.
  3:30 Discover shallow tidal pools and abstractions on the Brewster flats.
  5:30 Arrive early for chowder bisque and scallops at Brewster Fish House.
  8:00 Lick a fast-melting ice-cream cone from Brewster Scoop.

✳ To Do

BASEBALL ✍ The **Brewster Whitecaps** (508-896-7442; brewsterwhitecaps
.com), who joined the Cape Cod Baseball League in 1988 as an expansion team,
play behind the Stony Brook Elementary School, 384 Underpass Road, Brewster.
From mid-June to early August, games typically begin at 5 or 7 PM. The Whitecaps
also sponsor weeklong, weekday clinics in June and July for boys and girls age
6–13. Pick up registration forms at the Visitor Information Center, then meet at
the Stony Brook Elementary School, 384 Underpass Road, Routes 6A and 137 in
Brewster.

BICYCLING/RENTALS Because the Cape Cod Rail Trail runs through Brewster,
and Nickerson State Park (see the "Supreme State Park" sidebar) has its own network of bicycle trails linked to the trail, plenty of places rent bicycles. Look for
Rail Trail Bike & Kayak (508-896-8200; railtrailbikeshop.com), 302 Underpass
Road. It rents and sells bikes year-round. **Brewster Bike** (508-896-8149; brewster
bike.com), 442 Underpass Road, is open March through December. Both shops
also offer parking, sales, and repairs. In-season rates are about $18 for 4 hours, $28
for 24 hours, $56 for 3 days, $85 weekly. Helmets and locks included. Pick up the
excellent, free Nickerson trail map.

If you brought your own bikes, there is rail-trail parking on Route 137, on Underpass Road off Route 137, and at Nickerson State Park on Route 6A.

✍ Trailers and alleycats (rented above) for hauling kids are great for this stretch
because it's shady and fairly flat. Nickerson trails are a bit hillier.

BOATING/RENTALS See the sidebar
"A Supreme State Park" under *Green
Space.*

FISHING/SHELLFISHING Brewster
has almost 70 freshwater ponds, and
state fishing licenses are required. The
following ponds are stocked: **Sheep
Pond**, off Route 124, and **Flax**, **Little
Cliff**, and **Higgins ponds** within Nickerson State Park.

For shellfishing permits (and specifics
about where and when to find the
creatures), head to the Visitor Information Center in summer; head to the
town offices weekdays off-season. In
July and August shellfishing is permit-
ted only on Thursday and Sunday. Shellfish beds at **Saint's Landing Beach** (off
Lower Road from Route 6A) are seeded in summer. Quahogs and sea clams are
harvested in July and August on Thursday and Sunday; steamers are harvested
October to mid-April. Nonresident permits cost $15 weekly.

FOR FAMILIES ✍ **Summer camps** (508-896-3867; ccmnh.org), 869 Route 6A,
at the Cape Cod Museum of Natural History (see *To See*). Got an extra 2 hours or

5 days? Got children age 3–13? These classes explore "mud flat mania," "extreme science," tidal flats, archaeology, and Monomoy's barrier beach. The emphasis is on fun, outdoor adventure, and education. Call for a schedule.

❧ **Playground by the Bay**, Drummer Boy Park, Route 6A. Shaped like a packet ship to honor Brewster's seafaring history, this play structure has separate areas for toddlers and older children. Picnic tables. The **Eddy Elementary School** (2298 Main Street) has a playground as well.

See also **Cape Repertory Theatre** under *Entertainment* and **First Parish Church** under *To See*.

GOLF ❁ **Captain's Golf Course** (508-896-5100; 508-896-1716 pro shop; captainsgolfcourse.com), 1000 Freeman's Way off Route 6A. Rated among the top 25 public courses by *Golf Digest*; you'll find 36 holes (named for Brewster sea captains) at the Port and Starboard courses. The adjacent practice center is quite extensive.

❁ **Ocean Edge Golf Club** (508-896-5911; oceanedge.com), Ocean Edge Resort, 8320 Villages Drive off Route 6A. This 18-hole, tournament-caliber course underwent an $8.5 million overhaul by the Nicklaus Design Group in 2008.

HORSEBACK RIDING ❁ ❧ **Woodsong Farm Equestrian Center** (508-896-5800; woodsongfarm.com), 121 Lund Farm Way. Open daily by appointment. Established in 1967, Woodsong offers riding instruction, boarding, training, coaching for competitive riders, children's day programs (like "Horsemasters" for experienced riders age 9–18 and "Pony Kids," an introductory program for children age 5–14), horse shows, and an on-premises tack shop.

SAILING **Cape Sail** (508-896-2730; capesail.com), out of Upper Mill Pond and Harwich Harbors. Late May to mid-October. Captain Bob Rice has been offering customized sailing lessons and an overnight sailing school since 1983. The summertime price for instruction and an overnight to Nantucket (accommodations on board) for two people is $1,250; 3 days and 2 nights costs $1,875. Off-season is $200–300 less. Otherwise, a 3-hour lesson is $225 per person, or the 6-hour basic course costs $690 for two. Bob also offers great deals on custom charters, as well as sunset and moonlight cruises. Call him to discuss your interests.

TENNIS There are four public courts located behind the Fire Department near the town offices, Route 6A. Free.

Ocean Edge Resort (508-896-9000; oceanedge.com), 2907 Main Street, Route 6A, has four Plexipave and five clay courts open from mid-April to mid-September. Nonresort guests pay $20 for court time.

✳ Green Space

BEACHES Brewster has 8 miles of waterfront on Cape Cod Bay and eight public beaches, none of which is particularly spacious and all of which are located off Route 6A. Daily ($15), weekly ($50), and seasonal parking permits are purchased at the Visitor Information Center (508-896-4511). In other words, you cannot pay at the beach. No permit is required at any town beach after 3 PM.

A SUPREME STATE PARK

Nickerson State Park (508-896-3491; state.ma.us/dem), 3488 Route 6A. Open 8–8 daily during camping season, and dawn to dusk off-season. This former estate of Chatham native Roland Nickerson, a multimillionaire who founded the First National Bank of Chicago, contains just under 2,000 acres of pine, hemlock, and spruce and 11 to 14 kettle ponds, depending on water levels. Nickerson and his wife, Addie, who entertained such notables as President Grover Cleveland, had a fairly self-sufficient estate, with their own electric generator, ponds teeming with fish, vegetable gardens, and game that roamed the land. When the mansion that Roland's father, Samuel, built for him burned down in 1906, a disconsolate Roland died 2 weeks later. (The "replacement" is now the Ocean Edge Conference Center.) Addie ultimately donated the land in 1934 to honor their son, who died in the 1918 influenza epidemic.

Nickerson State Park has been developed with walking trails, bicycling trails, jogging paths, picnic sites, boat launches, and sandy beaches. Winter conditions often provide for ice-skating and ice-fishing and occasionally for cross-country skiing. (Snow rarely stays on the ground for more than a few days, though.) If you're at all interested in the out-of-doors, don't bypass Nickerson, one of the Cape's real treasures. Almost 500,000 people visit annually. During the summertime look for park programs like bay-side strolls, night walks, campfires, and "kid-diescope" bird watching. Day use is free.

Within the park you'll find:

Jack's Boat Rentals (508-896-8556), open mid-June to early September. Jack's rents canoes, kayaks, Sunfish, surf bikes, sea cycles, and pedal boats on Flax Pond. Rates $20–28 hourly, depending on what you rent; each additional hour about 40 percent less.

Flax Pond and **Cliff Pond**. Flax has Nickerson's best public beach, picnic area, and a bathhouse, but no lifeguard. Cliff Pond is ringed with little beaches, but bathers share the pond with motorized boats. (It's not really a problem, though.)

🍴 🏕 ✎ **Camping** (877-422-6762 reservations; reserveamerica.com; 508-896-3491 information), mid-April to mid-October. Since Nickerson is very popular, summer reservations are absolutely essential. They're also accepted 6 months in advance for all of the 418 available sites. There is a 14-day limit in summer. Fees $15–17; pets permitted; inquire about four- and six-person yurts $30–40.

See also *Bicycling/Rentals* and *Fishing/Shellfishing under To Do*.

Paine's Creek Beach, Paine's Creek Road off Route 6A. This is one of Brewster's most picturesque beaches because of the creek that feeds into it. Parking fee, restrooms, but no lifeguards.

PONDS Long Pond and **Sheep Pond**, both off Route 124, have freshwater swimming and sandy beaches. Long Pond has a summertime lifeguard. Long and Sheep ponds are among the best of Brewster's more than 50 ponds. Parking permits are required for residents and visitors. You'll find portable toilets at both.

See also the sidebar "A Supreme State Park."

WALKS Famed nature writer John Hay lives in Brewster. He's got plenty of places nearby to enjoy Mother Nature. You can follow in his footsteps.

Wing's Island Trail, **South Trail**, and **North Trail**, at the Cape Cod Museum of Natural History (see *To See*), 869 Route 6A. Named for Brewster's first settler, a Quaker forced to leave Sandwich due to religious persecution, the Wing's Island Trail (about 1.5 miles roundtrip) meanders past sassafras groves and salt marshes, which provide habitat for diverse plants and animals. Traversing a tidal island, it ends on the dunes with a panoramic bay view. South Trail is on the opposite side of Route 6A and extends for about a mile past Stony Brook, a beech grove, and the remnants of a cranberry bog. The short North Trail wends around the museum's immediate grounds, crossing a salt marsh. Naturalist-led walks depart from the museum daily in summer and most weekends in the fall. Call 508-896-3867 for times.

Punkhorn Parklands, at the end of Run Hill Road, off Stony Brook Road. Miles of scenic trails on 880 acres—some overlooking kettle ponds—traverse oak and pine forests, meadows, and marshes. Trails are used by birders and mountain bikers, even coyotes and foxes. Pick up a detailed trail and off-road map from the Visitor Information Center (see *Guidance*).

Spruce Hill Conservation Area, behind the Brewster Historical Society Museum, 3171 Route 6A. This trail, and the uncrowded little beach at the end of it, is a

---

TIDAL FLATS

At low tide, you can walk 2 miles out onto the tidal flats of Cape Cod Bay. During Prohibition, townspeople walking on the flats would often stumble onto cases of liquor thrown overboard by rumrunners. But encounters are tamer these days: Kids discover tidal pools, play in channels left by receding tides, and marvel at streaked "garnet" sand. On a clear day you can gaze from the Provincetown Monument to Sandwich. You can reach the flats from any bay beach.

secret treasure. The 30-minute, roundtrip trail (0.25 mile each way) follows an overgrown, old, clay dirt carriage road—probably used for off-loading fish and lumber and rumored to have been used by bootleggers during Prohibition—which runs from the museum to the bay and a private stretch of sandy beach. The Conservation Commission manages the 25-acre area.

See also the sidebar "A Supreme State Park."

✳ Lodging

Brewster has it all, from first-class inns and homey B&Bs to resort condos and family cottages.

RESORT TOWNHOUSES 🐚 **Ocean Edge Resort** (Booking agent: 800-626-9984; oceanedgebrewster.com), 2660 Route 6A. Town houses available seasonally through Great Locations booking agent. Once part of the vast Roland Nickerson estate (see the "Supreme State Park" sidebar), this 380-acre complex includes a Gothic and Renaissance Revival stucco mansion (now mainly a conference and event center) and 11 private, contemporary condominium "villages." Rental units are configured as apartments, two-story town houses (with one, two, and three bedrooms), and Cape cottages. Some units are bayside; the majority overlook the golf course. Most have "real" backyards and are within walking distance of resort facilities. Resort facilities include indoor and outdoor pools, a private 1,000-foot bayside beach (for bayside rentals only), four restaurants, two fitness centers, a playground, and organized programs for children age 4–10 (for a fee). Golf packages, without instruction, are available through the resort on a "pay-as-you-play" basis. WiFi is available in the café only. Weekly rates late May to mid-October: $950 one-bedroom, $1,300–1,750 two-bedroom, $2,500 three-bedroom.

INNS ✳ 🐾 🐚 ♿ "▼" **Old Sea Pines Inn** (508-896-6114; oldseapinesinn .com), 2553 Route 6A. I'm always impressed anew when I visit this delightful, period-perfect hostelry. In 1907 the building housed the Sea Pines School of Charm and Personality for Young Women. When Michele and Steve Rowan renovated it in 1981, they combined 1920s and '30s nostalgia with modern but unfussy comforts to create palpable authenticity. Few innkeepers work harder. All 24 rooms and three suites are pleasant, furnished with old brass or iron beds and antiques. The less expensive "classrooms" are small and share baths—it will be easy to imagine yourself as a young girl at boarding school. The rear annex has less charm but still feature the Rowan's attention to detail; family suites are quite economical. The inn is set on 3½ acres, and there's plenty of space to relax inside, too, including a large, comfy living room with fireplace that leads onto the wraparound porch set

OLD SEA PINES INN

with rockers. On Sunday evenings in summer, the Cape Repertory Theatre holds a well-received Broadway musical dinner revue here (see *Entertainment*). July and August $85–170; $10–40 less off-season; buffet-style breakfast included.

⚑ Chillingsworth (508-896-3640; 800-430-3640; chillingsworth.com), 2449 Route 6A. Open late May to late November. Overnight in Europe without a passport? Sure, if you stay here. This 1689 house, believed to be Brewster's second oldest, rents three European-style guest rooms above the restaurant (see *Dining Out*). The antiques-filled Stevenson Room boasts a private entrance and four-poster double bed—it's the largest and nicest of the rooms. The Foster Room has views of the back gardens and gazebo. Although the Ten Eyck Room is small and without a view, it's charming nonetheless. All have private bath, TV, and air-conditioning. Rates include afternoon wine and cheese, a continental breakfast, access to a private beach at the end of the street, and privileges at a private club with an indoor/outdoor pool, tennis courts, and golf. Rooms $110–165.

BREWSTER BY THE SEA AND SPA

BED & BREAKFASTS ❄ ⚑

Brewster by the Sea and Spa (508-896-3910; 800-892-3910; brewsterbythesea.com), 716 Route 6A. Nothing is ordinary here; everything is elevated to an art form. Let's start with the full breakfast served on the back deck (surrounded by splendid gardens and a hydrangea-ringed pool): from a fruitini glass of melon and mint to goat cheese, gruyere, and ham panini, Donna and Byron Cain (and their labradoodle mascot) set the tone for a perfect day. They've been excelling since 2003. Stay in the newer adjacent carriage house (aka the Old Orchard House) or the main Greek Revival farmhouse inn. Either way, you'll find English country decor in seven luxurious and spacious suites and stylish guest rooms. All feature flat-screen TVs and DVDs and luxurious amenities like thick towels, fine bedding, and nightly turndown with a truffle. One has a private deck; most have a fireplace; three have a whirlpool tub. Spa services (poolside in summer and fireside in winter) include a full range of massages, facials, reflexology, and body scrubs. Lots of packages and special weekends. The goodie bag on departure will remain a surprise. Late June to mid-October $205–325; off-season $135–225.

✿ ⚑ Old Manse Inn (508-896-3149; oldmanseinn.com), 1861 Route 6A. Open March through December. Innkeepers Karen and Rich Keevers, new in 2008, are putting their mark on this historic 1801 inn. Their ten guest rooms have period wallpapers, antique beds, air-conditioning, and refurbished bathrooms. Some have lots of light; others have little. My favorite third-floor rooms benefit from high, mansard-ceilinged rooflines. In Spring 2009 they added three top-of-the-line rooms in the adjacent barn; I have high hopes for them. On my last overnight, the full breakfast featured a burrito with peach mango salsa and a veggie frittata. Loaner bikes, beach towels, and concierge-like trip-planning services are also included. Children over 10 welcomed. Rooms $140–275.

❋ **Captain Freeman Inn** (508-896-7481; 800-843-4664; captainfreeman inn.com), 15 Breakwater Road. I was unable to see rooms for this edition, but here are the facts without much opinion: Rooms at this 1866 inn have four-poster canopy beds, sanded hardwood floors, designer window treatments, and air-conditioning. A private pool and full breakfasts are also big draws. Of the 12 rooms, 6 are upscale suites with fireplaces and a whirlpool bath on a private enclosed porch. One particularly secluded room (off the dining area) overlooks the garden. Some traditional quarters, many of which are large corner rooms, boast inlaid floors and oversized windows. All rooms have sitting areas, but there are also two living rooms, the cozier one with a working wood fireplace. Innkeepers Donna and Peter Amadeo, here since 2004, also offer free loaner bikes in-season. Children over 10 welcome. June through October $165–250; off-season $150–200.

COTTAGES AND APARTMENTS

❋ 🐾 ✐ ⁖¶⁖ **Michael's Cottages** (508-896-4025; 800-399-2967; michaelsin brewster.com), 618 Route 6A. I can't say enough complimentary things about Michael's, perhaps the most conscientious cottage owner on the Cape. Set back from the road, these five tidy and crisp cottages are a 15-minute walk from a bayside beach. They're a bargain, and proprietor Michael DiVito maintains them nicely. One is actually a **small house** that sleeps six and features a deck with a hot tub. Most others have a screened-in porch and

fireplace; all have air-conditioning and include linen service. Ask about Michael's two B&B rooms. July and August $840–915 weekly for two; large cottage $1,495–2,045 weekly for two; off-season $105–175 nightly.

🐾 **Ellis Landing Cottages** (508-896-5072; ellislandingcottages.com), off of Ellis Landing Road. Open June to mid-October. Only dune grasses and sandy lanes separate these six cozy waterfront cottages from the bay. Most of the refurbished housekeeping cottages were built by Gil Ellis's father and grandfather in the 1940s and 1950s. Some of the pine-paneled cottages are more rustic than others. All have kitchens, linens, cable TV, telephone, and a fireplace. My favorite is the cozy Rest Haven Cottage, once the East Brewster railroad station, with a private garden, screened-in porch, and three bedrooms. Late June to early September $1,400–2,500 weekly. Off-season, cottages go for $1,000–2,000 weekly or can be rented for $200–350 with a 3-night minimum. No credit cards.

MICHAEL'S COTTAGES

RENTAL HOUSES AND COTTAGES
Stonecroft-Abbott Real Estate (508-896-2290), Foster Square, 2655 Route 6A.

Vacation Cape Cod/Kinlin-Grover GMAC (508-896-7004; vacationcape cod.com), 1900 Route 6A.

See also **Ocean Edge Resort** under *Resort*.

CAMPGROUNDS See the sidebar "A Supreme State Park" under *Green Space*.

❝ĭ❞ Alternatives to Nickerson State Park include **Shady Knoll Camp-ground** (508-896-3002; capecamping .com), 1709 Route 6A at Route 137, which offers tent sites for $36–43 ($26–33 in off-season) from mid-June to mid-September, and **Sweetwater Forest** (508-896-3773; sweetwater forest.com), off Route 124, which is open April through October and set on 75 acres abutting a freshwater lake. Both accept reservations, but I like Sweetwater's 250 wooded sites a bit better. They also cost less: Expect to pay about $30–44 in-season, $27–35 off-season.

❋ Where to Eat

Brewster has a wide variety of really great restaurants.

DINING OUT 🍴 ☖ & **Brewster Fish House** (508-896-7867), 2208 Route 6A. Open for lunch and dinner (almost) daily, April to early December. This small roadside bistro doesn't look like much from the outside, but inside, owner Vernon Smith has created an intimate and pleasant atmosphere with fresh flowers, high ceilings, and a small bar. After all these years, it's still consistently excellent. Alongside creative and eclectic luncheon specials, you'll find grilled and broiled seafood and fish served on mod plates;

go for the catch of the day. Try the superlative chowder or lobster bisque, which has a nice spicy kick to it. For dinner, try innovative specials like the pan seared halibut with crispy polenta and sautéed summer vegetables. Save room for the crème brûlée. Arrive before 6 PM or expect to wait at least an hour. Put your name on the list and walk across the street to the beach; they'll honor your position on the list when you return. Lunch $8–15, dinner $15–30.

Chillingsworth (508-896-3640; chill ingsworth.com), 2449 Route 6A. Open for Sunday brunch and for lunch and dinner daily, mid-May to mid-October; dinner only until late November. If you can't fly to Paris for the weekend, you can at least dine at this special occasion restaurant. These small, candlelit dining rooms, filled with antiques, feel rather like European salons. The sophisticated service is well paced and discreet. Indulge in a six-course, prix fixe menu featuring superlative French/California-style haute cuisine—or dine more lightly with a different chef at Chill's Bistro, an airy greenhouse setting with a menu featuring grilled fish, pastas, pizzas, cobblers, and chocolate bread pudding. Or dine alfresco. À la carte luncheons in the greenhouse (or on the terrace) are always relaxing. Chef "Nitzi" Rabin

BREWSTER FISH HOUSE

❊ **Peddler's Restaurant** (508-896-9300; peddlersrestaurant.com), 67 Thad Ellis Road. Open for dinner nightly mid-June to mid-September, Thursday through Saturday off-season. Off Route 6A (turn at the Brewster Book Store), this small roadhouse completely covered in wisteria is an unlikely suspect in the local restaurant wars. And it's a winner. Chef Alain Hasson specializes in authentic, Paris bistro cooking, offering dishes like sole meuniere, duck a l'orange, steak au poivre and boeuf bourguignon. I've never met a blackboard specials that didn't delight. Dinner $26–30.

EATING OUT **El Guapo's Taqueria** (508-896-3338), 239 Underpass Road. Open 11–8 daily March through December. I spend a fair amount of time in New Mexico and I'd be happy eating every meal here. Try the chicken burrito: esta muy bien. As is their smoked street corn dip—wow. Look for all the usual Mexican dishes and

and his wife, Pat, proudly preside. Also look for a new shop with take-out pastries and cheeses. The wine cellar earns extraordinary marks! Bistro lunch $12–17, bistro dinner $25–30, prix fixe fine dining $65–69.

🦞 ❢ **Bramble Inn** (508-896-7644; brambleinn.com), 2019 Route 6A. Open for dinner on weekends May through October and Wednesday through Sunday in summer. After all these years, chef-owner Ruth Manchester's creativity still reigns. It's a real treat. Look for exceptional New American and internationally inspired cuisine like parchment-roasted chicken with grilled lobster, rack of lamb, and seafood curry. Along with gracious service and intimate dining rooms (or new courtyard dining), you'll find elegantly casual mix-and-match antique place settings. The broad, prix fixe menu changes every few weeks. On my last visit, I died and went to heaven at their hip little **Bayside Bistro Bar**, thanks to ceviche and pan seared day boat scallops with mushroom and truffle risotto. There's no entertainment, unless you consider Ruth's husband, Cliff; they've presided over the place since 1984. Four-course dinners $42–68, bistro menu $8–20.

look forward to them being a cut above. To boot: this place is on the Rail Trail. They also have a gringo menu for the kids, just in case. Dishes $6–13.

♪ "↑" **Bayside Seafood & Market** (508-896-5367; baysideseafoodand market.com), 2740 Route 6A. Open 8 AM–9 PM mid-May to mid-October, 8–3 Tuesday through Saturday off-season; no fresh fish off-season. This contemporary spot fills a niche for prepared seafood dishes to take away, sandwiches and panini, fresh fish and lobster, and some limited breakfast items. Feel like a clambake but don't want to go to all the trouble? Order one here. Eat here for $7–10, more for a clambake.

❄ ♪ **Café Alfresco** (508-896-1741), Lemon Tree Village, 1097 Route 6A. Open for all three meals in summertime, breakfast and lunch off-season. This modest café offers breakfast (eggs any style and croissants), lunch sandwiches, great soups and homemade bread, and nightly specials like fish-and-chips, scallop rolls, and chicken salad. But I generally only come for the lobster roll ($20) at lunchtime. There are a few outdoor tables where you hear trickling water fountains, but most people sit inside. Breakfast and lunch $5–8.

♪ **Cobie's** (508-896-7021; cobies.com), 3260 Route 6A. Open 10:30–9 daily late May to mid-September. Owner Rob Slavin has operated this old-fashioned summertime classic since 1984 and his staff is quite loyal, which says a lot. I like this seafood shack for its lobster rolls, onion rings, fried scallops, charbroiled burgers, and covered picnic tables near the pine trees. They also feature tasty all natural smoothies. Cobie's is convenient for rail-trail cyclists (see *To Do*). Some people prefer JTs across from Ocean Edge, but I'm a big Cobie's fan. Lunch $4–7, dinner $8–14.

Brewster Coffee Shop (508-896-8224), 1249 Route 6A. Open for breakfast and lunch mid-March through November. If you're renting a house or cottage, you'll end up at this friendly joint once—if you can get in at breakfast, that is. The place is always packed to the gills in the morning. Order up a short stack of pancakes, share some eggs Benedict, and then go for a walk. Dishes $4–10.

PICNICS, COFFEE & ICE CREAM

Satucket Farm Stand (508-896-5540), 76 Route 124 just off Route 6A. Open May to early September. An old-fashioned open-air stand with farm-fresh produce, including fantastic corn, pies, baked goods, jams, honey, and cheeses. It's a popular spot for local chefs.

Brewster Scoop (508-896-7824), 1935 Route 6A. Open noon–10 late May to early September. Behind the Brewster Store, this small shop is a purveyor of Bliss Dairy's sugar-free ice cream and nonfat frozen yogurt.

Also see **Great Cape Cod Herb, Spice & Tea Co**. under *Selective Shopping*.

THE BREWSTER SCOOP

✳ Entertainment

☿ **The Woodshed** (508-896-7771), 1993 Route 6A near The Brewster Store. Open nightly for live acoustic rock, late April to early September and on weekends to late October. This answers the question: Where do all the summer workers go on their night off? With wooden rafters and well-worn wooden floors (reeking of stale beer), this dark joint jumps with locals.

♪ **Band concerts**, Drummer Boy Park, 773Route 6A, 2.5 miles west of Route 124. Summertime concerts during July and August at 6 PM on Sunday at the gazebo. Bring a blanket and lawn chairs.

♪ **Cape Repertory Theatre** (508-896-1888; caperep.org), 3299 Route 6A. This company presents open-air theater in the woods (on the former Crosby estate), performances at their 129-seat indoor theater, and a summertime musical dinner revue at the Old Sea Pines Inn (see *Lodging*). Shows May through November; tickets $20–30. Children's productions Monday through Thursday mornings at 10 or 10:30 in July and August; tickets $8–10.

✳ Selective Shopping

❄ Unless otherwise noted, all shops are open year-round. The sweet **Lemon Tree Village** (Route 6A) has 15–18 shops and eateries worth poking around, if you're a real shopper.

ANTIQUES Dozens of antiques shops line Route 6A; only a tiny sampling follows.

Wysteria Antiques, Etc. (508-896-8650), 1199 Route 6A. The lavender exterior, the scent of wisteria as you cross the threshold, and three rooms filled top to bottom with amethyst glassware and porcelain add up to one unusual establishment. The owners, in business since the early 1980s, have a good eye for Limoges porcelain, mirrors, chandeliers, and Venetian glass, even if the presentation is over the top. Decide for yourself: if the stuff is good enough for Barbra Streisand, it might be right up your alley.

Countryside Antiques (508-896-1444; countrysideantiquesinc.com), 2052 Main Street. Owner Greg Mize carries English, Irish, Scandinavian,

European, Chinese antiques and fine reproductions. He also specializes in nautical and maritime antiques.

ART GALLERIES Underground Art Gallery (508-896-3757), 673 Satucket Road. Amazingly, this working studio sits beneath 100 tons of soil and is supported by 10 tree trunks. The gallery features the work of watercolorist Karen North Wells, who also uses oil and acrylic for her seascapes and landscape florals. Her husband, Malcolm Wells, who is also a painter, designs earth-covered solar buildings like this one and writes books on sustainable architecture.

Maddocks Gallery (508-896-6223; jamesmaddocksgallery.com), 1283 Route 6A. Open March through December. James Maddocks paints nostalgic traditional and representational Cape Cod scenes. His gallery, where you'll often find him painting and where he happily talks with visitors, is an 1840s carriage house attached to his home. He also offers less expensive limited-edition prints.

Ruddeforth Gallery (508-255-1056; ruddeforthgallery.com), 3753 Route 6A. Watercolors, oils, and limited edition prints of Cape Cod scenes, florals, and still lifes by Debra Ruddeforth (a signature member of the Copley Society in Boston). Husband Tom Ruddeforth's color and black-and-white photographs are also displayed.

Struna Galleries (508-255-6618), 3873 Route 6A. Working from copper plates to make dry-point engravings, artist Tim Struna creates sweet little renderings of Cape Cod scenes. They're a nice (and affordable) reminder of why life on the Cape is so special. Since his studio is here, you'll often find Tim hard at work (although there is also a gallery in Chatham). He also sells larger watercolors.

ARTISANS Heart Pottery (508-896-6189), 1145 Route 6A. Specializing in functional and decorative porcelain and raku, Diane Heart spends most days at her wheel here in the shop. Her raku, using an ancient Japanese firing technique, is particularly fine. Diane's husband, Mark Preu, offers nature and scenic photographs.

Clayton's Clayworks (508-255-4937), 3820 Route 6A. Clayton Calderwood makes large fish platters, more like wall elements that can be hung indoors or out.

The Woodwright (508-896-3393), 2091 Route 6A. Before you leave home, measure your needy window casings or door frames and have Leonard Courchesne replace them for you. He's an expert in restoration, reproduction, custom design, and millwork.

BOOKSTORES ✎ **Brewster Book Store** (508-896-6543; brewsterbookstore.com), 2648 Route 6A. Open daily. One of the Cape's better bookstores, this one features a large and excellent selection of children's books within a small space. Also Cape Cod titles, games, toys, book signings, and story time (Tuesday and Friday at 10 during the summer and Tuesdays at 10:30 off-season).

SPECIAL SHOPS Eve's Place (508-896-4914), 564 Route 6A. Eve Roulier learned all about pearls in Hawaii, where she lived for eight years. She buys directly from growers; she strings and sells pearls; and she's an authority on rare black Tahitian pearls, pearls from Kobe, Japan, and freshwater pearls from China. She'll tell you that injecting an irritant into an oyster's shell creates cultured pearls and that about 40 percent of the oysters die as a result of the injection. Those that don't die secrete a substance (nacre, the basis of the pearl) in reaction to the irritant. It then takes about three or four years for a good pearl to mature. Whether you're ready to buy, just want to learn about pearls, or need some pearls restrung, Eve is your woman. Everything is 20% off in June (officially "pearl month") and December.

Spectrum (508-385-3322; spectrum america.com), 369 Route 6A. This two-story shop, which opened in 1966, represents high-quality craftspeople from all over the country. I hesitate to itemize even a few of their pieces, because I don't want to limit your imagination.

Sydenstricker Galleries (508-385-3272; sydenstricker.com), 490 Route 6A. Glass-fusing demonstrations, using a technique developed by Brewster native Bill Sydenstricker (who died in 1994), are given from 9–2 on weekdays. Sydenstricker glass is used in two American embassies and displayed in museum collections around the country.

Spyglass (508-896-4423), 2257 Route 6A. Although this exceptional shop is best known for its telescope collection, there are all sorts of nautical antiques like barometers, sextants, maps, charts, and even a few paintings and sea cap-

tains' portraits. It's great to poke around and recapture a sense of the Cape's maritime glories.

Great Cape Herb Co. (508-896-5900), 2628 Route 6A. With more than 170 varieties of Western and Chinese herbs in stock, this herbal apothecary may well be the largest retailer of its kind in New England. Proprietor Stephan Brown (who opened the rustic shop in 1991) also stocks a selection of New Age literature on health and well-being, and many products from Thailand and China. Walk through the modest herb and community agricultural gardens before leaving, and revive yourself with a cup of strong espresso from Stephan's Cyber Café.

✳ Special Events

Mid-April–early May: **Herring Run**. Hundreds of thousands of alewives (herring) return from the salt water to lay their eggs in the same freshwater ponds where they were born (see **Stony Brook Grist Mill** and **Herring Run** under *To See*).

Late June: **Outdoor Antique Fair** sponsored by the Brewster Historical Society at Drummer Boy Park. Nominal admission fee.

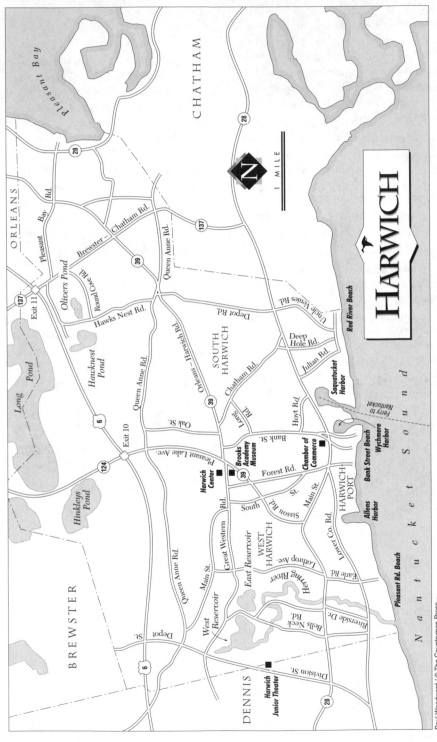

HARWICH

1 MILE

N

Paul Woodward / © The Countryman Press

HARWICH

Harwich isn't nearly as developed as its westerly neighbors, although its stretch of Route 28 does have its share of bumper boats, mini-golf courses, and go-carts. In fact, the town exudes a somewhat nonchalant air. It's as if the 12,700 year-rounders are collectively saying, "This is what we have and you're welcome to come and enjoy it with us if you wish"—which is not to say that Harwich doesn't attract visitors. It boasts a wide range of places to stay and eat, from humble B&Bs to family-friendly cottages, from exceptional New American fare to roasted chicken-on-a-spit. At the same time, while Harwich has more saltwater and freshwater beaches than any other town on the Cape, only a few have parking for day-use visitors.

Harwich, mostly blue collar and middle class, comprises seven distinct villages and is blessed with one of the most picturesque harbors on the Cape, Wychmere Harbor. Nearby, lovely Saquatucket Harbor is reserved for fishing charters and ferry service to Nantucket. It's worth poking around the quiet center of Harwich, with its historic homes standing in marked contrast to the heavily developed areas just a mile or so away. Harwich, which bills its annual Cranberry Harvest Festival as "the biggest small-town celebration in the country," lays claims to cultivating the first commercial cranberry bog.

GUIDANCE ⁗ ❀ **Harwich Chamber of Commerce** (508-430-1165; 800-442-7942; harwichcc.com) and **Harwich Information Center** (508-432-1600), Route 28, One Schoolhouse Road, Harwich Port. The latter is open 9–5 weekdays, 10–4 Saturday, 10–2 Sunday, late May to mid-September; also 9–5 weekdays off-season. Pick up their biking and walking-trail maps, as well as their very helpful (free) street map.

PUBLIC RESTROOMS At the chamber (see *Guidance*).

PUBLIC LIBRARY ❀ ✐ ☂ ⁗ **Brooks Free Library** (508-430-7562; brooks freelibrary.org), 739 Main Street, Harwich. Open Tuesday through Saturday.

GETTING THERE *By car:* From the Cape Cod Canal, take Route 6 to Exit 10 (Route 124 South and Route 39 South) to Route 28, or take Exit 11 to Route 137 for East Harwich. It takes 35 to 40 minutes to reach Harwich from the canal.

By bus: The **Plymouth & Brockton** bus line (508-778-9767; p-b.com) connects Harwich with Hyannis and other Cape towns, as well as with Boston's Logan Airport. The bus stops at the Park & Ride commuter lot near the intersection of Routes 6 and 124.

GETTING AROUND *By car:* Route 28 is also called Main Street. (This is not to be confused with the Main Street—aka Route 39—in the center of Harwich, which is inland.) Although most points of interest are located along or off developed Route 28, head inland to explore Harwich's ponds and conservation areas.

By shuttle: The **H₂O** (800-352-7155; capecodtransit.org) bus line, used by more locals than visitors, travels along Route 28 between the Hyannis Transportation Center and Orleans weekdays year-round and on weekends in summer. Flag it down anywhere along Route 28.

GETTING TO NANTUCKET There is seasonal passenger ferry service to Nantucket from Harwich Port. For many people, this service is more convenient than going into Hyannis to catch a boat. For complete information, see *Getting There* in "Nantucket."

MEDICAL EMERGENCY **Fontaine Medical Center** (508-432-4100), 525 Long Pond Drive, off Route 137, Harwich. Walk-ins July through September, 8–5 weekdays, 9–5 Saturday, and 9–1 Sunday. Registration window closes promptly at 4:30 Monday through Saturday, and at 12:30 on Sundays.

✳ To See

🌴 **Brooks Academy Museum** (508-432-8089; harwichhistoricalsociety.org), 80 Parallel Road, Routes 124 and 39 at Main Street. Open 1–4 Thursday through Saturday, late June to mid-October. This imposing 1844 Greek Revival schoolhouse was home to one of the country's early vocational schools of navigation, established by Sidney Brooks. Now operated by the Harwich Historical Society, the museum features a history of cranberry farming, historical photographs, and changing exhibits on Harwich's past. There is a permanent display of art by C. D. Cahoon. Genealogical resources and a significant manuscript collection round out the research facility. Also on the premises: a gunpowder house used from 1770 to 1864 and a restored 1872 outhouse. Adults $3; children up to 18 free.

First Congregational Church, Routes 124 and 39, Harwich Center. Built in the mid-1700s, this church is surrounded by a white picket fence and anchors the tiny town center.

Bird Carvings (508-430-0400), at the Cape Cod Five Cents Savings Bank, Route 28 in the center of Harwich Port. Check out a fine collection of carved miniature shore- and songbirds by hometown artist Elmer Crowell.

✳ 𝒮 **Harwich Junior Theatre** (508-432-2002; hjtcapecod.org), 105 Division Street, West Harwich. This semiprofessional theater—the country's oldest children's theater, established in 1951—produces up to twelve shows a year for both children and adults. In summer, children age 7–15 star in kids' roles, manage the sound and lighting, and sell refreshments. Whether your child is considering acting or you want to introduce him or her to theater, this is an imaginative alternative to another round of mini-golf. Classes or workshops are offered year-round. Tickets $12–20. Their **Harwich Winter Theatre** offers plays geared toward an older crowd off-season.

✳ To Do

All listings are in Harwich Center unless otherwise noted.

BASEBALL ✐ **The Harwich Mariners** (508-432-2000; harwichmariners.org) play baseball at Whitehouse Field behind the high school in Harwich Center, off Oak Street from Route 39. Most games begin at 7 PM and are played from mid-June to mid-August. Free. They also host weekly clinics (9:30–11) for children age 5–17 from late June to early August; $70–125. Sign up on Monday morning at the field. Private instruction also available.

BICYCLING/RENTALS About 5 miles of the Cape Cod Rail Trail run through Harwich; you can pick up the trail near the Pleasant Lake General Store on Route 124 and off Great Western Road near Herring Run Road. The chamber of commerce publishes a good biking map. **The Bike Depot** (508-430-4375; ccrailtrail .com), 500 Depot Street on the rail trail, is open May through October and rents equipment for $25 a day including helmets, locks, and maps.

BOATING **Saquatucket Harbor** (threeharbors.com), Route 28. With 200 berths, this is the largest municipal marina on the Cape; a few slips are reserved for transient visitors and a ramp pass costs $8. With a seasonal pass for $80, visitors can launch at both Saquatucket and Allens Harbor.

Wychmere Harbor, Harbor Road off Route 28. A fleet of sloops is often moored here, making it one of the Cape's most scenic (albeit human-made) harbors. In the late 1800s, Wychmere Harbor was simply a salt pond, around which a racetrack was laid. But locals, disapproving of horse racing, convinced the town to cut an opening from the pond into Nantucket Sound. A harbor was born.

Allens Harbor, on Lower County Road, is the town's other picturesque, well-protected, and human-made harbor; only seasonal ramp passes are available.

A PERFECT DAY IN HARWICH

  8:30 Order a famous melt-a-way-sweet bun and breakfast at Bonatt's.

10:00 Find the quiet center of Harwich Center.

10:30 Swim in a glacial kettle pond.

12:30 Dine outdoors at Brax, overlooking Saquatucket Harbor.

  1:45 Paddle up the Herring River with a kayak.

  4:00 Play a round at Harbor Glen Miniature Golf.

  5:00 Watch the light change on sailboats in Wychmere Harbor.

  6:00 Have a romantic New American dinner at Cape Sea Grille.

  8:00 Catch a Cape Cod League baseball game.

10:00 Enjoy an old-fashioned cone from the Sundae School.

The **Herring River**, which runs north to a reservoir and south to Nantucket Sound, is great for kayaking.

See also **Herring River/Sand Pond Conservation Area/Bells Neck** under *Green Space*.

FISHING/SHELLFISHING Shellfishing permits ($15 daily for nonresident families, $30 seasonally) are obtained from the harbormaster (508-430-7532) at Saquatucket Harbor 9–4 weekdays, June through September.

A number of charter fishing boats depart from Saquatucket Harbor, including the *Yankee* (508-432-2520), which departs twice daily Monday through Saturday and once on Sunday ($35 adults, $33 children) for 4 hours. Call ahead to confirm.

Try your luck casting from a jetty at **Red River Beach** (see *Green Space*) or the **Herring River Bridge** in West Harwich. And rent equipment from **Sunrise Bait and Tackle** (508-430-4117), 431 Route 28.

❋ **Fishing the Cape** (508-432-1200; fishingthecape.com), Routes 137 and 39, Harwich Commons. From May through August, the king of fly-fishing—Orvis— offers a 2-day saltwater fly-fishing course for $470. (The price includes equipment, lunch, and fishing.) Guided fishing trips, too. A full line of Orvis supplies, flies, and tackle is sold at the shop.

FOR FAMILIES ✐ **Grand Slam Entertainment** (508-430-1155; grandslam entertainment.com), 322 Route 28. Open weekends in April, then late May to mid-September (9 AM–10 PM daily in summer). Batting cages with varying degrees of difficulty and bumper boats for toddlers to teens. Also a radar pitching cage and one of the world's only (purportedly) Wiffle ball cages for kids.

✐ **Trampoline Center** (508-432-8717), 296 Route 28. Open daily July and August, weekends to mid-September . There are no age or height restrictions; the only limit at this outdoor center is that kids can't do flips.

✐ **Bud's Go-Karts** (508-432-4964), 9 Sisson Road, at Route 28. Open 9 AM–11 PM daily, mid-June to early

BUD'S GO-KARTS

September, and weekends only from mid-April to mid-June and early September to mid-October. Kids have to be more than 54 inches tall and at least 8 years old to drive without parents at this busy track. Five minutes cost $6.

🍃 **Castle in the Clouds**, behind the Harwich Elementary School, South Street. A fun playground. There are also picnic tables and a playground at Brooks Park, Route 39, Harwich.

GOLF **Cranberry Valley Golf Course** (508-430-7560; cranberrygolfcourse.com), 183 Oak Street, off Main Street, which turns into Route 39. Open March through December. An 18-hole, par-72 course with driving range and practice putting green.

❋ **Harwich Port Golf Club** (508-432-0250), South and Forest streets. A 9-hole, par-34 course.

MINI-GOLF 🍃 **Harbor Glen Miniature Golf** (508-432-8240), Route 28, West Harwich. Open April to mid-October. With fountains and imitation rocky water-falls, this place packs 'em in, especially at night. Perhaps it's due to the adjacent restaurant, which offers kids' meals and ice cream. Adults $6, children 11 and under, $4.

SAILING See **Cape Sail** under *Sailing* in "Brewster."

TENNIS Three public courts are located at **Brooks Park** (508-430-7553), Route 39 and Oak Street. Free. In summer there are morning programs for children.

❋ Green Space

BEACHES Weekly beach stickers ($55) are required for all but one of Harwich's 16 public saltwater beaches. If you're renting a cottage, purchase a parking sticker at the Community Center (508-430-7568), 100 Oak Street; open 8–3 daily, June to early September.

Red River Beach, off Depot Road from Route 28, is one of the few beaches with daily parking; $15 daily. Facilities include restrooms, concessions, and a lifeguard.

Pleasant Bay, off Route 28, is salt water, but calm, like a pond.

PONDS **Hinckleys Pond** and **Seymour Pond**, both off Route 124, are open to nonresidents. You can also swim at **Bucks Pond**, off Route 39. Limited parking; sticker required.

Long Pond has two beaches, although both require parking stickers $15. One is located off Long Pond Drive from Route 124, the other off Cahoons Road from Long Pond Drive from Route 137.

Sand Pond is off Great Western Road.

WALKS The chamber of commerce (see *Guidance*) publishes a good walking-trail map.

Herring River/Sand Pond Conservation Area/Bells Neck (park off Bells Neck Road from Great Western Road) in West Harwich. These 200-plus acres of marshland, tidal creeks, reservoir, and riverway are great for birding and canoeing. You may see cormorants, ospreys, and swans.

🐾 **Thompson's Field**, Chatham Road, south of Route 39. This 57-acre preserve, with dirt-road trails for you and your canine friends, is full of wildflowers in springtime. This gives you an idea of what the Cape probably looked like 100 years ago.

✳ Lodging

BED & BREAKFASTS Winstead Inn & Beach Resort (508-432-4444; 800-870-4405; winsteadinn.com), 4 Braddock Lane, Harwich Port. Open mid-January to mid-December. You'll pay dearly for this privileged perch because there's nothing between the decks and the ocean except a private beach. Gregg Winston has transformed this modest beachfront house into an upscale establishment with 18 simple but deluxe rooms and four suites. All rooms are off a central hallway; two offer a direct beach view; some have a private deck and Jacuzzi. All rooms have air-conditioning, TV, and refrigerator. The back porch, sheltered by *Rosa rugosa*, leads to multilevel decks set with lounge chairs. Extensive continental breakfast buffet included. WiFi is available for a fee. They also have an inland property with a pool. On my last visit, service was less than it should have been to my mind. Mid-June to mid-October $295–485 (4-night minimum); off-season $165–335.

✳ 🐾 **Lion's Head Inn** (508-432-7766; 800-321-3155; capecodinns.com), 186 Belmont Road, West Harwich. On a quiet residential street within walking distance of a beach, this modest B&B operated by Marilyn and Tom Hull (who exhibit great pride of ownership) has some nice attributes. Most of the six guest rooms can accommodate an extra person; one room has a private deck and original pine floors. The favored Huntington Suite is large, with a sitting area, TV, and private entrance to the pool. Nineteenth-century common rooms include two comfortable parlors (where guests watch TV since most rooms do not have one). The sunny breakfast room/terrace overlooks the nicely landscaped pool. Inquire about the two moderately priced **cottages**; they're a bit more rustic than the B&B, but fully equipped for family stays. Continental breakfast included. Unpredictable WiFi. Children over age 8 welcome in the B&B. Mid-June through August $120–195; off-season $100–190; cottages $775–875 weekly in-season.

✳ 🐾 🐾 **Barnaby Inn** (508-432-6789; 800-439-4764; barnabyinn.com), 36 Route 28, West Harwich. Although this rambling farmhouse is on busy Route 28, it's set well back from the road. Innkeeper Laurieann Galer, who is a licensed massage therapist, runs a relaxed and friendly ship. There's no standing on formality here. Of the six guest rooms, two are deemed deluxe rooms because they have a fireplace and Jacuzzi. Breakfast is delivered to those rooms; otherwise, a buffet is set up in the former bar and guests eat outdoors in the summertime. A two-bedroom **cottage**, with complete kitchen, is a bargain at $800–1,000 weekly in summer. Late May to mid-October $95–150; off-season $85–135.

❀ "ʏ" **Seadar Inn By-The-Sea** (508-432-0264; 800-888-5250; 508-842-4525 off-season; seadarinn.com), Braddock Lane, Harwich Port. Open mid-May through October. In a quiet neighborhood, just a short shuffle from Bank Street Beach, the rambling and shingled Seadar Inn is in need of attention, but just so you know, it has 23 air-conditioned rooms decorated in Early American style. A continental breakfast, served in the Colonial-style dining room, is included. Late June to mid-September $115–205; off-season $100–175.

MOTELS & MORE 🍴 ✎ ♿

Commodore Inn (508-432-1180; 800-368-1180; commodoreinn.com), 30 Earle Road, West Harwich. Open April to mid-November. For the money and more, this is the best value in Harwich. At first glance, Flora MacFarlane-Jones's complex looks like just another cluster of motel rooms set around a pool. But the delightful place is so much more than that. The large pool is heated; an excellent full breakfast buffet, prepared by daughter Fiona Rendon at **Raspberries**, is included (in summertime); and the 27 rooms are nicely outfitted with wicker furniture and white cotton bedspreads. There is real attention to detail here. Some have a Jacuzzi, gas fireplace, and a wet bar; all have microwaves; many can sleep four. Ask for a room with a vaulted ceiling; they feel much more spa-

cious. Located on 2½ acres in a quiet residential area, the Commodore is 75 yards from the beach, and there's a play area. Tour groups stay here in the fall, but don't let that dissuade you; there are too many other things going for it—including the best scones on the planet. Mid-June to mid-September $215–275 (3-night minimum); off-season $85–150.

❀ ✎ "ʏ" **Tern Inn** (508-432-3714; 800-432-3718; theterninn.com), 91 Chase Street, West Harwich. Hands-on owners David and Joan Bruce run a spotless operation and it pays off. A 10-minute walk from the beach, these six nicely maintained and renovated cottages and efficiencies (one of which is shaped like a gazebo) are set on a 2-acre wooded lot. They also rent eight **guest rooms** in a half-Cape house, where a bountiful, breakfast buffet is included. A pool, swings, and basketball court are on the premises, perfectly oriented toward family stays. Mid-June to mid-September $149–189 rooms, $875–1,395 weekly cottages; off-season $99–139 rooms, $150–250 cottages.

✎ "ʏ" **Sandpiper Beach Inn** (508-432-0485; sandpiperbeachinn.com), 16 Bank Street, Harwich Port. Open mid-April through October. New owner, Bryan Keenan, took over in 2008 and has a three-year plan to restore the inn's standing. Fronting its own private beach, this U-shaped building is constructed around a well-tended grassy courtyard. All 21 rooms have TV, refrigerator, telephone, and air-conditioning. Some can sleep three to five people; most have a private patio. The **duplex cottage** that opens directly onto the beach is practically perfect (and worth the money if you have it); call early as it's often booked a year in advance for July and August. Continental breakfast included. Mid-June to mid-September $200–485; off-season $130–325.

RENTAL HOUSES 🐾 "T" **Blue Heron** (508-430-0219), 464 Pleasant Lake Avenue, Harwich. Rents Saturday to Saturday, May to late September. The main draw for Susan Horvath's pleasant and homey 19th-century rental is its proximity to the Cape's largest freshwater lake and to the rail trail: Both are across the street. (The beach is private.) Off the beaten path, the house has five simple rooms with three baths, a fully equipped kitchen, wraparound porch, living room and den, and an outdoor shower. It sleeps up 10 people. No linens are provided. $3,200 weekly.

Waystack Realty (508-432-9922; 877-637-3684; newenglandvacationrentals .com), 565 Main Street, Route 28, Harwich Port.

✳ Where to Eat

Harwich has one of the Cape's best restaurants, a great hole-in-the-wall, and a bunch of places in between: You won't go hungry here.

DINING OUT ♿ **Cape Sea Grille** (508-432-4745; capeseagrille.com), 31 Sea Street, Harwich Port. Open for dinner mid-April through New Year's Eve. This contemporary bistro offers well-prepared, creative New American cuisine with a French Mediterranean influence. Because it's also served by twinkling candlelight in a lovely old sea captain's home, it's more like a grand slam. Outstanding signature dishes include pan-seared lobster with pancetta and asparagus and duck confit. Dishes change seasonally, but preparations always play with the classics. You'd better save room for strawberry shortcake or silky ginger crème brûlée. There is a three-course sunset

menu 5–5:45. Jennifer Douglas Ramler and her chef husband Douglas have presided since the day it opened in 2002. Dinner $20–34.

❋ **Buca's Tuscan Roadhouse** (508-432-6900; bucasroadhouse.com), 4 Depot Road. Open for dinner nightly. You might be hard-pressed to know which continent you're on at this cozy little trattoria. Both romantic and relaxing, with high-backed booths and red-and-white-checked tablecloths, they serve authentic and excellent *gamberetti ala toscana* (Tuscan herbed shrimp, goat cheese risotto, lemon butter sauce, and kale) as well as classic eggplant *parmigiana.* Furthermore, portions are generous, desserts are homemade by the owner, and there's a good selection of wines by the glass. Dishes $18–32.

❋ **L'Alouette Bistro** (508-430-0405; lalouettebistro.com), 787 Route 28, Harwich Port. Open for dinner nightly; closed Monday off-season. I didn't get a chance to eat here for this edition, but all gourmand innkeeper contacts assure me that it's up to snuff these days. Alan and Gretchen Champney's French country cuisine is simple but splendid, as rich as you might expect, but it's always a winner. Try the roast duck breast and duck confit in elegant but relaxed surroundings. Look for their bargain 3-course dinner with wine in June, estate-grown wines, and after-dinner tarts. Dinner $23–32.

EATING OUT ✐ ♟ ♿ **Brax** (508-432-5515; braxlanding.com), 705 Route 28, Harwich. Open for lunch, dinner, and Sunday brunch April through December. Bar open year-round. Overlooking Saquatucket Harbor, this popular and casual tavernlike restaurant has a varied menu. Look for fish and chicken sandwiches, fried seafood, seafood stew, and lobster rolls. For sure, their

BRAX LANDING

steamers are particularly renowned. A few indoor seats have choice views, but the real draw is outdoor seating by the tranquil harbor. A bountiful brunch buffet packs 'em in on Sunday. Regardless of the time of day, there is often a 45-minute wait. Lunch $7–19, dinner $13–20, brunch $15.

❋ **Andale Café** (508-432-0518; andale cafe.com), 703 Main Street, Harwich Center. Open for lunch and dinner daily June through September; closed Sunday off-season. This little place with outdoor seating, in the middle of little Harwich center, serves everything from carne asada and chile rellenos to enchiladas and burritos. There's something to suit every level of hunger. Dishes $7–16.

❋ **Hot Stove Saloon** (508-432-9911), 551 Route 28, Harwich Port. Open for lunch and dinner daily. Offering good-value pub grub since 2005, this place sports the requisite low lighting and boisterous quality you want in a (primarily) sports bar. The cheeseburgers are great, but you could also go for a thin-crust pizza, fish-n-chips, or any number of sandwiches (BLT, cheesesteak, or host pastrami for instance). A couple of picnic tables out front provide good watching on Main Street. Dishes $6–10.

❋ 🦞 ♂ ♿ **Bonatt's Restaurant & Bakery** (508-432-7199), 537 Route 28 at Sea Street, Harwich Port. Open for breakfast and lunch daily. A Harwich landmark since they created the melt-a-way sweet bun in 1939, Bonatt's is still well known for excellent breakfasts. The short-order kitchen specializes in lobster benedict and raspberry-stuffed french toast. Fortunately, breakfast is served all day. At lunchtime, look for blackboard specials, fish-and-chips, and open steak sandwiches. Bonatt's also provides box lunches for the beach (call an hour in advance in summer or be prepared to wait). Dishes $5–16.

❋ **The Mason Jar** (508-430-7600), 544 Route 28, Harwich Port. Open for lunch daily mid-May to mid-October and Tuesday through Saturday off-season. Chef-owner Guy Winialsk has been serving fine specialty sandwiches, homemade soups, prepared meals-to-go, and desserts since 2001. Patio seating. Dishes $5–10.

🦞 ♂ **Seafood Sam's** (508-432-1422; seafoodsams.com), 302 Route 28, Harwich Port. Open for lunch and dinner February to late December. Look for reliable, informally presented, reasonably priced fried or broiled seafood. Outdoor seating, chicken, burgers, and ice cream, too. Lunch specials $6–9, dinner $8–19.

SNACKS & COFFEE ❋ 🍴 **Harwich Central Café** (508-432-9801), 98 Parallel Street, Harwich Center. Open for breakfast and lunch daily. This funky little coffee shop-cum-café, just around the corner from little Harwich center, serves flavorful Indigo coffee from Northampton and more. It bills itself as a community place, and sure enough, you could hang out here for a while surfing the net, munching on some baked goods, and having a light sandwich or panini.

Sundae School Ice Cream Parlor (508-430-2444), 606 Route 28, Harwich

Port. Open late May to early October. This "olde" fashioned "shoppe" is the place to go for homemade ice-cream concoctions.

❄ **Pleasant Lake General Store** (508-432-5305), 403 Route 124, Harwich. Open daily. A good old-fashioned store, perfectly situated for cyclists on the rail trail (see *To Do*).

✳ Entertainment

♪ **Band concerts** are held Tuesday evening at 7 in Brooks Park, at Route 39 and Oak Street.

See also **Harwich Junior Theatre** under *To See*.

✳ Selective Shopping

❄ All establishments are open year-round unless otherwise noted.

SPECIAL SHOPS **Pewter Crafter of Cape Cod** (508-432-5858; cape codpewter.com), 791 Route 28, Harwich Port. Ron Kusins has been toiling at this ancient craft, creating traditional and contemporary designs, since the late 1970s. Finishes are either satin or shiny; forms are functional. This is one of only half a dozen pewter studios in the country (and the only one on the Cape), so now is the time to get an up-close view of pewter making.

Cape Cod Braided Rug Co. (508-432-3133), 537 Route 28, Harwich Port. In 1910 Romeo Paulus, great-grandfather of the current generation of rugmakers, was the first American to make these old-fashioned braided rugs on a machine. All sizes and shapes and color combinations are available—the in-store inventory is large, but you can also have them custom-make a rug in 4 weeks for about the same price. Visitors can also visit the factory warehouse outlet (4 Great Western Road, Harwich) and watch rugs being made.

Rose Cottage Shop (508-430-4610), 105 Route 137, East Harwich. Richard Morris, an expert at restoring and renovating old houses, also has a talent for decorating their interiors. This expansive showroom offers furniture, lighting, wall hangingsand unique home accessories. Richard travels to England several times a year, where he finds most of his pieces.

Cape Cod Tileworks (508-432-7346), 705 Main Street, Harwich Center. This colorful shop sells nothing but tile: ceramic, marble, limestone, and hand-painted. They do custom designs and installation, too.

Monahan & Co. Jewelers (508-432-3302; 800-237-4605), 540 Route 28, Harwich Port. Prices for high-end jewelry (manufactured, purchased from estate auctions, and left on consignment) range from the double digits to six digits. The largest jewelry shop on the Cape and America's oldest family-owned jewelry store (established in 1815), it has been in Michael Monahan's family for generations.

The Barn at Windsong (508-432-8281), 245 Bank Street, Harwich Port. Call for hours. Several dealers offer a variety of goods: quilts, silver, china, glassware, and furniture.

HARVESTING CRANBERRIES

✳ Special Events

Mid-May: **Toast of Harwich**, a formal evening of wine tasting, fine cuisine from the town's chefs, and live and silent auctions at the Wequassett Resort on Pleasant Bay; tickets $50.

July through September: **Guild of Harwich Artists** sponsors Monday "Art in the Park" at Doane Park, off Lower County Road. (Rain date is Wednesday.)

Early September: **A Taste of Harwich** (508-432-1600). This family-friendly, 1-day food-tasting event, at the Cape Cod Technical High School on Route 124, features almost 20 participating restaurants.

August: **Harwich Farm Fest**. Farms open for walking and tasting tours, demos, and other family fun. Maps available from the chamber.

Mid-September: **Harwich Cranberry Festival** (harwichcranberryfestival.org) at the Harwich High School off of Oak Street. Community spirit prevails at this popular celebration, which boasts an attendance of almost 40,000 people. Events include fireworks, a parade, a carnival, and hundreds of top-notch crafts displays.

Early December: **Christmas Weekend in the Harwiches**. Hayrides, strolling minstrels, a choral group, and merchant open houses.

CHATHAM

Although Chatham is less accessible from Route 6 than are its neighbors, even the most hurried Cape visitors stop here. Occupying the tip of Cape Cod's elbow, the town offers a good mix of archetypal Cape Cod architecture, a classic Main Street, a refined sensibility, plenty of excellent beaches and shops, and a rich seafaring history.

When Samuel de Champlain and his party tried to land at Stage Harbor in 1606, they were met with stalwart resistance from the Native inhabitants. Fifty years later, though, Yarmouth's William Nickerson purchased a great deal of land from Chief Mattaquason. By 1712, the permanent "settlers" had incorporated the town.

Today Chatham is known for its calm, genteel, independent spirit. The town's vigilant zoning commission has kept tourist-trap activity to a minimum. Bordered on three sides by water, the town is populated by descendants of its oceangoing founders, many of whom continue in their ancestors' footsteps. Despite the difficulty in navigating the surrounding waters, Chatham sustains an active fleet of fishermen and leisure-time sailors. Fishermen, sailors, shop owners, and an increasing number of retirees live quietly in this delightfully traditional village.

Chatham, along with the spectacularly desolate Monomoy National Wildlife Refuge, boasts 65 miles of shoreline. As such, Chatham's beaches are varied: Some are hit by pounding surf, sandbars shelter others; some are good for shell collecting, others are wide and sandy. A walk along the shore reveals gentle inlets and beautiful seafront homes. An inland drive or bicycle ride takes you past elegant shingled cottages and stately white houses surrounded by picket fences and boasting primroses and tidy lawns.

In the center of Chatham, Main Street is chock-full of upscale shops, offering everything from tony antiques and nautically inspired gifts to jewelry, clothing, and culinary supplies. This central part of town has excellent restaurants and inns, and some of the Cape's finest bow-shaped roof houses (so named because they're shaped like the bow of a ship turned upside down). North Chatham, primarily residential, is dotted with several picturesque inlets. West and South Chatham border the beaches; you'll find lots of rental houses, summer cottages, and piney woods here. Chatham's year-round population of 6,400 balloons to 30,000 to 40,000 in the summer.

GUIDANCE ⁰1⁰ **Chatham Chamber of Commerce and Visitor's Information Center** (508-945-5199; 800-715-5567; chathaminfo.com), 2377 Main Street, in the

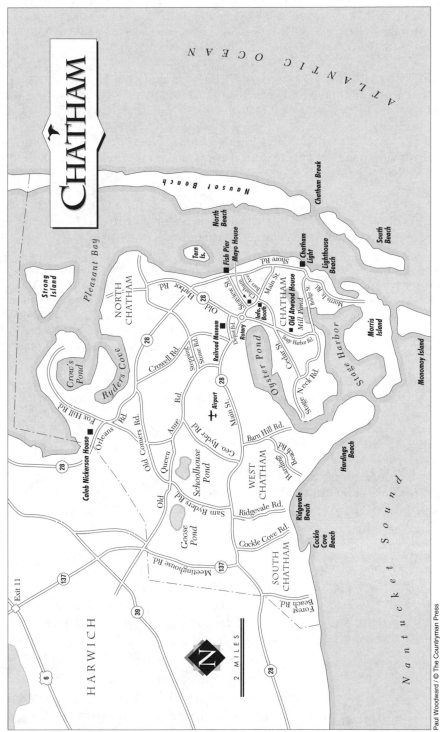

CHATHAM

historic Bassett House. Open 10–5 Monday through Saturday and noon–3 on Sunday, late May to mid-October; 10–2 weekdays off-season. The map-lined walls come in handy when you're planning an itinerary or looking for a specific place—as does the walking guide. There is also a **downtown welcome booth** at 533 Main Street with the same summertime hours as the main office.

PUBLIC RESTROOMS Year-round facilities are located at the town offices on Main Street and at the Fish Pier on Shore Road. Summertime restrooms are located behind Kate Gould Park (off Main Street).

PUBLIC LIBRARY ❊ ✐ ♆ ⁗ⴰ⁗ **Eldredge Public Library** (508-945-5170; eldredgelibrary.org), 564 Main Street. Open Monday through Saturday. One of the Cape's best libraries.

GETTING THERE *By car:* From the Cape Cod Canal, take Route 6 east to Exit 11 (Route 137 South) to Route 28 South. The center of Chatham is 3 miles from this intersection, about 45 minutes from either bridge.

GETTING AROUND Chatham is crowded in July and August, and you'll be happiest exploring Main Street on foot. It's about a 15-minute walk from mid–Main Street to the lighthouse and another 15 minutes from the light to the pier (one-way). There is free parking at Town Hall (off Main Street), the Colonial Building (off Stage Harbor Road), one block west of the rotary at the elementary school, and on Chatham Bars Avenue behind the Impudent Oyster restaurant off Main Street.

By shuttle: The **H₂O** (508-790-2613; 800-352-7155; capecodtransit.org) bus line, used by more locals than visitors, travels along Route 28 between the Hyannis Transportation Center and Orleans daily except Sunday year-round. It officially stops on Anchorage/Crowell Road and at the rotary in the center of Chatham, and

A PERFECT (JAM-PACKED) DAY IN CHATHAM
7:30 Have breakfast at the Lazy Lobster.
9:00 Drive back roads overlooking Pleasant Bay, Oyster Pond, and Stage Harbor.
10:00 Chase seagulls and peer through telescopes at the Chatham Break and lighthouse.
10:30 Stroll Main Street and duck into Odell's Studio.
12:30 Take a chicken potpie or bumbleberry pie from Marion's to Chase Park. OR Spare a bit more time (and money) to dine oceanfront at the Outer Bar & Grille or Beach House Grill.
1:30 Count personable seals on a cruise from Beachcomber.
4:00 Find your rhythm on a front-porch rocker at the Chatham Bars Inn.
5:30 Create memories with sophisticated cuisine at twenty-eight Atlantic.
8:00 Listen to crickets and catch the second half of a baseball game.

on Morton's Road in South Chatham, but will stop anywhere along Route 28; just remember to flag down the driver.

MEDICAL EMERGENCY Call **911**.

✳ To See

Chatham Light (508-430-0628), Main Street and Bridge Street. Built in 1808 and rebuilt in 1877, the lighthouse has a beacon visible 23 miles out to sea. The U.S. Coast Guard–operated lighthouse is open during July and August on Wednesday 1–3:30; no children under age 5 allowed. Parking limit of 30 minutes during the summer.

Fish Pier, Shore Road at Bar Cliff Avenue. Chatham's fleet of fishing boats returns—from as far away as 100 miles—to the pier daily about 2–4.

CHATHAM LIGHT

From the pier's second-floor observation deck you can watch fishermen unloading their catch of haddock, lobster, cod, halibut, flounder, and pollack. While you're at the pier, take a gander at the **Fisherman's Monument**. A 1992 call for designs attracted nearly 100 applicants from around the world. The committee chose Sig Purwin, a Woods Hole sculptor, to memorialize the town's fishermen. In recent years, as stocks have begun to dwindle, fishermen have increasingly turned to shellfish harvesting. (Local bay scallops harvested in late fall are like nothing you've ever tasted.) In fact, more commercial licenses are purchased yearly in Chatham than anywhere else on the Cape. With luck Kenny Eldrige will be on the pier. He's a colorful local character hired by the Commercial Hookfisherman's Association town to tell honest-to-goodness fish tales to tourists—stories about area seal colonies, local fishing conditions, and the like.

FROM THE FISH PIER

✐ ⊤ **Railroad Museum**, 153 Depot Road. Open 10–4 Tuesday through Saturday mid-June to mid-September. This carefully restored 1887 depot— on the National Register of Historic Places—features decorative "railroad gothic" architecture (unique to the US) from its turret to its gingerbread trim. In fact, this is such a good example of this architecture that students of architectural history come to Chatham to study it. On the track in front of the

station, you will find a 1910 New York Central train caboose (visitors are free to climb on the caboose and explore its interior); inside the museum are such treasures as photos, models, and equipment pertaining to the Cape's railroad history. Suggested donation $5.

✎ ⚓ **Old Atwood House** (508-945-2493; chathamhistoricalsociety.org), 347 Stage Harbor Road. Open 10–4 Tuesday through Saturday, July and August; 1–4 Tuesday through Saturday, June, September, and October. This gambrel-roofed house, built by a sea captain in 1752, has been maintained by the Chatham Historical Society since 1926. (Note the low doorways and how much we've grown over the last two centuries by eating our vegetables!) The museum complex includes a gallery devoted to the history of fishing on Cape Cod and seven additional galleries that display antique dolls, tools, toys, portraits of sea captains, seashells from around the world, Sandwich glass, and other Chatham seafaring artifacts. The adjoining train barn features a three-panel mural by Alice Stallknecht that depicts more than 130 townspeople with a "modern Christ." Adults $5; children under 12, free.

Mayo House (508-945-6098), 540 Main Street. Open 11–4 Tuesday through Thursday, late June to early September. Built in 1818 by Josiah Mayo (who served for 40 years as Chatham's first postmaster) and filled with period antiques, the Mayo House is owned and maintained by the Chatham Conservation Foundation. The tiny, grey-with-red-shutters, three-quarter Cape isn't the "best this" or the "oldest that"; it's just a nice little old house. Donations.

Caleb Nickerson House (508-945-6086), 1107 Orleans Road (Route 28). Open 9–1 Wednesday mid-June to late September. This near pristine full-Cape home, which dates to 1772, is a "jewel box of authentic Colonial architecture." Don't miss it. Although the house was moved from its original location overlooking Oyster River, it ended up on homestead land that originally belonged to the great, great, great, great grandfather of the founder of Chatham, William Nickerson. Donations.

SCENIC DRIVES Chatham is one of the most scenic Cape towns. Route 28 toward Orleans offers some of the loveliest scenery, with views of Pleasant Bay to the east. Shore Road passes handsome cedar-shingled houses. The causeway to Morris Island affords harbor views as well as views of the open ocean beyond tall grasses and sandy shores. And the road to Cockle Cove Beach from Route 28 in South Chatham runs along a picturesque salt marsh and tidal river.

CHATHAM BREAK

Coin-operated telescopes across from the lighthouse allow visitors to take a closer look at the Chatham Break. The main one was a result of a ferocious nor'easter on January 2, 1987. During the first historic storm in 1987, the barrier beach (the lower portion of Nauset Beach) that had previously protected Chatham Harbor from the open ocean was breached. As a result, low dunes were flattened, tidal waters rose, and waves and high winds forced a channel through Nauset Beach. Over the next few years, nine expensive waterfront homes were destroyed by the ensuing, unrestrained pounding of the fierce Atlantic Ocean. Although fishermen now have a more direct passage through the (formerly) long barrier beach, boating around the harbor's strong currents is more difficult than ever.

In a matter of hours in 1987 (rather than over the natural course of 50 years), the break altered Chatham's way of life. The effects are still felt and debated today. But ocean currents have a mind of their own; in 1846 a previous break in South Beach repaired itself. That hasn't happened to this breach yet. But some beachfront is returning, and some of

VIEWING CHATHAM BREAK

it belongs to folks who saw their lots washed away in the late 1980s. Sand, like birds, migrates south; Wellfleet's and Eastham's beach losses are Chatham's gain. Lighthouse Beach is directly below the lookout area; South and North beaches are visible across the harbor (see *Green Space*). Enjoy the view; it's a work in progress.

Sure enough, the work in progress continues: In April 19, 2007, another break developed in North and South Beach. Eight cottages washed into the sea, some were moved, and others could not be moved because of nesting piping plovers. Stay tuned.

✳ To Do

AIRPLANE RIDES ✳ ✿ **Cape Aerial Tours** (508-945-9000; chathamairport .com), Chatham Municipal Airport, 240 George Ryder Road. To really appreciate Chatham's shoreline and the fragility of the Outer Cape landscape, head 900 feet above it in a four-seater Cessna. These wonderful sightseeing rides are a bargain (25 minutes, $125; 55 minutes, $195). Prices are per ride, whether it's one person or three (max). Reservations recommended a day in advance in summer.

ART CLASSES ❋ **Creative Arts Center** (508-945-3583; capecodcreativearts .org), 154 Crowell Road. The center offers classes during July and August in pottery, drawing, photography, painting, jewelry making, and other fine arts. Work is shown at the center's on-site **Edward A. Bigelow Gallery**. Since 1971, the center has held an annual art festival in August (see *Special Events*), where you may meet the artists and purchase their work.

BASEBALL ✦ **The Chatham Athletics** (508-945-5511; capecodbaseball.org), one of 10 teams in the Cape Cod Baseball League, usually play ball at 7 PM from mid-June to early August at Veterans Park, Route 28, just west of the rotary. The information booth (see *Guidance*) has schedules. The A's sponsor weekly clinics for youngsters from mid-June to July. The cost is $60 for age 6–12, $90 for age 13–17. Register at Veterans Park on Monday morning at 8. And bring your own glove.

BICYCLING/RENTALS With gentle inclines, quiet lanes, and a well-marked 2.75-mile route around town, Chatham is nice for bicycling.

See **Rail Trail Bike & Kayak** under *Bicycling* in "Brewster."

Chatham Cycle (508-945-8981; brewsterbike.com), 193 Depot Road. Open mid-March through December. Convenient to the bike trail, this shop is staffed by experts who love to ride. Single and multiple speeds, alley cats, jogging strollers, and trailers are rented. FYI: It's 26.5 miles up to Coast Guard Beach and 16.5 miles to Nickerson State Park from here, but bicycling around town is also a smart option. Bikes $14–18 for 4 hours, $22–28 for 24 hours.

BOAT EXCURSIONS/RENTALS **Outermost Adventures** (508-945-5858; outermostharbor.com), 83 Seagull Road, Outermost Harbor Marine, off Morris Island Road. Late June to mid-September. This outfit offers continuous shuttles to pristine South Beach and Monomoy Island. Roundtrip South Beach shuttles costs $20 for adults, $10 children under 12; Monomoy is $20 per person; both run 8–5 daily.

Rip Ryder (508-945-5450; monomoyislandferry.com), at Monomoy Refuge headquarters off Morris Island Road. Boats run April through November; make reservations the night before. Regular launches to South Monomoy. When the captain drops you off, tell him what time you want to be picked up. Inquire about fly-fishing, birding, and seal trips.

Beachcomber (508-945-5265; sealwatch.com), from the Fish Pier and Ryders

---

✦ **Chatham Family Charters** (508-237-2628; chathamfamilycharters.com). Captains Story and Annie Fish (in Chatham since the 1980s and for a lifetime, respectively) know the waters of Pleasant Bay like your back lawn on a riding mower. They specialize in tours for kids with fishing gear that is sized just for them. My friend Jean's 7-year-old nephew had a ball pulling in a blue fish with a tiny little "fish harness" around his waist—just like the big boys! Four hours for $400 with a maximum of six people. Custom cruises at sunrise and sunset also available.

CLAM DIGGING IN PLEASANT BAY

Cove. Beach and fishing shuttles to North Beach. Like most other outfits, they also offer 90-minute seal trips ,$25 adults, $21 ages 3–15, but they use a faster boat so you spend more time watching seals and less time traveling. In this case it's the destination, not the journey.

Nauti Jane's Boat Rentals, at the Wequassett Inn Resort (508-430-6893), Route 28. You can rent kayaks, catamarans, powerboats, and Sunfish at this beachfront location from May to October. Make reservations for lessons. Their Ridgevale Beach location (508-432-4339) has sailboats from mid-June to early September.

FISHING/SHELLFISHING For freshwater fishing and shellfishing licenses, contact the Permit Department (508-945-5180) on 283 George Ryder Road in West Chatham.

✔ **The Fishin' Bridge**. Follow Stage Harbor Road to Bridge Street, where Mill Pond empties into Stage Harbor. You'll haul in crabs, small flounders, eels, and perhaps even a bluefish. Locals will certainly be there with long rakes, harvesting shellfish. Stop even if you don't fish; it's picturesque.

South Beach offers the best opportunity for surf-casting for striped bass, but **North Beach** is a close second.

Schoolhouse Pond (reached via Sam Ryders Road) and **Goose Pond** (off Fisherman's Landing) offer freshwater fishing for rainbow trout. In-season there is resident-only parking at Schoolhouse.

For sportfishing charters (May through November), try Bob Miller's ***Headhunter*** (508-430-2312; capecodfishingcharters.com) and Ron McVickar's ***Banshee*** (508-945-0403), both out of Stage Harbor Marine.

For custom tackle, supplies, rod rentals, and more charter information, stop in at **Top Rod Fly & Surf Fish Shop** (508-945-2256; capefishingcharters.com), 1082 Route 28, next to Ryders Cove in North Chatham.

See also **Beachcomber** under *Boat Excursions*.

FOR FAMILIES ✔ ♿ **Play-a-Round Playground**, on Depot Road behind Chatham Elementary School. This wonderful, multilevel wooden structure includes an area for disabled children and a fenced-in area for toddlers.

GENEALOGY **Nickerson Family Association** (508-945-6086; nickersonassoc .org), 1107 Orleans Road. Chatham's founder, William Nickerson, has over 350,000 descendants. Think you're one of them? This genealogical research center will help you find out. In addition to mapping the Nickerson family tree, the volunteer association casts a wide net, compiling information on folks associated with the Nickersons, and original settlers of Cape Cod and Nova Scotia.

GOLF ✳ **Chatham Seaside Links** (508-945-4774), 209 Seaview Street, next to the Chatham Bars Inn. Open March through November; a 9-hole, par-34 course.

KAYAKING For rentals see **Monomoy Sail & Cycle** under *Sailboarding*.

SAILBOARDING Monomoy Sail & Cycle (508-945-0811), 275 Orleans Road, North Chatham, rents sailboards and kayaks. Pleasant Bay enjoys easterly and northeasterly winds, while Forest Beach receives southwesterly winds.

SEAL CRUISES See the sidebar "Monomoy National Wildlife Refuge" under *Green Space*.

TENNIS Public courts are located on **Depot Road** by the Railroad Museum and at **Chatham High School** on Crowell Road. Free.

Chatham Bars Inn (508-945-0096; chathambarsinn.com), 297 Shore Road. Courts open mid-April to mid-November. CBI has three waterfront courts made of synthetic "classic-clay" (which play like clay but are much easier to maintain) that rent to nonguests for $35 an hour. Lessons are offered in the summer and cost $105 per hour plus court time for guests and $120 for non-guests.

✳ Green Space

Chase Park and **Gristmill**, on Cross Street, is a tranquil vest pocket of parkland just a couple of blocks from the summertime madness on Main Street. It's perfect for a picnic lunch and overlooks a tranquil gristmill built in 1797. The mill is open 10–3 weekdays, July to early September.

Hydrangea Walkway. Heading north on Shore Road from Main Street, the road is lined with stately private homes overlooking the ocean. One house on the left, in particular, is really eye-catching from mid-June to September, when its front walkway is awash with more than 25 blooming hydrangea plants.

BEACHES Cottage renters purchase weekly beach stickers for Hardings, Ridgevale, and Cockle Cove beaches (see below). Otherwise, from late June to early September, parking (508-945-5158) is $15 daily, $60 weekly.

PLEASANT BAY BEACH

Hardings Beach, on Nantucket Sound. From Route 28, take Barn Hill Road to Hardings Beach Road. One Explorer e-mails: "Hardings Beach is great mostly because it has a channel into a salt pond and marsh. You can tube or float in the channel depending on the tides, and the water's warm." Small dunes. Restrooms, lifeguard, and concession stand.

Ridgevale Beach, on Nantucket Sound. Take Ridgevale Road off Route 28. Restroom, lifeguards, and snack bar.

❧ **Cockle Cove Beach**, protected from Nantucket Sound by Ridgevale Beach. Take Cockle Cove Road off Route 28. Gentle waves and soft sand make this a good choice for families. Lifeguards and portable toilets.

❧ **Pleasant Bay Beach**, Route 28, North Chatham. The 7,000-acre inlet and bay has been called breathtakingly beautiful, and it is. It's also on the state's list of 25 areas of "critical environmental concern." This beach is narrow but great for children because the water is so shallow.

LIGHTHOUSE BEACH

North Beach, on the Atlantic Ocean. North Beach, which is actually the southern end of Nauset Beach, is accessible only by boat (see *To Do* for water-taxi services). It's well worth the effort and expense to get here.

Lighthouse Beach and **South Beach**, below the lighthouse, on the Atlantic Ocean. Parking is limited to 30 minutes, but you can bicycle or walk to the lane off Morris Island Road just beyond the lighthouse; a sign points the way to South Beach. It's a bit of a walk, but try parking on Bridge Street; from the lighthouse, keep going on Bridge Street until there are no more signs saying "No parking on either side of street." (You'll notice lots of other cars parked here too.) If you're day-tripping to Chatham, pay to park at the Eldredge Taxi parking lot, 365 Main Street, and take its taxi to the beach. The most desolate part of the beach requires quite a long walk, but the early sections are very nice, too. Many ferries (see *To Do*) take passengers to the farthest, most remote reaches of the beach. One of the best aspects of this beach is that you've got surf on the east side and calm bay waters on the west.

POND *❧* **Oyster Pond Beach**, off Stage Harbor Road, near the rotary. This inland saltwater pond is connected to Nantucket Sound by way of Oyster Creek and Stage Harbor. Good for families, its shores are calm and its waters are the warmest in town. Free parking; lifeguard.

WALKS **Chatham Conservation Foundation** (508-945-4084; chathamconser vationfoundation.org). With over 645 acres, the foundation has created three distinct walking areas traversing marshes, wetlands, and meadows. Contact the town information booth on Main Street (see *Guidance*) for directions to Frost Fish Creek, Barclay Pond, and Honeysuckle Lane.

🐾 **The Dog Runs**, as it's known locally. Walk 10 minutes along Bridge Street away from the lighthouse to find this forested coastal trail along Stage Harbor. Enjoy a picnic in the cattail marshes.

See also the sidebar "Monomoy National Wildlife Refuge."

MONOMOY NATIONAL WILDLIFE REFUGE

North and South Monomoy islands (monomoy.fws.gov), acquired by the federal government as part of a wildlife refuge in 1944, comprise a 7,600-acre habitat for more than 285 species of birds. Birds and seaside animals rule the roost; there are no human residents, no paved roads, no vehicles, and no electricity. (Long ago the island did support a fishing community, though.) It's a quiet, solitary place. Monomoy, one of four remaining "wilderness" areas between Maine and New Jersey, is an important stop for shorebirds on the Atlantic Flyway—between breeding grounds in the Arctic and wintering grounds in South America. Conditions here may well determine whether the birds will survive the journey. Some beaches are closed from April to mid-August to protect threatened nesting areas for piping plovers and terns. The lovely old lighthouse, built in 1823 and not used since 1923, was restored in 1988.

In the mid-1990s, the U.S. Fish and Wildlife Service embarked on a long-term management project to restore avian nesting diversity to Monomoy NWR by creating habitat for terns, which historically numbered in the thousands. Restoring the nesting space was controversial because the government considered it necessary to "remove" (with bread chunks laced with poison) about 10 percent of the aggressive seagulls that also nested here. As a result, by the late 1990s, the number of nesting terns, including 18 pairs of roseate terns, increased dramatically. Some protesters still maintain that the Fish and Wildlife Service took this action under pressure from off-road-

✴ Lodging

Generally, Chatham is one of the more expensive places to stay on Cape Cod. Its motels, though, are some of the best on Cape Cod. Two-night minimum stays in July and August are normal, and many of Chatham's most notable places are booked for July and August well before July 4. Unless otherwise noted, all lodging is in Chatham proper.

RESORTS & HOTELS ✴ 🍴 ♿ 🍸

Chatham Bars Inn (508-945-0096; 800-527-4884; chathambarsinn.com), 297 Shore Road. This grande dame's gracious elegance is rivaled by only a handful of places in New England.

Built in 1914 as a hunting lodge, it's now the quintessential seaside resort. And after extensive, multigazillion-dollar renovations (it changed hands most recently in June 2007), it's better than ever. Grounds are lushly landscaped, and the seaside setting nearly perfect. Scattered over 25 acres, the main inn and cottages have a total of 217 rooms and suites comfortably decorated in a traditional Cape Cod style—with wicker, hand-painted furniture, and understated florals. Some ocean-view rooms have private balconies or decks.

The complex includes a private beach, a heated outdoor pool, a spa, gift shop, three tennis courts, croquet, a health and wellness center, a nine-hole golf vehicle drivers, who are often banned from driving on mainland beaches because of nesting endangered birds. But by the late 1990s, Monomoy had become the second largest tern-nesting site on the East Coast, and the biggest between here and the Canadian Maritimes. In 1998, the refuge was dogged by another controversy: Dens of coyotes (and their pups) were feasting on newborn chicks. Management "removed" them as well. These days commercial clammers and crabbers are sparring with the refuge over the issuance (or lack thereof) of permits.

Monomoy was attached to the mainland until a 1958 storm severed the connection; a storm in 1978 divided the island in two. The islands are accessible only by boat (see *To Do*), and only under favorable weather conditions. Guided tours are available from the **Wellfleet Bay Wildlife Sanctuary** (508-349-2615; massaudubon.org; see the "Trails, Birds, Seals & Classes" sidebar in "Wellfleet"). Tours offered late May through September; must call to reserve since space is limited; adults only, $35; trip tour 3–4 hours. Groups of six or more must obtain a permit from the refuge headquarters on Morris Island (508-945-0594). The 40-acre Morris Island is accessible by car and foot: Head south from Chatham Light and turn left onto Morris Island Road, then take your first right and continue on Morris Island Road to the end.

About 300 gray and harbor seals summer off the shores of Chatham, and about 3,000 seals rally here in winter. While the Chatham shores have attracted seals since the early 1980s, Monomoy has been a haven only since the 1991 hurricane created a break in the barrier beach.

course, launch service to Nauset Beach, sailing lessons, seal and whale tours, Orvis flyfishing lessons and a full and complimentary children's program (for ages 4–18). Although prices don't include meals, a lavish buffet is available every morning ($28). A 10-minute walk from town, the hotel also has an expansive veranda and very comfortable, grand living rooms. Mid-June to mid-September $495–2,750; off-season $195–1,235 (serious minimum stays required in summer). Rates considerably higher for ocean-view rooms and

CHATHAM BARS INN

suites; off-season packages are available.

♂ ♿ ⁱⁱⁱ **Wequassett Resort and Golf Club** (508-432-5400; 800-225-7125; wequassett.com), 2173 Route 28. Open April through November. If CBI (see Chatham Bars Inn) appeals to a "new money" set, then the Wequassett (10 minutes north of Chatham on picturesque Pleasant Bay) appeals to "old money." Renowned for an attentive staff, exceptional service, and understated elegance, the complex consists of 23 buildings set on 22 beautifully landscaped acres. It also boasts an excellent restaurant (see *Dining Out*), four tennis courts, sailing, and an oh-so-suave pool renovated with aplomb in 2006 with cabanas, a Jacuzzi, and a waterfront bar, LiBAYtion. (There isn't a more perfectly situated pool on the Cape.) Other resort amenities include a fitness center, boat rentals, launch service to an uncrowded section of the National Seashore, baby-sitting, and summertime children's programs. The resort also offers guests playing privileges on the otherwise private Cape Cod National Golf Course, a challenging Silva course (golf packages available).

As for the 116 rooms (all renovated in 2007 with a more upscale look), some cottages have cathedral ceilings and their own decks, though not all have

SEASHORE LAUNCH AT THE WEQUASSET

views of boat-studded Round Cove. Triple sheeting, morning delivery of the newspaper, and turndown service are standard. Light lunches are served at the pool; nightcaps are soothing at the charming Thoreau's. June through September $320–675 non-water-view rooms, $665–1,450 water views; off-season $185–340 and $330–600 respectively.

❄ ⁱⁱⁱ **Chatham Wayside Inn** (508-945-5550; 800-391-5734; waysideinn .com), 512 Main Street. Dominating Main Street, this historic 1860 hostelry (which now looks brand new) was completely renovated and expanded in the mid-1990s. Its 46 guest rooms and five suites are furnished with flair and a decorator's sure touch. Triple sheeting, thick towels, and top-notch bathroom amenities are standard. Some rooms have a canopy or four-poster bed and reproduction period furniture, a fireplace, a whirlpool tub, or a private patio or balcony. As for views, choose between the town green, golf course, or parking lot. Whether in summer or winter, cocktails are served fireside in the pub. Swimming pool. Mid-June to early September $265–495 rooms and suites; otherwise $110–395; inquire about off-season packages.

BED & BREAKFASTS ❄ ⁱⁱⁱ

Captain's House Inn of Chatham (508-945-0127; 800-315-0728; captains houseinn.com), 369–377 Old Harbor Road. The epitome of traditional elegance, this Greek Revival inn enjoys a privileged position—with plenty of good reasons. Jill and James Meyer, innkeepers since 2006, preside over an enthusiastic British hotel management staff, 2 acres of well-tended gardens, 12 handsome rooms, and four sumptuous suites. It's easily among the top 10 places to stay in New England.

The Captain's Cottage contains one particularly historic room with wood-burning fireplace, walnut-paneled walls, and pumpkin-pine flooring; a hideaway attic suite; and a honeymoon-style room with a double whirlpool. Antiques-filled inn rooms are more traditional, but all have triple sheeting, luxe amenities, contemporary bathrooms, and flat-screen TV/DVD. Full breakfasts are served on linen, china, and silver in a wonderfully airy room. Smoked salmon graces the sideboard every morning; an authentic English tea is offered every afternoon; cookies always seem to be baking throughout the day; and the DVD library always has port in the evening. The inn also has an oh-so-exclusive-feeling swimming pool and a small but expert fitness room. Children age 10 and over welcome. Mid-May through October $250–475; off-season $185–305.

❋ **Carriage House Inn** (508-945-4688; 800-355-8868; thecarriagehouse inn.com), 407 Old Harbor Road. This superlative six-room B&B on the edge of town (and at a busy intersection) gets rave reviews—with good reason—from travelers across the board. Paula and Tim Miller, who've run it since 2006, offer sophisticated and contemporary decor with clean lines. I prefer the slightly pricier rooms in the adjacent carriage house because they have fireplaces, private outdoor sitting areas, and separate entrances. Lots of upscale amenities are included, making this an even better value than it already is. Don't miss the lemon blueberry crepes (if you're lucky) at breakfast. WiFi in main house only. Early June to early September $229–289; off-season $139–239.

❋ ⁗↑⁗ **Cranberry Inn** (508-945-9232; 800-332-4667; cranberryinn.com), 359 Main Street. A 10-minute walk from Chatham Light and the beach, this

CRANBERRY INN

renovated two-story inn has 18 traditional rooms off a long hallway. In attitude and decor, it more closely resembles an elegant small hotel than a B&B. Common space includes a traditional living room that also serves as a reception area and a small, handsome bar. Upscale guest-room furnishings—mixing period antiques with reproductions—might have a fireplace, private balcony (overlooking the parking lot), and wet bar; all have fridges. Behind the inn a little nature trail and an unharvested cranberry bog beckon, but most guests enjoy rocking in chairs on the long veranda. The innkeepers, Kay and Bill DeFord (and their daughter Jill and son-in-law Jeff), include a full breakfast of perhaps sweet potato pancakes or eggs Florentine, enjoyed at individual tables in a pleasant dining room. Children 12 and older welcome. Mid-June to early September $225–330; off-season $120–190.

❋ ❀ ✿ **Bow Roof House** (508-945-1346), 59 Queen Anne Road. One reader wrote to chide me for not changing this write-up from the last edition. But after another inspection, these thoughts stand, with one preface: This inexpensive place is more popular with Europeans than Americans because Americans tend to expect too much from a place that costs a hundred bucks *in Chatham in the summer*. A 5-minute walk from town—and a 2-minute walk from the town beach—

Vera Mazulis's late-18th-century B&B is a real find and feels authentic with its antique beds, skeleton keys, and latch doors. Of the six guest rooms, I prefer the first-floor ones. Room 1 features an old beehive oven, antiques, and two double beds. The living room is dark but comfy; a continental breakfast is served at one table. Vera has owned this B&B since 1975 and welcomes children; since she's getting up there in age, her daughter-in-law Maryann helps out. May through September $95–105, off-season $85–95. No credit cards.

COTTAGES **Metters' Cottages** (508-432-3535), Chatharbor Lane, West Chatham. Open late May through October. These three water-view cottages are more like homes than cottages. Talk with George and Donna Metter about your needs when reserving; there's probably a cottage with your name on it. July to early September $1,500–2,200 weekly for a water-view three-bedroom; off-season $900–1,300. 3 night minimum stay off-season. Reservations are taken after November 1 for the upcoming summer.

MOTELS 🐾 ♿ "🍴" **Chatham Tides Waterfront Motel** (508-432-0379; chathamtides.com), 394 Pleasant Street, South Chatham. Open mid-May to mid-October. I can't say enough about this favored place. Delightfully off the well-trodden path and about 4 miles from the center of town, this quiet beachfront complex of 24 rooms and suites is a real find. It stands out for its view—alone worth the price. In Ellen and Ed Handel's family since 1966, they still maintain it with impressive care, continually upgrading, renovating, and paying attention to guest's needs. After staying here once, you'll probably return again

CHATHAM TIDES

and again. Try booking in February after the repeat guests get their pick of the litter in January. Rooms come with kitchenette, air-conditioning, and decks. Late June through August $230–290 daily, $1,500–1,900 weekly; off-season $195–240 daily, $1,250–1,550 weekly. Town houses in-season $1,950–2,600 weekly.

🐾 "🍴" **Hawthorne Motel** (508-945-0372; thehawthorne.com), 196 Shore Road. Open mid-May to mid-October. Not wanting to sound like a broken record, I can't say enough complimentary things about Gil and Ellie Mucher's motel either! Every time I stop in,

HAWTHORNE MOTEL

it feels like coming home. A 10-minute walk from Main Street, this motel is popular because nothing stands between it and the ocean except grass and a path to their private beach. *Nothing.* To be sure, the 10 efficiencies and cottages (with kitchens) provide delightfully easy access to sunning, swimming, and lazing on the beach. The16 motel rooms, renovated in 2006 to feature bathrooms with spanking white wainscoting and tile, are a great bargain. I particularly like the corner rooms, since they're much larger. Mid-May to mid-June, and early September through October, $185–210 nightly for rooms/efficiencies; mid-June to early September $260–295; $4,200 weekly for cottage; off-season $125–145 for rooms/efficiencies, $2,800 weekly for cottage. Four-night minimum in-season.

♂ ⅙ "⊺" **Pleasant Bay Village Resort Motel** (508-945-1133; 800-547-1011; pleasantbayvillage.com), 1191 Orleans Road, Route 28. Open May through October. Three miles from town, this tranquil place will forever change your opinion of a motel complex. It's a horticulturalist's delight, making them green with envy. The 6 acres of lush, Japanese-style landscaping and tasteful heated pool with a Jacuzzi are reason enough to recommend it—as is the extensive selection of 58 well-maintained rooms. Some have a sundeck, others overlook a cascading waterfall; some are spacious, others are snug; some have grills, some have fully equipped kitchens with stainless appliances; most have fabulously tiled bathrooms. The spacious lobby is filled with Oriental carpets and it's a great place to hang out on a rainy day, as is the airy breakfast room. Walk across the street and down Route 28 to Pleasant Bay Beach (see *Green Space*). Don't make the mistake of guests who book for 2 or 3 days and want to stay

for 5 or 6 (and can't because of limited availability.) Hats off to Judy Gamsey, owner since 1953. Late June to early September $155–265 rooms, $215–235 efficiencies, $235–285 suites for four. Inquire about weekly rates.

🐾 ♂ ⅙ "⊺" **Chatham Highlander** (508-945-9038; chathamhighlander .com), 946 Route 28. Open April through November. An excellent choice for budget-minded travelers, this favored motel, operated by Sean and Lori O'Connell, is just a stone's throw from the center of town. The two adjacent buildings sit on a little knoll above a well-traveled road. Each of the 29 rooms has a TV, small refrigerator, newly tiled bathroom, and air-conditioning; the one-bedroom apartment has a bonafide kitchen. The cheery rooms are sparkling white, freshened with new mattresses and spreads in 2003; other aspects are charmingly retro. There are also two heated pools. Mid-July to early September $159–209; off-season $89–179.

LIGHTHOUSE South Monomoy Lighthouse (508-945-0594, ext. 19; lighthousefriends.com). At press time, overnights were not permitted, but it's worth checking for this season. Late May to late September. Administered by the Cape Cod Museum of Natural History (see *To See* in "Brewster"), this 30-hour Monomoy Island overnight includes transportation to and from the island and time with a naturalist, who will cook your dinner by kerosene lamp. Breakfast and a substantial lunchtime snack are also included. The rustic keeper's house has three bedrooms with air mattresses and cots. This overnight is very popular; make reservations after mid-February, if you can.

RENTAL HOUSES AND COTTAGES

Sylvan Vacation Rentals (508-945-7222; sylvanrentals.com), 1715 Route 28, West Chatham.

Chatham Home Rentals (508-945-9444; chathamhomerentals.com), 1370 Route 28.

✳ Where to Eat

Dining options in Chatham run the gamut, from elegant to child-friendly places. Reserve ahead in summer (especially at *Dining Out* eateries) or be prepared for a lengthy wait.

DINING OUT ✎ ⍭ ♿ **twenty-eight Atlantic** (508-430-3000; wequassett .com), at Wequassett Resort and Golf Club, 2173 Route 28, Chatham (just over the Harwich town line, actually). Open for breakfast and dinner April through November. Who says some places are reserved only for "special occasions"? Not me. Not this place. At the Wequassett Resort's signature restaurant, I can't decide whether it's the water views (come before sunset to enjoy the view through floor-to-ceiling windows) or the food that reigns supreme. Hard to say, since they both rise above lofty expectations. Executive

TWENTY-EIGHT ATLANTIC

chef Bill Brodsky oversees the regional and contemporary American menu, full of artfully presented dishes packed with great flourishes and flavors. The seasonal menu is served ever-so-graciously on Limoges china in a genteel, understated, open, and elegant dining room—which has a nice buzz to it as the evening wears on. Lengthy recitations by an-oh-so professional waitstaff accompany and elevate each course. Service is seamless. Seafood is a specialty, of course, and everything we tried was spirited and ambitious; also consider the signature New York strip steak. And enjoy jazz on Tuesday and Wednesday evenings. Dinner $21–46.

Pisces (508-432-4600; piscesofchatham .com), 2653 Route 28, South Chatham. Open for dinner nightly late April to mid-October. A foodie's delight (since it opened in 2001) lies tucked inside an inconspicuous yellow cottage. This charming and contemporary bistro offers Mediterranean and coastal cuisine dishes like local cod sautéed in a spiced cornmeal crust with lemon caper aioli, toasted orzo pasta, and summer vegetables. The simple decor features local art on the walls, but the plates are anything but simple. It's always crowded here, and if they had twice the space, twice as many people would be salivating. Start with a mouthwatering cosmo. Dinner $23–30.

✳ **RooBar** (508-945-9988; the roobar .com), 907 Route 28. Open for dinner nightly mid-May to mid-October, Wednesday through Sunday off-season. With outlets in Falmouth and Hyannis, you may already be familiar with Roo-Bar. If not, you're in for a treat. The buzz, lighting, and decor are hip and happening—downright urbane for Cape Cod. The contemporary menu features generous portions of seafood dishes like crab-encrusted, wood-roasted Chatham cod. If you're not *that* hungry, try an appetizer of a lobster

BLT and a Caprese salad. Or there's always pizza and a microbrew. Early specials. Dinner $15–28.

❋ ✏ 🍸 ♿ **Impudent Oyster** (508-945-3545), 15 Chatham Bars Avenue. Open for lunch and dinner daily. Ask around about great places in Chatham, and this places is still at the top of everyone's list—even though it's been around since the mid-1970s. The atmosphere is certainly pleasant and almost rustic: peaked ceiling with exposed beams, skylights, and hanging plants. And the extensive menu highlights internationally inspired fish and shellfish dishes. Try the deservedly popular spicy Portuguese mussels, Nantucket scallop sandwich, or beer-battered fish-and-chips for lunch. If those don't appeal to you, follow the lead of the regulars (of which there are many) and order from the daily specials. Or have a burger at the everybody-knows-your-name lower bar. Lunch $8–13, dinner $18–27.

♿ **Vining's Bistro** (508-945-5033), 595 Main Street (on the second floor). Open for dinner May through November; call for off-season schedule. This bistro, one of the more adventurous and creative restaurants in the area, specializes in wood grilling. Try the spit-roasted grilled pork loin. While the menu roams the world, it is strongly influenced by the West Coast. Look for signature seasonal staples like warm lobster tacos, Thai crab cakes, skillet roasted Portuguese scrod, Thai beef salad, and pan-roasted sea scallops. Given its inauspicious location (on the second floor of an almost mini-mall), it's surprisingly romantic and quiet. Dinner $19–29.

❋ ✏ 🍸 **Chatham Bars Inn** (508-945-0096; chathambarsinn.com), Shore Road. Open for breakfast and dinner. CBI offers a number of dining options. The grand hotel's **veranda**, overlooking the ocean, makes a picture-perfect setting for a late-afternoon drink and/or a light meal. As for the other draws, panoramic ocean views and grand Sunday-night buffets ($88 adults, $33 children 5–12) in the main dining room are legendary. If you normally avoid buffets, break that rule here. The family-friendly **tavern** serves fireside lunches and dinners daily in a more casual atmosphere; panini, sandwiches, and salads go for $10–14. Otherwise, breakfast buffet $28 adults, $12 children; dinner $15–45. Long pants and collared shirt requested at dinner.

EATING OUT 🐾 ❋ ✏ 🍸 ♿ **Chatham Squire** (508-945-0945 restaurant; 508-945-0942 tavern; chathamsquire.com), 487 Main Street. Open for lunch and dinner daily. A friendly place, Chatham's best family restaurant offers something for everyone—from burgers and moderately priced daily seafood specials to a raw bar, multi-ethnic dishes, and excellent chowder. Paisley carpeting, low booths, captains' chairs at wooden tables, exposed beams, and pool tables (off-season only) add to the family-den feel of the place. Drop in for a drink in the busy and colorful tavern (a rowdy watering-hole haven for 20-somethings in summer until locals take it back for the off-season). One reader called it "the perfect lunch

OUTER BAR & GRILLE

place for what it is," and I couldn't agree more. There's karaoke on Tuesday evenings at 9:30. Lunch $8–18, dinner $13–30.

☿ **Outer Bar & Grille** (508-432-5400; wequassett.com), Pleasant Bay Road, Route 28, North Chatham (just over the Harwich town line, actually). Open for lunch and dinner mid-June to mid-September. If for no other reason, you should come for unrivaled ocean views. At the Wequassett Resort, this sophisticated and "smart casual" eatery is one of the Cape's few oceanside eateries, and the grille's porch is a great place to enjoy a lunchtime lobster roll, salad, grilled pizza or panini, or sandwich. They also have a few more serious seafood choices. Be careful or prices can add up quickly and it might not be worth it. On my last visit, the tuna was terrific but the Caesar salad didn't pass muster. Still, those view . . . Dishes $10–28.

✍ **Beach House Grill** (508-945-0096; chathambarsinn.com), Shore Road. Open for lunch daily and theme dinners most nights mid-June to mid-September. One of the Cape's few alfresco oceanside eateries, the grill's deck is anchored in the sand, overlooking a wide, golden beach. It rarely gets much better. The overpriced menu features upscale seaside standards: burgers, summer salads, lobster rolls ($17), peel-and-eat shrimp, and fried seafood platters. Popular dinners revolve around family-friendly themes like clam and lobster bakes or Caribbean night (where folks dress up in pirate garb.) There's live music nightly. Lunch $10–26, dinner theme nights $69–78 adults, $17–38 children age 5–12.

❄ ❦ **Marion's Pie Shop** (508-432-9439; marionspieshopofchatham.com), 2022 Route 28. Open 8–4 or 6 daily in summer; closed Monday off-season. Cindy and Blake Stearns's pies are a delicious alternative. (Marion's gone, but the recipes are better than ever!) You can't go wrong with the savory potpies (chock-full of chicken), seafood pies, beefsteak pies, sweet fruit pies (the bumbleberry knocks my socks off), or any of the breakfast baked goods. This humble but humming little house only has takeout. Come once and you'll come often. I'm a convert. Careful with the children; misbehaving ones "will be made into pies."

❄ ✐ ♿ **Wild Goose Tavern** (508-945-5550; wildgoosetavern.com), 512 Main Street. Open daily for all three meals; closed Monday night off-season. Because of its prominent in-town location and a constant parade of strollers-by, this pleasant room really packs in visitors. The streetside patio is pleasant. Sandwiches, salads, pizzas, panini dominate the eclectic midday menu. The indoor bar has a flat-screen TV when you need to catch a game or some breaking news. Breakfast $6–13, lunch $6–20, dinner $17–28.

❄ **The Corner Store** (508-432-1077; cape-burrito.com), 1403 Old Queen Anne Road. Open 6–6 daily. Sit on the front benches (or take to the beach because there's no where else to sit) and partake in grilled panini (turkey, cheddar, bacon, sun-dried tomato aioli, and baby spinach), burritos (built to order). Dishes $7.

❋ ✑ **Carmine's** (508-945-5300), 595 Main Street. Open for lunch and dinner. Quick and inexpensive, Carmine's offers very good traditional and gourmet pizzas (slices and whole pies).

❋ **Chatham Village Café** (508-945-2525; chathamvillagecafe.com), 400 Main Street. Open for 6–3 daily (even in during a snowstorm!). This upscale deli beckons with creative sandwiches for $8 and excellent cranberry nut muffins. There are a couple of picnic tables in front.

❋ **New England Pizza** (508-945-9070; newenglandpizza.net), 1200 Route 28, heading towards West Chatham. Open for lunch and dinner daily; closed Tuesday mid-September to mid-May. Most people think this is the best pizza place in town and I have no reason to disagree. Pies $11–18.

Lazy Lobster (508-945-0032), 247 Orleans Road (heading north on Route 28 towards the rotary). Open for breakfast and lunch April through November. If you're renting a house and don't feel like cooking, this casual eatery has some of the best breakfasts in town. Dishes $4–18.

❋ ✑ ⟨¶⟩ **Box Office Café** (508-430-5211), 2642 Route 28, South Chatham. Open 6 AM–9 PM daily. This hangout appeals to teens and their families, 20-somethings, and others in search of a funky place for coffee, vegan and vegetarian alternatives, a large screen TV (for movie viewing), and creative sandwiches and pizzas.

See also **Concerts** (lobster roll suppers) under *Entertainment*.

SPECIALTY OUTLETS **High Tea at The Captain's House Inn** (508-945-0127; captainshouseinn.com), 369–377 Old Harbor Road. This inn serves an exceptional afternoon tea to non-guests by reservation. With a vast assortment of savories and sweets, all beautifully presented, it's well worth $18 per person.

Nickerson's Fish and Lobsters (508-945-0145), at the Fish Pier on Shore Road. Open 9 AM–8 PM daily May through September. Without going out on the day boats yourself, it's hard to get fresher fish! Fried seafood, including a mélange of choices as well as the humble fish sandwich, $14–21.

❋ **Chatham Fish & Lobster Company** (508-945-1178; chathamfishand lobster.com), 1291 Route 28, Cornfield Market Place. For those of you with cooking facilities: They hook 'em, you cook 'em.

Nantucket Wild Gourmet (508-945-2700; nantucketwildgourmet.com), 1223 Route 28. Open daily mid-June to early September; call for off-season hours. It's pricey at this luxury food purveyor, but I dare you to find better smoked salmon anywhere. They're as wildly helpful as their salmon is wild. Tuna, haddock, and bluefish are also smoked, as are their pates and dips.

❋ **Chatham Natural Market** (508-945-4139; capecodnaturalmarkets .com), 1218 Route 28. Open daily. Organic and whole food, vitamins, and other natural products and literature.

❋ Entertainment

Monomoy Theatre (508-945-1589; monomoytheatre.org), 776 Main Street. Performances mid-June through August. Operated by Ohio University, the Monomoy is among the Cape's better-known and oldest (1930) playhouses. A new production—anything from a Rodgers and Hammerstein musical to Shakespeare—is staged every week. There isn't a bad choice among the 263 seats. Evening curtain at 8 or 8:30 (Tuesday through Saturday), matinees at 2 (Thursday).

🦞 ♪ **Concerts (lobster roll suppers)**, First United Methodist Church (508-945-0474), 569 Main Street at Cross Street. The church sponsors free choral, jazz, big-band, light classical, and a cappella concerts Sunday summer evenings at 8. Since the mid-1960s, the church has also held popular Friday lobster roll suppers at 4:30. Lobster prices vary with market conditions.

Bands. Locals flock to the **Chatham Squire** (see *Eating Out*) to hear live music off-season.

✳ Selective Shopping

❉ Although merchants and visitors loyal to Provincetown's Commercial Street may have something to say about it, Chatham's Main Street might be the Cape's best shopping street. Instead of organizing shops by category as I usually do, I list them here in the order you'll encounter them while strolling. Unless otherwise noted, all shops are open year-round. *Note, though, that many places listed as open year-round are open only on weekends in winter.*

West of the rotary

Chatham Glass Company (508-945-5547; chathamglass.com), 758 Main Street. James Holmes designs and creates unique, colorful glass items—candlesticks, platters, bud vases, and marbles—which are sold at Barneys, Neiman Marcus, and Gump's. The working studio is just behind the brilliantly lit displays, so you can watch the creative process of glassblowing.

Munson Gallery (508-945-2888), 880 Main Street. Open April through December. In the Munson family for four generations, this space is the oldest gallery in New England and has been showing fine paintings and sculpture by contemporary artists since 1955. The collection, with something for everyone in both price and taste, is housed in a wonderfully restored barn. Even the horse stalls are hung with art.

Ivy Cottage Shop (508-945-1809), 894 Main Street, Munson Meeting Complex. Buyer Peggy DeHan has a good eye for both vintage and new stuff—place settings, decorative home accessories, framed prints, painted furniture, and antique collectibles—that would look perfect in a country cottage or summerhouse. Pieces are generally affordable (unlike at many shops in Chatham). She haunts flea markets and scours the countryside so you don't have to.

1736 House Home Furnishings (508-945-5690), 1731 Route 28, West Chatham. It's worth stopping here simply to walk through Chatham's oldest house. But watch out: It's tantalizingly easy to spend money on period antiques shown in a period house! The English owners have also filled a series of barns with antiques and other items

TAKING A BREAK ON MAIN STREET

CHATHAM POTTERY

West Chatham. Two miles east of Routes 28 and 137, this colorful shop sells dozens of varieties of homemade jams and jellies. Feel free to taste them before committing. Try the wild beach plum, elderberry, or damson plum.

Maps of Antiquity (508-362-7169; mapsofantiquity.com), 1409 Main Street. These folks carry rare antique and reproduction maps of the 19th century and earlier, from around the world. If you want to know what the Cape or a specific town looked like 100 years ago, this shop will have a reproduction map that will tell you. It's a treasure trove.

East of the rotary
Main Street Pottery (508-945-0128), 645C Main Street. Barbara Parent works here, so you can watch her making pots similar to the one you're purchasing.

Yankee Ingenuity (508-945-1288), 525 Main Street. This eclectic assortment of "cool things" extends from glass and jewelry to clocks and lamps. Prices run $2–1,500. If you don't get something here the day you see it, it may be gone tomorrow.

Yellow Umbrella Books (508-945-0144), 501 Main Street. Owner Eric Linder has gathered a fine selection of Cape Cod titles and some used books,

like sturdy lobster-pot chairs, a unique marriage of form and function invented by a Chatham commercial fisherperson.

Chatham Pottery (508-430-2191; chathampottery.com), 2058 Route 28, South Chatham. Gill Wilson and Margaret Wilson-Grey's large studio offers a wide array of functional, decorative stoneware—hand-thrown pots, pitchers, sinks, plates, bowls, tiles, and tables.

Chatham Jam and Jelly Shop (508-945-3052; chathamjamandjellyshop .com), 10 Vineyard Avenue, Route 28,

---

NOSTALGIA REIGNS

✒ **Band concerts at Kate Gould Park**, off Main Street. Every Friday night at 8, late June to late August, this brass-band concert is the place to be. Upwards of 6,000 lighthearted visitors enjoy music and people-watching as they have for the past 60 years. Dance and swing to Sousa marches, big-band selections, and other standards. The bandstand, balloons tied to strollers, bags of popcorn, blankets on the grass (set yours out at 10 AM for the best position), and the Star-Spangled Banner finale—it hasn't changed a "whit" since it began. (Except that beloved Whit Tileston, who led the band for almost 50 years, passed away in 1995.)

too, for all ages and interests. "Long-live-the-independents!"

Wynne/Falconer Gallery (508-945-2867), 492 Main Street. The gallery represents over 40 contemporary American artists, and many different Cape scenes are available in lithograph, and original oil paintings, too.

Mark August Designs (508-945-2600), 490 Main Street. Functional and fun, creative and artsy decorative items for your house. Jewelry, too.

Chatham Candy Manor (508-945-0825), 484 Main Street. They've been making hand-dipped chocolate, fudge, and liqueur-flavored truffles since 1955.

♪ **The Mayflower** (508-945-0065), 475 Main Street. Established in 1885, this venerable, old-time general store has joined the modern era (almost) on swanky Main Street.

Artful Hand Gallery (508-945-5681), 459 Main Street. This is one of the best artistic craft galleries in New England.

Demos Antiques, Ltd. (508-945-

DEMOS ANTIQUES, LTD.

1939), 447 Main Street. You can't miss this place; a trove of funky treasures spill out onto the front lawn. Run by Peter and Cynthia Demos, the shop has been a family-owned business since 1956. If they don't have it, you don't need it.

Odell's Studio and Gallery (508-945-3239), 423 Main Street. Tom and Carol Odell, metalsmith and painter, respectively, have lived and worked in their lovely old home since 1975. Carol does colorful nonobjective, multimedia paintings, monotypes, oils, and encaustic. Her work complements Tom's jewelry and sculpture, which he fashions from precious metals and alloys. Tom's recent work shows evidence of a Japanese aesthetic. This remains my favorite shop in town.

♪ **Mermaids on Main** (508-945-3179), 410 Main Street. Open late May through December. Kids love this colorful place, bursting at the seams with purple- and aquamarine-colored playthings. Books, bubble bath, candles, mobiles, mermaids, and stuffed and rubber creatures.

♪ "†" **Where the Sidewalk Ends** (508-945-0499; wherethesidewalkends.booksense.com), 432 Main Street. Open daily. This is one of the best independent bookstores I've encoun-

tered in years. From outdoor and fireside seating and children's story hours to coffee-with-the-author book signings and a great staff, this airy place has it all.

✳ Special Events

July 4: **Independence Day Parade** from Main Street to Veterans Field; **strawberry festival** with shortcake at the First United Methodist Church (16 Cross Street) post parade.

Late July/Early August: **Antique Show**. Since the mid-1950s; held at the Chatham Elementary School, Depot Road; $5.

Mid-August: **Chatham Festival of the Arts**, Chase Park. Since 1970. On the third weekend in August, the Creative Arts Center sponsors more than 100 exhibitors, from painters to quilters to sculptors (see *To Do*).

Late November–December: **Christmas by the Sea and Christmas Stroll**. This annual event includes a tree-lighting ceremony, candy-cane-making demonstrations, caroling, mulled cider

ODELL'S STUDIO AND GALLERY

served at the Mayo House (see *To See*), hayrides, open houses, and much more.

New Year's Eve: **First Night Celebration**. Fireworks over Oyster Pond. Chatham limits the number of buttons sold to residents and visitors so the town won't be overrun.

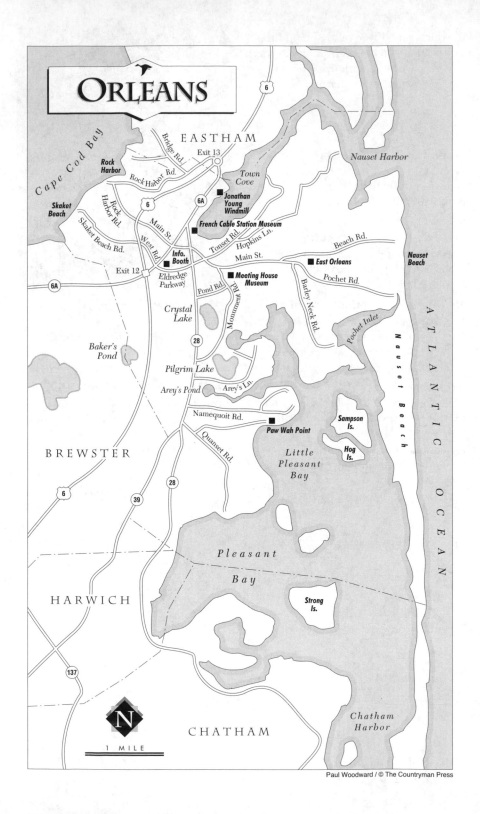

ORLEANS

EASTHAM

Cape Cod Bay

Rock Harbor

Skaket Beach

Exit 13

Town Cove

Nauset Harbor

Bridge Rd.

Rock Harbor Rd.

Jonathan Young Windmill

French Cable Station Museum

Rock Harbor Rd.

Main St.

West Rd.

Skaket Beach Rd.

Info. Booth

Exit 12

Eldredge Parkway

Crystal Lake

Baker's Pond

Pond Rd.

Monument Rd.

Pilgrim Lake

Arey's Pond

Arey's Ln.

Namequoit Rd.

Quanset Rd.

BREWSTER

Paw Wah Point

Little Pleasant Bay

Pleasant

Bay

HARWICH

Strong Is.

Tonset Rd.

Hopkins Ln.

Main St.

East Orleans

Meeting House Museum

Beach Rd.

Nauset Beach

Pochet Rd.

Barley Neck Rd.

Pochet Inlet

Sampson Is.

Hog Is.

Nauset Beach

ATLANTIC OCEAN

Chatham Harbor

CHATHAM

N

1 MILE

Paul Woodward / © The Countryman Press

ORLEANS

Many could argue, with some success, that Orleans's biggest draw is Nauset Beach, an Atlantic Ocean barrier beach more than 9 miles long. It can accommodate hundreds of sun seekers and sand-castle builders in summer. But in the off-season, you'll be practically alone, walking in quiet reflection, observing shorebirds and natural rhythms. It's a beautifully haunting place during a storm— so long as it's not a huge storm. Nauset Beach also has historical significance. Gosnold explored it in 1602 and Champlain in 1605. It was the location of the first recorded shipwreck on the eastern seaboard, in 1626, when the Sparrow Hawk ran aground near Pochet. It is the only place in the continental United States to be fired upon in the War of 1812 (by the British) and in World War I (in 1918 it was shelled by a German submarine). More recently, two Englishmen set off from nearby Nauset Harbor to row successfully across the Atlantic Ocean.

The real charm of Orleans, which has few historical sights, lies not in the sand but in the waters that surround the town. A large number of fingerlike inlets creep into the eastern shoreline from aptly named Pleasant Bay, dotted with tiny islands. And most of these quiet inlets are accessible via back roads and town landings. Excursion boats explore the rich habitat of Nauset Marsh to the north, while bayside, Rock Harbor is home to the Cape's most active charter fishing fleet.

Because Routes 6, 6A, and 28 converge in Orleans, traffic is heavy in summer; getting anywhere takes time. But Orleans straddles the two distinct worlds of the Outer Cape and the Lower Cape. On the one hand, Orleans serves as a year-round commercial and retail center for the area. It offers plenty of activities and a variety of dining and lodging options. On the other hand, Orleans has its share of exclusive residential areas and plenty of quiet, waterside spots. In the summer, Orleans balloons to a population of about 22,000 from its year-round count of 6,500.

Orleans is the only Cape town without a Native American or English name. Incorporated in 1797 after separating from Eastham, Orleans was named for Louis-Philippe de Bourbon, duke of Orléans (and later king of France), who sojourned here in 1797 during his exile.

GUIDANCE ⁱⁱⁱ Orleans Chamber of Commerce Information Booth (508-255-1386; 800-865-1386; capecod-orleans.com), Eldredge Park Way (exit 12 off Route 6A). Booth open 10–6 Monday through Saturday and 11–3 Sunday, late May to mid-October. The administrative office, at 44 Main Street, is open 10–2 weekdays year-round. Orleans publishes a helpful booklet and an excellent free map.

PUBLIC RESTROOMS At the information booth and 44 Main Street.

PUBLIC LIBRARY ❄ ✐ ⸙ '♦' **Snow Library** (508-240-3760; snowlibrary.org), 67 Main Street at Route 28. Open Monday through Saturday year-round and Sundays 2–4 from November to March.

See also **The Hot Chocolate Sparrow** under *Where to Eat.*

GETTING THERE *By car:* Take Route 6 east from the Cape Cod Canal for about 48 miles to Exit 12. Route 6A East takes you directly into town.

By bus: The **Plymouth & Brockton** bus line (508-778-9767; p-b.com) connects Orleans with Hyannis and other Cape towns, as well as with Boston's Logan Airport. It only stops at the CVS on Main Street.

GETTING AROUND East Orleans Village and Nauset Beach are 3 miles east of Orleans center (which stretches along Route 6A); Rock Harbor and Skaket Beach are 1.5 miles west of the center.

By shuttle: The **H₂O** (508-790-2613; 800-352-7155; capecodtransit.org) bus, used more by locals than visitors, travels Route 28 between the Hyannis Transportation Center and Orleans daily in the summer. It makes about five stops in Orleans; call for locations. It also will stop anywhere along Route 28 as long as you flag the driver down. It'll take about an hour to get from Orleans to Hyannis.

MEDICAL EMERGENCY Orleans Medical Center (508-255-9577), 225 Route 6A or Exit 12 off Route 6. Walk-ins 8–3:30 weekdays, 8–noon on Saturdays during the summer.

✹ To See

⸙ **Meeting House Museum** (508-240-1329; orleanshistoricalsociety.org), at Main and School streets. Open 10–1 Thursday through Saturday, mid-June through September. Built in 1833 as a Universalist meetinghouse, and now operated by the Orleans Historical Society, the museum contains artifacts documenting Orleans's early history. Among the items are an assessor's map of Orleans homes in 1858, photographs, Native American artifacts, and a bicentennial quilt. The building itself is a fine example of Greek Revival Doric architecture. Down at Rock Harbor,

the museum also has a Coast Guard rescue boat that was used during a 1952 shipwreck off the Chatham coast. That 32 people piled into this tiny boat is beyond belief. You can board the boat; a tour schedule is posted on-site. Free.

ʈ French Cable Station Museum (508-240-1735; frenchcablestation museum.org), Route 28 at Cove Road. Open 1–4 Thursday through Sunday, July and August; 1–4 Friday through Sunday, June and September. Before the advent of the "information super-highway" and wireless communications, there was the French Cable Station. Direct transmissions from Brest, France (via a 3,000-mile under-water cable), were made from this station between 1890 and 1941, at which time transmissions were automated.

JONATHAN YOUNG WINDMILL

Among the relayed news items: Charles Lindbergh's successful crossing of the Atlantic and his 1927 Paris landing, and Germany's invasion of France. Much of the original equipment and instruments are still set up and in working order. (Alas, the cable is no longer operational.) The displays, put together with the help of the Smithsonian Institution, are a bit intimidating, but someone is on hand to unravel the mysteries. Free.

Jonathan Young Windmill (508-240-1329; orleanshistoricalsociety.org), 27–33 Route 6A at Windmill Park Conservation Area. Open 11–3 daily, late June to early September. This circa-1720 gristmill was built in South Orleans, transported to the center of town in 1839, moved to Hyannisport in 1897, and returned to Orleans in 1987. Although it's no longer operational, the windmill is significant because of its intact milling machinery. Inside, you'll find interpretive exhibits including a display of a 19th-century miller's handiwork, as well as a guide who might explain the origins of "keep your nose to the grindstone." (Because grain is highly combustible when it's ground, a miller who wasn't paying close attention to his grain might not live to see the end of the day.) The setting, overlooking Town Cove, provides a nice backdrop for a picnic. Free.

ROCK HARBOR

Rock Harbor, on Cape Cod Bay, at the end of Rock Harbor Road from Main Street. This protected harbor, the town's first commercial and maritime center, served as a packet landing for ships transporting goods to Plymouth, Boston, and Maine. When

A PERFECT DAY IN ORLEANS

8:00 Get buttery delights from Cottage St. Bakery or The Hot Chocolate Sparrow.

9:00 Kayak around Pleasant Bay or Nauset Marsh.

12:00 Order a simple fish feast at Cap't Cass Rock Harbor Seafood.

1:00 Read a trashy novel (or existential poetry) at the 9-mile-long Nauset Beach on the Atlantic Ocean.

5:30 Enjoy a highly sophisticated, creative dinner at ABBA.

8:00 Listen to twilight at Rock Harbor while watching the fishing fleet return for the day.

10:00 Enjoy a nightcap at the convivial Joe's Beach Road Bar & Grille.

the harbor filled with silt, several old houses in the area were built from the lumber of dismantled saltworks. During the War of 1812, Orleans militiamen turned back Britain's HMS *Newcastle* from Rock Harbor. And what about those dead trees in the water? They mark the harbor channel that is dredged annually for the charter fishing fleet. This is a popular sunset spot for watching the boats come in, if you can tolerate the bugs.

SCENIC DRIVES Pleasant Bay, Little Pleasant Bay, Nauset Harbor, and Town Cove creep deep into the Orleans coastline at about a dozen named inlets, ponds, and coves. With the detailed centerfold map from the Orleans Chamber of Commerce guide in hand (see *Guidance*), head down the side roads off Tonset Road, Hopkins Lane, Nauset Heights Road, and Barley Neck Road to the town landings. After passing beautifully landscaped residences, you'll be rewarded with serene, pastoral scenes of beach grass and sailboats. Directly off Route 28 heading toward Chatham there are two particularly lovely ponds with saltwater outlets: **Arey's Pond** (off Arey's Lane from Route 28) and **Kescayogansett Pond** (off Monument Road from Route 28). There's a little picnic area with limited parking at **Kent's Point** near here, off Frost Fish Lane from Monument Road.

✳ To Do

BASEBALL ✐ **The Orleans Cardinals** (508-255-0793; orleanscardinals.com) play ball at Eldredge Park Field, off Route 28 at Eldredge Park Way, from mid-June to early August. Their clinics for boys and girls age 6–13 begin in late June. As many as 60 or 70 kids might show up, but there is always a good ratio of player-instructors to kids. The cost is $70 for the first week, $20 per day.

BICYCLING/RENTALS ✐ **The Cape Cod Rail Trail** runs near the center of town, right past **Orleans Cycle** (508-255-9115), 26 Main Street, which is open April through December. Expect to spend about $14 for 4 hours, $18 daily, $50 for 3 days; less for little kids' bikes.

BOAT EXCURSIONS 🦆 🐟 **Nauset Marsh Cruise** (508-349-2615; wellfleetbay.org), Town Cove, behind Goose Hummock, off Route 6A. Mid-June to mid-October. Sponsored by the Wellfleet Bay Wildlife Sanctuary, these 2-hour pontoon voyages do not depart daily, so it's best to call for departure times and days. Adult trips focus on birding and the natural history of the marsh and depart with high tides; kids' trips are synced with low tide, all the better for interactive exploration. Along with informative onboard interpretation, kids haul traps, unearth worms and steamers, and participate in scavenger hunts. Trips $25–40.

LOW TIDE ON NAUSET MARSH

BOWLING ❄ 🐟 ☂ **Orleans Bowling Center** (508-255-0636; orleansbowl.com), 191 Route 6A. Okay, so you didn't come to the Cape to go bowling, but if it's raining and you've got kids in the car, it's an idea.

FISHING/SHELLFISHING Pick up freshwater fishing permits at **Goose Hummock** (508-255-0455; goose.com), 15 Route 6A on Town Cove. Then head to **Crystal Lake**, off Monument Road (see *Green Space*), which has perch, trout, and bass. There are also a dozen fresh- and saltwater town landings in Orleans. Contact the town clerk (508-240-3755), Route 28, Orleans, about a shellfishing permit and regulations before you head out with your shovel, rake, and bucket.

❄ **Goose Hummock** (508-255-0455; goose.com), Town Cove, 15 Route 6A at the rotary. This outfitter fulfills all fishing-related needs, including rod rentals, fishing trips, instruction, and wintertime fly-tying seminars. Shellfishing equipment, too. The great staff offers lots of free advice and information.

🐟 **Rock Harbor Charter Fleet** (508-255-9757; rockharborcharters.com), Rock Harbor. Trips daily mid-May to mid-October. These 13, U.S. Coast Guard–licensed captains and boats make up the largest charter fleet in New England. All offer 4- and 8-hour trips for groups in search of bluefish and striped bass. Children welcome; call for prices.

ROCK HARBOR CHARTER FLEET

FITNESS CENTER ❄ 🐟 **Willy's Gym and Fitness Center** (508-255-6826; willysgym.com), 21 Old Colony Way, off West Road from Route 6A, Orleans Marketplace. Open daily. One of the Cape's best fitness centers,

Willy's has an extensive array of cardiovascular machines, free weights, sauna and steam rooms, classes, a juice bar, and supervised childcare. $17 daily, $59 weekly.

MINI-GOLF *⌗* **Cape Escape** (508-240-1791), 8 Canal Road, off Route 6A near the Orleans rotary. Open seasonally.

SAILING *⌗* **Arey's Pond Boat Yard** (508-255-0994, 508-255-7900 sailing school; areyspondboatyard.com), Arey's Lane off Route 28, South Orleans. Late May to early September. They offer 10 hours of beginning and intermediate sailing instruction over the course of five weekdays for $240. Group and private lessons by appointment.

SKATEBOARDING *⌗* **Jean Finch Skateboard Park**, located on the middle school fields, 70 Route 28; $5 fee; helmets required.

SKATING ✻ *⌗* **Charles Moore Arena** (508-255-2971; charlesmoorearena.org), 23 O'Connor's Way; look for signs near the information booth (see *Guidance*). Although this big arena is reserved most of the year, public skating times are set aside; call them. Every Friday 8–10 PM year-round is Rock Night, when the strobe-lit rink is reserved for 9- to 14-year-olds.

SPECIAL PROGRAMS ✻ *⌗* **Academy of Performing Arts** (508-255-5510; apa1.org), 5 Giddiah Hill Road. The academy offers instruction (to all ages) in dance, fitness, music, and theater. Their weekly July and August sessions (concentrating on musical theater, ballet, and drama production) culminate with a performance. Children's summer matinees are held Friday and Saturday at 10 AM at the playhouse.

Recreational Department (508-240-3785), 44 Main Street, offers instructional tennis for adults and children, swimming lessons, and more. Call for schedule details and registration.

SURFING **Nauset Surf** (508-255-4742; nausetsports.com), Jeremiah Square, Route 6A at the Orleans rotary. Open April through January, but rentals are only provided in-season: surfboards, paddleboards, skimboards, boogie boards, and wet suits.

TENNIS You'll find three public courts at **Eldredge Park** (off Route 28 at Eldredge Park Way) and three at the **elementary school** (off Eldredge Park Way). Seasonal fees.

See also the **Recreational Department** under *To Do*.

CANOEING AND KAYAKING

The protected, calm waters of northern **Pleasant Bay** offer delightful paddling opportunities. And the folks at **Goose Hummock** (508-255-2620; goose.com), off Route 6A on Town Cove, are the experts in this neck of the bay. Talk to them about Southern Pleasant Bay, for instance; it can be tricky for the uninitiated. Pick up the Nauset Harbor tide chart and rent a canoe or recreational kayak ($25 for 3 hours, $50 daily, $200 weekly; more for big touring sea kayaks). For 24-hour rentals, the center throws in a loaner roof rack. Parking is limited at the town landings, but it's free. If you're new to kayaking, take their 3-hour introductory course ($65) to learn basic paddle strokes and skills.

Otherwise, they have a huge array of other courses and specialty tours: intro to kayaking, tidal currents and navigation, open-water kayaking, sunrise tours, kids in kayaks, and more.

✳ Green Space

BEACHES ✍ ⅙ **Nauset Beach** (508-240-3780), on the Atlantic Ocean, off Beach Road, beyond the center of East Orleans. It doesn't get much better than this: good bodysurfing waves and 7 miles of sandy Atlantic shoreline, backed by a low dune. (Only about a half-mile stretch is covered by lifeguards; much of the rest is deserted.) A gently sloping grade makes this a good beach for children. Facilities include an in-season lifeguard on weekends, restrooms, a snack bar, a boardwalk over dunes, outside showers, chairs and umbrellas for rent, and plenty of parking (parking is rarely a problem). Parking costs $15 daily for nonresidents or renters, $50 weekly for Orleans renters, mid-June to early September; $5 late May to

NAUSET BEACH

PIRATE ADVENTURES

mid-June and off-season holiday weekends. It's free after 4:30.

Four-wheel-drive vehicles with permit are allowed onto Nauset Beach. Certain areas, though, may be restricted during bird breeding and nesting periods. Obtain permits at Old American Legion Hall, Main Street, 9–4 Thursday through Monday, in-season. Off-season, by appointment only, head to the Parks and Beaches Department (508-240-3775), 18 Bay Ridge Lane.

✍ ⚕ **Skaket Beach** on Cape Cod Bay, off West Road. Popular with families, as you can walk a mile out into the bay at low tide; at high tide the beach grass is covered. The parking lot often fills up early, creating a 30-minute wait for a space. Parking $15 daily from mid-June to early September. (The parking fee is transferable to Nauset Beach on the same day; free after 4:30.) Facilities include an in-season lifeguard, a bike rack, restrooms, a boardwalk, outside showers, and a snack bar.

Pleasant Bay Beach, Route 28, South Orleans. A saltwater bayside inlet beach with limited roadside parking.

PONDS Crystal Lake (off Monument Road and Route 28) and **Pilgrim Lake** (off Herring Brook Road from Route 28) are both good for swimming. Pilgrim Lake has an in-season lifeguard, restrooms, changing rooms, picnic tables, a dock, and a small beach; parking stickers only. At Crystal Lake, parking is free but limited; no facilities.

WALKS AND PICNICS Paw Wah Point Conservation Area, off Namequoit Road from Eldredge Park Way, has a loop trail leading to a nice little beach with picnic tables.

Rhododendron Display Garden, Route 28 and Main Street. A nice place for a picnic.

Sea Call Farm, Tonset Road, just north of the intersection with Main Street. Overlooking Town Cove, this is another fine picnic spot.

✳ Lodging

✤ Lodging in Orleans is a very good value. You'll find everything from super-stellar and friendly B&Bs to almost-beachfront motels and family motor inns.

RESORT MOTOR INN
✳ ✍ **The Cove** (508-255-1203; 800-343-2233; thecoveorleans.com), 13 Route 28, Orleans. This modest complex of 47 rooms and suites is situated on the waterfront along Town Cove and

close to bike paths. Pluses include a free boat tour of Town Cove and Nauset Beach; an outdoor heated pool; a dock for sunning and fishing; and picnic tables and grills that are well situated to exploit the view. Deluxe rooms (redecorated in 2003) have a sitting area and sofa bed; most waterfront rooms have a shared deck overlooking the water; two-room suites have a kitchen (some with a fireplace and private deck); all rooms have TV/DVD, fridge, and coffeemaker; and inn rooms have a bit more decor (some also have a fireplace and private deck). Children under 16, free in parent's room, but keep in mind that it's tough to fit more than four in a room. Late June through September $119–224; off-season $109–154.

BED & BREAKFASTS

⁋ A Little Inn on Pleasant Bay (508-255-0780; alittleinnonpleasant-bay.com), 654 Route 28, South Orleans. Open May to late October. Well, well, well. This marvelously and tastefully renovated place could easily be dubbed "A Little Slice of Heaven on High." The European innkeepers (Sandra, Pamela, and Bernd) have transformed this 1798 house into a priceless diamond with commanding views of Pleasant Bay and a thoroughly contemporary

6A LITTLE INN ON PLEASANT BAY

NAUSET HOUSE INN

aesthetic. Furthermore, no other B&B on the Cape comes close to matching their bountiful, European buffet breakfast—especially when it's taken outside in summer. Formerly a stop on the Underground Railroad, the main house has plenty of common space, including a big living room with windows all around. It's all quite conducive to luxuriating. Guest rooms feature white-washed barnboard and lovely bathroom tilework; some have private decks or patio. Blue stone patios grace the front and back yards, which are beautifully landscaped. The Bay Rooms (carved from a former paddock) and the Carriage House have also been renovated with similar doses of grace and style. Late-afternoon sherry and access to a private beach and dock are all included. Children over 10 welcome. Mid-May to early September $230–300 rooms; off-season $215–275 rooms.

⁋ Nauset House Inn (508-255-2195; 800-771-5508; nausethouseinn.com), Beach Road, East Orleans. Open mid-April through October. These 14 rooms (8 with private bath) have a lot going for them. The inn has genuinely hospitable hosts; it's half a mile from Nauset Beach; guest rooms are thoughtfully and tastefully appointed; afternoon drinks and cheese are a treat; and a greenhouse conservatory is just one of the many quiet places to relax. You'll have Diane Johnson, her daughter Cindy, and son-in-law John to thank: They've owned and constantly upgraded the 1810 farmhouse since 1982. Rooms in the carriage house are generally larger than inn rooms, while the rustic cottage, with peaked ceiling, is quite private and cozy. There's immense attention to detail here. Rooms $85–175; full breakfast included. One single room rents for $65.

✳ ❝❡❞ **Parsonage Inn** (508-255-8217; 888-422-8217; parsonageinn.com), 202 Main Street, East Orleans. Guests are quite happy here. This very pleasant, rambling, late-18th-century house has eight guest rooms comfortably furnished with country antiques. (Only two rooms have adjoining walls, so there is plenty of privacy.) Wide-pine floors, canopy beds, and newly redone bathrooms are common. Willow, the studio apartment, has a kitchenette and private entrance, while the roomy Barn, recently renovated with exposed beams and eaves, has a sitting area and sofa bed. Longtime innkeepers Elizabeth and Ian Browne, who hail from

PARSONAGE INN

England, serve a full breakfast at individual tables or on the brick patio. On my last visit, it was cheese soufflé, but you might also get lucky with ginger pancakes. Don't miss the convivial afternoon wine and cheese. June through September $135–180; otherwise $95–150.

✳ ❝❡❞ **Morgan's Way** (508-255-0831; morganswaybandb.com), Morgan's Way, Orleans. This is a quiet find, off the beaten path. Page McMahan and Will Joy opened their contemporary home, about a mile south of town, to guests in 1990. Lush landscaping extends across 5 acres, and a multilevel deck wraps around a 20-by-40-foot heated pool. The delightful poolside guesthouse is bright and modern, with a full kitchen and private deck. Inside the main house, one of the two guest rooms has a small, attached greenhouse, but both rooms share the second-floor living room, complete with TV, VCR, and wood-burning stove. Full breakfast included. Inquire about the Joy's 3-bedroom, 3½-bath custom-built **Hillsdale House** available weekly year-round; it's a bargain and includes use of the B&B pool. Otherwise, rooms $175 May through October. Cottage $1,400 weekly June through September; $1,100 May and October; $900 off-season. No credit cards.

✳ **Orleans Inn** (508-255-2222; 800-863-3039; orleansinn.com), 21 Route 6A. Near the Orleans rotary and with a crisp mansard roof, this inn commands a prominent position as you enter town. You can't miss it. Ed and Laurie Mass's 11 rooms and suites are a pleasant surprise, made more so by the inn's friendly policies: there is no cancellation fee, no deposit required, and they accept one-nighters in the summer. That might lead you to believe that there's something wrong with the rooms, but there isn't. Not at all. Rooms are located off a long hallway, and they're quite pleasant and include cable TV, refrigerator, and continental breakfast. Half overlook Nauset Bay; for $50 more, you obviously want one of these (which also have a fireplace)! Full breakfast included. Rooms $175–225, more for suites.

MOTELS ⟨ **Nauset Knoll Motor Lodge** (508-255-2364), 237 Beach Road, East Orleans. Open mid-April to mid-October. Nauset Knoll, a few steps from Nauset Beach, is often booked long before other places because of the expansive views of dune and ocean. You can watch the sun as it rises over the ocean from lawn chairs atop the lodge's namesake knoll. The 12 simply furnished rooms (à la 1950s) with large picture windows are in three separate units, distinctively modeled after a barn, shed, and Cape-style cottage. Mid-June to early September $185; off-season $120–145.

RENTAL HOUSES AND COTTAGES **The Real Estate Company** (508-255-5100; capecodvacation.com), 207 Main Street, East Orleans.

See also **Morgan's Way**, under Bed & Breakfasts.

✳ Where to Eat

Orleans has an excellent variety of restaurants.

DINING OUT ✳ ⟨ **ABBA** (508-255-8144; abbarestaurant.com), 89 Old Colony Way. Open for dinner. If I had to eat at only one restaurant for an *entire* week, I'd be thrilled if it were ABBA. It's my kind of food and my kind of setting—soothing. Serving contemporary and sophisticated Mediterranean food (with a Thai flair), ABBA would be perfectly at home in Boston's

TABLE FOR TWO AT ABBA

South End or New York's SoHo. Since it burst onto the scene in 2001, it's taken this part of the Cape by storm. Chef-owner Erez Pinhas and his front-of-the-house partner, Christina Bratberg, have a flair for creating mod spaces and inviting plates. The urbane menu changes quite often, but look for the luscious likes of black sea bass with fava beans, grilled foie gras with creamy lentils, or an ab-fab falafel with Israeli salsa in a tahini amba sauce. House specialties include a sublime shrimp, curries, or organic tofu pad Thai. The wine list is impressive and desserts are lovely: The poached strawberries and rhubarb in a shredded phyllo is killer. Dinner $8–34.

✳ ⟨ **Joe's Beach Road Bar & Grille** (508-255-0212; barleyneck .com), Beach Road, East Orleans. Open for dinner. Joe's *gets it*—both for atmosphere *and* cuisine. Joe's has a delightful split personality: One side has almost-formal dining, one is almost reserved for families, and the other is an hopping (upscale-ish) bar-happy place with barnboard walls and a large fieldstone fireplace. Your choice merely depends on your mood since both sides offer the same well-executed menu by Christian Schultz (a longtime renowned area chef.) I've eaten here often and always enjoyed it. As Joe and Kathi work the room with great ease, locals continue to flock here even as the summer crowds swell. That says all you need to know. Look for lobster prepared five different ways, lots of New American seafood dishes prepared with flair, as well as dishes featuring veggies from their organic garden. (Since my last visit, I still dream about their house vinaigrette and sublime beet salad.) Braised lamb shank with garlic mashed potatoes is always terrific. For lighter appetites and thinner wallets, there's pizza, pasta, soup, and main-course salads. Their crème brûlée defines perfection. Dinner $13–25.

❄ **Nauset Beach Club** (508-255-8547; nausetbeachclub.com), 222 Main Street, East Orleans. Open for dinner nightly. Neither a club nor on the beach, this buzzy bistro has a warm and welcoming feeling, thanks to proprietor Arthur Duquette and Chef Andrej Klimovsky. For Northern Italian cuisine, featuring local seafood, homemade pastas, and plenty of meat and game dishes, it has few rivals. On my last visit, the *ravioli di zuccaro et ricotta*, *risotto del giorno*, *carre d'agnello arrosto* (lamb), and daily special of sea bass were all executed with aplomb. Although tables are set with linens, crystal, and china, it has a relaxed atmosphere thanks to the warming fireplace and friendly service. The wine list is quite impressive. I enjoy this place more each season. Primi and Secondi $18–30.

❄ ✿ ￥ **Mahoney's Atlantic Bar & Grill** (508-255-5505; mahoneysatlantic .com), 28 Main Street. Open for dinner. Consistent and appealing across-the-board, this cozy storefront bistro serves a surprisingly sophisticated menu. It's firing on all cylinders. You can expect contemporary New Ameri-

can dishes like pan-roasted lobster, tuna sashimi, and roasted chicken. During my last visit the striped bass tasted like it was just off the boat. Salads, creative pasta dishes, and a few veggies dishes round out the choices. It's hard to go wrong here. Their lively and upscale martini bar (where you can get lighter dishes) also sports a few satellite TVs, all the better to catch a Sox game. The place is packed in the winter, which is always a good sign. Watch for live entertainment intermittently throughout the year. Bar menu $7–12, dinner $18–28.

🦞 **Captain Linnell House** (508-255-3400; linnell.com), 137 Skaket Beach Road. Open for dinner April tom mid-February. For a truly lovely dining experience, let chef-owner Bill Conway's fine fare match the gracious ease of this former sea captain's mansion. The traditional dining is romantic, with candles, fine china, and linens. One dining room overlooks a small water garden; the salon overlooks the side garden. Start with fabulous chowder or lobster bisque and move to scrod in parchment with crab and shrimp or roasted pork tenderloin. Rack of lamb specials are always popular. Chef Con-

CAPTAIN LINNELL HOUSE

way will also dish out small portions for children with refined palates. If you're seated by 5:30, you'll receive a complimentary lobster bisque or chowder and dessert with your dinner. It's one of the best deals in the land! Bill and his wife, Shelly, have owned and been restoring this gem since 1988. Dinner $21–32.

❄ 🐾 **The Beacon Room** (508-255-2211; beaconroom.com), 23 West Road. Open for lunch and dinner. For casual fine dining on the way to Skaket Beach, this intimate bistro offers sizable portions of well-presented dishes at reasonable prices. Dinnertime dishes range from pasta and lamb (quite popular) to seafood and chicken saltimbocca. Sandwiches and burgers are offered at lunch. Lunch $7–14, dinner $16–24.

EATING OUT Cap't Cass Rock Harbor Seafood, Rock Harbor. Open 11–2 and 5–8 daily except Tuesday in July and August; 11–2 and 5–8 on Friday and Saturday, 11–2 on Sunday, from mid-April to June and September to mid-October. Straight out of a movie set, with everything except the prices preserved, this classic harborside lobster shack is adorned with colorful buoys on the outside and checkered tables on the inside. As for

the food, it's a cut above: The lobster roll ($16) hasn't a shred of lettuce or breading in it; the she-crab stew ($7) is outrageously delectable; and the homemade chowder ($8) and fish-and-chips ($14) are pretty darn good, too. (On my last visit, though, the onion rings and "regular" fish weren't as good as other offerings.) The menu is posted on cardboard, as it has been done since 1958. There really is an 80-something-year old Captain Cass, by the way: George Cass, his wife, Betty, and their daughter Sue run the place. Lunch $9–18, dinner $15–30. BYOB. No credit cards.

❄ 🐾 ✂ 🍸 **Land Ho!** (508-255-5165; land-ho.com), 38 Route 6A. Open 11:30 AM—1 AM daily. A favorite local

CAP'T CASS ROCK HARBOR SEAFOOD

hangout since 1969 (with lines out the door in the summertime), John Murphy's place is very colorful (literally), from red-and-white-checked tablecloths, to old business signs hanging from the ceiling, to a large blackboard menu. Newspapers hang on a wire to separate the long bar from the dining area. Beyond club sandwiches, fried seafood dishes, and great burgers, look for specialties like fish-and-chips, barbecued ribs, stuffed clams, clam pie, and kale soup. With the addition of sashimi and grilled tuna, the menu is also going a bit upscale these days. But they'll always have draft beer. You'll find lots of families, college students, and old-time locals here. There's live music Thursday through Saturday. Lunch and dinner $10–20.

❋ ⓨ **Orleans Inn** (508-255-2222; orleansinn.com), 21 Route 6A. Open for lunch and dinner daily mid-May to mid-October, and Friday through Sunday off-season. This waterfront eatery has really upped its offerings to the caliper of "decent" lately and folks are flocking here because of the prime water views. Go easy with the expectations and you'll be thrilled. The traditional-feeling dining room offers surf and turf, sandwiches, fried seafood platters, and salads. Dine and have drinks on the deck and you'll be raving. Welcoming service is learned top down from the hands-on owners. Dishes $8–21.

THE LOBSTER CLAW

ℰ ♿ **The Lobster Claw** (508-255-1800; lobsterclaw.com), Route 6A, near the Orleans rotary. Open 11:30–9 daily April to mid-October. Since 1970 the Berig family has been dishing up seafood at their large, convenient, family-style restaurant. Proudly maintained and decorated with the requisite nautical motif, The Lobster Claw serves straightforward and consistent preparations like delicately broiled fisherman's platters, crab cakes, and fried clams. Lobster sandwiches and salads are popular at lunch. Early specials from 4 to 5:30, and a "waiting lounge" upstairs. Grape-Nut custard flies off the dessert menu. Lunch $6–20, dinner $12–23.

❋ ℰ ⓨ ♿ **Old Jailhouse Tavern** (508-255-5245; jailhousetavern.com), 28 West Road. Open 11:30–1 daily. Slightly boisterous by night, more sedate by day, the tavern is a good choice when everyone in your party wants something different: nachos, soup and salad, fish-and-chips, or a broiled seafood sampler. Or when you have late-night munchies. Eat in one of the booths, on the atriumlike terrace overlooking the garden, at the long oak bar, or within the rock walls of the old jail. In the early 1800s the town constable offered the use of his front bedroom, complete with bars on the windows, as an overnight lockup facility. Dishes $8–25.

❋ **Cape Cup** (508-255-1989; capecup.com), 54 Main Street. Open for breakfast and lunch daily. For a quick bowl of soup, salad, sandwich, this pleasant year-round place will keep you happy. Dishes $7.

❋ ✆ ℰ **Sir Cricket's Fish 'n Chips** (508-255-4453), 38 Route 6A. Open daily. This tidy hole-in-the-wall dishes out fast pints of fried seafood, British-style fish and chips, and mixed platters (scallops, oysters, and clams are the most popular). Kids might prefer chicken tenders and hot dogs. After the beach, plan on takeout, as there are only a couple of tables. Lunch and dinner $9–20.

❋ ✿ ♿ **The Hole** (508-255-3740; the holecapecod.com), 98 Route 6A within Main Street Square. Open 5 AM–2 PM. The Hole is a pleasant and airy place, a real local hangout for turkey subs or BLTs. It's packed at breakfast time, when eggs-your-way and a short stack of pancakes rule, and friendly all day. You gotta try their hand-cut donuts. Dishes $3–8.

SNACKS, ICE CREAM & COFFEE

❋ "☕" **The Hot Chocolate Sparrow** (508-240-2230; hotchocolatesparrow .com), Old Colony Way, behind CVS on Route 6A. Open 6:30 AM–9 PM weekdays (until 11 PM weekends). On the rail trail (with a convenient window for ice cream), this place is on my short list of never-miss-driving-by-without-stopping-in-for-something-anything! Proprietor Marje Sparrow sends her staff to "espresso lab" to make sure they know the hows and whys of making a consistent cup. Without a doubt, they make the best cappuccino, lattes, and hot chocolate between Beantown and Provincetown . . . not to mention frozen espresso

THE HOT CHOCOLATE SPARROW

drinks like "affogato" (with soft-serve ice cream), "the bash" (with fresh raspberries), and old-fashioned freshly squeezed lemonade. Come at 7 AM when the scones and croissants pour out of the ovens. Or come whenever, since all cookies are made on the premises. In addition to an overflowing blackboard menu, they also make luscious hand-dipped chocolates and sweet treats. The candy counter is filled with treats like "bark" chock full of pecans and cranberries or peppermint or a myriad of other temptations. Marje's big space is a terrific place to hang out.

❋ **Cottage St. Bakery** (508-255-2821; cottagestreetbakery.com), Cottage Street near Routes 6A and 28. Open 6 AM–4 PM Wednesday through Monday. This European-style bakery, buttering up the community since 1984, has a number of oddly named specialties, including "dirt bombs," an old-fashioned french doughnut recipe that requires baking, not frying; and "fly cemeteries," puff-pastry squares, knotted on top and filled with currants and nuts. Their breads are also great. Knead I say more? Okay, I will: You can get homemade soups, lasagna, chicken pies, and sandwiches here, too. There are a few indoor and outdoor tables.

❄ **Village Farm Market** (508-255-1949), 199 Main Street, East Orleans. Open daily. Not your average farm stand, you can assemble a gourmand's feast here with cold pastas, roasted chicken, sesame noodles, baked goods, and deli sandwiches. There's a salad bar and a full-service bakery, too.

❄ **Jo Mama's** (508-255-0255; jomamasnybagels.com), 125 Route 6A. Open 6–6 daily. Bagel sandwiches, smoothies, health tonics, and fair trade coffee. This mod little space has a few tables.

❄ **Phoenix Fruit & Vegetable** (508-255-5306), 14 Cove Street. Open daily. This tiny shop is a delight for foodies. If you have cooking facilities, you'll appreciate organic greens, locally made clam pies, and hearty Pain d'Avignon bread.

Sundae School (508-255-5473; sundaeschool.com), 210 Main Street, East Orleans. Open late May to mid-September. Try the sublime black raspberry or Grape-Nut ice cream.

See also **Orleans Whole Food Store** under *Selective Shopping*.

FISH MARKETS Young's Fish Market (508-255-3366), Rock Harbor. Open late May to early September. If you don't like to cook lobster, place your order here by 4:30 PM (the earlier, the better) and they'll do it for you. Their lobster rolls are also good. The market, by the way, has been in the Harrison family since 1962, when they bought it from the Youngs.

✳ Entertainment

❄ **Academy Playhouse** (508-255-1963; apa1.0rg), 120 Main Street. This 162-seat playhouse, in the 1873 Old Town Hall, and its resident theater company (established in 1975) host 10 to 12 dramas, comedies, and musicals each year. Think popular productions like Grease, Cinderella, and Biloxi Blues. Their eagerly awaited April event brings established and unknown Cape writers (who have been holed up working all winter) together with audiences. Tickets $20.

✳ Selective Shopping

❄ Unless otherwise noted, all shops are open year-round.

ANTIQUES Pleasant Bay Antiques (508-255-0930), 540 Route 28, South Orleans. Most of these high-quality, 18th- and 19th-century American antiques come from area residents rather than auctions. They're displayed in a lovely old barn.

Continuum (508-255-8513), 7 Route 28. Dan Johnson sells expertly restored antique lamps and fixtures from the Victorian to the art deco period.

ACADEMY PLAYHOUSE

ART GALLERIES **Left Bank Gallery** (508-247-9172), 8 Cove Road. One of the best galleries on the Cape, with ceramics, glass, jewelry, and furniture. The owner, Audrey Parent, has a good eye.

Addison Art Gallery (508-255-6200; addisonart.com), 43 Route 28. Helen Addison represents both new and established artists working in realistic and traditional realms. Look for oils, watercolors, limited-edition prints, egg tempuras, and sculpture. It's comfortable for browsing and buying, for serious collectors and novices. Saturday openings throughout the summer.

Tree's Place (508-255-1330; trees place.com), 60 Route 6A at Route 28. Tree's offers a vast collection of unusual gifts (like kaleidoscopes and antique jewelry) displayed throughout nine small rooms; an excellent collection of representational New England painters; and a tile shop. Meet-the-artist champagne receptions 5–7 Saturday in summer.

ARTISANS **Orleans Carpenters** (508-255-2646; shakerboxes.com), 8C Commerce Drive. These folks make magnificent reproduction Shaker nesting oval boxes, oval trays, oval carriers, and music boxes from cherry and bird's-eye maple. Custom engraving is possible on all items. These traditional oval boxes are so expertly made and durable that you could put your full weight on one and it would feel sturdier than a stepladder. The front of the unprepossessing shop has a small display of goods. The "seconds," that look perfect to all but the most expert eyes, go very quickly in summer. Orleans Carpenters is hard to find, off Finlay Road (from Route 28).

Nauset Lantern Shop (508-255-1009), 52 Route 6A. Michael Joly expertly handcrafts copper and brass

KEMP POTTERY

Colonial- and Early American–style lanterns. Most of the nautical and onion lanterns are for exterior use, but he also makes sconces and indoor accessories. Watch him work.

Kemp Pottery (508-255-5853; kemp pottery.com), 9 Route 6A near the Orleans rotary. Father Steven and son Matt Kemp create unusual designs utilizing Nauset Beach sand. They have functional porcelain and stoneware pieces like lamps, platters, mirrors, dinner sets and bathroom sinks, as well as less common decorative objects for home and garden, like pagodas and torsos. They also make fountains and tile.

BOOKSTORES **Booksmith/Music-smith of Orleans** (508-255-4590), Skaket Corners, Route 6A. Paperbacks and best sellers.

CLOTHING **Karol Richardson** (508-255-3944), 47 Main Street. Stylish women's clothing.

FARMER'S MARKET Orleans Farmer's Market, Old Colony Way near Depot Square. Pick up local produce 8–noon every Saturday from mid-May to October.

SPECIAL SHOPS Bird Watcher's General Store (508-255-6974), 36 Route 6A near the Orleans rotary. If it pertains to birds or watchers of birds, this store has it: bird feeders in every size and shape, birdseed in barrels (a ton of seed is sold daily), bird note cards, bird kitchen magnets, bird playing cards. As important as commerce is, though, this place is an invaluable resource for news of where and when birds have been sighted or will be sighted. (This place isn't just for the birds!)

Oceana (508-240-1414), 1 Main Street Square. Carol Wright stocks lovely household items, watercolors, glass, and jewelry inspired by the sea and nature.

Orleans Whole Food Store (508-255-6540), 46 Main Street, Orleans. Healthy foods, lunches-to-go, vitamins, books, and items that promote holistic living.

Baseball Shop (508-240-1063), 26 Main Street. The shop carries more than 1,000 caps, as well as trading cards, clothing, and other baseball paraphernalia.

Cape Cod Photo & Art Supply (508-255-0476), 38 Main Street. All things digital, 1-hour film processing, and painting supplies if the wonderful Cape Cod light inspires you.

✳ Special Events

Late May–November: **Fine Art and Crafts Shows**. At a few locations on various days; check at the information booth (see *Guidance*).

Late August: **Pops in the Park** (508-255-1386). The Cape Cod Symphony performs in Eldredge Park, off Route 28 at Eldredge Park Way; $18–20 adults, $5 children 6–17.

The Outer Cape 4

EASTHAM

WELLFLEET

TRURO

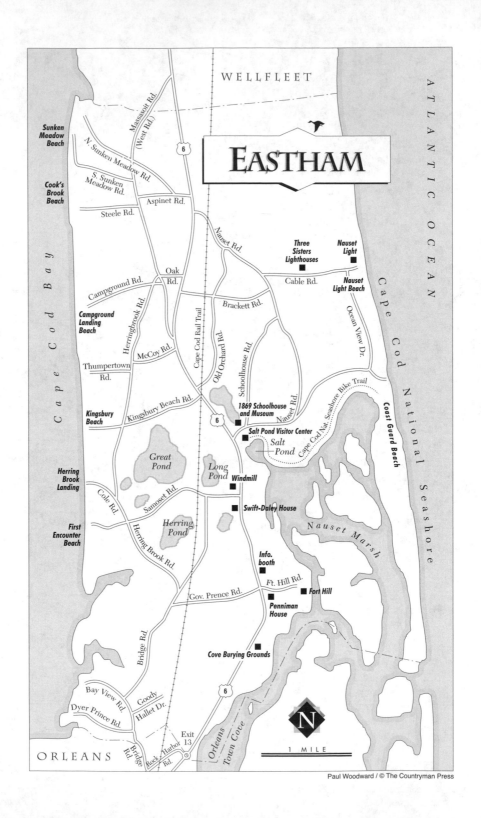

Paul Woodward / © The Countryman Press

EASTHAM

Settled by the Pilgrims in 1644, Eastham is content to remain relatively undiscovered by 21st-century tourists. In fact, although almost 18,000 folks summer here, year-rounders (fewer than 5,500) seem perfectly happy that any semblance of major tourism development has passed them by. There isn't even a Main Street or town center per se.

What Eastham does boast, as gateway to the Cape Cod National Seashore (CCNS), is plenty of natural diversions. There are four things you should do, by all means. Stop in at Salt Pond Visitor Center, one of two CCNS headquarters, which dispenses a wealth of information and offers ranger-guided activities and outstanding nature programs. Consider taking a boat trip onto Nauset Marsh, a fragile ecosystem that typifies much of the Cape. Hop on a bike or walking trail; a marvelous network of paths traverses this part of the seashore, including the Fort Hill area. And of course, head to the beach. The Cape's renowned, uninterrupted stretches of sandy beach, backed by high dunes, begin in earnest in Eastham and extend all the way up to Provincetown. One of them, Coast Guard Beach, is also where exalted naturalist Henry Beston spent 1928 observing nature's minute changes from a little cottage and recording his experiences in The Outermost House.

Eastham is best known as the site where the *Mayflower's* Myles Standish and a Pilgrim scouting party met the Nauset Indians in 1620 at First Encounter Beach. The "encounter," in which a few arrows were slung (without injury), served as sufficient warning to the Pilgrims: They left and didn't return for 24 years. When the Pilgrim settlers, then firmly entrenched at Plymouth, went looking for room to expand, they returned to Eastham. Led by Thomas Prence, they purchased most of the land from Native Americans for an unknown quantity of hatchets.

Although the history books cite these encounters as the beginning of Eastham's recorded history, the 1990 discovery of a 4,000-year-old settlement (see the sidebar "Coast Guard Beach") is keeping archaeologists and anthropologists on their toes.

GUIDANCE **Eastham Information Booth** (508-240-7211; easthamchamber .com), 1700 Route 6, near Fort Hill. Open 9–6 daily, mid-June to early September; 10–5 daily late May to mid-June and early September to mid-October.

❄ ☙ ⬆ ♿ **Salt Pond Visitor Center** (508-255-3421; nps.gov/caco), 50 Nauset Road, off Route 6. Open 9–5 daily in summer and 9–4:30 daily the rest of the year.

In 1961, newly elected President John F. Kennedy, Senator Leverett Saltonstall, and Representative Hastings Keith championed a bill to turn more than 43,000 acres into the **Cape Cod National Seashore** (CCNS), protected forever from further development. (About 600 private homes remain within the park.) Today, over 5 million people visit the CCNS annually. The excellent center shows short films on Thoreau's Cape Cod, Marconi, the ever-changing natural landscape, and the history of whaling and lifesaving. And the fine museum includes displays on the salt and whaling industries and the diaries of Captain Penniman's wife, Augusta, who accompanied him on several voyages. Rangers lead lots of activities during the summer, from sunset campfires on the beach to talks on tidal flats and bird walks. Two short loop trails depart from here around Salt Pond and are worth your time. Programs are also offered during spring and fall. Free.

OLDEST WINDMILL

PUBLIC RESTROOMS Salt Pond Visitor Center.

PUBLIC LIBRARY ❋ ✐ ↑ ᵗᵗᵗ **Eastham Library** (508-240-5950; eastham library.org), west of the windmill, 190 Samoset Road. Open Tuesday through Saturday. Story time and summer events for children; audio books for everyone.

GETTING THERE *By car:* Eastham is 40 miles from the Cape Cod Canal via Route 6.

A PERFECT DAY IN EASTHAM

7:30 Start the day simple: at The Sparrow (Orleans), a local hangout.

9:00 Bike the Cape Cod Rail Trail up to Wellfleet and down to Dennis.

12:30 Assemble a picnic from Box Lunch and enjoy it with panoramic views atop Fort Hill; walk the 1.5-mile Red Maple Swamp Trail afterward; tour the Captain Edward Penniman House.

2:00 Build sand castles at the shallow, bayside First Encounter Beach.

5:30 Beat the crowds at ABBA (Orleans) for exceptional cuisine.

8:00 Build a bonfire at the National Seashore (after having picked up a permit), or, on the second and fourth Saturday of the month, listen to acoustic, folk, and bluegrass at the First Encounter Coffee House.

By bus: The **Plymouth & Brockton** bus line (508-778-9767; p-b.com) connects Eastham with Hyannis and other Cape towns, as well as with Boston's Logan Airport. The bus stops across from Town Hall on Route 6 and at the Village Green Plaza at Bracket Road on Route 6 in North Eastham.

GETTING AROUND Eastham is only a few miles wide and 6 miles long. Most points of interest are well marked along or off Route 6. The CCNS is to the east of Route 6.

MEDICAL EMERGENCY Call **911**.

✳ To See

Edward Penniman House (508-255-3421), off Route 6 in the Fort Hill area, CCNS. Open early May to late October; one-hour tours at 11 on Tuesday and Saturday; house open for self-guided tours three to four days each week. At age 11, Penniman left Eastham for the open sea. When he returned as a captain 26 years later, he had this 1868 house built for him. Boasting indoor plumbing (the first in Eastham to make that claim) and a kerosene chandelier, this French Second Empire–style house has Corinthian columns, a mansard roof, and a cupola that once afforded views of the

EDWARD PENNIMAN HOUSE

bay and ocean. Ever-helpful National Park Service guides dispense lots of historical information. Even if it's closed, peek in the windows. Free.

Swift-Daley House and **Tool Museum** (508-240-0871; easthamhistorical.org), next to the post office on Route 6. Open 10–1 weekdays, July and August and 10–1 Saturday, September. In 1998 one of the seashore dune shacks (see Dune shacks under *To See* in "Provincetown") was

moved to this site. Although it's difficult to imagine what dune-shack life might have been like, this helps. As for the Swift-Daley House, it's a completely furnished full Cape Colonial built by ship's carpenters in 1741. It has wide floorboards, pumpkin-pine woodwork, narrow stairways, and a fireplace in every room on the first floor. The Tool Museum behind the house displays hundreds of old tools for use in the home and in the field. And the Olde Shop sells antiques and local arts and crafts. Donations.

SWIFT-DALEY HOUSE AND TOOL MUSEUM

1869 Schoolhouse and Museum (508-255-0788; easthamhistorical.org), off Route 6 across from the Salt Pond Visitor Center. Open 1–4 Tuesday, Wednesday, and Saturday and 10–4 Thursday and Friday, July and August; 1–4 Saturday, September. During the time when this former one-room schoolhouse served the town (1869 until 1936), there were separate entrances for boys and girls. Inside you'll learn about Henry Beston's year of solitude spent observing natural rhythms on nearby Coast Guard Beach. Thanks to the Eastham Historical Society, you can also learn about the town's farming history, daily domestic life, Native Americans, offshore shipwrecks, and the impressive Lifesaving Service. Donations.

Oldest windmill, on Route 6 at Samoset Road. Open 10–5 daily, June through August. Across from Town Hall, the Cape's oldest working windmill was built in Plymouth in the 1680s and moved to Eastham in the early 1800s.

First Encounter Beach, off Samoset Road and Route 6. A bronze marker commemorates where the Pilgrims, led by Captain Myles Standish, first met the Native Americans. The exchange was not friendly. Although arrows flew, no one was injured. The site goes down in history as the place where the Native Americans first began their decline at the hands of European settlers. On a more modern note of warfare history, for 25 years the U.S. Navy used an offshore ship for target practice. Until recently, it was still visible on a sandbar about a mile offshore. The beach, with its westward vista, is a great place to catch a sunset.

Doane Homestead Site, between the Salt Pond Visitor Center and Coast Guard Beach, CCNS. Only a marker remains to identify the spot where Doane, one of Eastham's first English settlers, made his home.

Cove Burying Grounds, Route 6. Many of these graves date back to the 1700s, but look for the memorial to the three *Mayflower* Pilgrims who were buried here in the 1600s.

Nauset Light (508-240-2612), at the corner of Cable Road and Ocean View Drive, CCNS. Tours Sunday, May through October; Wednesday in July and August. This light was originally built in Chatham in 1877, one of a twin, but was moved here shortly thereafter. In 1996, when Nauset Light was just 37 feet from cliff's edge, the large red-and-white steel lighthouse was moved—via flatbed truck over the course of 3 days—from the eroding shoreline. In 1998, the keeper's house (which dates to 1875) was also moved back. For now, the cast-iron behemoth sits a respectable 250 feet from the shoreline, its beacon still stretching 17 miles to sea. Free, but you may have to pay to park at Nauset Light Beach (see *Green Space*).

Three Sisters Lighthouses (508-255-3421), inland from Nauset Light, CCNS. Call about tours in-season. In 1838 this coastal cliff was home to three brick lighthouses that provided beacons for sailors. They collapsed from erosion in 1892 and were replaced with three wooden ones. When erosion threatened those in 1918, two were moved away; the third was moved in 1923. Eventually the National Park

Service acquired all three and moved them to their present location, nestled in the woods far back from today's coastline. (It's a rather incongruous sight: lighthouses, surrounded by trees, unable to reach the water.) Head inland from the beach parking lot along the paved walkway. Free, but you'll have to pay to park at Nauset Light Beach (see *Green Space*).

THREE SISTERS LIGHTHOUSE

✳ To Do

BICYCLING/RENTALS Cape Cod Rail Trail. This scenic, well-maintained, 26-mile (one-way) paved path winds from Dennis to Wellfleet. Park at the Salt Pond Visitor Center (see *Guidance*).

Nauset Bike Trail, CCNS. This 2.25-mile (one-way) trail connects with the Cape Cod Rail Trail and runs from the Salt Pond Visitor Center, across Nauset Marsh via a boardwalk, to Coast Guard Beach. The trail passes large stands of thin, tall black locust trees not native to the area—they were introduced to return nitrogen to the soil after overfarming.

Rent from the family-owned **Little Capistrano Bike Shop** (508-255-6515; cape codbike.com; 30 Salt Pond Road, open April through October), a superb shop right on the Rail Trail and across the street fro the Nauset Bike Trail. The owner, Melissa, is wonderful. It's across from the Salt Pond Visitor Center behind the Lobster Shanty. Rentals: $19 for 8 hours, $23 daily, $75 weekly; less for children's bikes. Repairs and sales too.

BOAT EXCURSIONS/RENTALS Castaways Marine (508-255-7751; castaways marine.com), 4655 Route 6. Along with surfing and kayaking lessons and rentals, these folks include free local delivery to and from the water. You can't miss them across from Willy's Gym. Single kayaks rent for $49, doubles $59.

FISHING/SHELLFISHING Purchase your required freshwater fishing license at **Goose Hummock** (508-255-0455; goose.com; 15 Route 6 at the rotary), and then head to the stocked, spring-fed **Herring Pond** (see *Green Space*). Contact the Sticker Office (508-240-5976), 555 Old Orchard Road (off Route 6 or Brackett Road), for shellfishing permits and

NAUSET BIKE TRAIL

regulations. Annual permits cost $65–75 for weekly. Most of Eastham's shellfishing areas are open daily; however, shellfishing is only permitted at Salt Pond (Route 6) and Salt Pond River on Sunday.

FITNESS CLUB ❋ **Willy's Gym** (508-255-6370; willysgym.com), 4730 Route 6. Open daily. Facilities include racquetball and squash courts, Nautilus and free weights, a lap pool, saunas and steam rooms, a whirlpool, six indoor tennis courts, four outdoor courts, a climbing rock wall, a three-story soft play structure, and aerobics, yoga, Pilates, and spinning classes. Daily pass $20. The also offer movie nights and food (see *Where to Eat*).

FOR FAMILIES ✎ **Recreational programs** (508-240-5974) are held 9–noon weekdays, late June to mid-August. Visitors and summer residents are encouraged to bring their children (age 5–12) to the playground at Nauset Regional High School (on Cable Road, North Eastham) for various programs. In the past they've included archery, arts and crafts, and soccer. Supervised swimming and instruction are offered at Wiley Park (see *Green Space*) for children age 2–13 on weekday mornings. Fees vary.

✎ **Poit's Place** (508-255-6321), 5270 Route 6. Open mid-May to early September. Families have stopped here since 1954 for mini-golf, ice cream, onion rings, hot dogs, and fish-and-chips. Will yours?

✎ **T-Time Family Sports Center** (508-255-5697), 4790 Route 6. Open daily in summer and weekends mid-May to mid-October. If you're desperately in need of a bucket of balls to belt out, this will suffice. The mini-golf is a bit run-down, but the Outer Cape has slim pickings.

✎ **Cedar Banks Links Adventure Golf** (508-255-2575), 3580 Route 6. Open 10–10 mid-May to mid-September. Forget T-Time, this attractive and waterfall-filled place attached to Arnold's makes waiting at Arnold's worth your time! Some holes are challenging and many are replicated historical landmarks.

TENNIS **Nauset Regional High School**, Cable Road. The public can use these eight courts for free, after school gets out.

See also *Fitness Club*.

LITTLE CAPISTRANO BIKE SHOP

BIKE SHOP

❋ Green Space

BEACHES **Nauset Light Beach**, CCNS, on the Atlantic Ocean. An idyllic, long, broad, dune-backed beach. Facilities include changing rooms, restrooms, and a lifeguard in-season. Parking $15 daily in-season (transferable to any CCNS beach; no charge after 4 PM); the lot fills by 10 AM in summer.

First Encounter Beach, Campground Landing Beach, and **Cook's Brook Beach**. These bayside town beaches are well suited to kite flying

NATIONAL SEASHORE BONFIRES

A beach bonfire, with or without a clambake, defines the essence of summertime on the Outer Cape. Here's the process you need to follow to secure a permit: In July and August head to the Salt Pond Visitor Center (508-255-3421; nps.gov/caco) three days before you want a permit and request one. For instance, if you want it for Wednesday, go on Saturday. Be there when the center opens. On the day of your big event, be at the visitor center at 3:30 sharp or you'll lose your permit to someone waiting in line. In the off-season, you can call three days ahead of your desired date without a problem. There are limits on the number of permits given out: 4 at Coast Guard Beach, 4 at Nauset Light Beach, and 4 at Marconi Beach; there are also limitations on the sizes of the groups allowed to congregate. Fires are permitted year-round.

and shelling. Because of the shallow water and gradual slope, they are also safe for children. At low tide, vibrant green sea grasses and rippled sand patterns are compelling. Parking $15 daily in-season. Weekly stickers ($55) are available from the Town of Eastham's Sticker Office (508-240-5976), 555 Old Orchard Road (off Route 6 or Brackett Road). The office is open 9–4 Monday through Saturday (except it closes at noon on Wednesday). No credit cards. First Encounter Beach has a bathhouse; the others are equipped with portable toilets. Daily parking $15.

PONDS **Herring Pond** and **Great Pond**, both west of Eastham center off Samoset, Great Pond, and Herring Brook roads. Great Pond has a fair amount of parking, a biggish beach, lifeguards, and two swimming areas (including Wiley Park, with a beach, playground, and bathhouse). Parking: $15 daily, $55 weekly.

WALKS **Fort Hill area**, CCNS; trailhead and parking off Route 6. The trail—one of my all-Cape favorites—is about 1.5 miles roundtrip with a partial boardwalk, some log steps, and some hills. It offers lovely views of Nauset Marsh, especially from Skiff Hill, but also winds through the dense Red Maple Swamp and past the Edward Penniman House (see *To See*). Birders enjoy this walk year-round, but it is particularly beautiful in autumn when the maples turn color. Pastoral Fort

NAUSET LIGHT

Hill was farmed until the 1940s, and rock walls still mark boundaries.

Nauset Marsh Trail, CCNS; trailhead behind the Salt Pond Visitor Center (see *Guidance*). About 1 mile roundtrip; some log steps. This trail runs along Salt Pond and yields expansive vistas of Nauset Marsh, which was actually Nauset Bay when French explorer Samuel de Champlain charted it in 1605. As the barrier beach developed, so did the marsh. Along those same lines, Salt Pond was a freshwater

COAST GUARD BEACH

This long **National Seashore** beach, backed by grasses and heathland, is perfect for walking and sunning. Facilities include changing rooms, restrooms, and in-season lifeguards. In summer a shuttle bus ferries visitors from a parking lot that fills by 10 AM; it's a mile from the beach and it's no use trying to drop off passengers at the beach *before* parking; the seashore banned it to control traffic and protect resources.) Parking $15 daily (good all day on any CCNS beach; no charge after 4 PM); fees in effect late June to early September and on weekends from late May to mid-October; seasonal pass $45.

At times during the winter, you might be lucky enough to spot gray seals and small brown harbor seals congregating at the southern tip of Coast Guard Beach. They feed on the ever-present sand eels. Take the walk at low tide and allow an hour to cover the 2 miles.

Henry Beston wrote his 1928 classic, *The Outermost House*, during the year he lived in a two-room bungalow on Coast Guard Beach. The book chronicles Beston's interaction with the natural environment and records seasonal changes. The cottage was designated a national literary landmark in 1964, but the blizzard of 1978 washed it into the ocean. Bundled up (tightly!) against the off-season winds, you'll get a glimpse of the haunting isolation Beston experienced.

After a brutal 1990 storm washed away a large chunk of beach, an amateur archaeologist discovered evidence of a prehistoric dwelling on Coast Guard Beach. It is one of the oldest undisturbed archaeological sites in New England, dating back 1,100 to 2,100 years to the Early and Middle Woodland cultures. Because Coast Guard Beach was then 5 miles inland, the site provided a safe encampment for hunters and gatherers.

In response to the thousands of ships that were wrecked off this treacherous coast, the Life-Saving Service established in 1872 morphed into the U.S. Coast Guard. After the Cape Cod Canal was built in 1914, and ships could pass through instead of going around the Cape, fatalities off this coastline decreased dramatically. And as such, by 1958, the Coast Guard Station at the top of the cliff could be decommissioned. It now serves as an educational center for the CCNS.

pond until the ocean broke through from Nauset Marsh. This complex ecosystem sustains all manner of ocean creatures and shorebirds.

Buttonbush Trail, CCNS, trailhead at the Salt Pond Visitor Center. The trail is half a mile (roundtrip), with some boardwalk, some log steps. It was specially designed with Braille markers for the blind and visually impaired.

❋ **Eastham Hiking Club** (508-255-3808). The club meets at 9 AM on Wednesday from September to late May for a vigorous 2-hour walk somewhere between Yarmouth and Provincetown. Generally about 45 to 50 people gather for the 4- to 6-mile hike along wooded trails and ponds. Call for the meeting place. Free.

❋ Lodging

Route 6 is lined with cottage colonies, but there are a few quite notable alternatives.

BED & BREAKFASTS ♿ ❢

Whalewalk Inn & Spa (508-255-0617; 800-440-1281; whalewalkinn.com), 220 Bridge Road. Open April to December. This upscale 19th-century whaling captain's home has been run like a tight ship by Elaine and Kevin Conlin since 2004. My hat's off to them. Expect a range of accommodations, including a romantic cottage, three suites, a luxuriously renovated carriage house, and the most romantic room, the spa penthouse. (Book it now!) Carriage house rooms are outfitted with four-poster beds and gas fireplace; all have a small private deck or balcony, and some have a large whirlpool. Inn rooms are decorated with country sophistication, a smattering of fine antiques, and breezy floral fabrics. I particularly like the brick patio where a full breakfast and afternoon hors d'oeuvres are served. On my last visit, daughter Heather was helping out by serving a mesclun salad with pecans, Gorgonzola, and pear slices, followed by a killer Grand Marnier oatmeal pie with vanilla yogurt. Not to be outdone, the inn also added a first-rate spa with an exercise facility, sauna, hot tub, and a resistance indoor pool; massage treatments can be arranged. As if you needed any more reasons to stay, the inn is also around the corner

from the Rail Trail and within walking distance of bay beaches. Late May to mid-October $240–420; off-season $190–365.

❋ ❢ **Fort Hill Bed and Breakfast** (508-240-2870; forthillbedandbreakfast.com), 75 Fort Hill Road. This B&B not only has car-stopping street appeal, it's insides live up to expectations. I could live out the rest of my days here. Perched on a little knoll overlooking Nauset Marsh, Jean and Gordon Avery's two suites and cottage enjoy one of the Cape's best locations. The casual, yet refined 19th-century Greek Revival farmhouse is a charmer—with absolutely wonderful hosts (who have separate guest

WHALEWALK INN

FORT HILL BED AND BREAKFAST

quarters). As for the guest rooms, the second-floor Lucille is sweet with slanted eaves, wide-pine floors, and a detached bathroom. The first-floor two-room Emma Suite features a little library, piano, and oversized tub. The *pièce de résistance*, though, is the ever-so-private Nantucket Cottage which boasts a secluded garden, distant marsh views, cathedral ceilings, and a sitting room with gas fireplace. Folks who stay tend to become serious repeat visitors. (All rooms have TV and AC.) A delectable full breakfast—perhaps zucchini quiche or piping-hot baked apples with "jammy" muffins—is relished by all. June to mid-October $235–325; off-season $200–275. No credit cards.

✿ ✑ ❝¶❞ **700 Samoset** (508-255-8748; 700samoset.com), 700 Samoset Road. Open May through October. The ever-resourceful Sarah Blackwell moved this abandoned 1870 Greek Revival farmhouse to its present location on the bay side of Route 6, on a quiet road near the bike trail. She also did a wonderful job restoring it, sanding floors and woodwork, and blending period pieces with contemporary accents like a painted checkerboard floor and tin lamps. It's all quite taste-

ful. Too bad for us: there are only two guest rooms (each with a private bath, queen beds, mini-fridge, and TV/DVD), but Eastham could use a dozen of them! From the open country kitchen, guests enjoy an expanded continental breakfast. Plan your day from the front-porch rocking chairs. July and August $125; off-season $70–85. No credit cards.

❊ ❀ ✑ ❝¶❞ **Inn at the Oaks** (508-255-1886; innattheoaks.com), 3085 Route 6. Innkeepers Pam and Don Andersen's big yellow Victorian house on the rail trail is delightfully hidden from Route 6 and across from the Salt Pond Visitor Center. Guests enjoy relaxing on the wide wraparound veranda or in the billiards room or parlor with velveteen curtains. All 10 guest rooms have lacy curtains and a smattering of antiques; some have cathedral ceiling and skylight. The Garden Room, my favorite, has a private porch and fireplace. An adjacent carriage house has three family-friendly suites (and one that accepts pets), but in fact, the whole place is family-friendly: witness the playground and little kids' playroom. Afternoon tea and dessert, as well as a full breakfast of ebleskivers (danish pancakes) or something equally good, are included. As a historical footnote, you might be interested to know that Henry Beston stayed on the property during bad weather while he was writing *The Outermost House*. June through October $155–280; off-season $125–240.

❊ ✑ ♿ ❝¶❞ **Penny House Inn & Day Spa** (508-255-6632; 800-554-1751; pennyhouseinn.com), 4885 Route 6. Since I was unable to see rooms for this edition, I can only tell you what I used to know: from the street, this shingled and bow-roofed Cape doesn't look nearly as old as it is. But sections date back to the mid-1700s. Check out the dining room's wide floorboards, original beams, and barnboard walls. The rest of the house has a newer feel: Each of the nine rooms (of varying sizes and styles) has comfortable furnishings. Each of the three suites boast a two-person whirlpool tub, gas fireplace, and balcony. The mother-and-daughter innkeeping team of Margaret and Becky Keith, presiding over the place since 1988, have created lots of common space, including a "great room," 2 acres of lawns, an outdoor pool, a day spa, and a garden-style brick patio. Kids 8 and up welcome. June through September $225–395; off-season $195–325.

COTTAGES 🐾 ✏ "🛈" **Fort Hill Cottages** (Cottage 1 (617-965-1002); Cottage 3 (202-320-8391); Cottage 4 (805-588-1341); forthillcottages.com), 45 Governor Prence, at the base of Fort Hill. Open January through November. I have great affection and admiration for this impressively designed and executed threesome. This cottage community is jointly owned by a group of old friends and is a place they enjoy visiting to connect with each other, relax, nap, read, and explore. Luckily for the rest of us, they're happy to share it when they're not there. Each has been recently remodeled from head to toe, designed for comfort, and appointed with simplicity. Each reflects the owner's tastes and personalities, but all are in keeping with the charm of the Cape. Cottage 1 features a soaring beach stone fireplace and sleeping loft. Cottage 3 has clean lines, a modern design, an eclectic art collection, and a blue slate fireplace. Cottage 4 incorporates salvaged architectural pieces to give it a charm and warmth. I bet you won't want to leave. They're spacious with well-appointed kitchens, large screened-in porches, private outdoor showers, and updated with air conditioning and cable. They're rented individually by owner. Mid-June to early September $1425- weekly; off-season rates nightly and weekly.

🐾 🐾 "🛈" **Cottage Grove** (508-255-0500; 877-521-5522; grovecape.com), 1975 Route 6. Open May through October. You can tell this is not your average cottage colony just by the unusually aesthetic fence that fronts Route 6. Although these are individually owned condos, they're expertly managed during the summer like rental units. No matter how you categorize them, I call them some of the most charming places to stay on the Outer Cape. The nine cozy cottages have been nicely renovated and are set back off the road on 3 acres. Cottages are rustic, with knotty-pine walls, but they have upgraded bathrooms and kitchens, firm new mattresses with cotton sheets, phones, and a smattering of antiques. Late May to mid-October $80–195 nightly, $1,000–1,575 weekly; off-season $95–195 nightly; in summer, most units have weekly or 3-night minimum stay requirements.

🐾 🐾 ✏ **Gibson Cottages** (508-255-0882; capecodtravel.com/gibson), off Samoset Road from Route 6. Open April to mid-October. Some of the

COTTAGE GROVE

Cape's best lakeside cottages are down a little dirt road marked only with GIBSON. Jerry and Mary Jane Gibson have owned these seven neat-and-tidy cottages since 1966 and take great pride in maintaining them. Each of the well-spaced one-, two-, and three-bedroom cottages (all freshly painted white) has a screened porch or deck and fully equipped kitchen. A swimming dock, a sailboat, rowboats, a kayak, a canoe, and a barbecue area are shared by all. There are also two bike trails on the other side of the pristine lake, which boasts a private, sandy beach. This is a gem; call early. Late June to early September $1,200–1,500 weekly; off-season $700–900 weekly (3-night minimum off-season). No credit cards.

✐ "1" **Midway Motel & Cottages** (508-255-3117; 800-755-3117; midway motel.com), Route 6. Open April through October. Pine and oak trees shield this reasonably priced complex from the road. The tidy grounds, over which the Knisely family has presided since 1983, feature a nice children's play area, shuffleboard, badminton, horseshoes, picnic tables, grills, and direct access to the Cape Cod Rail Trail (see *To Do*). All rooms have refrigerators, microwaves, TVs, and coffeemakers. Children under 16 are free. In-season $116–120 rooms, $960–1,085 weekly cottages; off-season $68–110 rooms, $575–730 weekly cottages.

✐ **Hidden Village** (508-255-1140), 1700 Bridge Road. Open late June through September. I've long known about this place spread out on 18 acres in the woods but have always been unable to stick my head into a vacant unit. The wait is over: Although some might think it's one step above camping, I happen to love these five, very rustic, 2-bedroom units. There's indoor plumbing and a very basic kitchen

(already it's better than camping!), along with 2-bedrooms and platforms in the room that serves as the living room, screened-in areas that serve as walls, and paper-thin real walls. You really feel like you're sleeping outdoors with a roof over your head (and a wood stove to ward against a chill.) They're not for everyone, but they're a real find for kindred souls. And they're all about quiet and privacy. No TV, WiFi, or pets. Late June to early September $805 weekly; off-season $560 weekly, $82 daily.

RENTAL HOUSES AND COTTAGES Anchor Real Estate (508-255-4949; capecodvacation.com), 4760 Route 6.

HOSTEL ✿ ✐ **Hostelling International Mid-Cape** (508-255-2785; hiusa.org; 888-901-2085 in-season; 617-536-9455 off-season), 75 Goody Hallet Drive, off Bridge Road. Open mid-May to mid-September. Located in a quiet residential neighborhood off the Orleans rotary, this hostel has about 46 beds in seven coed, same-sex, and family cabins. The hostel boasts no lockout times, assorted summertime events, a fully equipped common kitchen, bike shelter, outdoor shower, volleyball, and barbecue area. It's about a mile to the nearest bay beach. Reservations are essential in July and August. $32 weeknights, $35 on weekends for AYH members; $35–38 for nonmembers.

✳ Where to Eat

There aren't many restaurants—good or bad—in Eastham.

✿ ✐ ♿ **Arnold's Lobster & Clam Bar** (508-255-2575; arnoldsrestaurant .com), 3580 Route 6. Open 11:30–9:30 daily, mid-May to mid-September. Arnold's, under the same stewardship for years, offers a raw bar, lobster clambake dinners, excellent local clams (without the sand!), homemade ice cream, colorful salads, and the normal array of fried seafood baskets. Onion rings are excellent, too; they usually sell upwards of 4,000 pounds of them during any given summer!) Weekday lunch specials are an incredible bargain at $5. Abutting the rail trail, the neat-and-tidy Arnold's has a nice fenced-off area with tables under pine trees and an open-air patio. Expect to wait! Dishes $7–34. No credit cards.

❋ **Red Barn Pizza** (508-255-4500), 4180 Route 6. Open daily. It may not look promising, being a big red barn and all, but these folks make one heck of a great pizza. I'm particularly partial to the buffalo chicken with broccoli, which costs $21 for a large and also tastes great the morning after! Seriously.

Friendly Fisherman (508-255-3009), 4580 Route 6. Open mid-May to mid-October. This popular and rustic shack offers the requisite fish and chips, fried clams, and fish market, but I always gravitate to their very good lobster rolls ($17). Portions are large.

Brackett Farms & Sam's Deli (508-255-9340), 100 Brackett Rd. Right around the corner from Ben & Jerry's, these folks make great hot and cold sandwiches.

❋ **Willy's World Grille** (508-255-6370; willysgym.com), Route 6. Open 8–8 weekdays, 8–4 weekends. The gym and fitness center has a captive audience for salads, sandwiches, burgers, and a few entrées like veggie stir-fry and steak *frites*. (They even post nutritional data. They include a free movie (from new releases to foreign and independent flicks) on Wednesday and Friday evenings.

❋ 🎵 **Box Lunch** (508-255-0799; box lunch.com), 4205 Route 6. Open daily until 8 PM. If you've got a hungry family or have had enough fried food, stop at this inconspicuous strip mall. (In case you didn't know, they roll their sandwich meats in pita bread at this ubiquitous Cape franchise.) Sandwiches $5–12.

❋ Entertainment

First Encounter Coffee House (508-255-5438; firstencounter.org), 220 Samoset Road. Open year-round except December and May. Performances on the second and fourth Saturday of each month. Acoustic, folk, blues, and bluegrass reign here, attracting musicians with national reputations—including Wellfleet's Patty Larkin and Vineyarder Livingston Taylor. Home to the 1899 Unitarian Universalist church (aka Chapel in the Pines) since 1974, the intimate venue has only 100 seats, beneath stained-glass windows. Off-season, it's a very local affair, where everybody knows your name and knows to arrive early to get a good seat. Tickets $15–18; children under 13, free.

FIRST ENCOUNTER COFFEE HOUSE

See also **Willy's World Grille**, under *Where to Eat.*

✳ Selective Shopping

❋ **Collector's World** (508-255-3616), 4100 Route 6. Since 1974, Chris Alex has been selling an eclectic lineup of antiques, gifts, and collectibles like Russian lacquer boxes, scrimshaw, pewter, Civil War artifacts, and toy soldiers. It's one of the wackiest collections on the Cape.

❋ **Four Winds Leather** (508-240-7998), 5130 Route 6. You probably didn't come to the Cape in search of sheepskins and moccasins, but these are the real things. The store is piled high with Native American art, leather coats, wallets, and the like.

✳ Special Events

July–August: **Eastham Painters' Guild**, at the Old Schoolhouse Museum, Route 6 at the Salt Pond Visitor Center. Outdoor art shows are held here most Thursdays and Fridays, as well as over the Memorial Day and Labor Day weekends.

Early September: **Windmill Weekend**. This 2-day community festival is staged for locals and features a road race, a band concert, an arts-and-crafts show, square dancing, and a parade.

WELLFLEET

Although a whopping 70 percent of Wellfleet is conservation land, the town is perhaps best known as an art stronghold. Wellfleet's two principal thoroughfares, Main Street and Commercial Street, are dotted with 20 or so galleries representing a wide gamut of art: from souvenir works to images that transcend their media. Many artists and artisans who exhibit here call Wellfleet home, at least for a short time each year, gaining inspiration from pristine landscapes and an unrelenting ocean.

After art, Wellfleet's other main draw is nature. The outstanding Wellfleet Bay Wildlife Sanctuary offers practically unparalleled opportunities for observing marine and bird life through guided activities and self-guided walks. A mostly sandy, 8-mile-long National Seashore trail on Great Island yields solitude and commanding views of Wellfleet Bay. On the Atlantic side, dunes and cliffs back broad and uninterrupted beaches. Any of Wellfleet's meandering roads are perfect for cycling, leading you past ponds, salt marshes, heathlands, and scrub pines.

Wellfleet appeals to a distinct crowd, many of whom have returned year after year for decades. In fact, many nonnative families—wash-ashores—rent houses here for the entire summer. When shopkeepers and restaurateurs begin dusting off the shelves in early to mid-June, it feels like a real homecoming—old friends catching up over a coffee in a café, neighbors renewing relationships as they tend their gardens. And although Wellfleet is very popular with vacationing Freudian analysts, there's also a notable seasonal contingent of lawyers, professors, and writers. They've all come for the same purpose: to commune with their thoughts, recharge their batteries, and lead a simpler life (albeit only temporarily). Summer folks also venture out of their cocoons to dine on wonderful food in laid-back settings, to square dance outdoors, and to engage in lively conversation after a particularly spirited performance by the Wellfleet Harbor Actors Theater.

Wellfleetians are an independent bunch. Almost 30 percent of the 3,140 year-rounders are self-employed (proverbial Jacks and Jills of all trades), more than in any other Cape town, and almost 20 percent are unemployed in winter. (If you do visit midwinter, you'll find a few warm beds and the frozen bay—a romantic sight on an overcast day.) While most of the town rolls up its shutters from mid-October to mid-May, Wellfleet may also feel like a ghost town on a weekday in mid-June. But on any given summer day, about 17,500 folks will be overnighting in Wellfleet.

Wellfleet was most likely named for a town in England, which, like "our" Wellfleet, was also renowned for its oyster beds. As early as the 17th century, when

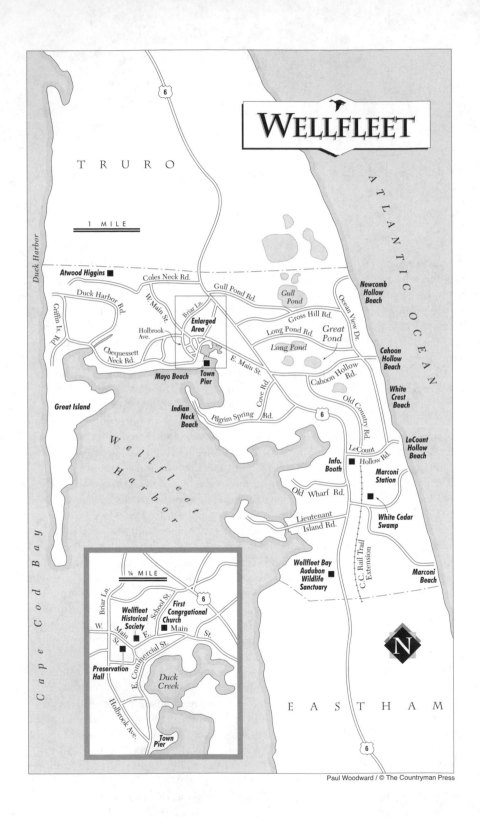

WELLFLEET

TRURO

1 MILE

Duck Harbor

Atwood Higgins

Coles Neck Rd.

Duck Harbor Rd.

W. Main St.

Griffin Is. Rd.

Chequessett Neck Rd.

Holbrook Ave.

Briar Ln.

Enlarged Area

Mayo Beach

Town Pier

Great Island

Indian Neck Beach

Pilgrim Spring Rd.

Cove Rd.

E. Main St.

Gull Pond Rd.

Gull Pond

Gross Hill Rd.

Long Pond Rd.

Long Pond

Ocean View Dr.

Great Pond

Newcomb Hollow Beach

Cahoon Hollow Beach

White Crest Beach

Cahoon Hollow Rd.

Old Country Rd.

LeCount Hollow Rd.

LeCount Hollow Beach

Info. Booth

Marconi Station

White Cedar Swamp

Old Wharf Rd.

Lieutenant Island Rd.

Wellfleet Bay Audubon Wildlife Sanctuary

C.C. Rail Trail Extension

Marconi Beach

Wellfleet Harbor

Cape Cod Bay

ATLANTIC OCEAN

6

6

N

¼ MILE

Briar Ln.

Wellfleet Historical Society

W. Main St.

School St.

First Congrational Church

E. Main St.

6

E. Commercial St.

Main St.

Preservation Hall

Duck Creek

Holbrook Ave.

Town Pier

EASTHAM

6

Paul Woodward / © The Countryman Press

Wellfleet was still a part of Eastham known as Billingsgate, the primary industries revolved around oyster and cranberry harvesting. Whaling, fishing, and other related industries also flourished until the mid-1800s. And by the 1870s, commercial markets had really opened up for littlenecks, cherrystones, and clams for chowder. Today, with the depletion of natural fish and shellfish stocks, year-round fishermen have turned to aquaculture. Currently about 50 or so aquaculturists lease 120 acres of Wellfleet Harbor; you'll see them off Mayo Beach at low tide. Shellfish like quahogs and oysters are raised from "seed," put out in "protected racks," and tended for two to three years while they mature. Since as many as 2 million seeds can be put on an acre of land, this is big business. For those looking for fishing charters, though, the harbor and pier are still centers of activity.

GUIDANCE Wellfleet Chamber of Commerce (508-349-2510; wellfleet chamber.com), Route 6. Open 9–6 daily, mid-June to mid-September, with additional but limited hours for one month prior to and after that. The information booth is well marked right off Route 6 in South Wellfleet.

PUBLIC RESTROOMS Seasonally at Bakers Field across from Mayo Beach (on Kendrick Avenue), as well as at the Town Pier and the marina (both at the end of Commercial Street). Year-round in the basement of Town Hall on Main Street.

PUBLIC LIBRARY ❋ ✄ ☂ ⁗ **Wellfleet Public Library** (508-349-0310; well fleetlibrary.org), West Main Street. Open daily. Housed within the former Candle Factory, this outstanding library offers children's story hour, and an impressive lineup of readings, screenings, and speakers.

GETTING THERE *By car:* Wellfleet is 50 miles beyond the Cape Cod Canal via Route 6.

By bus: The **Plymouth & Brockton** bus line (508-778-9767; p-b.com) connects Wellfleet and South Wellfleet with Hyannis and other Cape towns, as well as with Boston's Logan Airport. The bus stops in front of Town Hall on Main Street in Wellfleet, and at Farrell's Market on Route 6 in South Wellfleet.

GETTING AROUND *By car:* From Route 6, take Main Street to the town center or veer from Main to Commercial Street to the colorful harbor. There is free parking at the Town Pier (at the end of Commercial Street) and behind Town Hall on Main Street. As the seagull flies, the town is anywhere from 2 to 5 miles wide.

MEDICAL EMERGENCY Outer Cape Health Services (508-349-3131), 3130 Route 6. Not an urgent-care facility. Open daily in summer.

❋ To See

Marconi Wireless Station, CCNS, off Route 6 at the Marconi Area. In 1901 Guglielmo Marconi began construction of the first wireless station on the U.S. mainland, in little old Wellfleet. Two years later the first U.S. wireless transatlantic message was transmitted between this station and England: President Roosevelt sent King Edward VII "most cordial greetings and good wishes." (Canada beat the United States in sending a wireless transatlantic message by one month.) A mere

14 years later, the station was closed for wartime security reasons; it was dismantled and abandoned in 1920 because of erosion and the development of alternative technologies. There are few remains today, save the concrete foundation of the transmitter house (which required 25,000 volts to send a message) and sand anchors that held guy wires to the 210-foot towers.

The Cape Cod peninsula is at its narrowest here, and from a well-positioned observation platform you can scan the width of it—from Cape Cod Bay, along Blackfish Creek, to the Atlantic Ocean. (See the Atlantic White Cedar Swamp Trail under *Green Space*.)

Wellfleet Historical Society Museum (508-349-9157; wellfleethistoricalsociety .com), 266 Main Street. Open 10–4 Tuesday and Friday and 1–4 Wednesday, Thursday, and Saturday, late June to early September. The society has collected photographs, toys, shipwreck detritus, marine artifacts, displays on Marconi and oystering, and household items to illustrate and preserve Wellfleet's past. Join one of their historical walks around town on Tuesday and Friday at 10:15 in the summer; meet at museum; $3. Nominal admission.

First Congregational Church of the United Church of Christ (508-349-6877), 200 Main Street. Although the church was organized in 1721, this Greek Revival meetinghouse dates to 1850. The interior is graced with a brass chandelier, eggshell-yellow walls, curved pews, and a Tiffany-style stained-glass window depicting a 17th-century ship similar to the *Mayflower*. (The church office is open 9–noon weekdays year-round.) On Sunday evenings at 7:30 in July and August, try to catch a concert featuring the restored Hook and Hastings pipe organ. The bell-shaped cupola, by the way, was added in 1879 after a storm destroyed the traditional one. (It was thought that a bell-shaped tower would be sturdier—perhaps it has been.)

Town clock, First Congregational Church, 200 Main Street. According to the arbiter of strange superlatives, *Ripley's Believe It or Not*, this is the "only town clock in the world that strikes ship's time." Listen for the following chimes and try to figure out what time it is for yourself: Two bells distinguish 1, 5, and 9 o'clock; six bells signify 3, 7, and 11 o'clock; eight bells toll for 4, 8, and 12 o'clock. To make matters even more interesting, adding one chime to the corresponding even hours signifies the half hours. (After all these years of hanging out in Wellfleet, I still double-check my "newfangled" wristwatch!)

WELLFLEET'S WINTER "SKYLINE"

Preservation Hall (508-349-2222; wellfleetpreservationhall.org), 335 Main Street. On the occasion of the country's 1976 bicentennial, two troubadours expressed their thanks to the town after a long celebration by donating the handsome painted carvings attached to the doors. More recently, the town purchased the former church and rechristened it as a non-profit cultural center in 2007. Plans are afoot to use it as an art and music venue and for community functions. One random note: conversion of the hall from a church was briefly halted so that turtles, which decided to nest on the site, could give birth. To honor them, the hall will be topped with a turtle wind vane.

Samuel Rider House, Gull Pond Road. Although the house is not open to the public, it's a fine early-1700s Outer Cape farmstead.

Atwood Higgins House (508-255-3421), Bound Brook Island Road, off Pamet Point Road. Open for tours 11 on Wednesday) and open houses (1–4 Thursday) from late May to mid-October (by reservation only). The pastoral 5-acre home-stead, under the auspices of the CCNS, has a tour that focuses on the architecture and versatility of the 18th-century full Cape that was restored by its early-20th-century owners. Don't miss it. This is one of my favorite places on the entire Cape. Free.

SCENIC DRIVES **Ocean View Drive**. Take LeCount Hollow Road to Ocean View (despite its name, it has only limited views) and head back to Route 6 via Gull Pond Road or Long Pond Road. You'll pass heathlands, cliffs, and scrub pines.

Chequessett Neck Road. Cross the dike at Herring River and head to the end of the road for magnificent sunset views. Although there is room for only a few cars at the very end of the road, you can park near the Great Island Trailhead and walk down to the beach (about 15 minutes).

Pilgrim Spring Road. Not to be confused with the Pilgrim Spring Trail in Truro, where the Pilgrims got their first taste of fresh water, this quiet road offers lovely inlet and cove views; at the end of the road, look back toward Wellfleet Harbor.

✳ To Do

BICYCLING/RENTALS **Cape Cod Rail Trail**. It terminates in Wellfleet at LeCount Hollow Road (where there is parking), just east of Route 6.

Idle Times Bike Shop (508-349-9161; idletimesbikes.com), 2616 Route 6. Open mid-May to early September. A full line of bicycles for the whole family.

A PERFECT (JAM-PACKED) DAY IN WELLFLEET

7:00   Dip into Long Pond before resident-only parking begins (by 8 AM).

8:30   Savor an omelet at the funky Flying Fish Café

9:30   Trek trails, identify birds, cross tidal creeks, and beach yourself on the sand at the Wellfleet Bay Wildlife Sanctuary.

12:00   Dine alfresco at Winslow's Tavern.

1:30   Hike on the cool and primordial Atlantic White Cedar Swamp Trail.

3:00   Cruise the art galleries on Main and Commercial streets.

5:00   Join the boisterous 30- and 40-something crowd for reggae and frozen drinks at the open-air, surfside Beachcomber.

6:30   Enjoy Chatham day boat scallops from Moby Dick's or sushi from Mac's.

8:00   Catch a provocative show at Wellfleet Harbor Actors Theater.

See also **Cape Outback Adventures** under *Fishing/Shellfishing*.

BOAT EXCURSIONS/RENTALS

Jack's Boat Rentals (508-349-7553; jacksboatrental.com), Gull Pond. Open late June to early September. This friendly outfit rents canoes, pedal boats, sea cycles, surf bikes, kayaks, and Sunfish. If you want to paddle somewhere besides Gull Pond, pick up a boat at the shop (508-349-9808) on Route 6.

CAPE COD RAIL TRAIL

Funseekers (508-349-1429; fun seekers.org) offers guided kayak and canoe tours twice daily through estuary marshes, along the tidal Pamet and Herring rivers, and out to Great Island. Departures vary with the tides. Eric also offers instruction in surfing, kiteboarding, and windsurfing.

Wellfleet Marine Corp. (508-349-2233), Town Pier. From mid-June to mid-September, you can rent Stur-Dee Cat sailboats, sloops, and fishing skiffs by the hour or by the day.

FISHING/SHELLFISHING Obtain a freshwater fishing permit at Town Hall (508-349-0301) on Main Street. Freshwater fishing holes include **Great Pond**, **Gull Pond**, and **Long Pond** (see *Green Space*).

Shellfishing permits are required for the taking of oysters, clams, and quahogs. But the only time you can do it is to Wednesday and Sunday at Indian Neck. Expect to pay $40 for a four-month nonresident permit (valid January through September). Wellfleet's tidal flats are wondrous places at low tide. Contact the **Beach Sticker Booth** (508-349-9818) on the pier from mid-June through August or Town Hall (508-349-0300) off-season. Try your luck surf-casting early in the morning or at night at the following Atlantic beaches: **Newcomb Hollow**, **White Crest**, and **LeCount Hollow**, or at **Duck Harbor** on the bayside.

WELLFLEET HARBOR, LOW TIDE

Cape Outback Adventures (508-349-9801; capeoutback.com), 1446 Route 6. Open May to mid-October. One-stop shopping for surf rentals, outdoor maps, bike rentals, and kayaks, as well as kayak tours.

Naviator (508-349-6003; naviator .com), Wellfleet Harbor Marina. With more than 30 years of experience plying Cape Cod waters, Captain Rick Merrill offers morning and afternoon fishing trips in July and August but only one per day in June and September; $40 adults, $30 children under 12.

GOLF **Chequessett Yacht & Country Club** (508-349-3704; cycc.net), 680 Chequessett Neck Road. Open April through November, weather permitting. This nine-hole, par-35 course offers beautiful views of Wellfleet Harbor.

MINI-GOLF *⌘* **At the Wellfleet Drive-In** (508-349-2520; wellfleetcinemas .com), Route 6. Open late May through September. The only game in town is conveniently located next to the flea market, the drive-in, and a classic dairy bar.

SAILING *⌘* **Chequessett Yacht & Country Club** (508-349-0198; cycc.net), 680 Chequessett Neck Road, offers junior and adult sailing late June to late August. Group instruction by the week for youths; individual instruction by the hour. Call ahead for availability.

SEAL CRUISES See the "Trails, Birds, Seals & Classes" sidebar.

SPECIAL PROGRAMS See the "Trails, Birds, Seals & Classes" sidebar.

⌘ **Summer recreation programs** (508-349-0330), Bakers Field and Gull Pond. Weekdays 9–noon, early July to mid-August. Sports, arts and crafts, and swimming lessons. Nonresidents $120 for the six week session for the first child, $100 each additional child.

TENNIS Town courts are on **Mayo Beach**, Kendrick Avenue.

Oliver's Red Clay Tennis Courts (508-349-3330; oliversredclaytennis.com), 2183 Route 6. Open early June to late September. These seven courts cost $16 hourly; tennis lessons are available in July and August.

Chequessett Yacht & Country Club (508-349-3704; cycc.net), 680 Chequessett Neck Road. Open March through November, weather permitting. Five hard courts are available to the public for a fee.

✳ Green Space

BEACHES **Marconi Beach**, CCNS, on the Atlantic. A boardwalk and steep staircase lead to the long, narrow beach backed by dramatic dunes. In-season amenities include lifeguards, outdoor showers, and changing facilities. Parking $15 (permit valid all day at any CCNS beach; no charge after 4 PM).

Cahoon Hollow Beach and **White Crest Beach**, town beaches on the Atlantic Ocean. Sandy shoals create shallow, warmish (i.e., not frigid) pools of water here. Although each beach is wide and sandy, local townsfolk favor the sea grass and dunes of White Crest, and hang gliders and surfers

CAPE COD NATIONAL SEASHORE

TRAILS, BIRDS, SEALS & CLASSES

❊ **Wellfleet Bay Wildlife Sanctuary** (508-349-2615; massaudubon.org), 291 Route 6. Trails open daily sunrise to sunset; center opens daily 8:30–5, year-round, except closed Monday from early October to late May. This is one of my Top 10 places on Cape Cod. With almost 1,100 acres of pine, moors, freshwater ponds, tidal creeks, salt marsh, and beach, the Audubon sanctuary is one of New England's most active. Despite that, you'll appreciate the relative lack of human presence after a day of gallery hopping and sunbathing.

Three **trails** total more than 5 miles: Silver Spring Trail, a lovely, wooded walking trail alongside a long pond; Goose Pond Trail (an all-person accessible trail), past ponds, woodlands, a marsh, and heathland (a boardwalk leads to the bay from here); and Bay View Trail.

The sanctuary also offers a steady stream of **activities** throughout the summer (plenty year-round, for that matter): canoe trips, family seashore hikes, evening natural history talks, birding expeditions, and trips to Monomoy Island (see the sidebar under *Green Space* in "Chatham").

The popular July, August, and November **seal cruises** in the waters off Chatham last 90 minutes. Trips depart most weekends off-season and most weekdays in-season; call for the tide-dependent schedule. They also have a 2-hour Sea Bird and Seal Cruise in late fall, which goes out on an open commercial fishing vessel. Onboard naturalists will educate you about the habits and habitats of harbor and gray seals. Reservations required. Tickets: $25–30 for nonmembers, $5 less for children.

Wellfleet Bay Wildlife Sanctuary **Natural History Day Camps** are offered June through August. Geared toward children 4–14, these excellent

appreciate the surf. (Hang gliders are not allowed from mid-April to early October.) White Crest has more parking. Amenities include lifeguards and restrooms. Parking $15 daily, $30 for three days, $60 weekly.

Mayo Beach, Kendrick Avenue. Parking is free, but the beach is nothing to e-mail home about. From here you can see some of the offshore areas—marked by yellow buoys—where modern aquaculture thrives in the form of constructed shellfish farms.

The following beaches require a town sticker: **Maquire Landing** and **Newcomb Hollow Beach**, both off Ocean View Drive on the Atlantic Ocean; **Burton Baker Beach** (the only place in town where sailboarding is permitted) and **Indian Neck Beach**, both off Pilgrim Spring Road on the bayside; **Powers Landing** and **Duck Harbor**, both off Chequessett Neck Road on the bayside. Cottage renters may purchase a sticker at the well-marked Beach Sticker Booth (508-349-9818) on the weeklong programs are designed to "expand curiosity about and respect for the environment through hands-on outdoor experiences . . . and to develop skill in discovering the natural world using the principles of scientific inquiry." Indeed. $160–330 for members and nonmembers.

The sanctuary's summertime **Adult Field School** incorporates multiday, hands-on courses. Topics include Cape Cod natural history, ornithology, marine life, nature photography, local endangered habitats, and sketching in the field. Instruction is expert.

Before departing, don't miss the eco-friendly Esther Underwood Johnson Nature Center, and especially don't miss the environmentally friendly composting toilets, which save 100,000 gallons of water per season. It's a beautiful example of green architecture, with solar heating and gray-water planter beds.

Exhibits feature Cape Cod natural history as well as two 700-gallon aquariums displaying life beneath the water of salt marshes and tidal pools. Trails are free to members, $5 for adult nonmembers, $3 for children nonmembers. Members may **tent** in the wooded natural setting (call for fees and reservations).

Town Pier from July to early September, the only time you'll need a sticker. It's open 8:30–4 daily (until 8 PM on Friday and Saturday). $60 weekly.

In late January 2008, after a fierce mid-winter storm, a visitor washed ashore at **Newcomb Hollow Beach**: a mid- to late 19th century schooner that had ship-wrecked who knows when and had taken down who knows how many sailors with it (if any). The beached keel and ribs, upright in the sand, looked like the ribs of a 50-foot whale and it captured the attention of locals and visitors from 100 miles away. The National Park Service suggested the ship was the largest to wash ashore in 15 years; another marine specialist suggested it could have the *Logan*, a coal barge wrecked in 1920. What is known for sure is that 18 ships failed to navigate the treacherous shifting sand bars and shoals near the Cahoon Hollow Lifesaving Station between 1800 and 1927.

PONDS **Great Pond**, **Long Pond**, and **Gull Pond** offer freshwater swimming. If you're staying at an inn or cottage, you'll be eligible for the requisite parking sticker (available on the Town Pier; 508-349-9818). All ponds have lifeguards.

WALKS **Great Island Trail**, CCNS, off Chequessett Neck Road. About 8 miles roundtrip, this trail is relatively flat; but soft sand makes for a challenging 4-hour roundtrip trek. Walk at low tide when the sand is firmer. (Besides, Jeremy Point, the tip of land farthest out to sea, is covered at high tide.) You'll be rewarded with scant human presence and stunning scenery. Great for birders; best on a sunny spring day or a crisp autumn one. Bring plenty of water and sunscreen.

This area was once an island, hence its name. Over time Cape Cod Bay currents deposited sandbars that eventually connected it to the mainland. Long ago, Great Island was home to various commercial enterprises—oystering, cranberry harvesting, and shore whaling—and the land was dotted with lookout towers used to spot whales. There was even a local watering hole and overnight hostelry, the Great Island Tavern, built in 1690 and used until about 1740. But as shore whaling died, so did the Great Island community. By 1800 the island was deserted and deforested. (Pines have been planted in an effort to keep erosion under control.)

Atlantic White Cedar Swamp Trail, CCNS, roundtrip Marconi Area. One of the best Outer Cape trails, this swamp, navigable via a boardwalk, has a primordial feel. A dense overhead cover keeps it cool even on the most stifling of days. Nonetheless, the early and latter parts of this 1.2-mile trail traverse steep stairs and soft sand. This trail features one of the few remaining stands of white cedar on the Cape. Prized by settlers for its light weight and ease of handling, a century of overuse took its toll. While the swamp (in places, 24 feet deep with peat) has begun to recover, nature has its own cycles; red maples will eventually choke the white cedars out of existence. In August, trailside blueberries are ripe for the picking.

Uncle Tim's Bridge, East Commercial Street. The often-photographed wooden footbridge connects Commercial Street to a small wooded island, crossing a tidal creek (Duck Creek) and marshland. Short, sandy trails circle the island.

Wellfleet Conservation Trust (508-349-2162; wellfleetconservationtrust.org) is constantly purchasing and opening up new trails and tracts of land—including Bayberry Hill, Fox Island Marsh and Pilgrim Spring Woodlands, and Box Turtle Woods and Marsh. The easiest thing to do is go online and print trail maps.

See the "Trails, Birds, Seals & Classes" sidebar.

GREAT ISLAND TRAIL

✳ Lodging

Most summer visitors to Wellfleet stay in cottages and houses, rented by the week or, most probably, longer, but there are plenty of places for short-term guests.

BED & BREAKFASTS 🍴 "𝔶"
Aunt Sukie's Bayside B&B (508-349-2804; 800-420-9999; auntsukies.com),

AUNT SUKIE'S BAYSIDE B&B

525 Chequessett Neck Road. Open mid-June to mid-September. Hidden by a fence from a road less traveled, Sue and Dan Hamar's bayfront B&B is full of southward-facing picture windows. It takes just 30 seconds to walk from the shingled house, with a contemporary addition, across a boardwalk marsh to the inn's private bay beach. I'd live here all summer long, if I could. As for the rooms, two contemporary ones boast private decks and splendid southward bay views. The suite features wide-pine floors, Oriental carpets, a private patio, and a separate sitting room in the original 1830 section of the house. The common room, dotted with antiques, overflows with "Aunt Sukie's" history. An expanded continental breakfast is served on the bayside deck, weather permitting. Ask about the nearby, three-bedroom "House in the Woods," which comes with the use of the Aunt Sukie's private beach. B&B rooms $195–270, house $1,500–1,900 weekly.

❄ ✑ ⁝T⁝ **Oyster Cove B&B** (508-349-2994; oystercove.com), 20 Partridge Way. This B&B, in the heart of the National Seashore, offers a more personal alternative to many other lodging places. Hosts Sandy and Dick Nichol-

son, who built this spacious, three-story contemporary home in 1998, offer great views of Indian Neck, Great Island, Chipman Cove, and Wellfleet Harbor. And three levels of decks drink in those wonderful views. Further, the front beach is popular for walking or launching kayaks. At low tide you could even walk to town, although you have to watch it coming back! Guests have their choice of the romantic, upper Captain's Studio or the lower-level Beach Suite (with three good-sized bedrooms). The latter can be rented in its entirety or as one or two bedrooms. The inn is quite well suited to families and reunions. Sandy makes muffins and scones for breakfast, while Dick is most helpful in arranging outdoor adventures. June through September $265 studio, $495 suite for six people; off-season $225–395 and $125–390, respectively.

🐾 ✑ **Inn at Duck Creeke** (508-349-9333; innatduckcreeke.com), 70 Main Street. Open early May to mid-October. Half a mile from the town center, this rambling, old-fashioned 1800s inn is situated between an idyllic duck pond and a salt marsh (ask for one of the rooms overlooking it). Owners Bob "Moo" Morrill and Judy Pihl describe it as "friendly but not fussy." And that's just about right. Fine for active Explorers who won't be spending mornings lying around their rooms, the simple guest rooms serve both families and budget-conscious travelers. My favorite rooms are in the Saltworks Cottage (they share a homey living room) and the carriage house (they have a spiffed-up, romantic cabin feel). Continental breakfast included. In-season $110–135 private bath, $85–110 shared bath; off-season $65–120.

COTTAGES 🐾 **The Colony** (508-349-3761; thecolonyofwellfleet.com), 640 Chequessett Neck Road. Open late

May to mid-September. This is not your average cottage colony. In fact, no place on the Cape remotely resembles it. If I were going to spend a week or two anywhere, it'd be in one of these Bauhaus treasures, 1949 low-slung duplexes. Well-traveled guests flock here for quietude (you'll be speaking in hushed tones before you know it), communing with nature (fresh flowers adorn each cottage), and excellent service—including daily maid service. Eleanor Stefani purchased the low-key place in 1963, but Nathaniel Saltonstall (a trustee of Boston's Institute for Contemporary Arts) built it as a private club in 1949. Scads of original artwork grace the cottages, which are furnished in mod 1950s style. Cottages also feature galley kitchens, glass-enclosed dining porches, and terraces with furniture for dining al fresco. Each of the 10 charming units has decks and lots of picture windows, which bring the natural surroundings indoors. It's a real retreat, without TV or WiFi (for a reason), and plenty of books, journals, and magazines in each cottage. $1,295–2,375 weekly for one and two bedrooms, $195–350 nightly. No credit cards.

🐾 🐾 Surf Side Cottages (508-349-3959; surfsidecottages.com), 45 Ocean View Drive. Open early April through November. These 1950s-style housekeeping cottages are within a minute's walk of the dunes and ocean. Nothing separates them from the ocean except other Surf Side cottages and scrub pines; a few of the 18 units have ocean views. Come for the quiet and a family-friendly atmosphere. Most larger cottages have a roof deck; each has a screened-in porch (with that classic wooden door slamming sound) and wood-burning fireplace and a private outdoor shower. Modern kitchens, knotty-pine paneling, and tasteful rattan furnishings are the norm. Bring

sheets and towels (or pay $10 per person) and leave the cottage clean and ready for the next tenants. Reserve early. Pets accepted off-season. Since managers Armand and Lisa Audette took over in 2008 (they'd been the owners of The Even'tide for years), they've helped owners remodel and upgrade one third of their kitchens and bathrooms. Mid-June through August $1,150 for a one-bedroom, $1,850–2,500 for a two- or three-bedroom, weekly; off-season $95–168 daily, $655–1,175 weekly.

🐾 ¹⁰¹ The Even'tide (508-349-3410; 800-368-0007; eventidemotel.com), 650 Route 6. Open April through October. These nine cottages are a cut above. Wooded and set back from Route 6, the complex has a nice children's play area, a big heated indoor pool, an exercise room, a billiard table, mini-golf, shuffleboard, ping pong, badminton, horseshoes, basketball, direct access to the rail trail, and a walking trail to Marconi Beach. Phew! Is that enough for you? All cottages have TV, telephone, fully tiled bathroom, and full kitchen (except Tern). They also have some above-average motel rooms and suites that rent for $98–210 nightly in the summer and the Kingfisher House, a 5-bedroom place that rents for $2,000–2,700 weekly. Otherwise, cottages: July and August $1,200–2,700 for four to six people weekly; off-season $515–925 for four to six people weekly. Minimum summertime stays are 3–5 nights.

See also **Maurice's Campground** under *Campgrounds.*

MOTELS 🚻 ¹⁰¹ **Wellfleet Motel & Lodge** (508-349-3535; 800-852-2900; wellfleetmotel.com), 170 Route 6. Open mid-March through November. The bi-level, 1960s-style motel has 65 rooms and suites across from the Wellfleet Bay Wildlife Sanctuary. Rooms in the nicely landscaped lodge, built in 1986, are generally more spacious than the motel rooms and have balconies or patios with courtyard views. In addition to direct access to the Cape Cod Rail Trail, you'll find a gas grill, a Jacuzzi, and indoor and outdoor pools. No room goes more than three years without a "soft goods" renovation. July and August $160–300; off-season $70–165.

See also the **Even'tide** under *Cottages.*

CAMPGROUNDS 🌸 ✿ **Paine's Campground** (508-349-3007; camp ingcapecod.com), 180 Old County Road. Open late May to mid-September. At this tenter's haven there are designated areas for "quiet" campers, youth groups, and families, as well as sites to which you must lug your tent. Of the 150 sites, only six are reserved for big RVs. You can walk from the campground to the National Seashore. Freshwater swimming is found in nearby kettle ponds. Sites $40–50 for two.

🌸 ✿ **Maurice's Campground** (508-349-2029; mauricescampground.com), 80 Route 6. Open late May to mid-October. Maurice's has about 220 wooded sites for tents and trailers, four cottages that can sleep four, and cabins that can sleep three with a cot. Ask about the duplex cabin that sleeps four to six people. Direct access to the Cape Cod Rail Trail is a real plus for folks. Camping $36 for two; cottages $700 weekly for two, $750 for four; cabins $95–105 nightly and $575–635 weekly for 2 or 3 people.

See also the "Trails, Birds, Seals & Classes" sidebar.

RENTAL HOUSES AND COTTAGES **Kinlin Grover** (508-285-0118; chrisnagle.mykinlingroveragent

.com), 2548 Route 6. When you're looking to by something on the Outer Cape after renting, I have personal experience with this terrific agent. He can also direct you to rental specialists.

✳ Where to Eat

Wellfleet oysters are renowned: Legend has it that England's Queen Victoria served them at her state dinners (no others would do). According to aficionados, Wellfleet oysters taste better when harvested from the cooler waters in the off-season, but you'll have little choice if you vacation in July or August; order them anyway. Wellfleet is also known for its hard-shell quahog and steamer clams. In fact, these waters yield millions of dollars' worth of shellfish annually.

Although there are many restaurants reviewed here, *most are closed off-season.* Furthermore, most opening and closing dates are wholly dependent on weather and tourist traffic.

DINING OUT 🌸 ♈ **Winslow's Tavern** (508-349-6450; winslowstavern .com), 316 Main Street. Open noon– 1 AM daily May through October. Ahhh, alfresco dining overlooking a quiet town center in the summer. There are few things better. This upscale bistro and tavern, which opened in 2006 and recently started coming into its own, features New England classics, fresh fish, and imaginative specials. It's easy on the palette *and* the wallet—a perfect combination. Start with perfection in a bowl (fire-roasted gazpacho) or a lightly dressed creative salad and move on to oven-roasted Chatham cod, mussels, or pan-seared Colorado lamb chops with roasted artichokes, fava beans, beets, and a mint crème fraiche. On my last visit, the dense macadamia nut chocolate torte was served colder than it should have been. Within the casually elegant interior, meals are well paced and tables are well spaced. Come early for a drink upstairs in the cozy bar. Lunch $8–13, dinner $15–22.

✻ ☙ **Wicked Oyster** (508-349-3455; capecodchefs.com), 50 Main Street. Open for breakfast and dinner; call for off-season schedule. This place, both casual and elegant, gets sure high marks for service and food. When new owners Ken Kozak and Eliza Fitts took over management in 2008, they didn't miss a beat. For lunch in winter try pan-seared scallops on a bed of spinach salad or fried haddock with chips. At dinnertime in-season, venture towards the catch of day in a light crème broth with littlenecks, leeks, bacon and fingerling potatoes (for instance). The grilled black Angus tenderloin with bourbon caramel sauce is also quite worthy. And their oysters are deliciously buttery and soft. Either way, top it off with a chocolate peanut butter torte. Four course prix fixe dinner off-season. Otherwise, breakfast $6–10, dinner $15–30.

MOBY DICK'S

EATING OUT ☙ ☙ ♿ **Moby Dick's** (508-349-9795; mobydicksrestaurant .com), Route 6. Open 11:30–9 or 10 daily, May to mid-October. My high season on Cape Cod begins and ends with a meal at Moby Dick's. Since 1983 Todd and Migs Barry and their team have provided the best and largest portions of area seafood. Pride of ownership has its rewards. Although the place is always packed, would you really want to patronize an establishment that wasn't? Order off the blackboard menu, and then take a seat surrounded by weathered nautical paraphernalia or at a picnic table on the open upper level. You know the fare (it's just not normally this fresh and tasty)—Chatham steamers (clams) caught off Monomoy Island, lobsters, Wellfleet oysters and scallops, seafood rolls (with barely a hint of mayo), "dayboat hooked" cod, and unusually presented onion rings. The chowder, loaded with big chunks of clams, really tastes like clam chowder should. BYOB. Lunch $6–10, dinner $8–25.

✻ ☙ ☙ **Finely JP's** (508-349-7500; capecodchefs.com), 554 Route 6. Open for dinner nightly in July and August, Wednesday or Thursday through Sunday off-season. With very good reason, loyal vacationers return to JP's again and again. Chef-owner John Pontius gussied up the place in 2006 and 2007 with a new two-level building, complete with a small bar, a rooftop deck for outdoor dining, and better soundproofing. He's been reelin' 'em in since 1991 with large and satisfying portions of grilled scallops on linguine, poached salmon with ginger, and baked Wellfleet oysters. Call ahead and put your name on the waiting list, because if you arrive after 6 PM, you'll be waiting. His off-season 3-course, early dinner for $21 is, quite simply, the best deal on the Outer Cape; otherwise dinner $16–29.

Mac's Shack (508-349-6333; macssea
food.com), 91 Commercial Street.
Open for dinner nightly May to mid-
October. If you want to know the defi-
nition of summer, visit Mac's Shack.
Dine outside at the happenin' raw bar
in a crushed seashell parking lot. Or
join Wellfleetians in a long line to dine
(just as casually) inside this big post
and beam, colonial landmark. Order
up some fresh sushi or other creative
coastal cuisine brought to you by those
who own Mac's Seafood on the harbor.
Dinner $15–25.

♂ ♆ ♿ **Duck Creeke Tavern Room**
(508-349-7369; innatduckcreeke.com),
70 Main Street. Open for dinner and
late-night appetizers mid-May to mid-
October. Under the watchful eye of
chef-owner Judy Pihl since 1974, Wellfleet's oldest tavern is cozy, lively,
friendly, and fun. It offers well-priced,
less formal dishes like potted halibut, a
Mooburger, seafood stew, and a vegetarian hot pot. A fireplace, beamed
ceilings, greenery, and a bar fashioned
from old doors set the tone for live,
jazz entertainment Wednesday through
Sunday. As their tag line says, "where
lobster is sweet and jazz is cool." Dinner $12–17.

Mac's Seafood and Market Grill
(508-349-0404; macsseafood.com),
Town Pier. Open late May to mid-
October. Mac, who buys seafood direct
from boats throughout the day, offers
(among other seafood concoctions)
smoked pâté and mussels or littlenecks
with linguine in white wine sauce.
You'll also find decent fried seafood,
burritos, clambakes-to-go, and vegetarian dishes. Regardless of whether you
eat in or take out, it's the harborside
location and casual outdoor patio at
sunset that draw folks; BYOB. He's
been doing it since 1996, so you know
something's right! Dinner $10–15.

♣ **The Juice** (508-349-0535), 6 Commercial Street. Open for lunch and
dinner mid-May to mid-October. This
funky, archetypal Wellfleetian eatery
(which looks like it's falling down but
isn't) serves strong morning java, midday falafel and veggie burgers, and
nighttime Mexican food. Although the
service is slow, the twenty-something
clientele typically has time on their
hands. Ask them to blend you a specialty organic smoothie. Dishes $6–9.

♣ ♂ ♿ **Flying Fish Café** (508-349-
7292; theflyingfishcafe.com), 29 Briar
Lane, between Route 6 and Main
Street. Open May through October. All
three meals daily in summer, 3–10 PM
in the shoulder months. Chef-owner
(since 2004) Sarah Robbins presides
over a funky little place to eat, with
modest tables, local art, and a partially
visible kitchen. The café's vegetarian
and ethnic menu is much more interesting than the simple decor suggests.
For breakfast, try great omelets or a
burrito. Keep dinner simple with a
fancy pizza or a hot chicken parmesan
sub. Vegetarians do well here. Breakfast $5–8, lunch $5–8 and dinner
$10–20.

✍ ♿ **Marconi Beach Restaurant** (508-349-6025; marconibeachrestaurant.net), 545 Route 6. Open for lunch and dinner early April to late October. You won't find better southern-style, wood-fired barbecue on the Lower or Outer Cape. We're talking ribs, chicken, pulled pork, and beef brisket with all the fixin's. If you can't decide what to have, they'll help you with a barbecue platter. And if someone in your party can't do without a fried seafood plate or salad, they'll be fine here too. Look for the trail of smoke and follow your nose. Dishes $10–25.

✍ **Catch of the Day** (508-349-9090; wellfleetcatch.com), 975 Route 6. Open for lunch and dinner mid-April to late October. This seafood market and no-frills eatery features fresh catch (grilled or blackened); buckets of local shellfish (Wellfleet littlenecks, Eastham mussels, and Chatham steamers); and daily specials like fish tacos, fisherman's stew, or baked Chatham scrod. Bring it to the beach, cook it at home, or dine on their patio. Dishes $6–24.

✍ **Van Rensselaer's** (508-349-2127; vanrensselaers.com), 1019 Route 6. Open for breakfast and dinner early April to late October. This longtime community fixture packs in families with an all-you-can-eat breakfast buffet on weekends ($10 adults, $6.50 kids under 10), early specials (with a choice of six entrées plus a salad bar for $16), seafood, prime rib, vegetarian dishes, and a half-portion bistro menu. They've also been the brains behind Catch of the Day since 2006. Breakfast $7–13, dinner $12–50.

✍ ♿ **Bookstore & Restaurant** (508-349-3154; wellfleetoyster.com), Kendrick Avenue. Closed January. Since owner Carol Parlante raises oysters from family harbor shellfish beds, I recommend you come simply for oyster appetizers, preferably raw, as they're so fresh. Lobsters are okay, too.

If you can't get a table on the outside deck, dine elsewhere. Breakfast $3–14, lunch $4–19 and dinner $16–29.

✴ ♨ ✍ **Box Lunch** (508-349-2178; boxlunch.com), 50 Briar Lane. Open for breakfast and lunch daily. At proprietor Owen MacNutt's original branch of the ever-expanding chain, folks swear by "Porky's Nightmare." "Rollwiches" are perfect for the beach or to take on a Great Island hike. Dishes $3–7.

See also **Beachcomber** under *Entertainment*.

COFFEE See **The Juice** under *Eating Out*.

✳ Entertainment

♿ **Wellfleet Harbor Actors Theater** (508-349-6835; what.org), 1 Kendrick Avenue (Harbor Stage) and 2357 Route 6 (Julie Harris Stage). Performances March to November (8 PM nightly at the Julie Harris Stage, 7 PM at the Harbor Stage in July and August, Thursday through Sunday off-season; matinees and kids' shows); 90 seats. Known locally as WHAT, it's clear why this serious and experimental theater company doesn't receive federal government funding from the National Endowment for the Arts. WHAT

THE JUICE

AN OPEN-AIR SCREEN WITH STARS

Wellfleet Drive-In (508-349-7176; 508-349-2450 for a human being; 866-696-3532; wellfleetdrivein.com), Route 6. Shows late April to early October. One of the last holdouts of a vanishing American pastime, this drive-in has lured patrons since 1957, when the number of U.S. drive-ins peaked at 4,000. Today there are fewer than 800 left—only a handful in New England, no others on the Cape. Hence, it remains a treasured local institution. Late owner John Jentz, a former engineering professor at MIT, designed the screen with his MIT pals; perhaps that's why it's withstood hurricanes with winds up to 135 mph. Double features are shown nightly at dusk (about 8 PM in summer). Movies change about once a week, and there's a play area behind the reasonably priced **Intermission Bar & Grill**. The box office opens at 7. Films are generally family-oriented. Tickets $8 adults, $5 children 4–11.

produces plays by new writers and directors, established folks like David Mamet, and radical interpretations of Chekhov, too. A fixture in the community since 1985, WHAT can always be counted on to be provocative. Don't worry; their kid's shows are tamer! Artistic director Jeff Zinn, son of historian Howard Zinn, has great backing from the community. If you consider yourself cool, do yourself a favor and check out one of their shows. Tickets $22–32; $9 for kid's show; half-price "student rush" just prior to curtain time.'

❀ **Square dancing**, Town Pier or Mayo Beach parking lot. On Wednesday evening in July and August, the waterfront takes on a different tone. Dancing begins at 7:30, and the steps get progressively more difficult until 10 or so. I found myself in the middle of families, callers, and klieg lights on a hot summer night in August and had a blast. I have to admit.

❋ ❀ ↑ **Wellfleet Cinemas** (508-349-7176; wellfleetdrivein.com), 51 Route 6. Adjacent to the drive-in, this is the only Outer Cape cinema open year-round. First-run movies on four screens.

♈ **Beachcomber** (508-349-6055; the beachcomber.com), off Ocean View Drive on Cahoon Hollow Beach. Open weekends late May to mid-June, daily 11 or noon–1 AM, mid-June to early September. In its former incarnation, this 1890s structure was one of the Outer Cape's nine lifesaving stations. Today, perched on a bluff right above the beach, it's well known as a

restaurant *and* a bar and club. By day, shuffle from the beach to hang out with a thirty- and forty-something crowd on the outdoor deck, complete with a 40-foot-long, cabana-style raw bar. Burgers, seafood plates, and boneless buffalo wings also offered. Inside is dark, with wooden booths. Only appetizers and pizza are available after 9 PM. There's nothing else like it on the Cape, and it's simply amazing that it has survived this long, surrounded by National Park Service land. Be careful about wandering out onto the beach after a couple of drinks; the first step is a doozy! Hip Boston bands and national blues artists perform in the evenings, but the club is perhaps best known for its Sunday-afternoon concerts and reggae-filled happy hours (frozen mudslides are very popular). Dishes $6–20.

❋ Selective Shopping

Arts-and-crafts shows are held on many Mondays and Tuesdays in July and August at the Wellfleet Drive-In on Route 6. This is generally high-quality stuff, from oils and watercolors to pottery, jewelry, and objects de wood or glass. Free.

Wellfleet Flea Market (508-349-2520; 800-696-3532; wellfleetdrivein.com), at the Wellfleet Drive-In, 51 Route 6. Open 8–3 Saturday, Sunday, and Monday holidays mid-April through October; also Wednesday, Thursday, Saturday, and Sunday in July and August. With more than 300 stalls, there's more junk than treasure, but you never know what you'll find: name-brand clothing, a hat to ward off the summer sun, used and antique furniture, and trinkets, tea sets, and colored glasses. Wander in with the intention of spending a few minutes and a few dollars and you'll probably find that hours have passed and you've

bought more than you bargained on! It's the Cape's biggest and best. Admission $1–3 per car.

ART GALLERIES Wellfleet is an art town. The **Art Gallery Association** publishes a complete list of galleries, some of which are excellent, others of which cater to souvenir art. Pick one up at the Wellfleet Chamber of Commerce. In July and August, many galleries host wine-and-cheese openings on Saturday evening.

Cherry Stone Gallery (508-349-3026), 70 East Commercial Street. Open by appointment only. This long-established gallery carries works by Abbott and Atget, Motherwell and Tworkov (and local Cape artists). Unpretentious and friendly, it's for serious collectors.

❋ **Left Bank Gallery** (508-349-9451), 25 Commercial Street. Audrey and Gerald Parent's gallery is arguably the most interesting in town. Don't miss the crafts-filled potter's room behind the wonderfully diverse main exhibition area.

Nicholas Harrison Gallery (508-349-7799), 25 Bank Street. Open May through December. Owner Anna Besciak has catapulted contemporary crafts into the fine art category

LEFT BANK GALLERY

with this collection. In addition to excellent ceramics, their gallery shows an outstanding assortment of glass objects, metalwork, lighting, woodworking, jewelry, and other wearable art.

❋ **Left Bank Small Works & Jewelry** (508-349-7939), 3 West Main Street. Works on paper, contemporary jewelry, and clothing are highlighted.

Kendall Art Gallery (508-349-2482), 40 Main Street. Open May through October. These folks probably carry more sculpture in more media—bronze, aluminum, and marble—than any other gallery on the Cape. The sculpture garden is tranquil. In all, Walter and Myra Dorrell carry the work of about 40 artists and craftspeople, in addition to selling Walter's paintings. And they've been doing it since 1983.

Blue Heron Gallery (508-349-6724), 20 Bank Street. Open mid-May to mid-October. Royal Thurston packs contemporary fine art, pottery and sculpture into a seemingly endless series of small rooms. More than 40 representational contemporary artists and artisans are shown.

Cove Gallery (508-349-2530; cove gallery.com), 15 Commercial Street. Open late May to mid-October. This gallery has featured oils, pastels, and a full range of media since 1968; it also has a lively sculpture garden overlooking Duck Creek.

ARTISANS ❋ **Salty Duck Pottery** (508-349-6852), 115 Main Street. You never know whom and what you're going to find in this community of tolerant eccentrics—perhaps potters shaping their lives and clay alongside a salt marsh. Check out potter Maria Juster's blue-green stoneware pottery, tiles, mirrors, and tables.

❋ **Narrow Land Pottery** (508-349-6308), 2603 Route 6, adjacent to the service station. Joe McCaffery, who studied at the School of the Museum of Fine Arts, Boston, throws pots, vases, mugs, lamp bases, and plates. His glazes, porcelain, and stoneware come in a variety of colors.

BOOKSTORES **Herridge Books** (508-349-1323), 140 Main Street. Open late May to late September. Used books covering a wide range of subjects.

CLOTHING Style-conscious women are in luck (in-season) in Wellfleet. Loose-fitting designs in cotton, linen, rayon, and earth tones reign. Try **Hannah** (508-349-9884), 234 Main Street, with "curated," comfortable, classic fashions from around the world; **Eccentricity** (508-349-7554), 361 Main Street (ethnic designs featuring tactile fabrics); **Eccentricity's Off Center** (508-349-3634), across the street; and **Karol Richardson** (508-349-6378), nearby at 11 West Main Street.

FARM STAND **Hatch's Fish Market/Hatch's Produce** (508-349-2810), behind Town Hall on Main Street. Open 9–7 daily late May to mid-September. Although you might find better prices at the supermarket, the fish and produce here are fresh and beautifully displayed, and the location can't be matched. Hatch's smokes its own fish, pâté, and mussels.

SPECIAL SHOPS **Jules Besch Stationers** (508-349-1231), 15 Bank Street. Open daily May to mid-October; weekends mid-October to late November and April. This former 1873 bank building now features products that will make you want to take pen (perhaps an antique 1880s pen or a quill) to paper (perhaps some hand-made paper or a bound journal). It also sells unique wrapping paper, collectible postcards, artsy boxed note cards, specialty albums, and blank books. Parts of the shop resemble a study, set up with writing tables, leather blotters, and stylish desk lamps. Buy a blank card and ask Michael Tuck (aka Jules) to personalize it (overnight); he's known for his calligraphy and verse.

The Chocolate Sparrow (508-349-1333), 326 Main Street. Open late May to early September. As long as anyone can remember, Wellfleet has had a penny-candy store. The Chocolate Sparrow opened in 1990 to continue the tradition, and added rich, hand-dipped chocolates.

✳ Special Events

July 4: **Independence Day parade**.

Mid-October: **Oyster Festival** (well fleetoysterfest.org). An instant tradition since it began in 2001, this "aw shucks" weekend celebrates the famed local delicacy (and the men and women who make their livelihoods farming it) with oyster-shucking demonstrations, live music, art auction and more. Keep it simple with food and games, or get serious with shellfish education talks and demonstrations.

TRURO

Considered to be the last vestige of "old Cape Cod," Truro has no stop-lights, no fast-food outlets, no supermarket. It does have, though, the last working farm on the Outer Cape. And it has a lot of new construction—second homes that lie dormant during the off-season and lots of new year-round houses. Yes, Dorothy, the landscape is changing in Truro. Still, though, both Truro Center and North Truro consist of only a few shops. Nothing more, nothing less. And local folks, summer people (vacationing writers and urban professionals who have built large houses in the rolling hills and dunes), and even the newcomers are determined to keep it that way.

North Truro is also tiny but has blue-collar ties to Provincetown. Compare Dutra's Market (an institution) to Jams (a fancy food shop born in the '80s) and the differences are readily apparent. As you head toward Provincetown, the only real development—in a nod to the tourist industry—consists of hundreds of tiny cottages, motels, and houses lining a narrow strip of shore wedged between Cape Cod Bay and the dramatic parabolic dunes on Pilgrim Lake. It's an odd juxtaposition, but one I always look forward to.

There aren't many human-made sites to explore, except for Highland Light and the Truro Historical Museum, but there are plenty of natural ones. Almost 70 percent of Truro's 42 square miles (one of the largest towns on the Cape, in acreage) falls within the boundaries of the Cape Cod National Seashore (CCNS). There are hiking and biking trails as well as expanses of beach. Rolling moors and hidden valleys characterize the tranquil back roads east and west of Route 6. Windswept dunes, lighthouses, beach grass, and austere shorelines will inspire you, as they did Edward Hopper. The painter built a summer home in Truro in the 1930s and worked there until 1967. In 2007 a land dispute erupted between a developer-owner who wanted to build a trophy house on nine acres of what many view as sacred Hopper land and views. Neighbors wanted to preserve the landscape made famous by artist Edward Hopper. The Cape Cod Commission, arbiters of all things potentially contentious and historic, ruled in March 2008 that the Kline's could go ahead and build their 6,500 square foot house. Such is progress.

Truro, established in 1697, has endured many name changes. Originally it was called Payomet or Pamet, after the Native American tribe that inhabited the area before the Pilgrims. In 1705 it was known as Dangerfield because of the large number of offshore sailing disasters. Eventually it was named Truro, for a Cornish coastal town in England.

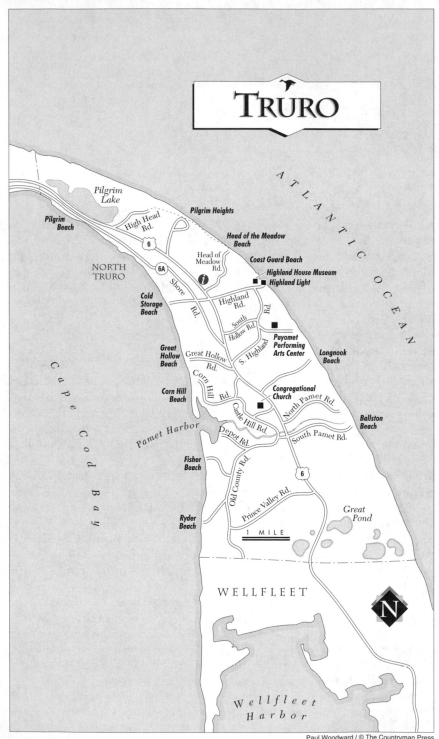

TRURO

ATLANTIC OCEAN

Pilgrim Lake

Pilgrim Heights

Pilgrim Beach

High Head Rd.

Head of the Meadow Beach

NORTH TRURO

6

6A

Head of Meadow Rd.

Coast Guard Beach

Highland House Museum

Highland Light

Shore Rd.

Cold Storage Beach

Highland Rd.

South Hollow Rd.

S. Highland Rd.

Payomet Performing Arts Center

Longnook Beach

Great Hollow Beach

Great Hollow Rd.

Corn Hill Rd.

Corn Hill Beach

Congregational Church

North Pamet Rd.

Ballston Beach

Cape Cod Bay

Pamet Harbor

Castle Hill Rd.

Depot Rd.

South Pamet Rd.

Fisher Beach

Old County Rd.

6

Ryder Beach

Prince Valley Rd.

Great Pond

1 MILE

WELLFLEET

N

Wellfleet Harbor

Paul Woodward / © The Countryman Press

Although today Truro is sleepy and rural, it has been, at times during the last few centuries, a hotbed of activity. The *Mayflower*'s Myles Standish spent his second night ashore in Truro. His band of 16 fellow Pilgrims found their first fresh water in Truro, as well as a stash of corn (which belonged to the Native Americans) from which they harvested their first crop. And although you wouldn't know it today, since Pamet Harbor choked up with sand in the mid-1850s, Truro's harbor once rivaled neighboring Provincetown as a whaling and cod-fishing center. By the late 1700s, shipbuilding was thriving and the harbor bustling. Vessels bound for the Grand Banks were built here, and a packet boat sailed from Truro to Boston. The whaling industry also owes a debt to early Truro residents, one of whom (Ichabod Paddock) taught Nantucketers how to catch whales from shore.

In 1851 the population soared to a rousing 2,000 souls. But in 1860 the Union Company of Truro went bankrupt due to declining harbor conditions, and townspeople's fortunes and livelihoods sank with it. Commercially, Truro never rebounded. Today, the year-round population is also about 1,800 (despite a recent housing boom); the summer influx raises that number tenfold.

GUIDANCE **Truro Chamber of Commerce** (508-487-1288;trurochamber.com), Route 6. Open 10–4 daily, late June to early September; 10–4 Friday and Saturday, noon–4 Sunday, late May to late June and early September to mid-October.

PUBLIC RESTROOMS Stop at the Pilgrim Heights area in summer.

PUBLIC LIBRARIES ❋ ✐ ⚓ "♪" **Truro Public Library** (508-487-1125; truro library.org), 5 Library Lane, off Standish Way, north of North Truro. Open Tuesday through Saturday. This contemporary library has programs for adults and kids. I often find myself here, working on the next edition of the Explorer's Guide (even sitting on a front porch bench using the WiFi when the library is closed).

GETTING THERE *By car:* The center of Truro is about 60 miles from the Cape Cod Canal via Route 6. Route 6A and Shore Road are synonymous.

By bus: The **Plymouth & Brockton** bus line (508-778-9767; p-b.com) connects Truro with Hyannis and other Cape towns, as well as with Boston's Logan Airport. The bus stops at Dutra's in North Truro and at Jams in Truro center.

GETTING AROUND *By car:* Beaches, sites, and roads are well marked off Route 6. Generally, the CCNS is east of Route 6. The Shore Road exit in North Truro takes you into North Truro and eventually to Beach Point, choked with motels as it approaches Provincetown. At its most narrow, Truro is only a mile wide, while it stretches for 10 miles north to south.

By shuttle: The excellent **Provincetown Shuttle** (800-352-7155; capecodtransit .org) operates daily late June to mid-September. The shuttles run from Horton's Camping Resort and Dutra's in Truro along Route 6A and up to the MacMillan Wharf in Provincetown. From there, another shuttle ferries folks to the Provincetown Inn, Beech Forest, and Herring Cove Beach. Buses run every 30 minutes 9 AM–midnight. Fares are $2 one-way (seniors 60 and up $1).

MEDICAL EMERGENCY Call **911**.

* **To See**

Cape Cod Light, or **Highland Light**, CCNS, 27 Highland Road, off South Highland Road, North Truro. The original lighthouse that guarded these treacherous shores was erected in 1797. It was the first on Cape Cod and had to be rebuilt in 1853, the year that a whopping 1,200 ships passed by within a 10-day period. Almost as important to landlubbers as mariners, the lighthouse provided shelter to Henry David Thoreau during one of his famous Outer Cape walks. The spot where he once stood and proclaimed that here a man could "put all America behind him" is thought to be 150 feet offshore now, thanks to erosion. One of only five working lighthouses on the Outer Cape, it was the last to become automated, in 1986. The original light shone with whale oil from 24 lamps, while later lamps were fueled with lard and kerosene. The modern light has a 110-watt halogen bulb. Visible 23 miles out to sea, it's the brightest lighthouse on the New England coast. And at 120 feet above sea level, it's aptly named Highland.

In mid-1996 the National Park Service, Coast Guard, Truro Historical Society, and the state joined forces to avert a looming disaster. Engineers cautioned that the lighthouse would crumble into the ocean. Erosion, at the rate of 3 to 4 feet per year, had chewed away the cliff upon which the lighthouse was built. (Thanks to ferocious storms in 1990, some 40 feet were lost in one year alone!) And when cliffs erode to within 100 feet of a lighthouse, it is too dangerous to bring in the heavy equipment needed to move it. So at a cost of $1.5 million, and over a period of 18 days, the 430-ton historic lighthouse and keeper's house was jacked up onto steel beams and pushed along steel tracks by hydraulic rams. At a rate of 25 feet per day, it was moved 450 feet west and 12 feet south (that is, inland), to a spot on the golf course. It should be safe for another 150 years, unless we get a lot of nor'easters.

Lighthouse tours (508-487-1121; trurohistorical.org), which include a short video and exhibit in the keeper's house, are offered daily mid-May through October, 10–5:30, for $4 per person. No children under 48 inches allowed. An observation deck, where the lighthouse recently stood, overlooks the ocean. Mark your calendar to ascend the lighthouse under the light of a full moon from April through December. It's quite something watching the sunset and moonrise from here. Reservations are required and occupancy is limited to 12 people; donations.

A PERFECT DAY IN TRURO

8:00 Start with cranberry pancakes high atop the bluffs at Adrian's.

9:00 Play the Scottish-style Highland Golf Links, the Cape's oldest course.

11:30 Tour the Cape Cod Light and historic Highland House Museum.

12:45 Assemble a picnic lunch from Jams.

1:00 Enjoy it at Truro Vineyards of Cape Cod, with tours and tastings.

2:00 Laugh at the irreverent Susan Baker Memorial Museum.

3:00 Catch afternoon rays at Head of the Meadow Beach on the Atlantic.

7:00 Indulge in creative New American and Italian specialties at Terra Luna.

Highland House Museum (508-487-3397; trurohistorical.org), 6 Highland Light Road, North Truro. Open 10–4:30 Monday through Saturday, 1–4:30 Sunday, June through September. Operated expertly by the Truro Historical Society and housed in the circa-1907 Highland Hotel, this museum is wholly dedicated to preserving Truro's maritime and agricultural past. Permanent items on display include a pirate's chest, fishing and whaling gear, 17th-century firearms, photos of Truro residents and places, toys, and ship models. In essence, all 12 of the former hotel rooms are set up as mini-museums furnished with period

pieces. One room is dedicated to Courtney Allen, the Truro Historical Society founder, artist, model maker, and wood-carver. Upstairs is reserved for rotating exhibits. The building is a fine example of the fashionable, once prominent, turn-of-the-20th-century summer hotels. Adults $4; children under 12, free.

Truro Center for the Arts at Castle Hill (508-349-7511; castlehill.org), 10 Meetinghouse Road at Castle Hill Road, Truro. Classes and workshops year-round, although the majority are held in summer. A nonprofit educational institute, Castle Hill was founded in 1972 and has evolved into an important cultural voice on the Outer Cape art scene. Classes and workshops are offered in a converted 1880s barn to people of all ages in painting, drawing, writing, printmaking, book arts, photography, clay, and sculpture. Castle Hill also sponsors lectures, concerts, and artist receptions. Nationally renowned artists and writers lead weeklong (and longer) classes.

Truro Vineyards of Cape Cod (508-487-6200; trurovineyardsofcapecod .com), 11 Route 6A, North Truro. Tastings 11–5 Monday through Saturday, 1–5 Sunday, late May through November; weekends in December and April. Tastings ($7) include five wines and a souvenir wineglass. Free tours at 1 and 3 PM daily. Feel free to bring lunch and enjoy a picnic amid the huge antique wine casks.

TRURO CENTER FOR THE ARTS

Jenny Lind Tower, CCNS, off Highland Light Road, North Truro. Between the Highland Golf Links and the former **North Truro Air Force Base**, this 55-foot tower of granite seems out of place. And in fact, it is. The short story goes like this: In 1850, P. T. Barnum brought Swedish singing

TRURO VINEYARDS OF CAPE COD

legend Jenny Lind to America. When Barnum oversold tickets to her Boston concert, and when Lind heard the crowds were going to riot, she performed a free concert from the roof tower for the people in the street. When the building was to be destroyed in 1927, a Boston attorney purchased the tower and brought it here (he owned the land at that time). The CCNS owns the property now and the entrance is blocked, but the granite tower still stands 150 feet above sea level, visible to passing ships and those of us on the ground.

Congregational church and **cemetery**, off Bridge Road, Truro. A marble memorial commemorates the terrible tragedy of the 1841 October Gale, when seven ships were destroyed and 57 crewmembers died. Renowned glassmakers of Sandwich made the church windows, and Paul Revere cast the steeple bell. Take Route 6 to Snow's Field to Meetinghouse Road to Bridge Road.

Payomet Performing Arts Center (508-487-5400; ppactruro.org), Old Dewline Road, off South Highland Road. Performances late June to mid-September, since 1998. This outdoor tent space hosts worthy alternatives (comedians, plays, concerts, films, children's shows) to reading trashy novels. Tickets $10–25.

SCENIC DRIVES It's difficult to find an unpicturesque Truro road. Both North and South Pamet roads, connected prior to a breach at Ballston Beach, wind past bayberry, beach plums, and groves of locust trees. From Truro center, Castle Hill Road to Corn Hill Beach is lovely. In North Truro, take Priest Road to Bay View Road to the bayside Cold Storage Beach for great bay views.

FIRST CONGREGATIONAL CHURCH

✳ To Do

BICYCLING **Head of the Meadow Bike Trail**, CCNS, off Route 6, North Truro. Just south of Pilgrim Lake, this 2-mile (one way) bikeway runs from High Head Road, past salt marshes and dunes, to Head of the Meadow Beach (see *Green Space*). Four-wheel-drive vehicles with proper stickers can enter the dunes here, too, depending on piping plover activity.

BOATING **Pamet Harbor**, at the end of Depot Road, Truro. If you have your own boat, contact the harbormaster (508-349-2555) for launching information.

FISHING/SHELLFISHING Permits for freshwater fishing and shellfishing are available from Town Hall (508-349-7004), 24 Town Hall Road, off Bridge Road from Route 6, Truro. Kids love fishing from the grassy shores off **Pond Road** (which leads to Cold **Storage Beach**); it's tranquil for picnicking and watching the sun set, too. Surf-fishing is good all along the Atlantic coastline. For freshwater fishing, try **Great Pond**, off Savage Road from Route 6 in southern Truro.

GOLF Highland Golf Links (508-487-9201), Highland Light Road, off South Highland Road, North Truro. Open April through November. Perched on a high windswept bluff, the Cape's oldest course (founded in 1892) is one of the country's oldest, too. At the turn of the 20th century, the course was part of the Highland House resort (now a museum; see *To See*), which drew Boston visitors by train. Today the museum sits between the eighth and ninth holes. The course exemplifies the Scottish tradition, with deep natural roughs, Scotch broom, heath, unirrigated open fairways, occasional fog, and spectacular ocean views. That's why golfers come to this 9-hole course. That, and for the dime-sized greens, whale sightings from the sixth tee in summer, and the view of Highland Light adjacent to the seventh hole. Avoid the crowds by playing on Sunday. It's the only public course between Orleans and Provincetown. $33 for 9 holes; $55 for 18 holes; clubs $15.

TENNIS Pamet Harbor Yacht & Tennis Club (508-349-3772; pametclub.com), 7 Yacht Club Road, on the harbor. When not reserved for club members, these three courts are available for rental to the public.

✳ Green Space

BEACHES Town parking stickers are required from July to August. Cottage renters may purchase parking stickers ($30 weekly) at the Beach Program Office (508-487-6983) behind the Truro center post office on Route 6A.

Head of the Meadow Beach, on the Atlantic Ocean. Half the beach is maintained by the town, half by the CCNS; both have lifeguards. The only difference is that the latter half has changing rooms and restrooms; otherwise, it's the same wide, dune-backed beach. Parking $15 in-season; no charge after 4 PM; $10 for the town half of the beach.

Corn Hill Beach, off Corn Hill Road, on Cape Cod Bay. This is the only other town-managed beach where nonresidents can pay a daily parking fee ($10). Facilities include portable toilets and a large parking area. Backed by a long, low dune. The width of Corn Hill Beach decreases measurably as the tide comes in. There's good sailboarding too.

Long Nook Beach, off Long Nook Road, on the Atlantic Ocean. Although this wonderful beach requires a town parking sticker, in the off-season anyone can park here.

Coast Guard Beach, off Highland Road, and **Ballston Beach**, off South Pamet Road; both on the Atlantic Ocean. Each is owned by the town and requires a resident sticker, but anyone can bicycle in for free. (This Coast Guard Beach is not to be confused with Henry Beston's Coast Guard Beach in Eastham, under the auspices of CCNS.) Lifeguard, no; portable toilets, yes. Note: Use caution because of the tricky undertow.

WALKS **Pilgrim Heights Area**, CCNS, off Route 6, North Truro. Two short walks yield open vistas of distant dunes, ocean, and salt marsh. As the name implies, the easy 0.75-mile roundtrip **Pilgrim Spring Trail** leads to the spot where the Pilgrims reportedly tasted their first New England water. Or so historians say; it's debatable. One subsequently penned: "We . . . sat us downe and drunke our first New England water with as much delight as ever we drunke in all our lives." A small plaque marks the spot.

Small Swamp Trail (about the same distance as the Pilgrim Spring Trail, above) was named not for the size of the swamp or trail but rather for the farmer (Mr. Small), who grew asparagus and corn on this former 200-acre farm. By August, blueberries are ripe for the picking. In spring, look for migrating hawks. There's a wooded picnic area.

Pamet Area/Bearberry Hill, North Pamet Road, Truro. You won't want to pick this tangy and sour fruit come late September, but take the lovely walk—to the top of Bearberry Hill for views of the Atlantic and the bog landscape. The trailhead is located at the parking lot below the youth hostel/education center.

✷ Lodging

BED & BREAKFAST ❄ 🏵 🐾 ✐ ((ı))
The Moorlands Inn (508-487-0663; themoorlands.com), 11 Hughes Road, North Truro. Laid-back and welcoming, this inn is a rarity in the modern world of commercial innkeeping. You'll be selecting books from the shelves and getting ice from the kitchen before you know it. On a back road, the massive sea captain's house is a great place for family reunions, children of any age, and a game of croquet. The house has two brightly colored suites and one room—each with antiques and most with TV. The third-floor aerie has its own deck. Innkeepers Skipper and Bill Evaul have filled the house with Bill's art and music (anyone up for a spur-of-the-moment jam session?). An adjacent two-story carriage house has a kitchen and private courtyard hot tub. An apartment, which occupies the inn's third floor, has a private entrance. Expanded continental breakfast included for inn guests. Late June to mid-September $155–185 rooms and suites, $175–185 apartment, $1,300–1,400 weekly carriage house. Call for nightly off-season rates.

COTTAGES AND EFFICIENCIES
✐ ((ı)) **Kalmar Village** (508-487-0585; 617-277-0091 in winter; kalmarvillage.com), Route 6A, North Truro. Open May to October. On a strip chock-full of cottage colonies, Kalmar stands out. It's particularly great for families, since Kalmar sits on 400 feet of private bay beach. The Prelacks have owned the place since 1968, and you can spot their care and attention in the details: well-tended lawns around the pool, freshly painted chimneys atop the shingled cottages, and six new waterfront cottages. All 45 cottages are delightfully roomy inside, with modern kitchens.

Other perks include daily housekeeping and a coin-operated laundry; each unit has its own picnic table and grill. There are also large and small efficiencies, as well as three motel rooms. July and August $1,289–2,475 weekly for one- and two-bedroom cottages, $635–1,145 weekly for efficiencies ($105–205 nightly); off-season cottages $640–1,400 weekly, $125–245 nightly; efficiencies $66–99 nightly.

✂ "!" **East Harbour** (508-487-0505; eastharbour.com), 618 Route 6A, North Truro. Open April to late October. Although Truro has dozens of small cottage colonies, Sonja Soderberg's is among the best. The tidy, tastefully wallpapered, two-bedroom beachfront and waterview cottages enjoy daily maid service and manicured lawns and gardens. In total, there are seven cottages (fully equipped), nine air-conditioned motel rooms (with microwaves and refrigerators), and one suite. Grills, deck chairs, and umbrellas are available. Although some guests have been coming for five generations, Sonja has kept up with the times. And last but not least, there are lots of birdhouses around, and guests love their antics. The place is generally noted for low-key laughter and for guests leaving *really* relaxed. Late June to early September $1,400–1,850 weekly; cottages rent nightly off-season, or $735–1,250 weekly. Motel rooms $150–175 in-season, $85–130 off-season. Make reservations in January if you can.

Day's Cottages (508-487-1062; dayscottages.com), 271 Route 6A, North Truro. Open May to late October. These little green-and-white cottages, all 23 of them lined up like ducks in a row, are something of a local icon. When you see them, you know you're just about to the tip of the Cape. Although each is only 20 feet from the

next, people love them. Perhaps because there's nothing between them and the ocean, except for a couple of lawn chairs (albeit on a cement slab). And perhaps because they face due west, toward the setting sun. Each cottage has a TV and a full kitchen. Linens provided. Late June to early September $1,050–1,250 weekly; autumn $740 weekly; May $600–670 weekly, $87–97 nightly. No credit cards.

MOTEL ✂ "!" **Top Mast** (508-487-1189; 800-917-0024; topmastresort.com), 217 Route 6A, North Truro. Open May to late October. Owned and operated by the Silva family since 1971, this nicely maintained, 72-unit motel flanks Route 6A well before the congestion begins. Beachfront units are built right on sandy Cape Cod Bay, and each has a sliding glass door that opens onto an individual balcony with Adirondack chairs. Choose among motel rooms, one- and two-room efficiencies, and 2-bedroom cottages with full kitchens. Poolside garden rooms rent by the night, even in high season. In 2008 they built a giant indoor pool complex with a large heated saltwater pool, kiddie pool, hot tub, sauna, aromatherapy steam room, weight fitness

ROUTE 6A COTTAGES

room, big screen TVs, and cocktail area. It's not enough to make you skip Provincetown (5 miles away), but it's a great perk. Late June to early September $1,195–1,615 weekly for beachfront efficiencies, $1,735 weekly for cottage for four people, $175–235 nightly for beachfront room; spring and fall $100–165 nightly, $665–1,105 weekly.

RENTAL HOUSES AND COTTAGES

Duarte/Downey Real Estate (508-349-7588; ddre.com), 12 Truro Center Road, in the center of town.

CAMPGROUNDS ✿ ✍ North of Highland Camping Area (508-487-1191; capecodcamping.com), Head of the Meadow Road, North Truro. Open late May to mid-September. On 60 acres of scrub pine forest within the CCNS, these 237 sites are suitable for tents and tent trailers only (no hookups, though) and are a 10-minute walk from Head of the Meadow Beach (see *Green Space*). There are strict quiet hours. From mid-July to mid-August, reservations must begin and end on a Saturday or Sunday. $30 nightly for two people.

✿ ⛺ "I" **Adventure Bound Camping Resorts** (508-487-1847; abcapecod .com), 46 Highland Road, North Truro. Open mid-April to mid-October. Within the CCNS, these 22 acres of wooded sites accommodate 330 tents and RVs. It's less than a mile to Coast Guard Beach (see *Green Space*), and only 6 miles to Provincetown. $35–39 daily for two, $41–50 for hookups.

HOSTEL ✿ Hostelling International, Truro (508-349-3889; hiusa.org; 888-901-2085 in-season reservations), 111 North Pamet Road, Truro. Open mid-June to early September. Originally a U.S. Coast Guard station, the hos-

tel commands a dramatic location—amid dunes, marshes, and a cranberry bog. The hostel is within the CCNS and just a 7-minute walk from Ballston Beach (see *Green Space*). National Park Service interpreters host special programs each week; they're free to all and not to be missed. Each of 42 dormitory beds rents for $35 for AYH members; $38 for non-members.

✳ Where to Eat

EATING OUT ✿ ✍ ♿ Adrian's (508-487-4360; adriansrestaurant.com), Route 6, North Truro. Open for breakfast and dinner daily, mid-June to early September; breakfast on weekends and dinner Thursday through Monday from mid-May to mid-June and early September to mid-October. Many people whiz by Adrian's because it's unceremoniously ensconced in the hilltop Outer Reach Motel. But if you're looking for a moderate price point and unpretentious food, you should stop. If you dine before sunset, sit on the outdoor deck with plastic chairs and tablecloths and drink in the spaciousness 270-degree views atop the bluff. If you dine after dark, dine inside at simple tables lit by candlelight and large picture windows. Chef Adrian Cyr and his wife, Annette, have wooed and won a decidedly loyal and ever-growing following since they opened their first area restaurant in 1985. They offer many fine, well-priced regional Italian choices: brick-oven pizzas, *linguine alle vongale*, a generous cold *insalate* and mixed antipasto, and specials like pistachio-encrusted local codfish in a lemon buerre blanc sauce with citrusy lentils. I always go for the catch of the day and am never disappointed. Clean flavors rule the day. Absolutely save room for the piping-hot blueberry-peach cobbler! For breakfast, try huevos rancheros, specialty omelets, and cranberry pancakes. Breakfast $3–8, pizzas $12–15, dinner $9–26.

🌸 ✑ **Terra Luna** (508-487-1019; theterraluna.com), 104 Route 6A, North Truro. Open for dinner nightly, mid-May to mid-October. All in all, this is one of the Outer Cape's best values. Peaked ceilings, large canvases, shellacked wooden tables, and candlelight transform this otherwise unassuming roadside eatery with barnboard walls into a very desirable place to spend a couple of hours (except when it's really hot, since there's no air-conditioning). Chef-owner Raina Stefani (at the helm since 1990) deftly executes New American and Italian dishes like *fra diavolo*. I particularly like the pan-seared salmon with lemon confit. And the wild mushroom ragout was rich, rich, rich. I dare you to finish it. Dipping oil infused with basil accompanying hearty bread sets an early tone, and warm polenta and blackberry custard caps it off nicely. The friendly service and low-key atmosphere are icing on the cake. Dinner $17–32.

Blackfish (508-349-3399), 17 Truro Center Road. Open for dinner May to late November. This refreshed taverny place, resurrected from its longtime incarnation as the Blacksmith Shop, has been under the direction of chef-owner Eric Jansen since Fall 2007. The menu is heavy on meat (pork, rabbit, duck) and locally caught fish dishes that are strongly but not overpoweringly flavored (think truffle chips). The dining room can feel crowded, but the crowd that is drawn here thinks of it more like a buzz. There's a good wine and beer selection too. All in all it reaches for gourmet-in-a-tavern. Dinner $19–33.

❄ ✑ **Sweet Escape** (508-487-2225), 316 Route 6. Open 6 AM–9 PM daily. You can't miss this big red building, and I bet you'll stop on your way to or from Provincetown more than once. From fabu ice-cream choices like Lavender Fig and Wicked Mud Flats (a chocolatey concoction) to stone-fired pizzas, grilled burgers, chicken breast sandwiches, and hand-cut fries (with vinegar), this big new place has the bases covered. Dine outside on Route 6 or at one of the long window stools. Ubiquitous paninis and wraps, too. At press time they were trying to make a go of staying open year-round, but that might change. No credit cards. Scoops $4, packed pints $5–6, dishes $7–18.

🌸 ♿ **Village Café** (508-487-5800), in the center of North Truro. Open 7 AM–9 PM daily in July and August, 7–3 daily May through June and September to mid-October. This pleasant and friendly sandwich place has a big brick courtyard where you can eat your Portuguese kale soup (a specialty) or H&H bagels. The extensive blackboard menu features hearty and creative sandwich combinations, pastries, espresso, desserts, and ice cream, too. Lunch $5–10. No credit cards.

❄ ✑ ♿ **Montano's** (508-487-2026; montanos.com), 481 Route 6, North Truro. Open nightly. This family restaurant serves dependable Italian favorites like seafood *fra diavolo* and steak *umbriago*, with unlimited refills on the garden salads, and early specials (4:30–6) for about $13–16. Montano's gets big points in my book for serving hungry Explorers in the dead of winter. Dinner $14–34.

SNACKS, ICE CREAM, AND COFFEE ✑ **Jams** (508-349-1616), 14 Truro Center Road, off Route 6 in Truro center. Open 6:30 AM–6 PM daily, late May to early September. Jams caters to those attached to their *New York Times*, tonic water, truffles, and pesto pizzas. Coffee aficionados take note: Jams serves rich espresso and lattes. Basic groceries share the stage with sun-dried tomatoes, rotisserie-roasted chicken and ribs, pizza-by-the-

JAMS

slice, and fresh mozzarella cheese. All the baked goods, including key lime pie and flan, are made from scratch. For those of you who don't live nearby, carry your picnic fixings to the small field across the street, perfect for bicyclists and the car-weary. Sandwiches $5–8 (lobster salad $11); salads by the pound.

See also **Sweet Escapes** and **Village Café** under *Eating Out*.

✳ Selective Shopping

Susan Baker Memorial Museum (508-487-2557; susanbakerart.com), 46 Route 6A, Truro. Open late May to mid-October and by appointment. One of the most irreverent painters on the Cape, Baker is a humorist at heart. She has a great body of work exploring the history of Provincetown and a recent one of European chapels and churches. She's perhaps best known for her sculptural, three-dimensional frames that take their cue from the architecture of whatever European building is in the painting. It's hard to keep a good woman in one medium.

✳ **Atlantic Spice Co.** (508-487-6100; atlanticspice.com), Route 6 at 6A, North Truro. Open daily. Culinary herbs and spices, botanicals, make-your-own potpourri, teas, spice blends, nuts, and seeds. They're here, they're

fresh, and they're in a cavernous warehouse. Although this is primarily a wholesaler, you can purchase small quantities (less than the usual 1-pound increments) of most products.

Whitman House Quilt Shop (508-487-3204), Great Hollow Road, off Route 6, North Truro. Open daily mid-April to mid-October. This former schoolhouse is packed with Amish quilts.

✳ Special Events

Mid-September: **Truro Treasures** (trurotreasures.org). Since 1992, this folksy 2-day weekend has features a crafts fair, antique car show, beach bash, treasure hunt, pancake breakfast, silent art auction, and many more fun events like a Dixieland concert at the winery.

SUSAN BAKER MEMORIAL MUSEUM

Provincetown 5

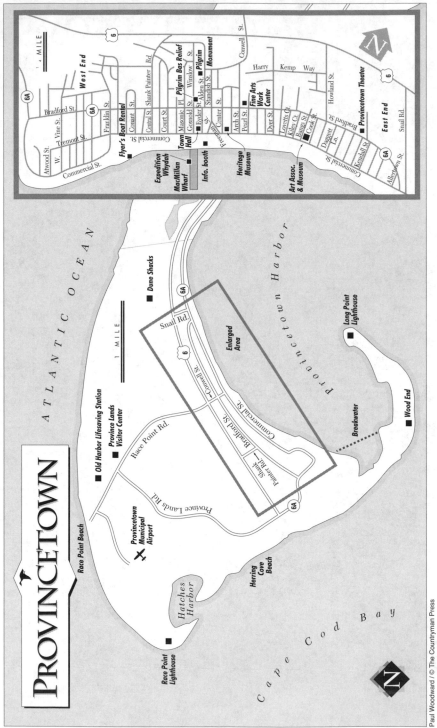

PROVINCETOWN

Paul Woodward / © The Countryman Press

PROVINCETOWN

As you cross into Provincetown, where high dunes drift onto Route 6, you begin to sense that this is a different place. This outpost on the tip of the Cape, where glaciers deposited their last grains of sand, attracts a varied population. Whether seeking solitude or freedom of expression in the company of like-minded souls, visitors relish Provincetown's fringe status. (Although it's becoming less "fringy" every day; but more on that later.) P-town, as it's often referred to by non-locals but not by locals, is perhaps best known as a community of tolerant individuals. Gay men and lesbians, Portuguese fishermen and families, artists, writers, all call it home and welcome those who are equally tolerant.

Visitors parade up and down Commercial Street, the main drag, ducking in and out of hundreds of shops and galleries. The town has a carnival-like atmosphere, especially in July and August, testing the limits of acceptability. As you might imagine, people-watching is a prime activity. On any given Saturday, the cast of characters might include cross-dressers, leather-clad motorcyclists, barely clad in-line skaters, children eating saltwater taffy, and tourists from "Anytown, USA," some of whom can't quite figure out what they've stumbled into and some of whom have come to scope out (gawk or relish) the alternative scene.

Provincetown's history began long before the *Mayflower* arrived. It's said that Leif Eriksson's brother, Thorvald, stopped here in 1004 to repair the keel of his boat. Wampanoag Indians fished and summered here—the tiny strip of land was too vulnerable to sustain a year-round settlement. In 1620 the Pilgrims first set foot on American soil in Provincetown, anchoring in the harbor for 5 weeks, making forays down-Cape in search of an agreeable spot to settle. By the late 1600s and early 1700s, only 200 fishermen lived here.

But from the mid–18th to the mid–19th century, Provincetown was a bustling whaling community and seaport. After the industry peaked, Portuguese sailors from the Azores and Cape Verde Islands, who had signed on with whaling and fishing ships, settled here to fish the local waters. The Old Colony Railroad was extended to Provincetown in 1873, transporting iced fish to New York and Boston. Upwards of four trains a day departed from the two-room station, located where the Duarte Motors parking lot is today, two blocks from MacMillan Wharf. But by the early 1900s, Provincetown's sea-driven economy had slowed. Trains stopped running in 1950. Today, although a small fishing industry still exists, tourism is the steam that drives the economy's train.

In 1899 painter Charles W. Hawthorne founded the Cape Cod School of Art.

He encouraged his Greenwich Village peers to come north and take advantage of the Mediterranean-like light. By 1916 there were six art schools in town. By the 1920s, Provincetown had become as distinguished an art colony as Taos, East Hampton, and Carmel. Hawthorne encouraged his students to flee the studio and set up easels on the beach, incorporating the ever-changing light into their work. By the time Hawthorne died in 1930, the art scene had a life of its own, and it continues to thrive today.

Artistic expression in Provincetown wasn't limited to painting, though. In 1915 the Provincetown Players, a group of playwrights and actors, staged their works in a small waterfront fish house. In their second season they premiered Eugene O'Neill's *Bound East for Cardiff* before moving to New York, where they are still based.

Provincetown's natural beauty isn't overshadowed by its colorful population. Province Lands, the name given to the Cape Cod National Seashore (CCNS) within Provincetown's borders, offers bike trails and three remote beaches, where, if you walk far enough, you can find real isolation. Most summertime visitors venture onto the water—to whale-watch or sail and sailboard in the protected harbor. A different perspective comes with a dune or aerial tour.

For all the history and natural beauty that doesn't change in Provincetown, the town itself is changing—like the rest of the United States. Condos have sprung up on every empty strand of sand, turning P-town into a bedroom community for Bostonians. Nightlife isn't *quite* as vibrant as it once was; more lesbians and gay men stay in, have dinner parties, and nest with their children. It's more expensive than ever for a new generation of gay youth, and the older generation is getting, well, older. And as gays move into the mainstream and gay marriage is legalized in Massachusetts, it's no longer quite *the* gay destination it used to be. When *Queer Eye* brings its aesthetic into everyone's households, when Ellen and Portia's wedding makes the cover of *People* magazine, and when *Will and Grace* has high ratings in the heartland, it becomes a little easier for gays to vacation anywhere they want. Straight folks are filling in around the edges and enjoying what gays and artists have long known: This is still one of the most unique destinations in North America.

Provincetown is a delight in late spring and fall, when upwards of 70,000 summer visitors return to their homes off-Cape. Commercial Street is navigable once again, and most shops and restaurants remain open. Tiny gardens bloom profusely, well into October. From January to March, though, the town is given back to the almost 3,300 hardy year-rounders—almost half of whom are unemployed during this time. Although about 80 percent of the businesses close during January and February, there are still enough guesthouses (and a handful of restaurants, especially on the weekends) open all winter, luring intrepid visitors with great prices and stark natural beauty. Steel yourself against the wind and take a walk on the

OPEN-AIR PAINTING CLASSES

beach, attend a reading at the Fine Arts Work Center, or curl up with a good book.

GUIDANCE/INTERNET ❄ "ℹ"
Provincetown Chamber of Commerce (508-487-3424; ptown-chamber.com), 307 Commercial Street at MacMillan Wharf and Lopes Square. Open 9–5 daily late May to mid-October; 10–4 off-season, when it's closed Wednesday and Sunday. This is the most informative and helpful on the Cape. The chamber offers free WiFi, but so do many cafés (see *Where to Eat*); Whaler's Wharf on Commercial Street has it; and you'll also find where two newspapers are located: at Commercial and Ryder and Commercial and Standish.

❄ **Provincetown Business Guild** (508-487-2313; 800-637-8696; ptown.org), 3 Freeman Street #2. The guild, established in 1978 to support gay tourism, promotes about 275 mostly gay-owned businesses.

🐾 ✿ ♿ **Province Lands Visitor Center** (508-487-1256; nps.gov/caco), Race Point Road, Cape Cod National Seashore (CCNS). Open 9–5 daily, early May to late October. First things first: Climb atop the observation deck for a 360-degree view of the outermost dunes and ocean. Second things second: the center offers informative exhibits on Cape history, local flora and fauna, and dune ecology, along with frequent short films. Organized summer activities include sunset campfires and storytelling, birding trips, dune tours, and a junior ranger hour for children age 8–12.

MORE WEB SITES Check out provincetownforwomen.com and provincetown.com.

MEDIA The *Provincetown Banner* (508-487-7400; provincetownbanner .com) will give you a sense of the town's local, fascinating politics as well as the latest on what to do. The weekly *Provincetown Magazine* (provincetown magazine.net) also has great information.

Tune in to **Outermost Radio** at **92.1 FM** (508-487-2619; WOMR; womr.org).

PUBLIC RESTROOMS ❄ Look behind the chamber of commerce (open daily mid-April to mid-October and weekends off-season), at the library (356 Commercial Street), and at Whaler's Wharf (237 Commercial Street).

LIFE MEETS ART, COMMERCIAL ST.

PUBLIC LIBRARY ❄ ✐ ⍑ ⁙ **Provincetown Public Library** (508-487-7094; ptownlib.com), 356 Commercial Street (at Center Street). Open daily. This magnificent facility is housed in the former Heritage Museum; it's never looked so good!

GETTING THERE *By car:* Provincetown is the eastern terminus of Cape Cod, 63 miles via Route 6 from the Cape Cod Canal and 128 miles from Boston and Providence. It takes almost 2½ hours to drive to Provincetown from Boston.

By boat from Boston: **Boston Harbor Cruises** (617-227-4321; 877-733-9425; bostonharborcruises.com) operates two or three daily fast boats (90 minutes) from Boston's Long Wharf to Provincetown from early May to mid-October. Roundtrip: adults $71, children $60, bikes $10.

Bay State Cruise Company, Inc. (508-487-9284 seasonally on MacMillan Wharf; 617-748-1428 on Boston's Commonwealth Pier, Northern Avenue; baystate cruisecompany.com), offers three trips daily, mid-May to mid October. Adult $79, child $58, roundtrip.

By boat from Plymouth: **Cape Cod Cruises (Capt. John's Boats)** (508-746-2643; captjohn.com), State Pier (next to the *Mayflower*) in Plymouth and at Fisherman's Wharf in Provincetown. The ferry schedule is designed so that you leave Plymouth at 10 AM, spend about 5 hours in Provincetown, and are back in Plymouth by 6 PM. You even get a narrated history of Plymouth Harbor as the boat pulls away from shore. Trips daily mid-June to early September. Roundtrip: adults $37, children $27, bicycles $5. Waterfront parking for a fee.

By boat from Gloucester: **Boston Harbor Cruises** (617-227-4321; 877-733-9425; bostonharborcruises.com) operates one daily ferry from Gloucester's Cruiseport to Macmillan Wharf. Departures late June to late August. Roundtrip: adults $80, children $70, bikes $10.

Photo by Lynette Molnar

By bus: The **Plymouth & Brockton** bus line (508-778-9767; p-b.com) connects Provincetown with Hyannis and other Cape towns, as well as with Boston's Logan Airport. The bus stops behind the chamber of commerce; purchase tickets on board. There are five buses a day in summer, two in the off-season from early September to early May. Travel time to Boston is 3½ hours and requires a bus change in Hyannis; $35 one-way, $63 roundtrip.

By air: **Cape Air** (508-487-0241; 800-352-0714; flycapeair.com) provides extensive daily, year-round service from Boston to Provincetown Municipal Airport. The flight takes 25 minutes, and the airport is 3 miles north of town. Summer fares from $180 roundtrip; $890 for a book of 10 one-way tickets.

East End. (Street numbers in the East End are higher than in the West End.)
Take the second exit for MacMillan Wharf and Town Hall, where street numbers
are in the 300s. Shank Painter Road, the third exit, leads to the West End. Follow
Route 6 to its end for Herring Cove Beach. A right off Route 6 takes you to the
Province Lands section of the CCNS.

Provincetown's principal thoroughfare, Commercial Street, is narrow, one-way, and
3 miles long. When you want to drive from one end of town to another quickly, use
Bradford Street, parallel to Commercial. There are no sidewalks on Bradford,
known as Back Street in the days when Provincetown had only a front and a back
street. About 40 narrow cross-streets connect Commercial and Bradford.

Finding free on-street parking is a problem. Meters require feeding from 8 AM to
midnight daily (with 3-hour limits), and meter maids are ruthless. There are
municipal lots next to the Pilgrim Monument off Bradford Street; on MacMillan
Wharf; off Commercial Street; off Bradford Street; and one at the end of Commercial Street near the Breakwater.

By shuttle: The excellent **Provincetown Shuttle** (800-352-7155; capecodtransit
.org) operates daily from late June to mid-September. Flag it down anywhere along
the route: Among other places, it stops at Herring Cove Beach, Beech Forest, the
Provincetown Inn, and MacMillan Wharf before heading down Route 6A to
Dutra's Market in North Truro. The shuttle runs every 30 minutes 9 AM–12:30 AM.
Fares are $2 one-way.

By boat: **Flyer's Boat Shop and Rental** (508-487-0898; flyersboats.com), 131A
Commercial Street. From mid-June to late September, a shuttle on the hour and

EXPLORING THE DUNES

Art's Dune Tours (508-487-1950; artsdunetours.com), 4 Standish Street at
Commercial Street, offers daily trips mid-April to mid-November. The Costa
family has expertly led tourists on these narrated, hour-long trips through
the CCNS dunes since 1946. I high-
ly recommend taking one. The
GMC Suburbans stop at least
once (on the beach or atop a
high dune) for photos, so you
can take in the panoramic
views. Trips cost $25–35
adults, $17–25 children; prices
vary depending on what time
of day you choose to go.
Reservations are necessary
for sunset trips. Ask about
sunset clambakes and surf-
fishing trips, too.

A PERFECT SUMMER DAY IN PROVINCETOWN

7:00   Stroll Commercial Street when everyone is still sleeping.

8:00   Secure a booth for your tribe by arriving early at Café Edwige.

9:30   Walk on the bayside flats during low tide.

10:30   Stroll Commercial Street again, now packed with drag queens and families. Pop into galleries and Marine Specialties.

12:30   Climb to the top of Pilgrim Monument or visit PAAM.

2:00   Enjoy a late brunch at Victor's.

2:45   Cruise the National Seashore backside dunes with Art's Dune Tours.

4:15   Get a delectable treat from Connie's Bakery.

5:00   Circle the serene Beech Forest Trail.

5:00   Or go to the Boatslip Tea Dance (if you're a dancer like me or a gay guy).

7:30   Watch the sunset at Herring Cove Beach.

8:00   Enjoy a late dinner at the Mews, Front Street, Edwige, or Devon's.

8:00   Or, catch a live show.

half hour takes bathers and picnickers to and from remote, unspoiled Long Point (see *Green Space*). Fare is $10 one-way, $15 roundtrip; children under 6, free. The boat runs from about 10 to 5:20-ish, when the last pickup is made at Long Point.

By trolley: **Provincetown Trolley, Inc.** (508-487-9483; provincetowntrolley.com), Commercial Street at Town Hall. These frequent 40-minute, narrated sightseeing trips depart May through October. You can get on and off at the Provincetown Art Association & Museum (see *To See*); the Provincetown Inn next to the breakwater (see *Green Space*), at the western end of Commercial Street; and the Province Lands Visitor Center (see *Guidance*). Adults $11; children 12 and under, $6.

Touring by foot: **Historic Walking Tour of Provincetown** (508-487-1310; pilgrimmonument.org). Led by a staff member from the Pilgrim Monument and Provincetown Museum (PMPM) and one from the CCNS, this 2-hour, 2-mile tour is a great introduction to art and architecture, to whalers and writers. Don't be too cool to take a walking tour in Provincetown. It departs at 9 AM sharp on Tuesdays at the PMPM; $5.

By taxi: Call **508-487-2222** to arrange a pickup. No, not that kind.

MEDICAL EMERGENCY ❋ **Outer Cape Health Services** (508-487-9395), 49 Harry Kemp Way. Open 8–5 weekdays, 9–2 Saturday.

Lyme disease. Ticks carry this disease, which has flu-like symptoms and may result in death if left untreated. Immediately and carefully remove any ticks that may have migrated from dune grasses to your body. Better yet, wear long pants, tuck pants into socks, and wear long-sleeved shirts whenever possible when hiking. Avoid hiking in grassy and overgrown areas of dense brush.

PROVINCETOWN ART ASSOCIATION & MUSEUM

❋ To See

Listings are organized from east to west.

Commercial Street. Until Commercial Street was laid out in 1835, the shoreline served as the town's main thoroughfare. Because houses had been oriented toward the harbor, many had to be turned around or the "front" door had to be reconstructed to face the new street. Some houses, however, still remain oriented toward the shore.

❋ ☂ **Provincetown Art Association & Museum** (508-487-1750; paam.org), 460 Commercial Street. Open 11–8 Monday through Thursday, 11–10 Friday, 11–5 weekends late May to early September; noon–5 Thursday through Sunday the rest of the year. Under the forward thinking stewardship of Director Chris McCarthy, PAAM is basking in the glow of a stunning new building and exhibit spaces. One of the country's foremost small museums, PAAM includes five sparkling galleries that feature established and emerging artists. Organized in 1914 by artists to "promote education of the public in the arts, and social intercourse between artists and laymen," PAAM has included Ambrose Webster, Milton Avery, and Marsden Hartley among its members. Selections from the permanent collection of 2,000-plus works change frequently. Special exhibitions, juried shows, and other events are sponsored throughout the year. The bookstore specializes in the local art colony. Adults $5; children, free; free for all Friday evening after 5.

MacMillan Wharf. By 1800 Provincetown was one of the country's busiest seaports; 50 years later it was second largest whaling port. By the 1880s, when cod fishing reached its peak and Provincetown boasted the Cape's largest population, MacMillan Wharf was just one of 56 wharves jutting into the harbor. (MacMillan Wharf, built in 1873, was originally called Old Colony Wharf after the railroad that met Boston packets, but was ultimately named for native son Admiral Donald MacMillan, who explored the North

MACMILLAN WHARF

Pole with Admiral Robert Peary.) The town bustled with herring canning, cod curing, whaling, and fishing. Although only a few wharves are still standing, MacMillan Wharf remains true to its original purpose: Even though the fishing industry has recently suffered because of overfishing, some boats still unload their afternoon catch here. And instead of whaling ships, the wharf now is lined with whale-watching boats. The view of town from the end of the pier has always been expansive, but now that the $2 million renovation is finished (in 2005), it's more impressive than ever.

EXPEDITION *WHYDAH*

⚓ ↑ **Expedition Whydah** (508-487-8899; whydah.com), 16 MacMillan Wharf. Open 9:30–7 daily, mid-April to late-October; weekends occasionally through November. This museum is devoted to chronicling the story of the *Whydah*, the only pirate ship ever salvaged. It sank 1,500 feet offshore from Wellfleet's Marconi Beach on April 26, 1717, and Cape Codder Barry Clifford discovered it in 1984. Adults $10; children 6–12, $8.

Provincetown Town Hall (508-487-7000; provincetowngov.org), 260 Commercial Street. Open 8–5 weekdays. Constructed in 1886, the building serves as the seat of local government and community agencies. The wonderful auditorium is also used for concerts and lectures. Look for an art collection throughout and for the Works Progress Administration (WPA)–era murals of farmers and fishermen by Ross Moffett and the portrait by Charles Hawthorne. FYI: the town hall will be closed and undergoing a two-year renovation through at least 2011 and possibly longer. The temporary location is 16 Jerome Smith Road.

Pilgrim bas-relief, Bradford Street, behind Town Hall. Sculptor Cyrus Dalin's memorial commemorates the *Mayflower* Compact, which has been called the "first American act in our history." After traveling from England for almost two months, the *Mayflower* sat in the harbor until the compact was drawn up. No one was allowed to go ashore until William Bradford signed the document, attesting to his willingness to abide by laws. One relief memorializes the five Pilgrims who died before reaching Plymouth. (Three Pilgrims are buried near the center of town.) The other relief contains the text of the compact and the names of the 41 people who signed it.

EXPEDITION *WHYDAH*

❄ ⚓ ↑ **Pilgrim Monument and Provincetown Museum** (PMPM; 508-487-1310; pilgrim-monument.org),

High Pole Hill Road, off Winslow Street from Bradford Street. Open 9–7 daily, mid-June to mid-September; 9–5 daily, April through June and September through November. Last admission is 45 minutes before closing. The 252-foot monument (the tallest all-granite U.S. monument) commemorates the Pilgrims' first landing in Provincetown on November 11, 1620, and their 5-week stay in the harbor while searching for a good place to settle. President Theodore Roosevelt laid the cornerstone in 1907, and President Taft dedicated it in 1910. Climb the 116 stairs of the monument—modeled after the Torre del Mangia in Siena, Italy—for a panoramic view of the Outer Cape. On a clear day you can see 42 miles to Boston.

One wing of the museum is devoted to early Pilgrim travails: the *Mayflower*'s first landing, finding corn and fresh water, the unsuccessful search for a place to settle. The other wing contains dioramas and changing exhibits dedicated to a whaling captain's life ashore, the birth of modern theater, shipwrecks, dolls and toys, the Lower Cape and the Outer Cape, and local art. Free parking with paid museum admission for the first 2 hours; then they start charging you. Beware: Your car will be towed if you linger or park illegally. Check out their walking tours too; see *Getting Around.* Adults $7; children 4–14, $3.50.

✳ **Universalist Meetinghouse** (508-487-9344; uumh.org), 236 Commercial Street. Generally open 9–1 Sunday through Thursday. This 1847 Greek Revival church contains trompe l'oeil murals (by Carl Wendte, who painted similar murals for Nantucket's Unitarian Universalist Church), a Sandwich glass chandelier, and pews made with Provincetown pine. The pews are decorated with medallions carved from whales' teeth.

Pilgrim plaque, at the western end of Commercial Street. Provincetown's version of Plymouth Rock—a plaque in the middle of a landscaped traffic circle—commemorates the Pilgrims' landing.

On the outskirts of town
Old Harbor Lifesaving Station (508-487-1256; nps.gov/caco), Race Point Beach. Call for hours. Open house 2:30–5 daily in July and August. This 1898 structure, one of nine original Lifesaving Service stations on the Outer Cape, was floated by barge from Chatham to its present location in 1977—just in the nick of time. One year later the great Nor'easter of 1978 blew through and wiped out its original location. The Lifesaving Service, precursor to the Coast Guard, rescued crews from ships wrecked by shallow sandbars and brutal nor'easters. The boat room contains the original equipment, but on Thursday at 6 PM (confirm the time before going), hour-long demonstrations are given using the old-fashioned techniques. "Surf-men" launch a rescue line to the wrecked ship and haul in the distressed sailors one at a time. Plaques lining the

PROVINCETOWN HARBOR

Dune shacks, beyond the end of Snail Road. In the dunes between Race Point and High Head in North Truro, along 2 miles of ridges and valleys, stand about 17 weather-beaten dune shacks. Constructed between 1935 and 1950 of driftwood and scavenged materials, the shacks are the subject of local legend. Over the years, notable writers and artists have called them home for weeks, months, even years: Among the tenants have been Jack Kerouac, e. e. cummings, Norman Mailer, Jackson Pollock, poet Harry Kemp, and Eugene O'Neill.

When the CCNS was created in 1961, the federal government set up 25-year or lifelong leases with squatters who were living in the shacks. (Only one of the inhabitants held a clear title to the land.) Some shacks are still occupied. In 1985, Joyce Johnson, a dune dweller since the early 1970s, founded the Peaked Hill Trust to oversee some of the shacks. Members of the trust can win stays through a lottery system; write to P.O. Box 1705, Provincetown 02657, for membership information. Since Province Lands was added to the National Register of Historic Places in 1989, the maintenance and fate of most of the historic shacks have fallen to the National Park Service. At this point, policies are decided from season to season. The park service still sets aside a few shacks, though, for an artist-in-residence program.

I've won weeklong stays in a shack owned by Hazel Hawthorne Werner. On my first visit, it took until the fifth day to shake the first thought that came to my mind after returning to the shack from a walk: I wonder who called while I was out? Remarkable. Remarkable that the shack felt so much like home and remarkable that it was such a deeply ingrained response to being away. I wrote many other impressions but didn't produce anything approaching Cynthia Huntington's *The Salt House*, which she wrote over many, many months of living in that shack. It's well worth reading.

There are a few off-road parking spots at the end of Snail Road. Take the short woodland trail and hike up the first steep dune, then over the next two crests; the shacks will appear in the distance. You can also reach the shacks by walking east from Race Point Beach. Remember, however, that most shacks are still occupied, and people live out there for privacy, to pursue the creative process uninhibited, to contemplate in isolation.

boardwalk to the museum explain how the service worked. Donation suggested, but you'll have to pay an additional $15 to park at Race Point Beach.

SCENIC DRIVES You must drive out Race Point Road from Route 6 and around Province Lands.

✳ To Do

BICYCLING/RENTALS **Province Lands**. Eight miles of hilly paved trails—around ponds, cranberry bogs, and sand dunes—wind through Province Lands' 4,000 acres. Spur trails lead to Herring Cove and Race Point beaches (see *Green Space*). Access is from Race Point Road near Route 6. There are parking areas at the Beech Forest Trailhead (see *Green Space*), Province Lands Visitor Center (see *Guidance*), and Race Point and Herring Cove beaches. That covers the logistics. What it doesn't cover is this: whatever you do, don't miss cruising around here. It's glorious and will be a highlight of your trip.

Rentals. Shops are open mid-April to mid-October, and bike rentals cost $12 for up to two hours, $22 daily, $85 weekly, depending on what kind of bike you get. **Ptown Bikes** (508-487-8735; ptownbikes.com), 42 Bradford Street, is my favored outfitter; **Galeforce Beach Market** (508-487-4849; galeforcebikes.com), 144 Bradford Street Extension, is on the western edge of town.

BOAT EXCURSIONS/RENTALS ✐ *Viking* **Princess Cruises** (508-487-7323; capecodecotours.com), MacMillan Wharf. Trips mid-May through late September. The *Viking* offers a number of trips, including a sunset cruise for $25 per person. Harbor tours (adults $15, children $10) head around one of the world's largest deepwater ports. Critter cruises (adults $21, children $16) are fun, hands-on educational trips. Privately chartered pirate cruises take folks on a treasure hunt. This outfit clearly offers something for everyone.

Bay Lady II (508-487-9308; sailcapecod.com) on MacMillan Wharf. Trips mid-May to mid-October. These 2-hour harbor sails into Cape Cod Bay are aboard traditionally gaff-rigged schooners. They offer four trips daily in-season, including a sunset trip. It's a really relaxing way to see the area. Adults $20–25; children under 12, $12.

Flyer's Boat Rental (508-487-0898; flyersboats.com), 131A Commercial Street. Open mid-May through September. Flyer's has been renting boats to suit your needs since 1965: Sunfish, sloops, kayaks, and powerboats. Sailboats cost $30–50 for first 2 hours, $60–125 daily; single kayaks cost $30 for 4 hours, $50 daily. Two-hour sailing instruction is also offered by reservation.

Kalmar Nyckel (302-429-7447; KalmarNyckel.org), docked at MacMillan Wharf. Trips mid-August to early September. This handsome boat is a replica of a 1638 ship that sailed from Sweden to Delaware and deposited 28 settlers in the new colonies. With an all-volunteer crew and a female captain, today's *Kalmar Nyckel* sails into Provincetown harbor for two weeks from its homeport in Wilmington. Daysailers like you and me can help hoist the main sail and more. Although the ship just goes a short way into the harbor to raise and lower her sails (quite slowly), it's authentic enough to make you feel like you've stepped back a few centuries in time. You also get to see the Provincetown skyline from the water, which is a treat. Peek your head below deck to see the ship's mascot cat, and check out the captain's quarters. The three-hour sail costs $60 adults, $40 children 17 and under.

FISHING Surf-casting is great on **Race Point Beach** (see *Green Space*) in the early morning or after sunset. Nonresidents are not permitted to shellfish.

Cee Jay (508-487-4330), MacMillan Wharf. From June to early September there are two daily departures on half-day excursions in search of bluefish, bass, fluke, and flounder. The third-generation crew will fillet your fish if you have a place to cook it. Adults $35, children 12 and under, $25.

Nelson's Bait & Tackle (508-487-0034; nelsonsbaitandtackle.com), 43 Race Point Road. Open daily mid-April to mid-October. If you're not hiring a charter boat (which supplies the necessary equipment), Nelson's is *the* source for rod rentals, live and frozen bait, and fresh- and saltwater tackle.

See also **Flyer's Boat Rental** under *Boat Excursions.*

FOR FAMILIES  **Playgrounds** are located at both ends of town: at Bradford and Howland streets (East End) and at Bradford and Nickerson streets (West End).

FITNESS CLUBS ❄ **Mussel Beach Health Club** (508-487-0001; mussel beach.net), 35 Bradford Street. The club has state-of-the-art equipment, free weights, and cardiovascular equipment. My spinning friends, Cricket and Catherine, also think it offers killer workouts. The day-use fee is $20.

❄ **Provincetown Gym** (508-487-2776; ptowngym.com), 81 Shank Painter Road. The cardiovascular machines and free weights here might feel less intimidating for women than Mussel Beach. The day-use fee is $15, or five visits for $60 (which can be shared between two people.)

SPECIAL PROGRAMS ❄ **Fine Arts Work Center** (508-487-9960; fawc.org), 24 Pearl Street. Open 9–5 weekdays. The center was founded in 1968 by a group of writers, artists, and patrons, including Robert Motherwell, Hudson Walker, Stanley Kunitz, and Myron Stout. And its intent was to provide a place for emerging artists to pursue independent work within a sympathetic community of their peers. In 1972 the center purchased Days Lumber Yard, where artists have worked in small studios since 1914. (Frank Days Jr., who had been concerned about the plight of artists, built 10 studios over his lumberyard. And Charles Hawthorne was one of the first tenants in 1914.) Writing and visual arts residencies, which include a monthly stipend and materials allowance, run October through April. Twenty candidates are chosen from a pool of about 1,000. Year-round readings, seminars, workshops, and exhibits are open to the public. There's also a great summer program for creative writing and visual arts, which offers weeklong and weekend workshops in printmaking, sculpture, fiction writing, and the like. Keep your eyes open for talks, presentations, and readings by visiting instructors like Kate Clinton.

❋ ✐ **Provincetown Museum School** (508-487-1750; paam.org), 460 Commercial Street at Bangs Street. Programs run year-round; galleries open 11–8 Monday through Thursday, 11–10 Friday, 11–5 Saturday in summer. Printmaking, painting, monotypes, and watercolor are just some of the classes taught by notable artists at the Provincetown Art Association & Museum (PAAM). Children's classes are also offered; some courses are accredited.

Center for Coastal Studies (508-487-3622; 800-826-9300 for whale-watching; coastalstudies.org), 115 Bradford Street. This independent, nonprofit, member-ship-supported institution is dedicated to research, public education, and conserva-tion programs for the coastal and marine environments. Among other things, researchers study the endangered right whale (there are only about 350 to 400 in the world) and maintain the largest population database of humpback whales in the Gulf of Maine. They have raised important environmental questions about Boston's Outfall Pipe and the overall health of the Cape Cod Bay. The center is also the only East Coast organization authorized to disentangle whales trapped in fishing gear. Educational offerings include whale-watching aboard a Dolphin Fleet boat (see the sidebar "Whale-Watching").

❋ ✐ **Provincetown Community Center** (508-487-7097), 44 Bradford Street. In addition to holding classes sponsored by the Provincetown Recreation Depart-ment, the center has a weight room, martial arts classes for adults and children, dance classes, and yoga classes.

SWIMMING POOL ❋ **Provincetown Inn** (508-487-9500; provincetowninn .com), 1 Commercial Street. This outdoor, Olympic-sized pool is free and open seasonally.

See also **Boatslip Beach Club** under *Entertainment*.

TENNIS Town courts are located at **Motta Field** off Winslow Street.

Provincetown Tennis Club (508-487-9574; provincetowntennis.com), 288 Brad-ford Street. Open mid-May to mid-November. Five clay and two hard courts.

Bissell's Tennis Courts (508-487-9512), 21 Bradford Street Extension. Open early May to late October. Five clay courts and lessons.

NATIONAL SEASHORE BONFIRES

A beach bonfire, with or without a clambake, defines the essence of sum-mertime on the Outer Cape. Here's the process you need to follow to secure a permit: In July and August head to the Province Lands Visitor Center (508-487-1256; nps.gov/caco) on Race Point Road three days before you want a permit and request one. For instance, if you want it for Wednesday, go on Saturday. Be there when the center opens. On the day of your big event, be at the visitor center at 3:30 sharp or you'll lose your permit to someone wait-ing in line. In the off-season, you can call three days ahead of your desired date without a problem. Fires are permitted when the center is open: early May to late October.

WHALE-WATCHING

For many people, seeing whales breech and frolic is one of the most exhilarating and sacred things they've ever done. There's something so inspiring about seeing these enormous and ancient creatures so close to the boat. If you've never done it, put it on your short list. On my most recent trip in 2008, the waters were thick with mothers and calves breeching in unison all around us. Even the naturalists were awed!

Located just 8 miles from Provincetown, the fertile feeding grounds of Stellwagen Bank attract migrating finback and humpback whales. Although the area was designated the country's first National Marine Sanctuary in 1992, the government's attempts to control the ocean's intricate ecosystem don't always work out as planned. For instance, whales feed on sand lance, which thrive when herring populations are small. (Herring eat sand lance larvae.) But since the government began protecting dwindling stocks of herring, the number of sand lance larvae has decreased. Some naturalists theorize that humpbacks are heading elsewhere in search of more abundant food supplies. Whale sightings vary each season. Some summers, sightings are a dime a dozen (although it never feels *that* blasé); other times, not. Although whale-watching outfits guarantee sightings (in the form of a free voucher for another trip), you may not have another afternoon to spare. Don't wait, as readers Doug and Lucyna Robertson did, until the last day of your trip. As they wrote to me, "d'oh!"

Most whale-watch cruises last about 3½ hours and have an onboard

✳ Green Space

BEACHES After you look at a map or take an airplane tour—to see the long spit of sand arching around the harbor—you won't doubt there are about 30 miles of beach within the CCNS in Provincetown.

Race Point Beach, CCNS, off Route 6. Race Point faces north and gets sun all day; it also has long breaking waves coming in off the Atlantic Ocean. Surrounded by dunes as far as the eye can see, Race Point feels as remote as it is. In spring, with binoculars, you might see whales spouting and breaching offshore. Facilities include lifeguards, showers, and restrooms. Parking late June to early September costs $15 daily (permit valid all day at any CCNS beach); a yearly pass is $45. The lot generally fills up by 11 AM in summer; there's rarely a charge to park after 5:30 PM.

Herring Cove Beach, CCNS, at the end of Route 6. The water here is calmer and "warmer" (it's all relative, isn't it?) than at Race Point. Because the beach faces due west, lots of folks gather for spectacular sunsets. (When I get a bonfire permit with friends it's always for Herring Cove.) Facilities include lifeguards, showers, and restrooms. Parking issues are identical to Race Point, above. The beach is also accessible by the Provincetown Shuttle.

Photo by Lynette Molnar

naturalist. Bring a sweater (even in summer), and sea-sickness pills if you think you'll need them. If you are prone to seasickness, do not stand out on the bow of the boat. Also, check the chamber of commerce brochure rack (see *Guidance*) or check with your lodging for money-saving coupons. **Dolphin Fleet Whale Watch** (508-240-3636; 800-826-9300; whalewatch.com), MacMillan Wharf. Trips mid-April through October. On board scientists, which will fill you with dozens of interesting facts, hail from the Center for Coastal Studies. Adults $37, children 5–12, $29; children under 5, free.

Before or after your trip, stop by the **Stellwagen Bank National Marine Sanctuary** (781-545-8026; stellwagen.noaa.gov), 205 Commercial Street at Carver Street. There's a small exhibit with touch screen computers offering images and information about local marine life, as well as two "video-scopes" that allow you to look into the underwater world of Massachusetts Bay. Free.

See also **Center for Coastal Studies** under *To Do*.

Harbor Beach is about 3.5 miles long and parallels Commercial Street. Although there is little beach at high tide, and few public access points, it's great to walk the flats at low tide. Really great.

Long Point. Long Point is easily accessible by boat in summer (see Flyer's Boat Rental under *Getting Around*), although relatively few people make the effort. You'll be rewarded if you do, but don't forget to pack a picnic and plenty of water. You can walk atop the breakwater (see *Walks*), but it takes about 2 hours. **Long Point Lighthouse**, at the tip of the spit, was built in 1826, two years before a community of fishermen began to construct homes out there. By 1846 there were 61 families on Long Point, all of whom returned to town during the Civil War. (Two Civil War forts were built on Long Point.) As you walk around town, notice which old houses sport a blue enamel plaque in the shape of a barge. This plaque identifies Long Point houses that were floated across the harbor on barges. (Locals call them "floaters.")

WALKS Beech Forest Trail, CCNS, off Race Point Road from Route 6. This sandy, 1-mile trail circles a freshwater pond before steep stairs cut through a forest of beech trees. Warblers migrating from South America pack the area from mid- to late May, but the trail is also beautiful in autumn. It's one of my all-time favorite Cape walks.

BREAKWATER

Breakwater, at the western end of Commercial Street (at the Provincetown Inn) and Bradford Street Extension, is a mile-long jetty that serves as a footpath to the secluded Long Point beach. Watch your footing. Even if you only walk out partway, it's a quintessential place to watch the tide roll in. Once you reach the beach, **Wood End Lighthouse** (1872) is to the north; **Long Point Lighthouse** is at the tip.

Hatches Harbor. From Herring Cove Beach, at the end of Route 6, walk about 10 minutes toward Race Point Light to the entrance of Hatches Harbor. There's a dike along the back of the salt marsh and tidal estuary that you can walk across.

See also **"Dune shacks"** sidebar under *To See* and **Province Lands** under *To Do*.

✳ Lodging

A few generalities: If you care about where you stay, don't go to Provincetown in summer without reservations. If you must wait until the last minute, there are often vacancies midweek in July. Most places have lengthy minimum-night stays during special events and holiday weekends—again, reserve early. (Rates for holiday weekends are always higher than I've reported.) Since the East End tends to be quieter than the West End, I've indicated where each lodging is located, unless it's in the middle of town. All guesthouses included below welcome everyone: gay and straight, although there are always more gay visitors in the summer.

BED & BREAKFASTS/ GUESTHOUSES

✳ ☐ ╏ The **Brass Key** (508-487-9005; 800-842-9858; brasskey.com), 67 Bradford Street. More like a luxurious private enclave—fenced in and gated—the Brass Key catapulted Provincetown accommodations to new heights. Purchased by the Crowne Pointe Inn in 2008, all 43 rooms surrounding the enclosed pool and court-yard are completely different. In addition to being elegant and sophisticated, rooms have vaulted ceilings, working fireplaces, whirlpool baths, upscale amenities, nightly turndown, and antiques. Some have balconies; all have access to a widow's walk and three living rooms. An expansive continental breakfast buffet is served in the country-inn-style Gatehouse. Complimentary wine and beer and cheese and crackers are offered each afternoon. No children. Mid-June to mid-September $195–475 (long minimums over weekends); off-season $100–275.

☐ ╏ The **Red Inn** (508-487-0050; 866-473-3466; theredinn.com), 15 Commercial Street (West End). Open April through December. Soothing and sophisticated, the Red Inn makes others green with envy. Not only is the waterfront location almost unequaled (and sunrises spectacular and semi-private waterfront decks), but the accommodations (four rooms, two suites, and two residences) are worthy of design and comfort awards, as well. A bed of down pillows (and 600-thread-count sheets) will cradle your body as a tranquil color palette lulls your spirit. Two waterfront "**residences**" are absolutely stunning, if you can afford them. But as my friend Tim said after a recent multi-night stay, " Some cosmetic upgrades are needed, it can be noisy from 6 PM until 11 PM while the restaurant is in full swing, and it has relatively few amenities for the price point." Still, they'd return for another stay. No children. Late June to mid-September $240–325 rooms (lengthy minimums in summer); off-season $135–265; residences $450–560 nightly; $2,835–2,637 weekly.

❄ "ꝉ" **White Porch** (508-364-2549; whiteporchinn.com), 7 Johnson Street. Run, don't walk to make reservations here! This completely remodeled guesthouse and carriage house burst onto the scene in 2007, and I couldn't be happier about it. The nine soothing and sophisticated rooms ooze a contemporary beach aesthetic and have been updated with iPod docking stations, flat-screen TVs, and luxe bedding. It's all quite stylin.' Although you might be tempted to cocoon here (at least you girls out there), gather for drinks with the gang on the front (white) porch. In and off-season, it's very mixed guesthouse, with all welcome, of course. Expanded continental breakfast included. Mid-June to early September $165–385; off-season $95–175.

🐾 ❄ "ꝉ" **Land's End Inn** (508-487-0706; 800-276-7088; landsendinn .com), 22 Commercial Street (West End). Open mid-May through November. Land's End has some of the best ocean views in town. And it's easily Provincetown's most unusual place to stay. That'll be readily apparent as you walk up the hidden path, catching glimpses of turrets and decks. (No description can really prepare you.) It's a visual feast, chock-full of Victoriana, woodcarvings, stained glass, and Oriental rugs atop floral carpets. Built in 1904, the inn offers 15 rooms and two apartments; the tower rooms and loft suite are spectacularly situated. Most theme rooms have access to decks; some rooms sleep four. It's all very tranquil and attracts a very diverse clientele. Be sure to return for wine, cheese, and beer in the afternoons; it's wonderfully relaxing since there is so much outdoor space. Continental breakfast. July and August $295–560; off-season $175–460.

❄ 🐾 ❄ "ꝉ" **Gabriel's at The Ashbrooke Inn** (508-487-3232; 800-969-2643; gabriels.com), 102 Bradford Street. This well-established guesthouse has fourteen units (five suites and nine guest rooms) in the heart of town; it's hard to beat them in quality of offerings and service. It's a first-rate place that features courtyards (with five levels of deck and lush landscaping) and plenty of amenities like flat-screen TVs, fireplaces, Jacuzzis. Not one to rest on its laurels, Gabriel's added new suites and a penthouse apartment in 2007. Families and those traveling with pets will be particularly happy here. Full breakfast. Mid-June to mid-September $210–380, off-season $120–250.

🐾 ♿ "ꝉ" **Benchmark Inn & Central** (508-487-7440; benchmarkinn.com), 6 and 8 Dyer Street. Open mid-February through December. Park and Jared's 14 rooms and penthouse (in two buildings) are welcoming and upscale. Service is supreme (think nightly turndown), amenities are top-notch (think marble bathrooms), and the aesthetic is simple but elegant with clean lines. Fireplaces, wet bars, outdoor space, and fresh flowers are the norm. Another big bonus? They have one of only three heated, outdoor pools in towns and theirs has more space per guest that the other two! On an annualized basis, the guesthouse is pretty evenly divided between gay men, lesbians, and straight couples. Late June to early September $190–485; shoulder seasons $120–385.

✻ ❀ "♈" **Fairbanks Inn** (508-487-0386; fairbanksinn.com), 90 Bradford Street. This Federal-style beauty, a 1770s sea captain's house, was the first house in town to have indoor plumbing. In the 1800s it was owned by the town's wealthiest individual, David Fairbanks, who began Seamen's Bank. Today it's a restored jewel, brought up to 21st-century standards without sacrificing historical integrity. Period antiques, wood-burning fireplaces, and wide-plank floorboards complement fine amenities and plush bedding. Although rooms in two adjacent buildings are less historic, they are still quite desirable. (The two least expensive rooms have a shared bath.) An expanded continental breakfast can be enjoyed in a wicker-filled, glassed-in porch or on the quiet brick patio. Owners Kathleen Fitzgerald and Alicia Mickenberg took over the centrally located 14-room inn in 2005. Mid-June to mid-September $145–275; off-season $99–165.

✻ ❀ **Inn at Cook Street** (508-487-3894; 888-266-5655; innatcookstreet .com), 7 Cook Street (East End). Owners Lisa Feistel and Doreen Bairdsell operate a mixed house (gay, straight, men, women), which is just the way they like it. The gracious 1836 Greek Revival sea captain's house offers four rooms, two suites, and two cottages. They are all very tasteful and highly recommended. Pick your room based on its sleigh bed (Garden Suite), how much sun it gets (the Retreat is very bright), or its deck access (some have a private deck). All have TV/DVD, fridges, and air-conditioning. Gas grilles in the private, shady backyard

are enticing and a rare amenity. Full breakfast. Mid-June to mid-September $229–319; off-season $115–205.

✻ ✐ "♈" **Beaconlight Guesthouse** (508-487-9603; 800-696-9603; beacon lightguesthouse.com), 12 Winthrop Street (West End). Innkeepers Keith Wilkinson and Mark Phillips preside over a warm and homey place. The living room has a grand piano begging to be played; the dining room and a country-style kitchen are the setting for an expanded continental breakfast and lively conversation. There's a big emphasis on organics here, from breakfast to bathroom products and cleaners. Of the 14 elegantly furnished rooms, Cape Ann is particularly spacious. All have TV and either a VCR or a dvd; some have a fireplace and separate sitting room. There are three decks (one of which is arguably the largest roof deck in town, with panoramic views) and an outdoor hot tub. Mid-May to late September $125–385; off-season $85–200; five night minimum in summer.

✻ "♈" **Oxford Guesthouse** (508-487-9103; 888-456-9103; oxfordguesthouse .com), 8 Cottage Street (West End). Innkeepers Stephen and Trevor opened this refined English-style B&B in 1998. I particularly like their front and back decks and gardens, a great place for coffee or just hanging out. Guests will definitely appreciate the lovely living room, furnished with plump sofas and a fireplace. As for the seven guest rooms (two with shared bath), they have central air, flat-screen TVs and DVDs, CD players, and 500-thread count sheets. A few have a gas fireplace. As for specific recommendations, Worcester has a private entrance, and the Trinity Suite is a particularly good value. An expanded continental breakfast is included, as is evening wine and time with their golden retriever, Potter. The inn transports guests to and from the ferry as needed. Mid-June through September $190–330; mid-season $120–250.

🐾 ♂ ⁗ᴵ⁗ **Tucker Inn** (508-487-0381; thetuckerinn.com), 12 Center Street. Open May through October. This cozy 8-room B&B, dating to 1872, is one of the most comfy, welcoming, and well-priced places to stay in town, thanks to owner Howard Burchman. He's constantly upgrading the offerings, with things like flat-screen TV and little gardens. Rooms are both soothing and simply decorated. One of the big pluses: the inn also offers arguably the best full breakfast in town, including eggs any style any morning, served on the brick patio in warm weather. Take time to hang out in the hot tub or relaxing garden and I bet you'll return. Inquire about the nice little **cottage**, which rents weekly. The inn is a mixed house of gay, straight, men, women. (Still, like most other places, it's more gay than straight.) July and August $175–265; off-season $155–195.

⁗ᴵ⁗ **Carriage House** (508-487-8855; thecarriaghse.com), 7 Central Street. Open April through February. Centrally located, this guesthouse offers something that most do not: each room has a private entrance and most have a private balcony. Completely renovated with a contemporary feel, the rooms are quite relaxing. In-season guests are about two-thirds men, one-third women; off-season, it's evenly divided between gay men, lesbians, and straight folks. Mid-June to mid-September $225–375; off-season $125–225.

APARTMENTS, COTTAGES & STUDIOS ❇ 🎈 🐾 ♿ ⁗ᴵ⁗ **Bay Shore & Chandler Houses** (508-487-9133; bayshorechandler.com), 493 Commercial Street at Howland Street (East

End). This six-building complex boasts 20 beachside units clustered around landscaped grounds. (Units across the street have access to the lawn and beach.) Most of the 25 units have a private deck or patio and a large picture window; all have a well-equipped kitchen; a few have a fireplace. The traditional exteriors belie individually and newly decorated interiors. I particularly like the Chandler House units, more contemporary and bright. All of these have a fireplace and "very good" or "spectacular" views. Although this is a condo complex, managers Ann Maguire and Harriet Gordon keep standards consistent and high. They also rent **two highly recommended units** (weekly) in the West End. Late June to early September $1,350–3,295 weekly; off-season $105–220 nightly.

❇ ⁗ᴵ⁗ **Watermark Inn** (508-487-0165; watermark-inn.com), 603 Commercial Street at Wiley Street (East End). These 10 contemporary suites are right at the water's edge. They feature triangular gable windows, skylights, spacious living areas, cable TV, and either a full kitchen or a kitchenette. (Two rooms have a fireplace.) Six suites have sliding glass doors that open out onto private decks—perfect for when high tide laps at the deck. It's a 20-minute

BAY SHORE & CHANDLER HOUSES

WATERMARK INN

walk from town, and they feature a rarity: on-site parking. Late June to early September $1,310–3,000 weekly; $205–470 nightly; off-season $85–350 nightly.

✳ ✎ "T" **The Masthead** (508-487-0523; 800-395-5095; themasthead .com), 31–41 Commercial Street (West End). At the far end of the West End, about a 15-minute walk from the center of town, the Masthead offers a superb variety of well-maintained (although distinctly old Provincetown) apartments, cottages, and rooms. The neatly landscaped complex, operated by the Ciluzzi family since 1959, has a boardwalk with lounge chairs and access to the 450-foot private beach below. Each cottage has a large picture window facing the water. Units, in buildings more than 100 years old, have fully equipped kitchens, low ceilings, pine paneling, and Early American furnishings that are a bit dated but nonetheless charming and comfortable. Although most units can accommodate four people; one sleeps eight. It's a great place for families; children under 12 stay free. July to early September $125–487 for two to four people; off-season $95–352.

Capt. Jack's Wharf (508-487-1450), 73A Commercial Street at West Vine Street (West End). Open late May to late September. On a rustic old wharf, these 15 colorfully painted bohemian apartments (condos, actually) transport you back to Provincetown's early days as an emerging art colony. Many units have whitewashed interiors, with skylights and lots of windows looking onto the harbor. Some first-floor units have narrow cracks between the planked floorboards—you can see the water beneath you! I particularly like Australis, a two-story unit with a spiral staircase and more than 1,000 square feet of space. The wharf is strewn with bistro tables, pots of flowers, and Adirondack chairs. Rates unavailable at press time.

✳ ✿ **White Horse Inn** (508-487-1790), 500 Commercial Street at Daggett Lane (East End). This low-key, artsy hostelry has been taking in guests since 1963, intent on providing clean, comfortable rooms at good prices. Mary Martin presides over six studio apartments that have been individually decorated with an eclectic, bohemian flair. Some are light and airy; some are dark and cozy. All defy

WHITE HORSE INN

description—although one bathroom is truly "postmodern nautical." Suffice it to say each is a work of art in progress. Although the 12 guest rooms are basic (most with a shared bath), they are filled with local art from the last 30 years. They're a real find and are very popular with Europeans. June through August $100–170 double ($60–75 single) rooms, $200 studio apartments. Off-season $80–100 double rooms, $125 studios; inquire about weekly studio rates. No credit cards.

MOTELS 🐾 🛁 ♿ ❝¶❞ **Surfside Hotel & Suites** (866-757-8616; surfsideinn.cc), 543 Commercial Street at Kendall Lane (East End). Open mid-April through October. Of these two, completely renovated buildings, one sits on a private harborfront beach and the other overlooks a large pool. After the complete transformation in 2008, we visitors ended up with 87 summery and fresh rooms (and three waterfront suites). Each has a TV, small refrigerator, and balcony. Inquire about two apartments, which sleep four to six people and have fully equipped kitchens. Packages available. Early July to early September $199–329 rooms, $650 suites; off-season $119–179 rooms, $250 suites.

🦞 ❝¶❞ **Inn at the Moors** (508-487-1342; 800-842-6379; innatthemoors.com), 59 Provincelands Road (West End). Open mid-May to late October. Perched at the edge of the moors, with unparalleled views of sand, sea, and sky, this 30-unit motel enjoys a spectacular perch. Upper-deck rooms, as you might imagine, have better views. Amenities include a heated pool and parking at your front door. It received an-almost extreme makeover in 2008, with new furnishings and more. It represents a terrific value. Late June to early September $159–225; off-season $99–179.

🛁 **Chateau Provincetown** (508-487-1286; chateauptown.com), 105 Bradford Street (West End). Open May through October. No longer affiliated with Best Western, but still with the same staff and owners, when you need a room in Provincetown, this 53-room place may have one. Rates unavailable at press time.

LIGHTHOUSE & MORE 🦞 🛁 **Race Point Lighthouse** (508-487-9930; racepointlighthouse.net). Open early May to mid-October. After the Coast Guard decommissioned this light in 1972, it stood empty for more than 20 years before a nonprofit foundation took over. Now that it's renovated, overnight stays are wonderful for families and groups. The **keeper's house** has three different-sized bedrooms (with a maximum occupancy of 11) that share 1½ baths as well as a living room. Solar energy powers appliances in the kitchen; bring your own food, water, and linens. It's glorious out here—with the Atlantic Great Beach on one side and Hatches Harbor, a tidal estuary with shallow warm water, on the other. First-time visitors tend only to come for 1 night, but those in the know come for 2 or 3. After making reservations (as early as possible), a volunteer will drive you out. Rates: $145–185 double. In 2007 they also opened up the remodeled **Whistler House**, which sleeps 8 people in 2 bedrooms. The only trick? You have to have your own 4WD to get there. Late July to early October $2,500 weekly.

CAMPGROUNDS 🐾 🛁 **Dune's Edge Campground** (508-487-9815; dunes-edge.com), off Route 6. Open May through September. Look for one hundred wooded lots, mostly for tents, on the edge of the dunes and within earshot of the highway. As my friends, Susan and Beth, said of a recent visit:

"It's a clean, well kept campground with a family atmosphere and overzealous night watchmen (bring battery powered lamps instead of torches unless you want a severe scolding). The sites can feel small if you've got more than one tent. Bike access to downtown with kids is scary because of cycling on Route 6. Ask for sites along the dunes and/or the back of the campground otherwise you may hear road traffic." Rates: $40 for two people tenting without electricity; $30 off-season.

❧ **Coastal Acres Camping Court** (508-487-1700; coastalacres.com), West Vine Street Extension. Open April through October. Wooded sites on the western edge of town; $27 for two in a tent, $43 with hookups. No credit cards.

RENTAL HOUSES AND COTTAGES

Across the Bay Real Estate (508-487-8888; acrossthebay.com), 132 Commercial Street. Ask for Leslie Parsons.

Pat Shultz Real Estate (508-487-9550; patshultz.com), 406 Commercial Street.

BUYING REAL ESTATE Kinlin Grover (508-285-0118; kinlingrover.com/chrisnagle), 162 Commercial Street. When you're looking to by something on the Outer Cape after renting, I have personal experience with this terrific agent.

CANINE ACCOMMODATIONS ❊ ❧ **KC's Animal Resort** (508-487-7900; ptownpets.com), 79 Shank Painter Road. Since so few hostelries accept pets, this kennel seemed an obvious idea to Karen and Custudio Silva Jr. in late 1998. Bring your dog on vacation, take her to the beach and on bike rides, drop her off overnight,

and then play together again after you've had breakfast the next day. Adjacent veterinary facilities.

✳ Where to Eat

The quality of Provincetown restaurants continues to impress me. In fact, Provincetown has the greatest concentration of fine restaurants of any town on the Cape. You'll have plenty of choices to suit your budget and taste buds. *Instead of listing places in order of preference (as I usually do), listings are from east to west relative to Commercial Street.* Opening and closing months listed here are only a guideline. Though many places are closed certain days of the week, I generally don't mention that because it's so changeable. If you have your heart set on a particular place, call ahead off-season, and always make reservations when you can, especially in summer.

DINING OUT ✎ ♈ **Ciro & Sal's** (508-487-6444; ciroandsals.com), 4 Kiley Court (at Commercial Street). Open for dinner nightly June through September, weekends off-season; closed January. The primary reason to eat here is historical, since it opened as a coffeehouse and sandwich shop for artists in the early 1950s. The ground floor still looks the same as it did back then—cozy with brick and plaster walls and chianti bottles hanging from the low rafters. Chef Larry Luster's extensive northern Italian menu has traditional signature dishes like veal marsala and seafood specials. My experiences here have always been "okay," but since Ciro & Sal's is open year-round, that almost qualifies it as a social service agency in my book. Dinner $15–37.

✳ ❧ ♈ ♿ **Mews Restaurant and Café** (508-487-1500; mews.com), 429 Commercial Street (between Kiley and Lovetts courts). Open for dinner night-

ly, as well as Sunday brunch from mid-May through October. One of Provincetown's most sophisticated restaurants, the beachfront Mews is elegant and romantic, awash in peach tones and bleached woods. Longtime chef Laurence deFreitas offers a popular mixed seafood grill and dishes like seared peppercorn crusted tuna. Sauces are rich and delicious. Servers are very knowledgeable. The more casual upstairs café, with the same water views and lower prices, also has great burgers, appetizers, salads, and pasta. It's a great place for a before-dinner drink or after-dinner dessert and coffee. (The Mews stocks over 200 types of vodka, the largest selection in New England.) There's also entertainment in winter. Dine before sunset to better appreciate the water view. Sunday brunch $12–18, dinner $18–34.

Bistro 404 (508-487-5404), 404 Commercial Street (at Washington Avenue). Open for dinner early May to late October. When Chester closed after the season ended in 2006, and Bistro 404 burst onto the scene in 2008, they had big shoes to fill. But fill them they did, with aplomb. Although I didn't get a chance to eat here for this edition, my reliable Provincetown contacts assure me that everything is more than up to snuff. Service, execution from the kitchen, and atmosphere (polished wood floors, artwork, and clean, con-

temporary lines) is all very new Provincetown. Creative seafood reigns. Dinner $25–40.

Devon's (508-487-4773; devons.org), 401½ Commercial Street (at Washington Avenue). Open for breakfast and dinner mid-May to mid-October. This little place harbors a big gem of a kitchen. Romantic and cozy, the waterfront eatery excels in contemporary cuisine. I particularly liked my organic, grilled black pearl salmon with miso tamari glaze, soba noodles, and baby bok choy. Look for 8 or 9 dishes nightly that rise to this level. Also come for one of the top three breakfasts in town. Sit outside on the enclosed front porch for a fancy omelet, tofu veggie scramble, organic vegan flax seed granola, or blueberry cornmeal pancakes. Arrive early or be prepared to wait. Breakfast $7–13, dinner $23–38.

🌸 **Edwige at Night** (508-487-4020; edwigeatnight.com), 333 Commercial Street (at Freeman Street). Open for dinner mid-May to mid-October. With sophisticated cuisine that even surpasses the lovely atmosphere, the Edwige is easily one of Provincetown's top places to dine. By night it's one big romantic dinner party, with subdued lighting, solicitous service, and closely spaced tables. The eclectic menu, a fusion of Mediterranean, Asian, and Latin cuisines, changes seasonally. Think duck confit spring rolls, native seafood cake, and *moqueca*, a northern Brazilian dish of scallops, halibut, and shrimp in coconut milk over basmati rice. The food and presentation are fun, the staff colorful, and the salads creative. You can't go wrong here. Edwige also mixes a killer cosmopolitan, concocted from homemade vodkas. Dinner $20–36.

❄ 🌸 🖊 ♈ ⅙ **Napi's** (508-487-1145; napis-restaurant.com), 7 Freeman Street (at Bradford Street). Open for dinner year-round, lunch October through April. The important thing about Napi's is their hours, for which I commend them heartily! Chef-owners Helen and Napi Van Dereck opened this unusual restaurant in 1973 and have filled it chockablock with local art, plants, stained glass, and lively objects to stir your imagination. The eclectic, international menu includes dishes made with Portuguese sausage (linguiça), organic salads, a large selection of vegetarian dishes (try the coconut-crusted tofu), pasta dishes, and stir-fry. Health-conscious Napi's also accommodates no-fat, vegan, and low-salt diets. A favorite of local artists, townsfolk, and the "Old Guard," Napi's is even more lively off-season. Free parking on the premises; early specials. Dinner $17–26.

❦ ☗ **Front Street** (508-487-9715; frontstreetrestaurant.com), 230 Commercial Street (between Gosnold and Masonic streets). Open for dinner May through December (closed Tuesday except in August). One of the Outer Cape's most consistent places, Front Street is also the best eatery in town for the money! Located in the cozy brick cellar of a Victorian house, it's a convivial place, made more so by small tables placed very closely together, antique booths, and local artwork. Service is provided by unobtrusive, attentive, and longtime waitstaff. Donna Aliperti, chef-owner since opening the restaurant in 1987, reigns over a kitchen creating much-lauded "Mediterranean-American fusion." The repertoire of Italian, French, and Continental dishes changes weekly, but signature dishes include herb-crusted rack of lamb, tea-smoked duck, and gorgonzola-stuffed filet mignon. The wine list is excellent. Leave room for pastry and sous-chef Kathy Cotter's delicious finales. Dinner $19–33.

❇ **Bistro at Crowne Pointe** (508-487-2365; crownepointe.com), 82 Bradford Street. Open for dinner. This bistro (within a hotel-inn) turns up the heat with refined dining. From filet mignon and seared duck breast to a specialty hot pot (with shrimp, scallops, and rice noodles) and a specialty seafood stew, dining isn't fly by night. The wine list is excellent. For this kind of cash, I prefer dining inside rather than on the porch. And I prefer a dozen other restaurants first. Dinner $24–32.

❇ ❦ ☗ **Lorraine's** (508-487-6074; lorrainesrestaurant.vpweb.com), 133 Commercial Street (between Pleasant and Franklin streets). Open for dinner, often until 12:30 AM. It's always nice when the warmth and generosity of a place match those of the owner. One of my all-time favorite restaurants, this authentic Mexican hideaway serves upscale south-of-the-border dishes like *carnitas enchiladas*, featuring the owner's third-generation recipe for pork tenderloin with mole sauce. Vegetarians will gravitate to Estelle's enchiladas—others for seafood with a twist, try specials like blackened tuna softshell tacos. There is a great margarita bar (with more specialty tequilas than you can imagine). I'd be tempted to eat here every night if I could. Dinner $19–28.

❇ ☗ **Victor's** (508-487-1777; victors ptown.com), 175 Bradford Street. Open for brunch, afternoon raw bar, and dinner. This is one hot and hoppin' restaurant; the tapas formula is a perfect concept for Provincetown. Mix and match little plates of stunning palate pleasers like lobster spring rolls, smoked ahi tuna pate, herbed chicken quesadilla, braised short ribs, miniburgers, and seafood cakes. We tried them all on repeated trips and registered euphoria each time. The open, airy, contemporary dining room is buzzy and convivial, and warm in the off-season thanks to a central stone fireplace. Kudos to owner Victor Depoalo and chef Mike Fennelly. Start off with a specialty cocktail like Too Hot Capriana (don't ask, don't tell) or something from the raw bar. Brunch $10–16, dinner $5–16.

🦞 ✐ ♿ **Sal's Place** (508-487-1279; salsplaceofprovincetown.com), 99 Commercial Street (at Cottage Street). Open for dinner early May to late October; long weekends in spring and fall. Reserve a waterside table on the deck covered in grapevines, and enjoy southern Italian dishes while listening to waves lap at the deck pilings. Sal's transports you to an earlier time a place and a space somewhere between Italy and Cape Cod. There's no better to way to spend a summer evening. One of the two indoor dining rooms is classic trattoria: Chianti bottles hang from the ceilings, and red-and-white-checked cloths cover the tables. Two or three nightly specials like *salmone alla grillia* or *calamari stufati* supplement

THE RED INN

classics like *melanzane alla parmigiana*. Service is friendly and leisurely, portions are large, and the tiramisu heavenly, thanks to longtime chef-owners Lora and Jack Papetsas (gregariously presiding since 1989). Dinner $16–25.

♿ ♿ **The Red Inn** (508-487-0050; theredinn.com), 15 Commercial Street. Open for brunch Thursday through Sunday, June through October; dinner nightly, April through October; dinner on weekends in November and December. This prime waterfront location is one of the hottest foodie destinations on the Cape. Decked out in white linens and soothing colors and perched on water's edge, the beautifully restored old house has sanded floors and huge picture windows—perfectly blending a contemporary aesthetic with a classic one. That about sums up the cuisine, too. The menu exudes finesse: herb- and dijon-crusted rack of lamb, pepper-crusted filet mignon with truffle mashed potatoes, and grilled duck breast with a passion fruit maple glaze. Then there's the specialty: a big porterhouse steak! History buffs take note: this circa 1800 inn is a few steps from where the Pilgrims landed in 1620. Dinner $26–46.

EATING OUT ❀ ❦ ∅ **Fanizzi's by the Sea** (508-487-1964; fanizzisrest aurant.com), 539 Commercial Street (between Hancock and Kendall streets). Open daily for lunch, dinner, and Sunday brunch. If you find yourself suffering from hunger pangs and lusting for a killer water view, fear not. Fanizzi's is also one of the rare places that serves throughout the afternoon. Enormous portions of comfort cuisine, seafood, and American dishes (from spinach salad to ribs and burgers) are offered at reasonable prices: Try the midday fish-and-chips and the evening buffalo chicken wings. When I consider the combination of price, offerings, execution, and its waterfront location, Fanizzi's is hard to beat. Early specials. Lunch $8–16, dinner $10–25.

❦ **Café Edwige by Day** (508-487-2008), 333 Commercial Street (at Freeman Street). Open for breakfast and lunch daily in July and August and weekends May and June and September to mid-October. This has to be one of the best breakfast places on the Eastern Seaboard. Proprietor Nancyann Meads has working her magic since 1974, dishing up lobster benedict, specialty omelets (perhaps with Boursin and asparagus), fruit crepes, steak and eggs, unbelievable French toast (covered with Fiji apples and toasted walnuts—think more along the lines of a baked casserole), spicy home fries, tofu casserole, and delectable danish. High-backed booths and small tables fill the lofty second-floor space, bright with skylights. Their signature poppy seed cream Danish is worth dying for. Take my word for it: Edwige

is a great place to fall in love. Breakfast and lunch $6–15.

Y **Patio American Grill & Cocktail Bar** (508-487-9465), 328 Commercial Street (between Freeman and Standish streets). Open throughout the day May to mid-October. I like this place simply because it's outdoors and Provincetown has relatively little streetside dining (or drinking). It's current incarnation (since 2005) is a primo people watching perch. Others like to eat here. Dishes $20–25.

∅ **Lobster Pot** (508-487-0842; ptown lobsterpot.com), 321 Commercial Street (between Freeman and Standish streets). Open daily for lunch and dinner April through November. This venerable waterfront institution, in the McNulty family since 1979, feels touristy and the service can be hurried. But the menu features a wide selection of fresh seafood, shore dinners, and truly great clam chowder. Look for the big neon red lobster sign and head down the long corridor, past the kitchens, and up the ramp. Lunch $9–19 dinner $10–30.

❀ ❦ ♿ **Ross' Grill** (508-487-8878; rossgrillptown.com), 237 Commercial Street (within Whaler's Wharf). Open for lunch and dinner; closed Tuesday. Overlooking the harbor from a second-floor vantage point, this casual American grill is a happening place, with good music, a structural steel ceiling, and an exposed kitchen. The menu is simple but good: arguably the best burgers in town, as well as shellfish risotto, a raw bar, and steak frites. There's also an impressive list of 50 wines by the glass and a dozen international beers. Because this place is tucked away, it feels like you need to be in the know to know, which is fun. Lunch $8–13, dinner around $30.

❦ **frapp066** (508-487-9066; frapp066 .com), 214 Commercial Street (at the

Art House Theatre). Open all day, mid-May to mid-October. New in 2007, this hopping place for casual eats and a cool vibe is one of my new faves. The concept is great: Hit the self-serve line for some fine, fine dishes like fillet of sole with lobster-corn stuffing, or grilled sirloin with fried leeks and a red wine sauce. And then take your food to a high bar table or outside. Or keep it more simple (hardly!) with a crispy goat cheese salad, grilled asparagus, and a curried chicken sandwich with snow peas and almonds. It's fast food with lots and lots of flair. Dishes $9–19.

♣ **Café Heaven** (508-487-9639), 199 Commercial Street (at Carver Street). Open for breakfast and lunch April through November; dinner June to early September. This very good storefront eatery with high ceilings is always lively, but sometimes it just feels noisy and cramped. (Peek in and decide for yourself.) Deservedly popular for late-day breakfasts, Heaven's specialties

CAFÉ HEAVEN

include create-your-own omelets, sweet cornmeal scones, fluffy banana pancakes, garlicky home fries, and crunchy granola. An extensive lunchtime selection of cold salads and sandwiches reigns midday, while dinner offerings seem to change annually. You can expect build-your-own burgers and pasta dishes and friendly service. Breakfast and lunch $5–8, dinner $10–18.

♈ **Jimmy's Hideaway** (508-487-1011; jimmyshideaway.com), 179 Commercial Street (at Carver Street). Open mid-April to mid-February. This cozy, casual, and hopping place on the water always seems to draw a crowd. Comfort food reigns on the tavern menu: think fish-and-chips and meat loaf. Also try the chef's specialty, peasant bouillabaisse. Then again, you can always get a burger for $10. Those are just a few of the reasons that folks come back again and again. Dinner $22–29, tavern specials $15.

♂ ♈ ♿ **Bubala's By The Bay** (508-487-0773; bubalas.com), 183 Commercial Street (at Court Street). Open 11 AM to "late" daily, May through October. Bubala's draws crowds because of its streetside tables and indoor bayside views. It's a moderately priced, fun, high-energy place with okay food. Live music, mostly jazz, almost every night. It's hard to beat the free parking! Brunch/lunch $8–15, dinner $14–26.

TAKEOUT ♣ **Karoo Kafe** (508-487-6630; karookafe.com), 338 Commercial Street (at Freeman Street). Open for lunch and dinner May to mid-October. One of my favorite, quick-bite places, this little take-out place (with patio seats) has terrific South African dishes, curries, pita sandwiches, burgers (with ostrich, buffalo, and turkey), veggie and vegan dishes, peri-peri chicken, and so much more. You can't go wrong here. Dishes $6–8.

 ♨ ◢ **Mojo's** (508-487-3140), Ryder Street, next to the MacMillan Wharf parking lot. Open 11–11 daily in summer and 11:30–5 in the shoulder seasons from May to mid-October. There are two important distinctions between this clam shack/fry joint and others of its type: The selection of dishes is extensive, and the fried foods are light and fresh. Try almost anything and you'll not be disappointed: fried mushrooms, baskets of fried shrimp or fish, chicken tenders, subs, french fries, burgers, Mexican dishes, salads, and vegetarian sandwiches. Take your enormous portions to the beach, pier, or, if you're lucky, to one of a few outdoor tables. Dishes $3–18.

 ♨ ◢ **Aquarium Mall** (no phone), 209 Commercial Street. Open seasonally. This little mini-mall is a warren of diverse, inexpensive eateries: come for quick and good burritos, gelato, Chinese food, bagels, and breakfast sandwiches. There are some picnic tables out back overlooking the water.

 ◢ **The Red Shack** (508-487-7422), 315A Commercial Street, Lopes Square/MacMillan Wharf. Open May to mid-October. New in 2008, from a family with longtime ties to Provincetown (see the Mayflower and Portuguese Bakery), this take-out window offers sandwiches, slices of pizza, hot sausages smothered in sautéed onions and peppers, and very good lobster rolls. It's perfect when you want something quick before the ferry or when you want to keep cruising Commercial Street. Grab a seat in front of Town Hall or on the wharf. Dishes $7–20.

 ◢ **Provincetown House of Pizza** (508-487-6655; ptownpizza.com), 50 Bradford Street. Open mid-April to late October. For fancy and plain pies, baked calzones, pasta, subs, and salads. You could feed an army here for less than most places in town. Dishes $8–20.

CAFÉS, COFFEE, DESSERT & MORE

"ℹ" **Connie's Bakery** (508-487-2167; conniesbakery.com), 43 Race Point Road. Open seasonally. What's Provincetown's morning hub? Find out at Connie and Richie's place, where they make everything from scratch. Try her delectable cakes, pastries, and pies or his unbeatable challah, cornmeal, and sesame breads. I dare you to leave Provincetown without going back for more. The magical mixture of flour, butter, and sugar (not to mention more exotic ingredients) never tasted so good. Also try their sandwiches made with Richie's fresh breads and prepared foods to take home. And dine at their communal table indoors or picnic tables outdoors.

✳ **Purple Feather Dessert Café** (508-487-9100; thepurplefeather.com), 334 Commercial Street (at Freeman Street). Open for lunch, dinner, and dessert. Just what Provincetown needed! It's a wonder no one thought of this satisfy-the-sweet-tooth-idea sooner. Sure they have panini, mac and cheese, and soups when you want to be good. But most everyone gets swept in for the sweets: gelato, homemade chocolates, fancy pies and cakes, cannolis, truffles, specialty fudge . . . you get the idea. Skip dessert at most restaurants and make a bee-line here. When the kids aren't looking, check out the adult candy.

SPIRITUS

⁰1⁰ **Spiritus** (508-487-2808), 190 Commercial Street (between Carver and Court streets). Open daily 11:30 AM–2 AM, April to mid-November (from 8 AM in summer). Everyone comes to Spiritus at least once during their time here, and some come once daily! If one of the front benches is empty, hang out and do some serious people-watching. This is *the* place to see and be seen after midnight (for gay guys anyway). Grab a slice of great thin-crust pizza or down a shake or freshly squeezed orange juice. Wooden booths are perfect for rainy or chilly days.

❄ **Joe** (508-487-6656), 148A Commercial Street (between Atlantic and Conant streets). Consistently exceptional coffee. When it opened, this tiny shop was so packed that one worker commented, "It was so busy I thought I was selling drugs." The beans are roasted by two women at Indigo, located in the tiny western Massachusetts town of Florence. There are fine pastries, too. My Left Coast friend Wayne knows no sweeter place for a ritualized cup of caffeine and a side of good, morning-after conversation.

⁰1⁰ **Wired Puppy** (508-487-0017; wiredpuppy.com), 379 Commercial Street (at Pearl Street). Open daily. Come for strong coffee, sweet treats, and good people-watching (pull up a bench alongside Lili Taylor, as we did for a week one summer).

Provincetown Portuguese Bakery (508-487-1803), 299 Commercial Street (between Standish and Ryder streets). Open daily, April through October. Short of hopping on a plane to Lisboa, you haven't tried Portuguese breads and pastries unless you've dropped into this classic sense of place: *pasteis de coco*, meat pies, *pasteis de nata* (a custard tart), and *tarte de Amendoa* (almond tart). In summer

WI-FI AT THE WIRED PUPPY

the ovens are cranking 24 hours a day, and the fried dough (*mallassadas*) flies out faster than they can make it. One last tidbit: It's the only place to get a fresh loaf of bread on Commercial Street.

❄ When you're in the middle of town, head to **Far Land Provisions** (508-487-0045), 150 Bradford Street (at Conwell Street). And when you need to see another human soul in winter,

STEPPING BACK IN TIME
Provincetown may be filled with second homes and condos purchased by baby boomers dining on $35 entrées and homemade vodkas, but there are still vestiges where you can step back three and more decades. Let's do the time-warp again: Head to the **Mayflower Café** (300 Commercial Street) or **Tip for Tops'n** (31 Bradford Street) for a quick meal; the **Portuguese Bakery** (299 Commercial Street; see above); **Sal's Place** (99 Commercial Street) for an outdoor, waterside Italian dinner; and the **Porchside Bar** at the Gifford House (9 Carver Street).

ANGEL FOODS

this is the hub. With or without hot coffee, lunchtime sandwiches with Boar's Head meats are killer when they're taken to Race Point with friends.

In the West End, no one does it better than **Relish** (508-487-8077), 93 Commercial Street. It's worth going out of your way for these higher end sandwiches, prepared salads to go, and amazing desserts—especially cupcakes.

In the East End with parking (!), the upscale **Angel Foods** (508-487-6666), 467 Commercial Street, has gourmet fixings that'll cost a pretty penny.

Farmer's Market, Ryder Street across from Town Hall. Great produce and more on Saturday and Sunday, 1:30–5:30 in summer. It's about time that Provincetown got a market like this. Seems a no-brainer now that it's here.

✳ Entertainment

THEATER ✳ **The Provincetown Theater** (508-487-9793; 238 Bradford Street; provincetowntheater.com), which flung open its doors in January 2006, is home to the Provincetown Repertory Theatre and the Province-

town Theatre Company. It's already hard to imagine life before the theater! **Provincetown Theatre Co. (PTC)**, founded in 1963 to further the goals of the early-20th-century Provincetown Players, is a collaborative of professional, semiprofessional, and amateur actors, writers, directors, technicians, teachers, and theater lovers. In addition to year-round theater, they also provide education for youth and adults and foster the development of emerging playwrights. **Provincetown Repertory Theatre**, a professional company, is dedicated to challenging audiences with creative, intelligent, and provocative American works. The REP draws upon and continues a long legacy of theater in Provincetown by rethinking and restaging American classics as well as fostering new voices and new plays.

✳ **Art House Theatre** (508-487-9222; ptownarthouse.com), 214 Commercial Street. Alongside the happenin' frapp066 (see *Eating Out*), this remodeled venue hosts some movies and a full line up of entertainment, including drag queens. Check out their schedule; it's usually a killer one.

MOVIES ✳ 🐾 ☂ **Whaler's Wharf Cinema** (508-487-4269), 237 Com-

ART HOUSE THEATRE

mercial Street (Whaler's Wharf). The only game in town for new releases, documentaries, and art films.

❄ 🐚 ↑ **Movies at the Cape Inn** (508-487-1711; capeinn.com), 698 Commercial Street. Open February through December; call for schedule. One of the quirkiest things to do in Provincetown, movie night here means an ever-changing group of about 40 locals getting together to watch a free movie and eat unlimited popcorn in the Whaler Lounge. Go for the experience of it, regardless of what's showing. (Movies change weekly.) Or go simply for the swivel cocktail lounge chairs, the camp, and the bar.

🍸 **NIGHTLIFE** Provincetown's after-dark scene can get rather spicy. There's something for everyone: gay, straight, and in between. Check the weekly *Provincetown Magazine* for live music. When the bars, clubs, and shows close at 1 AM, it seems like everybody ends up in front of the Provincetown Town Hall or Spiritus (see *Where to Eat*). It's rather extraordinary when you think about it: There can be 300 people hanging out in front of Spiritus in the middle of the night without any problems.

In addition to some of the places below, for live music head to: **Bubala's By The Bay** (see *Eating Out*) for an eclectic lineup, and **The Landmark** (508-487-6500; 269 Commercial Street) for its piano bar.

❄ **Crown & Anchor** (508-487-1430; onlyatthecrown.com), 247 Commercial Street (between Gosnold and Masonic streets). The diversity of entertainment is impressive here. The Crown features a men's dance club, disco, outdoor pool patio, popular drag shows, and cabaret acts. It draws a gay and mixed crowd. Check it out. It's home to some of the best entertainers in town,

including the incomparable comedian Kate Clinton. You can't miss it: Drag queens will be strutting up and down Commercial in the late afternoon, handing out flyers for their shows. Their **Central House Bar** is "safe" for straight people. And FYI: their restaurant is open almost all day every day! Off-season brings all-you-can-eat Taco Tuesday.

Cabo Lounge, **Vixen**, and **Madeira Room** (508-487-6424; thepilgrim house.com), 336 Commercial Street (between Freeman and Center streets), at the Pilgrim House. Open April through January. At press time, this bar and dance club was undergoing a major overhaul. Look for a wine bar, bigger name performers like Paula Poundstone and Sarah Bernhardt, a restaurant, and 180-seat theater.

Pied Bar (508-487-1527; piedbar .com), 193A Commercial Street (between Carver and Court streets). Open May through October. This waterfront bar and club has been around since 1971. These days it's best by day, when the waterfront bar is more geared to straight folks, although there is "after tea" dancing here when the Boatslip (see *For the Boys*) breaks up.

Grotta Bar at Enzo (508-487-7555; enzolives.com), 186 Commercial Street. Open April through December. This hip and hot spot has successfully managed something for everyone: live entertainment, sports on a giant plasma TV, pinball, jukebox tunes, DJs, and a killer line-up of signature drinks. It's a "cas" place to hang with friends, made more so by the fireplace in winter.

Post Office Cabaret (508-487-3892), 303 Commercial Street (between Standish and Ryder streets). Open mid-February to mid-January. Although this long, narrow room has too many pew-style seats, it hosts big-name female

impersonators like Jimmy James.

❄ **Governor Bradford** (508-487-9618), 312 Commercial Street (at Standish Street). To get a different but equally "real" flavor of Provincetown, stop into this townie and straight tourist tavern for a game of chess or backgammon or to listen to live music. Head upstairs for karaoke. From the game tables, you can watch people on the streets watching each other.

Bingo at the Unitarian Universalist Meeting House (508-487-9344), 236 Commercial Street (near Winslow Street). Call for schedule. When you need a dose of quirky Provincetown, nothing beats this mostly gay crowd.

Old Colony, 323 Commercial Street. Open April through December. For a really classic, old Provincetown experience, belly up to a bar stool here. Don't be scared.

The Red Inn, **Front Street**, and **The Mews Restaurant**, all under *Where to Eat*, all have nice little bars.

✳ Selective Shopping

Unlike other chapters, in which shops are arranged according to merchandise type, they're listed here from east to west along Commercial Street. (That's because there are upwards of 300 shops on the strip.) Shops not on Commercial Street are inserted in the text where you would naturally detour to them from Commercial.

A few more notes before we start: Most shops are open mid-April to mid-

---

FOR THE BOYS

The Boatslip Beach Club (508-487-1669; boatslipresort.com), 161 Commercial Street (between Central and Atlantic streets), is known around the world for its packed, oh-so-gay summertime "Tea Dance" from 4 to 7 PM daily (May to mid-October). Every gay person should experience the euphoria at least once. Last dance on Labor Day is particularly heady. If you like to dance, be here. You can also rent pool chairs for $4 and a towel for $2 if you're not staying here, as long as you depart by tea time.

✳ **Atlantic House** (508-487-3821; ahouse.com), 4 Masonic Place, more commonly referred to as the A-House, has three diverse bars: the so-called Macho Bar (a nationally known men's leather bar); the nautically decorated disco Dance Bar; and the Little Bar (more intimate, with a roaring fireplace in the off-season). I'm confident that no other 18th-century house sees such action. Open 365 days a year. There isn't a gay man in town who doesn't stop into the A-House off-season. Some credit the A-House with establishing Provincetown's "off-season" versus "closed for the season."

October, although some galleries keep a shorter season (mid-June to mid-September). Many shops stay open until 11 PM in July and August, and a number of them offer sales in mid-October. Even the shops designated with an "off-season" icon are usually only open on winter weekends. And just to keep it interesting, other shops that aren't "supposed" to be open year-round may open without notice in winter, depending on the weather.

Provincetown Arts (provincetownarts .org), a 150-page annual published in July, is Provincetown's bible of visual arts, literature, and theater. Look for it in bookstores.

Galleries hold Friday openings staggered between 5 PM and 10 PM, so patrons may stroll the street, catching most of the receptions, and meet with artists. Most galleries change exhibits every 2 weeks.

See also **Provincetown Art Association & Museum** under *To See* and **Fine Arts Work Center** and **Provincetown Museum School** under *Even More Things to Do.*

The Schoolhouse Center for Art and Design (508-487-4800; school

housecenter.com), 494 Commercial Street. Located in a mid-19th-century Greek Revival schoolhouse, this venture features four galleries, among them the **Schoolhouse Gallery**, with contemporary photography, paintings and sculpture, and the **Art Strand Gallery** (508-4870-1153; artstrand .com), with contemporary art made by a dozen Provincetown artists.

Berta Walker Gallery (508-487-6411; bertawalker.com), 208 Bradford Street (between Howland and Cook streets). This excellent gallery represents Provincetown-affiliated artists of the past, present, and future.

William-Scott Gallery (508-487-4040; williamscottgallery.com), 439 Commercial Street. This venue showcases contemporary art and preeminent regional artists like John Dowd and Will Klemm.

✳ **Harvey Dodd Gallery** (508-487-3329; harveydodd.com), 437 Commercial Street. Dodd has been painting and exhibiting his watercolors and pastels of Provincetown and other Cape Cod scenes since 1959. His gallery, opened in 1971, is the oldest in town.

✳ **Simie Maryles Gallery** (508-487-7878; simiemaryles.com), 435 Commercial Street. Maryles's vibrant landscapes sold so well in local galleries that the artist decided to open her own shop.

Rice/Polak Gallery (508-487-1052; ricepolakgallery.com), 430 Commercial Street. I always enjoy this gallery. Marla Rice, who assumed sole ownership in 2005, represents more than 40 contemporary artists working in painting, photography, assemblages, graphics, and sculpture. Biweekly exhibitions feature the work of two or three artists; the gallery offers art consulting, too.

Albert Merola Gallery (508-487-4424; albertmerolagallery.com),

424 Commercial Street. You'll find very fine contemporary art here, as well as notables like Milton Avery and Michael Mazure; it's always worth dropping in.

Packard Gallery (508-487-4690; packardgallery.com), 418 Commercial Street. Gallery director Leslie Packard showcases paintings by her sister Cynthia and her mother, Anne. In fact there are five generations of Packards who have painted in Provincetown: Anne's grandfather, Max Bohm, was an early member of the Provincetown Art Association. The gallery, by the way, is housed in a former Christian Science church, which Anne's grandmother used to attend. It's quite a family affair.

Utilities (508-487-6800; utilitieshome .com), 393 Commercial Street. They're purveyors of whimsical, colorful, summery, frivolous, and function items for the bath, home, and kitchen. Bed, Bath & Beyond they are not.

❋ **Womencrafts** (508-487-2501; womencrafts.com), 376 Commercial Street. In addition to books and music, this Provincetown institution features handcrafted items made by and for women.

Undercover Linen (508-487-4114; undercoverlinen.com), 361 Commercial Street. Look for beautiful linens and all the other layers required for the most sensual night's sleep, a scent shop, aromasensory bath products, and more. I dare you to get out of here without dropping some cash.

Small Pleasures (508-487-3712), 359 Commercial Street. Every shop has its niche: Here, it's antique jewelry for men and women.

❋ **Song of Myself** (508-487-5736; songofmyself.com), 349 Commercial Street. Brad Fowler's photographic studio is worth a visit regardless of whether or not you want a portrait. The walls are lined with his work, showcasing the diversity and pride of town residents and visitors alike.

❋ **Bradford Natural Market** (508-487-9784; bradfordnatural.com), 141 Bradford Street. They've got the market cornered for organic produce, homeopathic remedies, gluten-free this, dairy-free that, and much more.

❋ **Shop Therapy** (508-487-9387; shoptherapy.com), 346 Commercial Street. This landmark, psychedelic-swathed building proclaims: "Monsters attack P-town. Shop Therapy blamed." No doubt. Merchandise revolves around current alternative lifestyles and the retro look. It's a head shop without the dope, and it was opened in 1972 by the Vietnam vet who *still* owns it. Catherine and I always stop to visit their brilliantly reserved African gray parrot, Zella.

❋ **Land's End Marine Supply** (508-487-0784; landsendmarinesupply.com), 337 Commercial Street. It's amazing that this old-fashioned two-story hardware store continues to thrive. But it

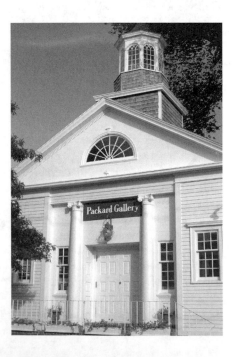

does, by selling beach chairs, umbrellas, coolers, suntan lotion, and more.

❋ **Hersheldon's Leather** (508-487-9046; hersheldonsleather.com), 317 Commercial Street. Hersh and Sheldon have a great knack for picking out just the right jacket (or briefcase or shoes) for your style and body type. Trust me, I have personal experience!

❋ ✎ **Cabot's Candy** (508-487-3550; cabotscandy.com), 276 Commercial Street. The Cicero family has made its own saltwater taffy here since 1969—it's the only shop on the Lower Cape or the Outer Cape to do so. Flavors range from peanut butter to piña colada to beach plum.

✎ **Outer Cape Kites** (508-487-6133), Ryder Street Extension (on the beach). There's no better place to fly a kite than the National Seashore dunes.

❋ **Julie Heller Gallery** (508-487-2169; juliehellergallery.com), 2 Gosnold Street. In a little beachfront shack, Heller offers work by luminaries who established this art colony, including Milton Avery, Ross Moffett, and Charles Hawthorne.

❋ **Provincetown Bookshop** (508-487-0964), 246 Commercial Street.

MARINE SPECIALTIES

A good selection of children's books, Cape titles, and cookbooks; established in 1932.

Whaler's Wharf, 237 Commercial Street. After a devastating fire in 1998 that burned the former building to the ground, Whaler's Wharf is better than ever. This three-story open arcade is filled with artisans, an artisan cooperative, shops, and a few restaurants. You're bound to find something interesting.

❋ **Marine Specialties** (508-487-1730; ptownarmynavy.com), 235 Commercial Street. One of the Cape's most unusual shops stocks an odd jumble of army-navy items in a warehouselike space: parachutes, wool blankets, candles, camel saddles, sand dollars, camping supplies, ships' salvage, and other random military surplus items. You'll undoubtedly walk out with some strange gewgaw you hadn't even thought of buying but you just couldn't pass up for the price. My friend, May Lily, always used to bang away on the piano here, offering passersby impromptu and impressive concerts and no one blinked an eye—just one more "expect the unexpected" at Marine Specialties.

❋ **WA** (508-487-6355; waharmony .com), 220 Commercial Street. This

CABOT'S CANDY

Japanese-inspired oasis carries teapots, ceramics, incense, and fountains as well as specialty items like antique suitcases covered with Chinese calligraphy.

Century (508-487-2332; century shopper.com), 212 Commercial Street. Whether or not you know what gifts you need, this place will bring out your inner generous nature.

Human Rights Campaign (508-487-7736; hrc.org), 205 Commercial Street. For all your equality T-shirt, jacket, jewelry, accessory, gift, and bumper sticker needs. And if you're not a member, consider becoming one.

Roots (508-487-2500; shoproots.com), 193 Commercial Street. Beautiful accessories for the home: stained-glass lamps, kilims, handmade furniture (indoor and outdoor), antiques, ceramics, and frames.

City Video (508-487-4493), 192 Commercial Street #6. This women-owned second floor shop fulfills all your rental needs. You're on your own for your emotional needs.

❋ **Impulse** (508-487-1154; impluseart gallery.com), 188 Commercial Street. This contemporary American crafts shop offers a large selection of kaleidoscopes, wind chimes, wood objets

HUMAN RIGHTS CAMPAIGN

Working for Lesbian, Gay, Bisexual & Transgender Equality

d'art, fragile and colorful glass creations, jewelry, and signed celebrity photos and letters.

Ruby's Fine Jewelry (508-487-9522; rubysptownjewelry.com), 167 Commercial Street. When it's time to get married, this quasi art gallery features elegant and unique silver and gold designs for men and women.

❋ **TJ Walton Gallery** (508-487-0170), 153 Commercial Street. Walton's large, bold canvases are a delight.

❋ **Tristan Gallery** (508-487-3939; tristangallery.com), 148 Commercial Street. Abstract and impressionistic paintings; some photography.

Provincetown Antique Market (508-487-1115), 131 Commercial Street. An engaging assortment of this and that: glass, toys, paper, books, tools, and ephemera.

❋ Special Events

Off-season, there are dozens of special event weekends geared toward single gay men, cross-dressers, lesbians, or whomever. If you want to be assured of a quieter off-season retreat, call the chamber of commerce (see *Guidance*) for an up-to-the-minute listing of events.

Mid-April: **Whale-watching** begins and **seasonal shops** begin to reopen.

Mid-May: **Single Women's Weekend** (girlpowerevents.com). Although the title is self-explanatory, the weekend is filled with more events than you can imagine.

Late May: **Memorial Day** weekend kicks off the summer season.

Early June: **A Night at the Chef's Table** (508-487-9445; asgcc.org). An annual benefit for Provincetown's AIDS Support Group. For $75 per person, you'll get a festive, multicourse gala dinner with champagne and wine at many of the town's finest restaurants. More than 50 restaurants from Falmouth to Provincetown participate. It's a real, local thing, but that doesn't mean you aren't welcome. **Women of Color Weekend** (girlpowerevents .com). Finally, a few days devoted to diversity.

Mid-June: **International Film Festival** (508-487-3456; ptownfilmfest .com). Established 1999, with special screenings, features, documentaries, international, and gay and lesbian shorts. Movies are shown at Whaler's Wharf, the Art House Theatre, School-house Center for Art and Design, and the Crown & Anchor.

Late June: **Portuguese Festival and Blessing of the Fleet**, MacMillan Wharf. Beginning on the Thursday before the last Sunday of the month, this 4-day celebration was developed to coincide with the Blessing of the Fleet (when the bishop blesses a parade of fishing boats decked out with flags and families aboard). Festivities include a swing-band concert, a kids' fishing derby, Portuguese menus at various restaurants, a food court and bazaar on Fisherman's Wharf, a parade, and competitions like lobster-pot pulls and codfish relays.

July 4: **Independence Day**. A spirited parade organized for and by the entire town, and a spectacular fire-works display.

Mid-July: **Secret Garden Tour** (508-487-1750). A popular and annual bene-fit for the Provincetown Art Association.

Late July: **Girl Splash** (girlpower events.com). A full week of women's events during fine summer weather! Think Dinah Shore East.

Late July to early August: **Family Week**. At this popular event, the defi-nition of *family* is expanded to include Heather and her two mommies as well as daddy-and-poppy nuclear families.

Mid- to late August: **Fine Arts Work Center Annual Benefit Auction** (508-487-9960; fawc.org). A benefit for the nationally recognized fellowship program for artists and writers (see *Even More Things to Do*); since 1969. This is an Art-with-a-capital-A event. **Carnival Week** (508-487-2313; 800-637-8696). A weeklong gala sponsored by the Provincetown Business Guild (see *Guidance*), capped by a New Orleans Mardi Gras–style parade that's very gay and very flashy . . . and very popular—folks from all over the Cape come to watch. Leave early and don't get stuck in traffic on the way.

Early September: **AIDS Support Group's Annual Silent and Live Auction** (508-487-9445; asgcc.org), at Fisherman's Wharf. It seems as if every artist in Provincetown donates work to this auction. Don't miss it.

Early September: **Swim for Life** (508-487-3684; swim4life.org). During this harbor swim from Long Point to the Boatslip Beach Club—to raise money for AIDS research—a "paddlers flotil-la" carries close to 300 swimmers across the bay so they can swim the 1.4 miles back to town. After the swim, the Boatslip holds a free "Mermaid Brunch" open to the public. The event often raises over $150,000; since its inception it's raised over $2 million. **The Great Provincetown Schooner Regatta** (provincetownschoonerrace .com). Two classes of sailing vessels parade along the waterfront (west to east) and then race.

Late September: **Tennessee Williams Theater Festival** (866-811-4111 for tickets; twptown.org). Four days of theater, dance, music, film, and fun sharing "the writer's vision of the heal-ing power of love."

Mid-October: **Women's Week** (womeninnkeepers.com). It all started back in 1984 with a small weekend clambake on the beach. These days it spreads over a 10-day period with hundreds of events, including "Meet other women who . . ." mixers and dance parties at the Pied Bar. A recent "Kiss-In"—the brainchild of Lynette Molnar—set a Guinness Book of World Records with 2,700 women smooching at once. Hosted by Women Innkeepers of Provincetown, the weeklong extravaganza features women artists and entertainers, but there's always a political component as well.

ART GALLERIES GALORE

Mid- to late October: **Fantasia Fair**. This 7-day event brings cross-dressers, transgendered persons, transsexuals, and others to town.

Late October: **Halloween**. This is a big event, as you might imagine, with lots of costumes and contests. The children's parade starts at the Pilgrim Monument and ends at the community center. **Festival of Lights** (508-487-3424). Nearly 5,000 white lights (4 miles' worth) illuminate the Pilgrim Monument on Thanksgiving Eve and remain lit until early January.

Early December: **Holly Folly Festival** (hollyfolly.com). A annual gay and lesbian festival featuring a concert by the Boston Gay Men's Chorus, seasonally decorated house tours, street caroling, shopping galore, special holiday menus, and general gay merriment and revelry.

December 31: **First Night**, ringing in the New Year.

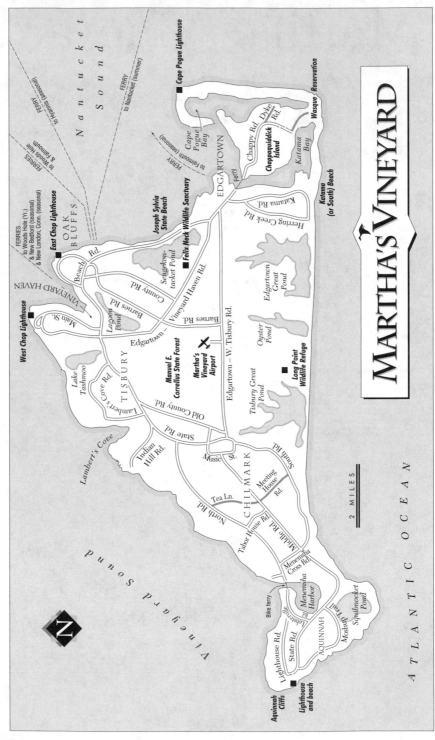

MARTHA'S VINEYARD

N a n t u c k e t   S o u n d

FERRY
to Nantucket (summer)

Cape Pogue Lighthouse

Cape Pogue Bay

FERRY
to Falmouth (seasonal)

Chappaquiddick Island

Chappy Rd.   Dyke Rd.

Wasque Reservation

Katama Bay

EDGARTOWN

Ferry

Katama Rd.

Katama (or South) Beach

Herring Creek Rd.

Edgartown Great Pond

FERRIES
to Hyannis (seasonal)

FERRY
to Falmouth
& Hyannis (seasonal)

FERRIES
to Woods Hole (Yr.)
& New Bedford (seasonal)
& New London, Conn. (seasonal)

East Chop Lighthouse

OAK BLUFFS

Joseph Sylvia State Beach

Felix Neck Wildlife Sanctuary

(Beach) Rd.

County Rd.

Sengekontacket Pond

Vineyard Haven Rd.

VINEYARD HAVEN

Barnes Rd.

Barnes Rd.

Lagoon Pond

West Chop Lighthouse

Main St.

Lake Tashmoo

Lambert's Cove Rd.

TISBURY

Manuel E. Correllus State Forest

Martha's Vineyard Airport

Edgartown — W. Tisbury Rd.

Oyster Pond

Long Point Wildlife Refuge

Tisbury Great Pond

Old County Rd.

State Rd.

Lambert's Cove

Indian Hill Rd.

Music St.

CHILMARK

South Rd.

Meeting House Rd.

Tea Ln.

North Rd.

Tabor House Rd.

Middle Rd.

Menemsha Cross Rd.

Bike ferry

Menemsha Harbor

Lobsterville Rd.

AQUINNAH

Squibnocket Pond

Moshup Trail

Lighthouse Rd.

State Rd.

Aquinnah Cliffs

Lighthouse and beach

V i n e y a r d   S o u n d

A T L A N T I C   O C E A N

2 MILES

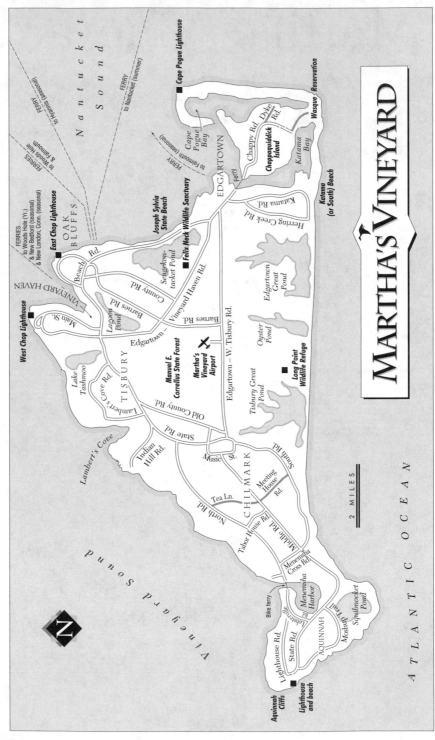

Paul Woodward / © The Countryman Press

MARTHA'S VINEYARD

Intrepid explorer Bartholomew Gosnold was the first European known to have visited Martha's Vineyard (in 1602), although Leif Eriksson may have done so earlier. Gosnold named the island for its bounty of wild grapes, but Martha's identity remains a mystery; she may have been Gosnold's daughter. The island was formally colonized in 1640, when a shipload of English settlers bound for Virginia ran short of supplies. They docked in Edgartown, found the resident Wampanoag friendly, and decided to stay.

The settlers converted the Wampanoag to Christianity with startling success, perhaps aided by the imported diseases that were killing Wampanoag by the thousands. A century after Edgartown was founded, the island's Native population had dropped from 3,000 to about 350. During that time, Vineyarders learned (from the surviving Wampanoag) how to catch whales. They also farmed in Chilmark and fished from Edgartown and Vineyard Haven.

During the American Revolution, islanders suffered extreme deprivation after British soldiers sailed into Vineyard Haven Harbor and looted homes and ships. Among their plunder were some 10,000 head of sheep and cattle from island farms. The island didn't fully recover until the 1820s, when the whaling industry took off. The Vineyard enjoyed a heyday from 1820 until the Civil War, with hundreds of whaling vessels sailing in and out of Edgartown. Whaling captains took their enormous profits from whale oil and built large Federal and Greek Revival homes all over the island. Many still stand today as gracious inns, renowned restaurants, and private homes.

After the Civil War, with the whaling industry in decline, tourism became the Vineyard's principal source of income. By 1878 the Methodist Campground of Oak Bluffs had become a popular summer resort, with 12,000 people attending annual meetings. Over the next 30 years, other travelers discovered the island and returned summer after summer to enjoy its pleasant weather, relatively warm water, excellent fishing, and comfortable yet genteel lifestyle. By the turn of the 20th century, there were 2,000 hotel rooms in Oak Bluffs alone—there aren't that many B&B or inn rooms on the entire island today! Summertime traffic was so high that a rail line was built from the Oak Bluffs ferry terminal to Katama. Daily ferry service ran from the New York Yacht Club to Gay Head (present-day Aquinnah).

Although the whaling industry rapidly declined, other sea-related businesses continued to reap healthy profits. In 1900, Vineyard Sound was one of the busiest sea-lanes in the world, second only to the English Channel. Heavy sea traffic continued until the Cape Cod Canal was completed in 1914. Tourism picked up again in the early 1970s. And when the Clintons began spending summer vacations here in the mid-1990s, they created a tidal wave of national and international interest in the island.

Today the year-round population of 15,000 mushrooms in July and August to about 105,000. Grumpy year-round Vineyarders are fond of saying that the island sinks 3 inches when ferries unload their passengers.

The terms *up-island* and *down-island* are holdovers from the days when the island was populated by seafarers—as you travel west, you move up the scale of longitude. *Up-island* refers to the less developed, hilly western end, including West Tisbury, Chilmark, Menemsha, and Aquinnah. Edgartown, Oak Bluffs, and Vineyard Haven, which are the most developed towns, are all *down-island*.

Elegant Edgartown is chock-full of grand white Greek Revival ship captains' houses, with fanlights and widows' walks. Many of these private homes are clustered on North and South Water streets, while elsewhere downtown you'll find chic shops, galleries, and restaurants.

Although it's less showy than Edgartown, Vineyard Haven maintains a year-round level of activity that Edgartown doesn't. It's the commercial center of the island, where "real" people live and work. The harbor is home to more wooden boats than any other harbor of its size in New England. For an experience straight out of the 19th century, stop in at Gannon and Benjamin Boatbuilders on Beach Road; it's one of the few remaining wooden-boat rebuilding shops in the country. Literary and journalistic personalities like Mike Wallace and Diane Sawyer (and her husband, Mike Nichols) have all called Vineyard Haven their second home.

Oak Bluffs today is at once charming and honky-tonk. A number of prominent African Americans have vacationed here over the years, including Spike Lee, Vernon Jordan, Dorothy West, and Charles Ogletree. In fact, Oak Bluffs has a long history of welcoming and attracting African Americans: In 1835, Wesleyan Grove was the site of the Methodist congregation's annual summer-camp meetings. The campers' small tents became family tents; then primitive, wooden, tentlike cottages; and finally, brightly painted cottages ornamented with fanciful trim. Cupolas, domes, spires, turrets, and gingerbread cutouts make for an architectural fantasyland. The whimsical, precious, and offbeat cottages are worlds away from Edgartown's traditional houses. So are Oak Bluffs' nightclubs and the baggy-pants-wearing, pierced youth.

West Tisbury is often called the Athens of the Vineyard because of its fine New England Congregational Church, Town Hall, and Grange Hall. Music Street, where descendants of the island's 19th-century ship captains still live in large houses, was so named because many of these families used whaling profits to purchase pianos. Over the years, West Tisbury summer residents have included *Washington Post* owner and Katharine Graham, cartoonist Jules Feiffer, and historian David McCullough. Other A-list celebs clamoring for their place in the Vineyard sun (in Hollywood East) have included Ted Danson and Mary Steenburgen, Larry David, film mogul Harvey Weinstein, John Cusack, and Michael J. Fox.

Chilmark is a peaceful place of rolling hills and old stone fences that outline 200-year-old farms. You'll find dozens of working farms up-island, some still operated by descendants of the island's original European settlers. Travel down North Road to Menemsha, a small (truly picturesque) village and working harbor that

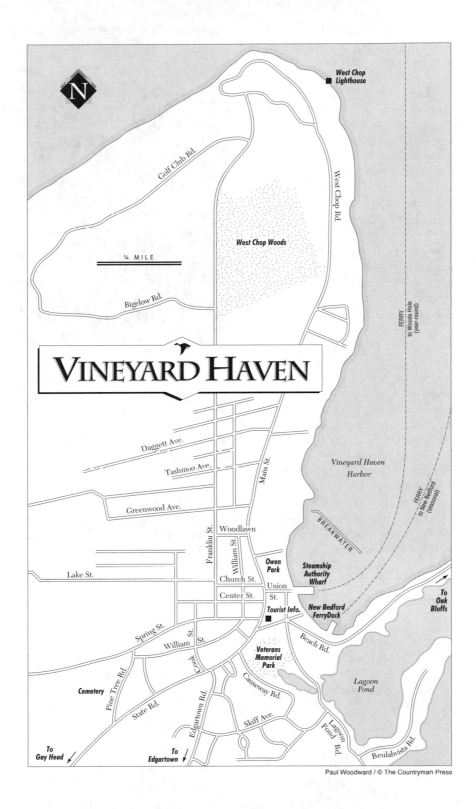

N

West Chop
Lighthouse

Golf Club Rd.

West Chop Rd.

West Chop Woods

¼ MILE

Bigelow Rd.

FERRY
to Woods Hole
(year-round)

VINEYARD HAVEN

Daggett Ave.

Tashmoo Ave.

Main St.

Vineyard Haven
Harbor

Greenwood Ave.

FERRY
to New Bedford
(seasonal)

Franklin St.

Woodlawn

William St.

BREAKWATER

Owen
Park

Lake St.

Church St.

Union
St.

Steamship
Authority
Wharf

Center St.

Tourist Info.

New Bedford
FerryDock

To
Oak
Bluffs

Spring St.

William St.

Cook St.

Beach Rd.

Veterans
Memorial
Park

Pine Tree Rd.

Cemetery

State Rd.

Edgartown Rd.

Causeway Rd.

Lagoon
Pond

Skiff Ave.

To
Gay Head

To
Edgartown

Lagoon
Pond Rd.

Beulahvista Rd.

Paul Woodward / © The Countryman Press

you may recognize as the location of the movie *Jaws*. The surrounding area is crisscrossed by miles and miles of unmarked, interconnected dirt roads, great for exploring. (Alas, many are private.) Chilmark is sparsely populated, to the tune of 1,050 or so year-rounders, and they aim to keep it that way. In order to limit growth they issue the island's only 3-acre-minimum building permits. Chilmark (among the 50 wealthiest towns in America; the median house price in mid-2007 was $2.337 million) has hosted such disparate personalities as photographer Alfred Eisenstaedt and John Belushi. (Belushi is buried on-island; "Eise's" photos are found in galleries and at his beloved retreat, the Menemsha Inn and Cottages.) Harvard Law School professor Alan Dershowitz is a denizen of Lucy Vincent Beach, one of the island's many residents-only beaches—and a nude one at that.

Aquinnah, a must-see destination, occupies the island's western tip. (If you haven't visited the Vineyard for a while, you may know Aquinnah as Gay Head. It was renamed Aquinnah, "land under the hill," in mid-1997 by a narrow 79–76 town vote.) Of the 1,100 members listed on the Wampanoag Indian tribal rolls, approximately 300 still reside on the Vineyard, half in Aquinnah. Tribal legend holds that the giant Moshup created the Vineyard, taught the Wampanoag how to fish and catch whales, and remains a protector. The Wampanoag own the brilliantly colored bluffs and the face of the Clay Cliffs of Aquinnah.

Martha's Vineyard has always attracted celebrity summer visitors. But in recent years many who visited decided they wanted to own a piece of it. Beginning in the late 1980s and continuing to this day, a tremendous building boom has changed the face of the Vineyard. While the Vineyard had been a place where the well-heeled and well-off came to escape notice, today the celebrities and power brokers come as much to see and be seen. Although residents are generally unfazed by their celebrity neighbors—movie stars, authors, journalists, musicians, financial moguls—many locals and longtime visitors agree that the Vineyard is no longer the quaint, tranquil island it was prior to the mid-1980s.

Martha's Vineyard is unlike most of the rest of America; people tend to get along pretty well with one another. They work hard to maintain a sense of tolerance and community spirit. Most lengthy debates center on land use and preservation rather than on race or religion. (Of course, there are notable exceptions.) Everyone relies, to some extent, on the hectic summer season that brings in most of the island's annual income, though residents do breathe a sigh of relief when the crowds depart after mid-October.

To experience the Vineyard at its best and still have a dependable chance for good weather, plan your visit from May to mid-June or from mid-September to mid-October. From January to March, the Vineyard is truly a retreat from civilization.

GUIDANCE ❋ Martha's Vineyard Chamber of Commerce (508-693-0085; mvy.com), 24 Beach Street, Vineyard Haven. Open 9–5 weekdays, 10–4 weekends early April through late November; and weekdays 9–5 the rest of the year. There are good, free street maps of Vineyard Haven, Oak Bluffs, and Edgartown available at all chambers.

Information booth (no phone), Steamship Authority terminal, Vineyard Haven. Open seasonally.

Information booth (508-693-4266), Circuit Avenue at Lake Avenue, Oak Bluffs. Adjacent to the Flying Horses Carousel, it's open 9–5 daily, mid-May to mid-October.

❋ Edgartown Information Center (no phone), Church Street, Edgartown. Around the corner from the Old Whaling Church, this minor center has restrooms and a post office, and serves as a shuttle-bus stop (see *Getting Around*).

MORE WEB SITES Vineyard.plumtv.com. On island, tune to Channel 79. On the Web you'll catch all sorts of fun videos about Nantucket, from the social scene, island life, and arts and entertainment to real estate, sports, and eating and drinking.

Mvol.com. A complete guide.

VineyardStyle.com. This glossy quarterly always has a few in-depth articles about artisans, gardening, trends, home, cuisine, interiors, or shopping.

MVInfo.com. Billed as the original Web site for vineyard and established in 1985.

MEDIA *Vineyard Gazette* (508-627-4311; mvgazette.com), 34 South Summer Street. The newspaper, which first rolled off the press on May 14, 1846, is a beloved island institution. Although its year-round circulation is only 10,000, the paper is mailed to island devotees in all 50 states and internationally. There's no single better way for an Explorer to get a handle on island life.

PUBLIC RESTROOMS In Vineyard Haven head to the top of the Stop & Shop parking lot (seasonal) and to the Steamship Authority terminal (year-round) off Water Street. In Oak Bluffs restrooms are next to the Steamship Authority terminal on Seaview Avenue; on Kennebec Avenue, one block from Circuit Avenue; and next to Our Market (seasonal) on Oak Bluffs Harbor. In Edgartown, they're at the visitors center (year-round) on Church Street. Seasonal facilities are also located near

the parking lot for the Clay Cliffs of Aquinnah, at Dutcher's Dock in Menemsha Harbor, and in West Tisbury, at the Grange Hall next to Town Hall.

LAUNDROMATS ❄ **Airport Laundromat** (508-693-5005), off the Edgartown–West Tisbury Road.

PUBLIC LIBRARIES ❄ ✎ ☂ "ꭲ" Most of these libraries have story times and Internet access; call ahead for hours and schedule vagaries:

Aquinnah (508-645-2314; aquinnahlibrary.vineyard.net), 1 Church Street at State Road.

Chilmark (508-645-3360; library.chilmark.ma.us.org), 522 South Road, Chilmark Center.

Edgartown (508-627-4221; edgartownlibrary.org), 58 North Water Street.

Oak Bluffs (508-693-9433; oakbluffslibrary.org), 56 R School Street.

Vineyard Haven (508-696-4210; vhlibrary.org), 200 Main Street.

West Tisbury (508-693-3366; westtisbury-ma.gov), 1042A State Road.

See also **Martha's Vineyard Museum** under *To See.*

GETTING THERE ❄ *By boat from Woods Hole:* **The Steamship Authority** (508-477-8600 for advance auto reservations; 508-548-3788 for day-of-sailing information; 508-477-7447 for last-minute day-of-sailing reservations, but don't count on getting lucky; steamshipauthority.com), Railroad Avenue. The Steamship is the only company that provides daily, year-round transport—for people and autos—to Vineyard Haven and Oak Bluffs. The Vineyard is 7 miles from Woods Hole, and the trip takes 45 minutes. About 9 boats ply the waters daily.

The Steamship annually carries upwards of 2 million people to the Vineyard. *Here's the biggest understatement of the entire book:* Make reservations as soon as possible. Call as soon as you know your dates, no matter when that is. Auto reservations are mandatory on weekends (Friday through Monday) between mid-May and early September. Otherwise, the Steamship has a standby policy that's first come, first served.

Roundtrip tickets from early May to late December cost $15 adults; $8 children; children under 5, free; $6 bicycles; $135–155 autos. Off-season, auto prices drop to $85–105. If you are not taking your car, the Steamship Authority provides free, frequent buses between the parking lots and the ferry dock. Each bus has a bike rack that holds two bikes. Parking is about $10–15 per calendar day.

STEAMSHIP AUTHORITY FERRY

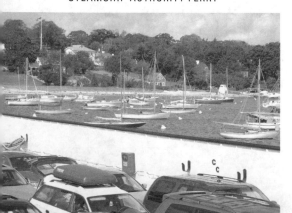

By boat from Falmouth: **Island Queen** (508-548-4800; islandqueen .com), 75 Falmouth Heights Road. This passengers-only service (smaller and more comfortable than the Steamship Authority's boat) operates late May to mid-October and takes

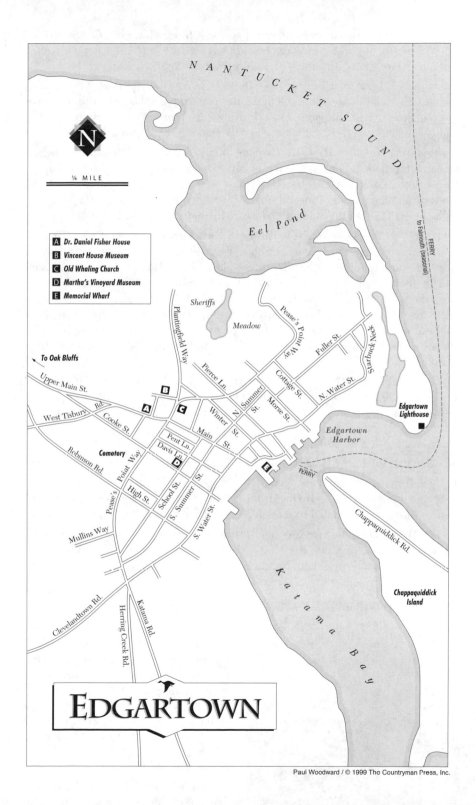

NANTUCKET SOUND

Eel Pond

FERRY to Falmouth (seasonal)

A Dr. Daniel Fisher House
B Vincent House Museum
C Old Whaling Church
D Martha's Vineyard Museum
E Memorial Wharf

Sheriffs
Meadow

Plantingfield Way

Pease's Point Way

Fuller St.

Starbuck Neck

To Oak Bluffs

Upper Main St.

Pierce Ln.

Cottage St.

N. Water St.

Edgartown Lighthouse

West Tisbury Rd.

Cooke St.

Winter St.

N. Summer St.

Morse St.

Edgartown Harbor

A C

B

Robinson Rd.

Pease's Point Way

Pent Ln.

Main St.

Davis Ln.

D

Cemetery

School St.

S. Summer St.

High St.

S. Water St.

F

FERRY

Chappaquiddick Rd.

Mullins Way

Chappaquiddick Island

Clevelandtown Rd.

Herring Creek Rd.

Katama Rd.

Katama Bay

EDGARTOWN

¼ MILE

N

about 35 minutes; departures are from Falmouth Inner Harbor to Oak Bluffs. There is plenty of parking near the *Island Queen's* dock ($15 per calendar day). Roundtrip fares cost $16 adults; $7 children age 3–12; $6 bicycles.

Falmouth–Edgartown Ferry (508-548-9400; falmouthferry.com), 278 Scranton Avenue. From late May to mid-October, this service plies the waters four to five times daily between Falmouth and Edgartown (Memorial Wharf). Roundtrip: adults $50; children 6–12, $30; bicycles $10. Parking is $25 per calendar day.

By boat from Hyannis: **Hy-Line Cruises** (508-778-2600; hy-linecruises.com), 220 Ocean Street Dock. Four to five passenger boats (1¾ hours) to and from Oak Bluffs from May to late October. If you haven't purchased advance tickets, it's wise to arrive an hour early in July and August. Roundtrip, in-season fares: adults $63 high-speed, $39 traditional ferry, children $45, and bicycles $12.

By boat from New Bedford: **New England Fast Ferry Co**. (866-683-3779; nefastferry.com) operates passenger boats from 49 State Pier to Vineyard Haven from late June to mid-October. The ferry takes 1 hour. Roundtrip fares: $72 adults, $42 children, $12 bicycles. Parking is $10 per calendar day. For visitors coming from the south, New Bedford is a more convenient departure point than Woods Hole. Even those driving from points north may wish to consider taking the New Bedford ferry to avoid Cape Cod Canal bridge traffic. From I-195, take Exit 15 (Route 18 South) to the second set of lights, turn left, and follow signs to ferry parking.

By boat from Nantucket: **Hy-Line Cruises** (508-778-2600 Hyannis; 508-693-0112 Oak Bluffs; 508-228-3949 Nantucket; hy-linecruises.com) offers interisland service between Oak Bluffs and Nantucket from mid-June to mid-September. The trip takes 1¼ hours; there is only one trip daily. One-way fares cost $28.50 adults, $17 children age 5–12, and $6 bicycles.

See also **Patriot Party Boats** under *To Do* in "Falmouth and Woods Hole."

By bus: **Bonanza/Peter Pan** (888-751-8800; peterpanbus.com) provides daily year-round service to Woods Hole from Boston, New York, Hartford, and Providence. Buses are scheduled to meet ferries, but ferries won't wait for a late bus.

By air: With a booming increase in jet-setting visitors, it's no wonder a new terminal was built in 1999. **Cape Air** (800-352-0714; flycapeair.com) flies to the Vineyard from Boston, Providence, Nantucket, and New Bedford.

EDGARTOWN LIGHTHOUSE

GETTING AROUND *By car:* The infamous Five Corners is the trickiest and most dangerous intersection on the island. It's also the first thing you'll encounter as you disembark from the Vineyard Haven ferry terminal. If you're going to Oak Bluffs, Katama, Edgartown, and Chappaquiddick, take the left lane. For West Tisbury, North Tisbury, Lambert's Cove, Menemsha, Chilmark, and Aquinnah, enter the right lane and turn right.

When making plans, consider these sample distances: Vineyard Haven to

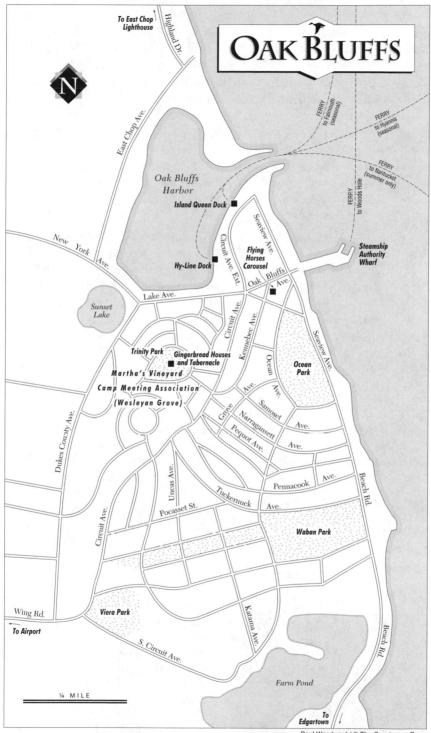

OAK BLUFFS

To East Chop Lighthouse

Highland Dr.

FERRY to Falmouth (seasonal)

FERRY to Hyannis (seasonal)

FERRY to Nantucket (summer only)

FERRY to Woods Hole

N

East Chop Ave.

Oak Bluffs Harbor

Island Queen Dock

Seaview Ave.

Steamship Authority Wharf

New York Ave.

Circuit Ave. Ext.

Flying Horses Carousel

Hy-Line Dock

Oak Bluffs Ave.

Sunset Lake

Lake Ave.

Circuit Ave.

Kennebec Ave.

Ocean Ave.

Ocean Park

Seaview Ave.

Trinity Park

Gingerbread Houses and Tabernacle

Martha's Vineyard Camp Meeting Association

(Wesleyan Grove)

Grove Ave.

Samoset Ave.

Narragansett Ave.

Pequot Ave.

Dukes County Ave.

Uncas Ave.

Pennacook Ave.

Beach Rd.

Circuit Ave.

Pocasset St.

Tuckernuck Ave.

Waban Park

Wing Rd.

To Airport

Viera Park

S. Circuit Ave.

Katama Ave.

Beach Rd.

Farm Pond

To Edgartown

¼ MILE

Paul Woodward / © The Countryman Press

Oak Bluffs, 3 miles; Vineyard Haven to Edgartown, 8 miles; Oak Bluffs to Edgartown, 6 miles; Vineyard Haven to Aquinnah, 18 miles.

Unfortunately, summertime traffic jams are commonplace in down-island towns. Try to park outside of town and take shuttles into town (see below). Why would you want to stop and crawl in a picturesque village on a vacation day?

In-season, expect to pay about $75–90 daily for the least-expensive rental car and $175–190 for four-wheel-drive. Off-season, rates go as low as $40–70 daily for a car.

Before heading out, invest $3.25 in the very detailed gold-and-orange Martha's Vineyard Road Map produced by Edward Thomas (508-693-2059). It's an excellent, accurate resource and even lists mileage between intersections. It's available at most bookstores, grocery stores, and liquor stores.

Note: It is illegal to pass mopeds in no-passing zones when you're moving at 20 mph.

Car rental companies include **Budget Rent-a-Car** (508-693-2232; budget.com), 45 Beach Road, Vineyard Haven; 12 Circuit Avenue Extension (at the ferry dock), Oak Bluffs; and at 71 Airport Road, Martha's Vineyard Airport. I've always found **Adventure Rentals Thrifty** (508-693-1959), 19 Beach Road, Five Corners, Vineyard Haven, helpful. By the way, gas is usually cheapest at the airport.

By moped: If most Vineyarders and emergency-room doctors had their way, mopeds would be banned. Once you've seen the face, arms, and legs of a fellow Explorer skinned, you'll know why. Sand, mopeds, winding roads, and speed do not mix. Take a look at the mopeds you might be renting; many of their plastic hulls have been cracked from accidents. Having said that and not wanting to appear maternalistic, here goes: Many rental agencies are located near the ferry terminals in Oak Bluffs and Vineyard Haven. **Adventure Rentals** (508-693-1959, 19 Beach Road, Vineyard Haven) and **Ride-on Mopeds** (508-693-2076, 9 Oak Bluffs Avenue, Oak Bluffs) have mopeds ($69–120). Extra training, yellow diamond road signs (at notorious intersections), and maps (with danger spots and distances between points) should help reduce casualties.

❇ ❦ *By shuttle:* **Martha's Vineyard Transit Authority (VTA)** (508-693-9440; vineyardtransit.com) operates an excellent system of buses. Twelve buses travel among Vineyard Haven, Oak Bluffs, Edgartown, West Tisbury, Chilmark, Menemsha, and Aquinnah year-round. Buses seem to stop everywhere you want to go; you can also flag them down. They even have bike racks. Get a copy of the very helpful VTA map with stops and routes clearly listed. Carry it with you wherever you go. One-day pass costs $6, 3-day $15, 7-day $25. Single tickets cost $1 per town (if you go from Vineyard Haven to Edgartown, for instance, it costs $3 because you have to go through Oak Bluffs). Exact change is strongly suggested since change is given only in the form of credit vouchers for future trips.

Edgartown Park & Ride. VTA has an alternative to wrangling for a parking place in Edgartown's car-choked streets. Leave your car at The Triangle (at the corner of Edgartown–Vineyard Haven Road and Oak Bluffs Road) and ride the shuttle. Parking and rides are free.

Tisbury Park & Ride (508-693-9440; vineyardtransit.com), State Road (across from Cronig's Market). Avoid the parking nightmare in Vineyard Haven and let the VTA shuttle drop you off downtown. The free shuttle runs year-round. Parking is $2, but you must purchase tickets in advance at the Cumberland Farms (at the Five Corners intersection) or Town Hall (William and Spring streets) in Vineyard Haven.

South Beach Trolley (508-693-9440). Early May to mid-October. The daily trolley ($1) runs from Edgartown's information building (near the corner of Church and Main streets) to three points at South Beach.

By bus tour: **Gay Head Sightseeing** and **M.V. Sightseeing** (508-693-1555; mvtour.com) offer daily, 2½-hour tours from mid-April to late October. The clearly marked buses meet ferries in Vineyard Haven and Oak Bluffs. The Gay Head tour covers all six towns, but makes only one stop—at the Clay Cliffs of Aquinnah—where there are small food stands, souvenir shops, public restrooms, and a wonderful view of the cliffs and the ocean. The only potential drawback: You may tire of hearing the constant running commentary about which celebrities live down which dirt roads. They also offer charter tours for large groups. Adults $26, children $14.

By taxi tour: Most taxis conduct island sightseeing trips for a price, but you don't want to go with just anyone. I highly recommend **Jon's Taxi** (508-627-4677). Trips with Jon or his assistant cost $75 per hour for one to six people. Schedule these private trips at your convenience.

❋ **Adam Cab** (508-627-4462; adamcab.com) is also very good and offers tours twice daily from Edgartown at 9:30 AM and 1 PM from late May to early September, less often during the off-season. This 3-hour, all-island tour costs $35 per person. If you'd prefer to arrange your own itinerary, hire them for $75 per hour.

🕭 *By bicycle:* Bicycling is a great way to get around, but it requires stamina if you're heading up-island (see *To Do*).

✿ 🌿 *On foot:* **Ghosts, Gossip, and Downright Scandals** (508-627-2529) is conducted by very knowledgeable folks from **Vineyard History Tours**. They basically take people by appointment any time of the year, except perhaps during a nor'easter. Their special tour focusing on Edgartown's whaling days, A-Whaling We Will Go, is also very good. Most tours cost $12 per person, with the exception of the Graveyard Tour, which is $20 per person.

HERITAGE TRAILS Aquinnah Cultural Trail (508-645-9265; wampanoagtribe .net). For those interested in something other than beaches and shops, look for the excellent and informative map once you're on-island. You can always find it at the Tribal Administration Building, 20 Black Brook Road, Aquinnah. It is full of interesting facts about the "first people of Noepe," place-name translations, Moshup legends, local government, and a schedule of events.

African-American Heritage Trail (508-693-4361; mvheritagetrail.org). Tours on request late May to early September. The brainchild of a M.V. Regional High School history teacher and NAACP archivist Elaine Weintraub, this developing trail currently has 22 sites devoted to telling the story of the island's strong association with African Americans. Weintraub researched the story of the Island's own African American whaling captain, William A. Martin and two generations of his family establishing an African American presence on Martha's Vineyard before the American revolution. Every town has sites, including abandoned graveyards; the home of Dorothy West, a Harlem Renaissance writer who lived on the island and died in 1999; a site dedicated to Rebecca Amos, the woman from Africa enslaved on the Vineyard; a decrepit "Gospel Tabernacle." The book *Lighting the Trail: The African American Heritage of Martha's Vineyard* is sold in all the Island bookstores.

MEDICAL EMERGENCY Martha's Vineyard Hospital (508-693-0410; mv hospital.com), 1 Hospital Lane, off Beach Road, Oak Bluffs. 24-hour emergency room. In 2008 the hospital broke ground on an impressive, long-overdue new facility.

Lyme disease. Ticks carry this disease, which has flu-like symptoms and may result in death if left untreated. Immediately and carefully remove any ticks that may have migrated from dune grasses to your body. Better yet, wear long pants, tuck pants into socks, and wear long-sleeved shirts whenever possible when hiking. Avoid hiking in grassy and overgrown areas of dense brush.

MENEMSHA HARBOR

✳ To See

In Vineyard Haven
Bank of Martha's Vineyard (508-696-4400), 75 Main Street. Open weekdays. This distinctive 1905 fieldstone building has lovely stained glass and great acoustics. On this site, incidentally, stood the harness shop where the Great Fire of 1883 started. The conflagration destroyed 60 buildings.

A PERFECT DOWN-ISLAND DAY ON THE VINEYARD

8:00 Order everything on the menu at Art Cliff Diner.

9:30 Watch quiet morning harbor activity from Owen Park.

10:30 Feel the whimsy of the gingerbread houses in Oak Bluffs.

11:45 Sit for a minute in the solid Old Whaling Church in Edgartown.

12:00 Have a quick (sidewalk) lunch at Alchemy.

1:30 Ride "On Time" to Chappy; take a Cape Pogue Natural History Tour.

6:00 Walk out to the Edgartown Lighthouse with a camera.

7:00 Dine at Lure (Edgartown) or Sweet Life Café (Oak Bluffs).

10:00 Resolve to visit the Vineyard longer next time.

William Street. The only street in town that survived the devastating 1883 fire boasts some fine examples of Greek Revival architecture. The **Richard G. Luce House**, near the corner of William Street and Spring Street, is prime among the carefully preserved sea captains' homes. Captain Luce never lost a whaling ship or a crew member during his 30-year career, and apparently his good fortune at sea extended to life on land.

Jirah Luce House, near the corner of South Main and Main streets. Built in 1804, this is one of the few buildings to survive the Great Fire of 1883.

Old Schoolhouse, Main Street at Colonial Lane. Built in 1829, the schoolhouse now houses a youth sailing program, but the Liberty Pole in front of it recounts the story of three courageous girls who defied British troops.

West Chop Lighthouse, at the western end of Main Street. Built in 1817 with wood and replaced with brick in 1838, the lighthouse has been moved back from the shore twice, first in 1848 and again in 1891. Today the lighthouse is inhabited by a family from the Menemsha Coast Guard base; it's not open for touring.

Katherine Cornell Theatre/Tisbury Town Hall (508-696-4200), 51 Spring Street at William Street. This 1844 performance center features murals by Stan Murphy depicting island scenes, whaling adventures, seagulls, and Native Americans.

WEST CHOP LIGHTHOUSE

In Oak Bluffs

East Chop Lighthouse (508-627-4441; marthasvineyardhistory.org). Telegraph Hill, off the Vineyard Haven–Oak Bluffs Road. Open Sunday 90 minutes prior to sunset and 30 minutes after, June through August; donations. This circa-1850 lighthouse was built by Captain Silas Daggett with the financial help of prosperous fellow seafarers who wanted a better system of relaying signals from the Vineyard to Nantucket and the mainland. Up to that point, they'd used a complex system of raising arms, legs, flags, and lanterns to signal that ships were coming in. In 1875 the government purchased the lighthouse from the consortium of sea captains for $6,000, then constructed the cast iron structure that stands today. There are nice ocean views from here.

Trinity Park Tabernacle, behind Lake, Circuit, and Dukes County avenues. The enormous, tentlike tabernacle was built in 1879 to replace the original meeting tent used by the Methodists who met here. Today the tabernacle is one of the largest wrought-iron structures in the country. There are community sing-alongs on Wednesday evening (at 8 PM) in summer.

Wesleyan Grove surrounds the tabernacle, which, in turn, is encircled by rows of colorful **"gingerbread" cottages**, built during the late 19th century to replace true tents. Owners painted the tiny houses with bright colors and pastels to accentuate the Carpenter Gothic architecture and woodwork. There are upwards of 320 cottages today, still leased from the Camp Meeting Association. Visitors are welcome to wander around the mainly Protestant (but always ecumenical) community. No bicycles are allowed in Wesleyan Grove, and quiet time is strictly observed after (11 PM).

Union Chapel, 55 Narragansett Avenue, at the corner of Kennebec and Samoset avenues. This 1870 octagonal chapel holds interdenominational services and hosts seasonal performing arts events.

Cottage Museum (508-693-7784), 1 Trinity Park. Open 10–4 Monday through Saturday; Sundays 1–4, early May to late October. The interior and exterior of this 1867 cottage are typical of the more than 300 tiny cottages in

EAST CHOP LIGHTHOUSE

Wesleyan Grove. Memorabilia and photographs span the ages from 1835 to present day. Adults $2, children 50¢.

𝄞 **Flying Horses Carousel** (508-693-9481), Circuit Avenue at Lake Avenue. Open daily when school is out and on weekends otherwise, mid-April to mid-October (10–10 in summer). The oldest operating carousel in the country, carved in New York City in 1876, is marvelously well preserved and lovingly maintained. It was brought by barge to the island in 1884, complete with four chariots and 20 horses (with real horsehair manes). Adults visit this national historic landmark even without a child in tow to grab for the elusive brass ring. (Here's a public service announcement: A few folks every year are not returning the brass ring when they grab it, and the carousel is getting precariously close to running out of them.) Rides $1.50, or a book of eight for $10.

In Edgartown

❋ 𝄞 **Martha's Vineyard Museum** (508-627-4441; marthasvineyardhistory.org), 59 Cooke Street at School Street. Open 10–5 Monday through Saturday, mid-June to early October; 1–4 Wednesday through Friday and 10–4 Saturday, mid-October to mid-December and mid-March to mid-June; 10–4 Saturday and by appointment Wednesday through Friday mid-December to mid-March. This excellent collection is housed in several buildings. Perhaps the most interesting exhibit is the Oral History Center, which preserves the island's history through more than 425 interviews with 450 or so of the island's older citizens. (The project was begun in 1993.) Other facilities include a fine pre–Revolutionary War house, which has undergone little renovation since the mid–19th century. Ten rooms at the Thomas Cooke House focus on various aspects of the island's history, including ethnic groups, architecture, natural history, and agriculture. The society also has a maritime gallery, a historical reference library, a tryworks replica, a carriage shed that houses boats and vehicles, and a historic herb garden. The enormous original Fresnel lens from the Aquinnah Lighthouse is here, too, and it's illuminated for a few hours Friday through Sunday. Adults $7; children 6–15 $4; children under 6, free.

Dr. Daniel Fisher House (508-627-8720), 99 Main Street. The island's best example of Greek Revival architecture, this 1840 house has an enclosed cupola (perhaps more correctly called a "lantern"), roof and porch balustrades, a shallow hipped roof, large windowpanes, and a portico, all exquisitely preserved. Dr. Fisher was a Renaissance man: doctor, whaling magnate, banker (he founded the Martha's Vineyard National Bank), merchant, and miller. He insisted that his house be constructed with the finest materials—with Maine pine timbers soaked in lime for two years, and brass and copper nails, for instance. The house is headquarters for the Martha's Vineyard Preservation Trust, which is charged with saving, restoring, and making self-sufficient any important island buildings that might otherwise be sold for commercial

FLYING HORSES CAROUSEL

purposes or radically remodeled. Combination tours with the Vincent House and Old Whaling Church (see below) are offered late May to mid-October; call for times; $10 per person.

Vincent House Museum (508-627-8720), behind the Old Whaling Church. Open noon–3 weekdays, late May through September. Dating to 1672, the Vineyard's oldest residence was in the same family until 1941, and was eventually given to the Preservation Trust in 1977. Reproduction and antique furniture in three rooms depicts how the residence looked in the 17th, 18th, and 19th centuries. Adults $4.

DR. DANIEL FISHER HOUSE

Old Whaling Church (508-627-8720 tours; 508-627-4440 events), 89 Main Street, at Church Street. Built in 1843, this thriving parish church also serves as a performing arts center, hosting plays, lectures, concerts, and films. Owned by the Martha's Vineyard Preservation Trust, the building originally housed the Edgartown Methodist Church and was constructed with the same techniques used to build whaling ships. Tours $10, including visits to the Dr. Fisher House and the Vincent House Museum.

Memorial Wharf, adjacent to the Chappy Ferry on the water. This two-story landing is a terrific spot from which to watch harbor boat traffic in one direction and stately manses in the other direction.

OLD WHALING CHURCH

North Water Street. Some of these fine Colonial, Federal, and Greek Revival houses may look familiar because many clothing companies, including Talbot's, have sent crews of models and photographers here to shoot their catalogs. Architectural detailing on these white houses trimmed in black is superb.

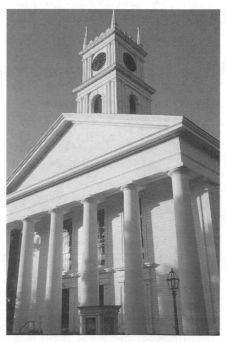

Edgartown Lighthouse (508-627-4441), at the end of North Water Street. The first lighthouse to direct boats into and around Edgartown Harbor was built in 1828 on a small island. Shortly after a new lighthouse replaced it in 1938, the island became connected to the "mainland" of the Vineyard by a spit of sand. Today the lighthouse (renovated in 2007) is accessible by

foot. Take note of the granite cobblestone foundation (dubbed the Children's Lighthouse Memorial), a tribute
to Vineyard children who have died.
Open to the public late May to mid-
October 11–5 Friday through Monday,
and Thursday 11 to half an hour after
sunset for the sunset tour. Adults $5,
children 12 and under free.

Up-island

Mayhew Chapel and **Indian Burial
Ground**, Christiantown Road, off
Indian Hill Road, West Tisbury. This
tiny chapel, burial ground, and memorial to the Praying Indians (who were
converted to Christianity by the Reverend Mayhew Jr. in the mid-1600s) is
a quiet place, owned by the
Wampanoag tribe of Aquinnah.

NORTH WATER STREET

Grange Hall (508-627-4440; mvp
reservation.org), State Road, West Tisbury. Open seasonally. The original Agricultural Society Barn now hosts functions and events.

Beetlebung Corner, at the intersection of Middle, South, State, and Menemsha
Cross roads; the center of Chilmark. The intersection was named for the grove of
beetlebung trees (the New England name for tupelos), which are unusual in this
region. Tupelo is a very hard wood, an excellent material for making mallets (also
called beetles) and the plugs (or bungs) that filled the holes in wooden casks and
barrels during whale oil days.

Abel's Hill Cemetery, South Road, about a half mile beyond Meeting House
Road, Chilmark. John Belushi, of SNL and Blues Brothers fame, was buried here
after a drug overdose in 1982 at the ripe age of 33. He'd been partying with
Robert DeNiro and Robin Williams at the Chateau Marmot in West Hollywood on
March 5th when a mainline cocktail of heroine and cocaine did him in. According
to legend, the only place Belushi ever
said that he got a good night's sleep
was on the Vineyard, where he and his
wife had some property. You'll easily
find the marked grave near the
entrance of the cemetery, but his body
lies in an unmarked grave about 11
feet north of the where his original
headstone was place.

JOHN BELUSHI

Menemsha Harbor, at Menemsha
Cross Road near Beetlebung Corner.
This working fishing village is filled
with small, sturdy docks and simple,
weathered boathouses. Some islanders

MENEMSHA HARBOR

still earn a living from the boats of Menemsha's fishing fleet. For the rest of us, the harbor is a great location from which to watch the setting sun. A few little shacks (shops and fast-food eateries) line the road to Dutcher's Dock.

Quitsa Overlook, off State Road. At Beetlebung Corner, bear left onto State Road, heading toward Aquinnah. After a mile or so, you'll pass over a bridge; Nashaquitsa Pond (also known as Quitsa) is on your right and Stonewall Pond is on your left. Just beyond, a spot overlooks Quitsa and Menemsha ponds. About half a mile farther locals fill water jugs from a fresh, sweet stream that's been siphoned off to run out of a pipe. Local lore attributes various cures to the water—from stress relief, to a flu antidote, to a hangover remedy.

Aquinnah Community Baptist Church (508-693-1539), Aquinnah. Turn left at the small red schoolhouse (now the town library) across the street from the Aquinnah Town Hall, Fire Station, and Police Department. The lovely church is the country's oldest Indian Baptist church. It may have the prettiest location, too, overlooking windswept grassy dunes, stone walls, and the Atlantic Ocean.

Aquinnah Tribal Administrative Building (508-645-9265; wampanoagtribe .net), 20 Black Brook Road, Aquinnah. Open 9–5 weekdays. Housed inside this eco-friendly building (made almost completely of recycled materials and run by solar power) are a number of interesting small displays about the Wampanoag tribe. Look for an elders gallery with pictures of the tribal elders past and present, traditional native gardens, and a wetu, a traditional native home. When visiting, be aware that this is a working environment for the government of the tribe, not just a tourist destination.

Clay Cliffs of Aquinnah. The brilliantly colored clay cliffs, a designated national landmark, rise 150 feet above the shore and were formed 100 million years ago by

AQUINNAH CULTURAL CENTER

glaciers. For a fine view of the full magnitude of this spectacular geological formation, and distant views of Noman's Land Island and the Elizabeth Islands, walk beyond the souvenir shops. A wooden boardwalk also leads to the beach, where you can appreciate the towering clay cliffs from sea level. It's important to note that the Wampanoag have lived here for more than 5,000 years and own most of this land (although most of the beach is public); only they may remove clay from the eroding cliffs.

Aquinnah Lighthouse (508-627-4441). This redbrick lighthouse was

CHERISHED INSTITUTION

Alley's General Store (508-693-0088; mvpreservation.org), State Road, West Tisbury. Open daily. Alley's is a beloved Vineyard landmark. "Dealers in almost everything" since 1858, the store has a wide front porch where locals have gathered over the decades to discuss current events and exchange friendly gossip. In the early 1990s, though, economic conditions almost forced Alley's to close. In true island spirit, the Martha's Vineyard Preservation Trust stepped in to renovate the building and ensure its survival. Alley's continues to feel like a country store, selling everything utilitarian: housewares, mismatched cups and saucers, and locally grown produce.

built in 1844 to replace a wooden lighthouse that had stood since 1799. In 1856 a powerful Fresnel lens was mounted atop the lighthouse, where it warned ships away from the perilous Aquinnah coast; it was used for almost 100 years. From late June to mid-September (on Friday, Saturday, and Sunday evenings), you can ascend the lighthouse to enjoy the sunset. It opens 90 minutes prior to sunset and closes 30 minutes after sunset; $3.

Aquinnah Cultural Center (vanderhoophomestead.org), Aquinnah. This 1880s homestead, which serves as a local museum and community cultural center, enjoys some of the most wonderful windswept vistas on the island. It's no wonder that their six acres are leased for weddings.

Moshup Beach Overlook, on the northern end of Moshup Trail and south of the parking lot for the lighthouse, off State Road. This scenic coastal road has nice views of wild, low heathlands.

SCENIC DRIVES Instead of making a beeline up-island, detour onto Lambert's Cove Road from State Road out of Vineyard Haven. Take North, South, or Middle roads up-island. I particularly like cutting between the roads on Tea Lane and Meeting House Road.

CHAPPAQUIDDICK

Accessible via the **"Chappy ferry,"** *On-Time III* (508-627-9427), at the corner of Dock and Daggett streets. The crossing between Edgartown and Chappy is completed in a blink of an eye. The ferry runs 6:45 AM–midnight, but doesn't really have a schedule; it just goes when it's needed, and thus it's always "on time." Since it's the only method of transportation between the two islands, and a surprising number of people live on Chappy year-round, the

MYTOI

ferry runs daily. Roundtrip for car and driver, $12; for passenger, $4; and bike, $6.

Chappaquiddick contains several lovely beaches and wildlife refuges, including the 516-acre Cape Pogue Wildlife Refuge, the 14-acre Mytoi, and the 200-acre

Wasque Reservation. Unfortunately, though, the beautiful island is perhaps best known because of Dike Bridge, the scene of the drowning incident involving Senator Edward Kennedy in July 1969. To reach Dike Bridge, stay on Chappaquiddick Road after you get off the ferry until the road turns into Dike Road. When the road takes a sharp turn to the right (in about a mile), continue straight on the dirt road until you reach the bridge.

When the bridge was rebuilt in 1995, pedestrians once again had direct access to Cape Pogue, a thin ribbon of sand that stretches along the east side of Chappaquiddick and the remote Cape Pogue Lighthouse. Four-wheel-drive vehicles can use the bridge when endangered shorebirds like the piping plover are not nesting. Cape Pogue is also accessible by foot or by four-wheel-drive vehicle, over the sand of Wasque Point, several miles south of the beach.

✒ **Cape Pogue Wildlife Refuge and Wasque Reservation** (508-693-7662; thetrustees.org). These adjoining tracts of land on the southeastern corner of Chappaquiddick are relatively isolated, so that even on summer weekends you can escape the crowds. This seaside wilderness contains huge tracts of dunes, the long and beautiful **East Beach**, cedars, salt marsh-

es, ponds, tidal flats, and scrub brush. Overseen by the Massachusetts Trustees of Reservations, Cape Pogue (516 acres) and Wasque (200 acres) are the group's oldest island holdings. Half of the state's scallops are harvested each autumn off the coast near the **Cape Pogue Lighthouse** (on the northern tip of the cape). The lighthouse was built in 1893 and automated in 1943. Limited East Beach parking $3; reservation entrance $3 per car, $3 per person (late May to mid-September). Note: It is dangerous to swim at Wasque Rip because of the forceful tide.

🦑 The outstanding 2½-hour **natural history tours** (508-627-3599; thetrustees .org) of Cape Pogue are naturalist led, in an open-air four-wheel-drive vehicle, and depart from Mytoi Garden (see below) at 9 AM and 2 PM. The fee is $40 for adults, $18 for children under 15. It'll be one of your best island adventures.

🦑 **Cape Pogue Lighthouse tours** (1½ hours), where you'll learn about the fascinating history of the light and the keepers who lived there, depart from Mytoi Gardens. Adults $25; children under 15, $12. Three trips are offered three times daily from late May to mid-October. Space is limited, so reserve early. Don't miss it.

Mytoi (508-693-7662; thetrustees.org), Dike Road. Open daily sunrise to sunset. This 14-acre Japanese garden, built by Hugh Jones in 1958, has camellias, irises, a goldfish pond, and a picturesque little bridge.

🦑 **Fishing Discovery Tour** (508-627-3599; thetrustees.org). Late May to mid-October. Operated by the Trustees of Reservations, these 4-hour guided surf-fishing trips (two trips, weekdays) drift along the Chappaquiddick shores at Wasque Point and Cape Pogue. Adults $60; children 15 and under, $25. Limited to eight people per trip. Only members may take this trip, but you can purchase a temporary membership for $22 per individual or $32 for a family.

🦑 **Poucha Pond** (508-627-3599; thetrustees.org), Dike Bridge. Early June to early October. Members of the Trustees of Reservations may take self-guided tours; rentals $25 per half day, $35 daily. Nonmembers must first purchase an introductory family membership for $32. Boats are available 9–5 daily.

As you approach Aquinnah, take a left onto Moshup Trail to the lighthouse and circle back via Lighthouse Road and Lobsterville Road (but do follow Lobsterville to the very end, across the cut from Menemsha).

✳ To Do

AIRPLANE RIDES **Classic Aviators** (508-627-7677; biplanemv.com), off Herring Creek Road at the Katama Airfield, Edgartown. Open seasonally. Open-cockpit rides in a 1941 Waco biplane, solo or with a friend, with Snoopy-like leather caps and goggles. Rates start at $149 for one or two people for a 10- to 12-minute flight.

BICYCLING/RENTALS Several excellent (albeit crowded) bicycle paths connect the main towns: Vineyard Haven to Oak Bluffs, Oak Bluffs to Edgartown, Edgartown to West Tisbury, and Edgartown to South Beach via Katama Road. Because the roads from West Tisbury to Aquinnah are rather hilly, you need to be in pretty good shape to tackle the ride. A less ambitious but rewarding journey would entail taking your bike to Aquinnah and then pedaling the hilly but scenic up-island circular trail that begins at the Aquinnah Lighthouse: Take Lighthouse Road to Lobsterville Road and backtrack up Lobsterville Road to State Road to Moshup Trail. The Manuel E. Correllus State Forest (see Green Space), off the Edgartown–West Tisbury Road, also has several bicycle paths.

Rubel Bike Maps (bikemaps.com) are the best, most detailed maps available. Rubel produces a combination map that covers both the Vineyard and Nantucket ($2), as well as another that includes the islands, Cape Cod, and the North Shore ($5).

The **Martha's Vineyard Commission** (508-693-3453) also produces a free map that tells you what to expect on major routes: for instance, narrow roadways (shared with cars), gently rolling terrain, steep rolling terrain, and so on. It does not give estimated times or exact mileage, though.

Bike Ferry (508-645-3511). Operates 9–5 (on demand) in July and August and weekends in the shoulder season from late May through September. Some people riding out to Menemsha and Aquinnah will be thrilled to know about Hugh Taylor's little ferry, which takes cyclists across Menemsha Creek (it separates the picturesque harbor from Lobsterville Beach and Aquinnah beyond). This 150-yard ferry ride saves cyclists a 7-mile bike ride. $10 roundtrip, $5 one-way.

MUST-SEE SUMMER EVENTS

Early August:
Possible Dreams Auction (possibledreamsauction.org), Harborside Inn, Edgartown. Given the celebrity involvement, it's not surprising that national publicity surrounds this event. Celebrities offer to fulfill "dreams" that vary from predictable to unusual. High bidders in the past have won a tour of the *60 Minutes* studios with Mike Wallace; a sail with Walter Cronkite on his yacht; a seat at a Knicks game with Spike Lee; a tour of Carnegie Hall with Isaac Stern; a walking tour of the Brooklyn Bridge with David McCullough; a song and a peanut butter sandwich from Carly Simon; and a lesson in chutzpah at the Five Corners intersection in Vineyard Haven with Alan Dershowitz. Longtime island celebrities see the auction as their chance to give back to the Vineyard—in 2008 the auction raised almost $570,000 for Martha's Vineyard Community Services. Even adjusted for inflation, that's a far cry from the $1,000 raised in 1979 when it began and folks bid in $5 increments for the privilege of helping lobstermen set out their pots. More than 1,000 people usually attend the event, and to date, the event has raised nearly $8 million. Fee.

Mid-August:
Illumination Night. The actual date is kept secret until a week prior to the event. The evening always begins with a community sing and is followed by an Oak Bluffs resident (usually the oldest) lighting a single Japanese lantern after all the electric lights in town are turned off. Then the rest of the "camp" residents illuminate their gingerbread cottages with lanterns and candles.

Mid-August:
Agricultural Fair (508-693-9549). Held at the Ag Hall and Fairgrounds on State Road in West Tisbury, this is arguably the island's most beloved summer event. It's certainly one of the oldest: It began during the Civil War! Fee.

Dozens of shops rent bikes, including: **R. W. Cutler Bikes** (508-627-4052) on the harborfront at 1 Main Street in Edgartown; and **Wheel Happy** (508-627-5928), 8 South Water Street in Edgartown. Expect to pay $20–25 daily in summer for a mountain or hybrid bike. (There are 3- and 7-day rentals, too.) Most shops are open April through October; ask about delivery and pickup service.

❋ **Cycle Works** (508-693-6966), at 351 State Road in Vineyard Haven, repairs bicycles. John Stevenson and his enthusiastic and helpful crew have the largest selection of cycling equipment (for sale and rent), accessories, and parts on the island. They've been here since 1975.

BOAT EXCURSIONS/RENTALS *Ayuthia* **Charters** (508-693-7245), Vineyard Haven. This traditional 48-foot, all-teak ketch takes a maximum of eight people on afternoon sails from early May to September. BYO food and drink; $75 per person for the afternoon trip. It's an excellent choice.

Magic Carpet (508-627-2889; sailmagiccarpet.com), Memorial Wharf, Edgartown. Departures four times daily June through September. Operated by Todd Bassett and Lee Taylor (a Vineyard native and his wife, respectively), this classic 56-foot wooden yahl comfortably accommodates 12 people on two hour charters along Cape Pouge. You'll learn some good island history and tales along the way. $60 per person.

Sea Witch (508-631-6535; seawitchsailingcharters.com), out of Vineyard Haven, offers highly recommended private charters.

Sail Ena (508-627-0848; sailena.com), Vineyard Haven. Day, sunset, and sailing for women aboard a 34-foot classic Alden sloop. $60 per person with a maximum of six people. Customized trips too.

Mad Max (508-627-7500; madmaxmarina.com), at the Seafood Shanty, Edgartown Harbor. This 60-foot catamaran sets sail twice daily (at 2 and 6 PM) from late May to September. Tickets for the 2-hour sail, which might have upwards of 40 people on board, cost $55 adults, $50 children under 10. Captain Bob Colacray knows these waters well.

Wind's Up! (508-693-4252; windsup mv.com), 199 Beach Road, at the drawbridge on Beach Road, Vineyard Haven. Rentals and instruction mid-May to late September. This full-service outfit (on-island since 1962) rents Sunfish and small catamarans and offers beginning, intermediate, and advanced instruction.

CANOEING AND KAYAKING
Wind's Up! (508-693-4252; windsup mv.com), 199 Beach Road, at the drawbridge on Beach Road, Vineyard Haven. Rentals and instruction mid-

May to late September. Rentals by the half and full day; private and introductory group instruction. If you're in the market to purchase a canoe or kayak, the well-priced fleet is sold at the end of each season.

🐾 **Long Point Wildlife Refuge Tour** (508-693-7392; thetrustees.org), led by Trustees of Reservations. This is a great way to learn basic paddling techniques and about the local ecology and natural history of Long Point.

Chilmark Pond Preserve (508-627-7141), access just before Abel's Hill Cemetery (where, incidentally, John Belushi and Lillian Hellman are buried) on South Road, Chilmark. When you paddle across Chilmark Pond, you'll be rewarded with a small ocean beach on the south shore. This local secret (well worth the effort) is accessed only by canoe or kayak, which you must supply.

See also **Cape Pogue Wildlife Refuge** under the sidebar "Chappaquiddick."

FITNESS CLUBS ❄ **The Vineyard Fitness Center** (508-693-5533), 155 State Road, Vineyard Haven–Edgartown Road, Edgartown. Open daily.

❄ **The Vineyard Fitness Center & Tennis Center** (508-696-8000; vineyard tenniscenter.com), off the Edgartown–West Tisbury Road, at the airport; a full-service center.

FISHING Fishing is excellent from most Vineyards **beaches and bridges**. The bridge between Oak Bluffs and Edgartown is perfect for anglers. There's also a wide area that hangs over the swiftly running channel between Nantucket Sound and Sengekontacket Pond. You're most likely to catch the island's prized striped bass and bluefish before sunrise. Surf-casting is best from south-facing beaches and the beaches at Aquinnah. On Chappaquiddick, **East Beach** at Cape Pogue Wildlife Refuge and **Wasque Point** (see the sidebar "Chappaquiddick" for both) are famed for fishing.

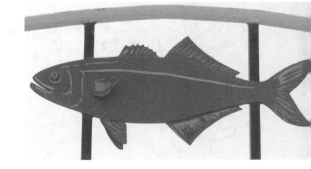

❄ **Coop's Bait & Tackle** (508-627-3909), 147 West Tisbury Road, Edgartown. This is your basic one-stop shopping for bait, tackle, boat charters, and information on "hot spots" for catching the big ones.

Dick's Bait & Tackle (508-693-7669), 108 New York Avenue in Oak Bluffs; and **Capt. Porky's** (508-627-7117), Dock Street, Edgartown, rent fishing rods, tackle, and other necessary equipment. Capt. Porky's also arranges charters.

Great Harbor Sportfishing Charters (508-627-3122 land; 508-627-2128 cell), Edgartown Harbor. May to late October. Captain Charlie uses light tackle, flies, and conventional means when he goes out sportfishing.

North Shore Charters (508-645-2993; bassnblue.com), out of Menemsha Harbor. May through October. Captain Scott McDowell takes anglers in search of bass and blues.

FOR FAMILIES ✐ There are so many family- and kid-friendly activities that I've interspersed them throughout this section. If I'd listed them under For Families, the other headings would have been decimated!

GOLF Farm Neck Golf Course (508-693-3057), off County Road, Oak Bluffs. Open April through December. Reservations are strongly suggested at this stately 18-hole course, but they're only taken 2 days in advance (4 days in advance off-season). A challenging course, but not long.

❋ **Mink Meadows** (508-693-0600), off Franklin Street, Vineyard Haven. A fairly long, but very subtle course; more challenging than you might think.

HORSEBACK RIDING ✐ ❋ **Crow Hollow Farm** (508-696-4554; crowhollow farm.com), New Lane, West Tisbury. Trail rides, lessons, and summer camp.

❋ **Red Pony Riding** (508-693-3788), 85 Red Pony Road, off the Edgartown–West Tisbury Road, West Tisbury. Private lessons and trails for experienced riders.

✐ **Nip-n-Tuck Farm** (508-693-1449), State Road, West Tisbury. Hayrides are offered Monday through Saturday during the summer (3–5 PM) for $6 per person; call to schedule one.

ICE-SKATING Martha's Vineyard Arena (508-693-4438; mvarena.com), Edgartown–Vineyard Haven Road, Oak Bluffs. Call for public skating hours. Who brings skates to the Vineyard? No one, but you can rent them here. Admission $5; children five and under are free.

MINI-GOLF Island Cove (508-693-2611), 386 State Road across from Cronig's Market, Vineyard Haven. Open daily May through September and weekends during April and October.

SAILBOARDING Wind's Up! (508-693-4252; windsupmv.com), 199 Beach Road, at the drawbridge on Beach Road, Vineyard Haven. Rentals and instruction mid-May to late September. Sheltered Lagoon Pond, where Wind's Up! has a facility, is a great place for beginners to learn sailboarding and sailing. The water is shallow and the instructors patient. Those more experienced can rent equipment, consult the shop's map, and head out on their own. Sailboarding is excellent all over the island, but experienced surfers should head to Menemsha, Aquinnah, and South Beach.

VINEYARD HAVEN HARBOR

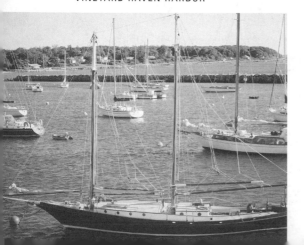

SPECIAL PROGRAMS ❋ **Vineyard Conservation Society** (508-693-9588; vineyardconservationsociety.org), Wakeman Conservation Center, 57 David Avenue off Lambert's Cove Road, Tisbury. Since it was established in 1965, this nonprofit group has protected thousands of acres from commercial and residential development by engaging in conservation land acquisition and advocacy. The society also sponsors a wide range of public activities, most of them free, including the Winter Walks program, a summer environmental lecture series, educational seminars and workshops on such topics as alternative wastewater treatment and solar-powered building technology, and the annual Earth Day all-island cleanup.

❀ ✿ **Featherstone Center for the Arts** (508-693-1850; featherstonearts.org), Vineyard Haven; off Barnes Road, half a mile north of the Edgartown–Vineyard Haven Road, West Tisbury. Gallery open daily noon–4. On 6 acres donated by the Martha's Vineyard Land Bank, this former horse barn and farm has been transformed into a community art center. **Classes** change seasonally but might include woodworking, stained glass, pottery, papermaking, printmaking, weaving, guitar lessons, and photography. Weekly summer art camps for kids, too. Continually searching for ways to be more responsive to its community, the center also stages a **flea market** on Tuesdays (9:30–2) in July and August with about 60 vendors; an **open pottery studio** on Wednesday; open **darkroom** on Monday nights; and "**Musical Monday**" evenings. About 20 of the surrounding acres are crisscrossed with so-called **Featherstone Trails** for hiking.

✿ **Farm Institute** (508-627-7007; farminstitute.org), 14 Aero Avenue, off South Beach and Katama Road, Edgartown. Open 9–5 Monday through Saturday. By now you hopefully are aware of the Vineyard's deep agricultural roots. Well, this is the place to milk goats, watch baby piglets or calves being born, explore vegetable gardens, or get lost in a 7-acre corn maze—for a day or a week or the whole season! This non-profit educational center offers summer programs for kids age 2 and older, Saturday morning farm chores, adult workshops, tons of fresh produce and meats, and more special events. It's a rare opportunity for most of us to connect to the natural world.

SWIMMING POOL ❀ **Mansion House Health Club & Spa** (508-693-2200; mvmansionhouse.com), Main Street, Vineyard Haven. Open 9–7 daily in-season; call for off-season hours. These folks have the only public pool on the island; the 75-foot heated mineral spring pool also has lap lanes. $16 adults, $11 children.

TENNIS Public courts are located at: **Church Street** (two clay) near the corner of Franklin Street in Vineyard Haven; **Niantic Avenue** (four hard) in Oak Bluffs; **Robinson Road** (four hard) near Pease's Point Way in Edgartown; **Chilmark Community Center** (508-645-3061) on South Road at Beetlebung Corner in Chilmark (available when members are not using them); **Old County Road** (two hard) in West Tisbury.

Island Inn Country Club Tennis Courts (508-693-6574), Beach Road in Oak Bluffs. Open mid-April to

mid-November. Three clay courts cost $24–28 per hour, depending on whether you are playing singles or doubles.

❋ ⌖ **The Vineyard Fitness Club & Tennis Center** (508-696-8000; vineyard tenniscenter.com), 22 Airport Road, off the Edgartown–West Tisbury Road, West Tisbury. When it's raining, this full-service indoor facility arranges matches, and offers lessons, tennis camps for all ages, and ball machines.

WATERSKIING **Martha's Vineyard Ocean Sports** (508-693-8476), Pier 44, Beach Road, Vineyard Haven, and Dockside Marina in Oak Bluffs. Open mid-June to mid-October. If you're over 4 years old, even if you're a self-described klutz, Mark Clarke can teach you how to water-ski, knee-board, tube, wakeboard, and parasail. He runs a safety-conscious outfit.

❋ Green Space

❧ **Martha's Vineyard Land Bank** (508-627-7141; mvlandbank.com), 167 Upper Main Street, Edgartown. The Land Bank was established in 1986 in order to purchase open space with funds raised by a 2 percent tax on real estate transactions. Today there are 61 parcels of land totaling more than 2,700 acres. I highly recommend getting this organization's map prior to your visit for a current look at the Vineyard's open land. Many of the island's conservation areas—ocean beach, moors, meadows, ponds, and woods—are free for all to enjoy. Maps are available at the six town halls, libraries, and the Land Bank office.

Manuel E. Corellus State Forest (508-693-2540; massparks.org), off the Edgartown–West Tisbury Road or Barnes Road. Comprising 5,146 acres of woodland and meadows in the center of the island, the forest's trails are used regularly by bikers, joggers, picnickers, and hikers. Park near the Barnes Road entrance.

In Oak Bluffs
Ocean Park, along Ocean Avenue. Fringed with some of Oak Bluffs' best-preserved gingerbread cottages, the park's centerpiece is a large white gazebo that serves as a bandstand for summer-evening concerts.

VINEYARD LAND BANK PROPERTY

In and near Edgartown
✿ **Felix Neck Wildlife Sanctuary** (508-627-4850; massaudubon.org), off Edgartown–Vineyard Haven Road, Edgartown. Trails open dawn–7 PM. Visitors center open 8:30–4:30 weekdays, June through August; 9–4 weekdays, 10–3 Saturday, 12:30–3 Sunday, September through May. The Vineyard is populated by many species of birds that flock to the island's forests and wildlife sanctuaries. This 350-acre preserve, affiliated with the Audubon Society, has 2 miles of easy trails that traverse thick woods, open meadows of wildflowers, beaches, and salt marshes. The interpretive exhibit center has tur-

A PERFECT UP-ISLAND DAY ON THE VINEYARD

7:45 Pick up fresh donuts from Humphrey's.

8:00 Take the scenic drive along Lambert's Cove Road.

9:30 Hike the crestline trail at Menemsha Hills Reservation.

11:30 Drive Tea Lane and Meeting House Road between North and South roads.

12:00 Sit on the front porch of Alley's General Store with a sandwich from Garcia's.

1:15 Interact with the joyful sculptures at Field Gallery.

2:30 Explore Polly Hill Arboretum.

4:00 Visit Chilmark Pottery or Martha's Vineyard Glass Works.

5:30 Stroll the beach beneath the Clay Cliffs of Aquinnah.

7:30 Watch the dusky light change color at Menemsha Harbor.

8:00 Enjoy clam chowder or lobster rolls at The Galley or The Bite.

10:30 Split a Mad Martha's ice-cream cone with your partner.

tles, aquariums, a gift shop, and a library. Year-round activities for children and adults include guided nature walks (almost daily during summer) and bird-watching trips for novices and experts alike. Inquire about weeklong children's day camps. Adults $4, children $3, free to Audubon Society members.

See also **Mytoi**, **Cape Pogue Wildlife Refuge**, and **Wasque Reservation**, and **natural history tours** under the sidebar "Chappaquiddick."

In West Tisbury and Up-island

Menemsha Hills Reservation (508-693-7662; thetrustees.org), off North Road, Chilmark. This exceptional Trustees of Reservations property makes for a great 2-hour hike. The 3-mile crestline trail, part of which runs along the island's second highest point, leads down to a rocky beach. This point was used during World War II as a military lookout. No swimming allowed.

Cedar Tree Neck Sanctuary (508-693-5207), off Indian Hill Road from State Road, West Tisbury. The 312-acre sanctuary, owned and managed by the Sheriff's Meadow Foundation, has trails through bogs, fields, and forests down to the bluffs overlooking Vineyard Sound.

Long Point Wildlife Refuge (508-693-7662 or 508-693-3678; thetrustees.org), off Edgartown–West Tisbury Road, West Tisbury. Open 9–5 daily, mid-June to mid-September; sunrise to sunset mid-September to mid-June. A long, bumpy, dirt road leads to a couple of mile-long trails, Long Cove Pond, and a deserted stretch of South Beach. Parking is limited at this 632-acre preserve, maintained by the Massachusetts Trustees of Reservations, so get there early. Parking: $10 per vehicle plus $3 per adult; bikes and walkers $3; free in winter.

Peaked Hill Reservation, off Tabor House Road from Middle or North roads, Chilmark. Turn left on the dirt lane opposite (more or less) the town landfill and then keep taking right-hand turns until you reach the trailhead. This 132-acre Land Bank property is the highest point on the island, at a whopping 311 feet above sea level. Good for hiking, picnicking, and mountain biking, this reservation also offers vistas of Noman's Land Island, Aquinnah peninsula, and Menemsha Bight.

Waskosim's Rock Preservation, North Road, just over the Chilmark town line. At almost 200 acres, this is one of the largest and most diverse of the Land Bank properties, with great hiking, bird-watching, picnicking, and mountain biking. The Waskosim boulder marks the start of a stone wall that ran down to Menemsha Pond, separating the English and Wampanoag lands in the mid–17th century.

Allen Farm Vista, South Road, Chilmark. On the south (or the left side) about 1 mile beyond Beetlebung Corner as you head toward Aquinnah. Practically the entire stretch of South Road in Chilmark once looked like this striking 22-acre field and pastureland, protected as a Land Bank property. Lucy Vincent Beach is just beyond the pond, grazing sheep, and moorlands.

AQUINNAH BEACH

Cranberry Acres, West Tisbury. This cranberry bog, on the south side of Lambert's Cove Road from Vineyard Haven, has walking trails.

❋ **Polly Hill Arboretum** (508-693-9426; pollyhillarboretum.org), 809 State Road, West Tisbury. Grounds open 5–5 year round; visitors center

open 9:30–4 daily late May to mid-October; tours at 2 during the summer. This is a magical place. Now totaling 70 acres, this former sheep farm was brought under cultivation by legendary horticulturist Polly Hill in order to preserve it as native woodland. The arboretum, opened to the public in 1998, is a not-for-profit sanctuary devoted to a mix of 1,600 native and exotic plants, many threatened by extinction. The arboretum is tranquil and beautiful from early spring well into fall. Wandering visitors will discover an extraordinary range of plants. Lecture series, too. Donations gratefully accepted: $5 adults.

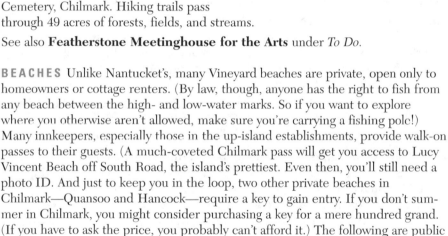

Fulling Mill Brook, off South Road, about 2 miles beyond the Chilmark Cemetery, Chilmark. Hiking trails pass through 49 acres of forests, fields, and streams.

See also **Featherstone Meetinghouse for the Arts** under *To Do*.

BEACHES Unlike Nantucket's, many Vineyard beaches are private, open only to homeowners or cottage renters. (By law, though, anyone has the right to fish from any beach between the high- and low-water marks. So if you want to explore where you otherwise aren't allowed, make sure you're carrying a fishing pole!) Many innkeepers, especially those in the up-island establishments, provide walk-on passes to their guests. (A much-coveted Chilmark pass will get you access to Lucy Vincent Beach off South Road, the island's prettiest. Even then, you'll still need a photo ID. And just to keep you in the loop, two other private beaches in Chilmark—Quansoo and Hancock—require a key to gain entry. If you don't summer in Chilmark, you might consider purchasing a key for a mere hundred grand. (If you have to ask the price, you probably can't afford it.) The following are public beaches.

In Vineyard Haven
Lake Tashmoo (or Herring Creek), at the end of Herring Creek Road, off Daggett Avenue from Franklin Street. This small beach offers good swimming, surf-fishing, and shellfishing. No facilities; limited parking; lifeguard.

❧ **Owen Park Beach**, on the harbor just north of the ferry. Good for small children and swimming. Parking.

In West Tisbury
❧ **Lambert's Cove Beach**, off Lambert's Cove Road. Although it's restricted to town residents and inngoers in-season, you can park here off-season to enjoy one of the island's top beaches. The sand is fine and the waters calm.

In Oak Bluffs
❧ **Oak Bluffs Town Beach**, on both sides of the ferry wharf, Oak Bluffs. This

AQUINNAH BEACH STAND

calm, narrow beach is very popular with Oak Bluffs families and seasonal visitors with small children. No facilities, although there are lifeguards, and public restrooms next to the ferry dock.

♂ **Joseph Sylvia State Beach**, along Beach Road between Edgartown and Oak Bluffs. The Edgartown end of this 2-mile-long barrier beach is also called Bend-in-the-Road Beach; this part of the gentle beach has lifeguards but no facilities. Park free along the roadside at the "people's beach." Good shore fishing and crabbing along the jetties, too.

In Edgartown

Lighthouse Beach, at the end of North Water Street, adjoining Fuller Street Beach. From Lighthouse Beach you can watch boats going in and out of the harbor. Rarely crowded with bathers because of seaweed, but always crowded with picture takers; gentle waves. No facilities. **Fuller Street Beach**, a favorite among college students, is a short bike ride from town and generally quiet.

Katama (or South) Beach, off Katama Road. A shuttle runs from Edgartown to this popular, 3-mile-long barrier beach, which has medium to heavy surf, a strong undertow, and high dunes. Children can swim in the calm and warm salt water of Katama Bay. There are lifeguards, but not along the entire beach. Facilities at the end of Katama Road and Herring Creek Road.

See also **Cape Pogue Wildlife Refuge** and **Wasque Reservation** in the "Chappaquiddick" sidebar; and **Long Point Wildlife Refuge**, above.

Up-island

Long Point Reservation, off Waldron's Bottom Road from the Edgartown–West Tisbury Road, West Tisbury. Owned by the Trustees of Reservations, this wide beach is isolated and beautiful, with good surf. From here you can also follow nature trails to **Tisbury Great Pond**. Lifeguard. Limited parking, for a fee.

♂ **Menemsha Beach**, Menemsha Harbor. This calm, gentle beach is also pebbly. Nearby restrooms. Sunsets from here can't be beat.

♂ **Lobsterville Beach**, off State and Lobsterville roads, Aquinnah. This beach is popular with families because of shallow, warm water and gentle surf. Limited parking along the road. Popular for fishing, too.

JOSEPH SYLVIA STATE BEACH

Lucy Vincent Beach, off South Road, is arguably the island's nicest beach. Although it's open only to residents and Chilmark inngoers (which is reason enough to stay in Chilmark), you can enjoy the wide, cliff-backed beach off-season. The farther east you walk, the less clothing you'll see. The farther west you walk, the more trouble you'll get in, since that stretch of beach is as private as they come.

Aquinnah Beach, just south of the Clay Cliffs of Aquinnah. Take the boardwalk and path through cranberry and beach plum bushes down to the beach, about a 10-minute walk. Resist the temptation to cover yourself with mud from the cliff's clay baths; the cliffs have eroded irreparably over the past century. (If that doesn't dissuade you, perhaps the law will: It's illegal to remove or use the clay.) Instead, walk along this 5-mile beach, called, from north to south, **Aquinnah Public Beach, Moshup** (the shuttle bus drops off here—otherwise, it's a 10-minute walk from paid Aquinnah parking), Philbin, and Zack's Cliffs. The cliffs are to the north, but the beaches are wider to the south. **Philbin** and **Zack's Cliffs** beaches are reserved for residents, but if you stick close to the waterline, you might not have a problem. Zack's fronts Jacqueline Kennedy Onassis's former estate. The farther south you walk, the fewer people you'll see. But those people you do see, you'll see more of—people come here specifically to sunbathe nude. It's not legal, but generally the authorities look the other way. Swimming is very good here; the surf is

ISLAND MYSTERIES

Vineyard mystery novelist Philip R. Craig writes page-turners that are perfect for beach getaways. In one of my favorites from this 20-plus-book series, *The Double Minded Men*, we first meet J. W. Jackson, a retired Boston cop, and his future wife, Zee, who tangle with a potentate, stolen necklace, and murder—all of which threaten their idyllic island home.

A big Craig fan who visited the Vineyard frequently, I always looked forward to the next installment of J. W.'s escapades, ones that took him to every nook and cranny of the island. When visiting, I'd always know with certainty that I'd just passed a little road that lead to one of his character's homes or a favorite fishing beach where he and Zee would catch blues when they were running. I recognized places from every page: street corners, shops, summertime traffic, Alley's General Store, or a specific beach on which we'd search for shells. The Vineyard becomes even more real to anyone who's read Craig's books.

J. W.'s friends and family are sometimes helpful in solving these cozy mysteries, but at other times he must protect them as he becomes involved in schemes by land developers, old-time gangsters, entertainers, environmentalists, and old pals. The characters who pop up become old friends we look forward to meeting in subsequent books. Sprinkled throughout, his love of cooking also becomes apparent with recipe riffs for smoked bluefish, clam cakes, and striped bass ("delish"). When reading the last sentence of his last book—**Vineyard Chill**, which was completed just before his death— I felt a sadness that I'd not read another J. W. case that would bring Martha's Vineyard even more to life than it already is.

—Martha Grant

usually light to moderate, and the shore doesn't drop off as abruptly as it does along the island's south shore. Facilities include restrooms and a few small fast-food shops at the head of the cliff. Parking is plentiful; $15 daily.

✏ **Uncle Seth's Pond**, off Lambert's Cove Road. A tiny (but public), freshwater pond on the side of the road. Good for children.

PICNICS Owen Park, off Main Street, north of the ferry dock, Vineyard Haven. This thin strip of grass runs from Main Street down to the harbor beach. It's a great vantage point for watching boats sail in and out of the harbor. You can usually get a parking space, and there are swings for the kids.

Mill Pond, West Tisbury. This wonderful place to feed ducks and swans is next to the simple, shingled West Tisbury Police Department.

✳ Lodging

With a few exceptions (primarily smaller B&Bs noted by our special value (✿) symbol), it is very expensive to stay on the Vineyard. Room rates have soared well, well beyond the rate of inflation since the late 1990s. Of all the towns, Edgartown is the most expensive by far; Oak Bluffs tends to draw younger visitors; and Vineyard Haven and West Tisbury are the most sensibly priced towns.

Reservations, made well in advance of your visit, are imperative during July and August and on weekends from September to mid-October. The *height of high season* runs, of course, from late June to early September, but many innkeepers define high season as mid-May to mid-October. In addition, many up-island inns are booked months in advance by hundreds of bridal parties, many with no ties to the island, who want meadows, stone walls, and spectacular ocean views as the backdrop for their photographs.

So many inns require a 2- or 3-night minimum stay in summer (and 2 nights on weekends in autumn) that I have omitted this information from the individual reviews. Assume it's true. Although there are quite a few year-round lodging choices, the island is incredibly quiet from January to March.

RESORT

In Edgartown
✏ **Winnetu Inn and Resort at South Beach** (508-310-1733; 866-335-1133; winnetu.com), South Beach, Edgartown. Open mid-April to late October. The Winnetu is easily one of the best family resorts on the Eastern Seaboard. But it also offers plenty of ways for romantics and more active folks to have a stellar holiday too. It has no rivals on the Vineyard, Nantucket, or Cape Cod. Three miles from Edgartown proper, and abutting South Beach (via a private pathway), this 11-acre resort offers tip-top service and plentiful amenities—an attractive and heated

FAMILY FRIENDLY WINNETU

WINNETU INN AND RESORT

pool, an first-rate tennis club and fitness center with an array of classes and massages, plenty of teen and children's programs (including a complimentary one in the mornings in-season), oversized chess pieces for playful fun, poolside bingo, a little pond with turtles, outdoor table tennis, a putting green, weekly clambakes, a library with fireplace, and a sublime restaurant (see Lure under *Dining Out*). A variety of accommodations suit a multitude of vacationer configurations: studios; one-bedroom suites with a combo living/dining area and a deck or patio (sleeping a family of five); and larger suites. Full kitchens are available. Furnishings are summery, contemporary, and upscale but not so precious that you can't enjoy the place after the beach. In the end, it's hard to say what's better—the facilities or the services, but they do go hand in hand. Tons of organized trips make it easy to relax here: kayak tours of Poucha Pond, private charters to Nantucket, whale watching, lighthouse and dune trips, and sunset water taxis to Edgartown. Concierges are ready to help with any and all requests and nary a staff member passes without a huge smile on their face and a ready hand. Late May to late August $230–2,135 nightly, with a 3-night minimum stay; off-season from $225 nightly; off-season packages offer a great value.

In Vineyard Haven

❄ ✿ ⁙ **Crocker House Inn** (508-693-1151; 800-772-0206; crockerhouseinn.com), 12 Crocker Avenue. With each return visit, I remain impressed by the value that Jynell and Jeff Kristal offer at their turn-of-the-20th-century B&B on a quiet side street near the center of town. And to boot, they're one of the few inns that takes one-nighters (although I certainly suggest staying longer). Each of the eight guest rooms has a fresh summer charm, retiled bathroom, cable TV/DVD, iPod docking station, and six pillows on the bed. The primo third-floor loft, tucked under the eaves with a gas fireplace and Jacuzzi, also has harbor views. Room 5 has good cross breezes and a private feeling; room 7 is larger, with a gas fireplace and strong morning sun; room 3 is good for three people traveling together and boasts a private entrance. A full breakfast daily served in the small combination living/dining room, is included. But many guests linger over a second cup of coffee and the newspaper on the front wrap-around porch set with rockers. You

CROCKER HOUSE INN

can't go wrong here. June through October $225–425; off-season $145–285.

❋ ♿ "♪" **Lambert's Cove Inn & Restaurant** (508-693-2298; lamberts coveinn.com), 90 Manaquayak Road. This place is quite something. The secluded country inn, a few miles from Vineyard Haven, has a setting that couldn't be more picturesque. The farmhouse estate once belonged to an ardent horticulturist, and the impressive formal gardens (and ancient rock walls) are nicely preserved. Common rooms, straight out of a magazine shoot (I swear), have the feel of a private gentleman's club; everything is just so, right down to the gilded mirrors and hunting prints. That said, service is quite friendly. Guest rooms are scattered throughout the inn and two outbuildings. They vary considerably, but each is distinctive and highly recommended. Some of the 15 rooms open onto sundecks; one especially comfortable room has a private sitting room. The grounds boast a heated outdoor pool and hot tub, around which are plenty of chaises and teak furnishings. Guests also receive parking passes to nearby Lambert's Cove, one of the island's prettiest beaches. Tennis courts, too, and full breakfast. No chil-

dren under 13. The **restaurant** (see *Dining Out*) is outstanding. Mid-May to mid-October $225–550; off-season $165–295.

❋ ♿ "♪" **Thorncroft Inn** (508-693-3333; 800-332-1236; thorncroft.com), 460 Main Street. Under the meticulous care of Karl and Lynn Buder since 1980, this elegant and conservative Craftsman-style bungalow sits on a 3½-acre wooded estate (about a mile out of town). All 14 guest rooms are decorated with Victorian and Colonial-period antiques and have plush carpeting. Amenities include thick robes, cable TV, air-conditioning, and the morning paper delivered to your door. Some rooms have hot tubs or Jacuzzis-for-two; many have wood-burning fireplaces. A complimentary full country breakfast is served at two seatings in the inn's two intimate dining areas, or you may opt for a continental breakfast in bed. Finally, there's afternoon tea and pastries and evening turndown service. It's all very sedate and harkens back to another era. Mid-June to early September $295–600; off-season $225–450; cottage $425–550.

🐾 **Marni's House** (508-696-6198; marnishouse.com), 122 Holly Tree Lane. Open late May through October. Off the beaten path near the center of town, Marni's is a warm and homey place, a throwback to the noncommercial era of innkeeping. It's a friendly and contemplative place, with 80 acres of conservation land abutting the property across the street. Shaded decks surround the house, and a combo living room/dining room/kitchen is warmed by a woodstove. As for the three guest rooms, Tower has a sleeping loft, an outdoor shower, and can accommodate an extra person; Sunlight gets great morning rays and has a Jacuzzi; Treehouse features a deep Japanese soaking tub. All have walk-

THORNCROFT INN

out decks. As for Marni's special breakfast breads, included with an extended continental breakfast, guests choose what they'd like Marni to bake. Rooms: $175–200 nightly; $1,050–1,200 weekly.

❋ 🐾 "𝖨" **Kinsman Guest House** (508-693-2311), 278 Main Street. Doreen Kinsman's shingled summer home is located a 10-minute walk from the center of town and a 20-minute walk to the West Chop Lighthouse. Built in 1880 as the original manse to the church across the street, it boasts high ceilings, an elegant staircase, and a proprietor who goes out of her way to accommodate guests. It has only three guest rooms, two of which share a newly tiled bath with modern fixtures. All rooms are gussied up with Laura Ashley accents, and two have four-poster beds. Breakfast is not included, but the front porch is so inviting many people pick up something in town to enjoy here. It's also hard to beat the price: $125 June through August; $100 off-season.

❋ 🐾 🍸 "𝖨" **The House at New Lane** (508-696-7331), 44 New Lane. Off the beaten path, this house is appealing to "real B&Bers," according to owners Ann and Bill Fielder. By that they mean the kind of guests who are happy to see family photos above the mantel and who don't need everything to be Martha-Stewart-perfect. Surrounded by 7 acres of woods and gardens, these three large rooms share two baths. One room has a private deck and entrance. Guests also have special access to a great beach, practically worth the cost of the room alone. Full breakfast included. Children are welcome, and futons ($20) are available. Rooms: $85–105.

In North Tisbury

🐾 "𝖨" **The Farmhouse** (508-693-5354; mvfarmhouse.com), 694 State

THE FARMHOUSE

Road, North Tisbury. Open May to late September. Drive 10 minutes from the ferry to this unpretentious B&B, and you'll be in another world. Dating to 1810, this warm house and its longtime innkeepers—Kathleen and Volker Kaempfert—are a delight. The five guest rooms (four with private bath) are furnished with country antiques and down comforters. The smallest room has a particularly unique feature: no indoor shower, but rather its own private outdoor shower! The combination living/dining room, where a decadent continental breakfast is served, features exposed beams and wide floorboards. Additional common space includes a quiet side deck. The Kaempferts are the kind of innkeepers who sit with guests at breakfast time (after they've poured your coffee). June through October $110–165.

In Oak Bluffs

🍸 "𝖨" **Oak Bluffs Inn** (508-693-7171; 800-955-6235; oakblufffsinn.com), 64 Circuit Avenue at Pequot Avenue. Open May through October. You can't miss the inn—it's the marvelously detailed pink building with an enormous third-floor cupola. It also has a great location: at the tip of Circuit, on the edge of the "campground," three blocks from a beach, and a 10-minute walk to the ferry. The friendly thirty-something innkeepers, Erik and Rhonda Albert, have done a great job

OAK BLUFFS INN

views; all have flat-screen TVs, air-conditioning, and refrigerators. Although the house sits on the main drag heading out of town and toward Edgartown, the traffic isn't a problem for city dwellers (who are at the beach and exploring during the days anyway.) Two big pluses: it's across the street from the expansive town beach and it's just a five minute walk to town from here. The wide front porch is also perfect for sunset cocktails. Buffet breakfast included. Late June to early September $250–395; off-season $150–295.

❄ ✿ 🐾 ﹔¹﹔ **Brady's NESW Bed & Breakfast** (508-693-9137; 888-693-9137; sunsol.com/bradys), 10 Canonicus Avenue. A 10-minute walk from the center of town and one block from the water, this refreshingly friendly place has been Brady Aikens's family home since 1929; he summered here in the 1940s and opened it as a B&B in 1991. Guest rooms are named according to direction: north, east, south, or west (hence the NESW appellation). The summery, whitewashed rooms have wood-slat walls and are decorated in soothing colors and designer linens. West (with sunset views) is the largest and nicest room. Two rooms boast a private balcony; one has a private bath; all have a ceiling fan. Start your day with an outdoor shower, followed by a continental breakfast on the wraparound porch with rockers, and end up back here with Brady as the sun sets. (He's here at 5 PM sharp every afternoon.) The comfy living room, decorated with southwestern influences, has a large video and CD collection. May through October $164–225 (including tax); November through April $101–160.

❄ ✿ ﹔¹﹔ **Nashua House** (508-693-0043; nashuahouse.com), Kennebec Avenue. Owned by the same folks who operate Zapotec Café (see *Eating*

freshening the place up. All ten guest rooms have small but newly redone baths, air-conditioning, cottage-style bedroom sets, and views of colorful neighboring cottages from every window. Make a bee-line for the soothing and contemporary **2-bedroom apartment** ($450 nightly) on the third floor; you could easily settle in for a week, especially given the balcony and kitchenette. Families are welcome in the carriage house or the first-floor room. An expanded continental buffet breakfast, enjoyed at individual tables, is included; guests may also eat on the wraparound porch. Mid-June to early September $215–300; off-season $140–300.

❄ ﹔¹﹔ **Isabelle's Beach House** (508-693-3955; 800-674-3128; isabelles beachhouse.com), 83 Seaview Avenue. This turn of the 20th century guesthouse was resurrected in 2008 by the namesake innkeeper, who has been associated with in-town inns for some time. Most of the 11, simply and tastefully decorated rooms have ocean

Out), the 1873 Nashua House has 15 breezy and simple rooms, all of which share five bathrooms. The guesthouse was completely renovated in 2000, and as a result, all its carpeted rooms are looking good. I particularly like the corner rooms (room 11 included). This guesthouse is perfectly situated in the thick of the action. Late May to early September $99–149; off-season $59–119.

🐾 **Attleboro House** (508-693-4346), 42 Lake Avenue. Open mid-May through September. This authentic gingerbread cottage faces Oak Bluffs Harbor and sits on the outer perimeter of the Methodist Camp Meeting Association. It's been taking in seaside guests since 1874, and it hasn't changed much since then. In Estelle Reagan's family since the 1940s, the guesthouse has 11 simple but tidy guest rooms that share five bathrooms. (Some rooms have a sink.) Most rooms have a porch, but if yours doesn't, there's a wraparound porch on the first floor. Rates: $95–125 rooms; $145–210 suites; third floor accommodates six people for $210.

In Edgartown

🐾 ✒ **Edgartown Inn** (508-627-4794; edgartowninn.com), 56 North Water Street. Open April through October. You don't find these kinds of places anymore because usually they've been gutted and gussied up. But this is the real deal, with an honest sense of place. A hostelry since the early 1800s, the inn has hosted such notables as Daniel Webster, Nathaniel Hawthorne, and then senator John F. Kennedy. Sandi, the inn's manager since 1985, has worked hard at maintaining and upgrading the inn's 20 (generally large) rooms with firm mattresses and homey antiques. The spic-n-span rooms are simply but nicely decorated and represent perhaps the best value in town. Bathrooms are nicely retiled. Three light and airy (but somewhat Spartan) rooms in the Garden House have private entrances. Breakfast is additional and served in the old-fashioned, charming period dining room or on the back patio. The inn is appropriate for children 8 and older. June through September $125–275; off-season $75–275. No credit cards.

❄ 🐾 "↑" **Shiverick Inn** (508-627-3797; shiverickinn.com), 5 Pease's Point Way. The Shiverick, a mere few blocks from the harbor, defines over-the-top grand elegance. From the four-poster beds and crisp bed linens to china and crystal breakfast table set-

OAK BLUFFS GINGERBREAD COTTAGE

EDGARTOWN INN

tings, you'll enter a bygone world at this graceful, period home. Dating to 1840 and built for the town's first doctor, the formal inn has a mere three rooms and two suites—that's a lot of house for a such a small number of guestrooms. Common space includes a drawing room, back yard terraces, gardens, a garden room, and a library. Oriental carpets, 18th and 19th century American and Continental antiques are places just-so, throughout. Interestingly, it also has nine working fireplaces! Only some rooms have a TV. Full breakfast included. Early June to mid-October $270–550; off-season $135–325.

❀ ⁱ¹ᵖ **Victorian Inn** (508-627-4784; thevic.com), 24 South Water Street. Winter season depends on demand and predilection of the owners. This centrally located B&B, well-presided over by Stephen and Karyn Caliri since 1993, has 14 luxurious guest rooms. Some have four-poster canopy beds; many have a private porch or balcony. While I particularly like room 10, with a slanting roofline and a steady stream of sunlight, all third-floor rooms are corner chambers with harbor and chimney views. Rooms are furnished with substantial, comfortable armchairs, sofas, loveseats, fresh flowers, and desks. Steve, a very gregarious innkeeper, presides over the morning meal, serving four courses on the flower-bordered back patio or indoors at individual tables in the formal breakfast room. Late May to mid-October $245–425; off-season $135–250.

❅ ⁱ¹ᵖ **Jonathan Munroe House** (508-627-5536; 877-468-6763; jonathanmunroe.com), 100 Main Street. Located in the heart of Edgartown, this inn has six antiques-filled guest rooms that welcome you with Bose radios, fresh flowers, and complimentary sherry. The bed and breakfast's trump card, though, is a secluded two-story **carriage house** that rents for $375 nightly from early May to mid-October. It offers exquisite privacy and a central location. A full breakfast served on the porch is included, as is afternoon wine and cheese. Early June through October $240–275; off-season $175.

❅ ⁱ¹ᵖ **Hob Knob Inn** (508-627-9510; 800-696-2723; hobknob.com), 128 Main Street. The exclusive-feeling Hob Knob was renovated from top to bottom in both furnishings and philosophy in late 1996 by Maggie White. The boutique property exudes a haughty sense of self and prides itself on attentive services. Just a few minutes' walk from the center of town (request a room off Main Street if you like to sleep in—otherwise you'll be awaked by truck traffic), this Gothic Revival house has 17 spacious guest rooms with down bedding, king-sized beds, fine antiques, and a very soothing and tasteful ambience. Afternoon tea and a full country breakfast, served at small tables, are included. Or have breakfast in bed. During inclement weather, you'll appreciate the enclosed porch, a private back patio, two sitting rooms, and a front porch with rockers. Exercise hounds will appreciate the fitness room and dry sauna. The nearby **Thaxter** and **Tilton houses**, luxury

CHARLOTTE INN

Lane. Within a short walk distance of Lighthouse Beach and just a block from the harbor, the five suites in the main house each have a separate sitting room and kitchen or kitchenette, and they share a covered patio with barbecue grill. None are fancy but they sure are comfortable. (East Chop boasts its own deck.) The separate cottage sleeps four. Mid-June to early September $275–375; off-season $125–225.

Up-island

 ♿ **Beach Plum Inn** (508-645-9454; beachpluminn.com), 50 Beach Plum Lane (off North Road), Menemsha. Open May through October. Secluded amid 6 wooded acres overlooking Menemsha Harbor in the near distance, the Beach Plum offers 11 luxurious guest rooms with fine bedding, first-class bathrooms (many with deep soaking or whirlpool tubs), stylish but unpretentious furnishings, and high-quality craftsmanship. A few inn rooms have small but private balconies with harbor views, and most rooms have some sort of water view. Practical in-room amenities like umbrellas, beach chairs, playing cards, and flashlights are not overlooked, either. The six cottages are each decorated with a simple but fresh style and grace. Facilities include beach access, a croquet court, and a tennis court. Because this is such a popular place for weddings, you'll find a large white lawn tent between the inn and the harbor in spring and fall. The inn also boasts very **fine cuisine** (see *Dining Out*). Off-island innkeepers Sarah and Bob Nixon (of soap opera Agnes Nixon fame) have owned the inn since 2006. Full breakfast included. Mid-June to mid-September $275–450; off-season $215–350 for rooms.

Outermost Inn (508-645-3511; outermostinn.com), Lighthouse Road,

rentals that accommodate 8 to 10 people ($12,000–20,000 weekly), are really quite extraordinary. Children over 7 welcome. Late May to late September $300–600; off-season $175–525.

✳ **Charlotte Inn** (508-627-4751), 27 South Summer Street. The Vineyard's highbrow grande dame is owned by Gery and Paula Conover, ardent Anglophiles who make frequent trips to the United Kingdom to purchase antiques. Without an ounce of hyperbole, it's fair to say that it has few equals in the U.S. Equestrian prints, elegant armchairs, and collections of beautifully bound classic novels have turned each of the 23 rooms (and two suites) into a luxuriously inhabitable museum. The Conovers' taste for all things English reveals itself on the inn's grounds, too: ivy-edged brick sidewalks, small croquet-quality lawns, impeccable flower beds. Continental breakfast included; full breakfast available for an additional charge. No children under 14. May through October $295–950; off-season $295–595.

✳ ☄ 🍷 **Lightkeepers Inn & Cottage** (508-627-4600; 800-946-3400; thelightkeepersinn.com), 25 Simpson's

Aquinnah. Open early May to mid-October. Hugh and Jeanne Taylor's 20-acre parcel of land has the island's second best ocean view. (The best view is just up the hill from the Aquinnah Lighthouse, where Jeanne's great-great-grandfather was born.) The inn's seven rooms (one with a whirlpool, two with views of the lighthouse) and one suite feature natural fabrics, wool rugs, and down duvets. Subdued colors and unpainted furniture emphasize the seaside light. Rooms are named for the wood used in each: beech, ash, hickory, oak, and cherry. (Speaking of wood, don't miss the outdoor bar made from one long, impressive hardwood tree.) Inquire about the adjacent lighthouse suite, added in 2006, which was booked when I visited. In keeping with the family's musical tradition, guitars, pianos, and other instruments are placed in the common areas. (You might get lucky and wander into an impromptu living-room concert given by Hugh's brother James.) Full breakfast included; there's also a full-service restaurant on premises; see *Dining Out*. Children over 11 welcome. Mid-June to mid-September $340–430; off-season $310–390.

✿ ✑ & **Inn at Blueberry Hill** (508-645-3322; 800-356-3322; blueberryinn.com), North Road, Chilmark. Open May through October. Part of Everlands, a worldwide consortium of preservation-style eco-properties, this secluded 56-acre retreat was completely overhauled in 1995 and has an intentionally exclusive feel to it. It recently came under new management, but during an overnight in 2008, service was a bit rough around the edges in many departments. Miles from anything but conservation land, walking trails, and stone walls, the 25 soothing rooms are scattered throughout six elegantly simple buildings. Privacy and connection to the natural

world is paramount here: Most rooms have a private deck or balcony. A wide array of spa treatments is available by advance request; cable TV is also available on request; box lunches are offered in-season. An expanded continental breakfast, use of fitness facilities (including a tennis court), and beach passes to a coveted beach are included. See **Theo's** under *Dining Out* for specifics about the inn's excellent dinners. Spotty WiFi. Mid-June through August $445–565; off-season $330–420.

❋ ✿ ✑ **The Duck Inn** (508-645-9018), 10 Duck Pond Lane, off State Road, Aquinnah. A throw back to the 70s, in that it feels like a hippie retreat, the Duck Inn is arguably the most unusual place to stay on the island. It's also only a 5-minute walk to Philbin Beach, one of the island's top two or three. You may be sleeping in a sleigh bed with a silk, hand-painted, feather duvet (in my favorite room, which also boasts a balcony). Another room has a brass bed, freestanding marble basin, little balcony, and one french door to the water closet. Ask longtime proprietor Elise LeBovit for a complete description of the eclectic rooms, especially the cave-like ground-floor room. The whole open first floor is a communal-style gathering space, complete with wax-covered candlesticks on the dining table, a central fireplace and Glenwood stove, and kilims and Native American carpets. There is a well-used game area and special breakfast table for kids, not to mention a hot tub and masseuse. A full organic breakfast is included. Ask about the sauna in the "Flintstone" room. July to early September $125–235; off-season $125–145.

COTTAGES & EFFICIENCIES

In Oak Bluffs

✿ ✑ ⊤ & "🐾" **Island Inn** (508-693-

2002; 800-462-0269; islandinn.com),
Beach Road. Open April through
November. If you want to avoid in-
town crowds, or let the kids run
around, this is a decent choice. Situated between Oak Bluffs and Edgartown, this 7-acre resort is also within
walking distance of two beaches and
adjacent to Farm Neck Golf Course.
In all there are 51 units with kitchenettes (in the form of **studios**, one-
and two-bedroom **suites**, **town houses**, and a **cottage** that can sleep up to
six) in several low-slung buildings.
For a quieter stay, choose a room in
the one-story buildings. Townhouse
units have a fireplace, a spiral staircase to the loft bedroom, and a separate bedroom. All rooms have cable
TV and air-conditioning. Facilities
include three well-maintained tennis
courts (a tennis pro is available in-season), a swimming pool, and plenty of
space to picnic and barbecue. WiFi is
available for a fee. Mid-June to early
September $220–405; off-season
$100–265.

In Edgartown

✓ "P" **Edgartown Commons** (508-
627-4671; 800-439-4671; edgartown
commons.com), Pease's Point Way.
Open May to mid-October. These 35
efficiencies—from studios to two-bedroom apartments—are near the center
of town and great for families. Most of
the individually owned units are in
very good condition; these are rented
first. Units in the main building have
high ceilings and thus feel more spacious. Many units surround the pool,
but all are comfortably furnished and
most feature new kitchens. Outside,
there are grills, picnic tables, and a
nice enclosed play area. Longtime
managers Rick and Janet Bayley keep
the place humming. Mid-June to early
September $195–315; off-season
$100–185.

MENEMSHA INN AND COTTAGES

Up-island

🏵 **Menemsha Inn and Cottages**
(508-645-2521; menemshainn.com),
North Road, Menemsha. Open May
through October. This secluded 14-
acre parcel of forest has some lovely
views of Vineyard Sound, a 4-minute
wooded path to Menemsha Beach, and
a friendly atmosphere. Over the years
(it was actually opened in 1923) it has
been continually upgraded and maintained with pride. There's an emphasis
on peace and quiet, rather than fussy
interior decorating. The complex
boasts six luxurious and crisp rooms in
the carriage house (with a "great
room" and fieldstone fireplace); nine
smaller but first rate "regular" rooms
with freshly retiled bathrooms; 11 tidy
seascape cottages; and one elegant,
two-bedroom suite. Cottages have a
screened-in porch, fully equipped
kitchen, outdoor shower, barbecue,
and wood-burning fireplace. Walk-on
passes to Lucy Vincent and Squibnocket beaches are provided. Reserve cottages in February if you can; this
well-manicured place has a loyal,
repeat clientele. Facilities include a
fitness center, bike rentals, and tennis
courts. Expanded continental breakfast
with smoked salmon quiche and the
like included. Mid-June to late

September $240–700 nightly for rooms, $2,500–3,400 weekly for cottages; off-season $175–425 rooms, $1,600–2,100 cottages.

See also **Island Inn** under *Hotels and Motels*.

HOTELS
In Vineyard Haven
❄ ♪ ⁕ï⁕ **Mansion House Inn** (508-693-2200; 800-332-4112; mvmansion house.com), 9 Main Street. Occupying the footprint of the former Tisbury Inn (which burned in late 2001), this professionally operated inn is one of the island's most full-service hostelries. Located just a few blocks from the ferry, the four-story hotel features 40 rooms and suites that range from cozy to spacious–with prices to match. Deluxe rooms have soaking tubs, plasma TVs, fireplaces, and balconies that afford views of Vineyard Sound (or Main Street). The basement health club and spa, with a 75-foot mineral spring pool, pampers guests with a wide array of services, including clay cliffs **Moshup Mud Wraps**. And the roof deck is a quiet place to escape. Full buffet breakfast included (see **Zephrus** under *Dining Out*). Late May to early September $279–519; off-season $99–369.

MANSION HOUSE INN

In Oak Bluffs
❄ ◕ 🐾 ♿ **Surfside Motel** (508-693-2500; 800-537-3007; mvsurfside.com), 7 Oak Bluffs Avenue. One of the few places open through the winter, the Surfside has above-average motel-style rooms near the ferry. The area can get a bit boisterous on summer evenings, but room rates reflect that. Each room has either a queen, two double beds, or two twin beds, cable TV, air-conditioning, and a small refrigerators; cribs and roll-away beds are available for a fee. Corner rooms are particularly nice and spacious. Mid-June to early September $155–240 rooms, $250–310 suites (up to four people); off-season $85–160 and $140–195, respectively.

In Edgartown
❄ ♪ ⁕ï⁕ **Harbor View Hotel and Resort** (508-627-7000; 800-225-6005; harbor-view.com), 131 North Water Street. This is one privileged perch, especially after the $77 million renovation was finished in 2008. Overlooking a lighthouse, grass-swept beach, and Chappaquiddick, the 1891 Harbor View Hotel is Edgartown's best-situated hostelry. This grande dame boasts 114 rooms and 21 suites. (The latter are privately owned but in a rental pool and feature deep soaking tubs and kitchenettes with granite countertops.) Tranquil harbor views from the hotel's spacious veranda (lined with rocking chairs) are reason enough to patronize the place. Some guest rooms enjoy these views; other rooms have porches overlooking the pool. The upscale guest rooms are generally large, and appointed with antique prints and watercolor landscapes by local artists. Facilities include room service, summertime children's programs, swimming pool, and concierge. Because of its size, the hotel caters to large groups. Children under 16 stay free in parent's room. Host Alan Worden has

HARBOR VIEW HOTEL

presided over the hotel since 2006.
June through September $575–1,600;
off-season $265–1,000.

Harborside Inn (508-627-4321;
800-627-4009; theharborsideinn.com),
3 South Water Street. Open mid-April
to mid-November. This seven-building
time-share condominium is one of the
few waterfront (harborfront, no less!)
accommodations on the island. And it's
the only one on Edgartown harbor.
Practically all rooms have some sort of
water view; most have a porch or patio.
The 90 rooms and four suites are well
appointed with standard hotel-issue
furnishings. Facilities include a heated
pool overlooking harbor boat slips.
Children under 12 stay free in parent's
room. June to early September
$200–465; off-season $160–400. Attention sailors: Inquire about transient
boat slips.

**RENTAL HOUSES AND COT-
TAGES** *Mattakesett Properties*
(508-310-1733; 866-335-1133; mattak
esett.com). South Beach, Edgartown.
Open mid-May to mid-October. These
exceptional properties, privately owned
and located all along South Beach, will
not disappoint. They're fully equipped
and offer access to their sister property, the Winnetu Inn and Resort at
South Beach (see *Resorts*) and Lure
(see *Dining Out*). Townhouses and

duplexes $4,225–6,310 weekly; 3- to 5-
bedroom homes $7,415–8,865 weekly.

Seacoast Properties (508-627-9201 x.
21; mvseacoast.com), Linda Bassett
Real Estate, 201 Upper Main Street,
Edgartown. Dozens of agencies handle
thousands of rentals, which vary from
tiny cottages to luxe waterfront homes,
from dismal and overpriced units to
great values. But I recommend
Stephanie Burke, who listens to what
you want and knows the island like the
back of her hand. She has about 600
properties in inventory and is well-
versed in all island towns.

CAMPGROUND 🐾 *Martha's Vineyard Family Campground* (508-693-
3772; campmvfc.com), 569 Edgartown
Road, Vineyard Haven. Open mid-May
to mid-October. In addition to shaded
tent and trailer sites, the campground
also has rustic one- and two-room **cabins** that sleep five or six people
($125–150). Tents and trailers $48–54
for two people; weekly rates, too.

YOUTH HOSTEL 🐾 *"ı"* **Manter
Memorial AYH Hostel** (508-693-
2665; usahostels.org; 888-901-2087 for
in-season reservations; 671-718-7990
for reservations prior to the start of the
season), Edgartown–West Tisbury
Road, West Tisbury. Open mid-May to
mid-October. This saltbox opened in
1955, and it remains an ideal lodging
choice for cycling-oriented visitors.
The hostel is at the edge of the
Manuel E. Correllus State Forest
(which is full of bike paths; see *Green
Space*) and next to the path that runs
from Edgartown to West Tisbury.
Bring your own linens or rent them for
the single-sex, dormitory-style bunk
beds. The large kitchen is fully
equipped, and the common room has a
fireplace. Reservations strongly recommended, especially from mid-June to
early September, when large groups

frequent the hostel. Beds: $32–35 nightly, an additional $3 for non-members; two private rooms available $150–200.

✳ Where to Eat

Most restaurants are open May to mid-October; some are open through Christmas; each year more and more operate year-round. Opening and closing days vary considerably from week to week, largely dependent on the weather and number of visitors, so it's impossible to tell you reliably which days any given restaurant will be open. Always call ahead after Labor Day and before Memorial Day.

There are a few more generalizations I can make. Vineyard Haven, Tisbury, and up-island towns are "dry," so BYOB of wine or beer. (Some restaurants charge a nominal corking fee.) I've tried to note when there is a chef-owner because generally these places provide the most reliable food. Many Oak Bluffs establishments are family-oriented and casual, though there are a few sophisticated options. The dress code in Edgartown is a bit more conservative, but most places don't warrant a jacket and tie. Dining options are scarcer up-island and require reservations well ahead of time. Otherwise, reservations are highly suggested at all *Dining Out* establishments.

DINING OUT

In Vineyard Haven
Lambert's Cove Inn & Restaurant (508-693-2298; lambertscoveinn.com), 90 Manaquayak Road. Open for dinner mid April to late December. Dine on exceptional New American cuisine far from the crowds in a rarified world that epitomizes genteel elegance. Wall sconces, floor-to-ceiling bookcases, fireplaces, and well-spaced tables set a deeply romantic tone. Tinkling piano

music in the summer furthers it. My last dinner, prepared by Chef Jose DaSilva, included black mission figs stuffed with bleu cheese and wrapped with proscuitto and was followed by sushi grade tuna with bamboo rice, Thai plum sauce, and black sesame haricot verts. It's almost unrivaled on island. BYOB; corkage $10. Dinner $28–40.

Mediterranean (508-693-1617; med-mv.com), 52 Beach Road. Open for dinner mid-April through October. New in 2004, chefs Douglas and Leslie Hewson preside over an excellent, two-story waterfront bistro. Featuring Mediterranean cuisine (with appetizers like cooked Moroccan salads and steamed mussels with saffron and curry) from countries where olives grow, I dined recently on sublime grilled lamb served with a rosemary pan reduction, grilled asparagus, and a goat cheese tomato tartin. The atmosphere is elegant without being stuffy. Get an outdoor second floor table if you can. Dinner $27–32.

✳ **Le Grenier** (508-693-4906; le grenierrestaurant.com), 96 Main Street. Open for dinner nightly. Chef-owner Jean Dupon's place opened in 1979 and is consistently *magnifique* and disarmingly unpretentious; forget what you know about French restaurants. Lyons-born, Dupon offers traditional French fare, including bouillabaisse, escargots, steak au poivre, and calf's brains Grenobloise. The menu is extensive, but each item is expertly prepared. As for desserts like crème caramel and banana flambé: *C'est bon.* Although the food is serious, the decor is relaxed and casual, conjuring a European indoor-garden style with twinkling lights, green-and-white accents, and hand-painted florals. Although it seems out of place at first, it's become a decidedly Vineyard institution. BYOB; corkage fee $5. Dinner (*plats de résistance*) $24–36.

❋ **Nicky's Italian Café** (508-696-2020; nickysitaliancafe.com), 395 State Road. Open for dinner. This neighborhoody place, on the lower level behind some storefronts near Cronig's Market, specializes in classic Italian comfort food like chicken marsala and pork scaloppini. It's not fancy but you'll sure feel away from the summertime crowds. BYOB. Dinner $12–24.

BLACK DOG TAVERN

ZEPHRUS

❋ ♪ ⵏ **Zephrus** (508-693-3416; mvmansionhouse.com), 9 Main Street. Open for lunch and dinner; off-season schedule varies. This casual bistro is contemporary and warm, with an eclectic menu that tries to offer something for everyone. As a consequence it can be uneven, but when you want to get in and out quickly, it's a decent choice. Except when the service is uneven. Come for light bites throughout the day (they don't close between lunch and dinnertime) or dine more seriously on a large pot of steamed mussels, free-range roasted chicken, or lobster ravioli. It's your call. Sidewalk tables are primo in the summer, but the exposed kitchen warms the main dining room too. BYOB. Dishes $12–32.

❋ ♪ **Black Dog Tavern** (508-693-9223; theblackdog.com), 21 Beach Street Extension. Open for all three meals daily. Longtime Vineyarder Bob Douglas became frustrated when he couldn't find good chowder within walking distance of the harbor, so he opened this place in 1971, naming it for his dog. These days the restaurant—and its ubiquitous T-shirts—is synonymous with a Vineyard vacation. And although the portions are smaller now that Bob's son is running the place, it's a fair place to eat. (Maybe you should just buy the T-shirt?) While you'll have to wait an hour for dinner, lunch won't be much of a problem. Interior decor is simple, with pine floors, old beams, nautical signs, and shellacked wooden tables packed close together. Best of all, the shingled saltbox is cantilevered over the harbor. Fresh island fish and locally grown vegetables dominate the menu. Although staff are often eager to hustle you out the door, don't be shy about finishing your coffee. BYOB. Breakfast $7–9, lunch $7–16, dinner $18–35.

✂ & **Saltwater** (508-338-4666; salt waterrestaurant.com), 79 Beach Road. Open for lunch and dinner February through December. New in 2008, this open, airy, newly constructed, contemporary dining room could not have a prettier setting overlooking Lagoon Pond. But my dinner of scallops with potato gnocchi, carrots, and corn (although fine) didn't quite live up to the setting. It may take a season or two to get its bearings, so do ask around when you're on island. The restaurant specializes in locally grown food, seafood, and homemade pastas, and the menu changes daily. Corkage fee $5. Lunch $9–15, dinner $25–32 (prix fixe $33 Tuesday through Thursday off-season).

In Oak Bluffs

Sweet Life Café (508-696-0200; sweetlifemv.com), 66 Circuit Avenue. Open for dinner May through October. When new owners Pierre and Susan Guerin took over the reigns in 2007 (along with chef Scott Ehrlich), they didn't miss a beat. Indeed, if I could

SWEET LIFE CAFÉ

eat only three dinners on the Vineyard, one would be here; it's as fabulous as always. Dine on a classical gourmet menu of fresh island seafood within a restored and airy Victorian house or outside on the twinkling garden patio. During my most recent dinner, their seared halibut with sweet pea risotto rose above my quite lofty expectations. The wine list is exemplary, thanks to Pierre. After leaving, you'll muse about how sweet life is, indeed! Dinner $30–44.

❋ & **Park Corner Bistro** (508-696-9922), 20H Kennebec Avenue (Circuit Avenue). Open for dinner and Sunday brunch; off-season schedule varies. This cozy, 10-table find has a rustic, European, and intimate feel. Featuring a wide range of New American dishes and a well-versed staff, Park Corner serves seasonal dishes like steak frites, chicken marsala and grilled pork. Early specials on Thursday and Friday off-season. Dinner $12–28.

🦞 ✂ ♈ & **Lola's Southern Seafood** (508-693-5007; lolassouthernseafood .com), Beach Road. Open for dinner and Sunday brunch ($16 adults, $8 children), April through October. Chef-owner Lola Domitrovich's place is a happening, lively, unusual joint with Cajun/Creole/southern cuisine. The atmosphere is a tad unusual, too: leopard-pattern napkins, brown paper tablecloths, cut-glass chandeliers, faux wrought iron, and a large multicultural mural (try to pick out Lola). Come for huge portions of BBQ ribs, a signature seafood jambalaya (or the vegan version), étouffée, and rib-eye steak. This is one place where a split-plate charge is worth it. There's also a less expensive, early-evening pub menu ($9–16). Otherwise, mains (served with biscuits and corn bread) are $20–40. Or better yet, come for a cosmo at the bar and listen to the bands that get the joint jumpin.'

JIMMY SEA'S PAN PASTA

Jimmy Sea's Pan Pasta (508-696-8550), 32 Kennebec Avenue. Open for dinner April through October. This small and casual place still serves enormous portions of delicious pastas, all cooked to order and served in the pan. Chef-owner Jimmy Cipolla's intensely garlic-infused place is an even better value if you have facilities to heat up your leftovers; it's virtually impossible to eat everything you're served. Better yet, get takeout and split the dishes at home yourself. Try the mussels in white wine sauce. And note the herb garden in front—you know the seasonings are fresh. No reservations are taken, so get there early or be prepared to wait. Dishes $20–28.

In Edgartown

✦ ♆ **Atria** (508-627-5850; atriamv.com), 137 Upper Main Street. Open for dinner April through October. Chef-owners Greer and Christian Thornton specialize in elegant, hip dining with a global flair. It's the kind of quiet and sophisticated place where celebs like to hangout. It's classy but casually romantic; tables are closely space and there's a rose garden patio too. Fish is a big deal here. Signature dishes include rare ahi tuna tempura as a starter and pan-seared Georges Bank scallops and cauliflower-goat cheese puree. The menu changes daily, but a vegetarian risotto is always available upon request. The burgers with onion rings are also great, as is the wok-fired lobster. Natural flavors come through loudly and clearly. As for dessert, try the gooey chocolate molten cake or traditional thin pecan tart. The bar (which hosts live jazz, folk, and blues on many nights) is a great place for solo diners and an even better place for a nightcap—try their martinis. Dinner $30–40.

♆ **Alchemy** (508-627-9999), 71 Main Street. Open for lunch May through October and dinner February through December. Owners Scott and Charlotte Caskey, so successful at Savoir Fare for so many years, have struck gold in this larger and more visible space. If you're lucky, you'll get one of a few sidewalk tables. For lunch try the excellent pressed Cuban sandwich or a lobster cake BLT. Fish and seafood specialties at dinner change regularly, but with luck you'll find seared salmon with creamed lentils, halibut meunière with lemon, and a traditional lobster clambake for one. The wine list is quite well chosen. In the evening, the open, rotunda-like two-story bistro and bar is loud and energetic; it's a great place for singles to nosh at the bar. Lunch $9–15, dinner $25–38.

L'Étoile (508-627-5187; letoile.net), 22 North Water Street. Open for dinner late April to late November. After all these years (since 1986 to be exact), chef-owner Michael Brisson is still the go-to guy for that singularly spectacular meal. There isn't a more elegant dining room on the island, nor more perfect contemporary French cuisine in New England. Although the garden patio is romantic too, I'm always bowled over by the soothing main dining room. Nothing short of spectacular, dishes like Dover sole, rack of lamb, and étuvée of native lobster are metic-

ulously prepared and artistically presented. Michael uses local fish and produce whenever possible, and you can taste the difference. If your wallet and appetite aren't quite up to the main event, a lighter bar menu has venison burgers, cheese paninis with roasted tomato soup, and the like. Start with a martini (aka a "startini.") And look for biweekly wine tastings and tapas on the lawn. Bar menu $14–23, dinner $37–48, tasting menu $95.

❄ 🍸 **Detente** (508-627-8810; detentewinebar.com), Winter Street. Open for dinner. This intimate and stylish restaurant, tucked back in Nevin Square, feels like a real find. Especially when you're inside with white linens and dark furniture. Especially when you dine on the summertime terrace. Especially when you grab a bite at the soapstone bar. It doesn't matter where you dine: it's candlelit, refined, romantic, and tickling to a modern palette. Owners Kevin and Suzanna Crowell get my warm thanks for superb New American cuisine. The menu, which features an abundance of locally procured ingredients, is thankfully limited to about six entrées, all executed with aplomb. Try the harpooned swordfish with sweet pea raviolis on spiced carrot slaw like I did, and you'll want to go back every night. The wine list is excellent. Dinner $30–36.

Lure (508-627-3663; winnetu.com), 31 Dunes Road (Katama Road). Open for all three meals, mid-April through October. Chef Mark Goldberg, who hails from Boston's fabu Mistral, has made his mark on Lure. Emphasizing the freshest of island ingredients, he walks tightrope of cooking for folks who return a few times in one week and pushing the envelope for foodies. The heirloom-like beet salad with goat cheese was deeply satisfying, as were the Katama bay oysters (plucked from waters just a stone's throw away.) And a month after delving into gigantic sea scallops with a corn and chanterelle succotash, I could still summon their memory. Live frivolity for dessert: with warm french doughnuts and an espresso pots du crème—or a s'more like you've never had them! To give you as many reasons as possible to return, children have their own menu and families have their own dining room. Brilliant idea. Snag a seat on the second-floor deck and enjoy the sunset during dinner. And don't forget to try a signature blackberry martini or island mojito. Lunch $12–21, dinner $26–45.

♿ **Chesca's** (508-627-1234), 38 North Water Street. Open for dinner early April to mid-October. Chef-owner Jo Maxwell offers a reliable menu of eclectic Italian-inspired seafood and pasta specials. She features a diverse menu where you can either eat affordably or drop a bundle. Try the grilled salmon with sweet Thai chili barbeque glaze, or lobster ravioli and seared sea scallops. It's noisy here—not good or bad noisy, just loud. Since reservations are accepted only for large parties, expect to wait (preferably at the sceney bar). Dinner $21–38.

❄ ♿ **Lattanzi's** (508-627-8854; lat
tanzis.com), Old Post Office Square,
off Main Street behind the brick courthouse. Open for dinner. Chef Albert
Lattanzi and his wife, Catherine, offer
sophisticated and traditional Italian
cuisine in conservative but not stuffy
surroundings. Tables are candlelit, covered with bistro paper and linen; the
staff are professional. As for the food,
it's prepared with flair: from wonderfully crusty tuscan bread and handmade pastas to lobster and
wood-grilled steaks and chops. Of
course the tiramisu is great, but so is
gianduja (flourless chocolate hazelnut
cake). There is some alfresco dining
too. Dinner $26–40.

❄ **Square Rigger** (508-627-9968), at
The Triangle. Open for dinner nightly.
You can tell right away that this place
is by and for locals: Patrons and servers
are friendly well into September! It's a
meat-and-potatoes kind of place; actually, it's a char-grilled meat, seafood,
and lobster kind of place—with an
emphasis on lobster. There's nothing
surprising—just good and casual, with
plenty of parking and a publike atmosphere. Dinner $24–50.

Up-island

♿ **Beach Plum Inn** (508-645-9454;
beachpluminn.com), 50 Beach Plum
Lane, off North Road, Menemsha.
Open for dinner, May through October. The focus is on food at this mini-
malist dining room devoid of
distractions. You may be drawn by the
distant sunset views of Menemsha
Harbor, but the menu features the
innovative seafood and locally grown
produce of chef James McDonough.
Although it changes nightly, the menu
might include pan-seared scallops with
sweet and spicy beets to start, followed
by hazelnut-crusted halibut with roasted shallot whipped potatoes. Portions
tend toward nouvelle (read: small).

And unless you're allergic to chocolate,
you'd be crazy not to order the chocolate quad cake. Service, by the way, is
friendly and low-key but professional.
A la carte $32–45; four-course, prix fixe
menu $78. BYOB; corkage $6.

🦞 ♫ ♿ **Theo's** (508-645-3322; blue
berryinn.com), 74 North Road,
Chilmark, at the Inn at Blueberry Hill.
Open for dinner May through October.
You don't hear much buzz about
Theo's, but chef Robin Ledoux-Forte
and her cooking deserve warm accolades for healthful, artful presentations
and hearty portions. The contemporary
menu emphasizes organic vegetables
from the garden and local seafood. Try
the butternut-squash-filled ravioli and
a cornmeal- and herb-crusted yellowtail flounder. Desserts, like a french
pear tart and triple chocolate tart, melt
in your mouth. As for the atmosphere,
candlelit tables glisten off multipaned
windows and cobalt glassware in a
quiet country setting. Four-course rustic Sunday suppers in May and October for $39 are worth every penny.
Otherwise, dinner $25–40; BYOB.

Outermost Inn (508-645-3511; outer
mostinn.com), Lighthouse Road,
Aquinnah. Open for dinner late May to
late August. Take the inn on its hippie
terms—or don't. It draws patrons
because it's exclusive (there are a limited number of tables), because they do
things their own funky way out here,
and because of dramatic sunsets over
the ocean. As for the New American
menu, it highlights fresh island ingredients. There are usually four or five
appetizer and entrée choices, perhaps
including Edgartown oysters and roasted halibut. By reservation only; two
seatings; $65 prix fixe.

♫ ♿ **HomePort** (508-645-2679; home
portmv.com), 512 North Road, Menemsha. Open for dinner seasonally. At
press time, Homeport's fate was uncer-

tain. It was unclear whether the town was going to purchase it and tear it down or whether a white night would swoop in and keep it exactly the same. Just in case the latter happens, here's what used to be true: Sunset views of Menemsha Creek are the big attraction at this local institution. It's an efficient surf-sun-and-turf kind of place, with long wooden tables and lobster cooked lots of different ways, thick swordfish, jumbo shrimp, and a raw bar. The servings are large and the clientele a bit older. Frankly, some prefer to get takeout from the back door and enjoy a view from the harbor. BYOB. Dinner $30–50.

EATING OUT

In Vineyard Haven
❄ 🦞 🍴 **Art Cliff Diner** (508-693-1224), 39 Beach Road. Open for breakfast and lunch daily. Great things come from this little package. Although it's not much to look at and the parking is limited in summer, the buzz is resounding and the dishes stellar. Chef-owner Regina Stanley (who was the pastry chef at Blair House, the guesthouse of the White House), a whirlwind of energy, meets and greets patrons. Breakfast is out of this world: fancy frittatas, a daily scone and eggs

ART CLIFF DINER

Benedict specials, tofu scramble, almond crusted French toast, breakfast tacos, and the bayou bundle. Anything-but-prosaic meat loaf is a terrific lunch choice. It's also family friendly, with crayons available for the kids. Dishes $8–13.

🍴 **Waterside Market** (508-693-8899; watersidemarket.com), 76 Main Street, Vineyard Haven. Open 6:30 AM–9 PM March through January. Stop by these spacious and casual digs for quick but filling lunchtime sandwiches and salads, as well as breakfast dishes like hash, croissant sandwiches, and buttermilk pancakes. There's always something appealing on the huge blackboard menu. Watch the street scene through large, street front picture windows. Dishes $5–15.

Black Dog Café (508-696-8190; the blackdog.com), 509 State Road. Open seasonally. The Black Dog began as a cottage industry, but now it's more like an industrial complex (figuratively speaking). About a mile out of town, you no longer have to fight traffic to fork over money for Black Dog pastries. Sandwiches under $10.

🦞 **Sandy's Fish & Chips** (508-693-1220), 455 State Road, Woodland Center. Open mid-May to mid-October. Located within John's Fish Market, this family-operated no-frills place has great fried fish sandwiches and fried clams. The fish market opened in the 1960s and the restaurant started in 1978.

❄ **Net Result Fish Market** (508-693-6071; mvseafood.com), 79 Beach Road. Sushi, lobsters, shellfish, smoked fish, and bay scallops (in-season) purchased on the spot or shipped home as a nostalgic reminder.

In Oak Bluffs
❄ 🦞 **Slice of Life Café** (508-693-3838; sliceoflifemv.com), 50 Circuit

Avenue. Open for all three meals. Brought to you by the same dynamic team that put The Sweet Life Café on the map originally, this wonderful and casual place offers savory and sweet treats to eat in or take out. Don't miss it. It's always one of the friendliest places on island. Try the chowder and a friend green tomato BLT for lunch. Dinner is fancier with, perhaps, roasted cod with sundried tomatoes or any number of nightly specials. You can always keep it simple with a thick burger too. Take out or dine in. Breakfast and lunch $7–14, dinner $14–22.

❀ ❈ ✆ ⚄ **Linda Jean's** (508-693-4093), 25 Circuit Avenue. Open 6 AM–8 PM daily. Established in 1979, this is a classic American diner without the chrome. Rehabbed in early 2002, the pleasant storefront eatery serves old-fashioned meals at old-fashioned prices, thanks to Lanie and Marc. Breakfast is still the best meal of the day here: Pancakes are thick but light, for instance. But the fish sandwich is quick and good, and the onion rings are crispy. Kids are happy with burgers and PB&J. And the waitstaff are friendly. What more could you ask for? If you haven't tried that famed New England "delicacy," Grape-Nut custard, this is the place to do it. Expect a wait for breakfast even in the dead of winter! Dishes $8–20.

❀ ❈ ✆ ⚅ ⚄ **Offshore Ale Co.** (508-693-2626; offshoreale.com), Kennebec Avenue. Open for lunch and dinner nightly. Not only is the food good—crispy, wood-fired, brick-oven pizzas, hefty burgers, grilled fish, fried calamari, and beer-batter fish and chips—but the place is fun, too. The front door is marked with a big barrel full of peanuts, and patrons toss the shells onto the wood floor already covered in cedar sawdust chips. But freshly fermented beer is reason enough to fre-

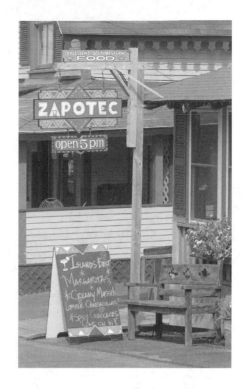

quent this dark, two-story barn—as is the homemade root beer. Check the blackboard for what's fresh from the shiny copper vats. Check out the frequent entertainment. Lunch $10–15, dinner $10–25.

✆ **Zapotec Café** (508-693-6800; zapotecrestaurant.com), 14 Kennebec Avenue. Open for lunch in summer, dinner May through October. Even if you're from New Mexico, this cozy place with twinkling chili pepper lights is festive and fun—as long as you're not old and stuffy. It serves huge

NET RESULT

portions of Mexican and southwestern dishes like chicken suiza in a tangy tomatillo sauce, marinated chicken with mole sauce, swordfish fajitas, and Mexican-style paella, as well as old standbys like burritos, chimichangas, and quesadillas. Flan and chocolate ganache pie are big desserts; sangria and Negro Modelo are the drinks of choice; the salsa is fresh; and the waitstaff friendly. *And . . .* they have crayons for the kids. Dishes $11–20.

🦪 🍴 ♿ **Giordano's** (508-693-0184; giosmv.com), 107 Circuit Avenue at Lake Avenue. Open for lunch and dinner May through September. This classic, family-style restaurant is run by fourth-generation Giordanos, who pride themselves on serving value-packed portions. Giordano's serves some of the best fried clams on-island (head to the take-out window), along with large portions of chicken cacciatore with spaghetti, chicken parmigiana, pizza, sandwiches, and fried seafood. The cocktails are also big. Dishes $10–20.

🍴 🍸 **Oak Bluffs Harbor Boardwalk** (aka **The Strip**). Among the many eateries that line the boardwalk, the

COOP DE VILLE

Coop de Ville (508-693-3420) has the best fry joint and raw bar. The oysters are excellent and fish-and-chips very good. Otherwise, you know the menu: seafood by the pint or quart; steamed lobster with corn; wings. With picnic tables and counters, this is a great location for fast food and people-watching. Open for lunch and dinner, mid-May to mid-October. Dishes $10–30.

🦪 🍴 ♿ **Farm Neck Café** (508-693-3560), off County Road. Open for lunch and limited breakfast April to mid-November; for all three meals June through September. When I ask locals to recommend a great, inexpensive lunch place, the Farm Neck Café inevitably pops up. Yes, the place is crawling with golfers, but the setting is lovely—with views of long, manicured fairways. While the atmosphere is clubby, it's public and very comfortable. You can get grilled shrimp and other seafood, soups, cob salad, sesame chicken wrapped in a flour tortilla, a burger, or a roast beef sandwich Philly style. Lunch $5–11, dinner $13–30.

❄ 🍴 **Seasons Eatery & Pub** (508-693-7129; seasonspub.com), 19 Circuit Avenue. Open for lunch and dinner. This is one of the few down-island places for a simple lobster dinner. Nightly entertainment in the summer. Dishes $10–22.

In Edgartown

🦪 🍴 **Among the Flowers** (508-627-3233), Mayhew Lane, off North Water Street. Open for breakfast and lunch May through October, and dinner in July and August. This small, friendly café has some of the most reasonable prices in Edgartown. There aren't many indoor tables, but there is an outdoor patio, enclosed and heated during inclement weather. Look for excellent omelets, lobster rolls, PB&J for the kids, crêpes, salads, quiches, corn chowder, and clam chowder. Lunch $5–15, dinner $12–30.

AMONG THE FLOWERS

❄ 🐾 ✎ ⊻ ♿ **The Newes from America** (508-627-4397; kelley-house.com), 23 Kelly Street. Open 11:30 AM–11 PM daily. The food is surprisingly good for pub grub—renowned burritos, as well as burgers and sandwiches. Stick to pub mainstays and don't order anything too fancy. At about $10 per person, lunch here is one of the better island values. The atmosphere is cozy, too: exposed beams, red brick, and a wood floor. Check out the selection of microbrews. When it's cold outside, this place will warm you to the core. Dishes $9–18.

❄ 🐾 ✎ ♿ **Main Street Diner** (508-627-9337), 65 Main Street, Old Post Office Square. Open 8 AM–10 PM (8–7 off-season). Glen Ward' nostalgic 1950s-style diner is a fun place for kids because there's plenty to look at—from old signs to a jukebox. As for the actual dining, you've got your basic comfort foods: eggs, pancakes, grilled cheese, meat loaf, PB&J, burgers, and some Italian. Parents won't mind the prices either: lunch $9–15, dinner $11–19.

❄ ✎ **Lattanzi's Pizzeria & Gelateria** (508-627-9084; lattanzis.com), Old Post Office Square, off Main Street behind the brick courthouse. Come here for the Vineyard's most excellent, creative, and moderately priced pizzas from a wood-burning stone oven—followed by authentic gelato. And while

you're at it, they also have homemade pastas, panini, salads, light appetizers, family fare, and wines by the glass, too. Main dishes $12–20.

✎ ⊻ **Seafood Shanty** (508-627-8622; theseafoodshanty.com), 31 Dock Street. Open for lunch and dinner seasonally. So you just want to nibble on something and have drinks on the water? Head here for lobster cakes, something from the raw bar or sushi bar, and a beverage of your choice. If you can't get a table on the rooftop deck, don't bother, though. Lunch $11–17, dinner $20–35.

Up-island

❄ **Fella's** (508-693-6924), 479 State Road, West Tisbury. Open daily 8-various late afternoon or early evening hours. Stop by this tiny, low-key take-out place for breakfast sandwiches, hearty sandwiches, hot pressed paninis, chili, and pizza. You can always count on them when you're hungry and heading up-island. Dishes $7–14, pizzas $14–25.

Faith's Seafood Shack (508-645-4080), on the path to the lighthouse, Aquinnah. Open seasonally. Of all the little shacks that line the path to the lighthouse overlook, this one is my favorite for fried seafood and the like.

AQUINNAH SHOP

♂ & **Aquinnah Shop** (508-645-3867), 27 Aquinnah Circle, Aquinnah. Open 8–5 mid-April to mid-October and until 9 PM in summer (but last table seated at 7:30). Come for the island's best sunset views rather than decent food and unbearably slow service. The Vanderhoop and Madison families, native Wampanoag, operate this homey restaurant, located near the Aquinnah Cliffs. Try the Tomahawk special at breakfast: homemade fish cakes covered with salsa atop poached eggs. Lunch is more prosaic: burgers, sandwiches, and salads. I'd go elsewhere for dinner, but just so you know, they dress up the place with sautéed shrimp, lobster with bérnaise sauce, fresh fish daily, and buffalo short ribs braised in cabernet. Lunch $10–20, dinner $20–40.

LIGHT MEALS, SNACKS & SWEETS

In Vineyard Haven

❋ **Vineyard Gourmet** (508-693-5181), 71 Main Street. This specialty food store carries picnic baskets and boxed lunches filled with smoked salmon, pâtés, and imported cheeses. Those with cooking facilities will find even more of interest. When the shop isn't too busy, call ahead and ask Helen and Diana what they've got, and have them pull something together so you can saunter right in and then be on your way. Most items are under $12.

❋ **Black Dog Bakery** (508-693-4786; theblackdog.com), 11 Water Street. Open daily. At the Five Corners intersection near the Steamship Authority parking lot, the Black Dog is well positioned to accommodate the hungry hordes that arrive each day. Indeed, it is many visitors' first stop—for a cup of strong coffee and a sweet pastry, muffin, or other goodies.

❋ ⊛ **Humphrey's** (508-693-1079), 455 State Road, West Tisbury. Pick up homemade soups and enormous sandwiches made with homemade bread, and save room for their jelly- or cream-filled doughnuts, affectionately called belly bombs. Two other seasonal operations are at 32 Winter Street in Edgartown and 1 Lake Avenue in Oak Bluffs.

In West Tisbury

❋ ♂ **Garcia's at Back Alley's** (508-693-8401), West Tisbury. Open 7–5 most days. Behind the general store, Back Alley's has sandwiches, salads, great chowder, soups, and baked goods—perfect for hungry bicyclists.

In Oak Bluffs

❋ **Mocha Mott's Good Coffee** (508-696-1922), Circuit Avenue. Open daily. This tiny, aromatic basement café has rich espresso that keeps me going well into the evening, and newspapers that keep me in touch.

See also **Slice of Life Café** under *Eating Out* and **Humphrey's** under *In Vineyard Haven.*

In Edgartown

❋ & **Soigné** (508-627-8489), 190 Upper Main Street. Open daily except closed for March. A connoisseur's deli just outside town, Soigné has all the makings for a gourmet picnic: the

SUNSET PICNIC ON MENEMSHA BEACH

island's best take-out sandwiches, soups, myriad cold salads, and boutique wine from around the world. Owners Ron and Diana, who have been at this since 1986, also sell "designer" pastas, pâtés, pastries, mousses, excellent clam chowder, dried fruits, imported cheeses, sauces, and select wines. It's a bit pricey, but worth every penny. By the way, something like "millions and millions" of brownies have been gobbled up here.

Espresso Love (508-627-9211), Old Post Office Square, behind the brick courthouse, Edgartown. Open daily March through December. Tucked back off Main Street, these folks make strong cappuccino and sweet pastries. A limited selection of soups and sandwiches are offered at lunch, when you can enjoy the outdoor patio.

See also **Morning Glory Farm** under *Farm Stands* and **Humphrey's** under *In Vineyard Haven*.

Up-island

❊ **Scottish Bakehouse** (508-693-6633), 977 State Road, Tisbury. Open 6:30–5 (or a bit longer in-season). Baking scones, meat pies, sweet breads, and more since the mid-1960s.

🦞 🐟 **The Galley** (508-645-9819), Chilmark. Open mid-May to mid-October. This tiny place has the best chowder on the island and great lobster rolls. Burgers and soft-serve ice cream, too.

🦞 🐟 **The Bite** (508-645-9239), Basin Road, Menemsha. Open seasonally. This tiny shack serves arguably the best fried clams on-island. Don't miss the chance to decide for yourself.

Chilmark Store (508-645-3739), State Road, near Beetlebung Corner, Chilmark. Open May through September. This general store offers great pizzas and baked goods (especially the pies) in addition to conventional general-store items. Do some people-watching from the front-porch rockers before you leave.

🦞 **Larsen's Fish Market** (508-645-2680), Dutcher's Dock, Menemsha. Open early May to late October. Down some oysters and cherrystones at the raw bar while you wait for your lobsters to be boiled. Or pick up some stuffed quahogs and head to the beach.

❊ **Menemsha Fish Market** (508-645-2282), Dutcher's Dock, Menemsha. This little place smokes their own fish and has a small raw bar, which is convenient for appetizers while you wait for your lobsters-to-go.

MENEMSHA FISH MARKET

Mad Martha's has irresistible home-made ice cream and many locations in all the right places (near the ferries, on Main Streets, and the like).

FARM STANDS Despite summer traffic, $45 dinner entrées, chichi boutiques, and a building boom, the Vineyard is an agricultural island at heart. With little effort, you'll find farms with produce so fresh you can almost taste the earth. Stop often; it will be one of the things most cherished about a Vineyard holiday.

Morning Glory Farm (508-627-9003), 120 Meshacket Road, off the West Tisbury Road, Edgartown. Open late May through December. Although their business card says Roadside Stand, this is a full-fledged farm with a large rustic barnboard building. You'll find farm-fresh eggs, a great salad bar,

VINEYARD WINTER

home-baked pies and breads, and homemade jellies, including especially tasty white grape jelly.

✳ Entertainment

ARTS AND MUSIC ✳ ♪ **Vineyard Playhouse** (508-693-6450; vineyard playhouse.org), 24 Church Street, Vineyard Haven. This small, community-based professional theater produces well-done plays and musicals; the main stage is within a former Methodist meetinghouse. They also host many special events; keep your eyes peeled. Tickets $25–38 ($25 for preview tickets, matinees on the first 3 performances of each show, and rush tickets.) Summer performances Tuesday through Saturday at 7 or 8 PM. Look for a varied and entertaining lineup at the troupe's Tisbury Amphitheater, Tashmoo Overlook, State Road, Vineyard Haven. The playhouse also offers educational programs, theater for young audiences, summer outdoor productions, and a theater arts camp.

❧ **The Yard** (508-645-9662; dancethe yard.org), Middle Road, near Beetlebung Corner, Chilmark. May through September. Founded in 1973, this colony of performing artists in residence is always engaging and appreciated. The choreography and dance are spirited. If you have a chance to go to one of their performances, by all means go. The Yard is one of those special organizations that make the Vineyard uniquely the Vineyard. Most shows are $25 adult, $15 seniors.

✳ **Chamber Music Society** (508-696-8055; mvcms.vineyard.net). Mid-July to mid-August. Performances at 8 PM; tickets $30. Monday concerts are held at the Old Whaling Church in Edgartown; Tuesday concerts are at the Chilmark Community Center.

Band concerts. The location alternates between Ocean Park in Oak Bluffs and Owen Park in Vineyard Haven, but the time remains constant: Sunday evening at 8 in July and August. If it's raining on the night of the concert in Oak Bluffs, head to the Tabernacle. If it's raining on the night of the concert in Vineyard Haven, you're out of luck.

Y NIGHTLIFE Outerland (508-693-1137; outerlandmv.com), 17 Airport Road, Martha's Vineyard Airport, Edgartown. Shows typically start at 9 PM, May through September. Formerly known as the Hot Tin Roof, Outerland is now under the ownership of Barry Rosenthal, an entertainment ad agency based on the Vineyard. When Carly Simon opened this club back in 1979, it was the coolest island nightspot. The star-studded shack attracted the likes of Keith Richards, Jimmy Cliff, and John Belushi. Since then, it's been up and down. The buzz returned when President Clinton, Prince Andrew, and Diane Sawyer hung out there. Then it was up and down again. Somehow, it remains a venerable island institution. As for the music, there is a diverse lineup of national and local R&B, reggae, and blues bands. Tickets $10–50.

❋ **The Newes from America** (508-627-4397), 23 Kelly Street, Edgartown. Open daily. This colonial-era basement tavern is atmospheric and cozy, with hand-hewn beams. The Newes features microbrews; try the specialty Rack of Beers, a sampler of five brews from the outstanding and unusual beer menu (see *Eating Out*).

Atlantic (508-627-7001), Two Main Street, Edgartown. Formerly the Navigator, this completely renovated waterfront restaurant and bar opened in April 2008. The setting couldn't be better, especially if you get an outdoor table on the porch. It's hip, urban, and loud. But it was working some kinks out when I dined there, so at this point, I can only recommend it for drinks. It's owned by Charlotte Inn proprietor, Gery Conover (see Inns & Bed & Breakfasts under Lodging), who also developed the oh-so exclusive and private Boathouse (above the Atlantic).

❋ ♪ **Sharky's Cantina** (508-693-7501; sharkyscantina.com), 31 Circuit Avenue. Open 11 AM–12:30 PM. Always packed and hopping, Sharky's is a fun place for wildly inauthentic Mexican food and margaritas—the watermelon version is a local legend. Dishes $7–16.

❋ **Ritz Café** (508-693-9851), 4 Circuit Avenue, Oak Bluffs. Open daily. Locals hang out at this funky blues bar, which, according to the *Improper Bostonian*, is: "seedy," "smokin'," "scary," "disgusting," "hilarious," and "a blast."

Lampost/Rare Duck (508-693-4032), Circuit Avenue, Oak Bluffs. On the second floor, the Lampost features dancing from early April to late October. The Rare Duck, open only in the height of the summer, is a frozen-drink kind of place, a smaller lounge with nightly summer entertainment.

❋ **The Wharf** (508-627-9966), Lower Main Street, Edgartown. A popular pub on the wharf.

❋ **Henry's Hotel Bar** (508-627-7000), 131 North Water Street, at the Harbor View Hotel. Open 11–11 daily. When you're in the mood for a sedate drink, there's no place better for a signature martini or mojito.

See **Lola's** under *Dining Out* and **Offshore Ale Co.** and **Farm Neck Café** under *Eating Out*, all in Oak Bluffs, and **Atria** under *Dining Out* in Edgartown.

MOVIES ❋ ↑ **Capawock Movie House** (508-627-6689), Main Street, Vineyard Haven. Built in 1912 the Capawock is the oldest continually operating movie theater in Massachusetts (if you don't count its recent shuttering in 2005 and 2006). As entertaining as movies can be, though, you may be just as entertained by conversations before the film begins: Off-season, this is a hot place to hear island gossip, real estate prices, and political scoops. You'll also pick up lots of pertinent info on where to eat and where not to go.

⬆ **Strand Theater** (508-696-8300), Oak Bluffs Avenue, Oak Bluffs.

⬆ **Island Theater** (508-627-6689), Circuit Avenue, Oak Bluffs.

⬆ **Entertainment Cinema** (508-627-8008), 65 Main Street, Edgartown.

See also **Grange Hall** under *To See*.

✳ Selective Shopping

These entries are truly "selective," for they do not begin to scratch the surface of America's most popular vacation activity: shopping.

ART GALLERIES For a super-complete listing of artists and galleries, look for the free and excellent *Arts Directory* available in many galleries.

Carol Craven Gallery (508-693-3535), off of Holmes Hole Road, Vineyard Haven. Open May through October. This contemporary gallery is bursting at the seams with incredible art. Framed pieces are stacked all over

SHAW CRAMER GALLERY

the place for you to flip through, and hung floor-to-ceiling and wall-to-wall with the likes of nationally acclaimed artists like Thomas Hart Benton and John Sloane. You'll find landscapes, watercolors and mixed media, photography, and drawings. What you won't find is any schlock. Check it out; Carol Craven is to be applauded for amassing such a great collection.

❅ ◗ **Shaw Cramer Gallery** (508-696-7323; shawcramergallery.com), 56 Main Street (second floor), Vineyard Haven. Nancy Shaw Cramer's exceptional gallery features classic contemporary crafts and paintings by about 15 islanders and 50 off-islanders. (Nancy is a tapestry weaver herself.)

Etherington Fine Art (508-693-9696; etheringtonfineart.com), 71 Main Street, second floor, Vineyard Haven. Open seasonally. Mary Etherington's contemporary gallery is like a secret society that you can't ignore. Do stop in; the gallery has a very distinctive feeling. Mary represents some 50 island and nonisland artists, some abstractionists.

Alison Shaw Gallery (508-696-7429; alisonshaw.com), 88 Dukes County

Avenue, Oak Bluffs. Open seasonally. This prolific shooter started in abstract black and white imagery (for the Gazette) before moving to highly graphic color imagery. Her work these days is more painterly than postcardy. Alison also teaches workshops.

❋ ♘ **Craftworks** (508-693-7463; craftworksgallery.com), 42 Circuit Avenue, Oak Bluffs. These folks have a mixed but usually affordable selection of contemporary American crafts that's worth a look and always visually interesting. Clay, metal, glass, paper, and wood.

Belushi Pisano Gallery (508-696-8989; belushipisanogallery.com); call for new location in Edgartown. Contemporary fine art by local and national artists working in a variety of mediums.

Old Sculpin Gallery and Studio School (508-627-4881; oldsculpin gallery.org), corner of Dock and Daggett streets, Edgartown. Open late May to mid-October. Operated by the nonprofit Martha's Vineyard Art Association, the building was originally Dr. Daniel Fisher's granary, then a boat-

builder's workshop. Look for the long, wide depression in the main room where boatbuilder Manuel Swartz Roberts's feet wore down the floor as he moved along his workbench during the early 20th century. Paintings, photographs and sculpture of varying degrees of quality are exhibited. Classes for all ages are offered throughout the season.

❋ **North Water Gallery** (508-627-6002; northwatergallery.com), 27 North Water Street, Edgartown. Regional and national artists emphasizing Vineyard landscapes, seascapes, maritime scenes, figurative works, photography, and still lifes are represented here.

Eisenhouer Gallery (508-627-7003; eisenhauergallery.com), 38 North Water Street, Edgartown. From realistic marine paintings to bold expressionism, and a new collection of antiques.

Edgartown Art Galleries (508-627-6227;edgartownartgallery.com), 19 South Summer Street, Edgartown. Original paintings, giclees, and prints by nationally acclaimed artists like Ray Ellis, Eric Conklin, and Marjorie Mason.

❋ **Granary Gallery at the Red Barn** (508-693-0455;granarygallery.com), Old County Road, West Tisbury. In addition to folk art and landscape paintings, this gallery carries old and new photography. Look for classic photos by the venerable photographer Alfred Eisenstaedt (who came to the island on assignment for *Life* in 1937 and vacationed here until his death in 1995). Most artists represented here have some affiliation with the island.

Field Gallery (508-693-5595; field gallery.com), 1050 State Road, West Tisbury. Open April to late December, weather depending. Tom Maley's field of joyfully dancing figures, which seem

OLD SCULPIN GALLERY

FIELD GALLERY AND SCULPTURE GARDEN

to be celebrating the surrounding beauty, is an icon of the Vineyard's cultural life. Other Vineyard artists are exhibited during summer months;

receptions are held 5–7 on many Sundays June through August.

See also **Featherstone Center for the Arts** under *To Do*.

ARTISANS ❄ **Tuck & Holand Metal Sculptures** (508-693-3914;tuckandholand.com), 275 State Road, Vineyard Haven. Although Travis Tuck died in 2002, his partner and former apprentice Anthony Holand carries on as the exclusive maker of Tuck's famed weather vanes. Holand also creates wonderful original designs of his own, too. Despite the prices ($12,000 and up) and time required to painstakingly produce one (weeks and weeks), Anthony is already booked for the next 18 months. The client list includes Steven Spielberg, who owns an animated velociraptor, and President and Senator Clinton.

"ARTISTS POINTING THE WAY"

Claudia Miller (a talented artist and sculptor) has converted her highly successful Point Way Inn in Edgartown into an exciting venture. Claudia believes that it's "of great importance for creative individuals to use their talents to help guide humanity toward greater peace and compassion." She goes on, "I believe the world is at an important crossroads and that messages of greater tolerance and understanding can be spread through the artistic media of writing, painting, sculpture, dance, music, and the spoken word.

"The Vineyard arts organizations enrich all of our lives with the talented artists they invite to Martha's Vineyard." It's her firm hope that 'Artists Pointing the Way' gives "artists a peaceful place to spend time together, foster a connection with fellow artists, and ultimately deepen the appreciation for the creative process."

Artists Pointing the Way (508-939-8478; pointway.com), 104 Main Street and Pease's Point Way, Edgartown, hosts visiting artists and lecturers in a lovely sea captain's home. N.B. The house is not open to the public in general. During their time there, artists teach, perform, exhibit, and share their craft with others on this beloved island. Claudia expresses her eloquent desire: "Just as the Point Way Inn contributed to the lives of so many of our guests, it is our hope that 'Artists Pointing the Way' will be another opportunity to give back to Edgartown and the island community."

You can see examples of their work around the island, too. Check out the weather vanes atop the new Agricultural Hall in West Tisbury (a Holstein cow); Cronig's Market on State Road (a grasshopper, as a public market symbol); the Tisbury and Edgartown Town Halls (a whale tail and whaling ship, respectively); and the Vineyard Gazette building (a quill pen).

❋ **Chilmark Pottery** (508-693-6476), 195 Field View Lane, off State Road, opposite Nip-n-Tuck Farm, West Tisbury. In 1982 artist Geoffrey Borr established his studio in a weathered shingled barn where he and his staff transform thoughtfully designed, wheel-thrown creations into hand-painted pottery with distinctive seascape, oxblood, and copper red hues. You'll find functional and sculptural mugs, vases, and plates, as well as more unusual sculptural pieces.

Martha's Vineyard Glass Works (508-693-6026; mvglassworks.com), 683 State Road, West Tisbury. Open April through January. Many designers share this dynamic studio, a colorfully bold visual feast where you can watch the artists and apprentices at work.

BOOKSTORES ✎ **Edgartown Books** (508-627-8463), 44 Main Street, Edgartown. Open February through December. This charming independent bookshop has everything from travel and local fiction to books and activities for children.

❋ **Bunch of Grapes Bookstore** (508-693-2291; bunchofgrapes.com), 44 Main Street, Vineyard Haven. Although a devastating fire ripped through the adjacent restaurant and forced the closing of this beloved general bookstore in 2008, the bookstore expects to be opened for the 2009 season.

❋ **Book Den East** (508-693-3946; bookden.com), 71 New York Avenue (Vineyard Haven–Oak Bluffs Road), Oak Bluffs. Open year-round (Thursday through Sunday off-season). This turn-of-the-20th-century two-story barn—complete with wood shelves, wood floors, and wood crates—is chock-full of used, rare, and out-of-print hard-covers and paperbacks. No haggling allowed. The barn has that great old-book smell, which tells me that if I look long enough, I'm going to find something I can't live without.

CLOTHING ❋ **Black Dog General Store** (508-696-8182; theblackdog.com), behind the eponymous bakery, 3 Water Street, Vineyard Haven. The Black Dog rakes in tens of thousands of dollars daily in merchandise (sweatshirts, towels, caps, and so on). And they have all the bases covered: there are a total of nine stores on the island.

Bryn Walker (508-627-7715), 23 Kelly Street, Edgartown. Open April through December. Upscale but affordable, mix-and-match women's linen, and cotton clothing in updated styles and colors.

EDGARTOWN BOOKS

The Great Put-On (508-627-5495), Dock Street at Mayhew Lane, Edgartown. Open May through October. One of the island's most fashionable clothing stores stocks an impressive selection of dressy clothing for women, more shoes for women than for men, and unisex accessories like leather backpacks, loose jackets, and sweaters.

Pandora's Box (508-645-9696), 4 Basin Road (off North Road), Menemsha. Open May to mid-October. The emphasis here is on comfortable, contemporary women's clothing.

HOME FURNISHINGS ❋ Bramhall & Dunn (508-693-6437), 23 Main Street, Vineyard Haven. Nesting instincts are satisfied with hand-hooked rugs, picture frames, clothing, and colorful ceramics.

❋ **Midnight Farm** (508-693-1997; midnightfarm.net), 18 Water- Cronwell Lane, Vineyard Haven. Carly Simon's home furnishing store is located between Main Street and the ferry terminal. There are some well-chosen items here.

LeRoux (508-693-0030), Main Street, Vineyard Haven. This store is devoted to kitchen items, home goods, and furnishings.

Pik-Nik Antiques and Vintage Housewares (508-693-1366), 99 Dukes County Avenue (off New York Avenue), Oak Bluffs. Open seasonally. Fine art gallery and designer apparel boutique.

JEWELRY ❋ C. B. Stark (508-693-2284; cbstark.com), 53A Main Street, Vineyard Haven. Goldsmiths Cheryl Stark and Margery Meltzer have designed gold and silver jewelry with island motifs since 1966. Cheryl created the original grape design that has become so popular on the island. The shop also carries locally made wampum from quahog shells. Look for a shop in Edgartown, too.

SPECIAL SHOPS Allen Farm Sheep & Wool Company (508-645-9064; allenfarm.com), 421 South Road, Chilmark. Call ahead for hours or take your chances. Engaging in sustainable and organic farming practices, the Allen family has been raising black and white Corriendale sheep on these rolling fields for over 200 years. Their wool is custom spun and hand dyed and used by islanders to make sweaters, scarves, mittens, and the like.

❋ **Island Alpaca** (508-693-5554; islandalpaca.com), 1 Head of the Pond Road, off the Edgartown–Vineyard Haven Road, Oak Bluffs. These gentle creatures, about 30 in this herd at last count, are raised for breeding, sales, and for their fleece. It's as soft as cashmere, four times warmer, comes in more than 20 natural colors, and is hypoallergenic. The farm store sells all things alpaca. Inquire about spinning and knitting classes.

❋ **The Golden Door** (508-627-7740), 18 North Summer Street, Edgartown.

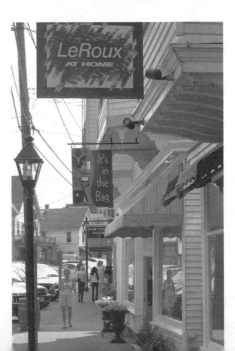

C. B. STARK

John Chirgwin spends half the year in Asia, leading tours and buying art. His Far East gallery is delightful; you'll find sculpture, furniture, jewelry, jade, and tribal objects.

Seaside Daylily Farm (508-693-3276; seasidelily.com), Great Plains Road, off Old County Road, West Tisbury. Open May to late September. These lilies are grown without the use of harmful chemicals that disrupt the ecosystem's natural balance.

Beadniks (508-693-7650; beadniks .com), 14 Church Street, Vineyard Haven. As they say, "Don't worry, bead happy" and "it's just a bead until you show up." Indeed, this fun place near the ferry can help you produce sophisticated, funky, or frivolous pieces of crafty custom jewelry.

Chilmark Chocolates (508-645-3013), State Road, near Beetlebung Corner, Chilmark. Open 11:30–5:30 Thursday through Sunday in summer; "closed for breaks in spring, winter, and fall." Good deeds and good products make an unbeatable combination. Not only will you love the creamy truffles and mouthwatering chocolates, it's nice to know that this chocolatier believes all members of society should be given a chance to be productive.

They hire people with disabilities to make and sell the chocolate. Try their Tashmoo Truffles or West Chomps or Squibnuggets.

❋ **Vineyard Photo** (508-627-9537), 20 Dock Street, Edgartown, and **Mosher Photo** (508-693-9430), 25 Main Street, Vineyard Haven.

❋ Special Events

The Vineyard has hundreds and hundreds of charming—great and small—special events throughout the year. A sampling of the larger, predictable, annual events follows. Contact the chamber of commerce (508-693-0085; mvy.com) for specific dates, unless an alternative phone number is listed below.

Mid-May through November: **Antiques at the Old Grange Hall** (508-696-7979). On most Fridays (9–3), but also on some Tuesdays and Saturdays.

Throughout the summer: **Vineyard Artisans Summer Festivals** (508-693-8989; vineyardartisans.com). Don't have time to pop into two dozen galleries? Then check this out. These excellent shows are held indoors and outdoors, rain or shine, weekly and biweekly at the Grange Hall in West Tisbury. Look for furniture, ceramics,

book arts, fiber arts, glass, jewelry, mixed media, painting, photography, printmaking, and sculpture. Shows are held 10–2 Sunday, June to early October, and on Thursday in July and August.

Early June–late August: **Flea in the Meadow Market**, West Tisbury School off of Old County Road, every Saturday and Wednesday from 8:30–3.

Mid-June–mid-October: **West Tisbury Farmer's Market** (508-693-8989), at Grange Hall, 9–noon Wednesday, late June to late August; and 9–noon Saturday, mid-June to mid-October.

Mid-June: **Oak Bluffs Harbor Festival** (508-693-3392). Since 1991.

July–August: **Community Sing** (508-693-0525). Singing and more at the Tabernacle, Methodist "campground," Oak Bluffs, every Wednesday at 8 PM. **Band concerts** every Sunday evening, alternating between Owen Park in Vineyard Haven and Ocean Park in Oak Bluffs.

Mid-July: **Edgartown Regatta**. Eleven different classes of boats have been racing since the mid-1920s.

Late July: **Book Sale** (508-693-3366). A benefit since the late '50s for the West Tisbury Library, held at the West Tisbury Elementary School on Old County Road.

Early August: **Edgartown House Tour** (508-627-7077). This event, sponsored by the Federated Church of Edgartown, opens up five antique houses in downtown Edgartown for tours every year. Tea and refreshments are served in the Old Parsonage at the end of the tour. $35.

Mid-September: **International Film Festival** (mvfilmfest.com). A laid but passionate, three-day celebration of films.

Mid-September–mid-October: **Striped Bass and Bluefish Derby**. When dozens of surf-casters begin furiously fishing from your favorite beach, you'll know it's derby time. Prizes are awarded for the largest fish caught each day, with a grand prize for the largest fish caught during the monthlong tournament. Weighing is done in Edgartown Harbor, just as it's been done every year since the mid-1940s.

Mid-September: **Tivoli Day** (508-696-7643). A lively street fair on Circuit Avenue in Oak Bluffs.

Mid-October: **Food & Wine Festival** (508-939-0880; mvfoodandwine.com), Edgartown. A three-day a fete of food and wine with cocktail parties, chef demonstrations, tastings, seminars, and a Sunday farmer's brunch.

Early–mid-December: **Christmas Events** (508-693-1151). Santa arrives by ferry in Vineyard Haven; there's also a chowder contest, horse and carriage rides, and "Christmas in Edgartown." **Vineyard Artisan Holiday Festival** (508-693-8989), at the Grange Hall, West Tisbury, from 10–4. More than 50 crafters and artists have gathered for this event since the mid-1960s.

New Year's Eve: **Last Night, First Day**. An alcohol-free, family-oriented celebration. Events in Vineyard Haven and Edgartown begin in the afternoon on December 31 and end with Edgartown Harbor fireworks.

Nantucket 7

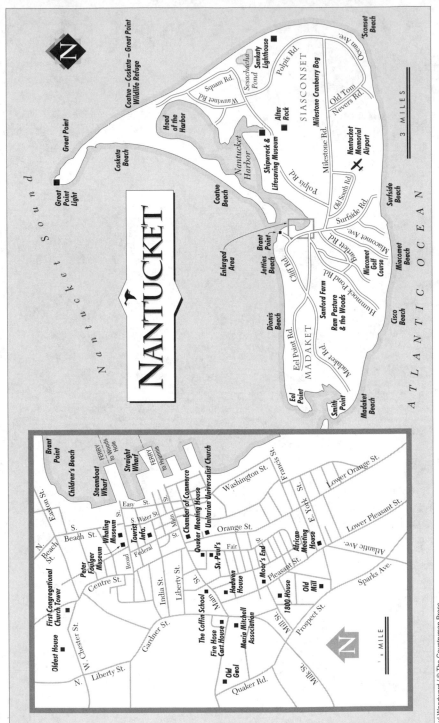

NANTUCKET

Coatue – Coskata – Great Point
Wildlife Refuge

Great Point

Nantucket Sound

Great Point Light

Coskata Beach

Head of the Harbor

Squam Rd.

Sesachacha Pond

Wauwinet Rd.

Sankaty Lighthouse

Polpis Rd.

'Sconset Beach

Ocean Ave.

SIASCONSET

Milestone Cranberry Bog

Nantucket Harbor

Shipwreck & Lifesaving Museum

Altar Rock

Old Tom Nevers Rd.

Milestone Rd.

Nantucket Memorial Airport

Coatue Beach

Enlarged Area

Jetties Beach

Brant Point

Cliff Rd.

Polpis Rd.

Old South Rd.

Surfside Rd.

Surfside Beach

Dionis Beach

Eel Point Rd.

Sanford Farm

Bartlett Rd.

Miacomet Golf Course

Miacomet Beach

ATLANTIC OCEAN

Eel Point

Madaket Rd.

MADAKET

Ram Pasture & the Woods

Hummock Pond Rd.

Cisco Beach

Smith Point

Madaket Beach

3 MILES

Brant Point

Easton St.

Children's Beach

Steamboat Wharf

FERRY to Woods Hole

Straight Wharf

FERRY to Hyannis

Washington St.

Francis St.

Lower Orange St.

N. Beach St.

S. Beach St.

Easy St.

S. Water St.

Chamber of Commerce

Unitarian Universalist Church

Whaling Museum

Tourist Info.

S. Main St.

Quaker Meeting House

Orange St.

E. York St.

Lower Pleasant St.

Peter Foulger Museum

Broad

Federal

St. Paul's

Fair

African Meeting House

Atlantic Ave.

First Congregational Church Tower

Centre St.

India St.

Liberty St.

Moor's End

Pleasant St.

Old Mill

Sparks Ave.

Oldest House

N. W. Chester St.

Gardner St.

The Coffin School

Fire Hose Cart House

Maria Mitchell Association

Hadwen House

1800 House

Prospect St.

Mill St.

N. Liberty St.

Old Gaol

Quaker Rd.

Milk St.

⅛ MILE

NANTUCKET

Thirty miles out to sea, Nantucket was called "that far away island" by Native Americans. Just 14 by 3.5 miles in area, Nantucket is the only place in America that is simultaneously an island, a county, and a town. In 1659 Thomas Mayhew, who had purchased Nantucket sight unseen (he was more interested in Martha's Vineyard), sold it to Tristram Coffin and eight of his friends for £30 and "two Beaver Hatts." These "original purchasers" quickly sold half shares to craftsmen whose skills they would require to build a community.

When Mayhew arrived, there were more than 3,000 Native American residents, who taught the settlers which crops to farm and how to spear whales from shore. By the early 1700s, the number of settlers had grown to more than 300, and the number of Natives had shrunk to less than 800, primarily because of disease. (The last Native descendant died on-island in 1854.)

In 1712, when Captain Hussey's sloop was blown out to sea, he harpooned the first sperm whale islanders had ever seen. For the next 150 years, whaling dominated the island's economy. The ensuing prosperity allowed the island's population to climb to 10,000. In comparison, there are also about 11,000 year-rounders today.

Nantucket sea captains traveled the world to catch whales and to trade, and they brought back great fortunes. By the late 1700s, trade was booming with England, and in 1791 the *Beaver*, owned by islander William Rotch, rounded Cape Horn and forged an American trade route to the Pacific Ocean. Fortunes were also made in the Indian Ocean—hence, Nantucket's India Street.

In its heyday, Nantucket Harbor overflowed with smoke and smells from blacksmith shops, cooperages, shipyards, and candle factories. More than 100 whaling ships sailed in and out of Nantucket. But when ships grew larger, to allow for their longer voyages at sea, they couldn't get across the shallow shoals and into Nantucket Harbor. The industry began moving to Martha's Vineyard and New Bedford. At the height of the whaling industry in 1846, the "Great Fire," which began in a hat shop on Main Street, ignited whale oil at the harbor. The catastrophic blaze wiped out the harbor and one-third of the town. Although most citizens began to rebuild immediately, other adventurous and energetic souls were enticed to go west in search of gold in 1849. When kerosene replaced whale oil in the 1850s as a less expensive fuel, it was the final blow to the island's maritime economy. By 1861 there were only 2,000 people on-island.

Although tourism began soon after the Civil War and picked up with the advent of the railroad to 'Sconset, the island lay more or less in undisturbed isolation until the 1950s. Perhaps it was the sleepiness of those 100 years that ultimately preserved the island's architectural integrity and community spirit, paving the way for its resurrection. In the late 1950s and early 1960s, islander and S&H Green Stamp heir Walter Beinecke Jr. organized a revitalization of the waterfront area, replacing decrepit wharf buildings with cottages. He also declared the premise that guides tourism to this day: It is preferable to attract one tourist with $100 than 100 tourists with $1 each. In accordance with the maxim, strict zoning laws were adopted, land-conservation groups were launched, and Nantucket's upscale tourism industry began in earnest.

By the late 1990s, the well-to-do set was forgoing the Hamptons and similar enclaves for Nantucket. By 2000 it had become too popular for its own good and was placed on the list of Most Endangered Historical Places, as decreed by the National Trust for Historic Preservation. In contrast to the Vineyard's showy excess and celebrity allure, Nantucket is a restrained haven for behind-the-scenes power brokers. In the recent past, mammoth multimillion-dollar trophy houses (and to be fair, some of the more understated ones, too) have belonged to people like the Gambles of Procter & Gamble, the Du Ponts, R. H. Macy, R. J. Reynolds, Bill Blass, David Halberstam, Graham Gund, Jack Welsh, Tommy Hilfiger, John Kerry, and Russell Baker. And now, downtown properties like the former Harbor House Hotel are being converted into one- to three-bedroom residences (aka condos) with hefty price tags. It was only a matter of time, I suppose, although many islanders are up in arms with dismay at what their island is fast becoming: a gated theme park for the rich. It's no longer enough to be a millionaire on Nantucket. Billionaires are the new millionaires.

In 1966 Nantucket was declared a national historic landmark: It boasts more than 800 buildings constructed before 1850—the largest concentration of such buildings in the United States. The historic district is picture-perfect: paved cobblestone streets, brick sidewalks, electrified "gas" street lamps. Gray-shingled houses are nestled close together on narrow lanes, which wind as you amble beyond the downtown grid of streets. Elegant white residences are trimmed with English boxwood hedges, white picket fences, and showcase flower gardens.

With a daily summer population that swells to 56,000, today's tourist industry is about as well oiled as the whale industry once was. It's difficult to find a grain of sand or a seashell that hasn't been discovered.

Most sites in Nantucket are within a mile of the historic center—you'll probably walk more than you're accustomed to. In addition to historic houses and museums, Nantucket prides itself on offering world-class dining. Although there are little pockets of settlements around the island, the only real "destination" is 'Sconset, an utterly quaint village with rose-covered cottages. Elsewhere on the island, more than 45 percent of the island's 10,000 acres are held by conservation trusts; you'll be able to explore places where

NANTUCKET HISTORICAL ASSOCIATION

most tourists don't venture. The island boasts excellent bicycle paths and almost limitless public beaches.

Nantucket is a year-round destination. Millions of daffodils blanket the island in yellow as the earth reawakens each April. The weather in May and June is slightly less predictable than in fall, but if you hit a nice stretch, you'll probably muse that life just doesn't get any better. Gardens are brightest in May and June. Where once there were whaling ships, yachts now fill the harbor in summer. Warm ocean water and beach barbecues beckon, wild roses trail along picket fences, and many special events are staged. Come September (my favorite month on-island), the crowds recede a bit. You can swim in the still-temperate ocean by day and not have to wait for a table at your favorite restaurant at night. Skies turn crisp blue, and cranberry bogs, heathlands, and the moors blaze red, russet, and maroon. Many restaurants that close in mid-October (at the end of Columbus Day weekend) reopen for the long Thanksgiving weekend. The first 3 weeks of November are very quiet indeed. Before the monochrome days of winter set in, there is one last burst of activity: Nantucket Noel and Christmas Stroll (see *Special Events*). In January, February, and March you'll discover why whaling captains called the island the "little grey lady"—she is often shrouded in fog. It's a time of reflection and renewal for year-rounders and visitors alike.

GUIDANCE ✳ **Nantucket Visitor Services & Information Bureau** (508-228-0925; nantucket-ma.gov), 25 Federal Street. Open 9–5 daily mid-April to early December, 9–5 Monday through Saturday off-season. The bureau also maintains seasonal kiosks at Straight Wharf.

✳ **Nantucket Island Chamber of Commerce** (508-228-1700; nantucketchamber .org), Zero Main Street. The second-floor chamber is open 9–5 weekdays. It produces a glossy book, *The Official Guide: Nantucket*, which is free on-island but costs $7 to mail in advance of your visit.

Nantucket Historical Association (508-228-1894; nha.org), 15 Broad Street. The NHA, which owns 23 historic properties representing island life from its farming beginnings to its prosperous whaling days, is a fabulous source of historical information. Generally, NHA properties are open 10–5 Monday through Saturday and noon–5 Sunday, late May to mid-October. Hours are shortened in winter and change from year to year. Most properties require a History Ticket ($18 adults,

$9 children 6–14), valid for admission to all properties. Purchase one at the Nantucket Whaling Museum (see *To See*).

MORE WEB SITES **Artsnantucket.com**. Look for their free color guide to the island's visual and performing arts.

Nantucketonline.com. Look for their 8 x 10 inch glossy publication, The Nantucket Guide & Travel Planner.

Nantucket.net. A complete guide.

Nantucket.plumtv.com. On-island, tune to Channel 22. On the Web you'll catch all sorts of fun videos about Nantucket, from the social scene, island life, and arts and entertainment to real estate, sports, and eating and drinking.

MEDIA The venerable *Inquirer and Mirror* (ack.net) has been published on Thursday since 1821.

The free weekly *Yesterday's Island* (yesterdaysisland.com) is useful for entertainment listings.

The Nantucket Independent (acknews.com) is a weekly newsprint for news, business, and the arts.

On-island, tune into **Channel 22** (508-228-8001, 4 North Water Street) and **Channel 17** (508-292-2203) to learn more about the island.

WNAN 91.1 (508-548-9600; cainan.org) is the NPR affiliate.

PUBLIC RESTROOMS Visitor Services & Information Bureau at 25 Federal Street (open year-round); Children's Beach (see *Green Space*) and Straight Wharf (both open seasonally).

PUBLIC LIBRARY See **Atheneum** under the sidebar "Quiet Time."

ATM Short on greenbacks? In town, look for automatic teller machines at the Pacific National Bank (61 Main Street), The Pacific Club (15 Main Street), the Steamship Authority terminal (Steamboat Wharf), and Nantucket Bank (2 Orange Street).

GETTING THERE With high-speed ferry service, day-tripping to Nantucket from Hyannis is more feasible than ever. Although I still recommend spending a few days on Nantucket, you are no longer shut out if you can't.

By bus: **Peter Pan/Bonanza** (508-775-6502; 888-751-8800; peterpanbus.com) travels from points south to Hyannis, where you can catch the boats. **Plymouth & Brockton** (508-778-9767; p-b.com) runs from Boston to Hyannis.

❊ *By boat from Hyannis:* **The Steamship Authority** (508-477-8600 for information and advance auto reservations; 508-771-4000 for day-of-sailing information in Hyannis; 508-228-0262 for day-of-sailing information on Nantucket; steamship authority.com), South Street Dock, Hyannis. The Steamship, established in 1948, carries autos, people, and bikes to Steamship Wharf year-round. Make car reservations in the spring for the summer if you can; no reservations are needed for passengers. There are six high-season sailings daily and three off-season. Parking in Hyannis is $10 to $15 per calendar day, depending on the time of year. The voyage takes 2¼ hours. Roundtrip fares: adults $33; children 5–12, $17(free under age 5);

PULLING INTO NANTUCKET HARBOR

bicycles $12. Cars cost a whopping $380 mid-May to late October, $260 off-season—but you really don't need one. Take it from me, a my-car-is-my-home-when-I-travel nut.

Steamship Authority's *Flying Cloud* **High Speed Passenger Boat** (508-495-3278; 508-477-8600), South Street Dock, Hyannis. Dock-to-dock in 1 hour. The boat sails early May through December and makes four to five trips daily; adults $65, children 5–12, $49. Reservations strongly suggested.

❋ **Hy-Line Cruises** (508-778-2600 in Hyannis; 508-228-3949 on Nantucket; 888-778-1132 for advance sales; hy-linecruises.com), Ocean Street Dock, Hyannis. Passengers and bicycles to Straight Wharf, mid-May to mid-October. There are three summertime boats daily, one to three daily off-season. Roundtrip fares are adults $39; children 5–12, $20; bicycles $12. Parking in Hyannis is $10–15 per calendar day.

❋ **Hy-Line's** *Grey Lady II* **High Speed Passenger Boat** (508-778-0404; 800-492-8082; hy-linecruises.com), Ocean Street Dock. This high-speed luxury catamaran costs a bit more, but it operates year-round: adults $71; children 12 and under, $50. Reservations are strongly recommended. There are five to six boats daily, with the last one departing at 7 or 8:45 PM, depending on time of year.

By boat from Harwich: **Freedom Cruise Line** (508-432-8999; nantucketisland ferry.com), Saquatucket Harbor in Harwich Port, provides daily passenger service to Nantucket, mid-May to early October and during the Christmas Stroll (see *Special Events*). During the summer, two of the three trips are scheduled so that you can explore Nantucket for about 6½ hours and return the same day. In spring and fall, there is only one morning boat daily. Reservations are highly recommended; make them 3 to 4 days in advance. Roundtrip prices: adults $64; children 2–12, $51; bicycles $12. Free parking for day-trippers; $15 daily thereafter. The trip takes 80 minutes each way.

By boat from Martha's Vineyard: **Hy-Line Cruises** (508-778-2600 in Hyannis; 508-228-3949 on Nantucket; 508-693-0112 in Oak Bluffs, Martha's Vineyard; hy-linecruises.com). One daily, interisland departures from mid-June to mid-September. The trip takes 90 minutes. (There is no interisland car ferry.) One-way: adults $31.50; children 5–12, $20; bicycles $9.

By air: **Cape Air** and **Nantucket Airlines** (508-771-6944; 800-352-0714; flycapeair.com) offer dozens of daily flights direct from Boston, Hyannis,

HY-LINE'S *GREY LADY II*

New Bedford, Providence (T. F. Green), and Martha's Vineyard. Frequent-flier coupon books for 10 one-way trips are available. **Island Air** (508-228-7575; 800-248-7779; islandair.net) offers daily, year-round flights from Hyannis.

GETTING AROUND *By shuttle:* 🏵 **NRTA Shuttle** (508-228-7025; shuttle nantucket.com). Buses daily 7 AM–11:30 PM late May to early October. This is an economical and reliable way to travel to 'Sconset (two routes) and Madaket, but the schedule is too complicated to disseminate here. Pick up a route map on-island. Shuttles have a bike rack, so you can take the bus out to 'Sconset, for instance, and ride back. The Surfside Beach and Jetties Beach buses run on a shorter season, from mid-June to early September. Tickets cost $1–2, depending on the route. Ask about multiday passes at the NRTA office at 3 East Chestnut Street.

By car or 4WD: There isn't a single traffic light in Nantucket, and Nantucketers intend to keep it that way. You don't need a car unless you're here for at least a week or unless you plan to spend most of your time in conservation areas or on outlying beaches. Even then, a four-wheel-drive vehicle is the most useful, as many of the stunning natural areas are off sandy paths. Nantucket is also ringed by 80 miles of beaches, most of which are accessible via four-wheel drive. Four-wheel drives are rented faster than the speed of light in summer, so make reservations at least a month in advance in summer. And lastly, parking is severely restricted in the historic center. Rent from my favorite company, **Affordable Rentals** (508-228-3501), 6 South Beach Street, early April through late December. Expect to pay $100–130 for a compact during the summer, $200–270 for a 4WD Jeep. **Nantucket Windmill Auto Rental** (508-228-1227; 800-228-1227) is based at the airport but also offers free pickup; **Hertz** (800-654-3131; hertz.com) is also based at the airport. Prices drop by almost half in the off-season.

If you get stuck in the sand, call **Harry's 24-hour Towing** (508-228-3390). Once you do call him, though, wait with your vehicle so he doesn't make the trek out to fetch you, only to find that you've been helped by a friendly local.

Contact the Police Department (508-228-1212), South Water Street, for **overland permits** ($125) required for four-wheel, oversand driving.

The Coatue–Coskata–Great Point nature area (see *Green Space*) requires a separate permit, available from the **Nantucket Conservation Foundation** (508-228-2884 information; 508-228-0006 gatehouse, where permits are purchased) mid-May through October ($125).

Most beaches are open to four-wheel-drive traffic, except when terns are nesting.

By taxi: Taxi fares can add up, but cabs are a useful way to get to the airport or to an outlying restaurant.

Try **All Point Taxi** (508-228-5779) or look for one when you disembark from the ferry. Taxis usually line up on lower Main Street and at Steamboat Wharf. Flat rates are based on the destination:

$19 to 'Sconset, $10 the airport, and $8 within town, for instance. Rates are for one person; add $1 for each additional passenger.

By bicycle: Bicycling is the best way to get around (see *To Do*).

By moped: **Nantucket Bike Shop** (508-228-1999; nantucketbikeshop.com), Steamboat Wharf, rents scooters April through October; $70 single, $90 double, daily.

On foot: ✒ **Architectural Walking Tours** (508-228-1387), by the Nantucket Preservation Trust. June through September, $10 adults, children free.

✒ See the Nantucket Whaling Museum for great walking tours sponsored by the **Nantucket Historical Association**.

By van or bus tours: ❋ **Ara's Tours** (508-228-1951; 508-221-6852; arastours.com) offers a 90-minute island tour for $20 that make stops for photography. On a clear day you can see all three lighthouses. For those that have more time and money (like $300 per carload, for 6 to 8 people), ask about the 3-hour barrier beach tours of Great Point (see *Green Space*).

🐾 **Trustees of Reservations** (508-228-6799; thetrustees.org) offers excellent 2½-hour natural history tours of Great Point from mid-May to mid-October. Tours depart at 9:30 AM and 1:30 PM and culminate with an ascent of the Great Point Lighthouse. Adults $40; children 12 and under, $15; reservations strongly recommended.

Barrett's Tours (508-228-0174), 20 Federal Street, and **Nantucket Island Tours** (508-228-0334), Straight Wharf, offer 75-minute narrated mini-bus tours May through October. Adults $20, children 5–12, $8. 4 and under free.

MEDICAL EMERGENCY **Nantucket Cottage Hospital** (508-228-1200), 57 Prospect Street. Open 24 hours.

Lyme disease. Ticks carry this disease, which has flu-like symptoms and may result in death if left untreated. Immediately and carefully remove any ticks that may have migrated from dune grasses to your body. Better yet, wear long pants, tuck pants into socks, and wear long-sleeved shirts whenever possible when hiking. Avoid hiking in grassy and overgrown areas of dense brush.

❋ To See

ON THE HARBOR **The wharves** (from north to south). The Steamship Authority is based at **Steamboat Wharf**, but from 1881 to 1917, steam trains, which met the early steam-powered ferries and transported passengers to Surfside and

A PERFECT DAY TRIP TO NANTUCKET

8:15 Board a high-speed ferry in Hyannis.

9:30 Get fresh-squeezed concoctions and treats from The Juice Bar.

10:00 Take a walking tour with the Nantucket Historical Association.

11:45 Learn the island's rich history at the Nantucket Whaling Museum.

1:15 Split an oversized sandwich from Provisions with your companion.

2:00 Take an island driving tour with Nantucket Island Tours.

3:15 Shop and stroll along cobblestone streets; pop into the Atheneum.

6:15 Enjoy regional cuisine at American Seasons, Oran Mor, or the Boarding House.

8:40 Take the last high-speed ferry back to Hyannis.

'Sconset, originated here. **Old North Wharf** is home to privately owned summer cottages. **Straight Wharf**, originally built in 1723 by Richard Macy, is a center of activity. It was completely rebuilt in the 1960s (except for the Thomas Macy Warehouse; see below) as part of a preservation effort. The wharf is home to Hy-Line, a few T-shirt and touristy shops, restaurants, a gallery, a museum, a nice pavilion area, and charter boats and sailboats. Straight Wharf was so named because folks could cart things from here "straight" up Main Street. **Old South Wharf** houses art galleries, crafts shops, and clothing shops in quaint little one-room "shacks" (see *Selective Shopping*). **Commercial Wharf**, also known as Swain's Wharf, was built in the early 1800s by Zenas Coffin.

Thomas Macy Warehouse, Straight Wharf. Built after the Great Fire of 1846, when the wharves were completely destroyed and more than 400 houses burned, the warehouse stored supplies to outfit ships.

Main Street

The lower three blocks of Main Street were paved in 1837 with cobblestones, purchased in Gloucester, that proved quite useful—they kept carts laden with whale oil from sinking into the sand and dirt as they were rolled from wharves to factories. After the Great Fire swept through town, Main Street was widened considerably to prevent future fires from jumping from house to house so rapidly. In the mid-1850s Henry and Charles Coffin planted dozens of elm trees along the street, but only a few have survived disease over the years. The former drinking fountain for horses, which today spills over with flowers, has been a landmark on Lower Main since it was moved here in the early 1900s.

Pacific Club, Main Street at South Water Street. This three-story, Georgian brick building was built as a warehouse and countinghouse for shipowner William Rotch, owner of the *Beaver* and *Dartmouth*, two ships that took part in the Boston Tea Party. In 1789 it served as a U.S. Customs House. In 1861 a group of retired whaling captains purchased the building for use as a private social club, where they swapped stories and played cribbage. Descendants of these original founders carried on the tradition of the elite club. Until the 1980s.

Pacific National Bank (508-228-1917), 61 Main Street at Fair Street. This 1818, two-story, Federal-style brick building is one of only four to survive the Great Fire. It's no coincidence that the two important buildings anchoring Main Street are named "Pacific" for the fortunes reaped from the Pacific Ocean: This bank almost single-handedly financed the wealthy whaling industry. Step inside to see the handsome main room, original teller cages, and murals of the port and street scenes.

Thomas Macy House, 99 Main Street. Many think this is Nantucket's most attractive doorway, with its silver doorplate, porch railing that curves outward, and wooden fanwork. This NHA (Nantucket Historical Association) property is open to the public on special occasions.

"Three Bricks," 93, 95, and 97 Main Street. These identical Georgian mansions were built in 1836 for the three sons (all under the age of 27) of whaling-ship magnate Joseph Starbuck. Joseph retained the house titles to ensure that his sons would continue the family business. When the sons approached age 40 (firmly entrenched in the business), Joseph deeded the houses to them. One house remains in the Starbuck family; none is open to the public.

ONE OF "THREE BRICKS"

Hadwen House (508-228-1894; nha .org), 96 Main Street. Taken together, 94 Main (privately owned) and 96 Main are referred to architecturally as the Two Greeks. Candle merchant William Hadwen married one of Joseph Starbuck's daughters and built the Greek Revival house (at No. 96. Starbuck's two other daughters also ended up living across the street from their brothers—at 92 and 100 Main Street—creating a virtual Starbuck compound). Docents point out gas chandeliers, a circular staircase, Italian marble fireplaces, silver doorknobs, and period furnishings. Don't overlook the lovely historic garden in back. The "other" Greek (No. 94) was built in the mid–19th century for Mary G. Swain, Starbuck's niece; note the Corinthian capitals supposedly modeled after the Athenian Temple of the Winds. This is another NHA property (see *Guidance* for hours and fees). Combo pass for the museum, Hadwen House, and Quaker Meeting House is $18 for adults, $9 children.

Henry Coffin House and **Charles Coffin House**, 75 and 78 Main Street. The Coffin brothers inherited their fortunes from their father's candle-making and whaling enterprises and general mercantile business. They built their houses across the street from each other, using the same carpenters and masons. Charles was a Quaker, and his Greek Revival house (No .78) has a simple roof walk and modest brown trim. Henry's late-Federal-style house (No. 75) has fancy trim around the front door and a cupola. Neither is open to the public.

John Wendell Barrett House, 72 Main Street. This elegant Greek Revival house features a front porch with Ionic columns and a raised basement. Barrett was the president of the Pacific National Bank and a wealthy whale oil merchant, but the house is best known for another reason. During the Great Fire, Barrett's wife, Lydia, refused to leave the front porch. Firefighters wanted to blow up the house in order to deprive the fire of fuel. Luckily for her, the winds shifted and further confrontation was averted. Not open to the public.

North of Main Street

⚓ **Nantucket Whaling Museum** (508-228-1736; nha.org), 15 Broad Street. Open daily, late May to early October; weekends, early spring and late autumn; Saturday in winter for a lecture and self-guided tour at 1:30. This 1846 brick building, another NHA property (see *Guidance* for hours), is a must-see on even the shortest itinerary. It began life as Richard Mitchell's spermaceti candle factory, and as such, it now tells the story of the candle factory and preserves a bit of Nantucket's whaling history (in Gosnell Hall—see below). Spermaceti, by the way, is a substance found in the cavity of a sperm whale's head; it was a great source of lamp and machine oil. During the restoration of the original candle factory in 2004, the NHA discovered an original beam press and the base of the factory triworks. (It's the only one in the world still in its original location.) So, the story the museum can tell grows even richer. You can also see the lens from the Sankaty Head Lighthouse, as well as an entire exhibit about the *Essex* whaling ship. **Gosnell Hall** houses a 46-foot sperm whale skeleton and a fully rigged whale boat—which will

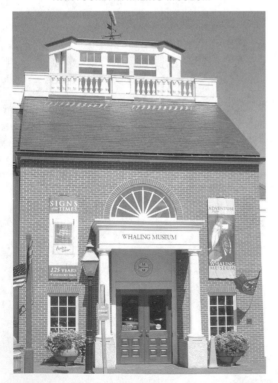

NANTUCKET WHALING MUSEUM

help you envision the treacherous "Nantucket sleigh ride." When the small boat harpooned a mammoth whale and remained connected by a rope, the boat was dragged through the waves until the whale tired. **Peter Foulger Gallery** is named for one of the island's first settlers who acted as an interpreter when the settlers purchased the island from Native Americans in 1659. Peter's daughter Abiah was Ben Franklin's mother. Adults $15, children $8; History Tickets with guided walking tours are an additional $10 for adults and $4 for children. Combo pass for the museum, Hadwen House, and Quaker Meeting House is $18 for adults, $9 children.

Centre Street was referred to as Petticoat Row during the whaling era, when men went out to sea and women were left to run the shops and businesses. It's still chock-full of fine shops.

FIRST CONGREGATIONAL CHURCH

First Congregational Church Tower (508-228-0950; nantucketfcc.org), 62 Centre Street. Church open 10–4 Monday through Saturday, mid-May to mid-October; tower open "weather permitting." This church is known for its 120-foot steeple, from which there are 360-degree panoramic views of the island and ocean. The climb to the top is 94 steps—not that I've counted or anything. On a clear day you can see from Eel Point to Great Point (see *Green Space*), and all the moors in between. Serious photographers shouldn't get too excited, though, because they'll have to shoot through dirty storm windows.

The present steeple was built in 1968; the previous one was dismantled in 1849 when it was deemed too shaky to withstand storms. The church was built with whaling money at the industry's apex in 1834. Note the things money could buy: a 600-pound brass chandelier and trompe l'oeil walls. The rear wing of the church contains the simple vestry, the oldest church building on the island (circa 1720). Donation suggested for climbing the steeple: $2.50 adults, 50¢ children.

⚘ Oldest House (508-228-1894; nha.org), Sunset Hill Road. Also known as the **Jethro Coffin House**, this 1686 home was built as a wedding present for Jethro Coffin and Mary Gardner by their parents. Peter Coffin cut and shipped timbers from his land in Exeter, New Hampshire, for the house. The marriage joined two prominent island families—the Coffins were "original purchasers" while the Gardners were "half-share men." Features include small, diamond-shaped, leaded windows, sparse period furnishings, and a huge central chimney decorated with an upside-down horseshoe. When lightning struck the house in 1987, the NHA (see *Guidance* for hours and fees) decided it was time to restore it.

Brant Point Lighthouse, off Easton Street. In 1746 the island's first "lighthouse" (and the country's second oldest, after Boston Light) guarded the harbor's northern entrance. It was rather primitive, consisting of a lantern hung on rope between two poles. The lighthouse standing today is small in size but large in symbolism. Folklore and tradition suggest that throwing two pennies overboard as you round the point at the lighthouse ensures your return. Many throw two pennies, and many return. Don't pass up the chance to catch a sunset from here; it's the reason you came to Nantucket in the first place.

Near or Off Upper Main Street

Quaker Meeting House (508-228-1894; nha.org), 7 Fair Street. Open late April to mid-October. This small, simple building with wooden benches and 12-over-12 windows began as a Friends school in 1838. NHA property (see *Guidance* for hours). Combo pass for the museum, Hadwen House, and Quaker Meeting House is $18 for adults, $9 children.

Nantucket Historical Association Research Library (508-228-1894; 508-228-1655 library; nha.org), 7 Fair Street. Open 10–4 weekdays. Behind the Meeting House, this library contains Edouard A. Stackpole's collection of manuscripts, photographs, ships' logs, and other items. $5 per visit.

St. Paul's Episcopal Church (508-228-0916), 20 Fair Street. Stop in to admire this granite church's Tiffany windows.

❋ **Unitarian Universalist Church** (508-228-5466), 11 Orange Street. Open 10–2 weekdays, July and August, or by appointment during the rest of the year; the office is also open weekday mornings the rest of the year, so you're welcome to stop in. This 1809 church, also called **South Church**, is known for its tall spire (quite visible at sea and a distinct part of the Nantucket "skyline"); a wonderfully illusory trompe l'oeil golden dome; and a mahogany and ivory 1831 Goodrich organ. Orange Street was once home to more than 100 whaling captains, and for years, a town crier watched for ships (and fires) from this tower.

🐚 **The Coffin School** (508-228-2505; eganmaritime.org), 4 Winter Street, one block off Main Street. Open 10–4 daily, late May to mid-October. The school was founded in 1827 by Admiral Sir Isaac Coffin, English baronet and a descendant of Tristram Coffin, one of the island's first settlers. It was established to provide a "good English education" for Coffin descendants. (In the early 19th century, more than half of Nantucket's children were Coffin descendants.) The impressive brick Greek Revival building now serves as home for the **Egan Maritime Institute**, displaying special exhibits related to Nantucket history. A fine collection of 19th-century paintings portraying significant Nantucket events is featured, including works by Elizabeth R. Coffin, a student of Thomas Eakins.

BRANT POINT LIGHTHOUSE

Historical lectures on the school and maritime subjects are given year-round.
Admission $5 adults, $3 students; price also includes admission to the Nantucket
Shipwreck and Lifesaving Museum (see *Around the Island*).

See also **Lightship Basket Museum** under the sidebar "Lightship Baskets."

Beyond Upper Main Street

Fire Hose Cart House (508-228-1894; nha.org), 8 Gardner Street. Open daily.
This small 1886 neighborhood fire station is the only one of its kind remaining on-
island. As you can imagine, lots of stations were built after the Great Fire. On display are leather buckets and an old hand pumper, used more than a century ago.
NHA property (see *Guidance* for hours); self-guided.

Old Gaol (508-228-1894; nha.org), 15R Vestal Street. This 1806 penal institution,
built of logs bolted together with iron, was used until 1933. It had only four cells.
The first incarcerated felon escaped (a 15 year old climbed out the chimney), but
others weren't so lucky. Well, perhaps they were—it's said that the last prisoners
got to sleep at home rather than on the planks that served as beds. NHA property
(see *Guidance* for hours); self-guided.

❀ ♪ **Maria Mitchell Association** (MMA; 508-228-9198; mmo.org), 4 Vestal
Street. Open 9–5 weekdays. Founded in 1902, the association owns six properties
that celebrate the life and continue the work of Maria (pronounced *mar-EYE-a*)
Mitchell, born on-island August 1, 1818. At age 13 Maria helped whaling captains
set their navigational devices, with the aid of astronomical projections. At 18 she
became the librarian at the Atheneum, where she served for the next 20 years. At
29 Mitchell was the first woman to discover a comet (which was dubbed Mitchell's
comet)—from atop the Pacific National Bank, where her father (bank president
and amateur astronomer) had set up an observatory. Maria was also the first
woman to be admitted to the American Academy of Arts and Sciences and the first
woman college professor of astronomy. (She taught at Vassar from 1865 until her
death in 1888.)

The association hosts a number of children's programs that foster an appreciation
of the connection between science and "beauty and poetry." Also, look for postings
of special lectures and walks sponsored by the group; I've never been to one that
was less than excellent. A combination ticket (available at any of the properties)
costs $10 adults and $8 children 6–14, but tickets may also be purchased separate-
ly ($5 and $4, respectively).

❀ ♪ **Maria Mitchell Science Library** (508-228-9219; mmo.org), 2 Vestal Street.
Call for hours. This library, which has a children's section, houses 19th-century science books, current scientific periodicals, Maria's own papers, and natural history
and astronomy books. Maria's father taught navigation by the stars in this former
schoolhouse. Free.

Maria Mitchell Birthplace (508-228-2896; mmo.org), 1 Vestal Street. Open
10–4 Monday through Saturday, mid-June to early September; Friday and Saturday until mid-October. Built in 1790, Mitchell's birthplace contains family memorabilia and the telescope she used to spot her comet. Tour the house and check out
the island's only public roof walk. Adults $5, children $4.

♪ **Natural Science Museum & Shop** (508-228-0898; mmo.org), 7 Milk Street.
Open 10–4 Monday through Saturday, mid-June to early September; Friday and
Saturdays only, early September to mid-October. See displays of Nantucket's natu-

ral history and visit the live animal room to meet frogs, turtles, snakes, spiders, insects, fish, and other island creatures. Adults $5, children $4.

❊ **Loines Observatory** (508-228-9273; mmo.org), 59 Milk Street Extension. Open on clear Monday, Wednesday, and Friday evenings year round (call to confirm days), when lectures and telescope viewings are held at 9 PM. Climb a ladder to the eyepiece of a fine, old telescope and sample the sights of the distant heavens. You'll also have the opportunity to see MMA's new, 24-inch research telescope as well. Adults $10, children $6.

✐ **Maria Mitchell Aquarium & Museum Shop** (508-228-5387; mmo.org), 28 Washington Street. Open 10–4 Monday through Saturday, mid-June to mid-September. Once a railroad station ticket office for the Nantucket Railroad, the MMA Aquarium has grown into a much-loved island resource. Visitors have the opportunity to learn about Nantucket's marine ecology through firsthand experience with many of the organisms that inhabit our coastal areas. The expanded aquarium complex contains twenty saltwater tanks in three buildings, an orientation area for dry exhibits and small group instruction, and two large "touch tanks" for curious hands. Visitors might count the eyes of a scallop, watch a channeled whelk feeding on a mollusk, or see baby squid hatching. Call about the wildly popular Marie Ecology and Beachcombing Walks. Adults $6, children $5.

Old Mill (508-228-1894; nha.org), South Mill and Prospect streets. Reputed to be made with salvaged wood, this 1746 Dutch-style windmill has canvas sails and a granite stone that still grinds corn in summer. A reminder of when the island's principal activity was farming, this windmill is the only remaining of the four originals. (It's in its original location, too.) NHA property; tours on the hour and half hour. (See *Guidance* for hours and fees.)

African Meeting House (508-228-9833; afroammuseum.org), 29 York and Pleasant streets. Open to the public July and August, 11–3 Tuesday through Saturday, 1–3 Sunday. Built as a church and a schoolhouse in the 1820s, when Black children were barred from public school, this house is thought to be the second oldest such building in the country. Boston's Museum of Afro-American History presents cultural programming and interpretive exhibits on the history of African Americans on Nantucket. They also publish a very good pamphlet with a walking tour of the island's Black heritage sites.

Moor's End, 19 Pleasant Street. This large 1830s Georgian house—the first island house made with brick—belonged to Jared Coffin. Although today it's among the island's finest, Mrs. Coffin was not satisfied with its location. She wanted to be closer to

THE OLD MILL

GREAT POINT LIGHT

town, and so Jared built another at 29 Broad Street (see Jared Coffin House under *Lodging*). A beautiful garden lies behind the tall brick wall, but unfortunately for us, like the house, it's private.

Around the Island

Great Point Light, Great Point, is accessible by four-wheel-drive vehicle, by boat, or by a difficult 5-mile (one-way) trek through soft sand. A 70-foot stone structure guarded the island's northeastern tip for 166 years, until a ferocious storm destroyed it in 1984. This new one was built to withstand 20-foot waves and 240 mph winds.

Madaket. When Thomas Macy landed here in 1659, he found poor soil and didn't stay long. Today there is a large summer community and many rental houses. On the western coast, Madaket is a great place to enjoy a sunset, do some bluefishing, or get a boat repaired in the boatyard. The picturesque creek is best viewed from the little bridge to the right of the main road.

✒ ⌂ **Nantucket Shipwreck & Lifesaving Museum** (508-228-1885; nantucket lifesavingmuseum.org), 158 Polpis Road on Folger's Marsh. Open 10–4 daily, early July to mid-October. This building replicates the original 1874 Surfside Lifesaving Service station that survives today as the Nantucket Hostel (see *Lodging*). Instead of being at water's edge, however, it's scenically situated on a salt marsh—perfect for a picnic. Dedicated to humanity's dramatic efforts against the relentless sea, this museum houses equipment used in the daring rescues of sailors stranded in their sinking offshore boats. You'll find one of three Massachusetts Humane Society lifesaving surfboats and the only surviving beachcart still used for demonstration drills. You'll also find photographs, accounts of rescues, Nantucket's three Fresnel lighthouse lenses, and artifacts from the *Andrea Doria*, which sank off Nantucket almost half a century ago. $5 adults, $3 children 6 and older.

LIFESAVING STATION

✳ To Do

BICYCLING/RENTALS ✒ Excellent paved, two-way bicycle paths lead to most major "destinations." If you're riding on the street, ride in the direction of traffic or you'll be fined. Or walk your bike.

Madaket Bike Path begins on Upper Main Street. This 6-mile (one-way) road takes you to the western end of Nantucket in 45 minutes. Although the route is a bit hilly and winding, it's beautiful. There are rest areas along the way and a water fountain at the halfway point, picnic tables at Long Pond (see *Green Space*), and usually elegant swans, too.

Dionis Bike Path is a 1-mile spur trail off the Madaket Bike Path that runs to Dionis Beach. Getting to the beach has never been easier.

'Sconset (or Milestone) Bike Path begins at the rotary east of the historic district. This 6.5-mile (one-way) route with slight inclines parallels Milestone Road; it takes about an hour to get to 'Sconset. (Visually, the ride is a bit dull.) There's a water fountain at the rotary.

DECIDING THE WAY IS EASY (OR HARD?)

Surfside Bike Path. Take Main Street to Pleasant Street and turn right onto Atlantic Avenue to Surfside Road. This flat path is very popular in summer; it takes about 20 minutes to get to the beach. And just in case you want to pause, there are benches along the 2.5-mile (one-way) route.

Polpis Road Path. The loop from the 'Sconset Bike Path to Polpis Road and back to town is about 16.5 miles. It's definitely worth the detour, especially in spring-time when it's lined with thousands of daffodils.

Cliff Road Bike Path begins on Cliff Road from North Water Street. This 2.5-mile, slightly hilly road passes large summer homes.

With more than 2,500 rental bikes on-island, companies offer competitive rates. Average prices: $25 daily for adult bikes, $100 weekly; kid's bikes, trailers, zipper strollers, and trail-a-bikes, too. Inquire about discounts for family rentals. The following shops rent bicycles: **Young's Bicycle Shop** (508-228-1151; youngsbicycle shop.com), 6 Broad Street, Steamboat Wharf; **Nantucket Bike Shop** (508-228-1999; nantucketbikeshop.com), 4 Broad Street, Steamboat Wharf; and **Cook's Cycles** (508-228-0800), 6 South Beach. Young's has the longest season, but Cook's is often a bit less expensive.

See also **Eco Guides** under *Outdoor Adventure*.

BIRD-WATCHING **Maria Mitchell Association** (508-228-9198; mmo.org), 1 Vestal Street, offers a regular schedule of birding walks all over the island, late spring to early fall, and by appointment in the off-season. Adults $10, children $6. Some people think that Nantucket offers the best wintertime bird-watching on the East Coast. I wouldn't argue.

See also **Eco Guides** under *Outdoor Adventure*.

BOAT EXCURSIONS/RENTALS *Endeavor* (508-228-5585; endeavorsailing .com), Slip 15, Straight Wharf. May through October. Captain Jim Genthner and his wife, Sue, operate a 31-foot Friendship sloop that departs on at least three daily harbor tours and a sunset cruise. Adults $25–35 for a 90-minute sail; $15 for a 60-minute sail. Custom sails may include pirating for children and an onboard fiddler or storyteller.

Nantucket Boat Rentals (508-325-1001), Straight Wharf, Slip 1. You don't have to be macho to handle one of these little boats that can take you across the harbor to Coatue, where you can sunbathe and picnic in relative quiet. Leave in the morning when there's less wind. Jeff has been renting runabouts and powerboats daily or weekly in-season since 1990.

✍ **Nantucket Island Community Sailing** (508-228-6600; nantucketcommunity sailing.org), Jetties Beach, rents Windsurfers, Sunfish, kayaks, and large sailboats, and it holds youth, sailboard, sailing, and racing classes. For really unique thing to do, take a class in how to sail a replica 19th-century whaleboat. Mid-June to early September.

COOKOUTS Contact the **Fire Department** (508-228-2324), 131 Pleasant Street, for the requisite permits for charcoal cookouts.

QUIET TIME

❋ ✍ ☂ ⁱ **Atheneum** (508-228-1110; nantucketatheneum.org), 1 India Street. Open 9:30–5 Monday, Wednesday, Friday, and Saturday; 9:30–8 Tuesday and Thursday; closed Monday off-season. Public Internet access. This fine Greek Revival building with Ionic columns was designed by Frederick Coleman, who designed the "Two Greeks" (see Hadwen House under *To See*). When the library and all its contents were lost in the Great Fire (1846), donations poured in from around the country and a new building replaced it within six months. The Great Hall on the second floor has hosted such distinguished orators as Frederick Douglass, Daniel Webster, Horace Greeley, Henry David Thoreau, Ralph Waldo Emerson, and John James Audubon. (The hall seats about 100 people; there are numerous free readings and lectures here.) Maria Mitchell (see Maria Mitchell Association under *To See*) was the first librarian. Since then there have been, amazingly, only seven other librarians in its long history. In addition to comfortable reading rooms on both floors, the Atheneum has an excellent children's wing and a nice garden out back. Some of the more than 50,000 volumes include town newspapers dating from 1816, early New England genealogy, and ships' logs. Portraits of whaling captains grace the space, while display cases are filled with scrimshaw and other historical artifacts. This is one of the island's most special places. It's a quiet refuge from the masses in the height of summer, as well as a delightful place to spend a rainy day. Call for information about special events and story hours.

FISHING/SHELLFISHING Permits for digging clams, mussels, and quahogs are obtained from the Marine Department and shellfish warden (508-228-7261), 34 Washington Street. Scalloping season opens October 1, after which you'll see fishermen in the harbor and off nearby shoals of Tuckernuck Island; local scallops harvested from mid-October through March are delicious.

Try your luck freshwater fishing at **Long Pond** (see *Green Space*). Nantucket blues, which run in schools from May to October, are caught from the southern shore. Fishing isn't as good in July and August when the waters are warmer; but if that's the only time you're here, toss out a line anyway. No fishing licenses are needed for Nantucket.

Mike Monte (508-228-0529), a year-round islander, takes people surf-fishing and fly-fishing May through October. His daily trip generally goes out with "first light" at sunrise, and he has folks back in time to have breakfast with their friends and family. He'll take from one to four people, and he provides all equipment.

Bill Fisher Tackle (508-228-2261), 3 Polpis Road, rents a full line of equipment, supplies daily fishing reports, and provides guide service.

Most charters in search of striped bass and bluefish are located on Straight Wharf, including ***Herbert T*** (508-228-6655), Slip 14, and ***Just Do It Too*** (508-228-7448), Slip 13.

GOLF Siasconset Golf Club (508-257-6596), Milestone Road. Open late May to mid-October. This nine-hole public course, encircled by conservation land, dates to 1894.

❋ **Miacomet Golf Course** (508-325-0333), off Somerset Road. This flat, eighteen-hole course is owned by the Land Bank and has views of Miacomet Pond, heathland, and the coastline.

Sankaty Head Golf Club (508-257-6655), 100 Polpis Road, 'Sconset. Although this links-style, 18-hole course is private, the public may play from mid-April to late May and from mid-October to early December. There are magnificent lighthouse views. This course operates the country's only caddy camp (for boys age 13–17), and it has done so since the early 1930s.

Nantucket Golf Club (508-257-8500), 250 Milestone Road (there's no sign). One of the most exclusive clubs anywhere. Many members, like gazillionaire Bill Gates, do not own property on-island, but rather jet in, play golf, and jet out. Memberships cost hundreds of thousands of dollars, plus annual dues. The membership list is

FISHING CHARTERS ARE PLENTIFUL

closely guarded, of course, but it has its share from the Forbes 400 Wealthiest Americans list. As for the golf, the par-72, links-style course rolls with the naturally undulating landscape, within sight of Sankaty Head Light, on the moors with scrub oak and pitch pine. Generally appreciated by island conservationists, who realize that it could have been developed in less favorable ways, the 350-acre course was designed by Rees Jones.

IN-LINE SKATING Summertime skating is prohibited in town. You can skate on bike paths and at the skateboarding park at Jetties Beach; helmets and pads are required.

OUTDOOR ADVENTURE ❊ ✿ **Eco Guides** (508-228-1769; strongwings.org). Casual, customized adventure instruction and guided group trips, for novices and experts, in birding, climbing, mountain biking, sea kayaking, and natural history. After settling on a trip, price, and meeting time with John, be absolutely sure that you confirm and reconfirm your trip. There is also a large youth organization geared toward year-rounders, but vacationing kids can participate, too.

SCUBA DIVING ❊ **The Sunken Ship** (508-228-9226; sunkenship.com), 12 Broad Street. Perhaps because the *Andrea Doria* sank off Nantucket's treacherous shoals in July 1956, the island attracts Atlantic Ocean divers. This full-service dive shop has the market cornered with charters, lessons, rentals, and even fishing referrals.

SEAL CRUISES ❊ **Shearwater Excursions** (508-228-7037; explorenantucket .com), Straight Wharf, Slip 1011, has daily departures, weather permitting, to see lounging seals on the outer island of Muskeget. Tours are 2½ hours; adults $90, children under 12, $70.

SURFING **Force 5 Watersports** (508-228-0700), 6 Union Street, a retail surf shop with a knowledgeable staff, is a good source of information, too. Surfing is best on the southern beaches.

TENNIS Free, public courts are open at **Jetties Beach** (see *Green Space*) from early September to mid-June; from mid-June to late August the courts cost $20 an hour. Sign up at the **Parks and Recreation Building** (508-228-7213), North Beach Street, for one of six courts. Clinics and lessons are offered for adults and children.

Great Harbor Yacht Club (508-228-3700), 23 Nobadeer Farm Road. Open May to mid-October. A full-service place, with nine clay courts, a pro shop, round-robins (in summer), and rentals.

✳ Even More Things to Do

FITNESS CLUB ✳ **Nantucket Health Club** (508-228-4750), 10 Young's Way. Open daily. A full array of machines, free weights, classes, and personalized training sessions. $25 day-use fee; $180 for 10 visits.

FOR FAMILIES ✎ **Strong Wings Summer Camp** (508-228-1769; strongwings .org), late June to late August. This weekly action-filled day camp for kids age 5–15 has a 5-day option that might include sea kayaking, rock climbing, snorkeling, biking, ghost stories, crafts, and nature exploration—depending on the child's age.

✳ ✎ **Nantucket Babysitters Service** (508-228-4970; nantucketbabysitters.com) provides parents a respite. Ronnie Sullivan-Moran assesses your needs, matches a sitter to your kids (all ages), and then sends the sitter to wherever you're staying. She also picks up groceries, provides "lifestyle management" and "new home helper" services, and rents equipment for traveling with kids.

SPECIAL PROGRAMS ✳ ✎ **Nantucket Island School of Design and the Arts** (508-228-9248; nisda.org), 23 Wauwinet Road. Founded in 1973, the NISDA presents an extraordinary range of classes and lectures for adults, youths, and kinders. Summerlong, weeklong, or daylong classes might include drawing, design, textile, folk art, floor cloth painting, puppet making, garden tours, yoga, modern dance, clay and sculpture, painting, and photography. Affiliated with Massachusetts College of Art in Boston, the school offers college graduate and undergraduate summer sessions in a converted dairy barn. Individuals attending classes may rent the school's studios and one-bedroom cottages on the harbor.

✳ ✎ **Artist's Association of Nantucket** (508-228-0722; nantucketarts.org), Gardner Perry Lane. Offering seasonal workshops and classes in a variety of disciplines for adults and children, the association also maintains a fine art library on Gardner Perry Lane and a gallery at 19 Washington Street (see *Selective Shopping*).

✳ ✎ **Nantucket Community School** (508-228-7257), 10 Surfside Road. Offers adult-education classes and programs and camps for kids.

SWIMMING POOL ✳ ✎ **Nantucket Community Pool** (508-228-7262), Atlantic and Surfside avenues. An Olympic-sized pool at the Nantucket High School is open daily for swimming; adults $8, children $6 daily; ten visit passes, too. Swimming lessons for a fee.

'SCONSET

This charming village on the eastern shore is the island's only real "destination," 7 miles from town. (Well, for the adventuresome, Great Point—see *Green Space*—is the other "destination.") The village is renowned for its tiny rose-covered cottages, all a few feet from one another. Some of the oldest are clustered on Broadway, Centre, and Shell streets. You won't have any problem finding them since the town consists of only a post office, a liquor store, a market, and a few restaurants. Of course, 'Sconset also has its share of grand summer homes—along Ocean Avenue and Sankaty and Baxter roads (on the way to Sankaty Head Lighthouse; see below). Recently, the combination of severe winter storms and the absence of offshore shoals to break incoming waves has created extreme beach erosion. Beachfront homes have been moved after several were engulfed by the sea.

Siasconset, which means "land of many bones," was probably named after a right whale was found on the beach. The 17th-century village was settled by and used as a base for fishermen in search of cod and whales. When wives began to join their husbands here in summer, the one-room shanties were expanded with additions called warts. (Perhaps early summer visitors wanted to escape the oil refineries in town, too.) When the narrow-gauge railway was built in 1884, it brought vacationing New York City actors who established a thriving actors' colony. Today 150 hardy souls live here year-round.

A few "sites" in 'Sconset include the **'Sconset Pump**, an old wooden water pump dug in 1776, and the **'Sconset Union Chapel**, the only place of worship in town. Despite its name, the **Siasconset Casino**, built in 1899 as a private tennis club, has never been used for gambling. Turn-of-the-20th-century actors used it for summer theater; movies are now shown in summer (see *Entertainment*).

Sankaty Head Light, 'Sconset. Partially solar powered, this red-and-white-striped light stands on a 90-foot-high bluff about 300 feet from the shoreline—it was relocated in 2007 thanks to community action and should be safe for the foreseeable future. Its light is visible 24 miles out to sea.

WINE, BEER & SPIRITS ✵ **Nantucket Vineyard, Cisco Brewers & Triple Eight Distillery** (508-325-5929; ciscobrewers.com), 5 Bartlett Farm Road, about 2.5 miles south of town off Hummock Pond Road. Open 10–6 Monday through Saturday, noon–5 Sunday in summer; then by appointment. Imagine a warm summer afternoon, sitting at an outdoor café in the interior of the island, surrounded by Bartlett farmland, sipping a frosty beer or icy vodka. Well, imagine no longer. This three-beverage destination is a fun diversion. Come to sample fresh, traditionally brewed ales, porters, stouts, and seasonal concoctions like Celebration Libation. Look for the excellent Cisco beer at island restaurants and package stores. It's more satisfying (and cheaper) than most bottles of restaurant wine. And look for the clean tastes of 888 vodkas, flavored with vanilla, cranberry, and orange. (In tastings, the pure 888 outscored Kettle One.) I didn't get a chance to sample their boutique Hurricane Rum, Gale Force Gin, or Nor'Easter Bourbon (hey, someone has to do the research!), but I encourage you to sip to your heart's content. As for wine, since vinifera grapes don't grow particularly well on Nantucket, this vineyard imports grapes for its wines.

✳ Green Space

Nantucket is renowned for the amount of open, protected land on the island. In fact, thanks to the efforts of various conservation groups, more than 45 percent of the island is protected from development. Two organizations deserve much of the credit: **Nantucket Conservation Foundation** (508-228-2884; nantucketcon servation.org), 118 Cliff Road; and the **Nantucket Land Bank** (508-228-7240; nantucketlandbank.org), 22 Broad Street. The Conservation Foundation was established in 1963 to manage open land—wetlands, moors, and grasslands. It's a private, nonprofit organization that's supported by membership contributions. Since then, the foundation has purchased or been given more than 8,600 acres on the island. Because the foundation is constantly acquiring land, call for a map of its current properties, published yearly; free. The Land Bank was created by an act of the state legislature in 1983, granting permission to assess a 2 percent tax for all real estate and land transactions. With the tax receipts, property is purchased and kept as conservation land.

🐚 **Maria Mitchell Association** (508-228-9198; mmo.org) leads informative nature walks around the island (see *To See*) for $5 adults, $4 children; half price for members.

Coatue–Coskata–Great Point, at the end of Wauwinet Road, accessible only by four-wheel-drive vehicle and on foot. The narrow strip of very soft sand leading to Great Point is about 5 miles long. Note the "haulover," which separates the head of the harbor from the Atlantic Ocean. This stretch of sand is so narrow that fishermen would haul their boats across it instead of going all the way around the tip of Great Point. During severe storms, the ocean breaks through the haulover, effectively creating an island. (Sand is eventually redeposited by the currents.) The spit of sand known as Coatue is a series of concave bays that reaches all the way to the mouth of Nantucket Harbor.

There's a wealth of things to do in this pristine preserve: birding, surf-casting, shellfishing, sunbathing, picnicking, and walking. Since the riptides are dangerous, especially near the Great Point Lighthouse (see *To See*), swimming is not recommended. These three adjacent wildlife areas, totaling more than 1,117 acres, are owned by different organizations, but that doesn't impact visitors. The Conservation Foundation owns both Coatue and the haulover. But the world's oldest land trust, the Trustees of Reservations, also manages part of the land. Ara's Tours and the Trustees of Reservations offer tours of Great Point; see *Getting Around* for tours and for information on getting your own four-wheel-drive permits.

Eel Point, off Eel Point Road from the Madaket Bike Path (see *To Do*), about 6 miles from town. Leave your car or bicycle at the sign that reads 40th Pole Beach and walk the last half mile to the beach. There aren't any facilities, just unspoiled nature, good birding, surf-fishing, and a shallow sandbar. Portions of this beach are often closed to protect nesting shorebirds. For in-depth information, pick up a map and self-guided tour from the **Nantucket Conservation Foundation** (see above).

Sanford Farm, **Ram Pasture**, and **the Woods**, off Madaket Road. These 700-plus acres of wetlands, grasslands, and forest are owned and managed by the Conservation Foundation and the Land Bank. Ram Pasture and the Woods were one of the foundation's first purchases (for $625,000) in 1971. Fourteen years later, Sanford Farm was purchased for $4.4 million from Mrs. Anne Sanford's estate. A 6.5-mile (roundtrip) walking and biking trail goes past Hummock Pond to the ocean, affording great views of heathlands along the way. Interpretive markers identify natural and historic sites. There is also a popular 45-minute (1.6-mile) loop trail as well as the Barn Trail (1½ hours, 3 miles), which affords beautiful expansive views of the island's southern coastline.

Milestone Bog, off Milestone Road on a dirt road to the north, about 5 miles from town. When cranberries were first harvested here in 1857, there were 220 acres of bogs. Today, because of depressed prices and a worldwide cranberry glut, very few bogs are still harvested. The land was donated to the Conservation Foundation in 1968.

Windswept Cranberry Bog, off Polpis Road to the south. This 40-acre bog is also partially owned by the Conservation Foundation.

BEACHES Nantucket is ringed by 50 miles of sandy shore, much publicly accessible. In general, beaches on the south and east have rough surf and undertow; western and northern beaches have warmer, calmer waters. There is limited parking at most beaches; NRTA (508-228-7025) provides a special beach bus to Jetties Beach and Surfside Beach from mid-June to early September, and regular buses to Madaket and 'Sconset beaches.

BEACHES RING THE ENTIRE ISLAND

Northern beaches

𝒮 **Children's Beach**, off South Beach Street on the harbor. A few minutes' walk from Steamboat Wharf, this is a great place for children (hence its name). Facilities include a lifeguard, restrooms, bathhouse, playground, food, picnic tables, bandstand, and a grassy play area.

Brant Point, off Easton Street. A 15-minute walk from town, and overlooking the entrance to the harbor, this scenic stretch is great for boat-watching and surf-fishing. Swimming conditions aren't great: There's a strong current and a beach that drops off suddenly.

𝒮 **Jetties**, off Bathing Beach Road from North Beach Road. Shuttle buses run to this popular beach—otherwise it's a 20-minute walk. (There is also a fairly large parking lot with lots of bike racks.) This is a great place for families because of the facilities (restrooms, lifeguards, showers, changing rooms, a snack bar, chairs for rent) and the activities (volleyball, tennis, swings, concerts, a playground, an assortment of sailboats and kayaks). The July 4 fireworks celebration is held here. Look for the skateboarding park, for which helmets and pads are required.

Francis Street Beach, a 5-minute walk from Main Street, at Washington and Francis streets. This harbor beach is calm. There are kayak rentals, portable restrooms, and a small jungle gym.

Dionis, off Eel Point Road from the Madaket and Dionis bike paths (see *To Do*). Nantucket's only beach with dunes, Dionis is about 3 miles from town. The beach starts out narrow but becomes more expansive (and less populated) as you walk farther east or west. Facilities include lifeguards and a bathhouse.

Southern beaches

Surfside, off Surfside Road; large parking lot. Three miles from town and accessible by shuttle bus, this wide beach is popular with college students and families with older kids because of its proximity to town and its moderate-to-heavy surf. Kite flying, surf-casting, and picnicking are popular. Facilities include restrooms, lifeguards, showers, and a snack bar.

Nobadeer, east of Surfside, near the airport and about 4 miles from town. There are no facilities at Nobadeer, but there is plenty of surf.

Madaket, at the end of the scenic Madaket Bike Path (see *To Do*). About 5 miles west of town (served by shuttle bus), Madaket is perhaps the most popular place to watch sunsets. This long beach has heavy surf and strong currents; there are lifeguards, portable restrooms, and very little parking.

☙ **Cisco**, off Hummock Pond Road from Milk Street. About 4 miles from town, this long beach is popular with surfers. There are lifeguards and surfing lessons for kids, but very little parking.

"Nude Beach," an unofficial beach, certainly, is unofficially located between Miacomet and Cisco.

Eastern beaches

'Sconset (aka Codfish Park), at the end of the 'Sconset Bike Path; turn right at the rotary. About 7 miles from town, accessible by shuttle bus, this narrow, long beach takes a pounding by heavy surf. Seaweed lines the beach when the surf whips up. Facilities include lifeguards, a playground, and very limited parking.

PONDS **Long Pond**. Take Madaket Road from town and, when you reach the Hither Creek sign, turn left onto a dirt road. This 64-acre Land Bank property is great for birding. A mile-long path around the pond passes meadows and a cranberry bog.

Miacomet Pond, Miacomet Avenue (which turns into a dirt road), off Surfside Road. This long, narrow, freshwater pond next to the ocean has a sandy shore and is surrounded by grasses and heath. This Land Bank property is a pleasant place for a picnic, and the swans and ducks make it more so.

Sesachacha Pond. Take Polpis Road to Quidnet Road. A narrow barrier beach separates the pond and ocean. There's a nice view of the Sankaty Head Lighthouse from here.

WALKS **The Moors and Altar Rock**, off Polpis Road, to the south, on an unmarked dirt road. When you want to get away from the summertime masses, head to the Moors (preferably at dawn or dusk, when they're most magical). From Altar Rock, the third highest point on the island (rising a whopping 103 feet above sea level), there are expansive views of lowland heath, bogs, and moors. It's stunning in autumn. The Moors are also crisscrossed with trails and deeply rutted dirt roads.

Lily Pond Park, North Liberty Street. This 6-acre Land Bank property supports lots of wildlife and plant life, but the trail is often muddy. You may find wild blackberries, grapes, or blueberries.

✳ Lodging

Consider making summertime reservations in February. No kidding. Also keep in mind that the historic district, while convenient, has its share of foot traffic (and boisterous socializers) late into the evening and that houses are also very close together. A 10-minute walk from Straight Wharf will put you in quieter surroundings. Most lodgings require a 2- or 3-night minimum stay in-season; I indicate only minimum-night-stay policies that go beyond that norm. Much to my chagrin, many places charge more for weekends than weekdays. Lastly, most places are not appropriate for small children. More and more folks are renting houses rather than staying in guesthouses. Which means that, even though the number of B&B rooms dwindles every year, it's worth calling at the last minute to check on availability—even at the primo places.

IN A CLASS BY THEMSELVES

On the outskirts of town

♂ "1" **Cliffside Beach Club** (508-228-0618; 800-932-9645; cliffsidebeach.com), Jefferson Avenue. Open late May to mid-October. *Stylish simplicity, understated elegance*, and *breezy beachside living* are the watchwords at this low-key luxe inn. You can't get a bed closer to the beach than this: Decks sit on the beach, and a boardwalk over the sand connects the low-slung, weathered-shingle buildings. A private club when it opened in 1924, it has been in Robert Currie's family since 1958. Family pride of ownership knows no bounds here. Improvements are constant. The lobby is large and airy, decorated with white wicker furniture, local art, and quilts hanging from the rafters. The dedicated breakfast room is sunny and window-filled. The 22 contemporary guest rooms (most with ocean views) feature handcrafted woodwork and granite bathrooms. Five newer suites, with outstanding views of dunes and sunsets, offer the most privacy. There is also a luxuriously simple three-bedroom apartment that almost defies description. If it were possible, I'd live in this unit forever. For meals, shuffle to the excellent beachside Galley Restaurant (see *Dining Out*) or walk 15 minutes into town. For exercise, nothing on-island compares their impressive health club, an oh-so-private 60-foot lap pool, leisure pool, Jacuzzi, and saunas. If you get the impression that I'm smitten with this place, you are correct. It's pricey but it's worth every penny. Mid-June to early September $450–710 rooms and studios, $875–1,745 suites, apartment, and cottages; off-season $275–390 and $525–960, respectively. Add 5.3 percent service charge.

Around the island

& **The Wauwinet** (508-228-0145; 800-426-8718; wauwinet.com), 120 Wauwinet Road. Open May through October. When privacy and extraordinary service are of utmost concern, this Relais & Châteaux property is *the* place. Nine miles from town, it occupies an unparalleled location between oceanside dunes and a beach-rimmed harbor. The 28 guest rooms and six cottages feature luxe linens and toiletries, pine armoires, Audubon prints, and sophisticated decorating touches. Public rooms are awash in chintz, trompe l'oeil, fresh flowers, and bleached woods. There's practically no reason to leave the enclave. Facilities include tennis courts, spa, boating, mountain bicycles, croquet, a DVD library, lobstering demonstrations, and Great Point nature trips. All are included in the room rates. Topper's (see *Dining Out*) offers truly outstanding dining. In the morning, enjoy as much from the complimentary breakfast menu as you'd like. Mid-June to mid-September $700–1,220 rooms, $1,020–1,450 cottages (4-night minimum in July and August); off-season $380–1,120 rooms, $710–1,250 cottages.

HOTELS

In town

White Elephant Hotel (508-228-2500; 800-475-2637; whiteelephant hotel.com), Easton Street. Open early May to late October. After a total renovation in early 2000 and another in 2006, the sedate White Elephant is more sedate than ever. A 10-minute walk from the center of town and on the edge of the harbor, many of the spacious 65 rooms, suites and garden cottages have prime water views framed by shuttered white windows. Most have a balcony or deck; many suites have a fireplace. Decor is a sophisticated blend of leather armchairs and white wicker, of crisp linens and textured, neutral fabrics, of antique prints and contemporary art-

THE WAUWINET

work. Bathrooms boast fine toiletries, lots of white tile, and marble counters. Common space includes a handsome library, a fitness room, extensive spa, and broad lawns that reach a harborside dock. Inquire about the in-town Loft, a 3-bedroom place that sleeps eight with a fully equipped kitchen. June through August $600–1,300 (5-night minimum), suites more; off-season $260–1,000 rooms.

Near the Airport

⁰ɪ⁰ **Nantucket Inn** (508-228-6900; 800-321-8484; nantucketinn.net), 1 Miller's Way. Open mid-May to mid-October. The main reason I'm including this tasteful but undistinguished motor inn, near the airport, is because it has 100 rooms, which is a lot of rooms for this small island. Other amenities include an indoor pool, tennis courts, and a complimentary full breakfast. Mid-June through August $290–390; off-season $150–310.

INNS AND BED & BREAKFASTS

In town

⁰ɪ⁰ **Union Street Inn** (508-228-9222; 888-517-0707; unioninn.com), 7 Union Street. Open April through October. The island's best run B&B, a circa 1770 hostelry, is run by innkeepers Ken and Deb Withrow with a sense of understated hospitality. You want to know perfection? Stay here. There are a variety of rooms, many with fireplace and all with air-conditioning and TV. The two-room suite and room #3 (with pine-paneled wall and wing chairs in front of the fireplace) are the premier rooms, but smaller chambers aren't slighted in any way. (Value-conscious shoppers should inquire about the inexpensive room with a detached bath.) After a new round of redecorating and renovating, the 12 rooms are more luxurious than ever, with fine linens, plush bathrobes, and fluffy

UNION STREET INN

duvets. On my last visit the full break-fast, served on the side patio, was a choice between an omelet with goat cheese and dill or bagel and smoked salmon. (It's the only B&B that's allowed to serve a full "B.") The art of providing attentive service remains a strong suit here. June through October $395–515, more for suites; off-season $160–445.

✄ ⁗ **The Veranda House** (508-228-0695; theverandahouse.com), 3 Step Lane. Open mid-May to mid-October. This upscale guesthouse, with 15 guest rooms and three suites, was completely renovated in 2007 to reflect a "retro chic" vibe—awash in black, white, and neutral tones (with a splash of red here or there). No expense seems to have been spared. And it could certainly hold its own in SoHo. Gracious "extras" are the norm here: balconies overlooking the harbor, goose down comforters, spanking new bathrooms with hip tile, and Frette linens make for a most hospitable stay. Fortunately, the owners kept one of the best features: three wraparound porches that offer spectacular views of Nantucket Harbor. For this reason and more, they're to be seriously applauded. An ultra-sophisticated continental break-fast is served on the patio by over solicitous servers; and the terraced garden is a welcome respite. Resident

manager, Scott Allen, and his staff provide excellent concierge services. Children 10 and over welcome. Mid-June to mid-September $309–599; off-season $129–219.

✳ **Anchor Inn** (508-228-0072; anchor-inn.net), 66 Centre Street. This friendly B&B, one of the best values in town, has been innkeeper-owned and operated since 1983. Charles and Ann Balas, and their cracker-jack staff, offer 11 guest accommodations in a historic 1806 house; the most spacious rooms are corner ones with a queen canopy bed. All have tiled bathrooms, telephone with voice mail, TV, air-conditioning, and comfortable period furnishings. One has a private porch. The less expensive rooms are snug but inviting, tucked under the eaves in the back of the house. A continental break-fast is served on the enclosed porch or carried to the tranquil side garden. Beach towels and ice packs are available in-season. The Balases also have five additional rooms at 72 Centre

THE VERANDA HOUSE

Street (72centre.com). Eliza can accommodate a couple and a child and has a summer sleeping porch. Phoebe has only an old-fashioned tub but can sleep three. Essex, Lydia, and Aurora are popular larger rooms. Their ever-growing empire also extends to A Cottage in Town: cozy, simple, with a kitchenette, and family-friendly. WiFi on porch. Mid-June to mid-September $185–275; off-season $75–155.

⁰**1**⁰ **Pineapple Inn** (508-228-9992; pineappleinn.com), 10 Hussey Street. Open late April to late October and on Christmas Stroll weekend. This 1838 whaling captain's house led the surge towards luxury B&B renovations in 1997 with a refined and understated elegance. And six years later it was acquired by the Summer House in their march toward the acquisition of fine properties around the island. Historic grace and modern conveniences coexist comfortably here. First-class touches surround you, including white marble bathrooms and custom-made four-poster beds fitted with Ralph Lauren linens and down comforters. The 12 rooms have air-conditioning, TV, and telephone with voice mail. I particularly like the enclosed back patio, complete with trickling water fountain; it makes for a nice respite from the crowds. Complimentary use of the Summer House Beach and Pool Club is included. Mid-June through October $215–375; off-season $145–250.

⁰**1**⁰ **Arbor Cottage at 6 Step Lane** (508-228-0695; arborcottage.com), 6 Step Lane. Open mid-May to late October. Longtime innkeepers and Nantucket residents John and Sandy Knox-Johnston offer three rooms with personalized service. It's all about a sense of calm, style, and privacy here. Sandy's rooms have a fresh summery feel, with clean lines, a pale palate of

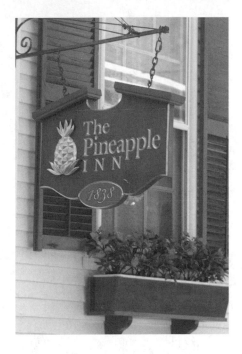

whites, and a liberal dose of sisel and linens. Twenty-first-century amenities include flat-screen TVs, DVD players, spa-like toiletries, and great bathroom shower heads. You'll long remember tucking into a decadent bed dressed in Frette linens. Mid-June to mid-September $195–429; off-season $119–189.

⁰**1**⁰ **Ship's Inn** (508-228-0040; shipsinn nantucket.com), 13 Fair Street. Open May through October. Beyond the bustle of Main Street, a 10-minute walk from Straight Wharf, the Ship's Inn is a largely unsung and very comfortable choice for lodging as well as fine dining (see *Dining Out*). The three-story 1831 whaling captain's house was completely restored in 1991. Its 13 large guest rooms, named for Captain Obed Starbuck's ships, all have refrigerator, telephone with voice mail, air conditioning, and TV. Many are bright corner rooms. Like the living room, they're large and airy, and sparsely furnished to create a summery feel. Expanded continental breakfast included. Mid-May to mid-October

$195–275 double ($90–125 single with shared bath); off-season $175–210 double, $75–110 single.

❄ ✐ ((↑)) **Nantucket Whaler Guest House** (508-228-6597; 888-808-6597; nantucketwhaler.com), 8 North Water Street. With the exception of a traditional 1850 Greek Revival exterior, nothing about this guesthouse is conventional. Proprietors Calli Ligelis and Randi Ott have upped the island's already considerable ante with their luxe suites and large studios, each with a private entrance and deck or patio. Furnishings are a blend of country American and English antiques; beds are dressed in linens and down comforters; towels and robes are plush; and the color palettes are soothing. Other amenities include flat-screen TV, DVD and CD players, cordless phone (with a private number), continental breakfast, movie snacks, limited room service, light bite baskets, wine and cheese, coffeemaker, refrigerator, microwave, and toaster oven. Who wants to leave the room? Children over 10 welcome. Mid-June to mid-October $325–425 rooms, $425–795 one- and two-bedroom suites; off-season $275–395 and $375–650, respectively.

❄ 🐾 ((↑)) **Vanessa Noel Hotel (VNH)** (508-228-5300; vanessanoelhotelgreen.com), 5 Chestnut Street. Noted shoe designer Vanessa Noel opened this chic boutique property in 2002 to offer guests her vision of perfection: simplicity paired with the sophistication and luxuries of the best European hotels. An example? The wide-planked lobby is graced with a Baccarat chandelier. Though most rooms are small, this trendy property compensates with custom features like plasma TVs, Frette linens, feather beds, Bulgari toiletries, and Italian marble bathrooms. I'm particularly fond of the two spacious attic rooms. Organic breakfasts are offered at **Café V**, on the first floor. It seats a mere 27 trendy types at leopard-print banquettes and offers a caviar and champagne bar with imported delights. You might also look into Vanessa's adjacent venture, **Hotel Green**; no children allowed. Mid-June to mid-September $340–580; $200–300 off-season.

❄ ((↑)) **Martin House Inn** (508-228-0678; martinhouseinn.com), 61 Centre Street. Resident innkeeper Skye Schuyler presides over this 1803 mariner's house, an elegantly comfortable and relaxed place. The side porch is decked out with white wicker; on cooler days you can curl up in front of the fire or in a window seat in the large living room. Many of the 13 guest rooms (4 with shared bath) have canopy bed, period antiques, and fireplace. Some bright third-floor singles are tucked under the eaves. A continental buffet breakfast is served at one long table, or you can take a tray table to the porch or your room. Mid-May to mid-October $180–385 double, $120 single (more for the suite); off-season $135–275 double, $95 single.

⁏ Centerboard Guest House (508-228-9696; centerboardguesthouse.com), 8 Chester Street. Open April through December. A 5- to 10-minute walk from the ferry, Centerboard has a generally light Victorian sensibility. The second floor rooms are romantic, with feather beds, luxurious linens, stripped floors and woodwork, and gleaming bathrooms. The two-room master suite features inlaid floors, rich woodwork, a working fireplace, marble bathroom, deep Jacuzzi tub, and pencil-post canopy bed. Two garden rooms are decidedly different. One is reminiscent of a houseboat, with built-in carpentry, a galley kitchen, a matching pair of raised double beds, and a snug twin berth; it can sleep five. Modern amenities include mini-refrigerators and flat-screen TVs. Resident innkeeper James Blunt presides. Mid-June to mid-October $275–325 rooms, $365–450 suite; off-season $135–155 rooms, $249–295 suite; expanded continental breakfast included.

⁏ Century House (508-228-0530; centuryhouse.com), 10 Cliff Road. Open mid-May to mid-October. The oldest continuously operating inn on Nantucket, dating to 1835, has 16 rooms and suites that are just far enough from the center of town to be quiet and just close enough for a pleasant walk. Innkeepers Gerry Connick and Jean Ellen Heron, hands-on owners since 1984, have created a homey and luxurious getaway, complete with an abundant Berry Buffet Breakfast (enjoyed on the wrap-around verandah or garden patio.) Beach towels and tote are provided for the nearby sands. Mid-June to late August $255–595 rooms, $625 suites; off-season $195–325 and $425, respectively.

❋ ✐ ⁏ The Chestnut House (508-228-0049; chestnuthouse.com), 3 Chestnut Street. Not many old-fash-ioned guesthouses remain, and this one has been in the Carl family since the early 1980s. The family-friendly place is busy and eclectic, with local art taking up almost every inch of wall space. (See Hawthorn House, below, for more about familial contributions to decor.) Two-room suites can sleep four people if they are good friends, or a family. Otherwise, they are nice and roomy for two people. One suite is particularly quiet, and there is only one "regular" guest room. All have TV, a small refrigerator, air conditioning; most have a DVD. The freestanding **cottage** is more like a suite, with a Murphy bed and separate kitchen. You'll find added value in the additional bathrooms, which allow for post-beach showering and late departures. Mid-June to mid-October $210 room, $250–300 suites; off-season $100 room, $125–145 suites; includes a breakfast voucher for $9 per person per day, valid at two good restaurants; cottage $375 daily for four people, off-season $250.

❋ ⁏ The Hawthorn House (508-228-1468; hawthornhouse.com), 2 Chestnut Street. A guesthouse since the mid-1940s, this simple B&B was built in 1849, so the rooms are small. Seven of nine guest rooms and suites

MARTIN HOUSE INN

are upstairs off a casual common area; all rooms have a private bath. Because the B&B is in the historic district, the two ground-floor rooms can be a tad noisy in the evening. Innkeepers Mitchell and Diane Carl came to Nantucket on their honeymoon and loved it so much they returned three years later to purchase the inn and have operated it since. Mitchell's father made the hooked rugs; Diane made the needlepoint pillows; and his mother did most of the paintings. Mitchell is responsible for the lovely stained-glass panels. Inquire about the **efficiency cottage** and two-room suite. Mid-June to mid-September $180–255; off-season $85–125; includes a breakfast voucher for $9 per person per day, valid at two good restaurants.

🦞 🦀 🐾 ⑪ **Nesbitt Inn** (508-228-0156), 21 Broad Street. Open late April to early December. The Nesbitt Inn, built in 1872, exemplifies Nantucket's simpler lodging roots. Many furnishings are original to the house. A favorite among Europeans, the inn's 10 double and 2 single rooms (which share only three baths and have in-room sinks) are Victorian in style. For inclement days, the living room has a

fireplace, games, and TV. Otherwise, guests can people-watch from the front porch, relax on the back deck, and make use of the outdoor grill, guest refrigerator, and beach towels. Two **cottages** with full kitchens and private baths are available in-season for $260 nightly. Otherwise, late-May to mid-October $115–190, off-season $75–120; includes continental breakfast.

Jared Coffin House (508-228-2400; 800-248-2405; jaredcoffinhouse.com), 29 Broad Street. The island's first three-story house, topped with a cupola and slate roof, was built in 1845 by a wealthy ship owner for his wife. Made of brick, it was also one of the few buildings to survive the Great Fire of 1846. One year later, after Coffin's wife refused to live here, it was converted to an inn. In its current state, I simply note it for its historical value.

Around the island

⑪ **Summer House 'Sconset** (508-257-4577; thesummerhouse.com), 'Sconset. Open late April to late October. The brochure's photograph is almost too idyllic to believe: Honeysuckle vines and roses cover a shingled cottage with tiny windows; the double dutch door opens to a white, skylit interior that's cozy and simple. But it's true! Dating to the 1840s, these enchanting cottages surround a colorful garden set with Adirondack chairs. The Munchkin-like cottages have been updated with marble Jacuzzi bathtubs, English country-pine antiques, and hand-painted borders; some have a fireplace and kitchen. All have off-season heat. Shuffle across the street to the eastern beach or to the inn's pool, nestled in the dunes just below the bluff. (Drinks and lunch are served in their well-regarded dining room, as well as pool- and oceanside; see *Dining Out*.) Continental breakfast included.

NESBITT INN

Early June to mid-September $575–675, more for two- and three-bedrooms; off-season $250–325, more for multi-bedroom cottages.

COTTAGES

In town

✱ ⁺¹⁺ **The Cottages** (508-325-1499; 866-838-9253; thecottagesnantucket .com), 24 Old South Wharf. Open early May through November. These 29 snug cottages are fun for a change, although they'll cost a pretty penny for all that fun! Occupying a unique location—jutting out on wharves in the midst of harbor activity—most have private decks and water views; all have fully equipped kitchens, TV/VCR/ DVDs, and daily maid service. Although the cottages are small and rather rustic by Nantucket standards, they're efficiently designed and crisply decorated in yellows, whites and blues. It can be noisy on the pier, but that's part of the fun of staying here. WiFi for a fee. (What did you expect at these prices?) July and August $490–720 for a one-bedroom; two and three bedroom run from $590–1,200, and studios are $490–570; off-season from $200.

See also **The Chestnut House**, **Hawthorne House**, **Anchor Inn,** and **Nesbitt Inn** under *Inns & Bed & Breakfasts.*

Around the island

♂ ♿ **Wade Cottages** (508-257-6308; 212-989-6423 off-season; wadecottages .com), 'Sconset. Open late May to early October. There's nothing between the property and the ocean here except a broad lawn and an ocean bluff. Parents will appreciate the play area and swings for kids. Ocean views are de rigueur. The five apartments have from 1- to 3-bedrooms. A portion of this private estate is still used by Wade family members. July and August $1,600–2,350 weekly; about half off-season.

See also **Summer House 'Sconset** under *Inns and Bed & Breakfasts.*

RENTAL HOUSES Many islanders are opposed to the residential building boom that began in earnest in the mid-1990s because the island's infrastructure just can't handle it. But there's no going back. There are thousands of new three- and seven-bedroom rental houses on the market. Expect a nice two-bedroom house to rent for an average $3,000 weekly in August.

Congdon & Coleman (508-325-5000; congdonandcoleman.com), 57 Main Street.

Jordan Associates (508-228-4449; jordanre.com), 8 Federal Street.

❊ ⁺¹⁺ **Barntucket** (508-228-4835; barntucket.com), 73 North Liberty Street. A five-bedroom, three-bath beauty built in the early 1800s. These prices are actually quite reasonable if you're splitting them among five other couples or individuals. $7,500–8,500 weekly in summer, $1,000 nightly for first two nights, $500 for additional nights (with a 2- or 3-night minimum) throughout the year.

TimeAndPlace.com. A stellar site with premier homes for rent.

CAMPGROUNDS Camping is not permitted.

HOSTEL ✱ ♂ **Nantucket Hostel** (508-228-0433; usahostels.org; 800-909-4776 for in-season reservations; 617-531-0459 for reservations prior to the start of the season), 31 Western Avenue. Open mid-May to late September. Originally built in 1873 as the island's first lifesaving station, and now on the National Register of Historic Places, this Hostelling International hostel is 3 miles from town on Surfside Beach (see *Green Space*) and steps from the NRTA beach shuttle. Facilities include a kitchen, barbecue and picnic area, and volleyball. Dormitory-style, gender-separated rooms accommodate about 49 people. Reservations are essential in July and August and on all weekends. Continental breakfast included. $32–35 for dorm beds, $178 for a private room.

✳ Where to Eat

The dining scene here is highly evolved. Enough Nantucket diners are passionate about haute cuisine that the island supports one of the densest concentrations of fine-dining establishments in the country. And one of the most expensive: $50 entrées are commonplace even as patrons shake their heads in disbelief. Some restaurants offer less expensive, bistro-style fare in addition to their regular menu. Prices aside, many of Nantucket's 60-some restaurants would hold their own in New York or San Francisco. It's rare to be served a bad meal in Nantucket, but some restaurants do offer more value (note the symbol for value ✿) than others.

A few more details: Unless otherwise noted, reservations are highly recommended at all *Dining Out* establishments. Additionally, you might need to reconfirm your reservation on the day of or you'll lose it. There are perhaps 10 restaurants (not all are reviewed here) that serve the year-round community. Generally, you can assume that all places below are open daily late June to early September. But I have not included shoulder-season hours of operation because they are dependent on weather, number of tourists, and owner's whim.

By the way, don't pass up the opportunity to have bay scallops after mid-October (when the scalloping season begins). The experience might explain why Nantucketers are so passionate about food.

DINING OUT

In town

✿ & **American Seasons** (508-228-7111; americanseasons.com), 80 Centre Street. Open for dinner April to mid-December. *Consistency* is the watchword here; year after year, this place remains at the top of my dining list. While inspired by America's regional traditions, Executive Chef Michael LaScola's menu is both inviting and innovative. The ever-changing menu is broken down into: Down South (chili-glazed organic salmon with fried green tomatoes), Pacific Coast (braised pork cheek and miso glazed shrimp), and New England (creamed spinach and leek tart). Mammoth portions of vertically presented food are balanced with savory and sweet tastes, crunchy and smooth textures. If the food weren't so good, I'd suggest simply coming for dessert. Although there is patio dining, I like the candlelit bistro-style dining room that features folk art murals and checkerboard tables. Dinner $24–38.

MAIN STREET

Y & **21 Federal** (508-228-2121; 21federal.com), 21 Federal Street. Open for dinner mid-October to early December. Loyal patrons return year-after-year for sophisticated New and traditional American cuisine served in an elegant and reserved dining room. These days Executive Chef Russell Jaehnig stands at the helm. To some the food is "pretentious"; to others it's "venerable." No matter; 21 reigns as one of the top five places year after year. Although the ever-changing menu highlights seafood, you might also enjoy grilled Colorado rack of lamb with fava bean falafel or a dry aged sirloin with parmesan shoestring potatoes. The dark-paneled bar is convivial; there is also a lighter bistro menu and garden dining. The bar remains as popular as ever. Dinner $35–40.

❋ Y & **Boarding House** (508-228-9622; boardinghouse-pearl.com), 12 Federal Street. Open for dinner daily May through December and brunch on weekends June through August. Chef-owners Seth and Angela Raynor's contemporary, sexy, Euro- and Asian-inspired cuisine stands center stage at one of Nantucket's most consistent and superior restaurants. An award-winning wine list accompanies signature dishes (aka BoHo Classics) like grilled lobster tails. Organic ingredients from local farms are used whenever possible. (I'm partial to pan-seared sea scallops.) As for atmosphere, with brick and plaster arched walls, the main dining room is cozy. At street level, there's a lively bar packed with locals and thirty-something visitors; it's a real scene (especially with an extensive appetizer menu). But in good weather, the patio—surrounded by flowers and a white picket fence—is the place you'll want to be. It's common for folks to line up in summer at 4 PM for one of these seats. Dinner $26–38, brunch $15–20; late-night menu available Wednesday through Sunday.

Y **The Pearl** (508-228-9701; boarding house-pearl.com), 12 Federal Street. Open for dinner May through October. From the attitude to the oh-so-trendy-bar to the whole scene, don't look now: You just might be in Miami's South Beach. Executive Chef-Owner Seth Raynor (see Boarding House, above) has furthered his winning formula of coastal cuisine prepared with an Asian flair. The atmosphere and cuisine here are sophisticated, relaxing, and dramatic. (Note the onyx bar, huge fish tanks filled with brilliant fish and coral, pearl-shaped ceiling, and pale blue lighting.) Although the menu changes frequently, you can always count on creatively prepared native seafood and local fish. Patrons are particularly fond of tuna martinis (nonalcoholic) and Chef Seth's wok-fried lobster. Dinner $30–50.

Oran Mor (508-228-8655; oranmor bistro.com), 2 South Beach Street. Open for dinner mid-April to early December. Chef-owner Chris Freeman, formerly of Topper's fame (see below), has an intimate restaurant

AMERICAN SEASONS

inconspicuously located over an antiques shop near the waterfront. Once you find it, you'll probably return more than once. I do. Chris's cuisine defines true inspiration. His refined execution never falls short of perfection, whether he's preparing striped bass, yellowfin tuna, or scallops. It'd be downright foolhardy to bypass it. The seasonal New American menu ranges from roasted rack and grilled loin of lamb to its featured Wolfe's Neck Farm beef. Specials are always tempting. The Gaelic phrase oran mor, by the way, means "great song." Dinner $26–38.

Company of the Cauldron (508-228-4016; companyofthecauldron .com), 7 India Street. Open for dinner late May to mid-October and on Christmas Stroll weekend (see *Special Events*). Peer through ivy-covered, small-paned windows and you'll see what looks like an intimate dinner party. Sure enough, since the tables are so close together, you'll probably end up talking to your neighbors before the

THE PEARL

night is over. It's a warm and inviting place, with low-beamed ceilings and plaster walls illuminated by candlelight and wall sconces. Longtime chef-owner Al Kovalencik's New American menu is set a week in advance, but it might go something like this: a trio of crab, lobster, and salmon cakes with three luxurious sauces; a mesclun salad with caramelized shallot vinaigrette; ginger- and herb-crusted rack of lamb with blackberries and pine nut couscous; and a pear almond tart to top it all off. One or two seatings; prix fixe $59 per person.

♣ ⅄ **Ship's Inn Restaurant** (508-228-0040; shipsinnnantucket.com), 13 Fair Street. Open for dinner May through October. Longtime chef-owner Mark Gottwald, who graduated from La Varenne in Paris and apprenticed at Le Cirque and Spago, serves American brasserie-style cuisine in a romantic, subterranean, bistro-style space. He also catches his own seafood. I always leave here very satisfied. Many dishes are healthful (that is, sans butter or cream) without sacrificing taste or creativity. I particularly like the signature sautéed halibut with a cognac lobster ragout. Save room for the chocolate soufflé. They have an award-winning wine list; sit at the old dory boat bar and enjoy a glass. Dinner $23–38.

⅄ **Straight Wharf Restaurant** (508-228-4499; straightwharfrestaurant .com), 6 Harbor Square. Open for dinner June through October, as well as lunch and brunch in July and August. When given the choice, I prefer the more casual dining, reasonable price points, and first come-first served nature of the bar. It's also pleasantly upbeat and zippy. No matter where and when you dine, though—whether it's on the deck overlooking the harbor or in the lofty main dining room with exposed rafters—the New American dishes are well prepared and elegantly presented. Look for the likes of wood grilled sirloin, dayboat scallops and a clam bake with buttered lobster, sweet corn, chorizo and potatoes. Desserts are decidedly rich. Lunch $10–24, dinner $25–44.

✳ ᛉ **Lola 41** (508-325-4001; lola41 .net), 15 South Beach Street. Open for dinner. This is one hip eatery. I mean, really. Walk through the doors and you'll forget you're on Nantucket. Along with boasting a "global bistro menu," Lola 41 specializes in sushi, sashimi, and designer rolls. Try the excellent gnocchi Bolognese, or go for one of the house specialties these days: sesame crusted calamari with Korean chili dipping sauce or a house-ground rib eye, served on an English muffin. Bring a fun attitude and live it up. Dinner $19–37.

ᛉ **Brant Point Grill** (508-325-1320; whiteelephanthotel.com), at the White Elephant Hotel, 50 Easton Street. Open for all three meals early May to early December. There's no more pleasant place to have an alfresco luncheon than this harborside terrace. (Heaters and awnings keep it warm well into autumn.) Look for Thai beef salad and mouthwatering lobster BLT served on challah bread with crispy fried onion rings. The handsome grill, with attentive service, specializes in steamed and grilled lobsters and thick, juicy steaks. Nothing is too fussy or overdone. Check out the raw bar, too. Breakfast $6–17, lunch $16–25, dinner $30–45, and Sunday brunch, $38 for adults, $19 for children; bar menu available 3–11.

✦ ᛉ ♿ **Ropewalk** (508-228-8886; theropewalk.com), 1 Straight Wharf. Open for lunch and dinner mid-May to mid-October. Night or day, try to get an outdoor patio table at Nantucket's only harborside (*yacht-side* might be more apt) restaurant. If you can't,

though, don't worry; the interior is open to sea breezes and rolling fog banks. Although the casual ambience might suggest standard seafood fare, the cuisine is really quite good and the menu extensive. Ropewalk also has an excellent raw bar and frozen drinks. Light, eclectic lunch choices include salads, sandwiches—a little bit of everything, really. No reservations are taken, but you can call ahead for preferred seating. As for the bar, you can pick out the locals: They're often pitching ice (or bottle tops) at their friends passing by in boats. Early specials in the fall. Lunch $12–20, dinner $28–38.

✳ ᛉ **Queequeg's** (508-325-0992; queequegsnantucket.com), 6 Oak Street. Open for dinner. Henri Laaksonen, who was the Executive Sous Chef at The Wauwinet for years, opened this cozy, comfortable, and contemporary place in 2001. He characterizes has diverse dishes as American eclectic; you might come for jambalaya, braised short ribs, or lobster ravioli with sage cream. The small bar is nice for before- or after-dinner drinks, as is the outdoor patio. All in all it's a welcome relief from the attitude at other fine dining places. Dinner $24–29.

ᛉ **DeMarco** (508-228-1836; demarco restaurant.com), 9 India Street. Open for dinner mid-May to mid-October. Light northern Italian cuisine is offered in this restored sea captain's home. Downstairs has a taverny feel with a bar, wood beams, brick, and curtains, while upstairs is more airy. Start with a rich antipasto, followed by pasta with wild mushrooms, prosciutto, tomato, sage and cream. The menu changes regularly, although homemade pasta and grilled seafood are house specialties. Don DeMarco, who has owned his namesake restaurant since 1979, has amassed an outstanding wine cellar. Dinner $26–48

☗ **Club Car** (508-228-1101; theclub
car.com), 1 Main Street. Open for
lunch and dinner mid-May through
October; also Thanksgiving and on
Christmas Stroll weekend (see *Special
Events*). While the kitchen has put out
fabulous Continental cuisine since
1972, the menu hasn't really changed
since then, either. The off-season beef
Wellington Sunday-evening specials
are classic, though, best enjoyed in the
elegant and somewhat haughty dining
room, set with linen and silver. I prefer
to come simply for a seafood salad and
chowder at lunch—and to enjoy the
only remaining club car from the narrow-gauge train that used to run
between Steamboat Wharf and 'Sconset. Depending on the time of night,
be prepared for sing-alongs to old Billy
Joel tunes at the piano bar. Lunch
$10–15; dinner $30–45.

❄ ♿ **Fifty-Six Union** (508-228-6135;
fiftysixunion.com), 56 Union Street.
Open for dinner. Since they opened in
2003, chef-owners, Peter and Wendy
Jannelle, have succeeded in creating a
friendly find away from tourists roam-
ing the more well-known haunts downtown. It's one of the more playful and
lighthearted "serious" restaurants in
town—to wit, you can't miss the man-
nequin out front. Seasonal menus
reflect what's fresh in the world of
global cuisine: Curried mussels and
day-boat summer fluke are personal
favorites. There are two seatings (at
5:30 and 8:15) at banquettes as well as
patio dining. Inquire about the outdoor chef's table. Dinner $30–50.

Water Street (508-228-7080; water
streetnantucket.com), 21 South Water
Street. Open for dinner early April to
early January. Unpretentious, comfortable, and sophisticated, this two-for-
one bistro has a bakery on site that
specializes in organic breads, sandwiches, and salads ($8–10). Upstairs,
you'll find casual bar meals (like burgers and fish tacos) and specialty cocktails. Chefs Jason and Robert try to use
organic local ingredients as much as
possible. I'm particularly fond of their
crispy-skin striped bass with gazpacho
and a cucumber avocado emulsion. Bar
menu $12–16; otherwise, dinner
$26–40.

♨ ✐ **Cioppino's** (508-228-4622;
cioppinos.com), 20 Broad Street. Open
for dinner mid-May to mid-October.
Continental and New American cuisine—seafood stew, filet and lobster
combo with *pommes frites*, and grilled
lobster tails with shrimp and pesto
pasta—is featured, and cioppino is an
obvious specialty. There's also a different prime steak every week. Tracy
Root's dining room is quiet and the bar
cozy, but in good weather the garden
patio is even more tempting. Cioppino's offers an excellent "summer
fling" menu ($20) and a good wine list.
The key lime pie is lip-pursingly tart.
Early specials. Dinner $18–27.

On the outskirts of town
❄ ♨ ♿ **Sfoglia** (508-325-4500; sfoglia

restaurant.com), 130 Pleasant Street. Open for dinner. A mile from the center of town, this regional Italian restaurant is charmingly rustic, with mismatched table settings and the like. Look for ultracreative and homemade pasta dishes by the husband-and-wife team of Ron and Colleen Suhanosky, both Culinary Institute of America grads, who opened the place in 2000. Dinner $16–32.

& **Galley Beach** (508-228-9641), at the end of Jefferson Avenue. Open for lunch and dinner late April to late October. At the Cliffside Beach Club (but no with relation to it), you'll literally dine beachside, drinking in sunsets along with your cosmos. But this isn't a sand-in-your-shoes kind of place—it's elegant, candlelit dining under an awning on Nantucket Sound. The coastal cuisine menu features sea scallops, other local seafood, and organic greens. A restaurant with this kind of location might be content to pass, but the Galley Beach is absolutely stellar in all ways. Lunch $17–29, dinner $35–48.

Around the island

🦞 & **Topper's** (508-228-8768; wauwinet.com), 120 Wauwinet Road, Wauwinet. Open for lunch, dinner, and Sunday brunch May through October. You could break the bank here and Topper's would still be worth every penny. All the superlatives in the dictionary just can't do the place justice. The setting and service are luxurious, indulgent, and sophisticated, yet relaxed. Regional dishes are downright sublime: New American cuisine is matched by outstanding pairings from a French and California wine list. (Topper's consistently wins the just-about-impossible-to-win *Wine Spectator* Grand Award. And to quote myself in *National Geographic Traveler*, "Their wine pairing is unrivaled on the

eastern seaboard.") On my most recent visit, I splurged on the prix fixe menu *with* wine pairing. Each dish and wine comes into its own when paired with the other: one plus one equals three. It's an ungodly amount of money for most people reading this book, but it's an uncommonly rare dining experience. Dishes and wines ascend in boldness, telling a story, exuberantly, and come back down to earth. For lunch (served on the bayside porch) Topper's offers a two-course menu for $21. Topper's offers complimentary van service from town, as well as transportation aboard the *Wauwinet Lady*, which takes guests from Straight Wharf to the restaurant's private dock in-season. Kudos to chef David Daniels and the whole staff. Brunch $16–40, lunch $21, dinner $40–50, prix fixe $89.

'Sconset Café (508-257-4008; sconset cafe.com), Post Office Square, 'Sconset. Open for lunch and dinner mid-May to mid-September, breakfast in summer. This tiny place is always great. It's known for its chowder with herbs, but you'll also find creative salads and sandwiches at lunch. Chef-owner Rolf Nelson's dinners really shine and tend toward sophisticated New American dishes. The menu changes constantly, but chocolate volcano cake is often the dessert specialty. Reservations accepted for 6 PM seating only. No credit cards; BYOB; $4 corkage fee. Rolf owns the wine shop next door where he recommends wines that go with his menu. (Customers typically buy their wine there for dinner. Convenient.) Breakfast $8–10, lunch $10–15, dinner $25–36.

🍸 **Summer House Beachside Bistro** (508-257-9976; thesummer house.com), 17 Ocean Avenue, 'Sconset. Open for lunch and dinner early June to mid-September and into the autumn as weather permits. Ocean-

and poolside light lunches of salads and sandwiches here are the epitome of a relaxed Nantucket summer. Specialties include mussels, fish dishes, lobster rolls, and clam chowder. Nestled into the dunes and wedged between sand and shore, it's the most idyllic place on Nantucket to dine. Lunch $11–29, dinner $25–39.

♿ **The Chanticleer** (508-257-4499; thechanticleer.net), 9 New Street, 'Sconset. Open for lunch and dinner May through October. When Susan of Black-Eyed Susan's took over this venerated institution, those who didn't know about the change in ownership wouldn't have known. That's a serious compliment. French inspired nouveau cuisine is served in the courtyard of a rose-covered cottage, in small dining rooms overlooking the courtyard through small-paned windows, or in the more formal main dining room with low ceilings. Local fish, local produce, and game birds are highlighted. I suspect that dining here will live on

SUMMER HOUSE BEACHSIDE BISTRO

in your memory for years. The wine list is outstanding. Lunch $12–32, dinner $12–43.

EATING OUT

In town

❇ ⚜ **Centre Street Bistro** (508-228-8470; nantucketbistro.com), 29 Centre Street. Open for breakfast on weekends, lunch on weekdays, and dinner nightly. Chef-owners Ruth and Tim Pitts, who have been cooking on-island since 1989, have cultivated a deservedly loyal following. Perhaps it's because they serve exceedingly good food at even better prices. Their ever-evolving menu might include dishes like cheeseburger tortilla, but I often can't help myself and revert to their signature smoked salmon taco or crispy shrimp pad Thai. Or start your day with their "Nantucket Breakfast"—scrambled eggs, bacon, potato pancake, and blueberry pancake. There are only a couple of dozen seats (and a small bar) within this Mediterranean-style space, but that's fine, as people enjoy the summertime patio. Breakfast and lunch $6–9, dinner $18–28.

Black-Eyed Susan's (508-325-0308; black-eyedsusans.com), 10 India Street. Open for breakfast and dinner mid-April to mid-October. This small place with pickled walls is part bistro, part glorified lunch counter with open kitchen. Hip, funky (in a good way), mellow, and homey, the downscale decor belies the stylishly presented plates. The global menu changes frequently, but look for complex fish preparations and dishes like North African spiced chicken with seasonal veggies. Breakfasts run the gamut from bagels and grits to Pennsylvania Dutch pancakes and a veggie scramble with pesto (made with eggs or tofu). BYOB. No credit cards. Breakfast averages $10, dinner $18–26.

💧 ✿ ❖ **Arno's 41 Main** (508-228-
7001; arnos.net), 41 Main Street. Open
for breakfast, lunch, and dinner, April
to early January. Chris Morris's two-
story storefront eatery is an atmospheric spot, with hurricane lamps on
the tables, high ceilings, and large canvas artwork on brick walls. Around
since the early 1960s, Arno's is known
for bountiful breakfasts featuring
French toast from Portuguese sweet
bread, "bananza" pancakes, and eggs
Benedict. It's also the island's only
wine bar and offers—surprise—41
wines by the glass. Moderately priced
lunch fare includes sandwiches, Thai
peanut noodles, large portions of pasta,
salads, and a few vegetarian dishes.
Dinner is a bit pricier; specialties
include lobster bisque, crabcakes, and
scampi florentine. Off-season specials,
wine dinner, and three-course prix fixe
dinners. Breakfast $9–16, lunch
$10–24, dinner $20–40.

❄ 💧 ✿ ❖ **Brotherhood of Thieves**
(508-228-2551; brotherhoodofthieves
.com), 23 Broad Street. Open for
lunch and dinner, until late at night.
The 1840s former whaling tavern feels
like an English pub: brick walls,
beamed ceilings, and few windows. It's
a convivial place—helped along by an
extensive coffee and drinks menu—
frequented by locals chowing on good
chowder, burgers, cheddar cheese
soup, shoestring fries (long and curly),
and thick sandwiches. Open until late
at night. Expect a line in summer;
patio dining available until mid-October. Lunch $10–19, dinner $10–25.

❄ 💧 ✿ **Fog Island Café** (508-228-
1818; fogisland.com), 7 South Water
Street. Open for breakfast and lunch.
Anne and Mark Dawson preside over
one of the top two or three breakfast
joints on island. Casual and inviting
with wooden tables and booths, they
offer food that you can relate to:

burgers, quesadillas, and specialty
sandwiches at lunchtime, and grilled
salmon and roasted pork loin at dinner.
I love the thick cut brioche French
toast and Nantucket fishcakes in the
morning (as long as I'm skipping
lunch.) Breakfast $8–13, lunch $10–15.

💧 ✿ ❖ **Cambridge Street Victuals**
(508-228-7109; cambridgestreet
nantucket.com), 12 Cambridge Street.
Open for dinner April through
December. Proprietors Trish Gallen,
Meghan McCutchean, and Tim Col-
lette preside over a casual place where
restaurant workers flock on their sole
night off. It's a jumping place with a
dark blue, barlike joint (three-deep in-
season) and a section devoted solely to
eating. Don't be fooled by the good
selection of fresh draft beers and
microbrews at the bar: Cambridge
Street serves a constantly changing
menu of very worthy food. Though it's
particularly known for monster portions of Dixie-style barbecue (smoked

on the premises), you can also get a whisper-thin veggie pizza, pulled-pork sandwich, schwarma, and baba ghanoush. Look for 99¢ ribs in the off-season on Thursday and entertainment on weekends. Dinner $22–24.

❋ **Sushi by Yoshi** (508-228-1801; sushibyyoshi.com), 2 East Chestnut Street. Open for lunch and dinner daily. When you tire of eating fancy gourmet preparations, this small place offers fresh sushi and sashimi, "Aloha" rolls with yellowtail tuna from Japan, "dynamite" rolls, and noodle dishes. For dessert, consider banana tempura or green tea ice cream. They do a brisk take-out business. BYOB. Dishes $8–20.

❋ ✐ ☿ ♿ **Atlantic Café** (508-228-0570; atlanticcafe.com), 15 South Water Street. Open for lunch and dinner. The AC's lively front section is a happening place if you don't mind the boisterous pitch from the bar as the evening progresses. Families enjoy the low-key atmosphere, large portions of pub grub, and good prices. The crispy, house-battered onion rings and flavorful clam chowder are worth the visit. Otherwise, stick to burgers, sandwiches, and salads. There are always lots of grazing dishes like onion rings, zucchini sticks, nachos, wings, and BBQ. Dishes $8–21.

❋ ✐ ☿ ♿ **Rose & Crown** (508-228-2595; the roseandcrown.com), 23 South Water Street. Open for lunch and dinner mid-April through September. This hopping place with live entertainment (nightly in-season) serves American fare—sandwiches, pastas, chicken wings, steak, and seafood—in a traditional pub atmosphere. Formerly a carriage livery, the large, barnlike room is decorated with signs from old Nantucket businesses. Lunch $8–15, dinner $10–25; early specials in spring and fall.

❋ ✐ ♿ **Starlight Café** (508-228-4479; starlightnantucket.com), 1 Union Street. Open for lunch and dinner. I like to come to this low-key spot for live music in the summer, a glass of wine, and their house specialty: lobster macaroni and cheese. The arbor patio is perfect on a warm summer night. Lunch $8–14, dinner $18–24.

❋ ✐ **Even Keel** (508-228-1979; even keelcafe.com), 40 Main Street. Open for all three meals and Sunday brunch. Nothing here is going to surprise you—except the relatively modest prices. Because of its location on Main Street, long hours, and price points, you'll probably end up here once during your visit. It's part bistro, part diner and offers American cuisine. Head to the back patio for quieter dining. Breakfast $7–19, lunch $9–16, brunch $8–15, dinner $9–26.

✐ ♿ **Nantucket Lobster Trap** (508-228-4200; nantucketlobstertrap.com), 23 Washington Street. Open for dinner May to mid-October. If you've got a hankering for lobster, plain and simple, head to this casual eatery with barn-board walls and booths. (I recommend only the basic lobster here.) Large patio and outdoor bar; delivery and takeout. Dinner from $25.

⌁ ⍦ Cap'n Tobey's Chowder House (508-228-0836), 20 Straight Wharf. Open for lunch and dinner mid-May to mid-December. I can make a meal here out of a steaming bowl of chowder. But others come for "real" food like succulent sea scallops, lobster salad, baby back ribs, or halibut (grilled, baked, or blackened). Chef Jon Roche also prepares a specialty lobster pasta that will knock your socks off (even if you're only wearing sandals). This local spot dates back to the 1950s, but Chris Roche (the chef's brother) has updated the menu and atmosphere. The game room and family-friendly dining room upstairs are well away from the noise of the downstairs pub. Lunch $xx–xx, dinner $13–31.

On the outskirts of town
✳ **Sea Grille** (508-325-5700; theseagrille.com), 45 Sparks Avenue. Open for lunch weekdays and dinner daily. Despite having plenty of parking, this attractive restaurant is overlooked by nonlocals (except in winter, when it's one of a handful open). Every kind of seafood and fish is prepared practically every way: as bouillabaisse (a specialty), grilled, blackened, steamed, fried, and raw (there's an extensive raw bar). Light meals at the bar are a good alternative. Lunch $11–25, dinner $20–40; bar menu $12–20.

⍦ **Cinco** (508-325-51515; cinc05.com), 5 Amelia Drive. Open for dinner early April through December. When you don't want to commit to one pricey entrée, try a few little ones here. New since 2004, this warm and inviting tapas restaurant offers mini-burgers, oysters on the half shell, skirt steak, sea scallops, and salt cod fritters. They also have outdoor music on the patio in the summertime. Then again, dining at the bar, with a long menu of specialty cocktails is always fun too. Dishes $6–20.

In town
Provisions (508-228-3258), 3 Straight Wharf at Harbor Square. Open late April to early October. Even in the height of summer, when this island institution is cranking, they make excellent sandwiches (big enough to feed two people), salads, and soups. Hot and cold vegetarian dishes, too. Since 1979.

✳ **The Bean** (508-228-6215), 29 Centre Street. This funky little café has strong coffee, specialty teas, and baked goods. Grab a local newspaper, play some board games, and watch this rarified world go by.

⌁ **Henry Jr's** (508-228-3035), 129 Orange Street. Open mid-May to mid-October. Downright excellent sandwiches with fast, efficient service.

⌁ **"The Street."** The first block of Steamboat Wharf is lined with fast-food shops appreciated by families and those catching ferries. Take-out eateries are generally open May to mid-October. You'll find **Easy Street Cantina** (Home of Tacos Tacos and Joe's Broad Street Grill), the excellent **Lola Burger**, **Steamboat Pizza**, and sandwiches at **Walter's**.

The Juice Bar (508-228-5799), 12 Broad Street. Open late May to mid-October. Yes, they offer fresh juices like carrot, lemonade, and orange, but they also make their own low-fat ice cream and nonfat yogurts, and breakfast baked goods. In fact, they make everything from scratch.

✳ ⌁ **The Soda Fountain at the Nantucket Pharmacy** (508-228-0180), 45 Main Street. This old-fashioned drugstore soda fountain, complete with swivel stools at Formica counters, offers egg creams, milk shakes, inexpensive soups, sandwiches, and New York City–style hot dogs.

NANTUCKET

On the outskirts of town

🎵 ⚅ **Downy Flake** (508-228-4533), 18 Sparks Avenue. Open 6 AM–2 PM daily (except 6 AM–noon Sunday); closed March. Order justifiably famous doughnuts (there are only three kinds, but who cares?) and pancakes (but not on the same morning, please) from this island institution. Light lunches, too.

Nantucket Bake Shop (508-228-2797; nantucketbakeshop.com), 79 Orange Street. Open April through November. Its advertisement claims more than 100 different items baked daily, including Portuguese breads, desserts, muffins, croissants, quiches, cakes, and pastries. You can take Jay and Magee Detmer's word for it; they've been baking the goodies since 1976.

🎵 ⚅ **El Rincon** (508-332-4749), 17 Old South Road. Open for all three meals, early February to mid-November. This great little place dishes up Salvadoran delights. Breakfast $7–11, lunch and dinner $7–17.

❄ **Pi Pizzeria** (508-228-1130; pipizzeria.com), 11 West Creek Road. Open for lunch (take-out only) and dinner. Excellent, wood-fired, thin-crust pizza for take-out and dining in. Pies $12–20.

Around the island

Claudette's (508-257-6622), Post Office Square at Main Street, 'Sconset. Open daily mid-May to mid-October. Known primarily for catering (perhaps the best catered clambakes on Nantucket), John Pearl's tiny shop's raisons d'être are box lunches and lemon cake. Although there are a few indoor tables, most people take their sandwiches to the beach or ice cream to the front deck.

✳ Entertainment

MUSIC 🎵 **Band concerts** (508-228-7213) at the Children's Beach bandstand (off South Beach Street). They're mostly held on Thursday and Sunday 6–7:30 PM in July and August.

Noonday concerts (508-228-5466), 11 Orange Street at the Unitarian Universalist Church. These concerts, featuring ensembles, soloists, and an 1831 Goodrich pipe organ, are held on Thursday in July and August. $5 donation requested.

Nantucket Musical Arts Society (508-228-1287), 62 Centre Street at the First Congregational Church. Look for concerts with world-renowned musicians on most Tuesday evenings at 8:30 from July to August. On the night before the concert, there is a meet-the-artist event hosted at the Unitarian Universalist Church, 11 Orange Street. $15 adults.

THEATER/SLIDE SHOW ✳ **Theatre Workshop of Nantucket** (508-228-4305; theaterworkshop.com), Bennett Hall, 62 Centre Street. Since 1956, this community-based group has staged a variety of plays and musicals. Call for perform locations.

🎞 ☂ **MOVIES/FILMS Dreamland Theatre** (508-228-5356; nantucketdreamland.org), 17 South Water

Street. This institution has a long and beloved history. It began as a Quaker meetinghouse, was converted to the Atlantic Straw Company, and was eventually moved to Brant Point to serve as part of a hotel before it was floated back across the harbor in 1905 on a barge. More recently it shuttered its doors in 2005 to first-run movies and was headed for demolition. But thanks to a powerhouse of locals (hedge fund managers, the wife of Google CEO, the former CEO of Starwood Hotels, and more), it was purchased for almost $10 million in 2007 and now it's back on track to open in Summer 2010 (with some luck) after an enormous renovation. It's just another little example of summer folks pitching in to help preserve a little of Nantucket's history.

❋ **Starlight Theatre and Café** (508-228-4435; starlightnantucket.com), 1 North Union Street, shows first-run movies. Drop by the café for a drink before or after the show. See *Eating Out*.

Siasconset Casino (508-257-6661; siasconsetcasino.com), New Street, 'Sconset, shows first-run movies in July and August.

♀ **NIGHTLIFE** See **Rose & Crown** (dancing or live bands) under *Eating Out*, as well as **Summer House Beachside Bistro** (live piano in 'Sconset) under *Dining Out*.

Chicken Box (508-228-9717; thechickenbox.com), 16 Daves Street off Lower Orange Street. This divey, boxy bar and music club is very laid-back. When things quiet down in town, take a cab out to "The Box" to extend your night—if you're into pool tables and live tunes. No, you can't get chicken here, but you could in 1948 when it opened as a restaurant-club.

The Muse (508-228-1471), 44 Surfside Road. This roadhouse has DJs, techno music, live bands (the Dave Matthews Band cut their teeth here), pool tables, table tennis, and a big-screen TV. It's on the shuttle circuit ad has take-out pizza, too.

The West End (508-228-5100), 326 Madaket Road. Stay tuned for new changes here, since it was purchased by a new owner in 2008 who vowed to return it to its former glory. What glory? Come at sunset—along with half the rest of the island (it seems)—and down some rum-based Madaket Mysteries and you'll know glory.

Many *Dining Out* restaurants have bars that, when diners depart for the evening, become happenin' places to socialize. Look for the ♀ symbol.

✳ Selective Shopping

❋ The principal shopping district is bordered by Main, Broad, and Centre streets. Straight Wharf shops cater more to the middlebrow tourist market, while Old South Wharf (see below) is more upscale. About 90 percent of Nantucket's shops remain open year-round, but in the winter that usually means they're open only on weekends. In the summer, many shops are open late into the night. Look for these free brochures: *Nantucket Guide to Antique Shops* and the *Guideline to Buying a Nantucket Lightship Basket*. *Nantucket Arts*, a glossy annual (with paid advertisements) found in galleries, is useful for its profiles of artists, artisans, and craftspeople.

ANTIQUES Tonkin of Nantucket (508-228-9697), 5 and 7 Teasdale Circle. Purveyors of English and French antiques (both country and formal), brass and silver items, militaria, and marine objects.

Weeds (508-228-5200), 14 Centre Street. Featuring 19th-century English country home and garden furnishings, Weeds is also an exclusive dealer in Wedgwood "Nantucket" fine bone china.

Paul La Paglia (508-228-8760), 38 Centre Street. Antique prints of Nantucket, whaling, botanicals, and game fish.

Nina Hellman Antiques (508-228-4677), 48 Centre Street. Nautical items, folk art, Nantucket memorabilia, and work by scrimshander Charles A. Manghis, who gives demonstrations on premises.

J Butler Collection (508-228-8429), 36 Centre Street. Open June to mid-October. Antiques and reproduction furnishings, collectibles, and dishware in a homey setting.

Antiques Depot (508-228-1287), 14 Easy Street. An interesting collection of furniture and fine decorative arts.

Manor House Antiques Cooperative (508-228-4335), 31½ Centre Street. This basement-level shop carries porcelain, tea services, glassware, crystal, sterling, rugs, ivory, estate jewelry, original art, and lamps. Phew. It's the island's only multidealer shop.

Salt Meadows Antiques (508-228-0230), 78 Union Street. Located on the edge of town in the so-called Cavendish neighborhood, this treasure trove of antiques, folk art, and crafts carries a particularly fascinating collection of copper weather vanes. They also specialize in reconditioning 100- and 150-year-old steamer trunks.

ART GALLERIES **Artist's Association of Nantucket Gallery** (508-228-0294; nantucketarts.org), 19 Washington Street. Open April through December. This association of 200 artists was founded in 1945 to showcase members' work. Changing AAN member exhibits, juried shows, demonstrations, and special events conspire to make this a vital venue for the local arts scene.

Old South Wharf. Generally open mid-May to mid-October. Lined with small galleries, clothing stores, artisans, and a marine chandlery, Old South is located in the boat basin just beyond the A&P parking lot. Definitely wander over.

Art Cabinet (508-325-7202; artcabinet.com), Studio 18, Dukes Road. Open May to late September. If you blink as you round the corner of Union and Main streets, you might miss this little gem of a gallery, so keep your eyes peeled. Owner Dorte Neudert showcases European contemporary artists.

Dane Gallery (508-228-7779; danegallery.com), 28 Centre Street. An outstanding shop, with a dazzling array of sophisticated glass sculpture by artists like shop owner Robert Dane.

BOOKSTORES ✒ **Nantucket Bookworks** (508-228-4000; nantucketbookworks.com), 25 Broad Street. This

MAKING HYDRANGEA WREATHS

shop has a very well-chosen selection of travel, literature, children's books, and biographies—along with an incredibly helpful staff.

Mitchell's Book Corner (508-228-1080; mitchellsbookcorner.com), 54 Main Street. This icon, which has anchored Main Street since the late 1960s, was sold in early 2008 to Wendy Schmidt, a philanthropist, wife of Eric Schmidt (Google CEO), and seasonal visitor to the island. The former owner, Mimi Berman, a descendant of astronomer Maria Mitchell, vowed to stay on for matchmaking (books to people, that is.) There's a great selection of maritime, whaling, and naturalist books. Sit and browse titles in the small "Nantucket Room," which features all things Nantucket.

CLOTHES Hepburn (508-228-1458), 3 Salem Street. Open April through January. A chic boutique with designs for women executed in crushed velvet, satin, silk, and wool.

Johnston's Cashmere (508-228-5450; johnstonscashmerenantucket.com), 4 Federal Street. Scottish cashmere, with a nice selection of classic women's sweaters, dresses, and scarves.

Pollack's (508-228-9940), 5 South Water Street. Open mid-May through December. The personable proprietor, Bob Pollack, stocks comfortable, sophisticated clothing for men and women.

Murray's Toggery Shop (508-228-0437; nantucketreds.com), 62 Main Street. This shop "invented" and owns the rights to Nantucket Reds, all-cotton pants that fade to pink after numerous washings—almost as "Nantucket" as lightship baskets. This is the only shop that sells the real thing, and has since 1945.

Peter Beaton Hat Studio (508-228-8456; peterbeaton.com), 16½ Federal Street and on Straight Wharf. Open April through December. Down a little walkway, this fun little shop has finely woven straw hats. Custom fitting and trimming, of course.

Zero Main (508-228-4401), Zero Main Street. A women's store for classic and contemporary clothes and shoes.

CRAFTS SHOPS Stephen Swift Furniture (508-228-0255; stephenswiftfurnituremaker.com), 23 Federal Street. Beautifully handcrafted chairs, benches, stools, beds, dressers, and other furnishings.

Erica Wilson Needle Works (508-228-9881; ericawilson.com), 25 Main Street. Featuring namesake designs by Wilson, an islander since 1958. And also featuring the Nantucket Knot Bracelet made by local goldsmith Heidi Weddendorf.

Nantucket Looms (508-228-1908; nantucketlooms.com), 16 Federal Street. Features weavers at work on their looms, and their creations. Although customers are not allowed into the work area, they can watch the weavers through a window in the shop.

OLD SOUTH WHARF

Claire Murray (508-228-1913; claire murray.com), 11 South Water Street. Murray came to Nantucket in the late 1970s as an innkeeper and began hooking rugs during the long winter months. She has since given up the B&B business to concentrate on designing and on opening more stores; her staff now makes the rugs. She sells finished pieces as well as kits.

Four Winds Craft Guild (508-228-9623; sylviaantiques.com), 15 Main Street, off Fair Street. Baskets, lightship purses, scrimshaw, and marine items.

FARM PRODUCE Main Street at Federal Street. Local produce is sold from the backs of trucks daily except Sunday, May through October. It doesn't get any fresher than this.

Farmer's Market, Nantucket New School. Late June to mid-October, Saturdays, 9–noon, weather permitting.

Bartlett's Ocean View Farm & Greenhouse (508-228-9403; bartletts farm.com), Bartlett's Farm Road, off Hummock Pond Road. Bartlett's boasts a 100-acre spread run by an eighth-generation islander family.

SPECIAL SHOPS Sweet Inspirations (508-228-5814; nantucketclipper .com), 26 Centre Street. Purveyor of

Nantucket Clipper Chocolates, displayed in luscious mounds in the glass cases. Of particular note are cranberry-based confections such as cranberry cheesecake truffles and chocolate-covered cranberries.

Nantucket Natural Oils (508-325-4740; nantucketnaturaloils.com), 5 Centre Street. A treat for the senses, this shop deals in essential oils and perfumes and looks like an old apothecary. Take a seat at the bar and let master perfumer John Harding custom-mix you an original fragrance. Gorgeous handblown glass perfume bottles, too.

L'Ile de France, The French General Store (508-228-3686; french generalstore.com), 8 India Street. This charming little shop features the best of France, from crockery to olive oil, from pâté to real French bread. No kidding: owners Joyce and Michel Berruet take orders and fly in fresh-baked loaves from Paris!

The Camera Shop (508-228-0101; nantucketposters.com), 32 Main Street. Extensive greeting card collections; island prints and posters.

Vanderbilt Collection (508-325-4454), 18 Federal Street. Open April through December. An eclectic assemblage of oil paintings, glitzy handbags, sculpture, lightship baskets, and classic custom jewelry.

LIGHTSHIP BASKETS

Although it is thought that Nantucket's first famed baskets were made in the 1820s, they didn't get their name until a bit later. When the first lightship anchored off the Nantucket coast to aid navigation around the treacherous shallow shoals, crewmembers were stationed on board for months at a time. In the spare daylight hours, sailors created round and oval rattan baskets using lathes and wooden molds. Stiff oak staves were steamed to make them more pliant; the bottoms were wooden. They were made to withstand the test of time. There are perhaps 20 stores and studios that sell authentic lightship baskets, which retail for hundreds to thousands of dollars and require at least 40 hours of work to produce. Among the shops that make them and take custom orders are **Michael Kane Lightship Baskets** (508-228-1548; michaelkaneslightshipbaskets.com), 18A Sparks Avenue, and **Bill and Judy Sayle** (508-228-9876), 112 Washington Street Extension.

Make it a point to visit the **Lightship Basket Museum** (508-228-1177; nantucketlightshipbasketmuseum.org), 49 Union Street. Open 10–4 Tuesday through Saturday, late May to mid-October. This informative little museum has re-created a workshop with simple tools that helps visitors understand the simple techniques artisans employed to make exquisite baskets. With baskets from the 1850s to the present, the museum certainly helps promote the art form. Adults $4, kids $2.

If you want to try making lightship baskets on your own, purchase kits and materials from **Peter Finch Basketmaker** (508-228-2267), 5 Polliwog Pond. Since it's a long walk to the shop, take the South Loop shuttle in summer.

The Golden Basket (508-228-4344; thegoldenbasket.com), 44 Main Street, sells miniature gold versions of the renowned baskets.

⚓ **The Toy Boat** (508-228-4552; the toyboat.com), Straight Wharf 41. An old-fashioned children's toy store selling great wooden boats, a wooden ferryboat and dock system, rocking boats, cradles, handmade toys and puzzles, marbles, and books.

✳ Special Events

Contact the chamber of commerce (508-228-1700; nantucketchamber.org) for specific dates, unless an alternative phone number is listed below. Also, remember that this is *just a sampling* of the larger, predictable annual events. The chamber produces an excellent Events Calendar.

Late April: **Daffodil Festival**. In 1974 an islander donated more than a million daffodil bulbs to be planted along Nantucket's main roads. It is estimated that after years of naturalization, there are now more than 3 million of these beauties. The official kickoff weekend to celebrate spring includes a vintage-car parade to 'Sconset, a tailgate picnic in 'Sconset, and a garden-club show. *This is a Very Big Weekend.*

May: **Historic Preservation Month** (508-228-1387). This celebration of Nantucket's rich local history and heritage includes discussions about

preservation and education efforts. **Wine Festival** (508-228-1128; nantucketwinefestival.com). Look for Grand Tastings at the Nantucket Yacht Club, as well as winery dinners at local restaurants.

Late May: **Figawi Boat Race** (508-771-9615). A famed race over Memorial Day weekend that goes from Hyannis to Nantucket; since 1972.

Mid-June: **Nantucket Film Festival** (212-708-1278; nantucketfilmfestival .org). It's been an intimate and important venue for new independent films and filmmakers since 1996. Screenings, Q&A seminars, staged readings, panel discussions on how screenplays become movies and on the art of writing screenplays. The festival has attracted the Farrelly brothers and Natalie Portman and included readings by Rosie Perez and Jerry Stiller.

July 4: **Independence Day** (508-228-0925). Main Street is closed off in the morning for pie- and watermelon-eating contests, a 5K run, a dunk tank, puppets, face painting, fire-hose battles, and more. Festivities are capped off with fireworks from Jetties Beach off Norton Beach Road.

Late July–early August: **Billfish Tournament** (508-228-2299). A weeklong event on Straight Wharf since 1969.

Mid-August: **House Tour** (508-257-4434). Sponsored by the Nantucket Garden Club since 1955 and featuring a different neighborhood every year; preregistration is required. **Sandcastle & Sculpture Day**. Jetties Beach off Norton Beach Road, since 1974.

Mid-September: **Island Fair** (508-228-7213). At the Tom Nevers Recreation Area; a 2-day event with puppet show, flea market, music, food, pumpkin weighing contest, and more.

Late November–December: **Nantucket Noel** begins the day after Thanksgiving with a Christmas-tree-lighting ceremony; live Christmas trees decorated by island schoolchildren line Main Street; special concerts and theatrical performances heighten the holiday cheer and merriment.

Early December: **Christmas Stroll**. Begun in 1973 and taking place on the first Saturday of December, the Stroll includes vintage-costumed carolers, festive store-window decorations, wreath exhibits, open houses, and a historic house tour. Marking the official "end" of tourist season, like the Daffodil Festival this is a *Very Big Event.* Make lodging reservations months in advance.

INDEX